T0271313

CHALLENGES AND OPPORTUNITIES FOR INNOVATION IN INDIA

About the Conference

The 7th international conference on challenges & opportunities for innovation in india (COII 2024) is organized on 23rd & 24th february 2024. It aims to providing a platform to experts, specialists, practitioners and researchers working in the field of technological and managerial innovation to share their views. The COII-2024 would be instrumental in meeting the challenges and opportunities of technology and its application in today's tech world. It will provide an excellent international forum to exchange the knowledge resulting into the application of technological innovations and managerial practice. Eminent scientists and researchers across the country would be presenting their work and discuss the future prospects of innovative ideas in the field of science, engineering and management. Authors are solicited to contribute to the conference by submitting research papers from various fields.

CHALLENGES AND OPPORTUNITIES FOR INNOVATION IN INDIA

**Proceedings of International Conference on
Challenges and Opportunities in Innovation in India (COII-2024)**

Editors
**Dr. Shweta Mishra
Dr. Avneesh Kumar Singh
Dr. Pankaj Prajapati**

CRC Press
Taylor & Francis Group
Boca Raton London New York

CRC Press is an imprint of the
Taylor & Francis Group, an **informa** business

First edition published 2024
by CRC Press
4 Park Square, Milton Park, Abingdon, Oxon, OX14 4RN

and by CRC Press
2385 NW Executive Center Drive, Suite 320, Boca Raton FL 33431

British Library Cataloguing-in-Publication Data
A catalogue record for this book is available from the British Library

ISBN: 978-1-032-99840-4 (hbk)
ISBN: 978-1-032-99842-8 (pbk)
ISBN: 978-1-003-60626-0 (ebk)

DOI: 10.1201/9781003606260

Typeset in Times LT Std
by Aditiinfosystems

Contents

Challenges and Opportunities for Innovation in India – Dr. Shweta Mishra et al. (eds)
© 2024 Taylor & Francis Group, London, ISBN 978-1-032-99842-8

List of Figures

Challenges and Opportunities for Innovation in India – Dr. Shweta Mishra et al. (eds)
© 2024 Taylor & Francis Group, London, ISBN 978-1-032-99842-8

List of Tables

Challenges and Opportunities for Innovation in India – Dr. Shweta Mishra et al. (eds)
© 2024 Taylor & Francis Group, London, ISBN 978-1-032-99842-8

About the Authors

Dr. Shweta Mishra is a seasoned editor with 10 years of experience in Master of Business Administration. She has worked with a range of authors, from emerging voices to established writers, helping to shape compelling narratives and ensure clarity and coherence in their work.

Holding a Ph.D. degree from B.H.U. Varanasi. Dr. Shweta Mishra has a keen eye for detail and a passion for research and writing. This proceeding of COII-2024 is collection of research papers from national and International writers and research scholars from reputed institutes. She has a strong track record of enhancing manuscripts through comprehensive editing processes.

Dr. Avneesh kumar Singh, Ph.D. from Lucknow University in the field of Liquid crystals, has experienced of more than 20 years in teaching and research field. He has taught Physics in UG and PG classes and published more than 10 research papers in various international journals of repute.

Addition to this he has involved in conducting and organizing research conferences and seminars from 20 years.

Dr. Pankaj Prajapati is a distinguished researcher and academic in the field of electronics, holding a PhD in Electronics. With over 12 years of experience, Dr. Prajapati specializes in semiconductor technology, embedded systems, contributing significantly to both academic research and industry applications.

Dr. Prajapati has authored numerous papers published in reputable journals and presented at international conferences. His work focuses on Digital Signal Processing, where he has made notable advancements that bridge theoretical concepts with practical implementations.

Challenges and Opportunities for Innovation in India – Dr. Shweta Mishra et al. (eds)
© 2024 Taylor & Francis Group, London, ISBN 978-1-032-99842-8

Nanotechnology Along with the Tools of RDT can Provide Sustainable Solutions for Future

1

Naveen Sharma,
Pradeep Tripathi, Sushil Kumar Singh Tomar
Ambalika Institute of Management and Technology,
Lucknow

Abstract

Bio-nanotechnology is the term that came in the existence through the combination of various aspects of nanotechnology and biology. In this new emerging field of technology, we applied tools of nanotechnology to give effective, long term and sustainable solution for many biological problems. Bio-nanotechnology usually involved manipulation of various specific materials that ranges from micrometer (μm) to nanometer (nm) with the machinery of living beings, so that their outcomes are beneficial for the society. Outcomes of above concept helps us "how does the cell act at the molecular level". By using biotechnology at nano-scale we can able to understand the mechanism by which human body or immune system get interact with the foreign particle or pathogens and how these disease are cured easily, cost effective solutions are provided. As well as better drug delivery system can also be designed by using above technique that have high targeting ability and less side affect. The basic idea, behind the combination of two fields is to increase the effective interaction among various bio-susceptible materials and how they can be beneficial for the living beings However; this chapter tries to cover basic techniques of biotechnology along with the principles of biology applied at nano-scale which not only allow scientist to imagine but also they can create a new healthy system that can be used for biological research and make promise with the future to give cheap and targeted drug delivery system that can be more effective and efficient.

Keywords

Nanotechnology, Biology, Micrometer (μm), Nanometer (nm), Various bio-susceptible materials, Ex-vivo, Delivery system

Nano is a prefix that means "one-billionth." The nanometer is one-billionth of meter — much too small to see with the naked eye or even with a conventional light microscope. **Nanotechnology** involves creating and manipulating materials at the nano scale. This is a relatively new area for researchers, with rapidly growing commercial applications. By the end of 2011 there were more than 1,300 consumer products using some form of nanotechnology.

Corresponding author: pkt07880@gmail.com

DOI: 10.1201/9781003606260-1

1. NANOTECHNOLOGY

Nanotechnology is a field of research and innovation concerned with building 'things' - generally, materials and devices - on the scale of atoms and molecules. A nanometer is one-billionth of a meter: ten times the diameter of a hydrogen atom. The diameter of a human hair is, on average, 80,000 nano-meters. At such scales, the ordinary rules of physics and chemistry no longer apply. For instance, materials' characteristics, such as their color, strength, conductivity and reactivity, can differ substantially between the nano-scale and the macro. Carbon 'nano-tubes' are 100 times stronger than steel but six times lighter.

2. NANOTECHNOLOGY CAN DO A LOT

Nanotechnology is hailed as having the potential to increase the efficiency of energy consumption, help clean the environment, and solve major health problems. It is said to be able to massively increase manufacturing production at significantly reduced costs. Products of nanotechnology will be smaller, cheaper, lighter yet more functional and require less energy and fewer raw materials to manufacture, claim nanotech advocates.

3. EXPERTS VIEWS ABOUT NANOTECHNOLOGY

In June 1999, Richard Smalley, Nobel laureate in chemistry, addressed the US House Committee on Science on the benefits of nanotechnology. "The impact of nanotechnology on the health, wealth, and lives of people," he said, "will be at least the equivalent of the combined influences of microelectronics, medical imaging, computer-aided engineering and man-made polymers developed in this century."

Fig. 1.1 Nanotechnology and its role

The goal of this chapter is to help students understand the basic technique to biotechnology and their application at nano scale and out comes may increase the effectiveness drug delivery and targeting. This chapter may help many emerging explores to explore new possibilities in this exciting field.

The term "nanotechnology" was first coined by Eric Drexler in 1981, while a graduate student at MIT.

A nanometer is about three to five atoms wide.

The idea behind nanotechnology—manipulating atoms to build things—was actually first proposed by Noble-prize winning physicist Richard Feynman in 1959.

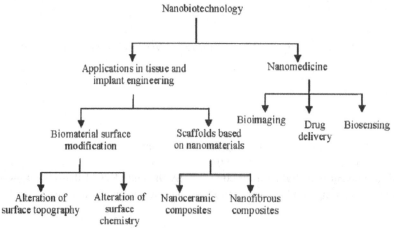

Fig. 1.2 Classification of nanobiotechnology

Nanobiotechnology is an emerging field of research at the crossroads of biotechnology and nanoscience, and involved in many different disciplines, including physicists, chemists, engineers, information technologists, and material scientists, as well as biologists.

Nanoscale materials (nanoparticles, nanopores, nanoshells, nanostructures, etc) allow highly sensitive detection by specific interactions with various biomolecules on both the surface and inside the cells.

Nano-biotechnology, **bio-nanotechnology**, and **nano-biology** are terms that refer to the intersection of nanotechnology and biology. Given that the subject is one that has only emerged very recently, bio-nanotechnology and nano-biotechnology serve as blanket terms for various related technologies. This discipline helps to indicate the merger of biological research with various fields of nanotechnology. Concepts that are enhanced through nano-biology include: nano-devices (such as biological machines), nano-particles, and nano-scale phenomena that occurs within the discipline of nanotechnology. This technical approach to biology allows scientists to imagine and create systems that can be used for biological research. Biologically inspired nanotechnology uses biological systems as the inspirations for technologies not yet created. However, as with nanotechnology and biotechnology, bio-nanotechnology does have many potential ethical issues associated with it.

The most important objectives that are frequently found in nano-biology involve applying nano tools to relevant medical/biological problems and refining these applications. Developing new tools, such as peptoid nano-sheets, for medical and biological purposes is another primary objective in nanotechnology. New nano-tools are often made by refining the applications of the nano tools that are already being used. The imaging of native biomolecules, biological membranes, and tissues is also a major topic for nano-biology researchers. Other topics concerning nano biology include the use of cantilever array sensors and the application of nano photonics for manipulating molecular processes in living cells. Recently, the use of microorganisms to synthesize functional nanoparticles has been of great interest. Microorganisms can change the oxidation state of metals. These microbial processes have opened up new opportunities for us to explore novel applications, for example, the biosynthesis of metal nano materials. In contrast to chemical and physical methods, microbial processes for synthesizing nano materials can be achieved in aqueous phase under gentle and environmentally benign conditions. This approach has become an attractive focus in current green bio-nanotechnology research towards sustainable development.

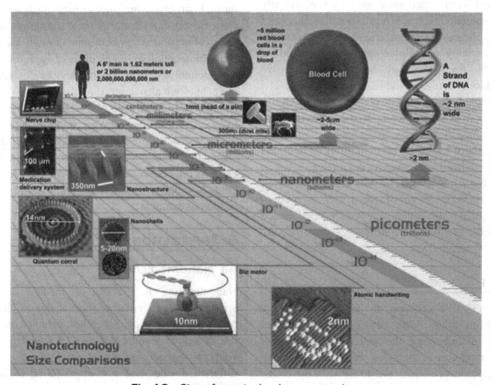

Fig. 1.3 Size of nanotechnology comparison

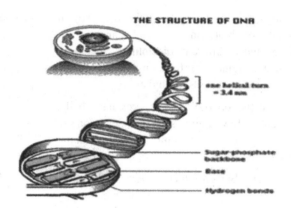

Size Ranges of Biological Material

- Cells: 100um – 10um

- Cell organelles (nucleus, mitochondrion): 10um – 1um

- Viruses: 100nm – 50nm

- Cell material (proteins, lipids, DNA, RNA): 10nm – 0.1nm

Fig. 1.4 Structure of DNA

4. RMINOLOGY

The terms are often used interchangeably. When a distinction is intended, though, it is based on whether the focus is on applying biological ideas or on studying biology with nanotechnology. Bio-nanotechnology generally refers to the study of how the goals of nanotechnology can be guided by studying how biological "machines" work and adapting these biological motifs into improving existing nanotechnologies or creating new ones. Nano-biotechnology, on the other hand, refers to the ways that nanotechnology is used to create devices to study biological systems. In other words, nano-biotechnology is essentially miniaturized biotechnology, whereas bio-nanotechnology is a specific application of nanotechnology. For example, DNA nanotechnology or cellular engineering would be classified as bio-nanotechnology because they involve working with biomolecules on the nano-scale. Conversely, many new medical technologies involving nanoparticles as delivery systems or as sensors would be examples of nano-biotechnology since they involve using nanotechnology to advance the goals of biology. The definitions enumerated above will be utilized whenever a distinction between nano-bio and bio-nano is made in this article. However, given the overlapping usage of the terms in modern parlance, individual technologies may need to be evaluated to determine which term is more fitting. As such, they are best discussed in parallel.

5. CONCEPT

Most of the scientific concepts in bio-nanotechnology are derived from other fields. Biochemical principles that are used to understand the material properties of biological systems are central in bio-nanotechnology because those same principles are to be used to create new technologies. Material properties and applications studied in bio-nanoscience include mechanical properties (e.g. deformation, adhesion, failure), electrical/electronic (e.g. electromechanical stimulation, capacitors, energy storage/batteries), optical (e.g. absorption, luminescence, photochemistry), thermal (e.g. thermo-mutability, thermal management), biological (e.g. how cells interact with nano-materials, molecular flaws/defects, bio-sensing, biological mechanisms such as mechanosensation), nano-science of disease (e.g. genetic disease, cancer, organ/ tissue failure), as well as computing (e.g. DNA computing) and agriculture (target delivery of pesticides, hormones and fertilizers. The impact of bio-nanoscience, achieved through structural and mechanistic analyses of biological processes at nano-scale, is their translation into synthetic and technological applications through nanotechnology. Nano-biotechnology takes most of its fundamentals from nanotechnology. Most of the devices designed for nano-biotechnological use are directly based on other existing nanotechnologies. Nano-biotechnology is often used to describe the overlapping multidisciplinary activities associated with biosensors, particularly where photonics, chemistry, biology, biophysics, nano-medicine, and engineering converge. Measurement in biology using wave guide techniques, such as dual-polarization interferometry, is another example.

6. APPLICATIONS

6.1 Nanomedicine

Nanomedicine is a field of medical science whose applications are increasing more and more thanks to nano-robots and biological machines, which constitute a very useful tool to develop this area of knowledge. In the past years, researchers have made many improvements in the different devices and systems required to develop nano-robots. This supposes a new way of treating and dealing

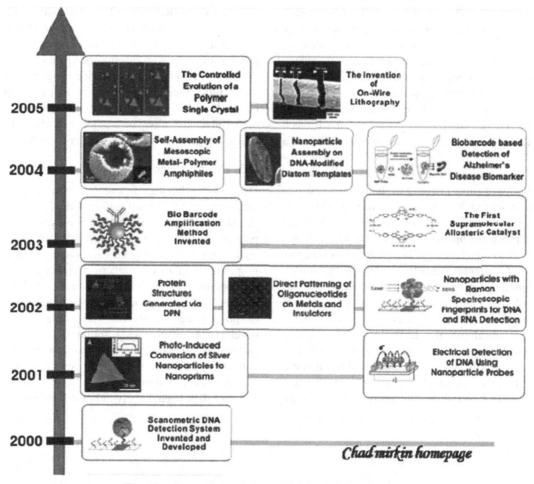

Fig. 1.5   Chronological approach of nanobiotechnology

with diseases such as cancer; thanks to nano-robots, side effects of chemotherapy have been controlled, reduced and even eliminated, so some years from now, cancer patients will be offered an alternative to treat this disease instead of chemotherapy, which causes secondary effects such as hair loss, fatigue or nausea killing not only cancerous cells but also the healthy ones. At a clinical level, cancer treatment with nanomedicine will consist of the supply of nano-robots to the patient through an injection that will search for cancerous cells while leaving the healthy ones untouched. Patients that will be treated through nanomedicine will not notice the presence of these nano-machines inside them; the only thing that is going to be noticeable is the progressive improvement of their health. Nano-biotechnology is quite important for medicine formulation. It helps a lot in making vaccines as well.

6.2 Nano-biotechnology

Nano-biotechnology (sometimes referred to as nano-biology) is best described as helping modern medicine

progress from treating symptoms to generating cures and regenerating biological tissues. Three American patients have received whole cultured bladders with the help of doctors who use nano-biology techniques in their practice. Also, it has been demonstrated in animal studies that a uterus can be grown outside the body and then placed in the body in order to produce a baby. Stem cell treatments have been used to fix diseases that are found in the human heart and are in clinical trials in the United States. There is also funding for research into allowing people to have new limbs without having to resort to prosthesis. Artificial proteins might also become available to manufacture without the need for harsh chemicals and expensive machines. It has even been surmised that by the year 2055, computers may be made out of bio-chemicals and organic salts. Another example of current nano-biotechnological research involves nano-spheres coated with fluorescent polymers. Researchers are seeking to design polymers whose fluorescence is quenched when they encounter specific molecules. Different polymers would detect different metabolites. The polymer-coated spheres could become part of new biological assays, and the technology might someday lead to particles which could be introduced into the human body to track down metabolites associated with tumors and other health problems. Another example, from a different perspective, would be evaluation and therapy at the nano-scopic level, i.e. the treatment of Nano-bacteria (25-200 nm sized) as is done by Nano-Biotech Pharma. While nano-biology is in its infancy, there are a lot of promising methods that will rely on nano-biology in the future. Biological systems are inherently nano in scale; nanoscience must merge with biology in order to deliver bio-macro-molecules and molecular machines that are similar to nature. Controlling and mimicking the devices and processes that are constructed from molecules is a tremendous challenge to face for the converging disciplines of nano-biotechnology. All living things, including humans, can be considered to be nano-foundries. Natural evolution has optimized the "natural" form of nano-biology over millions of years. In the 21st century, humans have developed the technology to artificially tap into nano-biology. This process is best described as "organic merging with synthetic." Colonies of live neurons can live together on a biochip device; according to research from Dr. Gunther Gross at the University of North Texas.

Self-assembling nano-tubes have the ability to be used as a structural system. They would be composed together with rhodopsins; which would facilitate the optical computing process and help with the storage of biological materials. DNA (as the software for all living things) can be used as a structural proteomic system - a logical component for molecular computing. Ned Seeman - a researcher at New York University - along with other researchers are currently researching concepts that are similar to each other.

6.3 Bio-nanotechnology

DNA nanotechnology is one important example of bio-nanotechnology. The utilization of the inherent properties of nucleic acids like DNA to create useful materials is a promising area of modern research. Another important area of research involves taking advantage of membrane properties to generate synthetic membranes. Proteins that self-assemble to generate functional materials could be used as a novel approach for the large-scale production of programmable nano-materials. One example is the development of amyloids found in bacterial biofilms as engineered nanomaterials that can be programmed genetically to have different properties. Protein folding studies provide a third important avenue of research, but one that has been largely inhibited by our inability to

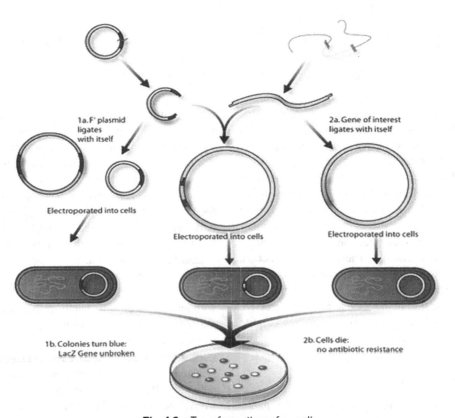

Fig. 1.6 Transformation of e- coli

predict protein folding with a sufficiently high degree of accuracy. Given the myriad uses that biological systems have for proteins, though, research into understanding protein folding is of high importance and could prove fruitful for bio-nanotechnology in the future.

7. RECOMBINANT DNA TECHNOLOGY

- Recombinant **DNA** technology refers to the joining together of DNA molecules from two different species that are inserted into a host organism to produce new genetic combinations that are of value to science, medicine, agriculture, and industry.
- Recombinant DNA (rDNA), on the other hand is the general name for a piece of DNA that has been created by the combination of at least two strands.
- They are DNA molecules formed by laboratory methods of genetic recombination (such as molecular cloning) to bring together genetic material from multiple sources, creating sequences that would not otherwise be found in the genome.
- Recombinant DNA in a living organism was first achieved in 1973 by Herbert Boyer, of the University of California at San Francisco, and Stanley Cohen, at Stanford University, who used *E. coli* restriction enzymes to insert foreign DNA into plasmids.

8. STEPS OF GENETIC RECOMBINATION TECHNOLOGY

1. Isolation of Genetic Material

- The first step in rDNA technology is to isolate the desired DNA in its pure form i.e. free from other macromolecules.
- Since DNA exists within the cell membrane along with other macromolecules such as RNA, polysaccharides, proteins, and lipids, it must be separated and purified which involves enzymes such as lysozymes, cellulase, chitinase, ribonuclease, proteases etc.
- Other macromolecules are removable with other enzymes or treatments. Ultimately, the addition of ethanol causes the DNA to precipitate out as fine threads. This is then spooled out to give purified DNA.

2. Restriction Enzyme Digestion

- Restriction enzymes act as molecular scissors that cut DNA at specific locations. These reactions are called 'restriction enzyme digestions'.
- They involve the incubation of the purified DNA with the selected restriction enzyme, at conditions optimal for that specific enzyme.

- The technique 'Agarose Gel Electrophoresis' reveals the progress of the restriction enzyme digestion.
- This technique involves running out the DNA on an agarose gel. On the application of current, the negatively charged DNA travels to the positive electrode and is separated out based on size. This allows separating and cutting out the digested DNA fragments.
- The vector DNA is also processed using the same procedure.

3. Amplification Using PCR

- Polymerase Chain Reaction or PCR is a method of making multiple copies of a DNA sequence using the enzyme – DNA polymerase in vitro.
- It helps to amplify a single copy or a few copies of DNA into thousands to millions of copies.
- PCR reactions are run on 'thermal cyclers' using the following components:
    1. Template – DNA to be amplified
    2. Primers – small, chemically synthesized oligonucleotides that are complementary to a region of the DNA.
    3. Enzyme – DNA polymerase
    4. Nucleotides – needed to extend the primers by the enzyme.
- The cut fragments of DNA can be amplified using PCR and then ligated with the cut vector.

4. Ligation of DNA Molecules

- The purified DNA and the vector of interest are cut with the same restriction enzyme.
- This gives us the cut fragment of DNA and the cut vector that is now open.
- The process of joining these two pieces together using the enzyme 'DNA ligase' is 'ligation'.
- The resulting DNA molecule is a hybrid of two DNA molecules – the interest molecule and the vector. In the terminology of genetics this intermixing of different DNA strands is called recombination.
- Hence, this new hybrid DNA molecule is also called a recombinant DNA molecule and the technology is referred to as the **recombinant DNA technology**.

5. Insertion of Recombinant DNA Into Host

- In this step, the recombinant DNA is introduced into a recipient host cell mostly, a bacterial cell. This process is 'Transformation'.
- Bacterial cells do not accept foreign DNA easily. Therefore, they are treated to make them 'competent' to accept new DNA. The processes used may be thermal shock, Ca^{++} ion treatment, electroporation etc.

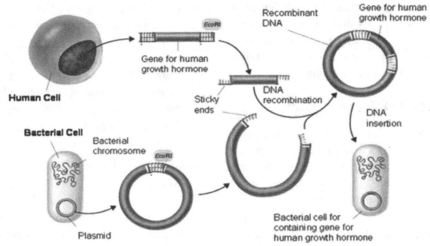

Fig. 1.7 Transformation and production of recombinant product

6. Isolation of Recombinant Cells

- The transformation process generates a mixed population of transformed and non-trans- formed host cells.
- The selection process involves filtering the transformed host cells only.
- For isolation of recombinant cell from non-recombinant cell, marker gene of plasmid vector is employed.
- For examples, PBR322 plasmid vector contains different marker gene (Ampicillin resistant gene and Tetracycline resistant gene. When pst1 RE is used it knock out Ampicillin resistant gene from the plasmid, so that the recombinant cell become sensitive to Ampicillin.

Application of Recombinant DNA technology

- Recombinant DNA is widely used in biotechnology, medicine and research.
- The most common application of recombinant DNA is in basic research, in which the technology is important to most current work in the biological and biomedical sciences.
- Recombinant DNA is used to identify, map and sequence genes, and to determine their function.
- Recombinant proteins are widely used as reagents in laboratory experiments and to generate antibody probes for examining protein synthesis within cells and organisms.
- Many additional practical applications of recombinant DNA are found in industry, food production, human and veterinary medicine, agriculture, and bioengineering.

    1. DNA technology is also used to detect the presence of HIV in a person.

    2. Application of recombinant DNA technology in Agriculture – For example, manufacture of Bt-Cotton to protect the plant against ball worms.
    3. Application of medicines – Insulin production by DNA recombinant technology is a classic example.
    4. Gene Therapy – It is used as an attempt to correct the gene defects which give rise to heredity diseases.
    5. Clinical diagnosis – ELISA is an example where the application of recombinant DNA is possible.

Limitations of Recombinant DNA technology

- Destruction of native species in the environment the genetically modified species are introduced in.
- Resilient plants can theoretically give rise to resilient weeds which can be difficult to control.
- Cross contamination and migration of proprietary DNA between organisms.
- Recombinant organisms contaminating the natural environment.
- The recombinant organisms are population of clones, vulnerable in exact same ways. A single disease or pest can wipe out the entire population quickly.
- Creation of superbug is hypothesized.
- Ethical concern about humans trying to play God and mess with the nature's way of selection. It is exaggerated by the fear of unknown of what all can be created using the technology and how is it going to impact the civilization.
- Such a system might lead to people having their genetic information stolen and used without permission.
- Many people worry about the safety of modifying food and medicines using recombinant DNA technology.

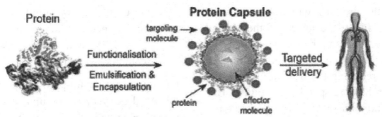

Fig. 1.8 Target of nanoparticles in human body

9. NANO-SCALE DRUG DELIVERY SYSTEMS

A Nano-capsule is a Nano-particle that is spherical, hollow structure with a diameter less than 200nm in which desired substance may be placed. They can be filled with a solvent, either polar or non polar

Nano-capsules can be distinguished from other Nanoparticles because they have well defined core and shell, whereas the latter do not. When it is made from polymers, Nano-capsules can be referred as hollow polymer nanostructures[1]. Technologies for microencapsulating materials have been around for several years, primarily for applications involving minimization of hygroscopic and chemical interactions, elimination of oxidation, and controlled release of nutraceuticals

10. THE PROPERTIES OF POLYMERIC NANO-CAPSULES

Polymeric nano-capsules can be made in specific sizes, shapes, and in reasonable quantities. Nano-capsules can be made to function in various ways. They can be produced as mono-disperse particles with exactly defined biochemical, electrical, optical, and magnetic properties. They can be tailored to suit the complexity of whatever application they are intended for, such causing the release of the contents in response to a particular bimolecular triggering mechanism in targeted drug-delivery systems.

The Use of Nano-capsules as Smart Drugs: Nano-capsules can be used as smart drugs that have specific chemical receptors and only bind to specific cells. It is this receptor that makes the drug 'smart,' allowing it to target cancer or disease. The advantages of nano-encapsulation technologies for pharmaceutical applications include:

• Higher dose loading with smaller dose volumes

• Longer site-specific dose retention

• More rapid absorption of active drug substances

• Increased bioavailability of the drug

• Higher safety and efficacy

• Improved patient compliance

11. APPLICATIONS OF NANO-CAPSULES

Nano-capsules as Drug Delivery Systems: Dispersed polymer Nano-capsule can serve as nano-sized drug carriers to achieve controlled release as well as efficient drug targeting. The dispersion stability and the primary physiological response are mainly determined by the type of the surfactant and the nature of the outer coating. Their release and degradation properties largely depend on the composition and the structure of the capsule walls. Nano-capsules can be prepared by four principally different approaches: interfacial polymerization, interfacial precipitation, interfacial deposition, and self assembly procedures. The most important capsule parameters such as capsule radius distribution, the capsule surface, the thickness and the permeability of the capsule membrane and its thermal or chemical decomposition, are discussed.

Nano-capsules for Drug Delivery: Scientists in Australia have developed minute Nano-capsules which can be used to target anti-cancer drugs to tumors, sparing other healthy tissue from side effects. The capsules, which measure about 1 micron across - or 1 thousandth of a millimeter - can be coated with an antibody which directs them from the bloodstream to a tumor. Once they are in the tumor, a quick blast with a harmless skin-penetrating laser producing near-infrared light causes the capsules to open up, discharging their contents. To make them, a polymer which when added to a suspension of drug particles forms a sphere enclosing the drug, several layers thick [3]. They then add tiny gold particles 6 nanometers - that's 6 millionths of a millimeter across - which stick onto the surface of the polymer, rather like the speckles on a bird's egg. It's these gold particles which are sensitive to the laser light and allow the capsules to deploy their drug cargo at the desired time. When near-infrared light hits the gold spots they instantaneously melt, rupturing the capsule, but without harming the contents.

Future Nano-capsule Bandages to fight infection: Conventional dressings have to be removed if the skin becomes infected, which slows healing and can be distressing for the child. This advanced dressing will speed up treatment because it is automatically triggered to release antibiotics only when the wound becomes infected, meaning that the dressing will not need to be removed, thereby increasing the chances of the wound healing without scarring. The color change acts as an early warning system that infection is present, meaning we can treat it much faster, reducing the trauma to the child and cutting the time they have to spend in hospital". This Nano-capsules bandage might also be used for other types of wounds, such as ulcer and even by the military on the battlefield.

The medical dressing will release antibiotics from Nano-capsules, activated by the presence of disease-causing pathogenic bacteria, targeting treatment before the infection aggravates. The advanced wound dressing will also change color when the antibiotics are released, thus alerting doctors that an infection is present. This bandage will only be activated by disease-causing bacteria. The toxins that it produces will break open the capsules containing the antibiotics coloring the dressing. This way, the antibiotics will only be released if needed, thus reducing the risk of the evolution of antibiotic-resistant microbes, such as MRSA (Methicillin-resistant *Staphylococcus aureus*).

12. NANO-CAPSULES FOR DRUG DELIVERY

Drug delivery and related pharmaceutical development in the context of nanomedicine should be viewed as science and technology of nanometer scale complex systems (10–1000 nm), consisting of at least two components, one of which is a pharmaceutically active ingredient, although nano-particle formulations of the drug itself are also possible. The whole system leads to a special function related to treating, preventing or diagnosing diseases sometimes called smart-drugs or theragnostics. The primary goals for research of nano-bio-technologies in drug delivery include:

- More specific drug targeting and delivery,
- Reduction in toxicity while maintaining therapeutic effects,
- Greater safety and biocompatibility, and
- Faster development of new safe medicines.

The main issues in the search for appropriate carriers as drug delivery systems pertain to the following topics that are basic prerequisites for design of new materials. They comprise knowledge on

(i) Drug incorporation and release,
(ii) Formulation stability and shelf life
(iii) Bio-compatibility,
(iv) Bio-distribution and targeting and
(v) Functionality. In addition, when used solely as carrier the possible adverse effects of residual material after

the drug delivery should be considered as well. In this respect biodegradable nanoparticles with a limited life span as long as therapeutically needed would be optimal.

The aims for nano-particle entrapment of drugs are enhanced delivery to, or uptake by, target cells and/or a reduction in the toxicity of the free drug to non-target organs. Both situations will result in an increase of therapeutic index, the margin between the doses resulting in a therapeutic efficacy (eg, tumor cell death) and toxicity to other organ systems.

Table 1.1

Particle class	Materials	Application
Natural materials or derivatives	Chitosan Dextrane Gelatine Alginates Liposomes Starch	Drug/Gene delivery
Fullerenes	Carbon based carriers	Photo-dynamics Drug delivery
Quantum dots	Cd/Zn-selenides	Imaging In vitro diagnostics
Various	Silica-nanoparticles Mixtures of above	Gene delivery

13. OVERVIEW OF NANOPARTICLES AND THEIR APPLICATIONS IN LIFE SCIENCES

So far, the use of CNTs in oral drug delivery – which is one of the most common and convenient route of therapeutics administrations – has not been possible to achieve. During oral delivery a drug must survive the harsh conditions of the gastrointestinal tract and retain its potency to be effective, and CNTs must be released with their cargo at a specific gastrointestinal site.

The team used single-walled CNTs, which they functionalized with hydrophilic carboxylic acid and hydroxyl groups, and then embedded them in the core of alginate microcapsules or coated them on their surface. By using an automated micro-encapsulator they were able to obtain highly uniform capsules.

"The nano-tubes on the capsule surface can be functionalized with antibodies to promote adhesion of the capsules to specific target sites *in vivo*, thereby facilitating targeted delivery while the embedded CNTs can be functionalized with suitable biomolecules for drug/gene delivery at the site of adhesion upon degradation of the capsule at the target site,".

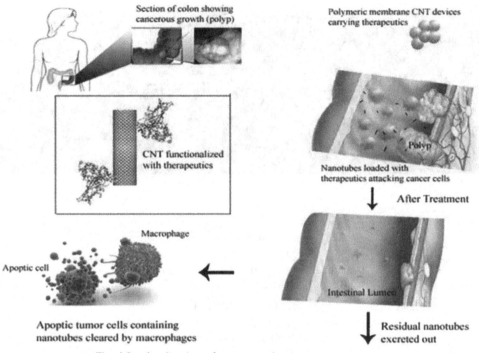

Fig. 1.9   Application of nanoparticles in cancer treatment

■ REFERENCES ■

1. Prospects and applications of nanobiotechnology: a medical perspective, MdFakruddin, Zakir Hossain &HafsaAfroz Journal of Nanobiotechnology volume 10, Article number: 31 (2012).
2. Nanotechnology from particle size reduction to enhancing aqueous solubility, DoaaHasan Alshora, Fars Kaed Alanazi, in Surface Chemistry of Nanobiomaterials, 2016.
3. Editorial: Applications of Nanobiotechnology in Pharmacology, by Baowen Qi1, Chao Wang2*, Jianxun Ding1,3* and Wei Tao1* EDITORIAL ARTICLE Front. Pharmacol., 04 December 2019.
4. Chapter 10: Bionanotechnology, by David E. Reisner The Nano Group, Inc., USA Samuel Brauer Nanotech Plus, LLC, USA WenweiZheng University of California, Berkeley, USA Raj Bawa Rensselaer Polytechnic Institute, USA &Bawa Biotech, LLC, USA Jose Alvelo Vector Consulting Group, LLC, USA MariekieGerickeMintek, South Africa Chris Vulpe University of California, Berkeley, USA Article, January 2014 DOI: 10.4018/978-1-4666-5125-8. ch003
5. Brenner, S. The Revolution in the Life Sciences. Science 338, 1427–1428 (2012).
6. Schrödinger, E. What is Life? Cambridge University Press, 1944. [Free PDF]
7. Rothemund, P. W. K. Folding DNA to Create Nanoscale Shapes and Patterns. Nature 440, 297–302 (2006).
8. Rothemund, P. W. K., Papadakis, N., &Winfree, E. Algorithmic Self-Assembly of DNA Sierpinksi Triangles. PLoS Biology 2, e424 (2004). [Open Access]
9. Ke, Y. et al. Three-Dimensional Structures Self-Assembled from DNA Bricks. Science 338, 1177–1183 (2012).
10. Adleman, L. M. Molecular Computation of Solutions to Combinatorial Problems. Science 266, 1021–1024 (1994).

Note: All the figures and table in this chapter were made by author

Challenges and Opportunities for Innovation in India – Dr. Shweta Mishra et al. (eds)
© *2024 Taylor & Francis Group, London, ISBN 978-1-032-99842-8*

Circular Flow Number of Unbalanced Edge Connected Signed Graph

2

Mohd. Izhar[1]

Research Scholar,
Department of Applied Science and Humanities,
MUIT, Lucknow (India)

Bal Govind Shukla[2]

Department of Applied Science and Humanities,
SRIMT, Lucknow (India)

Chinta Mani Tiwari[3]

Department of Applied Science and Humanities,
MUIT, Lucknow (India)

Abstract

The concepts of circular flow first introduce by F. Jaeger [1] in 1984 and proposed a conjecture for circular flow. In 1998 Goddyn and etal [4] gives the concept of circular flow number as the dual of circular chromatic number, recently Tao-Ming Wang and etal [5] show in 2012 Zero sum flow numbers of regular graphs. Andre Respoud and Xudin Zhu [7] gives the new concept of circular flow number for signed graph, after that Xudin Zhu[8] in 2012 gives the result for circular flow number of highly edge connected signed graphs. Now in this paper we show that for any positive integer $kk > 1$, every essentially $2k-1$-unbalanced $12k-1$-edge connected signed graph has circular flow number at most $2+1k$.

Keywords

Flow number, Factorization of graph, Signed graph, Circulation

1. INTRODUCTION

In case of path factorization of complete bipartite graph we give the various different models for the disjoint path of graphs in [9], [10], [11]. Here in this paper we discuss the circular flow number of un-balanced edge connected signed graph.

Suppose G is a graph. Then circulation in graph G is an orientation D of G together with a mapping $f: E(G) \to R$, Circulation in a digraph D is a function $f: A \to R$, which satisfies the conservation condition at every vertex:

$$f^+(v) - f^-(v) \ \forall v \in V(G).$$

[1]iamizhar1@gmal.com, [2]bgshukla12@gmail.com, [3]cmtiwari@muit.in

DOI: 10.1201/9781003606260-2

The boundary of a circulation f is a map $\partial f: V(G) \to R$, which is defined as

$$\partial f(v): \sum_{e \in E_D^+(v)} f(e) - \sum_{e \in E_D^-(v)} f(e).$$

Here $E_D^+(v)$ and $E_D^-(v)$ is the set of direct edges D in the form (v, u) and (u, v) respectively.

A flow in G is circulation in G with $\partial f = 0$. If r is real number and f is a flow with $1 \le f(e) \le r - 1$ for every edge e, then f is called circular rflow inG. The circular flow number $\Phi_c(G)$ of G is the least r such that G admits a circular r – flow. If r is an integer and $1 \le |f(e)| \le r - 1$ are integers then f is called a nowhere zero r – flow, The flow number $\Phi_c(G)$ of G is the least integer r such that G admits a nowhere zero r – flow. It is known that[7] that $\Phi_c(G) = \lceil \Phi_c(G) \rceil$ for any bridge less graph G. Integer flow was basically introduced by Tutte in 1949 and 1954[12, 13]. Tutte propose the three conjectures as a generalization of map coloring, these three conjecture motivated most of the studies on integral flow graph which are as follows:

Every bridge less graph has a nowhere zero 5-flow.

Every bridge less graph without 3-edge cut has nowhere zero 3-flow.

Every bridge less graph containing no Peterson minor has nowhere zero 4-flow.

First in 1979 Jaeger[2] studies circular flow in graph and proposed a conjecture that for any positive integer k, if G is 4k – edge connected, then flow number $\Phi_c(G) \le 2 - \dfrac{1}{k}$.

Luis A. Goddyn and etal in 1998[4] introduce circular flow number as the dual of chromatic number, and as a refinement of the flow number. L. M Lovasz and etal in 2013[6] proposed that for any positive integer k, if a graph G has odd edge connectivity at least 6k + 1, then $\Phi_c(G) \le 2 + \dfrac{1}{k}$.

In this paper we prove an analog of this result for signed graph.

A signed graph (G, σ) consist a graph G and a function σ from the set of links and loops (A link has two distinct end point and a loops has two coinciding end points) i.e. $\sigma: E(G) \to \{1, -1\}$ assign to each edge to a sign: an edge e is either a positive edge $(\sigma(e) = 1)$ or a negative edge $(\sigma(e) = -1)$.

An orientation e of (G, σ) assignes "Orientations" to the edges of G as follows:

if e = xy is a positive edge, then the edge is oriented either from xtoy or from ytox. In thefirst case, $e \in E_\tau^+(x) \cap E_\tau^-(y)$ and in the second case, $e \in E_\tau^-(x) \cap E_\tau^+(y)$. If e = xy is

a negative edge then the edge is oriented either from both xandy or towards both xandy. In the first case, $e \in E_\tau^+(x) \cap E_\tau^+(y)$ then edge is called sink edge and in the second case, $e \in E_\tau^-(x) \cap E_\tau^-(y)$ edge is called source edge. If H(G) denote the set of half edges of G as in [2 Flow on bidirected graph, Matt de vos], then an orientation τ of (G, σ) is a map $\tau: H(G) \to \{\pm 1\}$ with the property that $\tau(h_e^1)\tau(h_e^2) = \sigma(e)$ for every edge e. If h is a half-edge incident with the vertex v and $\tau(h) = +1$, then h is directed towards the vertex v. If $\tau(h) = -1$ then h is directed away from v.

Following figure shows the orientation of signed graph,

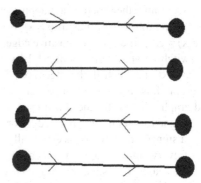

Fig. 2.1 Orientation of signed graph

Source: Author

An oriented signed graph is called a bidirected graph. If all the edges of a graph G are positive, then an orientation of (G, σ) is a directed graph. So the concept of signed graph is a generalization of graph, and a bidirected graph is a generalization of digraphs. All the concepts concerning flow in graphs can be naturally extended to signed graph.

The concept of flow, circular r – flow, nowhere zero r – flow, circular flow number and flow number are extended to signed graph in the same way. In case of signed graph (G, σ) does not admit a nowhere zero k – flow for any k, then let

$$\Phi(G, \sigma) = \Phi_c(G) = \infty.$$

There are not more conjecture in signed graph Bouchet [3] in 1983 prove that if a signed graph admits nowhere zero flow, then its flow number at most 216. In 1987 A. Khelladi[14] improve that for 4-edge connected graphs the upper bound can be reduced to 18, and R. Xu and C. Zhang in 2005 [15] proved that for 6-edge connected graphs, the upper bound can be reduced to 6. The above mentioned results shows that highly edge connected graphs have circular flow number close to 2. One naturally wonders if a similar result holds for signed graph. By applying the main result in [7], we show that the answer to this question is positive, provided that an additional minor necessary condition is satisfied. If (G, σ) is a signed graph and v is a vertex of G, then by switching at v, we obtain another signed graph (G, σ') such that

$$\sigma'(e) = \begin{cases} -\sigma(e), & \text{if } e \in E(v) \\ \sigma(e), & \text{otherwise.} \end{cases}$$

Here $E(v)$ is the set of edges incident to v. Two signed graphs (G, σ) and (G, σ') with the same underling graph G are equivalent if one can be obtain from the other by sequence of switches. It is easy to see that equivalent signed graphs have the same flow number and the same circular flow number. A signed graph (G, σ) is called a balanced signed graph if each circuit of (G, σ) is balanced. If (G, σ) is a balanced signed graph, then there is a mapping $c : V(G) \rightarrow \{1,2\}$ such that the following holds: If $e = xy$ is a negative edge, then $c(x) \neq c(y)$; If $e = xy$ is a positive edge, then $c(x) = c(y)$. By switching at all vertices in $c^{-1}(1)$, we obtain a signed graph (G, σ') in which all the edges are positive, i.e., (G, σ') is a graph. It is easy to see that converse is also true. So a signed graph (G, σ) is balanced if it is equivalent to a graph, i.e., a signed graph in which all edges are positive. Here we say a signed graph (G, σ) is essentially $(2k-1)$ – unbalanced if every signed graph equivalent to (G, σ) has at least $2K - 1$ negative edges, and say (G, σ) is essentially $(2k-1)$ – unbalanced if every signed graph (G, σ) has either an even number of negative edges or at least $2K - 1$ negative edges. For a signed graph to have circular flow number at most $2 + \dfrac{1}{k}$, being highly edge connected is not sufficient. Since if a highly edge connected signed graph may have exactly one negative edge then in this case it does not admit a nowhere zero flow. It is also easy to verify that a signed graph $2K - 1(K > 1)$ negative edges, then its circuit flow number is at least $2 + \dfrac{1}{k}$.

So here it is important to show an essentially $(2k-1)$ – unbalanced (for $K > 1$) highly edge connected signed graph has circular flow number closer to 2.

In this paper, we prove the following result:

Theorem (1):

Let k be a positive integer $(k > 1)$. If a signed graph (G, σ) is $(12k - 1)$ – edge connected an essentially $(2k-1)$ – unbalanced, then $\Phi_c(G) \leq 2 + \dfrac{1}{k}$.

2. MODULO $(2K - 1)$ – ORIENTATIONS AND Z_{2k-1}-FLOW

Give an orientation τ of a signed graph (G, σ). The out degree and in degree of signed graph(G, σ) of τ in each vertex x is defined as:

$$d_\tau^+(x) = \left| E_\tau^+(x) \right| \text{ and } d_\tau^-(x) = \left| E_\tau^-(x) \right|.$$

Fix a positive integer $k(k > 1)$. Give a mapping

$$\beta : V(G) \rightarrow Z_{2k-1}.$$

An orientation τ is called β orientation for every vertex x of G, if

$$d_\tau^+(x) - d_\tau^-(x) \equiv \beta(x) \bmod (2k - 1).$$

If $\beta(x) = 0$, then a β orientation of (G, σ) is called modulo $(2k - 1)$ – orientation.

A mapping $\beta : V(G) \rightarrow Z_{2k-1}$ is called a Z_{2k-1} –boundry if,

$$\sum_{x \in \gamma} \beta(x) = 0 \bmod (2k - 1).$$

For any orientation D of ordinary graph G:

$$\sum_{x \in V(G)} [d_D^+(x) - d_D^-(x) \equiv 0 \bmod(2k - 1).$$

Thus for a graph G to have β orientation, one necessary condition is that β be a Z_{2k-1} – boundry.

Below in theorem (2), L.M. Lovasz and etal in[6], says that if G is highly edge connected, then the converse is also true.

Theorem (2) For any positive integer $k(k > 1)$, $6(k - 1)$ – edge connected graph has a β– orientation for any Z_{2k-1} – boundry β of G.

First we prove the analog of theorem 2 for signed graphs. Note that for an orientation τ of a signed graph (G, σ), the summation $\sum_{x \in V(G)} [d_D^+(x) - d_D^-(x)$ not necessarily zero.

Theorem (3) For any positive integer $k(k > 1)$, for any mapping $\beta : V(G) \rightarrow Z_{2k-1}$, every $(2k - 1)$ – unbalanced $(12k - 1)$ – edge connected signed graph (G, σ) has a β– orientation.

Proof. Let (G, σ) is a $(2k - 1)$ – unbalanced $(12k - 1)$ – edge connected signed graph and β is a mapping such that:

$$\beta : V(G) \rightarrow Z_{2k-1}.$$

It may be assume that the graph (G, σ) has the minimum number of negative edges among all signed graphs equivalent to (G, σ). Otherwise let (G, σ') be the one with minimum number of negative edges. Let (G, σ') is obtained from (G, σ) by switching vertices in x.

Let β' be the mapping in G such that:

$$\beta' . V(G) \rightarrow Z_{2k-1}.$$

Where β' is defined as

$$\beta'(v) = \begin{cases} -\beta(v) \, if \, v \in X \\ \beta(v) \, \text{otherwise.} \end{cases}$$

We shall show that (G, σ') has a β' – orientation, which is same as (G, σ) has a β – orientation.

Consider the mapping

$$\beta : V(G) \to Z_{2k-1}.$$

Let $0 \le t \le 2k$, be the integer such that

$$\sum_{x \in V(G)} \beta(x) \equiv 2t \bmod(2k-1).$$

Let Q be the set of negative edges in the graph (G, σ). If $t \equiv |Q|(\bmod 2)$, then let τ be the orientation of Q with $\dfrac{(|Q|+t)}{2}$ sink edges, and $\dfrac{(|Q|-t)}{2}$ source edges.

Let

$$\beta'(x) \equiv \beta(x) - \Big(d_\tau^+(x) - d_\tau^+(x)\Big) \bmod (2k-1).$$

Since each sink edge or source edge contribute 2 or -2 to the summation

$$\sum_{x \in V(G)} \Big(d_\tau^+(x) - d_\tau^-(x)\Big),$$

We conclude that

$$\sum_{x \in V(G)} \Big(d_\tau^+(x) - d_\tau^-(x)\Big) = (|Q|+t) - (|Q|-t)$$

$$= 2t$$

$$\equiv \sum_{x \in V(G)} \beta(x) \bmod(2k-1)$$

Thus

$$\sum_{x \in V(G)} \beta'(x) \equiv \sum_{x \in V(G)} \beta(x) - \sum_{x \in V(G)} \Big(d_\tau^+(x) - d_\tau^-(x)\Big) \bmod(2k-1)$$

$$\equiv 0 \quad \bmod(2k-1)$$

Hence it shows that β' is Z_{2k-1} – boundry of G.

If

$$t \equiv |Q| - 1 \; (\bmod 2),$$

Then let τ be an orientation of Q with $\left(\dfrac{(|Q|+t-2k+1)}{2}\right)$ sink edges and $\left(\dfrac{(|Q|-t+2k-1)}{2}\right)$ has source edges. The same calculation show that β' is a Z_{2k-1} boundary of G.

Let R be the sub graph of G induced by the positive edges of graph (G, σ).

Claim 1. The graph R is $(6k-6)$ – edge connected.

Proof. We prove above by contradiction that R has an edge cut $E_R[X, X']$ of size at most $(6k-7)$. since G is $(12k-1)$ edge connected, we have

$$\Big|E_Q(X, \overline{X})\Big| \ge 6k-7 > \Big|E_R(X, \overline{X})\Big|.$$

Let (G, σ') is obtained from (G, σ) by switching at all vertices in X. Then

$$\sigma'(e) = \begin{cases} -\sigma(e) \text{ if } e \in E_G[X, \overline{X}] \\ \sigma(e) \text{ otherwise} \end{cases}.$$

Thus (G, σ') has less number of negative edges then (G, σ). Which is the contradiction to our choice of (G, σ). Hence graph R is $(6k-6)$ – edge connected.

By theorem 2, graph R has a β' –orientation D, i.e.

$$[d_D^+(x) - d_D^-(x) \equiv \beta'(x) \bmod(2k-1).$$

for every vertex x.

The union of this orientation of R and the previously chosen orientation τ of Q is an orientation τ' of (G, σ), with

$$d_{\tau'}^+(x) = d_\tau^+(x) + d_D^+(x)$$

and

$$d_{\tau'}^-(x) = d_\tau^-(x) + d_D^-(x).$$

Hence for every vertex x,

$$d_{\tau'}^+(x) - d_\tau^-(x) = \Big(d_\tau^+(x) + d_D^+(x)\Big) - \Big(d_\tau^-(x) + d_D^-(x)\Big)$$

$$= \Big(d_\tau^+(x) - d_\tau^-(x)\Big) + \Big(d_D^+(x) - d_D^-(x)\Big)$$

$$\equiv \beta'(x) + \Big(d_\tau^+(x) - d_\tau^-(x)\Big) \bmod (2k-1)$$

$$\equiv \beta(x) \bmod (2k-1)$$

i.e. τ' is a β orientation of (G, σ).

For theorem 3, the condition that (G, σ) be $(2k-1)$ – unbalanced is needed. For example if β is not a Z_{2k-1} – boundry, and (G, σ) has no negative edges then (G, σ) cannot be β orientation. To prove the above result, if $|Q| < 2k-1$, then the number $|Q| - t$ and $|Q| + t - (2k-1)$ appeared in the proof might be negative. Also if we restrict to modulo $(2k-1)$ – orientations in graph (G, σ), then this situation can be not strong. Given following theorem can be proved in the same manner as above in Theorem 3 can be proved.

Theorem 4. For any positive integer $k(k > 1)$, every $(12k-1)$ – edge connected and essentially $(2k-1)$ – unbalanced signed graph (G, σ) has a modulo $(12k-1)$ – orientation.

Let (G, σ) be a signed graph and let A is an abelian group. An A – circulation of (G, τ) is an orientation τ of (G, σ) together with a mapping $f: E(G) \to A$. The boundary of an A – circulation f of (G, σ) is defined in the same way as before, i.e.

$$\partial f(x) = \sum_{e \in E^+(x)} f(e) - \sum_{e \in E^-(x)} f(e).$$

Here the summation is a group operation, and an A – flow of (G, σ) is an A – circulation f with $\partial f(x) = 0$ for every vertex x. Let $k(k > 1)$ be a positive integer, we consider the group Z_{2k-1}. A special Z_{2k-1} – circulation is a signed graph (G, σ) is a Z_{2k-1} – circulation f with $f(e) \in \{k - 1, k\}$ for every edge e.

Corr.-1: For any positive integer $k(k > 1)$, every $(12k - 1)$ – edge connected and essentially $(2k - 1)$ – unbalanced signed graph (G, σ) admits a special Z_{2k-1}– flow.

Proof. From theorem (4) signed graph (G, σ) admits a modulo $(2k - 1)$ – orientation τ. Let the function $f(e) = k$ for all edges e of G. Then f is a special Z_{2k-1}– flow in signed graph (G, σ).

3. CIRCULAR FLOW NUMBER.

Let a and b be two integers such that $0 < b \le \dfrac{a}{2}$. A (a, b) – flow in a signed graph (G, σ) is called an integral flow f with $f(e) \in \{\pm b, \pm (b + 1), \ldots, \pm (a - b)\}$ for every edge e. i. e.

$$f: E(G) \to \left\{\pm b, \pm (b + 1), \ldots, \pm (a - b)\right\} \cup \{0\}.$$

If signed graph (G, σ) admits (a, b) – flow f, then $g(e) = \dfrac{f(e)}{b}$ is a circular a/b – flow in (G, σ).

Hence $\Phi_c(G,\sigma) \le \dfrac{a}{b}$. (Converse is also true: if $\Phi_c(G,\sigma) \le \dfrac{a}{b}$, then (G, σ) admits a (a, b) – flow. But we shall not use that.).

Thus to prove $\Phi_c(G,\sigma) \le 2 + \dfrac{1}{k}$, it is sufficient to prove that (G, σ) admits a $(k, 2k - 1)$ – flow for $k > 1$.

In 2005 Rui Xu and Cun-Quan Zhang [13] prove that if (G, σ) is a cubic signed graph which admits a special Z_3 – flow, then (G, σ) admits a nowhere zero 3-flow if and only if G has a perfect matching. Nevertheless, we shall prove that the condition of Corollary 1 implies that (G, σ) admits a $(k, 2k - 1)$ – flow and hence (G, σ) has circular flow number at most $2 + \dfrac{1}{k}$.

Theorem 5. If a signed graph (G, σ) is $(12k - 1)$ – edge connected and essentially $(2k - 1)$ – unbalanced for $k > 1$, then (G, σ) admits a $(k, 2k - 1)$ – flow.

Proof. Let (G, σ) is $(12k - 1)$ – edge connected and essentially $(2k - 1)$ – unbalanced. Let us assume that (G, σ) has the minimum number of negative edges among all signed graphs equivalent to (G, σ). Let S and T be the subgraphs of (G, σ) which induced by the set of positive edges and by the set of negative edges, respectively.

Now we construct a $(k, 2k - 1)$ – flow in (G, σ) in two steps. In first step, we construct a special Z_{2k-1} – circulation f in the sub graph T. In the second step, we construct a special Z_{2k-1} – circulation g in the sub graph in S, so that $f + g$ is a $(k, 2k - 1)$ – flow. In taking the sum $f + g$, here f and g is a circulation in (G, σ) with $f(e) = 0$ for every positive edge e, similarly for every negative edge e we have $g(e) = 0$.

Given a special Z_{2k-1} – circulation f in T. For a subset X of V(G). Let $E_G[X, \overline{X}]$ is the set of edges in G with one end vertex in X and the other in $\overline{X}$, where $\overline{X} = V/X$. Let

$$\partial f(X) = \sum_{v \in X} \partial f(v),$$

$$\varphi(X) = k|E_S [X, \overline{X}]| + \partial f(x).$$

We say that the circulation f is balanced if the following hold:

(1) $\displaystyle\sum_{v \in V(G)} \partial f(x) = 0.$

(2) For any subset X of V,

$$\varphi(X) \ge k - 2.$$

The special Z_{2k-1} – circulation f in T we construct in the first step will be a balanced circulation. Lemma 1 below show that such a circulation exists.

Lemma 1. There exists a balanced special Z_{2k-1}-circulation f in T.

Proof. By Claim 1, S is $6k$ – edge connected. From Nash –Williams' Theorem, S contains 3k edge disjoint spanning trees, $T_1, T_2, \ldots, T_{3k}$. Let G' be the sub graph of G induced by $Q \cup T_1 \cup T_2$. It is well known that any spanning tree of G' contains a parity sub graph F of G', i.e. for each vertex x,

$$d_F(X) \equiv d_{G'}(x) \bmod 2.$$

Let F be the parity sub graph of G' contained in T_2. Then $G' - F$ is connected and every vertex has an even digree, and hence has an eulerian cycle W. We orient the edges in T alternately source edge and sink edge. In other word, assume we traverse the eulerian cycle W, the negative edges encountered on the way are $e_1, e_2 \ldots e_q$. Then e_{2i-1} are source edges and e_{2i} are sink edges. In particular, if $|T|$ is odd, then the number of sink edges is one less than edges. This completes the construction of orientation τ of T.

If $|T|$ is even then let $f(e) = k$ for every edge $e \in T$. If $|T|$ is odd then the number of sink edges is one less than the source edges that is, $|T| \ge 2k - 1$. Let T' be the set of k sink edges. Let $f(e) = k - 1$ if $e \in T'$ and $f(e) = k$ if $e \in T/T'$. this completes the construction of the special Z_{2k-1} – circulation f in Q.

Now from the construction we prove that f is a balanced special Z_{2k-1} – circulation. i.e.

$$\sum_{e \in S} f(e) = \sum_{e \in T} f(e).$$

As each sink edge and source edge contributes $2f(e)$ and $-2f(e)$ respectively to

$$\sum_{e \in V} \partial f(x),$$

we have

$$\sum_{e \in V} \partial f(x) = 0.$$

Now we shall show that for any subset X of V, $\varphi(X) \geq k - 2$.

Starting from a vertex in $\overline{X}$, we traverse the eulerian cycle W. Each time we enter X and leave X, we traversed throw a segment of W contained in X, and the two edges in $E[X, \overline{X}]$.

Let the set of edges $(e_1', e_2' \ldots e_b')$ be such a segment, with $e_1', e_b' \in E[X, \overline{X}]$, and $e_i' \in G(X)$ for $i = 1, 2, 3, \ldots, b - 1$.

Now we calculate the contribution of these edges to $\varphi(X)$.

From the definition of $\varphi(X)$ it follow the following:

If $e_i' \in G(X)$ is a source or sink edge, then e_i' contributes $-2f(e_i') = -2k$ or e_i' contributes $2f(e_i') \geq 2k$ to $\varphi(X)$.

If $e_i' \in G[X]$ is a positive edge, then e_i' contributes 0 to $\varphi(X)$.

If $i \in \{1, b\}$ and e_i' is a source or sink edge, then e_i' contributes $-k$ or $e_i' \geq k$ to $\varphi(X)$.

If $i \in \{1, b\}$ and e_i' is a positive edge, then it contributes k to $\varphi(X)$.

By our orientation the negative edges in W are alternately source edge and sink, except that in case |T| is odd, there are two consecutive source edges.

We claim that the contribution of the edges in this segment to $\varphi(X)$ is non-negative, except that when the segment contains two consecutive source edges, the contribution of this segment is at least $-2k$.

For the proof of this claim we need to consider a few cases according to whether e_1', e_b' are positive edges, or one positive and the other is a source edge, or one is positive and the other is sink edge, etc.

However, each case is straightforward. We just consider two cases, and for simplicity, we assume that the segment does not contain two consecutive source edges.

If both e_1', e_b' are positive edges, then the number of source edges in this segment is at most one more than the number of sink edges. Since each of e_1', e_b' contributes k to $\varphi(X)$,

we conclude that the total contribution of this segment to $\varphi(X)$ is non-negative. If both e_1', e_b' are sink edges, the number of source edges in this segment is one more than the number of sink edges. Since each of e_1', e_b' contributes k to $\varphi(X)$, we conclude that the total contribution of this segment to $\varphi(X)$ is non-negative.

Add up the contribution of all the edges in the eulerian cycle W, we conclude that the total contribution is at most $-2k$, where $-2k$ is contributed by the segment containing two consecutive source edges. Now each spanning tree T_i for $i = 3, 4, \ldots, 3k$ contains at least one edge in $E_S[X, \overline{X}]$, and hence contributes at least k to $\varphi(X)$.

$$\varphi(X) \geq 3k - 2 - 2k$$
$$= k - 2.$$

This is the complete proof of Lemma 1.

Let f be a balanced special Z_{2k-1} – circulation f in Q.

Claim 2. There is a special $(2k - 1)$ – circulation g of R such that $f + g$ is a special Z_{2k-1} – flow in (G, σ).

Proof. Let $\beta: V(G) \to Z_{2k-1}$ be defined as

$$\beta(x) \equiv 2\partial f(x) \bmod (2k - 1).$$

Then

$$\sum_{x \in V(g)} \beta(x) \equiv 0 \bmod (2k - 1).$$

Since S is 6k – edge connected, by theorem 3, R has a β – orientation D. Let $g(e) = k$ for $e \in R$. Then for each vertex x,

$$\partial g(x) \equiv k\beta(x) \bmod (2k - 1)$$
$$\equiv 2k \, \partial f(x) \bmod (2k - 1)$$
$$\equiv -\partial f(x) \bmod (2k - 1).$$

Hence

$$\partial(f + g)(x) = \partial f(x) + \partial g(x) \equiv 0 \bmod (2k - 1)$$

for each vertex x, i. e., $f + g$ is a special Z_{2k-1} – flow in (G, σ).

For a Z_{2k-1} – flow ϕ in (G, σ), let

$$\|\phi\| = \sum_{x \in V(G)} |\partial \phi(x)|.$$

Thus a special Z_{2k-1} – flow ϕ is a $(k, 2k - 1)$ – flow if and only if $\|\phi\| = 0$.

Among all the special Z_{2k-1} – flow ϕ in (G, σ) of the form $f + g$, choose one for which $\|(f + g)\|$ is minimum. If $\|f + g\| = 0$, then $f + g$ is a $(k, 2k - 1)$ – flow in (G, σ), and we are done.

Assume this is not the case.

Let

$$V^+ = \{x: \partial(f + g)(x) > 0\}$$

and

$$V^- = \{x: \partial(f + g)(x) < 0\}.$$

Since

$$\sum_{x \in V(G)} \partial(f + g)(x) = 0,$$

$$V^+ \neq \varnothing \text{ and } V^- \neq \varnothing.$$

Let D be the orientation of R associated with with the circulation g. We say a vertex y of G is reachable if there is a directed path in D from y to a vertex $x \in V^-$. In particular, every vertex in V^- is reachable. Let Y be the set of all reachable vertices.

Assume first that

$$Y \cap V^+ \neq \varnothing.$$

Let P be a directed path in D from $x \in V^+$ to $x \in V^-$.

We reverse the orientation of the edges in P, and let $g'(e) = 2k - 1 - g(e)$ for $e \in P$ and $g'(e) = g(e)$ for $e \notin P$.

Then $f + g'$, is a special Z_{2k-1} – flow in (G, σ) along with

$$\partial(f + g')(v) = \begin{cases} \partial(f + g)(v) - (2k - 1), \text{ if } v = y, \\ \partial(f + g)(v) + (2k - 1), \text{ if } v = x, \\ (f + g)(v), \qquad \text{Otherwise.} \end{cases}$$

As $f + g$ is a Z_{2k-1} – flow, $\partial(f + g)(x) < 0$ and $\partial(f + g)(y) > 0$ imply that $\partial(f + g)(x) = -a(2k - 1)$ for some positive integer a, and $\partial(f + g)(y) = b(2k - 1)$ for some positive integer b.

Therefore

$$\|(f + g')\| = \|(f + g)\| - 2(2k - 1),$$

Which is contradiction to our choice of g.

Let us assume $Y \cap V^+ \neq \varnothing$. Since $X^- \subseteq Y$, we have

$$\sum_{v \in Y} \partial(f + g)(v) \leq -(2k - 1).$$

If there exist $y' \in \overline{Y}$ and $y \in Y$ such that (y', y) is a directed edge of D, then y' would be reachable vertex, a contradiction. Thus all edges in $E_D[Y, \overline{Y}]$ are oriented from Y to $\overline{Y}$. Observe that

$$\sum_{v \in Y} \partial(f + g)(v) = \sum_{v \in Y} \partial f(v) + \sum_{v \in Y} \partial g(v).$$

Since each edge in $E_D[Y, \overline{Y}]$ contribute k to $\sum_{v \in Y} \partial g(v)$

And every other edge contributes 0 to

$$\sum_{v \in Y} \partial g(v),$$

We conclude that

$$\sum_{v \in Y} \partial(f + g)(v) = \varphi(Y).$$

By Lemma 1, $\varphi(Y) \geq k - 2$, contrary P to the conclusion that

$$\sum_{v \in Y} \partial(f + g)(v) \leq -(2k - 1).$$

This is the complete proof of Theorem 5. Hence if a signed graph (G, σ) is $(12k - 1)$ – edge connected and essentially $(2k - 1)$ – unbalanced for $k > 1$, then (G, σ) admits a $(k, 2k - 1)$ – flow.

Jaeger's $\left(2 + \dfrac{1}{k}\right)$ – flow conjecture is sharp: there are $(4k - 1)$ – edge connected graph G for which $\Phi_c(G) > 2 + \dfrac{1}{k}$.

Corresponding to Jaeger's conjecture it is very clear that there exist an integer k such that every essentially $(2k - 1)$ – unbalanced $(12k - 1)$ – edge connected signed graph (G, σ) have $\Phi_c(G) > 2 + \dfrac{1}{k}$.

4. CONCLUSION

Hence from the above results we have conclude that a signed graph (G, σ) is $(12k - 1)$ – edge connected and essentially $(2k - 1)$ – unbalanced for $k > 1$, then (G, σ) admits a $(k, 2k - 1)$ – flow and a special $(2k - 1)$ – circulation g of R such that $f + g$ is a special Z_{2k-1} – flow in (G, σ), also there exists a balanced special Z_{2k-1} -circulation f in T.

■ REFERENCES ■

1. F. Jaeger, On circular flow sin graphs, in Finite and Infinite Sets, Eger, 1981, in: Colloquia Mathematical Societatis János Bolyai, vol. 37, North-Holland, 1984, pp.391–402.
2. F. Jaeger, Flows and generalized coloring theorems in graphs, J.Combin. Theory Ser. B 26(1979) 205–216.
3. A. Bouchet, Nowhere-zero integral flows on a bidirected graph, J. Combin. Theory Ser. B 34 (3) (1983) 279–292.
4. L. A. Goddyn, M. Tarsi and C.-Q. Zhang, On (k; d)-colorings and fractional nowhere zero flows, Journal of Graph Theory, 28 (1998), 155–161.
5. T. M Wang and etal, Zero sum flow numbers of regular graphs. FAW-AAIM 2012, LNCS 7285, pp. 269–278, 2012. Springer-Verlag Berlin Heidelberg 2012.
6. L. M. Lovasz and etal, Nowhere-zero3-flows and modulo k-orientations. Journal of Combinatorial Theory, Series B 103 (2013) 587–598.
7. A. Respoud and X. Zhu, Circularflow on signed graphs, J. Combin. Theory Ser. B 101(2011), no. 6, 464–479.
8. Xudin Zhu, Circular flow number of highly edge connected signed graph. arXiv:1211.3179v1 [math.CO] 14 Nov 2012.

9. U. S. Rajput and Bal Govind Shukla: P_9 – factorization of complete bipartite graphs. Applied Mathematical Sciences, volume 5(2011), 921–928. →

10. U. S. Rajput and Bal Govind Shukla: P_5 – factorization of complete bipartite symmetric digraph. .IJCA(12845-0234) Volume 73 Number 18 year 2013. →

11. U. S. Rajput and Bal Govind Shukla: P_7 – factorization of complete bipartite symmetric digraph. International Mathematical Forum, vol. 6(2011), 1949–1954.

12. W.T.Tutte, On the imbedding of linear graphs in surfaces, Proc.London Math.Soc., Ser.251 (1949) 474–483.

13. W.T.Tutte, A contribution on the theory of chromatic polynomial,Canad. J.Math. 6(1954)80–91.

14. A. Khelladi, Nowhere-zero integer chains and flows in bidirected graphs, Journal of Combin. Theory Ser. B., 43 (1987), 95–115.

15. R. Xu and C. Zhang, On flows in bidirected graphs, Discrete Mathematics,299(2005) 335–343.

Challenges and Opportunities for Innovation in India – Dr. Shweta Mishra et al. (eds)
© 2024 Taylor & Francis Group, London, ISBN 978-1-032-99842-8

Teaching and Learning Technical English for Engineers

3

Mohit Kumar Tiwari[1]
Associate Professor in English,
Ambalika Institute of Management & Technology,
Lucknow

Prabha Shanker Dixit[2]
Assistant Professor,
Ambalika Institute of Management & Technology,
Lucknow

Abstract

Teaching and acquaintance of Technical English for Engineers is an crucial aspect for employability where linguistics expertise are sharpen to excel in ones career along with technological subjects. This paper emphasize more upon the applied part of communication skill, so that it may prove useful to them later on too in their professional life. I also draw attention to the need of sub skills at technical pinnacle and its importance in campus placements where the linguistic skills are tested in the form of group discussion or oral presentations and its practices towards learning Technical English.

Keywords

Employability, Technological, Linguistic, Technical pinnacle

1. INTRODUCTION

English is considered as an international language as it is widely spoken language of the world. English language enjoys the status of lingua franca and has been widely accepted as the most widespread language in the world. English began to emerge as a global language. English has a great acceptance at socio- economical, political and industrial levels. English is cited as the major language of international business, diplomacy, science & Technology and IT enabled professions, the outlook behind the usage of English has been changing significantly accordingly.

2. SUMMARY

In this article the main focus is on the importance of English particularly for the engineers who come across the English Subject as Technical or Professional English. English is

[1]mohitkrtiwari@gmail.com, [2]prabhashanker.dixit@gmail.com

DOI: 10.1201/9781003606260-3

an international language. Many people around the world use English. Many technologies are available in English. So, English become an important language beside native language. Technologies made by engineers. Therefore, English language is very important for an engineer and engineering student.

3. Need of Communication Skills for Engineering Students

Nowadays English is the language of science, aviation, computers, diplomacy and tourism. It is the language of international communication, the media and the internet. Whether it is for professional or personal reasons, understanding the importance of English will help you reach your goals. English is the Language of International Communication. It gives access to more entertainment and more access to the Internet. It also makes it easier to travel and can make you 'smarter' Engineering student is a person that study about engineering and technologies. Besides studying about engineering and technologies, engineering students must study about English. We must study English because English is very important in our studies and career. Engineering students need to read many literatures to maintain our knowledge of engineering. Many references and literatures about engineering are available in English. Most of the theories are though in English language. So, we must know English to help them understand what we read.

4. Engineer's Language should be Refined

Engineering students need to communicate with others. We can share our ideas or problems. We can communicate by text, but not all are good at writing. Engineering students also use technologies in our studies and daily activity. In this era, many technologies are available in English language. For example, someone can know about information from internet. Besides that, engineering students will make new technologies in the future. We must use English language for our technology; in order people around the world can use our invention. Engineers are highly skilled, knowledgeable creative workforce and yet fail in communicating their expertise in their profession. English language often proves to be a fatal and futile experience by while the potential engineers and experts of the industry fail in writing, publishing, participating in conferences among their peer professionals. This brings a great fall in the ones career and one should refine their English skills of their profession to be a complete professional.

5. Engineers English Syllabus

The Technical English for Engineers syllabus should focus mainly on the communication skills to function effectively with the people, by the people and to the people, principle strictly so that the language would work in all shades of the subject concern.

6. English for Industry

English is important to information technology for various reasons. IT is used in businesses and is very crucial for the commercial world at the moment. English is the international language of trade currently, and so the two are interlinked In terms of being able to operate many systems. English is an international language of communication and also allows communication via electronic means in a single language, which avoid confusion. A vast majority of information on the internet is in English and so in many ways it's necessary to be able to understand English to understand a lot of that.

The five communication skills are as below

- Technical writing
- Public speaking
- Working with individuals
- Working with groups
- Talking with people

7. Nicholas D. Sylvester in his Book Engineering Students

He has given data under the title **"Engineering Education must improve the communication skills of its Graduates."** From the data, it is observed: "75% of engineering undergraduates takes jobs in industry, where at least 25% of an engineer's time is spent in the reporting process. As the engineer moves to higher position in his profession, this time could increase to as much as 80%."

8. Scientific and Technical Terminology should be Simple

Writers of scientific and technical writing should produce sentences that readers can easily understand, and they should place those statements in contexts, paragraphs or larger units. Hence people of technical fields are expected to study significant amount of both oral and written work and learn to communicate in a variety of forms, especially shorter forms using technical terms for non-specialists helping non-technical people understand technical terminology in ease.

Writers could present in intelligent way if the terms are easy to comprehend.

For Example:

The full meaning of a term can often be expressed by simply 'unwinding' it from right to left and inserting the appropriate preposition. Like in the term – "wall stress" could be explained as "stress on a wall", "stress inside a wall", "stress produced by a wall", etc. only the Civil Engineering Department personnel can be sure that "stress inside a wall" is exact meaning. The correct interpretation of the term depends heavily on the reader's prior knowledge of the subject being discussed the non-specialists would be able to guess the intended meaning of the compound term as a whole.

9. TECHNICAL WRITING: A PROMISING CAREER

Technical writing is a form of communication, a style of formal writing used in fields as diverse as computer hardware, software, chemistry, Aerospace industry Robotics, finance consumer electronics an biotechnology. Technical writing is communication written for and about business and industry. Technical writers explain technology and its-related ideas to technical and non- technical audiences. Technical writing department is often known as information development user assistance, technical documentation or technical publications.

11. CONCLUSION

This article concludes with a good note that engineering students should earn by practicing the entire sub skills of language in an application based either by listening to audio files, reporting or presentations, writing through plans, procedures and presenting by seminars would develop the linguistic skills of a language learner. All the sub skillsof English language can be interpreted in an integrated form by using creativity, innovative and thinking logical, lateral and critically. This is purely practice based skill where the mastery of a language would solely depend on theory and skill practice in any field of the profession.

■ REFERENCES ■

1. Jeff Butterfield (2014), Softskills for Everyone, Cengage Learning, Delhi.
2. Lakshminarayanan K.R, English For Technical Communication, 2nd Edition, Scitech.
3. Rizvi, Ashraf M (2005), Effective Technical Communication, Tata Mc Graw Hill, New Delhi.

Suggested Reading:
1. Sylvester, Nicholas. D. Engineering Education. "Engineering Education must improve the Communication Skills of its Graduates". 1980
2. Crystal David, "English as a Global Language", 2nd Edition. Great Britain, Cambridge University Press 2003

Challenges and Opportunities for Innovation in India – Dr. Shweta Mishra et al. (eds)
© 2024 Taylor & Francis Group, London, ISBN 978-1-032-99842-8

Liquid Crystals with its Gigantic Potentials

4

Avneesh Kumar Singh*

Associate Professor,
Department of Applied Science
Ambalika Institute of technology and Management,
Lucknow (India)

Abstract

Liquid crystals are the unique substance those are exist in-between the liquid and solid states. Liquid crystals have distinct molecular configuration than the liquids and solids. The liquid crystalline phase may occur either due to heating of solids (thermotropic LC) or due to dissolving an amphiphilic mesogen in a suitable solvent (lyotropic LC). There are various types of liquid crystals based on distinct internal arrangement of molecules in lattice. They acquire lots of properties of a liquid, as high fluidity, incapability to support shear, creation of droplets however they show crystalline behavior as anisotropy in their optical, electrical, and magnetic properties. Due to its unique structure and performance it has a large number of applications in various areas. This review paper discusses the exclusivity of LCs, its types, properties and vast applications in various fields such as displays, medical, pharmaceutical industries, cosmetic industry, sensor. Application of LCs in new fields based on latest research and its remarkable potential is also discussed.

Keywords

Liquid crystals (LCs), Mesophase, Displays, Recent applications

1. INTRODUCTION

The liquid crystal technology is one of the important inventions of twentieth century that has found many applications as a visualization tool and other areas [1,2,3]. Liquid Crystal is accidently invented by Austrian Chemist Friedrich Reinitzer and Otto Lehmann in (1888). Liquid Crystals are intermediary state in-between solid and liquid state of matter. It is generally known as mesomorphic state which is a state of matter in which the degree of molecular order lie between the perfect three dimensional, long-range positional and orientational orders found in crystalline solid and the absence of long-range order found in isotropic liquids, gases, and amorphous solids [4].

The liquid crystals can be mainly categorized as Thermotropic and Lyotropic liquid crystals. Lyotropic liquid crystals are induced by the presence of solvent, and

*Corresponding author: aksphy@gmail.com

DOI: 10.1201/9781003606260-4

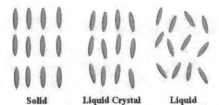

Fig. 4.1 Molecular arrangements

have been broadly illustrated in the context of emulsion technology and pharmaceutics. Thermotropic liquid crystals are induced by a temperature change and are basically free of solvent. Liquid crystals (LC) are liquids characterizing a certain level of orientational order. Molecules in liquid crystals tend to point to a certain direction, while they still have translational (positional) freedom. Even though they are well-known for their application in displays, liquid crystals are also an essential part of all life forms. Lyotropic liquid crystals are natural organic substances.

Depends on the shape of the molecules involve in liquid crystalline material, liquid crystals are rod like (calamitic), discotic and banana shaped as shown in figure. Their behavior and order parameter vary with shape of molecules.

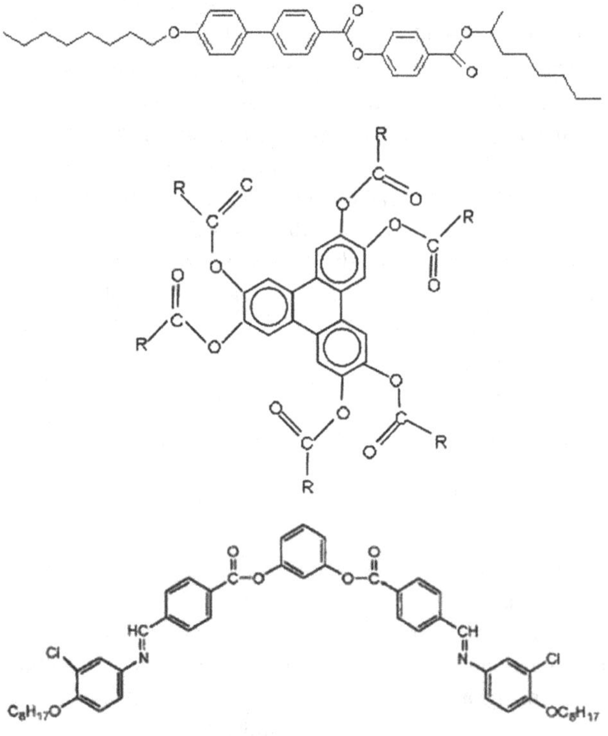

Fig. 4.2 Cholesteric liquid crystal molecules

Most important category of liquid crystals is the phases of calamitic liquid crystals depends on their molecular arrangement as

1.1 Nematic Phase

The least ordered phase is the nematic which has only long-range orientational order (i.e.: no positional order). In this case, the long axes of the molecules point on the average in the same direction, which is defined by a unit vector commonly known as "the director" (n).

The macroscopic optic axis lies along the same direction as the director. The nematic phase can also be considered as centro-symmetric since the physical properties are indistinguishable with an inversion of the director. This mesophase has complete rotational symmetry about the director. As the temperature is decreased the order of the phase is increased. Due to the microstructure of the nematic phase, many of the macroscopic properties are anisotropic. For example, nematics exhibit a birefringence, because for polarised light, the refractive index in a direction along the long axis of the molecules (ordinary refractive index) is different to the refractive index in the orthogonal direction across the width of the molecules (extraordinary refractive index). Furthermore, the molecules can undergo a reorientation (electro-optic switching) due to an anisotropy in the distribution of electrical charge across the molecule (i.e.: the anisotropy in dielectric permittivities). Therefore, nematic liquid crystals possess a number of useful material properties such as a high birefringence, sensitivity to low frequency electric fields and structural flexibility. This combination forms the basis of operation of many of the liquid crystal devices in production today.

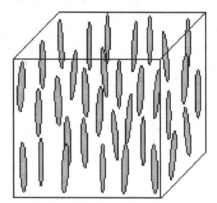

Fig. 4.3 Nematic phase

1.2 Chiral Nematic Phase - (Cholesteric)

A variant of the nematic phase is the chiral nematic (also known as the cholesteric phase) which is a spontaneously forming macroscopic helical structure. This phase was first observed by Reinitzer in 1888 in derivatives of cholesterol. Consequently, the phase is often referred to as cholesteric.

The presence of chiral molecules causes the director profile to assume a twisted configuration through the medium. In

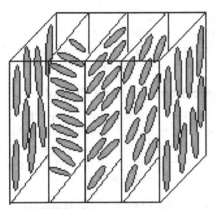

Fig. 4.4 Chiral nematic phase

the figure below, a somewhat naïve picture illustrates the rotation of the director about a single axis, the helix axis. The revolution of the director results in a macroscopic helix. There is actually no layered structure and the local ordering is identical to that of the nematic phase. The defining length scale of this phase is the pitch, the distance for which the director rotates through an angle of 2π. However, due to the fact that this phase is also non-polar, the invariance with director values of n and -n means that the periodicity is only half the pitch. Unlike the nematic phase, the optic axis is aligned along the helix axis. Macroscopically, they are therefore uniaxially negative.

1.3 Smectic Phase (SM)

Higher order liquid crystal phases are the so-called smectic phases which combine orientational order with positional order. Unlike the nematic and chiral nematic phases the density is not uniform as there is some correlation between the molecules' centre of mass. This results in a diffuse layered structure. However, the interlayer forces are weak in comparison to the intralayer forces between the molecules and therefore the layers have some degree of freedom to move. Due to the layered structure smectics

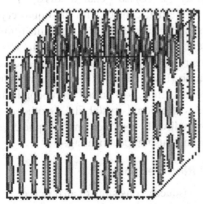

Fig. 4.5 Smectic A phase

are usually more viscous than conventional nematics and tend to appear at lower temperatures. There are a number of different smectic phases and these are characterised by the packing formation and the tilt angle with respect to the layer normal. Each phase being classified by a different letter of the alphabet in the order they were discovered (eg: SmA, SmB, SmC, etc, ranging from A to K). The most commonly used smectics used in research and applications are SmA and SmC.

1.4 Chiral Smectic (SM*)

Helical smectic phases are also known to exist such as the chiral smectic C phase (SmC*). This is similar to the chiral nematic structure except that the molecules are tilted at an angle to the layer normal and it is the precession of the tilt that gives rise to the macroscopic helical structure. Smectic C* liquid crystals exhibits ferroelectric qualities, including bistabilityand fast switching speeds. In the case of liquid crystal molecules that possess an electric dipole, each molecular layer within the smectic structure will have a net electrical polarisation. The polarization vector will rotate from one layer to the next, resulting in a material with overall zero electrical polarisation.

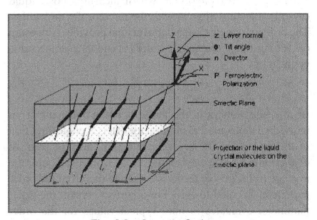

Fig. 4.6 Smectic C phase

We call such liquid crystals **'ferroelectric'** (FLC). **Antiferroelectric** structures are also possible, in which the director is orientated to either one side of the cone or the other in every alternate layer, resulting in the electric polarisation reversing itself from one layer to the next. Meanwhile, as one observes every other layer, the directors continue to precess around the cone. A third form is also possible, whereby only occasional layers have the reverse electric polarisation. More layers are therefore located on one side of the cone than the other, and the material has a net electrical polarisation. We call this a **'ferrielectric'** liquid crystal.

2. PROPERTIES OF LIQUID CRYSTALS

2.1 Mechanically Similar to Ordinary Liquids

Flow Normally the liquid crystals are fluid in nature, in mesomorphic phase.

Similar densities Liquid crystals posses more or less similar densities to that of ordinary liquids. *Approximately constant volume* The variation of the volume of the liquid crystals with temperature is almost negligible as in the case of liquids.

2.2 Posses Some Properties Similar to Solids

X-ray diffraction The liquid crystals give the X-ray pattern like crystals when diffracted by X-ray beam. *Long range order* The liquid crystalline state can be described through its positional, orientational and conformational order. While positional order is important to characterize the various liquid crystalline state (nematic, smectic A, Smectic C etc.) i.e. predictability of the position of the molecular centers, the conformational order is measure of how the rings and functional groups with in a molecule are oriented. These degrees of order can be qualitatively measured in terns of order parameter. From the application point of view it is usually the orientation order parameter S which is most important, which measures how liquid crystal molecules aligned with the director the molecules. The order parameter S of a liquid crystal provides a measure of its long-range orientation order [5] and its average value is given by

$$S = \frac{1}{2}\langle 3\cos^2\Theta - 1\rangle$$

In this equation Θ is the angle between the axis of an individual molecule and the director that is average direction of the molecule. The brackets denote an average over all of the molecules in the sample. In an isotropic liquid, the average of the cosine terms is zero, and therefore the order parameter is equal to zero. For a perfect crystal, the order parameter evaluates to one. Typical values for the order parameter of a liquid crystal range between 0.3 and 0.9, with the exact value a function of temperature, as a result of kinetic molecular motion. A change in order parameter from zero to one is accompanied by a reduction in entropy of the system; hence, order parameter theories are useful for calculating thermodynamic quantities of liquid crystals.

Anisotropic properties Liquid crystal has a number of unique characteristics that makes it very suitable for use in displays. Most of these characteristics stem from the fact that liquid crystal is an anisotropic material, meaning that the properties of the material differ depending on what direction they are measured. Liquid crystal behaves differently depending on what direction electric or magnetic fields are applied relative to the director. Since light is an electromagnetic wave, what happens to light as it passes through the liquid crystal will also depend highly on the direction of its propagation and polarization with respect to the director of the crystal.

2.3 Applications of Liquid Crystal

Liquid crystals are very important because they are easily affected by surfaces, electric and magnetic fields; they are well controllable and consume lesser power in devices. Based on these properties, there are several applications of liquid crystals as discussed below.

2.4 Indicator and Measuring Devices

Thermal Devices

Liquid crystal thermometers represent the most direct application of the temperature dependent selective reflection. Special mixtures of cholesteric liquid crystals are commercially available that allow the user the design of thermometric films that can be adjusted for a large variety of temperature intervals and operating temperature. The application range from encapsulated liquid crystal thermometers designed for desks, swimming pools, and fish tank to temperature-limit indication [6,7].

Mechanical Devices

A Liquid crystal pressure sensor device has been use, which indicates pressures [8] from 500-5000 bars as a red shift of the selective reflection maximum at constant temperature.

Electrical Devices

Voltage and rms current meters have been made, which consist of restive films supporting a liquid crystal layer. The measuring current shifts the temperature distribution and thus the location of the colour band.

D. Optical Devices

The temperature dependence of the selective reflectance is utilized in a variety of displays. They consists of an electrically xy- addressed penal of dissipative elements which are in thermal contact with the liquid crystal film. These dissipative elements can be thin film resistors [9], magnetic memory elements (transfluxors) [10], or microtransistrs [11]. Other displays are addressed by input radiation (UV, visible, or IR), which modulates the electrical conductivity of biased photoconductive layer sandwiched with a liquid crystal film. In other displays the information is directly inscribed on the liquid crystal by an electron beam, causing local heating.

2.5 Radiation Sensors

Radiation transducer, consisting of an observer sandwiched with a liquid crystal film or suspended in the liquid crystal and of the appropriate optical components, may be the most versatile and inexpensive devices for the conversion of invisible to visible radiation that is ionizing, ultraviolet, infrared, microwave, and ultrasonic radiations.

2.6 Non-Destructive Testing

Thermal mapping conducted with temperature-sensing films, which are the direct contact with the test item, may be most important application of the cholesteric liquid crystals. This technique can solve many problems because both temperature level and temperature interval of the colour band can be adjusted over a wide range by selecting the mixture of appropriate compounds. This temperature pattern can be thermally mapped in the steady and in the transient state. The steady-state approach is limited by the lateral heat conduction, which tends to wash out those characteristic details of the pattern that are associated with tiny cracks, minute in homogeneities, and other small structure deviation in the test piece [12].

2.7 Medical Application

In medicine, thermal mapping is used to detect those defects and malfunction in human beings that can generate temperature patterns on the skin. The correct interpretation of these patterns can represent a formidable medical problem because the exact correlation between medical cause and the observed temperature effect is difficult to quantify. Expensive infrared thermographs, equipped with sophisticated electronic signal processors, are used to quantitative thermal mapping, while rather an inexpensive liquid crystal are primarily applied to qualitative and comparative thermal mapping. In addition, liquid crystals serve as temperature monitors of medical equipment. Several patents describe the use of cholesteric liquid crystals in clinical thermometry. The temperature range of the liquid crystal thermometers can be extended without a loss of sensitivity by imbedding different liquid crystals in close proximity. For example, a plastic sensing patch has been proposed in which liquid crystal, contained in a radial segment, selectively reflects in a different temperature region. Mixtures of Cholesteryl Oleyl Carbonate, Cholesteryl Nonanoate, and carbon black confined to small pockets in special wrist strap have been proposed as optical fever indicators[7]. Liquid crystals in different forms are used successfully in the vast area of medical sciences like Dentistry [13], Gynecology [14,15], Neurology [16,17], Oncology [18,19], Ophthalmology [20], Pediatrics [21], Surgery [22] and Urology [23] etc

2.8 Solitary Wave Propagation In Liquid Crystals

A high intensity laser beam injected in a liquid crystal can produce a local reorientation of the director molecules. In this way the light produces its own waveguide and the laser light will not diffract but stays confined in a narrow beam. The solation application can lead to an addressable liquid crystal waveguide to switch light between several optical fibers.

2.9 Hollow Liquid Crystal Fibers

Hollow optical fibers have already proved their use. If we fill them with liquid crystals, they can give interesting controllable behaviour to the optical fibers.

2.10 Liquid Crystal Solar Cell

A new and promising application of liquid crystals has been in the form of liquid crystal semiconductor. Liquid crystals are organic molecules similar to polymers. In polymers containing conjugated systems (alternating single and double bond) the creation of a higher and lower pi-bond leads to the creation of a band gap similar to semiconductors. The use of such a liquid crystal in a device similar to the Grätzel cell can lead to new types of solar cells.

2.11 Characterization of Liquid Crystals

Various techniques have been employed to characterize liquid crystals. The main factors to be considered for describing liquid crystalline structure involve their order. By taking into consideration these parameters, one can recognize the proper phase as well as the interactions between molecules of liquid crystals. Polarizing Optical Microscope (POM) is a standard tool in the identification of liquid crystal phases and phase transitions but requires considerable experience, particularly in the study of new and less familiar materials. POM equipped with standalone temperature controller is employed to investigate the textural information and thermal span of the liquid crystal phases. Differential Scanning Calorimeter (DSC) provides excellent clues that help characterize the LCs. Melting point and transition points, which are often more spread than in low mass materials, can usually detected. It also employed to investigate the phase transition temperatures, enthalpy values and order of the corresponding phase transitions. Dielectric studies through impedance gain phase analyzer provide information about important parameters used in various application of liquid crystals. Further, electrical characterization is extremely potent tool in identifying the mesophases which are not clearly noticed either by POM or by DSC. Nuclear Magnetic Resonance Spectroscopy (NMR) is very useful technique for identifying of parts of molecues. The order within the liquid crystals can also be determine. Fourier Transform Infrared Spectroscopy (FTIR) has been used extensively to study polymers whose ability to exhibit liquid crystalline phases may be due to hydrogen bonding. Small Angle Light Scattering has been used to study the shear flow textures that occur during flow of lyotropic systems. Small Angle Neutron Scattering (SANS) has been used to study polymer chain conformation and order parameter in lyotropic.

■ REFERENCES ■

1. B. Bahadur (Editor), *Liquid Crystals: Application And Uses*, Vol. 1 (Singapore World Scientific) (1991).

2. B. Bahadur (Editor), *Liquid Crystals: Application And Uses*, Vol. 2, 3 (Singapore World Scientific) (1994).

3. T. D. Wilkinson, W. A. Crossland, S. T. Warr, T. C. B. Yu, A. B. Davey & R. J. Mears, *Liquid Crystals: Today* **4(3)**, 1 (1994).

4. IUPAC Compendium of Chemical Terminology IUPAC Gold book 2005.

5. W. Tsvetkov, *Acta Physicochim (USSR)* **16**, 132 (1942).

6. R. Parker, U. S. Patent 3,861,213 (1975).

7. H. Seto, M. Veda & H. Segawa, U. S. Patent 3,704,625 (1972).

8. P. Pollmann, *Ber. Bunsenges. Phys. Chem.* **78**, 374 (1974); *J. Phys. E* **7**, 190, (1975).

9. J. L. Fergason & A. E. Anderson, U. S. Patent 3,410,999 (1968).

10. J. A. Asars, British Patent 1,119,253 (1968).

11. S. A. Hadjistavros, U. S. Nat. Tech. Inform. Sorv., Rep. AD 734 442 (1971).

12. W. E. Woodmansee, *Appl. Opt.* **7**, 1721 (1968); E. Sprow, *Mach. Des.* **41(2)**, 37 (1969).

13. R. M. Howell, R. C. Duell & T. P. Mullaney, *Oral Surg.* **29**, 763 (1970).

14. T. W. Davison, K. L. Ewing, H. Sayat, N. P. Mulla & J. L. Fergason, *Obstet. Gynecol.* **42**, 574 (1973).

15. T. W. Davison, K. L. Ewing, J. L. Fergason, M. Chapman, A. Can & C. C. Voorhis, *Canser* **29**, 1123 (1972). A. Benjamin, *Image Dyn.* **3(5)**, 10 (1968).

16. J. T. Crissey, E. Grody, J. L. Fergason & R. B. Lyman, *Roche Med. Image Comment.* **11**, 6 (1969).

17. M. Gautheric, *J. Phys. (Paris)* **30**:C4, 122 (1969).

18. K. L. Ewing, T. W. Decision & J. L. Fergason, *Ohio. J. Sci.* **73**, 55 (1973).

19. J. B. Kinn & R. A. Tele, *IEEE Trans. Biomed. Eng.* **20**, 387 (1973).

20. R. T. Hall & T. K. Oliver, *J. Amer. Med. Ass.* **218**, 1700 (1971).

21. B. Y. Lee, F. S. Trainor & J. L. Madden, *Arch. Phys. Med. Rehab.* **54**, 96 (1973).

22. K. D. Panikrotov, Yu. M. Gerusuv, G. G. Maidachenko & V. A. Vorontsov, *Coll. Rep., All-Union Sci. Conf. Liquid Cryst., Acad. Sci. USSR*, 1st, 1970, 309 (1972).

Note: All the figures in this chapter were made by the author

Prevalence and Technology Advancements at Work Place to Enhance Occupational Health and Safety of Employees

5

Navya Sharma, Priyakshi Sharma,
Vijay Bhalla, Poonam Arora*

SGT College of Pharmacy, SGT University,
Gurugram, Haryana

Abstract

Occupation has always been a major source of health challenges in the workers. An occupational disease is a health condition caused by the environment or activities at work place. The workplace related diseases occur as a result of continual exposure to industrial environmental hazards and are observed at a higher frequency in people than rest of the population. Amongst various health challenges, respiratory disorders including asthma, lung diseases and Chronic Obstructive Pulmonary Diseases (COPD) have highest propensity to occur at work place. Therefore, understanding, analyzing and adopting ways to minimize the impact of hazards on the workers is immediate need of the time. Emerging technologies such as, assessing particulate matter floating at work place, wearable devices, digitization in occupational health, could prevent contracting infection, exposure to noxiuos substances and oxidative stress, insuring safety of workers. Moreover, e-consultations, bringing telemedicine into practice is getting approachable technique providing onsite and immediate advice. This state-of-the-art technologies could provide key metrics allowing industries to maximize employee engagement and reduce morbidity and mortality. Here, we aim to identify risk factors, their prevalence about which employees need to be warned off to avoid any workplace induced fatalities.

Keywords

Occupational disease, Respiratory disorders, Digitization, Wearable devices, Telemedicine

1. INTRODUCTION

An occupational disease is a health condition that is caused by the environment or activities at work place. These diseases are observed at a higher frequency in people than the rest of the population with similar exposures in their occupational environment. According to the Protocol by Occupational Safety and Health (OSH) Convention, laid down in year 2002, during General Conference of International Labour Organization, the term "occupational disease" refers to disease that develops as a result of exposure to risk factors arising from and in surroundings of work activity, such as allergens, dust mites etc. (Garus-Pakowska et al, 2022, Keogh et al, 2022). Work place is

*Corresponding author: PoonamArora_FPHS@sgtuniversity.org

DOI: 10.1201/9781003606260-5

also reported as one of the major reasons for increasing trend of sucidal attempts. Epidemiologists have estimated an annual data of 36,700 fatalities, 1,83,00,000 injuries and 18,50,000 diseases related to occupational hazards till date. Lately, outbreak of coronavirus disease (COVID-19) pandemic has been a breakthrough example, where 23% of healthcare workers globally suffered depression and anxiety and 39% workers suffered insomnia showing higher risks of work-related psychiatric disorders (Coleman et al, 2021). Major occupational diseases can be exemplified as occupational dermatoses, such as Dermatitis, Vitiligo, Urticaria; respiratory illnesses such as Asthma, lung disease and Chronic Obstructive Pulmonary Diseases (COPD), Siderosis, Bronchopulmonary disease, Pneumoconiosis caused by fibrogenic mineral dust (Silicosis, Asbestosis); musculoskeletal disorders (MSDs) such as chronic tenosynovitis; hearing loss; Cancer; neurologic and psychiatric disorders such as PTSD; infection causing diseases such as Hepatitis, Tuberculosis, HIV/AIDS; reproductive and development disorders, cardiovascular disorders, haematologic disorders, hepatic disorders, renal and urinary disorders (Kim et al, 2013). A study by WHO considers 19 occupational risk factors, including exposure to long working hours and workplace exposure to air pollution, asthmagens, carcinogens, ergonomic risk factors and noise. The key risk factor is recognised as exposure to long working hours which was linked to approximately 7,50,000 deaths. Workplace exposure to air pollution (particulate matter, gases and fumes) are responsible for about 4,50,000 deaths globally (Espitia-Pérez et al, 2020).

2. RISK FACTORS ASSOCIATED WITH COMMON TYPES OF OCCUPATIONAL DISORDERS

The workplace related diseases occur as a result of continual exposure to industrial environmental hazards that are intricately linked to health complications in people working there. The major risk factors contributing to occupational disorders can be categorised as mechanical factors (including heat, noise, vibration, radiation), chemical factors (such as solvents, pesticides, heavy metal dust such as lead in the workplace causing lead poisoning), biological factors (which include bacteria, fungi, parasites, viruses causing Tuberculosis, Hepatitis B and C), psychosocial factors (for instance, lack of control over work, bullying, stress, harassment, lack of recognition, inadequate personal support in the workplace) and sometimes, ergonomic factors (like repetitive motion, improper designed tools and equipment). These factors in the work environment are predominant and essential in the etiology of any occupational disease. For instance, Occupational Asthma, occupational silicosis, occupational dermatoses, occupational musculoskeletal disorders, occupational haemotological diseases, Occupational urinary and renal disorders etc. predominantly observed in workers who inhale powder from latex gloves or other chemicals (Lim et al, 2014), in workers working in manufacturing of building construction materials, in agricultural industries, production of incense sticks etc. (Mah Jephcote, et al. 2020, Kumar et al. 2019, Bhatia et al. 2017) (Table 5.1).

Table 5.1 Common occupational disease and associated risk factors

S.No	Name of Disease	Affected population	Causative factors
1	Occupational Asthma	Workers like Farmers, grain millers, who inhale powder from latex gloves or other chemicals, especially the animal handling laboratory workers.	Plant products, mites, fruit and vegetable pollen, juices, latex, preservatives, amides, epoxy resins, isocyanates, acrylate monomers, animal skin, persulfates etc.
2	Occupational Silicosis	In workers working in manufacturing of building construction materials, tunnelling, sculpturing, foundries industries.	Chromate, epoxy resin, cobalt, nickel and rubber chemicals, thiazole etc.
3	Occupational dermatoses	Workers working in coffee plantation, incense stick production, carpet weavers	Plant products, animal products and dander, latex gloves, epoxy resins etc.
4	Occupational musculoskeletal disorders	Operators, fabricators, and labourers (38%) and precision production, craft, and repair technical, sales, and administrative supporters.	Latex gloves, cement dust (chromium), enzymes etc.
5	Reproductive and development disorders	Sawmill workers, chemical workers, petroleum and gas workers.	Wood dust, isocyanates like diisocyanate, anhydrides, amides etc.
6	Occupational haemato-logical disorders	Petrochemical industry, synthetic rubber manufacturing plants, plastics manufacturing industries.	Isocyanates, adhesives anhydrides, solvents like toluene etc.
7	Occupational urinary and renal disorders	Mining workers, agricultural workers, chemical industry workers.	Plant products, animal products and dander etc.

Source: Author

3. GLOBAL PREVALENCE OF OCCUPATIONAL DISORDERS

According to the data reported by International Labour Organisation (ILO), every year over 2.3 million women and men succumb from an occupational injury and almost 2 million deaths are caused by fatal work-related diseases. In addition, over 313 million workers are involved in non-fatal occupational accidents causing serious injuries and absences from work. The ILO also reckons that approximately 160 million cases of non-fatal work-related diseases occur annually. These estimates demonstrate a major burden of work related health challenges irrespective of modernisation in world.

3.1 United States

In the United States, people who open bales of cotton during the first stage of processing are at the highest risk of byssinosis disease. Another type of byssinosis that appears in people who work with grains called grain worker's lung (Nafees et al, 2023). As per reports from the U.S. Bureau of Labor Statistics, in united states, private industry employers report 2.8 million non-fatal workplace injuries and illnesses in 2022, with increase of 7.5 percent from 2021. This spike in casualties is driven by a rise in illnesses upto 26.1 percent with total of 460,700 cases. The increase in illnesses was driven by respiratory disorders that further increased to 35.4 percent (365,000 cases) in 2022. These estimates are given by Survey of Occupational Injuries and Illnesses (SOII) (Soo et al, 2023).

3.2 India

A comprehensive review of literature suggests that majority (85%) of Indian workers engaged in unorganised sector lack access to occupational health services (OHS). India contributes (17%) of the global total of occupational diseases casualties, accounting for 1.9 million out of 11 million cases worldwide. Heavy burden and poor concern for occupational disease is reflected in respiratory disease in workers, e.g., Silicosis, 4.1%–54.6% among miners and Byssinosis, 28%-47% in textile workers. (Meena et al, 2023). As per NIMH, chest radiographs revealed the prevalence of pneumoconiotic opacities in open cast mine workers were 5.7-12% and 5.3-13%, in 2005 and 2011, respectively. In addition, 85% of people suffers from musculoskeletal disorders which is commonly associated with back, shoulders, knees, neck. In India, prevalence of silicosis varies among occupational groups: (34%) in mica miners, 4.1 % in manganese miners, 30.4% in lead and zinc miners, 9.3% in deep and surface coal miners, 27.2% in iron foundry workers, and 54.6% in slate-pencil workers. Whereas the prevalence of asbestosis was extended from 3% in asbestos miners to 21% in mill workers. 28-47% textile workers suffer from Byssinosis a brown lung disease caused due to inhaling hemp, flax, and cotton. The economic impact of adverse occupational factors ranges from 2% to 14% of the gross national product (GNP).

3.3 United Kingdom

As per HSE Annual Report, about 1.8 million workers suffered from work-related ill health, which was almost more than 6% in 2021/22 compared to previous year. Annual statistic on work related ill-health and workplace injuries published by the Health and Safety Executive (HSE) for 2022/23 period, 1.8 million cases are related to work illness, out of which, 875,000 suffer from work-related stress, depression or anxiety, 473,000 cases were of work-related musculoskeletal disorder. About 35.2 million working days were lost due to workplace injuries and illness and the estimated cost of injuries and ill health from current working conditions accounted to be £20.7 billion was. (Harrison, 2022; Renwick et al, 2016). Recent outbreak of coronavirus pandemic in 2021/22, resulted in increased work-related illness (Chen et al, 2023).

3.4 China

Various industries in China account for the large cases of occupational disease particularly, skin diseases, occupational tumours, occupational eye disease and occupational radiation diseases (Wei et al, 2023). The two primary hazardous chemicals CO, lead, H_2S, arsenic poisoning account for more than 50%, 27.11%, 29.2%, 19.73%, respectively. Between 2006 and 2020 over 6037 new cases of pneumoconiosis were reported, which gradually declined since 2013. The majority of cases occurred within the small scale and domestic funded enterprises, constituting 71.75% and 96.97% respectively. When analysing the industry distribution, the cases were mainly concentrated in mining (37.12%), manufacturing (31.11%) and public administration and social organisation (23.94%) industry. Among cases of pneumoconiosis, the average age at diagnosis was 55.44 years and median exposure duration was 11.00 years. Significantly older diagnosis age and longer exposure duration were found in females, coal workers pneumoconiosis cases, cases with the first year of dust exposure earlier and cases from large-scale companies. The top three cities reporting the most pneumoconiosis cases in Zhejiang Province were Taizhou, Quzhou and Hangzhou. (Wei et al, 2023).

3.5 Australia

In any industry or occupation, the impact of work-related injuries and illnesses are felt by workers, their families and the community. The latest findings from the 2023 Key Work

Health and Safety Statistics in Australia's Research shows an increase in work related mental health conditions. In 2022, three industries, Transport, postal and warehousing accounted for 71% of fatalities including, (34%, 67 fatalities), followed by fatalities in the agriculture, forestry and fishing industry (23%, 44 fatalities) and construction industry (14%, 27 fatalities). The agriculture, forestry and fishing industry had fatality rate at 14.7 fatalities per 100,000 workers, followed by the transport, postal and warehousing industries with 9.5 fatalities per 100,000 workers (Espitia-Pérez et al, 2020).

3.6 Malaysia

In Malaysia, Occupational risks were identified to contribute to the overall chronic disease, where the 37% cases are of the back pain, 16% of hearing loss, 13% of chronic obstructive pulmonary disease, 11% of asthma, 8% of injuries, 9% of lung cancer, 2% of leukemia, and 8% of depression. (Maria et al, 2023). Almost two million deaths in 2016 were attributable to occupational risks estimating to 2.7% of the disease burden worldwide. The newly added occupational risk factor is exposure to long working hours.

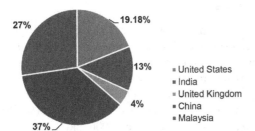

Fig. 5.1 Pie chart representing global prevalence of leading occupation related lung diseases

Source: Author

4. Occupational Lung Diseases

Major work-related lung diseases that are caused or made worse by materials such as irritants when exposed in the workplace include:

4.1 Pneumoconiosis

There has been recent increase in prevalence and severity of pneumoconiosis in the United States. As on 7 November 2022, approximately 54% of health workers in low- and middle-income countries were found to have latent tuberculosis, which is 25 times higher than the general population. When people are exposed to high-level coal mine dust than they are mainly associated with pneumoconiosis. It was the most prevalent occupational lung disease after the Second World War. Increased mechanisation and automation in the mining industries and

foundries and the implementation of efficient preventive exposure control measures then reduced dust exposure levels and thus, the associated respiratory disease burden. Due to recent climate change mitigation policies aimed to decrease environmental fossil-fuel carbon emissions in most European countries. Even in countries with strict occupational health and safety regulations such as the USA worryingly, indications exist of a resurgence of pneumoconiosis in coal workers, because of lack of exposure control measures increasing in number of small private mines. As a supporting recent example, diacetyl (2,3-butanedione), a volatile butter-flavored diketone, was identified as a new cause of serious disabling bronchiolitis obliterans because several workers from popcorn-producing industries ended up on lung transplant lists, (Wei et al, 2020). The major cause of occupational respiratory infections is bacterial, viral, and fungal pathogens. Transmission can occur from co-workers or patients, animals, or the environment and in any industries or workplaces. Transmission of infectious pathogens, include disease factors such as mode of transmission air, water, penetration through dermal absorption, some workplace factors such as conditions or practices, and itself worker factors such as impaired immunity.

a) Silicosis

Silicosis is a fibrotic respiratory disease which is caused by the inhalation and deposition of respirable crystalline silica. It is a severe occupational hazard that is caused by long-term inhalation of crystalline-free silica dust which affects the lungs (Li et al, 2022). When the particle size is less than 5 μm in diameter, which is small enough to reach the distal airways and alveoli is termed as silica particles (Tan et al, 2021). The most important factor in the development of silicosis is the cumulative dose of silica exposure. They are basically identified by alveolar macrophages in the lungs leading to cell signaling cascade regulated by macrophage scavenger receptors such as SR-AII and macrophage receptor with collagenous structure. Ultimately cytotoxic effect of silica causes macrophage death, which further releases inflammatory cytokines and other substances that cause proliferation of fibroblasts. In China, silicosis is treated by tetrandrine, which has been already approved inhibits lung inflammation and lung fibrosis to improve pulmonary function. (Tan et al, 2021). Out of 101 workers in 2011, workers working in stone mining suffers from respiratory diseases whereas 73 suffered from silicosis, of whom 16 had silicosis with progressive massive fibrosis (PMF).

b) Asbestos-linked disease

Asbestos, a naturally occurring fibrous silicate material found in construction and various manufacturing industries that includes brake linings and pads, tiles, bricks, insulation materials, and furnace oven linings. According to the Global Burden of Disease (GBD) project approximately 125 million people worldwide are exposed to asbestos annually, with chrysotile accounting for more than 95% of all the asbestos used globally. Widely use of asbestos fiber can increase the risk of non-malignant inflammatory, malignant pulmonary diseases, lung cancer. (Anonymous, 2023)

4.2 Occupational Asthma

Occupational asthma is defined as a disease characterised by variable airflow limitation and inflammation in lungs due to conditions attributable to a particular occupational environment and not to stimuli encountered outside the workplace. Occupational Asthma, with an incidence of 2–5 cases per 1,00,000 population per year, represent approximately 15–20% of the overall adult-asthma, which is mainly associated with allergies triggered by respiratory sensitising agent that includes high molecular weight substance such as wheat flour in baking.

A detailed history need to be taken where exposure to certain (frequently uncommon) irritants may be present in working environment (Sara et al, 2017). Work-related asthma should become part of the differential diagnosis of every case of adult-onset asthma or declining expiratory air flows in an individual with preexisting but previously clinically quiescent asthma (Murgia et al, 2022).

4.3 Chronic Obstructive Pulmonary Disease

Chronic obstructive pulmonary disease (COPD) stems from exposure to harmful particles and gases. Occupational contact with vapours, gases, dust, and fumes plays a role in the initiation and advancement of COPD, representing a population attributable fraction of 14%. Specifically, workplace pollutants, particularly inorganic dust, can trigger airway damage and inflammation, serving as key elements in the pathogenesis of COPD (Murgia and Gambelunghe, 2022). COPD is referred as a progressive airflow limitation that is not fully reversible, which is associated with an abnormal inflammatory response of the lungs to toxic particles or gases. Destruction of alveolar walls causes Emphysema, which leads to reduced gas exchange, permanent airspace enlargement, loss of elastic recoil, hyperinflation, and expiratory flow limitation. Changes in collagen- and elastic-fiber organization mainly occurs by destruction of fibers by metalloproteinases (Murgia et al, 2022). Appropriate use of bronchodilators and corticosteroids helps in the management of COPD. Bronchodilators relaxes the muscles around the airways which usually occurs in inhalers which can help in relieving in coughing and shortness of breath and make breathing easier (Vogelmeier et al, 2022).

4.4 Occupational Lung Cancer

One of the most common causes of deaths from cancer in the world has been found to be from lung cancer, causing about 1 in 5 (18.4%) cancer deaths. In most countries, including low-income, middle-income, high-income nations, it is mostly a predominant cause of cancer death for men and the most frequent cause among women in the United States, China, Australia, Scandinavia, and Canada. The most common cause of lung cancer is Tobacco, the maturity of the cigarette smoking epidemic, and the adoption of smoking cessation determines much of the geographic and gender variation in lung cancer incidence and mortality. Lung cancer is caused by exposures in the workplace that account for about 50% or more of occupational cancers. Occupational exposures cause or contribute to 10-15% of lung cancers. This attributable fraction, obtained by combining estimates of the prevalence of exposure to recognised occupational lung carcinogens with relative risk estimates for each agent, has been remarkably consistent across studies over the past two decades, despite variation in agents, study populations, available exposure data, and modelling assumptions. A recent analysis by the British Occupational Cancer Burden study group applied estimates of working populations exposed to 21 occupational lung carcinogens to estimates of lung cancer relative risks concluded that approximately 15% of all lung cancers in the United Kingdom are related to work place climate (Anonymous, 2023) A prospective cohort study in the Netherlands estimated that about 12% of cases of lung cancer in men were attributable to lifetime occupational asbestos exposure. Moreover, a recent large, pooled analysis of mainly European case–control studies showed that the joint effect of asbestos and smoking exposure was more than additive in all lung cancer subtypes. The total burden of lung cancer cases attributable to work-related exposure to respiratory carcinogens in Europe has been estimated to be 400 cases per year. Many etiological factors of lung cancer, other than cigarette smoking, have been ascertained as exposure to environmental cigarette smoke (including passive smoking), occupational exposure to agents like asbestos and hard metals, exposure to radiation, especially radon; and exposure to indoor and outdoor air pollution, silica, and diesel engine exhaust.

5. POLICIES AND LEGAL ACTS RELATED TO HEALTH WELFARE IN INDIA

The Government firmly believes that building and maintaining national preventive safety and health culture is the need of the hour. However, so far only 26 out of the 195 Member States of WHO have in place policy instruments and national programmes for managing occupational health and safety of health workers. (Saha et al, 2018). With a view to develop such a culture and to improve the safety, health and environment at workplace, it is essential to meet the following requirements: - 1) providing a statutory framework on Occupational Safety and Health (OSH) in respect of all sectors of industrial activities including the construction sector, designing suitable control systems of compliance, enforcement and incentives for better compliance. 2) Promoting inclusion of safety, health and environment, improvement at workplaces as an important component. Since 2003, April 28 is celebrated as World Day for Safety and Health at work with aim to promote the prevention of occupational accidents and disease in the workplace and raise public awareness about the importance of occupational health and safety. (Anonymous, 2023) In India, two legislative acts containing the main provisions for legal measures for the protection of health and safety of workers are the Factories Act (1948) and the Mines Act (1952). The Ministry of Health and Family Welfare is responsible for providing health and medical care to workers through its facilities. The DGMS (Directorate General of Mines Safety) and the DGFASLI (Directorate General – Factory Advisory Services and Labour Institutes) that assist the Ministry in technical aspects of occupational health and safety in mines, ports and factories respectively. (Anonymous, 2023) Standards that must be set under REACH for chemical substances and that describe safe levels of these substances in the air have now been increasingly derived by employers. Such effective and efficient tools will help healthcare professionals correctly identify the causes of respiratory diseases, if made accessible for routine clinical practice.

6. CONCLUSION

Unsafe working conditions resulting in occupational illness, injuries and absenteeism constitute a significant financial cost for the health sector and is estimated up to 2% of health spending, however, the count is on surge due to increasing construction sites and need of cotton and raw materials in market. This should highlight the need for new paradigm for introducing advanced technologies that could help to minimize not only on occupational injuries but associated health challenges occurring as a result of work place.

■ REFERENCES ■

1. Aichouni M, Touahmia M, Alshammari S, et al. (2023) An Empirical Study of the Contribution of Total Quality Management to Occupational Safety and Health Performance in Saudi Organizations. Int J Environ Res Public Health; 20(2):1495.

2. Anonymous, 2023. https://www.ccohs.ca/oshanswers/chemicals/how_do.html (assessed on December 3, 2023)

3. Anonymous, 2023. https://www.who.int/news-room/fact-sheets/detail/occupational-health--health-workers (assessed on December 3, 2023)

4. Anonymous, 2023. www.cdc.gov/workplacehealth promotion/health-strategies/musculoskeletal-disorders/index.html (assessed on December 4, 2023)

5. Anonymous, 2023. www.epa.gov/pm-pollution/health-and-environmental-effects-particulate-matter-pm (assessed on December 5, 2023).

6. Anonymous, Global burden of chronic respiratory diseases and risk factors, 1990–2019: an update from the Global Burden of Disease Study 2019. 2023; 59(10): 101936.

7. Awaluddin S. Maria, MM, Lim KK, Shawaluddin NS, Lah T. M. A. T., "Occupational Disease and Injury in Malaysia: A Thematic Review of Literature from 2016 to 2021". Journal of Environmental and Public Health, 2023; 1–32.

8. Bhatia R, Sharma VK. Occupational dermatoses: An Asian perspective. Indian J Dermatol Venereol Leprol. 2017 Sep-Oct;83(5):525–535.

9. Coleman, B., Casiraghi, E., Blau, H., Chan, L., Haendel, M., Laraway, B., Callahan, T. J., Deer, R. R., Wilkins, K., Reese, J., & Robinson, P. N. (2021), Increased risk of psychiatric sequelae of COVID-19 is highest early in the clinical course. medRxiv: the preprint server for health sciences, 2021.11.30.21267071.

10. De Matteis S, Heederik D, Burdorf A, Colosio C, Cullinan P, Henneberger PK, Olsson A, Raynal A, Rooijackers J, Santonen T, Sastre J, Schlünssen V, van Tongeren M, Sigsgaard T; European Respiratory Society Environment and Health Committee. (2017 Nov); Current and new challenges in occupational lung diseases. Eur Respir Rev. 15;26(146):170080.

11. EPA United States Environmental Protection Agency (assessed on December 4, 2023)

12. Espitia-Pérez L, Jiménez-Vidal L and Espitia-Pérez P (2020) Particulate Matter Exposure: Genomic Instability, Disease, and Cancer Risk. Environmental Health - Management and Prevention Practices. IntechOpen.

13. Garus-Pakowska A. (2022, May); Biological Factors in the Workplace-Current Threats to Employees, the Effects of Infections, Prevention Options. International Journal of Environmental Research and Public Health.19(9):5592. (assessed on December 3, 2023)

14. Harrison J. (2012). Occupational safety and health in the United kingdom: securing future workplace health and wellbeing. *Industrial health, 50*(4), 261–266.

15. Jang Leikauf GD, Kim SH, Jang AS. Mechanisms of ultrafine particle-induced respiratory health effects. Exp Mol Med. 2020 Mar ;52(3):329–337.

16. Jumat MI, Hayati F, Syed Abdul Rahim SS, Saupin S, Awang Lukman K, Jeffree MS, Lasimbang HB, Kadir F. Occupational lung disease: A narrative review of lung

conditions from the workplace. Ann Med Surg (Lond). 2021 Mar 23; 64:102245.

17. Keogh SA., Leibler JH, Sennett Decker, CM. et al. (2022) High prevalence of chronic kidney disease of unknown etiology among workers in the Mesoamerican Nephropathy Occupational Study. BMC Nephrol 23, 238.

18. Kim, E. A., & Kang, S. K. (2013). Historical review of the List of Occupational Diseases recommended by the International Labour organization (ILO). Annals of occupational and environmental medicine, 25(1), 14.

19. Kumar S, Sharma A, Kshetrimayum C. Environmental & occupational exposure & female reproductive dysfunction. Indian J Med Res. 2019 Dec;150(6):532–545.

20. Leikauf, G.D., Kim, SH. & Jang, AS. (2020) Mechanisms of ultrafine particle-induced respiratory health effects. *Exp Mol Med* 52, 329–337.

21. Li T, Yang X, Xu H, Liu H. Early Identification, Accurate Diagnosis, and Treatment of Silicosis. Can Respir J. (2022) Apr 25; 2022:3769134.

22. Lim J.W., KOH D, (2014) Chemical Agents that Cause Occupational Diseases.he Wiley Blackwell Encyclopedia of Health, Illness, Behavior, and Society, First Edition. Edited by William C. Cockerham, Robert Dingwall, and Stella R. Quah. Published by John Wiley & Sons, Ltd.

23. Madeleine K, Scammell DSc*, Caryn M, Sennett MPH, Zoe E, Petropoulos BS, Jeanne Kamal MD, James S, Kaufman MD "Environmental and Occupational Exposures in Kidney Disease" 2019.

24. Mah Jephcote C., Brown D., Verbeek T. *et al.* A systematic review and meta-analysis of haematological malignancies in residents living near petrochemical facilities. *Environ Health* 19, 53 (2020).

25. Mohammadi, H., Rabiei, H., & Dehghan, S. F. (2023). Editorial: Emerging technologies in occupational health and safety. Frontiers in public health, 11, 1117396. https://doi.org/10.3389/fpubh.2023.1117396

26. Meena JK*. Geetanjali Medical College and Hospital, Udaipur, Rajasthan, India occupational health in india: Present scenario, challenges and way forward. April 2018. Occupational and Environmental Medicine 75(Suppl 2):A144.1–A144

27. Murgia N, Gambelunghe A. Occupational COPD-The most under-recognized occupational lung disease? Respirology. (2022 Jun); 27(6):399–410.

28. Murgia N, Gambelunghe A. Occupational COPD-The most under-recognized occupational lung disease? Respirology. 2022 Jun; 27(6):399–410.

29. Murgia, N., & Gambelunghe, A. (2022). Occupational COPD-The most under-recognized occupational lung disease?. *Respirology (Carlton, Vic.)*, 27(6), 399–410.

30. Nafees AA, Muneer MZ, Irfan M, *et al.* Byssinosis and lung health among cotton textile workers: baseline findings of the MultiTex trial in Karachi, Pakistan. *Occupational and Environmental Medicine* 2023;**80:**129–136.

31. Renwick, L., Lavelle, M., Brennan, G., Stewart, D., James, K., Richardson, M., Williams, H., Price, O., & Bowers, L. (2016) Physical injury and workplace assault in UK mental health trusts: An analysis of formal reports. *International journal of mental health nursing*, 25(4), 355–366.

32. Saha R. K. (2018). Occupational Health in India. Annals of global health, 84(3), 330–333.

33. Samanta S, Gochhayat J, (2023) Critique on occupational safety and health in construction sector: An Indian perspective. Materials Today: Proceedings, Volume 80, Part 3, Pages 1703.

34. Soo SY, Ang WS, Chong CH, Tew IM, Yahya NA. Occupational ergonomics and related musculoskeletal disorders among dentists: A systematic review. Work. 2023;74(2):469–476.

35. Tan S, Chen S. The Mechanism and Effect of Autophagy, Apoptosis, and Pyroptosis on the Progression of Silicosis. Int J Mol Sci. 2021 Jul 28;22(15):8110.

36. Vogelmeier CF, Miguel Román-Rodríguez b, Dave Singh c, MeiLan K. Han d, Roberto Rodríguez-Roisin e, Gary T. Ferguson. (May 2020) Goals of COPD treatment: Focus on symptoms and exacerbations. Respiratory Medicine, Volume 166, 105938

37. Wei, F., Xue, P., Zhou, L. et al. Characteristics of pneumoconiosis in Zhejiang Province, China from 2006 to 2020: a descriptive study. *BMC Public Health* 23, 378 (2023).

Challenges and Opportunities for Innovation in India – Dr. Shweta Mishra et al. (eds)
© 2024 Taylor & Francis Group, London, ISBN 978-1-032-99842-8

Simulation-Based Learning: The Key Elements Growth of Cloud Kitchen and Behavior's Ordering Patterns in the Post-Covid Era

6

Arun Kumar Singh*

Student (Executive MBA),
BML Munjal University, NH 48, Kapriwas,
Haryana

Chirag Malik

Professor,
BML Munjal University, NH 48, Kapriwas,
Haryana

Abstract

This study intended to investigate how simulation technologies are beneficial to management and higher education. Buzzwords like immersive settings, participatory learning, experiential learning, experimental learning, etc. are commonly used in modern educational practice.

E-learning and virtual learning environments are only two examples of the cutting-edge educational techniques that have evolved as a result of the swift growth in the information and communication technology industry. New educational technologies are widely used, particularly in higher education. Institutions of higher learning exist to train future professionals. A disruptive aspect of the food service industry is the concept of a cloud kitchen, also known as a virtual or ghost kitchen. In contrast to conventional restaurants, Cloud Kitchens don't have actual eating areas and instead provide meal preparation and delivery services. The operational paradigm, advantages, and influence of Cloud Kitchens on the food industry are all covered in this abstract. Overall, the findings show that Cloud Kitchen simulations are helpful for achieving learning objectives. The main benefits of a simulation include fostering new learning relationships with the students, offering them new roles to play, and improving their capacity for active learning. This essay examines the notion of simulation as well as how simulation is viewed by the general public in management education.

Keywords

Cloud kitchen, Simulation, Post-Covid era, Operational paradigm

*Corresponding author: arunkumar.singh.21emb@bmu.edu.in

DOI: 10.1201/9781003606260-6

1. INTRODUCTION

A restaurant without a physical location where food is prepared for various deliveries is known as a Cloud Kitchen or Delivery Kitchen. Orders are taken via websites and online ordering aggregators. Additionally, different restaurants or brands may operate in the same establishment. They are primarily focused with preparing food for online orders sent through several platforms for food delivery. The population of India is under 30 years of age and if we calculate the median age it comes out to be 28.7 years which makes it the youngest amongst the BRICS countries. As per the CIA refund of 2020,43.82% of the population is under the age of 24 years and the working age population makes it a significant chunk of population[1].

Rising urbanization, an increase in nuclear families, changing consumer tastes and preferences, increased food experimentation, awareness of and access to market offerings, and an increase in the proportion of women in the workforce all contributed to the post-millennial era's transformation of India's population and family structure.

1.1 Relevance of Cloud Kitchen

Cloud Kitchen operates on the hub-and-spoke model. Food is delivered to the outlets (the spokes) from a sizable central kitchen (the hub), where it is then served to the proper customers. A cloud kitchen is a restaurant that only serves takeaway.

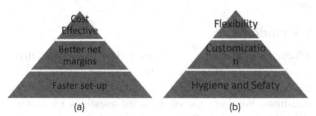

| (a) | (b) |

Fig. 6.1   (a) Benefit of supply side (b) Benefit of demand side

1.2 Growth of Indian Cloud Kitchen Market

In India, the $15 billion meal delivery market is currently rising significantly. There has been a nearly 150 percent increase in the online food delivery system since 2018. Of the $300 million market for internet meal delivery services, $200 million goes toward cloud kitchens. The market for internet food delivery will bring in $8,167 million in 2019. From 2019 to 2023, the online delivery market's revenue is projected to grow at a 9.1% CAGR[2].

As with any revolutionary idea, there can be difficulties and issues to work through, such as maintaining food quality during delivery, effectively managing various brands, and navigating the market. How these challenges are handled and solved may also affect how well stakeholders embrace a solution.

1.3 Essential Traits of Cloud Kitchens

Reference sources published in the Restaurant Times "Know About Cloud & Delivery Kitchens" https://www.posist.com/restauranttimes/resources/cloud-kitchen-delivery-kitchen.html[5]several essential traits are required.

Some essential trails of cloud kitchens are required as per below summary: -

a) **Dining in with multiple brands:** Cloud kitchens are delivery-only businesses; consumers cannot eat there. Online orders: meal is delivered to customers' doorsteps after they make orders through meal delivery apps, websites, or other online platforms. Under one roof, cloud kitchens frequently house several virtual restaurant businesses. the requirement for separate physical locations is not required, a single kitchen can cook a variety of foods or even different restaurant designs.

b) **Cost effectiveness with Flexibility and Scalability:** Cloud kitchens can dramatically lower overhead expenses by replacing conventional restaurant setup. They don't need expensive infrastructure for customers. To run their businesses more efficiently, cloud kitchens frequently use data and analytics. To increase customer satisfaction and expedite production, they may identify popular dishes, peak ordering periods, and other information.

Cloud kitchens give restaurant operators and food entrepreneurs a more flexible way to try new ideas and increase their product offers without major upfront costs.

c) **More opportunity to try new ideas:** The advantages that cloud kitchens gave restaurant owners and entrepreneurs led to a number of them accepting the idea. For individuals seeking to grow their business without taking on the risk of launching a conventional brick-and-mortar restaurant, the cheaper start-up costs, lower overhead, and flexibility to experiment with various virtual restaurant brands appealed. Cloud kitchens were accepted broadly by food delivery platforms since they gave their clients more culinary options. Delivery platforms might broaden their selection and serve a larger consumer base by housing several virtual restaurant brands in a single location. It's crucial to keep in mind, though, that views and acceptance among stakeholders can differ depending on factors including region, market saturation, and general openness to innovative business models. Venture capitalists and investors were interested in the idea of cloud kitchens. Cloud kitchens were a desirable investment due to their potential for cost reductions, scalability, and the rising popularity of food delivery services [4].

1.4 Top Requirements that Stakeholders have for Cloud Kitchens

a) **Food Quality and Consistency:** The size of the household has a significant impact on purchasing power. Worldwide, there is a tendency toward more single-person homes, particularly in India, where growth of this kind will be increasing by 128% between 2000 and 2030. While there are no appreciable differences in the amount spent on food orders by single (88.3%) and married (89.3%) consumers, the percentage for married parents is relatively high (98.1%) [3]. Quality of the food is the most important factor. Customers, investors, and delivery platforms are just a few of the stakeholders who want cloud kitchens to provide consistently excellent meals. Building a loyal customer base requires maintaining the same standard of presentation and taste over orders.

b) **Food Safety and Hygiene Practices:** It is crucial to ensure food safety and follow stringent hygiene standards. Customers in particular demand that their food be cooked in a sanitary and secure setting to reduce the danger of foodborne illnesses. Order administration, data analytics, and delivery planning are all largely reliant on technology in cloud kitchens. Platforms with user-friendly interfaces, smooth integration with well-known delivery apps, and insightful data that helps to optimize operations are valued by stakeholders. Because customers value variety, stakeholders want cloud kitchens to provide a menu that takes into account a variety of tastes and dietary requirements. This can be accomplished by having several virtual restaurant brands using the same kitchen.

c) **Communication transparency:** It's crucial for customers, restaurant owners, and cloud cooking and delivery systems to communicate effectively with one another. Stakeholders like openness on order progress, delivery schedules, and any possible delays. As environmental concerns are becoming more widely recognized, stakeholders may favour cloud kitchens that employ sustainable practices. This can involve using environmentally friendly packaging, cutting back on waste, and obtaining materials ethically. Restaurant owners and investors want cloud kitchens to be commercially successful and provide a

respectable return on their investments. Effective cost control, pricing tactics, and scalability all play a role in the model's overall performance and appeal. The fundamental factors influencing the development of cloud kitchens in the post-COVID era are discussed in depth in this research. The consequences on their position in the worldwide market are also examined in this study, with any substantial changes in market share being highlighted. The study also reveals the key factors that buyers use to decide whether or not to buy food online. These observations should give us a full understanding of how the food industry is developing, how consumers behave when ordering from Cloud Kitchen through an online platform and whether or not Cloud Kitchen cuisine is more hygienic than home-cooked food.

2. RESEARCH METHODOLOGY

It is a self-directed study whereas sampling techniques are used is non-Probability sampling method in which research go with the" Purposive sampling" or we can say the "Judgemental Sampling". In the Indian context, trustworthy market research studies from a number of sources are used to compile qualitative assessments. As per the questionnaire set for the sampling is the Categorical based whereas we asked for the education background, profession, manage any order from Cloud kitchen or not, customers placing the orders more after covid or before etc.

2.1 Findings

When evaluating non-numerical (quantitative) components, no properties of numbers are present. Close-ended questions are what we're using for the survey's questions. We don't use open-ended questions for making the Cloud Kitchen Survey. Close-ended questions are ones in which the experts present options from which the participants must select their responses in their overview questions. However, open-ended questions are those to which a simple "yes" or "no" cannot be the answer. These questions are expressed as a clarification that calls for a suitable response. Below is the Questionnaire which was circulated to collect responses from different consumers:

1. Name
2. Age
2. Gender
3. What is your profession?
4. Have you heard about the Cloud Kitchen or Ghost Kitchen?
5. Did you make any order from the Cloud Kitchen?

6. Have you placed any Food order from Cloud Kitchen before Covid or after Covid?

7. When would you prefer to make an order from the Cloud Kitchen?

8. Do you think Food from the Cloud Kitchen is more Hygienic than conventional Kitchen?

9. Does the Food from the Cloud Kitchen is comparable to Home cooked food?

10. Have you heard of any Cloud Kitchen locations close to your location? Please provide the name and address of that Cloud Kitchen.

11. Which Online Platform for food ordering (app) would you prefer?

12. How much amount do you prefer spending on your Online food ordering in a single month?

13. How many orders do you place in a single month?

14. Would you prefer ordering from any recognized Cloud Kitchen brand only?

On the basis of these Questionnaires, we conducted a survey in which we selected a sample of about 100 people from a large population that ranges from age bracket of (18 to 40 above) and consist of different qualifications in order to establish a relationship between different variables affecting the Cloud Kitchen advertising appeal and Consumers purchase intention in India. Additionally, this sample includes a mix of male and female respondents who have purchased food from Cloud Kitchen. This study explains how many characteristics and factors influence consumers' intentions to buy from Cloud Kitchen. To address this, we have developed the below Hypothesis theory: -

H0: There is no significant relationship since more food orders are put online following the COVID 19 pandemic.

H0: There is no significant relationship between gender and purchase intention of Cloud Kitchen food by consumers.

Using these hypothesis different tests will be performed according to the type of variables and conclusion will be established.

2.2 Research Limitations/Implications

Due to a lack of time, lack of broad network data, we were only able to collect up to 100 samples for the survey for this report.

Future research could think about asking for consumer input to better understand how eating patterns would change in a post-pandemic scenario.

2.3 Huge Support by Smart Network & Gadgets

India has over 859 million people by 2023, according to market intelligence firms' projections (PwC-ASSOCHAM,

2018). It's fascinating that the 97% of Internet consumers in India use phones specially smartphones to access the web (Mumbai Bureau, 2019).By the middle of 2020, India's digital revolution would have entered a new stage as rural Internet users would have surpassed urban ones (Mishra and Chanchani, 2020).

3. ANALYSIS

The study's intended sample size was 56 participants. To gather replies, well-crafted questionnaires in the form of Google Forms were distributed to a variety of sectors or companies including the food and service, automotive, IT and college student sectors.

3.1 Demographic Characteristics of the Respondents

A. Age Distribution of the Respondents

The above Table 6.1. A represents the age distribution of the respondents. It is found that majority of the respondents, i.e., 36.8% of the respondents belong to age group of 31-40years, 29.8% of 17 the respondents belong to age group 18-25 years, 17.5% belong to age group of above 40 years and 15.8% belong to age group 26-30 years.

Table 6.1 A: Age distribution of the respondents

Age (in Years)	No. of Respondent	Percentage
18-25 Years	17	29.8%
26-30 Years	09	15.8%
31-40 Years	21	36.8%
Above 40 Years	10	17.5%
TOTAL	57	100%

Source: Survey, N=57 Respondents

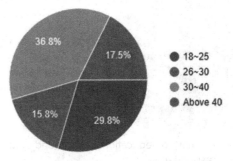

Fig. 6.2 Pi chart of age distribution of the respondents

B. Gender Distribution of the Respondents

The gender breakdown of the respondents is seen in Table 6.2 above. Male participants represent 77.2% of the total participants, while female participants make up 22.8%.

Table 6.2 Gender distribution of the respondents

Age (in Years)	No. of Respondent	Percentage
Male	44	77.2%
Female	13	22.8%
Other	0	0%
Total	**57**	**100%**

Source: Survey, N=57 Respondents

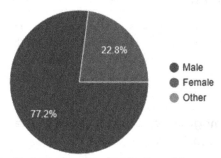

Fig. 6.3 Pi chart of gender distribution of the respondents

C. Education Background Data of the Respondents

The educational background information for the respondents is shown in Table 6.3 above. The majority of respondents 27 or 47.4% are graduate students followed by 22 respondents who are postgraduate students and account for around 38.6% of the total.

Table 6.3 Education background data of the respondents

Education Background	No. of Respondent	Percentage
Higher Secondary	04	7.0%
Graduate	27	47.4%
Post Graduate	22	38.6%
Other than PG	04	7.0%
TOTAL	57	100%

Source: Survey, N=57 Respondents

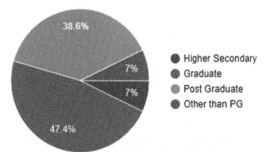

Fig. 6.4 Pi chart of education background data of the respondents

D. Find out the Significant Relationship since more Food Orders are Put Online Following the Covid 19 Pandemic

Table 6.4 above displays the ordering of Cloud kitchen before Covid vs. after Covid responders.

Table 6.4 Placing order from cloud kitchen before Covid and after Covid respondents

Order placed Background	No. of Respondent	Percentage
Before Covid	06	10.5%
After Covid	21	36.8%
Not Yet Placed Any Order	30	52.6%
Total	57	100%

Source: Survey, N=57 Respondents

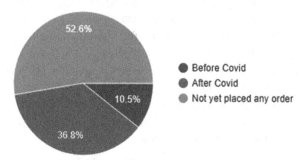

Fig. 6.5 Pi chart of placing order from cloud kitchen before Covid and after Covid respondents

The majority of respondents 21 or 36.8% placed their orders for food after Covid, followed by 6 or 10.5% of those who did order before Covid and 30 or 52.6% of those who haven't yet done so.

3.2 Analysis of Objective

The response to all of the information gathered for the study is divided into five degrees of agreement using the scale shown in Table 6.5 above: Strongly Agree, Neutral, Disagree, and Strongly Disagree. Any response that includes the option Strongly Agree is categorized as level 1. Similar to this, the number for "agree" is 2, then "neutral" is 3, then "disagree" is 4, and lastly "strongly disagree" is 5.

Table 6.5 A: Scale

S No.	Scale
1	Strongly Agree
2	Agree
3	Neutral
4	Disagree
5	Strongly Disagree

Chi Square Test for further Analysis: -

The statistical significance of the difference between the two categorical variable groups is assessed using a Chi square. When constructing the null and alternative hypotheses with regard to both variables, we additionally consider the p-value to demonstrate its significance.

Before doing a Chi square test, a null hypothesis and an alternative hypothesis must be constructed. A test was used to examine the significance of the following null hypotheses.

3.3 Since More Food Orders are Being Placed Online as a Result of the COVID 19 Pandemic, Is there a Link Between the Two?

Null Hypothesis:

H0: There is no significant relationship since more food orders are put online following the COVID 19 pandemic.

Alternative Hypothesis:

Ha: There is statistical significant relationship between more food orders are put online following the COVID 19 pandemic.

Row Labels	Count of Have you placed any Food order from Cloud Kitchen before Covid or after Covid?
After Covid	21
Before Covid	6
Not yet placed any order	30
Grand Total	57

		Frequency data					
	BC	AC	NY				
Actual	21	6	30				
Expected	19	19	19				

k	3
df	3

Test Statistic

χ^2 | 15.474

p-value | 0.0015

Fig. 6.6 Chi square test compare the meal orders before and after the Covid

As we can see from the data above, the Chi Square test has used for compare the meal orders before and after the covid toward simulation-based learning. Therefore, 0.0015 is the significance p-value between the given variables. As p-value for above hypotheses is less than 0.05, so the null hypothesis is rejected (False and have relationship). Hence, we can say that there is significant relationship between more food orders are put online following the COVID 19 pandemic.

3.4 Is there a Relationship between Consumers' Intentions to Purchase Cloud Kitchen Meals and Their Gender?

Null Hypothesis:

H0: There is no significant relationship between gender and purchase intention of Cloud Kitchen food by consumers.

Alternative Hypothesis:

Ha: There is statistical significant relationship between the gender and purchase intension of Cloud kitchen food by consumers.

Row Labels	Count of Did you make any order from the Cloud Kitchen?
Female	13
Male	44
Grand Total	57

		Frequency data					
	F	M					
Actual	13	44					
Expected	29	29					

k	2
df	3

Test Statistic

χ^2 | 16.586

p-value | 0.0009

Fig. 6.7 Chi square test for compare between gender and purchase

As we can see from the data above, the Chi Square test had used for compare the relationship between gender and purchase intention of Cloud Kitchen food by consumers. The Gender and the purchase intension of Cloud kitchen food simulated by the Chi square test. Therefore, the significance the p-value is 0.0009 between the given variables. As p-value for above hypotheses is less than 0.05, so the null hypothesis is rejected (False and have relationship).

Hence, we can say that there is significant relationship between the gender and purchase intension of Cloud kitchen food by consumers.

4. FINDINGS

4.1 Research Design and Methodology Overview

Based on first-hand information collected from respondents at BML Munjal University with a range of educational backgrounds, as well as from a range of industries or businesses, including the food and service, automotive, IT, and college student sectors. This research is descriptive in nature. With the guidance of the Chirag Sir and dependable factors and items chosen from previously published library articles, a standardized questionnaire was developed to collect data. The data is collected using a simple random method.

4.2 An Overview of the Conclusions from the Data Gathered for the Objective is as Follows

According to our research, educational background significantly affects attitudes, awareness, and perceptions of simulation-based learning, particularly when it comes to comprehending the analysis of categorical data using the Chi square test.

Our study's findings lead us to the conclusion that eating habits have a big impact on attitudes toward, awareness of, and perceptions of simulation-based learning, as well as how food is ordered following Covid.

5. LIMITATIONS

This research has several limitations just like any other study or articles. We made every effort to ensure that there were no errors at every stage of this research, from examining the literature to developing the survey's questions to collecting and analysing the data to eventually drawing the appropriate conclusions. We encountered the following restrictions when conducting our research: -

1. The sample size we were able to collect was just 57 numbers, which is insufficient to validate descriptive and statistical results. A larger sample size is required for statistical tests to ensure that the sample is truly representative of the population. We were limited to using the institution as our primary point of contact.

2. Another limitation is that we did not ask the respondent what program they used to solve the simulation.

3. There is no guarantee that the responses provided by the respondents are accurate; some responses may be biased as many respondents may not be very familiar with Cloud Kitchen and his line of business.

4. The final but not least limitation is that we have less time as a working professional which left us with insufficient time to cover all of the course content and various perspectives on simulation-based learning.

6. CONCLUSION

Virtual reality technology offered consumers a more realistic simulation tool experience in addition to a way to evaluate various scenarios. Simulators were developed with the intention of standardizing the education sector, notably in higher education, telecom, and I.T. sectors, as new technologies arose as instruments for problem-solving after new Internet technological transition. Following

COVID, consumers' top priorities have changed from price to cleanliness and safety. Those who want to limit their exposure to the public while still enjoying restaurant-quality food have a reassuring choice in Cloud Kitchens, which were created with streamlined operations and rigorous adherence to health and safety rules.

Although simulation has been used for some time in the technological domains, it has developed more in the business and economics sectors. Students pick up the principles being taught more quickly, efficiently, and in a way that will be useful in everyday life.

■ REFERENCES ■

1. Kishore Thomas John (2021,15 July),"Disruption: the hyperlocal delivery and cloud kitchen driven future of food services in post-COVID India". https//www.emerald.com/insight/2516-8142.htm

2. Nita Choudhury (2019,25 Sept) "Strategic Analysis of Cloud Kitchen-A Case Study". https://www.researchgate.net/publication/336419009

3. SanjuktaPookulangara (2022, 28 Sept), "Consumer attitudes toward ordering from cloud kitchens: a gender and marital status perspective".https://www.emerald.com/insight/0959-6119.htm

4. Claudio Nigro and EnricaIannuzz (2022, 26 Oct) "Food delivery, ghost kitchens and virtual restaurants: temporary or long-lasting game changers?:https://www.emerald.com/insight/0007-070X.htm

5. https://www.posist.com/restauranttimes/resources/cloud-kitchen-delivery-kitchen.html

6. BRM_Division-1_Group-8

7. https://www.emerald.com/insight/2516-8142.htm

8. https://www.emerald.com/insight/0959-6119.htm

9. https://economictimes.indiatimes.com/tech/technology/food-delivery-platforms-see-tepid-demand-in-first-half-of-india-pak-match/articleshow/104428911.cms

10. https://www.thehindu.com/news/national/rise-of-cloud-kitchen-concept-in-india/article34787157.ece

Note: All the figures and tables in this chapter were made by the author

Revitalizing Innovation in Education as per NEP 2020

7

K K Pandey*

Librarian,
NNM Deemed University, MoC; GoI,
Nalanda, Bihar

Abstract

Highlights special features of India that is Bharat. Defines innovation and states its importance in education. Describes research and innovation in the higher education system in India based on New Education Policy 2020. Enumerates some examples of innovation in education. Discusses about establishment of the National Research Foundation (NRF) to enable a culture of research in the country through suitable incentives for and recognition of outstanding research and establishment of the Higher Education Commission of India (HECI) to ensure the distinct functions of regulation, accreditation, funding, and academic standard setting.

Keywords

Higher education, Innovation, New education policy 2020

India is a vast country. Unity in diversity is its unique feature. It is one of the oldest civilizations in the world with rich and diverse cultural heritage. Like cultural heritage of India, Indians are being inherited their education including science, technology and medical educations from their ancient ancestors. There were several world famous ancient higher education institutions in India such as *Nalanda, Takshasila, Vallabhi, Vikramasila, Ujjain* etc. They set the highest standards of multidisciplinary teaching and research and hosted scholars and students from across backgrounds and countries. The Indian education system produced great scholars such as *Charaka, Susruta, Aryabhata, Varahamihira, Bhaskaracharya, Brahmagupta,* *Chanakya, Chakrapani Datta, Madhava, Panini, Patanjali, Nagarjuna, Gautama, Pingala, Sankardev, Maitreyi, Gargi and Thiruvalluvar,* among numerous others, who made seminal contributions to world knowledge in diverse fields such as mathematics, astronomy, metallurgy, medical science and surgery, civil engineering, architecture, shipbuilding and navigation, yoga, fine arts, chess, and more. Indian culture and philosophy have had a strong influence on the world. These rich legacies to world heritage must not only be nurtured and preserved for posterity but also researched, enhanced, and put to new uses through our education system. The teacher must be at the centre of the fundamental reforms in the education

*Corresponding author: kkpandey65@gmail.com

DOI: 10.1201/9781003606260-7

system. Actually, India that is Bharat has rightly been considered *'Vishva Guru'* in ancient past. It has achieved all round socio- economic progress since independence in 1947. As the 7th largest country in the world, India stands apart from the rest of the Asia. Higher education is the most powerful tool to build a knowledge-based society. But today higher education is faced with many challenges. One of them is maintenance of quality of education & research leading to innovation skill. Improvement in the quality of teachers, students, course contents and infrastructures are essential. New Education Policy 2020 describes in detail about all these issues. NEP 2020 is built on the foundational pillars of *Access, Equity, Quality, Affordability and Accountability.* The Policy envisages that the curriculum and pedagogy of our institutions must develop among the students a deep sense of respect towards the Fundamental Duties and Constitutional values, bonding with one's country, and a conscious awareness of one's roles and responsibilities in a changing world. The new education policy must help re-establish teachers, at all levels, as the most respected and essential members of our society, because they truly shape our next generation of citizens. It must do everything to empower teachers and help them to do their job as effectively as possible. The new education policy must help recruit the very best and brightest to enter the teaching profession at all levels, by ensuring livelihood, respect, dignity, and autonomy, while also instilling in the system basic methods of quality control and accountability. It insists on that Higher Education must form the basis for knowledge creation and innovation thereby contributing to a growing national economy. One of the fundamental principles of NEP 2020 for guiding the education system is the nurturance of creativity and critical thinking in learners to harbour innovation. Innovation in education is increasingly important for the success of learners. Traditional educational models are not sufficient to prepare students for the challenges they'll face in the future. In order to prepare students with the skills needed to succeed at university and beyond, schools need to be hubs of innovation. Innovative educators are exploring new approaches to teaching and learning that can help students develop critical thinking, problem-solving, and collaboration skills. Innovation in education comes from identifying problems, watching and learning from others, to develop new methods to address these problems, and iterating on them when these experiments don't necessarily give the expected results. To innovate means to make changes or do something a new way. To innovate does not require one to invent. Innovation gives emphasis on creativity and adaptability. Innovation in education isn't a specific term with fixed definitions. The spirit of innovation in education is an openness to look

with fresh eyes at problems and to address them in new different ways. It is a recognition that we don't have all the answers and are open to new approaches to improve such as methods of knowledge transfer with innovative teaching strategies. Innovation in education, actually, refers to the development and implementation of new ideas, methods and technologies that enhance the learning experience and improve educational outcomes. It includes everything from new teaching techniques and curriculum design to the use of digital tools and online resources. The goal of innovation in education is to make learning more individualized, engaging, and effective for students at all levels. By embracing innovation in education, educators can create more dynamic and effective learning environments that help students develop the knowledge, skills, and competencies they need to succeed in rapidly changing world of today. With the speed at which technology is developing now, there are plenty of examples of innovation in education. Some of these include:

- **Project-Based Learning (PBL)** – This approach helps students identify a real-world problem and develop a solution for it. Including PBL in lessons can have a big impact on developing a number of vital skills such as creative thinking, problem-solving, and teamwork.

- **Blended learning (BL)** – This came about with the explosion of online platforms such a Blackboard and has been adopted by schools and universities worldwide. Blended learning combines online learning with traditional classroom learning. The benefits of such an approach mean students experience both ways of learning – in a physical classroom setting, and a more flexible online setting. The online aspects mean they are able to develop and use the tools that they'll find common in the workplace while they begin their professional careers.

- **Educational Technology (EdTech)** – It typically refers to any software, application or service developed to enhance education. Innovative classroom technologies often mirror the innovations outside of education. So, the more students engage with technologies in the classroom, the better prepared they will be to engage with and through technology in the workplace.

- **Artificial intelligence (AI)** – The latest development in education, as in many other sectors, is the use of artificial intelligence (AI). While it is still in its infancy, in the education setting, it is already being used to revolutionise numerous aspects including grading, plagiarism detection, recommending individual learner paths, and more.

Aims and objectives of New Education Policy is to embrace change, innovation, and technological disruption and to ensure the students are best prepared to enter the world of work with the skills necessary to succeed in their life and mission. Regular visits from guest speakers and leaders in industry may also be ensured to present to students about the latest updates in various sectors, helping them to be aware of the latest trends. Knowledge creation and research are critical in growing and sustaining a large and vibrant economy, uplifting society, and continuously inspiring a nation to achieve even greater heights. Despite this critical importance of research, the research and innovation investment in India is, at the current time, only 0.69% of GDP as compared to 2.8% in the United States of America, 4.3% in Israel and 4.2% in South Korea. In addition to their value in solutions to societal problems, any country's identity, upliftment, spiritual/intellectual satisfaction and creativity is also attained in a major way through its history, art, language, and culture. Research in the arts and humanities, along with innovations in the sciences and social sciences, are, therefore, extremely important for the progress and enlightened nature of a nation. Research and innovation at education institutions in India, particularly those that are engaged in higher education, is critical. Evidence from the world's best universities throughout history shows that the best teaching and learning processes at the higher education level occur in environments where there is also a strong culture of research and knowledge creation; conversely, much of the very best research in the world has occurred in multidisciplinary university settings. India has a long historical tradition of research and knowledge creation, in disciplines ranging from science and mathematics to art and literature to phonetics and languages to medicine and agriculture. This needs to be further strengthened to make India lead research and innovation as per the National Education Policy 2020. Thus, this Policy envisions a comprehensive approach to transforming the quality and quantity of research in India. This includes definitive shifts in school education to a more play and discovery-based style of learning with emphasis on the scientific method and critical thinking. This includes career counselling in schools towards identifying student interests and talents, promoting research in universities, the multidisciplinary nature of all HEIs and the emphasis on holistic education, the inclusion of research and internships in the undergraduate curriculum, faculty career management systems that give due weightage to research, and the governance and regulatory changes that encourage an environment of research and innovation. All of these aspects are extremely critical for developing a research mindset in the country. In order to build on these elements in a synergistic manner and thereby to grow and catalyse quality research in the nation, the new education policy envisions the establishment of a National Research

Foundation (NRF) with the goal to enable a culture of research to permeate through our universities. In particular, the NRF will provide a reliable base of merit-based but equitable peer-reviewed research funding, helping to develop a culture of research in the country through suitable incentives for and recognition of outstanding research, and by undertaking major initiatives to seed and grow research at State Universities and other public institutions where research capability is currently limited. The NRF will competitively fund research in all disciplines. Successful research will be recognized, and where relevant, implemented through close linkages with governmental agencies as well as with industry and private/philanthropic organizations. Institutions that currently fund research at some level, such as the Department of Science and Technology (DST), Department of Atomic Energy (DAE), Department of Bio-Technology (DBT), Indian Council of Agriculture Research (ICAR), Indian Council of Medical Research (ICMR), Indian Council of Historical Research (ICHR), and University Grants Commission (UGC), as well as various private and philanthropic organizations, will continue to independently fund research according to their priorities and needs. However, NRF will carefully coordinate with other funding agencies and will work with science, engineering, and other academies to ensure synergy of purpose and avoid duplication of efforts. The NRF will be governed, independently of the government, by a rotating Board of Governors consisting of the very best researchers and innovators across fields. The functioning of all the independent verticals for Regulation (NHERC), Accreditation (NAC), Funding (HEGC), and Academic Standard Setting (GEC) under the overarching autonomous umbrella body (HECI) will be based on transparent public disclosure, and use technology extensively to reduce human interface to ensure efficiency and transparency in their work. The underlying principle will be that of a faceless and transparent regulatory intervention using technology. Strict compliance measures with stringent action, including penalties for false disclosure of mandated information, will be ensured so that Higher Education Institutions are conforming to the basic minimum norms and standards. HECI itself will be resolving disputes among the four verticals. Each vertical in HECI will be an independent body consisting of persons having high expertise in the relevant areas along with integrity, commitment, and a demonstrated track record of public service. HECI itself will be a small, independent body of eminent public-spirited experts in higher education, which will oversee and monitor the integrity and effective functioning of HECI. Suitable mechanisms will be created within HECI to carry out its functions, including adjudication **Thus, it may be concluded that, New Education Policy of India**

is designed to reform and equalize education standards according to today's need. The vision of the Policy is to instil among the learners a deep-rooted pride in being Indian, not only in thought, but also in spirit, intellect, and deeds, as well as to develop knowledge, skills, values, and dispositions that support responsible commitment to human rights, sustainable development and living, and global well-being, thereby reflecting a truly global citizen. This policy envisions an education system rooted in Indian ethos that contributes directly to transforming India, that is Bharat, sustainably into an equitable and vibrant knowledge society, by providing high-quality education to all, and thereby making India a global knowledge superpower on the basis of fundamental research and creative innovation.

■ REFERENCES ■

1. https://www.education.gov.in/sites/upload_files/mhrd/files/NEP_Final_English_0.pdf
2. https://theglobalcollege.com/blog/what-is-innovation-in-education/
3. https://www.unicef.org/education/strengthening-education-systems-innovation
4. https://standtogether.org/news/innovation-in-education/
5. https://corp.kaltura.com/blog/what-is-innovation-in-education/

Convection-Reaction Flow in a Square Enclosure Filled with Porous Medium—A Review

8

Sunil Kumar Singh*
Research Scholar, GLA University, Mathura

Abhishek Kumar Sharma
Assistant Professor,
BN College, Patna University, Bihar

Archana Dixit
Associate Professor, GLA University, Mathura

Abstract

This paper provides a literature review of the double-diffusive convection-reaction of a binary mixture in a square enclosure filled with a porous media, with constant temperatures and concentrations at the two vertical walls and adiabatic and impermeable horizontal walls. The boundaries of the enclosure are under chemical equilibrium. The porous medium is assumed to be in local thermal equilibrium (LTE) state and the solubility of the dissolved salts depends on temperature. The two dimensional steady-state flow rate is determined by a non-Darcy (Darcy–Brinkman) model, and the entire governing equations are solved using the usual SIMPLE-R finite-volume methodology. It has been found that as the reaction rate increases in the system the salt precipitation also increases, causing a decrease in overall mass transfer rate. Also, the chemical reaction tends to decrease the overall heat transfer-rate.

Keywords

Darcy–brinkman model, Double-diffusive convection-reaction, Simple-R algorithm, Porous medium, Heat and mass transfer

1. INTRODUCTION

A double-diffusive convection flow in a porous medium is a highly complicated process where both temperature and dissolved solute affect the buoyancy of underlying fluid. It is characterized by the different rates of diffusion of heat and solute in the system (Phillips, 1991). The double-diffusive convection in a fluid-saturated porous medium has been studied widely by many researchers across the globe as it has applications in geological processes, i.e., soil salinization (Gilman and Bear, 1994; Wooding et al., 1997), heat transfer in geothermal reservoirs (Oldenburg and Pruess, 1998), petroleum engineering, marine sciences, contaminant transport in saturated soil, underground

*Corresponding author: jmisunil@gmail.com

DOI: 10.1201/9781003606260-8

disposal of nuclear wastes, liquid reinjection, the migration of moisture in fibrous insulation, electro-chemical processes, and many other industrial applications (Nield and Bejan, 2013; Vafai, 2000; Mamou et al., 1996; Mamou and Vasseur, 1999; Phanikumar and Mahajan, 2002). The thermal field diffuses rapidly as compared to the solute field. They may contribute in the same sense or in the opposite sense to the buoyancy gradient. Some interesting studies have been conducted to study the double-diffusive flow of a binary mixture (Griffiths, 1981; Khan and Zebib, 1981; Mamou and Vasseur, 1999); where both thermal and solutal buoyant forces influence the flow dynamics. Nield and Bejan (2013) and Vafai (2000) evaluate all of the considerable volume of work in this field. A host of researchers have conducted studies on convection in porous enclosure where the side walls are maintained at constant temperature and concentration (Trevisan and Bejan, 1985; Goyeau et al., 1996; Nithiarasu et al., 1996; Angirasa et al., 1997; Karimi-Fard et al., 1997; Bera et al., 1998; Bennacer et al., 2001; Chamkha, 2002; Sankar et al., 2012). Trevisan and Bejan (1985), after having conducted a parametric study of double-diffusive flow in a square enclosure, found that the heat transfer is minimum at buoyancy ratio N = 1 for the set of fluid they had considered in their study. A numerical study by Angirasa et al. (1997) has confirmed the scale analysis result obtained by Trevisan and Bejan (1985) which is then extended by Bennacer et al. (2001) by considering an anisotropic medium. Similar observations were also made by other researchers using different models (Angirasa et al., 1997; Nithiarasu et al., 1996; Bera et al., 1998). The heat and mass transfer rates are determined by the fluid's thermal diffusivity to solutal diffusivity (Lewis number, Le) and other corresponding parameters. Sankar et al. (2012) have found that the heat-transfer rate and mass transfer rate attain their minimum at different values of buoyancy ratio N when Le = 5. In the presence of a discrete heat and solute source in a vertical porous annulus. Chamkha (2002) has studied the cooperating temperature and concentration gradients and heat generation or absorption effects to understand the impact of temperature-dependent heat source or sink on the double-diffusive flow in a porous enclosure. A significant effect of heat generation (source) or absorption (sink) on the flow rate is observed. It is found that the point of minimum for heat and solute transfer rate is N = 1 when Le = 1.

In many geological systems, the solute is not conserved due to its varying solubility. The solubility of solute in general depends on temperature, pressure, and the chemical composition of porous matrix. When the solute gets dissolved or precipitated onto the porous matrix then the buoyancy of the fluid and its vertical circulation gets affected in the porous medium. This can also happen due to

chemical reactions on the surface of porous matrix. When a reactive binary fluid is made to flow through a porous medium certain reactions can occur in the resulting double-diffusive convection flow influencing the dissolution and precipitation of dissolved solute (Pritchard and Richardson, 2007; Gatica et al., 1989; Malashetty and Biradar, 2011; Raffensperger and Garven, 1995a,b). Pritchard and Richardson (2007) have determined that the precipitation and dissolution of the mineral may have a substantial impact on the stability of the conductive base state and the convection patterns that ensue. Malashetty and Biradar (2011) have studied the effect of increasing the Damkohler number and found that it advances the onset of stationary convection and delays the onset of oscillatory and finite amplitude convection. Gatica et al. (1989) and Viljoen et al. (1990) considered exothermic-reaction term and concentrated on the limiting case where the Lewis number Le = 1, so that the thermal and solutal diffusion rates are identical. This study aims to address the effect of chemical reaction on thermosolutal convection in a two-dimensional porous enclosure as it has received relatively little attention. We will consider reaction-convection in a square porous enclosure, where the vertical walls are maintained at different constant temperatures and concentrations. The thermal contribution of the reaction is neglected and chemical equilibrium is assumed on the bounding surfaces. Some important applications relevant to the present geometry are heat transfer in geothermal reservoir, cleaning and drying processes, liquid-gas storage; solidification, oxidation, and crystal growth in materials processing. We will not confine ourselves to particular regimes of the Lewis number, buoyancy ratio, or reaction rate; instead, we will investigate more thoroughly how the reaction-convection affects the dynamics of considered double-diffusive flow. To the best of our knowledge, no one has examined double-diffusive reaction-convection flow in an enclosure under local thermal equilibrium (LTE). The specific goal of this paper is to comprehend the combined buoyancy effects under LTE conditions on the physics of the previously discussed problem. The plan of our paper is as following: Section 2 describes the mathematical formulation and the governing equations, whereas Section 3 shows the numerical technique of solution. In Section 4 we have discussed the results and findings. Finally, conclusions and some remarksare reported in Section 5.

2. RELATED WORK

Double-Diffusive Convection in Slender Anisotropic Porous Enclosures: This article reports an analytical solution for steady natural convection in a slender rectangular porous cavity with hydrodynamic, thermal, and solute anisotropy, and uniform flux of heat and mass on the vertical sides. The principal directions of the permeability, thermal diffusivity, and solute diffusivity tensors are taken independently oblique to the gravity vector. The assumptions inherent in the derivation of the analytical solution are validated by comparison with numerical solutions. A thermal non-equilibrium approach on double-diffusive natural convection in a square porous-medium cavity: In this manuscript the influence of local thermal non-equilibrium state on double-diffusive natural convection in a square cavity filled with fluid-saturated porous medium has been addressed numerically. The two dimensional steady state flow is induced due to maintenance of constant temperature and concentration on the vertical walls and insulation of both horizontal walls of the cavity. Non-Darcy (Darcy–Brinkman–Forchheimer) model has been taken and the complete governing equations are solved by standard SIMPLER algorithm. A comparative study of the effect of the presence of Brinkman term in the momentum equation showed that results under the Darcy model are very close to those for the non-Darcy Brinkman model for relatively low permeable medium. Natural convection in a square cavity filled with ananisotropic porous medium due to sinusoidal heat flux on horizontal walls: In this article, a comprehensive numerical investigation of the natural convection in a hydro-dynamically as well as thermally anisotropic porous enclosure with insulated side walls is presented. The two different cases, (I) same heat flux on the top as well as bottom walls and (II) heat flux on the top wall being negative of the heat flux on the bottom wall, are considered. A non-Darcy model that includes Darcy and Brinkman terms have been adopted and the coupled governing equations are solved numerically by SIMPLER algorithm. A thermal non-equilibrium approach for 2D natural convection due to lateral heat flux: Square as well as slender enclosure: This paper reports the influence of local thermal non-equilibrium state between solid porous matrix and saturated fluid on natural convection in enclosure. The two dimensional steady flow is induced by constant heat flux on side walls of the enclosure, when both horizontal walls are insulated. The governing equations are solved numerically by ADI method and analytically by using parallel flow assumption valid for slender enclosure. A comparative study has been made between convection in square cavity and the same in slender enclosure. Numerical experiments indicate that in comparison with square cavity, where a sharp decrease of local heat transfer rate for fluid (Nuf) takes place up to a certain small value of interface heat transfer coefficient (H), in slender enclosure a smooth decrease of Nuf has been observed in the entire range of H when conductivity ratio (c) is very small. However, for relatively high values of c (e.g., c = 10), Nuf is almost independent of H in both geometries. For a given c, when

the value of H is relatively very high, up to a certain value of Ra the difference between both solid as well as fluid temperature rates is negligible. Natural Convection in an Anisotropic Porous Enclosure Due to Nonuniform Heating From the Bottom Wall: A comprehensive numerical investigation on the natural convection in a hydrodynamically anisotropic porous enclosure is presented. The flow is due to nonuniformly heated bottom wall and maintenance of constant temperature at cold vertical walls along with adiabatic top wall. Brinkman-extended non-Darcy model, including material derivative, is considered. The principal direction of the permeability tensor has been taken oblique to the gravity vector. The spectral element method has been adopted to solve numerically the governing conservative equations of mass, momentum, and energy by using a streamfunction vorticity formulation. Influence of periodicity of sinusoidal bottom boundary condition on natural convection in porous enclosure In this paper, natural convective flow within a rectangular enclosure has been investigated numerically. All the walls of the enclosure are adiabatic except the bottom wall, which is partially heated and cooled by sinusoidal temperature profile. Both situations: medium is hydro-dynamically isotropic and anisotropic are considered. The governing equations are written under assumption of Brinkman-extended non-Darcy model, including material derivative, and then solved by numerically using spectral element method (SEM). Main emphasize is given on effect of periodicity parameter (N) on local heat transfer rate (Nux) as well as flow mechanism in the enclosure.

3. METHODOLOGY

Involved in Convection-reaction flow in a square enclosure filled with porous medium We have reviewed numerous articles to examine the distinct method to solve numerically.

Table 8.1 Summarized description of methodology involved in convection-reaction flow in a square enclosure filled with porous medium

S. No.	Authors Name	Method
1	P. Bera, Sarita Pippal, Abhishek K. Sharma	SIMPLE-Revised (Semi-Implicit Method for Pressure Linked Equations) algorithm
2	Harish Chandra, P. Bera & Abhishek K. Sharma	Standard SIMPLE Revised (Semi-Implicit Method for Pressure Linked Equations)
3	Sarita Pippal, P. Bera	Alternate direction implicit method (ADI)
4	Ashok Kumar P. Bera	Spectral element method (SEM)
5	P.Bera, V. Eswaran, P. Singh	Spectral element method (SEM)

Source: Author

4. CONCLUSION

This paper presents a literature review of The problem of double-diffusive reaction-convective flow of binary mixtures inside a square porous enclosure with different but fixed temperature and concentration at the vertical walls in the presence of chemical reaction was studied numerically using the SIMPLER algorithm. The results for streamline, temperature, and concentration contours and representative velocity, temperature, and concentration profiles at the midsection of the enclosure for various sets of parameters were presented and thoroughly discussed. The present results show the effect of contribution of the chemical reaction to buoyancy in the system. It was found that the rate of heat transfer, mass transfer, and the flow characteristics depended strongly on the product of Rayleigh and Darcy numbers ($Ra' = RaDa$) and chemical reaction parameter, i.e., Damkohler number (k). The effect of increasing the Damkohler number k is to decrease the maximum value of stream function. One effect of reaction is to increase the rate of mass transfer in the porous enclosure. It is found that the effect of buoyancy ratio N is to either increase or decrease the intensity of the flow depending on the value of N. In addition, it was concluded that the average Nusselt number decreased and Sherwood number increased as a result of chemical reaction. The thermosolutal reaction-convection system discussed here offers several options for more theoretical investigation. Consideration of additional boundary conditions at the upper and lower surfaces, such as heat-flux conditions.

■ REFERENCES ■

1. Angirasa, D., Peterson, G.P., and Pop, I., Combined Heat and Mass Transfer by Natural Convection with Opposing Buoyancy Effects in a Fluid Saturated Porous Medium, Int. J. Heat Mass Transf., vol. 40, pp. 2755–2773, 1997.

2. Bennacer, R., Tobbal, A., Beji, H., and Vasseur, P., Double Diffusive Convection in a Vertical Enclosure Filled with Anisotropic Porous Media, Int. J. Therm. Sci., vol. 40, pp. 30–41, 2001.

3. Bera, P., Eswaran, V., and Singh, P., Numerical Study of Heat and Mass Transfer in an Anisotropic Porous Enclosure Due to Constant Heating and Cooling, Numer. Heat Transf., Part A., vol. 34, pp. 887–905, 1998.

4. Chamkha, A.J., Double Diffusive Convection in Porous Enclosure with Co-Operating Temperature and Concentration Gradients and Heat Generation or Absorption Effects, Numer. Heat Transf., Part A, vol. 41, pp. 65–87, 2002.

5. Gatica, J.E., Viljoen, H.J., and Hlavacek, V., Interaction between Chemical Reaction and Natural Convection in Porous Media, Chem. Eng. Sci., vol. 44, pp. 18–53, 1989.

6. Gilman, A. and Bear, J., The Influence of Free Convection on Soil Salinization in Arid Regions, Transp. Porous Media, vol. 23, pp. 275–301, 1994.

7. Goyeau, B., Songbe, J.P., and Gobin, D., Numerical Study of Double-Diffusive Natural Convection in a Porous Cavity Using the Darcy–Brinkman Formulation, Int. J. Heat Mass Transf., vol. 39, pp. 1363–1378, 1996.

8. Griffiths, R.W., Layered Double-Diffusive Convection in Porous Media, J. Fluid Mech., vol. 102, pp. 221–248, 1981.

9. Karimi-Fard, M., Charrier-Mojtabi, M.C., and Vafai, K., Non-Darcian Effects on Double Diffusive Convection within a Porous Medium, Numer. Heat Transf., Part A, vol. 31, pp. 837–852, 1997.

10. Khan, A.A. and Zebib, Z., Double Diffusive Instability in a Vertical Layer of Porous Medium, ASME J. Heat Transf., vol. 103, pp. 179–181, 1981.

11. Malashetty, M.S. and Biradar, B.S., The Onset of Double Diffusive Reaction-Convection in an Anisotropic Porous Layer, Phys. Fluids, vol. 23, p. 064102, 2011.

12. Mamou, M. and Vasseur, P., Thermosolutal Bifurcation Phenomena in Porous Enclosures Subject to Vertical Temperature and Concentration Gradients, J. Fluid Mech., vol. 395, pp. 61–87, 1999.

13. Mamou, M., Vasseur, P., and Bilgen, E., Analytical and Numerical Study of Double Diffusive Convection in Vertical Enclosure, Int. J. Heat Mass Transf., vol. 32, pp. 115–125, 1996.

14. Nield, D.A. and Bejan, A., Convection in Porous Media, New York: Springer-Verlag, 2013. Nithiarasu, P., Seetharamu, K.N., and Sundararajan, T., Double-Diffusive Natural Convection in an Enclosure Filled with FluidSaturated Porous Medium: A Generalized Non-Darcy Approach, Numer. Heat Transf., Part A, vol. 30, pp. 413–426, 1996.

15. Oldenburg, C.M. and Pruess, K., Layered Thermohaline Convection in Hypersaline Geothermal Systems, Transp. Porous Media, vol. 33, pp. 29–63, 1998.

16. Patankar, S.V., Numerical Heat Transfer and Fluid Flow, Washington, DC: Hemisphere Publishing Corporation, 1980.

17. Phanikumar, M.S. and Mahajan, R.L., Non-Darcy Natural Convection in High Porosity Metal Foams, Int. J. Heat Mass Transf., vol. 45, pp. 3781–3793, 2002.

18. Phillips, O.M., Flow and Reactions in Permeable Rocks, Cambridge, UK: Cambridge University Press, 1991.

19. Pritchard, D. and Richardson, C.N., The Effect of Temperature-Dependent Solubility on the Onset of Thermosolutal Convection in a Horizontal Porous Layer, J. Fluid Mech., vol. 571, pp. 59–95, 2007.

20. Raffensperger, J.P. and Garven, G., The Formation of Unconformity-Type Uranium Ore Deposits. 1. Coupled Groundwater Flow and Heat Transport Modelling, Am. J. Sci., vol. 295, pp. 581–636, 1995.

21. Raffensperger, J.P. and Garven, G., The Formation of Unconformity-Type Uranium Ore Deposits. 2. Coupled Hydrochemical Modelling, Am. J. Sci., vol. 295, pp. 639–696, 1995.

22. Sankar, M., Kim, B., Lopez, J.M., and Do, Y., Thermosolutal Convection from a Discrete Heat and Solute Source in a Vertical Porous Annulus, Int. J. Heat Mass Transf., vol. 55, pp. 4116–4128, 2012.

23. Trevisan, O.V. and Bejan, A., Natural Convection with Combined Heat and Mass Transfer Buoyancy Effects in Porous Medium, Int. J. Heat Mass Transf., vol. 28, pp. 1597–1611, 1985. Vafai, K., Handbook of Porous Media, New York: Marcel Dekker, 2000.

24. Viljoen, H.J., Gatica, J.E., and Hlavacek, V., Bifurcation Analysis of Chemically Driven Convection, Chem. Eng. Sci., vol. 45, pp. 503–517, 1990.

25. Wooding, R.A., Tyler, S.W., and White, I., Convection in Groundwater below an Evaporating Salt Lake: 1. Onset of Instability, Water Resour. Res., vol. 33, pp. 1199–1217, 1997

Challenges and Opportunities for Innovation in India – Dr. Shweta Mishra et al. (eds)
© 2024 Taylor & Francis Group, London, ISBN 978-1-032-99842-8

Enhancement of Heat Transfer through Fins 9

Chandra Kr. Dubey[1], Vandana Pathak[2]
Assistant Professor,
Department of Mechanical Engineering,
Ambalika Institute of Management and Technology,
Lucknow

Madhur Prakash Srivastava[3]
Ambalika Institute of Management and Technology,
Lucknow

Abstract

Various industries nowadays use extended surfaces, better known as fins, to increase the heat transfer rate wherever required. Fins are easy to construct and provide more effective heat transfer when used. The heat transfer through fins depends upon several parameters that are obtained from several experiments by different researchers. Factors such as the number of fins, geometry and spacing, fin thickness and material to be used, and the environment of an application decide the overall functionality of the fins. Moreover, surface operations such as perforations can further increase the fin effectiveness by substantially increasing the heat transfer rate. Also, along with actually reducing the weight of an individual fin, this can increase the surface area engaged in the heat transfer process without having to alter its dimensions. So, in this paper, various parameters have been discussed that are responsible for the enhancement of the overall performance of the fins.

Keywords

Heat transfer, Effectiveness, Perforations, Geometry, Fins

1. INTRODUCTION

Generally in engines, boilers, transformers, air-conditioners, radiators, and several other engineering equipments in industries, a tremendous amount of heat is generated during the conversion of energy from one form to the other, which is said to be heat loss. If the health of the machine is taken into concern, the heat generated might become a vulnerable aspect for the machine. As a result, either the machine will have its breakdown or stops working due to overheating issues. It became necessary to stop the overheating phenomena as it was becoming hazardous for the industry itself, keeping the equipment's performance on the line. In order to bring the temperature

---
[1]ckd96niec@gmail.com, [2]vp9415809167@gmail.com, [3]madhurprakashsrivastava@gmail.com

DOI: 10.1201/9781003606260-9

down of engineering equipment, there are generally two ways, either by reducing the loss of energy (thermal energy) or by releasing the waste thermal energy in the open atmosphere. Since the reduction was not possible in excess and the temperature was still high, the engineers came up with the concept of extended surfaces, which are now called fins. Fins are extended surfaces that are used to increase the rate of heat transfer from a solid surface to a surrounding fluid (air), which are attached externally over the periphery of the heat transfer equipment. There are two ways for enhancing the heat transfer rate known as active and passive methods. Active methods are more complex compared to the passive methods as they require some extrinsic power input in order to improve the heat transfer rate and thus its applications are limited in the present scenario. On the other hand for improving the heat transfer rate via passive methods, which require geometrical or surface modifications. Fins belong to the passive methods of increasing the heat transfer rate [1].

1.1 How Does the Fin Work?

Heat transfer through fins is done by combination of two basic modes of heat transfer, conduction and convection. Though heat transfer through radiation is not dominant since it requires a temperature difference more than 10^4 °C which can easily melt the fin material if ever achieved. Hence it plays a less dominant role in the process. Firstly, the heat gets conducted into the fin from the base wall to its root where the heat gets conducted further by the mechanism of lattice vibrations throughout the fin material along its length. While the heat gets conducted along the fin, it is simultaneously convected from the surface area exposed to the atmosphere.

$$Qfin = \sqrt{(hPKA)} \tanh(ml) (Tb-T\infty) \qquad (i)$$

In the above equation (i), 'Q' is the heat transfer rate through fin, 'h' is the convective heat transfer coefficient, 'P' is the perimeter of the cross-section of the fin, 'K' is the thermal conductivity of the material, 'A' is the cross-section area, 'l' is the length of fin, 'Tb' is the temperature of the base wall, 'T∞' is the temperature of the ambient atmosphere, 'm' is a constant whose value is given by the expression $\sqrt{(hP/KA)}$. If value of 'm' increases then the there is a high drop of temperature from the base wall to the tip of fin, hence fin will be much more effective in that case.

1.2 Effectiveness of Fin

Effectiveness of fin is defined as the ratio of heat transfer rate using fin to the heat transfer rate without fin. It depends upon various parameters such as thermal conductivity of fin material (K) should be high, spacing between the fins should

be less, thickness should be low and the length of the fin should be moderately short. Above are the predetermined factor which are used to increase the effectiveness of the fin some other factors such as perforations, quantity of perforations, geometry of fin, geometry of perforations also plays a vital role in enhancing the performance of the fin arrangement

2. LITERATURE REVIEW

Fin Material Pankaj Rao et al. In the case of improving the performance of the overall fin arrangement, fins made up of aluminum or its alloy will have the upper hand as compare to other fins made up of copper, brass, mild steel etc. It has arbitrated the parameters regarding the circular fin using different materials such as mild steel, brass, and aluminum both in natural as well as forced convection. In natural convection, the aluminum fin has less heat transfer coefficient, less Nusselt number, and has high efficiency than brass and mild steel fin. In forced convection, the aluminum fin has a high heat transfer coefficient, high Nusselt number, and high efficiency compared to brass and mild steel fin. If comparing the efficiency between natural convection and forced convection for a particular material, the efficiency in the case of forced convection is lesser than in natural convection [2]. An alloy of aluminum, copper, manganese and magnesium, known as 'duralumin' might prove as a great asset in the process. Duralumin possesses more thermal conductivity (approx. 160 W m^{-1} K^{-1}) as compare to mild steel and stainless steel, hence it becomes much more performative than stainless steel, both having similar geometrical parameters [3].

2.1 Fin Spacing and Notches

G.P. Lohar et al. In order to improve the heat transfer rate spacing between the fins must be improved or optimized since fin's height and its spacing can have a major effect on heat transfer rate. It should be kept in mind that the heat transfer coefficient can be enhanced by even providing narrow spacing between the fins [6].

Yazicioglu, B. et al. If the spacing between the fins is kept fixed then there is a bland increase of the heat transfer rate along with the fin height and the temperature difference between the base wall and the ambient fluid. But in the case of smaller fin spacing keeping the temperature difference fixed between the base wall and surrounding fluid, the heat transfer rate experiences a sharp increment with fin height. As there are high number of fins present in the fin arrangement with smaller fin spacing, hence the increase in the height of the fin leads to large surface area and also a greater amount of convective heat transfer rate [7].

In the formula

$$\frac{S_{\text{opt}}}{L} = 3.94 Ra_L^{-1/4}$$

Where

s_{opt} = Optimal fin spacing (in meters).
Ra = Rayleigh number
L = Fin Length (in meters)

By the above formula it become possible to find optimum fin spacing in the fin arrangement [7].

Shebab et. al. If the fin have notches then it will provide a better performance as compare to the un-notched one as it has higher heat transfer coefficient when compared to the un-notched fin. Also, there is a increment in the value of average heat transfer coefficient as the removed area of fin increases that is about 20% [9].

2.2 Geometry of Fin

Sandhya Mirapalli et. al. On changing the length of fin keeping the base temperature constant, the heat dissipation rate in the case of the triangular fin is more as compared to the rectangular fin. The effectiveness of the triangular fin is the best if compared with the rectangular fin. The triangular fin has more efficiency than the rectangular fin. As base temperature changes for a particular length of fin, the rectangular fin gives better efficiency than the triangular fin. The rectangular fin is also more effective than the triangular fin [17].

Devendra J. Waghulde et. al. With changing the thickness of the fin, there is variation in temperature distribution along the fin. The temperature distribution is less in the case of a fin having a thickness of less than 2.5mm and it is maximum for the fin having thickness greater than 3mm. If comparing the geometry of fins keeping the thickness of the fin constant, the heat dissipation is maximum in triangular fins then in rectangular fins, and least in circular fins [20].

2.3 Perforations

Raaid R. Jassem. at a particular heat transfer rate through fin, the lowest temperature distribution is in triangular perforation and the highest in circular perforation. The RAF value (It is the ratio of the surface area of the perforated fin to the non-perforated fin) is maximum for triangular perforated fin and minimum for circular perforations. The heat transfer rate also depends on the dimension of perforation and lateral spacing. If the dimension of perforation decreases, the rate of temperature drop along the length of the perforated fin decreases. Heat transfer coefficient also plays a major role in increasing

heat transfer through fins. The heat transfer coefficient for perforated fins containing many perforations is higher than for fins with a small number of perforations. If comparing the geometry of perforations regarding heat transfer coefficient, the heat transfer coefficient is maximum for triangular perforations and is minimum for rectangular perforations [18].

Chandra Kr. Dubey et. al. The temperature drop between the base and tip of the fin increases with the percentage of perforation. The heat dissipation rate also depends on the shape of the perforation as well as the perforation dimension. The advantage of increasing the number of perforations is not limited to increasing heat dissipation but they also help in decreasing the weight of fins. In the case of elliptical perforation (a/b>3) maximum temperature drop was 32.2% and the Maximum average heat flux i.e. 68.42% more than fin without perforation was found. The elliptical-shaped perforation gives the best result [19].

Awarasamol and Pise. Since the perforations can be made up of different sizes as per requirement. It has seen that the fin which has been perforated with perforations sized 12mm and have 45 ° angle of orientation or inclination, it results in remarkable increase of about 31% of heat transfer rate and while decreasing the weight of material by 30%[21].

3. INCLINATIONS

Sometimes for a better heat transfer rate in the devices with a change in orientation or compact size, fins are adjusted in their orientation as well, like providing some inclination to the fins instead of keeping them vertical or horizontal.

Fujii and Imura, It was observed that for both, a horizontal plate carrying heat as well as that with a small inclination, the Nusselt number and Ra number both were related, with the Nusselt number being proportional to the one-fifth power of Ra number [22].

Mittelman et. al., Illustrated a considerable increment in the overall heat transfer rate when the fin arrangement was kept tilted at and beyond a certain angle, or as advised by the researcher, more than 10° [11].

Khudheyer and Hasan, On experimentally studying the rectangular fins with different figures such as interrupted and inclined fins which under natural convection heat transfer, concluded that the heat transfer coefficient of the interrupted fins was of a higher impact to heat transfer rate when compared to that of the inclined fins [12].

Naidu et. al., Further, the impact of inclination of an arrangement of fins on heat transfer rate, as experimented by was seen in the form of an increase in convective heat transfer rate with a further increase in the inclination angle for a particular tested limits [13].

Lee et. al., To study and observe the electronic devices that use tilted fins for cooling applications, resulting in the fact that an inclination angle of 60° of the fins showed 6% higher cooling performance when compared with solid rectangular fins. Furthermore, a significant 9.2 times downfall was experienced in the cooling performance when no fin at all was used [14].

Degao et. al., Noticed that there was no notable reduction in the convection heat transfer rate by the inclination of rectangular fins of vertical cross section [16].

4. Conclusions

1. Fins are in most cases are used under the influence of natural convection. There is a direct impact on the heat transfer rate due to fin height and fin spacing. Fin spacing which is sufficiently narrow can easily enhance the heat transfer coefficient and hence performance, in which duralumin (an alloy of aluminum), might be a perfect material example for applications, which have the property to increase the heat transfer rate as well as the strength of the arrangement.

2. A rectangular notched fin has higher potential to enhance the heat transfer rate as compare to the other notch geometries. If the material selected as aluminum for the production of fins with notches there is a growth up to 20% in the value of heat transfer coefficient.

3. Perforations play a major role in order to enhance the heat transfer rate by increasing the area of expose of the fin. If the shape of the perforations is made circular then there is a increase of 16.7 % in heat transfer rate. For triangle shape perforations the heat transfer rate is maximum. Less fin with more perforations will show improved performance as compare to large quantity of fin with less perforations.

4. Fins arrangement which are inclined at an angle like 30°, 45° ,60° or 90° etc. in which the rectangular fin arrangement at 60° shows a 6% more cooling performance as compared to the regular arrangement. In order to have an enhanced heat transfer rate it has been suggested that the inclination angle must be greater than 10°

■ REFERENCES ■

1. Ambarish Maji, Gautam Choubey, Improvement of heat transfer through fins: A brief review of recent developments, DOI: 10.1002/htj.21684

2. Experimental Analysis on Pin Fin Heat Exchanger using Different Circular Fin Material Mr. Pankaj Rao Prof. Anand Prakash Rakecha, ISSN (online): 2321–0613

3. Ko, Y. M., Leung, C. W. & Probert, S. D. (1989). Steady-state free convective cooling of heat exchangers with vertical rectangular fins: Effect of Fin Material. Alied Energy, 34, 181–191.

4. Babus'Hag, F. R., Probert,F. S. & Taylor, R. C. (1993). Heat transfer effectiveness's of shrouded. rectangular fin arrays, Alied Energy, 46, 99–112.

5. G.P. Lohar and Dr. S.G. Taji , Experimental Investigation for Optimizing Fin Spacing in Horizontal Rectangular Fin Array for Maximizing the Heat Transfer under a Natural and Forced Convection (2014), ISSN: 2278–0181.

6. Starner, K. E. & McManus, JR.H.N. (1963). An experimental investigation of free convection heat transfer from rectangular fin arrays. Journal of Heat Transfer, Series C,85, 273–278.

7. Yazicioglu, B. & Yüncü, H. (2007). Optimum fin spacing of rectangular fins on a vertical base in free convection heat transfer. Heat and Mass Transfer, 44, 11–21

8. Dogan, M. & Sivrioglu, M. (2009). Experimental investigation of mixed convection heat transfer from longitudinal fins in a horizontal rectangular channel: in natural convection dominated flow regimes. Energy Conversion and Management, 50, 2513–2521

9. Shebab, S. N. (2017). Experimental study of free-convection from rectangular fins array on a heated horizontal plate with notch effect. AlNahrain Journal for Engineering Sciences, 20(1), 140–148.

10. Umesh V. Awasarmol, Ashok T. Pise, An experimental investigation of natural convection heat transfer enhancement from perforated rectangular fins array at different inclinations, Experimental Thermal and Fluid Science 68 (2015) 145–154.

11. Mittelman, G., Dayan, A., Turjeman, K. D. & Ullmann, A. (2007). Laminar free convection underneath a downward facing inclined hot fin array. International Journal of Heat and Mass Transfer, 50(13-14), 2582–2589.

12. Khudheyer, A. F. & Hasan, Z. H. (2015). Effect of the fin's configuration on natural convection heat transfer experimentally and numerically. International Journal of Energy and Environment, 6(6), 607–628.

13. Naidu, S. V., Shorma, K. V., Rao, B. G., Sombabu, A. & Sreenivasulu, B. (2010). Natural convection heat transfer from fin arrays-experimental and theoretical study on effect of inclination of base on heat transfer. Journal of Engineering and Alied Sciences, 5(9), 7–15

14. Rocha, A. D. & Ganzarolli, M. M. (2005). Natural convection in an arbitrary inclined plate with protruding heated elements, 18th International Conference of Mechanical Engineering, Brazil.

15. Lee, J. B., Kim, H. J. & Kim, D. K. (2017). Thermal optimization of horizontal tubes with tilted rectangular fins under free convection for the cooling of electronic devices. Alied Sciences, 7(4), 352.

16. Degao, H., Xiaofeng, X. & Qian, J. (2020). Analysis of natural convection heat transfer from vertical and inclined plate fin heat sinks. Proceedings of the Seventh Asia International Symposium on Mechatronics, 479–487.

17. Heat Transfer Analysis on a Triangular Fin, Sandhya Mirapalli, International Journal of Engineering Trends and Technology (IJETT) – Volume 19 Number 5 – Jan 2015.

18. Effect The Form Of Perforation On The Heat Transfer In The Perforated Fins, Raaid R. Jassem, ISSN-L: 2223–9553, ISSN: 2223-9944, Vol. 4 No. 3 May 2013.

19. Effect Of Perforation Shapes On The Heat Transfer Characteristic Of Perforated Fins, Chandra Kumar Dubey, Anand Kumar Singh, Shailendra Sinha, International Journal of Recent Technology and Engineering (IJRTE), ISSN: 2277-3878, Volume-8 Issue-4, November 2019.

20. Effect of Fin Thickness and Geometry on Engine Cylinder Fins, Devendra J. Waghulde, Prof. V H Patil, Prof. T. A. Koli. e-ISSN: 2395–0056, p-ISSN: 2395–0072.

21. Awasarmol, U. V. & Pise, A. T. (2015). An experimental investigation of natural convection heat transfer enhancement from perforated rectangular fin arrays at different inclinations. Experimental Thermal and Fluid Science, 68, 145–154.

22. Fujii, T. & Imura, H.(1972). Natural-convection heat transfers from a plate with arbitrary inclination. International Journal of Heat and Mass Transfer, 15 (4), 755–764

Challenges and Opportunities for Innovation in India – Dr. Shweta Mishra et al. (eds)
© 2024 Taylor & Francis Group, London, ISBN 978-1-032-99842-8

An Introduction of Game Theory using Its Application

10

Puneet Shukla*, Vipul Srivastava, Suresh Maithani
Department of Applied Sciences,
Ambalika Institute of Management & Technology,
Lucknow

Abstract

The research paper describes the basic concepts of "Game Theory "by using the historical background of game theory. This topic focuses on the appropriate definition of relevant terms that will be used to this theory like a game, nash equilibrium, and dominance which form the basis of the theory concept. This concept also covers mixed strategies, extensive games with both perfect and imperfect information, auction bidding, and their relevant practical application of the concept as applied in the field of economics.

Keywords

Game theory, Zero-sum game, Nash equilibrium, Economics

1. LITERATURE REVIEW

This theory has been of great importance in various fields, especially those of social sciences dating back to more than fifty years ago. It first looked into zero-sum games where one person's gains are equal to the losses of the other player [1]. Game theory may be defined as a decision-making process in formal studies where various players make choices that directly or indirectly affect the other players' interests. The first application of the game theory was during the study duopoly by Cournt back in the year 1838. Other scholars like Camerer highlight the application of game theory in 1713 through a letter from James Waldegrave [2]. John Neumann, through his study of the theory of polar games, puts to the spotlight the application of this theory in the 20th century. Neumann, together with other neo-classical economists, brought with them a fresh way of looking into the theory as a competitive process with economic players applying strategic interactions. The first published material on game theory was authored by John Forbes Nash in his thesis in 1949. The thesis was entitled 'Non-Cooperative Games,' where he introduced the widely used phenomenon of Nash Equilibrium or equilibrium point [1], [2]. Nash Equilibrium is noted to be a concept based on the principle where strategy combinations the players are most likely to choose represents one that none of the other players could do better if they chose other different strategy keeping in mind the strategy choice of the others. Game theory is commonly used in economics, psychology, biology, and political science. Its application is majorly in

---

*Corresponding author: puneetshkl78@gmail.com

DOI: 10.1201/9781003606260-10

studies of competitive scenes. As such, the stated problems are referred to as games while the participants are referred to as the players. A player may be defined as a person, or a group of persons that are involved in the decision-making process as Osborne describes it [2]. Camerer adds on this definition and outlines specific assumptions stating that all players form beliefs with their basis on the actions of others, make the best response concerning the made beliefs, and finally adjust these responses until a point of equilibrium is achieved or until the beliefs are equal. He also notes that these assumptions are sometimes undermined and violated in the sense that some players tend to behave irrationally as the situation gets di cult [3]. The basic and most fundamental assumption that encourages game theory is that players are rational and have strategically reasoned. Players are also believed to be aware of the various alternatives available, and their choice of action is mostly after an optimization process. Osborne views game in the light of the strategic interaction including all constraints on the player actions that may be taken by a player taking into consideration the interests of such a player but does not de ne the actions the decision-makers could take. Although most descriptions show a game as a situation involving at least two players, there exists one player game referred to as a decision problem [3]. It is important to note that the players could be individuals, firms, nations, or a combination of any of these. Game theory could be summarized as a language enabling structure formulation, analysis, and strategic scenario understanding. With numerous possible strategies to choose, games follow a sequence of moves where individual moves are considered crucial due to their contribution to the overall strategy [4]. A perfect example, as Pindyck and Rubinfeld states, is a situation where firms compete alongside each other through the setting of prices or a situation of auction bidding by a group of consumers.

2. GAME THEORY

Game theory is best applied in circumstances where various agents are interdependent [4]. This section mainly focuses on game theory with great emphasis on the dominance, Nash equilibrium, mixed strategies, max-min strategies, and extensive games, both with perfect and imperfect information, bidding in auctions, computation, and lastly, zero-sum games.

2.1 Games Definition

Since the major purpose of this study of game theory is the game, decision-makers involved are arranged according to their information, preferences, strategic actions availed to these players, and their respective influence on the outcome. By description, a game only specifies the payoffs of each player or group of players may achieve with its various member arrangement [5]. Game theory can be broken down into two broad categories, namely non-cooperative and cooperative game theory, with the distinction of these categories being whether the decisionmakers are in a position to communicate with each other or not. Non-cooperative game theory majorly looks into choices emanating from economic interactions among decision-makers. Every player independently and strategically makes choices intending to maximize their utility [6]. This simply means that players explicitly have their interests at heart without considering the interest of any other party. This model of noncooperative game theory, the timing of players' choices, and the details of orders are of utmost importance while determining the outcome of the game. Concepts such as Nash Equilibrium are applicable in solving non-cooperative games. The concept, as described by Lim, may be used both in the Normal and strategic form and only gives a solution in circumstances where each decision-maker tends to earn maximum payoff considering strategies applied by the other players. Unlike non-cooperative game theory, which majorly dwells on scenarios with competition, cooperative game theory applies analytical tools in the study of the behavior of rational players in the event where they cooperate [6]. Mainly, these games describe the formation of cooperating groups of decision-makers that make better the position of the players in a game. Lim, in this case, views cooperative game theory scenarios as combination payoff sets satisfying group as well as individual rationality [7]. Cooperative game theory is most appropriately applied in events developing from international relations and political science, where the key focus is power.

2.2 Dominance

Assuming that all the players in a game are deemed rational, their made choices must result in their desired outcome given the actions of their opponents. In such a case, the said players are said to have dominant strategies. Dominant strategies refer to the most suitable choice for any player given every choice by the opponent player [7]. Payoffs in a dominant strategy are in such a way that despite the choices made by other players, there be no other strategy with a higher payoff. Dominance in game theory is best brought out in the concept of Prisoner's Dilemma first introduced in the mid-20th century by Tucker. The game, according to Kerk, shows the major tensions with both individuals and group actions and their respective outcomes, which are more likely than not a result of their actions. In the scenario of the prisoner's dilemma, Davis explains it where two criminals thought of committing a crime together after their arrest are taken into different police cells. The police gather enough evidence for their duo conviction unless either party informs on the other party. This means that each party is faced with the option of either confessing or remaining silent, and every party knows the consequence of their action. The police give the two of them the option that if they both agree and confess, they both serve a ten-year jail-term while if only one confesses, he gets one-year jail term and the other twenty- five years. In the case where none of them confesses, then they both face a jail term of 3 years. This scenario narrated by Avinash and Nalebu in 1991 may be best tabulated and summarized as follows [8]

Table 10.1 Prisoner's dilemma

	Admit	Hold out
Prisoner 1	10 years	25 years
Prisoner 2	1 year	3 years

Source: Author

The table shows prisoner one getting a 10-year jail term upon confession and 25 years if he does not. This means that if the second prisoner decides to admit, then the best option is for the first prisoner to confess as well. Conversely, if the second prisoner holds out, the first prisoner's best choice is to confess still to get the minimum time of one year. These decision-makers have dominant strategies where, despite the choice made by other players in the game, none of the other strategies would give a higher payoff. In this case, the optimal solution does not lie in the scenario where both prisoners admit.

2.3 Nash Equilibrium

This is an economics theoretic game solution concept involving two or more players where each decision-maker has ultimate knowledge on the equilibrium strategies of the other players, and there's nothing gain by alteration of individual strategy. Any game may have several Nash equilibriums as described by Myerson, although there may be considered unreliable in comparison to the expected outcome of any game [9]. Several studies show that this equilibrium major concern is the expected choice of actions by players in any game. Decision-makers have to have perfect knowledge of opponents' choices, and for this to be possible, the concept of the rationality of all the players becomes inapplicable. Alternatively, when statistical information of the previous playing circumstance is available and reliable, then the game falls in place perfectly. Another example of the prisoner's dilemma and Nash Equilibrium is in cases of buyer and seller transactions. Buyers, in this case, are seen to only transact once or repeatedly and anonymously with any seller. Each buyer's action is based on their belief in the other party's actions.

2.4 Mixed Strategies

According to Turocy and Von (2001), strategic form games may not necessarily have a Nash equilibrium whereby one of the parties gets to choose one of the strategies. However, decision-makers have to utilize certain probabilities as a basis of their random strategic selection. Simply, this can be described the distribution of probabilities over the specified combination of actions. Alternatively, some scholars viewed this strategy as other players' belief in a specific player's action [10]. A perfect example of the application of mixed strategies is seen in drunk driving. Police officers decided to put up roadblocks with a probability of one third. When an individual drinks Coca Cola he gets zero, with wine consumption the same individual gets -2 with 1/3 probability and 1 with the probability of 2/3, so, In this case, the decision-maker is torn between taking a Cola or Wine, putting all probabilities in mind. With wine consumption with the probability of 1/2, the expected payoff is 1 while he decides not to then; Consequently, the officers are indifferent about whether to set up roadblocks with any mixed strategy. As such, the mixed strategy equilibrium is achieved. This equilibrium discourages players in a strategic game to introduce behavioral randomness since decision-makers are known to randomize events in a bid to influence the opponents' behavior. This emphasizes the absence of Nash equilibrium in mixed strategies. In this view, the mixed strategy is seen to be opportunities for common knowledge since most positive probability actions are deemed most ideal.

2.5 Perfect Information Extensive Games

These games refer to the representation of all moves in any game and are best described in the form of a decision tree. Players in this scenario get to choose their various preferred strategies without any prior knowledge of the other players' choices [11]. However, with time, players may get information about the actions of fellow decision-makers, and hence a scenario of perfect information arises over time as all players become aware of opponents' previous choices. In this form of interaction, only one player moves at a time in a bid to avoid simultaneous movement. Players in this scenario have the opportunity not only to learn the opponent's moves at the beginning but also at any point in the game. There is a restriction in the observation of ongoing game since every player chooses their action plan once and for all, and hence one is unable to reconsider their initial decision on the plan of action.

2.6 Imperfect Information Extensive Games

Since one player's payoff is affected by the action of the other, then the preferred strategy of each player may also be dependent on the other decision-makers. Therefore, these are games that are believed not to be fully observable [12]. A player, in this case, needs not to know the actions of that their fellow players have previously taken in the case of extensive games with imperfect information. According to Gilpin and Sandholm (2007), decisions on the actions to be taken at any given time may not be optimally decided while not considering other decisions at all points in time because such decisions impact immensely on the probabilities of different states at present.

2.7 Zero-sum Games and Computation

This mathematical representation refers to the scenario where a player's utility gain or loss balances with the gains and losses of the competing participant. It is the case whereby upon the summation of all gains and negation of all losses of a certain participant total up to zero, and hence the zero-sum game title [13]. A case of two players with completely conflicting interests demonstrates and extreme case of this game. In this case, one team must win while the other completely lose without any in-betweens and hence a closed system, as stated by the theory by Neumann and Morgenstern. In a mathematical representation of a two-player game, every set of payoffs sums to zero.

2.8 Auction Bidding

One of the greatest accomplishments of game theory is seen in the analysis and design of the auction process. Theory on Auction, which was stipulated by the economist William Vickrey, assisted in auctions generating billions of dollars in mobile telecommunication. The Combination of strategies emanating from a set of decision-makers apply set strategies presented to every individual and come up with a payoff vector enhancing maximum utility and profits. Practically, in auctions, a valuable object is placed where bidders signal their willingness to pay with perfect knowledge of the set rule of assigning the object. The object is assigned to the optimal bidder following the set rules, about which all bidders had perfect information. Von Stengel describes an English auction or an open ascending auction as the situation where an object is put up for sale in the presence of all buyers and price keeps rising as long as there are at least two or more interested bidders [14]. The winning bidder gets the object at the last price at which the last bidder dropped.

3. Application of Game Theory

In economics, game theory is widely applied in areas such as oligopolies, market equilibrium, general equilibrium, auctions, amongst other applications [15]. The major application lies in oligopolistic competition and hence the major concern in this research paper. Oligopoly market

may simply be defined as the scenario where a small group of huge companies in unison acquires control of a large market share well informed on the effects of their nature of correlation on the profits and market shares. Due to this oligopolistic structure, decision-making in this case heavily relies on game theory. A dynamic model in which companies and buyers regularly interact in identical circumstances can be named the best application of game theory. The Below illustration describes a situation where two companies with three strategies achieve their payoff's demonstrating game theory application.

Table 10.2 Prisoner's dilemma

Minimum (mi)	15, 15 5, 21 5, 10
Median (me)	21, 5 12, 12 2, 5
Maximum (ma)	10, 3 5, 2 0, 0

Source: Author

From the above diagram, (mi, mi) (me, me) (ma, ma) combinations may be shown to indicate a monopoly event while (me, me) describes a single-period game Nash Equilibrium.

4. Conclusion

It is evident from this paper that game theory goes beyond mathematical representations to the description of the real world events where decisions made by other players affect other players' interests. Game theory may not be very efficient in the prediction of behavior like in the case of sciences though in some unique cases, it might take up that role as described (Vorob'ev 1994, p. 14). Game theory in this essay is looked at as a conceptual analysis applicable in the decision-making process as well as conflict resolution. Immense emphasis has been put on auction bidding a set of decision-makers achieve a payoff through strict observance of a set of laid out strategies that all players have perfect information about (Vorob'ev 1994, p. 16-17). In an attempt to bridge the gap between theory and real-life situations, game theory is seen being applied in sales and marketing and through observation of people's behavior by the choices they make. Game theory is shown in companies' management strategies where important decisions need to be made. With game theory knowledge, managers can make sound decisions while maximizing industry payoff. This paper also describes the role of Nash equilibrium in describing the concept of the prisoner's dilemma that forms the basis in the illustration of game theory (Owen 2013, p. 31). The only challenge with game theory lies in the tradeoff between realism and solvability in the real world, a problem that the common assumptions of rationality and common knowledge try to smoothen out.

■ REFERENCES ■

1. FUDENBERG, D., & TIROLE, J. (2002). Game theory. Cambridge, Mass, MIT Press.
2. CAMERER, C. F. (2011). Behavioral Game Theory: Experiments in Strategic Interaction. Princeton, Princeton University Press.
3. BINMORE, K. G. (2007). Game theory: a very short introduction. Oxford, Oxford University Press.
4. DRESHER, M., SHAPLEY, L. S., & TUCKER, A. W. (1964). Advances in game theory. Princeton, Princeton U.P.
5. ROMP, G. (1997). Game Theory: Introductions and Applications. Oxford, Oxford University Press.
6. OWEN, G. (2013). Game theory. Fourth edition, Emerald Group Publishing.
7. STRAFFIN, P. D. (2010). Game theory and strategy. ICMECE 2020 IOP Conf. Series: Materials Science and Engineering 993 (2020) 012114 IOP Publishing doi:10.1088/1757-899X/993/1/0121147
8. Avinash, D. & Nalebu , B., 1991. Thinking Strategically. New York: Norton & Co.
9. DAMME, E. V. (1983). Re nements of the Nash equilibrium concept. Berlin, SpringerVerlag
10. HEIFETZ, A. (2012). Game theory: interactive strategies in economics and management. Cambridge, Cambridge Univ. Press
11. ZAGARE, F. C. (1986). Game theory: concepts and applications. Beverly Hills, Sage Publications.
12. RAPOPORT, A., ORWANT, C. J., & CHAMMAH, A. M. (1965). Prisoner's dilemma: a study in con ict and cooperation. Ann Arbor (Mich.), University of Michigan Press.
13. CARMONA, G. (2012). Existence and stability of Nash equilibrium. Singapore, World Scienti c.
14. ICHIISHI, T. (1983). Game theory for economic analysis. First edition, New York: Academic Press.
15. FINK, E. C., GATES, S., & HUMES, B. D. (1998). Games theory topics: incomplete information, repeated games, and N-player games. Thousand Oaks, Sage.
16. VOROB'EV, N. N. (1994). Foundations of Game Theory: Noncooperative Games. Basel, Birkhauser Basel.

Challenges and Opportunities for Innovation in India – Dr. Shweta Mishra et al. (eds)
© 2024 Taylor & Francis Group, London, ISBN 978-1-032-99842-8

Thermophysical Study of Poly (Propylene Glycol) Monobutyl Ether340 (PPG MBE 340) with Toluene, Benzene and Benzyl Alcohol

11

Rahul Singh

Department of Humanities and Applied Sciences,
Ambalika Institute of Management and Technology,
Lucknow, India

Laxmi Kumari

Department of Humanities and Applied Sciences,
School of Management Sciences,
Lucknow, India

Abhishek Mishra, and Manisha Gupta*

Department of Physics, University of Lucknow,
Lucknow, India

Abstract

Binary mixtures of Poly (propylene glycol) monobutyl ether 340 (PPGMBE 340) with toluene, benzene and benzyl alcohol using density, viscosity and refractive index data at varying temperatures and concentrations. The excess molar volume (VmE), deviation in viscosity ($\Delta\eta$) and deviation in molar refraction (ΔRm) and many other derived parameters such as optical dielectric constant (ε), polarizability (α) and interaction parameter (d) at varying concentrations of PPGMBE340 have also been calculated. Results have been analyzed in the light of molecular interactions between like and unlike molecules with respect of their polarities.

Keywords

Molecular interaction, Excess molar volume (VmE), Deviation in viscosity ($\Delta\eta$), deviation in molar refraction (ΔRm), optical dielectric constant (ε)

1. INTRODUCTION

Poly (propylene glycol) monobutyl ether 340 (PPGMBE340) is a unique synthetic polymer, among other polyalkylene glycols having the structure,

*Corresponding author: guptagm@rediffmail.com, laxmi.05.laxmi@gmail.com

DOI: 10.1201/9781003606260-11

PPGMBE340 is inexpensive, biodegradable, insoluble in water [1], and is widely used as lubricant for automobile engine in cold climates [2, 3]. This fluid shows the expected low carbon and low sludge, as well as cleans engine parts and satisfactory cranking at low temperature down to -60°F. PPGMBE340 does not readily crystallize. Instead, it becomes too thick to flow at a temperature known as pour point. The pour point for this polymer is very low (-56°C). Even at temperatures below its pour point, it does not crystallize but forms glass like solid. It is also used as fire-resistant fluid, brake fluid, compressor lubricant, textile lubricant, metalworking fluid, refrigeration lubricant, two-cycle engine lubricant, crankcase lubricant etc. PPGMBE340 is also used as hydraulic fluid, metal working fluid, heat transfer fluid, solder assist fluid, plasticizer and foam control agent. The pendent methyl group on each repeat unit in poly(propylene oxide) led to a lower cohesive energy density and surface tension that reduces the intermolecular interaction between polymer segments, resulting in a higher solubility of poly(propylene oxide) verses poly(ethylene oxide) [4]. The solubility of a PPGMBE340 is determined by its structure. It is a polar molecule and according to solubility rules it should dissolve in polar solvents. The solubility derived from the presence of propylene oxide group in its molecule is responsible for its water insolubility and solubility in nonpolar solvents to some level [5]. In a dilute solution, the properties of polymer are characterized by the interaction between the solvent and the polymer. In a good solvent, the polymer appears swollen and occupies a large volume. When a polymer is added to given solvent, attraction as well as dispersion forces becomes active between its segments, according to their polarity, chemical characteristics and solubility parameters. If the polymer-solvent interactions are higher than its intramolecular attraction forces, the chain segment of the polymer start to entrap solvent molecules, increasing the volume of the polymer matrix and loosening out their coiled shape. A rigorous literature survey reveals that molecular interaction studies on binary liquid mixtures in PPGMBE340 are almost lacking [4]. Seeing the importance of PPGMBE340, in the present study, it is proposed to initiate with the molecular interaction studies on binary mixtures of PPGMBE340 with non-polar aromatic hydrocarbons namely benzene, toluene and a polar aromatic liquid benzyl alcohol at three temperatures 293.15, 303.15 and 313.15 K over the entire range of composition. Density, viscosity and refractive index of these mixtures were experimentally measured at

several mole fractions of PPGMBE340 and thermodynamic properties namely excess molar volume V_m^E, deviation in viscosity $\Delta\eta$ and deviation in molar refraction ΔRm were calculated and fitted to Curve Expert 1.3 linear regression polynomial equation. The results have been discussed in terms of molecular association occurring between the components. Using various semi empirical mixing rules proposed by Lorentz-Lorenz (L-L), Gladstone-Dale (G-D), Wiener (W), Heller (H), Arago-Biot (A-B), Newton (N), Eykman (E) and Oster (O), refractive index was also theoretically calculated. A comparative study has been made between the experimental and theoretical values of refractive index at all the three temperatures and results have been discussed in terms of average percentage deviation (APD).

2. CHEMICALS

Poly(propylene glycol)monobutyl ether 340 (grade analytical standard) was supplied by Sigma-Aldrich Pvt. Ltd. Toluene (mass fraction $\geq$ 0.995) was supplied by Ranbaxy Laboratories Ltd, benzene (mass fraction $\geq$ 0.995) and benzyl alcohol (mass fraction $\geq$ 0.990) were supplied by Qualigens Fine Chemicals, India. All these solvents were stored under moisture free conditions to avoid the alterations of their specifications. The measured density, viscosity and refractive index of pure liquids along with their literature values are given in Table 11.1 and are in good agreement.

3. RESULTS AND DISCUSSION

The values of density, viscosity and refractive index measured for PPGMBE340 + toluene, PPGMBE340 + benzene and PPGMBE340 + benzyl alcohol mixtures over the entire range of compositions at three temperatures, 293.15, 303.15 and 313.15 K are given in Table 11.2. The calculated excess parameters like excess molar volume (V_m^E), deviation in viscosity ($\Delta\eta$) and deviation in molar refraction (ΔR_m) are given in Table 11.3. Table 11.4 displays the values of the Curve Expert 1.3 linear regression polynomial coefficient, ai evaluated by Curve Expert 1.3 software along with their standard deviations. The Table 11.5 shows optical dielectric constant (ε), polarizability (α) and interaction parameter (d) of the systems PPGMBE340 + toluene, PPGMBE340 + benzene and PPGMBE340 + benzyl alcohol. APD of theoretically estimated values of refractive index are listed in Table 11.6

Table 11.1   Density (ρ), viscosity (η) and refractive index (n) of pure liquids at temperatures, (293.15, 303.15, 313.15) K with their literature data

Component	Temp.(K)	Density ρ (gm.cm^{-3})		Viscosity η (cp)		Refractive index n	
		Expt.	Lit.	Expt.	Lit.	Expt.	Lit.
PPGMBE340	293.15	0.9593	–	21.1855	–	1.437	1.44[18]
	303.15	0.9515	–	14.2792	–	1.433	–
	313.15	0.9438	–	9.7252	9.6[18]	1.429	–
Toluene	293.15	0.8668	–	0.6120	–	1.498	–
	303.15	0.8574	0.85754[19] 0.8578[20]	0.5459	0.526[20]	1.492	1.4907[21]
	313.15	0.8484	0.84815[19]	0.5146	0.4662[21]	1.486	1.4837[21]
Benzene	293.15	0.8789	–	0.6440	–	1.501	–
	303.15	0.8682	0.86828[19] 0.8682[22]	0.5626	0.5632[22]	1.494	1.4942[22]
	313.15	0.8581	0.85797[19]	0.5012	0.4991[21]	1.487	1.4886[21]
Benzyl alcohol	293.15	1.0462	–	6.3490	–	1.539	–
	303.15	1.0384	1.0365[22] 1.0371[23]	4.5161	4.5042[22] 4.5250[23]	1.536	1.5188[22] 1.5352[23]
	313.15	1.0313	–	3.4252	–	1.533	–

Table 11.2   Experimental values of density (ρ_m), viscosity (η_m), refractive index (n_m) for the systems, PPGMBE340 + Toluene, PPGMBE340 + Benzene and PPGMBE340 + Benzyl alcohol at 293.15, 30315 and 313.15 K with respect to the mole fraction x_1 of PPGMBE340

x_1	ρ_m (g.cm^{-3})	η_m (cp)	n_m	ρ_m (g.cm^{-3})	η_m (cp)	n_m	ρ_m (g.cm^{-3})	η_m (cp)	n_m
		293.15K			303.15K			313.15K	
				PPGMBE340 + Toluene					
0.0000	0.8668	0.5912	1.497	0.8574	0.5229	1.491	0.8484	0.4656	1.484
0.1000	0.8924	1.2590	1.481	0.8836	1.2157	1.476	0.8751	1.1567	1.470
0.1999	0.9099	1.9671	1.470	0.9014	1.6177	1.465	0.8931	1.3998	1.460
0.3987	0.9318	4.5747	1.457	0.9236	3.6469	1.452	0.9156	2.9292	1.447
0.4998	0.9391	6.3857	1.452	0.9310	4.8809	1.447	0.9231	3.9171	1.442
0.7000	0.9495	11.1892	1.445	0.9416	8.0306	1.441	0.9339	6.0125	1.437
0.7995	0.9533	14.2769	1.442	0.9455	10.0847	1.438	0.9378	7.3323	1.434
1.0000	0.9593	21.1855	1.437	0.9515	14.2792	1.433	0.9438	9.7252	1.429
				PPGMBE340 + Benzene					
0.0000	0.8789	0.6440	1.501	0.8682	0.5626	1.494	0.8581	0.5012	1.487
0.0999	0.9044	1.3311	1.481	0.8947	1.1159	1.475	0.8854	0.9838	1.469
0.1996	0.9204	2.3659	1.468	0.9113	1.8915	1.463	0.9023	1.6090	1.457
0.3993	0.9389	5.3998	1.454	0.9304	4.1370	1.449	0.9222	3.3878	1.444
0.4997	0.9446	7.4116	1.449	0.9363	5.6441	1.445	0.9282	4.3712	1.440
0.6989	0.9524	12.2148	1.443	0.9443	8.6993	1.439	0.9365	6.9243	1.435
0.7997	0.9551	15.0933	1.441	0.9472	10.4602	1.436	0.9394	7.6927	1.432
1.0000	0.9593	21.1855	1.437	0.9515	14.2792	1.433	0.9438	9.7252	1.429

x_1	ρ_m	η_m	n_m	ρ_m	η_m	n_m	ρ_m	η_m	n_m
	(g.cm^{-3})	(cp)		(g.cm^{-3})	(cp)		(g.cm^{-3})	(cp)	
		293.15K			303.15K			313.15K	
				PPGMBE340 + Benzyl alcohol					
0.0000	1.0462	6.3409	1.539	1.0384	4.5161	1.536	1.0313	3.4252	1.533
0.0999	1.0284	9.8835	1.516	1.0206	7.1884	1.511	1.0131	5.3218	1.506
0.2919	1.0027	15.2119	1.483	0.9951	10.6429	1.479	0.988	7.7353	1.474
0.4983	0.9854	18.4084	1.464	0.9775	12.7436	1.459	0.9699	9.0482	1.455
0.5994	0.9769	19.1286	1.448	0.9689	13.1168	1.452	0.9613	9.2941	1.456
0.6990	0.9732	20.0505	1.451	0.9650	13.9241	1.447	0.9571	9.7559	1.443
0.8901	0.9636	20.8891	1.442	0.9552	14.0952	1.438	0.9478	10.0073	1.434
1.0000	0.9593	21.1855	1.437	0.9515	14.2792	1.433	0.9438	9.7252	1.429

Table 11.3 Excess Molar Volume (V_m^E), Viscosity Deviation ($\Delta\eta$) and Molar Refraction Deviation (ΔR_m) for the systems, PPGMBE340 + Toluene, PPGMBE340 + Benzene and PPGMBE340 + Benzyl alcohol at293.15,303.15 and 313.15 K with respect to the mole fraction x_1 of PPGMBE340

x_1	V_m^E	$\Delta\eta$	ΔR_m	V_m^E	$\Delta\eta$	ΔR_m	V_m^E	$\Delta\eta$	ΔR_m
	(cm^3 mol^{-1})	(cp)		(cm^3 mol^{-1})	(cp)		(cm^3 mol^{-1})	(cp)	
		293.15K	303.15K	313.15K					
				PPGMBE340+To uene					
0.0000	0.0000	0.0000	0.0000	0.0000	0.0000	0.0000	0.0000	0.0000	0.0000
0.1000	-0.0874	-1.3916	-10.5103	-0.1219	-0.6828	-10.4578	-0.1541	-0.2349	-10.4359
0.1999	-0.1821	-2.7409	-15.7223	-0.2269	-1.6551	-15.6883	-0.2610	-0.9168	-15.6263
0.3987	-0.2883	-4.2275	-17.8084	-0.3279	-2.3606	-17.8248	-0.3692	-1.2282	-17.8299
0.4998	-0.2832	-4.4985	-16.5437	-0.3170	-2.5174	-16.5889	-0.3585	-1.1765	-16.6288
0.7000	-0.2169	-3.8180	-11.3610	-0.2530	-2.1217	-11.3202	-0.3097	-0.9348	-11.2799
0.7995	-0.1504	-2.7794	-7.9605	-0.1948	-1.4364	-7.9388	-0.2331	-0.5364	-7.9125
1.0000	0.0000	0.0000	0.0000	0.0000	0.0000	0.0000	0.0000	0.0000	0.0000
				PPGMBE340+Benzene					
0.0000	0.0000	0.0000	0.0000	0.0000	0.0000	0.0000	0.0000	0.0000	0.0000
0.0999	-0.1061	-1.3650	-13.8282	-0.1323	-0.8170	-13.7788	-0.1525	-0.4389	-13.7359
0.1996	-0.2174	-2.3782	-20.0485	-0.2595	-1.4089	-19.9641	-0.2618	-0.7333	-19.9519
0.3993	-0.3367	-3.4464	-21.9028	-0.3772	-1.9026	-21.8868	-0.4315	-0.7965	-21.8830
0.4997	-0.3364	-3.4970	-20.1362	-0.3750	-1.7727	-20.0421	-0.4139	-0.7392	-20.0701
0.6989	-0.2705	-2.7857	-13.6620	-0.2789	-1.4498	-13.6037	-0.3319	-0.0236	-13.5600
0.7997	-0.1738	-1.9777	-9.4133	-0.2057	-1.0716	-9.5402	-0.2286	-0.1849	-9.5098
1.0000	0.0000	0.0000	0.0000	0.0000	0.0000	0.0000	0.0000	0.0000	0.0000
				PPGMBE340+Benzylalcohol					
0.0000	0.0000	0.0000	0.0000	0.0000	0.0000	0.0000	0.0000	0.0000	0.0000
0.0999	-0.7687	2.0596	-10.4872	-0.7821	1.6970	-10.5885	-0.7662	1.2672	-10.6912
0.2919	-1.3026	4.5378	-17.7203	-1.3613	3.2769	-17.7515	-1.4503	2.4712	-17.8919
0.4983	-1.4781	4.6704	-16.4930	-1.4809	3.3626	-16.6124	-1.5003	2.4837	-16.6281

x_1	V_m^E	$\Delta\eta$	ΔR_m	V_m^E	$\Delta\eta$	ΔR_m	V_m^E	$\Delta\eta$	ΔR_m
	(cm³ mol⁻¹)	(cp)		(cm³ mol⁻¹)	(cp)		(cm³ mol⁻¹)	(cp)	
		293.15K	303.15K	313.15K					
0.5994	-0.8907	3.8891	-15.2704	-0.8546	2.7482	-14.2164	-0.8728	2.0924	-13.1665
0.6990	-1.2047	3.3332	-11.3485	-1.1100	2.5836	-11.3196	-1.0523	1.9270	-11.3057
0.8901	-0.4340	1.3351	-4.3904	-0.2351	0.8889	-4.3351	-0.3380	0.9745	-4.3608
1.0000	0.0000	0.0000	0.0000	0.0000	0.0000	0.0000	0.0000	0.0000	0.0000

Table 11.4 Coefficients a_i of curve expert 1.3 linear regression polynomial equation for excess parameters and their standard Deviation for the systems PPGMBE340 + Toluene , PPGMBE340 + Benzene and PPGMBE340 + Benzene alcohol at three temperatures

Functions	a_1	a_2	a_3	a_4	a_5	(Y^E)
PPGMBE340 + Toluene						
T=293.15 K						
V_m^E (cm³.mol⁻¹)	0.0022	0.9602	-0.2044	2.6627	-1.5009	0.0067
$\Delta\eta$(cp)	0.0095	-15.0971	4.6043	19.6398	-9.1517	0.0619
ΔR_m	-0.0784	-130.6644	311.3614	-280.9301	100.3344	0.2086
T=303.15 K						
V_m^E (cm³.mol⁻¹)	0.0027	-1.4956	1.8748	-0.3799	-0.0029	0.0083
$\Delta\eta$(cp)	0.0299	-8.5609	1.3117	14.9836	-7.7592	0.1225
ΔR_m	-0.0757	-129.8190	306.5289	-272.8679	96.2541	0.2009
T=313.15 K						
V_m^E (cm³.mol⁻¹)	0.0007	-1.8443	3.0471	-2.1229	0.9196	0.0076
$\Delta\eta$(cp)	0.0452	-4.2814	-1.6378	14.2784	-8.4044	0.1339
ΔR_m	-0.0819	-128.9217	301.8472	-265.3111	92.4866	0.2141
PPGMBE340 + Benzene						
T=293.15 K						
V_m^E (cm³.mol⁻¹)	0.0015	-1.1403	-0.1765	2.9830	-1.6671	0.0090
$\Delta\eta$(cp)	-0.0045	-15.0938	15.4829	3.1895	-3.5707	0.0249
ΔR_m	-0.1492	-172.4886	436.0236	-417.1125	153.7709	0.3936
T=303.15 K						
V_m^E (cm³.mol⁻¹)	0.0031	-1.5712	1.1797	1.3747	-0.9874	0.0082
$\Delta\eta$(cp)	0.0109	-10.2669	18.3727	-12.7059	4.5878	0.0489
ΔR_m	-0.1372	-172.3802	437.5350	-421.5178	156.5344	0.3448
T=313.15 K						
V_m^E (cm³.mol⁻¹)	-0.0009	-1.5224	0.3587	2.7632	-1.5986	0.0134
$\Delta\eta$(cp)	0.0155	-5.9102	11.4574	-3.6242	-1.9567	0.1532
ΔR_m	-0.1334	-171.8478	434.4071	-416.0924	153.6989	0.3371
PPGMBE340 + Benzene alcohol						
T=293.15 K						
V_m^E (cm³.mol⁻¹)	-0.0056	-9.5379	22.7942	-22.5227	9.2882	0.2284
$\Delta\eta$(cp)	-0.0524	26.4539	-43.2401	18.8465	-1.9805	0.1538
ΔR_m	-0.1898	-124.3702	276.5099	-226.1148	74.2906	0.6238

Functions	a_1	a_2	a_3	a_4	a_5	(Y^E)
T=303.15 K						
V_m^E (cm³.mol⁻¹)	-0.0116	-9.1527	18.3793	-12.2965	3.1084	0.2325
$\Delta\eta$(cp)	0.0039	20.5235	-38.8121	25.7250	-7.4693	0.1673
ΔR_m	-0.1438	-128.5535	297.4733	-255.4266	86.7509	0.3165
T=313.15 K						
V_m^E (cm³.mol⁻¹)	0.0140	-10.1499	22.3052	-17.6329	5.4636	0.2022
$\Delta\eta$(cp)	-0.0267	17.1574	-39.9463	38.8862	-16.0539	0.0909
ΔR_m	-0.0717	-134.3170	326.2352	-296.9372	105.1592	0.5113

Table 11.5 Optical dielectric constant (ε), polarizabilities (α) and interaction parameter (d) for the systems, PPGMBE340 + Toluene, PPGMBE340 + Benzene and PPGMBE340 + Benzyl alcohol at 293.15, 303.15 and 313.15 K with respect to the mole fraction x_1 of PPGMBE340

		293.15K			303.15K			313.15K	
x_1	ε	α(cm³g⁻¹)	d	ε	α(cm³g⁻¹)	d	ε	α(cm³g⁻¹)	d
PPGMBE340+Toluene									
0.0000	2.2410	0.0806	-	2.2231	0.0807	-	2.2023	0.0806	-
0.1000	2.1934	0.0762	4.4225	2.1786	0.0762	5.6997	2.1609	0.0762	6.7343
0.1999	2.1609	0.0732	3.0432	2.1462	0.0733	2.9278	2.1316	0.0733	3.0839
0.3987	2.1229	0.0698	2.5829	2.1083	0.0698	2.6015	2.0938	0.0697	2.6172
0.4998	2.1083	0.0686	2.3637	2.0938	0.0686	2.3231	2.0794	0.0685	2.4433
0.7000	2.0880	0.0669	2.0729	2.0765	0.0670	1.9838	2.0650	0.0670	2.0517
0.7995	2.0794	0.0663	2.0143	2.0678	0.0663	1.9670	2.0564	0.0663	2.0394
1.0000	2.0650	0.0652	-	2.0535	0.0652	-	2.0420	0.0652	-
PPGMBE340 +Benzene									
0.0000	2.2530	0.0801	-	2.2320	0.0801	-	2.2112	0.0801	-
0.0999	2.1934	0.0752	4.1934	2.1756	0.0752	4.0233	2.1580	0.0751	4.2056
0.1996	2.1550	0.0721	3.7803	2.1404	0.0722	3.5494	2.1229	0.0721	3.5957
0.3993	2.1141	0.0689	3.0498	2.0996	0.0689	2.9343	2.0851	0.0688	3.0302
0.4997	2.0996	0.0678	2.7899	2.0880	0.0679	2.7591	2.0736	0.0678	2.7358
0.6989	2.0823	0.0665	2.3816	2.0707	0.0665	2.2724	2.0592	0.0666	2.6289
0.7997	2.0765	0.0660	2.2516	2.0621	0.0659	2.1010	2.0506	0.0660	2.2446
1.0000	2.0650	0.0652	-	2.0535	0.0652	-	2.0420	0.0652	-
PPGMBE340 + Benzyl alcohol									
0.0000	2.3685	0.0715	-	2.3593	0.0717	-	2.3501	0.0719	-
0.0999	2.2983	0.0702	3.5958	2.2831	0.0701	3.8903	2.2680	0.0701	3.7411
0.2919	2.1993	0.0680	2.5300	2.1874	0.0681	2.5217	2.1727	0.0679	2.4675
0.4983	2.1433	0.0669	1.8588	2.1287	0.0668	1.8551	2.1170	0.0668	1.8056
0.5995	2.0967	0.0655	1.5870	2.1083	0.0665	1.5667	2.1199	0.0675	1.5521
0.6990	2.1054	0.0661	1.4640	2.0938	0.0661	1.5272	2.0823	0.0662	1.5079
0.8901	2.0794	0.0656	1.2112	2.0678	0.0656	1.1607	2.0564	0.0656	1.4647
1.0000	2.0650	0.0652	-	2.0535	0.0652	-	2.0420	0.0652	-

Table 11.6 Average percentage deviation (APD) of various theoretical mixing rules used for evaluation of refractive index (n) at varying temperatures

Temp. (K)	Lorentz-Lorenz	Gladstone-Dale	Wiener's relation	Heller's relation	Arago-Biot	Newton	Eykman's relation	Oster's relation
PPGMBE340 + Toluene								
293.15 K	0.0108	0.0253	0.0293	0.0369	0.0253	0.0144	0.0004	-0.0025
303.15 K	0.0039	0.0239	0.0277	0.0348	0.0239	0.0136	-0.0001	-0.0074
313.15 K	-0.0111	0.0143	0.0178	0.0245	0.0143	0.0046	-0.0012	-0.0204
PPGMBE340 + Benzene								
293.15 K	-0.0451	-0.0244	-0.0201	-0.0124	-0.0244	-0.0359	-0.0041	-0.0582
303.15 K	-0.0484	-0.0225	-0.0186	-0.0115	-0.0224	-0.0331	-0.0043	-0.0590
313.15 K	-0.0589	-0.0287	-0.0251	-0.0187	-0.0287	-0.0383	-0.0050	-0.0674
PPGMBE340 + Benzyl alcohol								
293.15 K	-0.0142	0.0931	0.1033	0.1222	0.0931	0.0666	-0.0018	-0.0323
303.15 K	0.0299	0.1321	0.1426	0.1620	0.1321	0.1049	0.0016	0.0099
313.15 K	0.0687	0.1712	0.1819	0.2018	0.1712	0.1433	0.0047	0.0476

4. EXCESS PARAMETERS

Non-ideal liquid mixtures show considerable deviation from the linearity in their physical parameters with respect to concentration and these have been interpreted in terms of the presence of weak or strong interactions. The excess properties provide valuable information about microscopic and macroscopic behavior of liquid mixtures [6, 7], and can be used to test and improve thermodynamic models for calculating and predicting the fluid phase equilibria. These excess properties are fundamentally important in understanding the intermolecular interactions and nature of molecular agitation in dissimilar molecules. These functions give an idea about the extent to which a liquid mixture deviates from ideality [8, 9]. The variation of V_m^E values with x1 at three temperatures are shown graphically in Fig. 11.1. The V_m^E values are negative for all the three mixtures over whole composition range at all the temperatures. The extent of negative deviation in V_m^E on mole fraction follows the sequence: toluene < benzene < benzyl alcohol. Negative values of V_m^E are an indication for presence of specific intermolecular interaction in these systems. V_m^E values are found to be more negative for PPGMBE340 + benzene system in comparison to PPGMBE340 + toluene system (Fig. 11.1) probably due to the strong non-polar interaction between benzene and non-polar chain of PPGMBE340, whereas the interaction of toluene with polymer is less due to the $+I$ effect of $-CH_3$ group of toluene. Polymer size and structure also play an important role to understand the interaction in solution. The structural contributions are mostly negative and arise from several effects, especially from interstitial accommodation and changes in the free volume. The actual value of excess parameters would depend on the relative strength of these effects. The experimental values of V_m^E suggest that H-bonding and interstitial accommodation both are leading to the negative values while increase in negative values with temperature suggest that structural effect is more prominent than chemical effect in these solutions due to the fitting of smaller molecules of benzene, toluene and benzyl alcohol into the voids created by bigger molecules of PPGMBE340 and the large difference in molar volumes of components (molar volumes of PPGMBE340, toluene, benzene and benzyl alcohol are 354.43, 106.29, 88.87 and 103.36 cm3 mol-1 respectively at 293.15K. The actual value of excess parameters would depend on the relative strength of these effects. Hansen [10] proposed that the cohesive energy has three components, corresponding to the three types of interactions;

$$E = E_D + E_P + E_H$$

Dividing the cohesive energy by the molar volume gives the square of the Hildebrand solubility parameter as the sum of the squares of the Hansen dispersion (D), polar (P) and hydrogen bonding (H) components;

$$E/V_m = E_D/V_m + E_P/V_m + E_H/V_m$$
$$\delta^2 = \delta^2_D + \delta^2_P + \delta^2_H$$

where δ, δ_D, δ_P and δ_H are total Hildebrand solubility parameter, Hansen dispersive solubility parameter, Hansen polar solubility parameter and Hansen hydrogen bonding solubility parameter respectively. Solubility parameters for toluene, benzene and benzyl alcohol are shown below,

Table 11.7 Variation of total Hildebrand solubility parameter for various components

Component	δ	δ_D	δ_P	δ_H
Toluene	18.2	18.0	1.4	2.0
Benzene	18.6	18.4	0.0	2.0
Benzyl alcohol	23.8	18.4	6.3	13.7

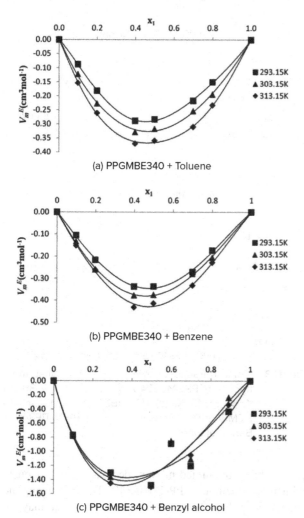

Fig. 11.1 Excess molar volume (V_m^E) against mole fraction of PPGMBE340 (x_1): ■, 293.15 K; ▲, 303.15 K; ♦, 313.15 K. (a) PPGMBE340 + Toluene, (b) PPGMBE340 + Benzene and (c) PPGMBE340 + Benzyl alcohol

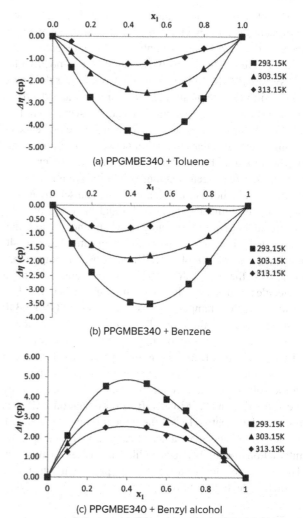

Fig. 11.2 Deviation in viscosity ($\Delta\eta$) against mole fraction of PPGMBE340 (x_1): ■, 293.15 K; ▲, 303.15 K; ♦, 313.15 K. (a) PPGMBE340 + Toluene, (b) PPGMBE340 + Benzene and (c) PPGMBE340 + Benzyl alcohol

Viscosity is also an important bulk property that provides a measure of the internal friction of a fluid and is closely related to the self-association of molecules in liquids. The viscosity deviations $\Delta\eta$ are negative for the systems PPGMBE340 + toluene and PPGMBE340 + benzene, over the entire composition range at all the three temperatures and increase with rise in temperature as can be seen from Figs. 11.2(a) and 2(b). From the above discussion total

Hildebrand solubility parameter (δ) of toluene and benzene are highly dependent upon Hansen dispersive solubility parameter (δD) indicating that the interaction between polymer and benzene / toluene is because of dispersive forces. Dispersive forces are weak intermolecular forces which give negative deviation in PPGMBE340 + toluene and PPGMBE340 + benzene. Figures 11.2(a) and 11.2(b) show that, $\Delta\eta$ values are more negative in PPGMBE340 + toluene than PPGMBE340 + benzene mixture, which implies that benzene is comparatively more interactive with PPGMBE340 than toluene. Negative deviation in $\Delta\eta$ values may also be on account of the difference in the molecular size of the component molecules. Similar conclusions have also been reported by other workers [11, 12]. Furthermore, the $\Delta\eta$ values become less negative and tend towards zero with rise in temperature indicating that the system approaches ideal behavior at higher temperatures meaning thereby the thermal energy enhances the molecular order in the mixture. The viscosity deviation, $\Delta\eta$, is positive for the system PPGMBE340 + benzyl alcohol, over the entire composition range at all three temperatures and decrease with increase in temperature as can be seen from Fig. 11.2(c). The positive values of $\Delta\eta$ indicate the presence of strong intermolecular interaction between the components of the mixture. From above solubility parameter table, the Hansen hydrogen bonding solubility parameter (δH) of benzyl alcohol is sufficiently high. Hansen hydrogen bonding solubility parameter (δH) and presence of –OH group on both polymer and benzyl alcohol shows that moderate hydrogen bonding occurs between PPGMBE340 and benzyl alcohol molecule. The increase in temperature decreases the strength of H-bonding between unlike molecules. Consequently the values of $\Delta\eta$ become less positive as the temperature is raised in PPGMBE340 + benzyl alcohol mixture. Refractometry is one of the earliest techniques used to study polymer dissolution [13]. The basic of this technique is that during the dissolution process, the polymer concentration increases continuously in the solvent and this concentration can be measured by the refractive index. Molar refraction deviation (ΔR_m) is found to be negative for all the three mixtures (Fig. 11.3). The observed negative values of ΔR_m support that specific interactions occur between unlike molecules in mixture. The effect of temperature is not prominent in molar refraction deviation study.

5. Thermophysical Parameters

Optical properties of liquids and liquid mixtures have been widely studied to obtain information on their physical, chemical and molecular behavior. Maxwell's theory for electromagnetic materials [14-17] gives the following relation between optical dielectric constant and refractive index assuming that for non-magnetic materials permeability approximately approaches unity.

$$= n^2$$

The permittivity ε, of nonpolar solvents can be explained by considering, both, the properties of the isolated molecules and the effects of the molecular interactions. Table 11.5 reveals that optical dielectric constant (ε) for the systems PPGMBE340 + toluene, PPGMBE340 + benzene and PPGMBE340 + benzyl alcohol varies non-linearly with mole fraction of PPGMBE340 (Fig. 11.4). It indicates that benzyl alcohol is more interactive with PPGMBE340 than benzene and toluene. Polarizability (α) of the mixture as given in Table 11.5 shows that the

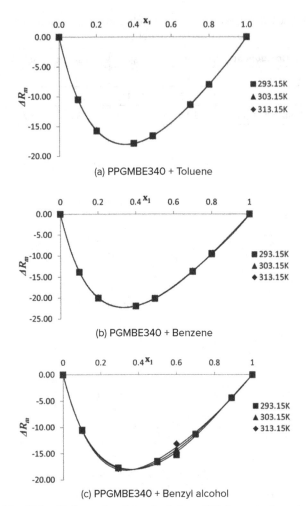

Fig. 11.3 Molar refraction deviation (ΔR_m) against mole fraction of PPGMBE340 (x_1): ■, 293.15 K; ▲, 303.15 K; ◆, 313.15 K. (a) PPGMBE340 + Toluene, (b) PGMBE340 + Benzene and (c) PPGMBE340 + Benzyl alcohol

polarizability of studied mixture decreases monotonously with mole fraction of PPGMBE340. There is negligible change in polarizability with temperature that may be due to small permanent electric dipole moments of the components and their mixtures, as orientation of molecular dipoles is slightly disturbed by temperature. The values of interaction parameter (d) in all the three systems under investigation are positive. These large and positive values of interaction parameter indicate specific interaction to be present in the solutions under study. Table 11.6 shows the results of estimation of refractive index in terms of average percentage deviation (APD) for all the three mixtures. It may be seen from Table 11.6 that all the mixing rules are best suited for estimation of refractive index in these mixtures.

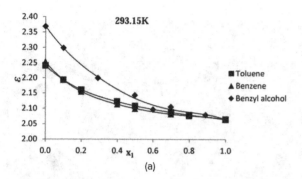

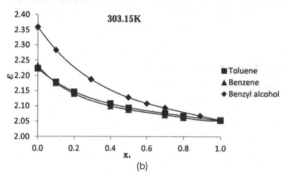

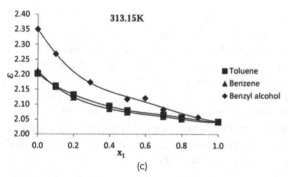

Fig. 11.4 Optical dielectric constant (ε) against mole fraction of PPGMBE340 (x_1): ■, toluene ▲, benzene; ◆, benzyl alcohol. (a) 293.15K, (b) 303.15K and (c) 313.15K

6. CONCLUSION

Significant specific intermolecular interactions are observed in all the three systems. From observed experimental data and calculated excess parameters, it is found that the interaction is strongest in the system PPGMBE340 + benzyl alcohol. The difference in molar volumes of the components is much large hence the structural effect is prominent in these mixtures. Derived parameters (ε, α and d) also support that intermolecular interactions are present between solvents and polymer. The effect of temperature on the strength and extent of interaction among the component molecules of liquid mixtures seems to be significant. Comparison of experimental and estimated values of refractive index in terms of average percentage deviation exhibits the suitability of semi empirical relations.

■ REFERENCES ■

1. Union Carbide Corp., UCON Fluids and Lubricants, booklet P5-2616(**1996**).
2. B. Rubin and E. M. Glass, SAE Q. Trans., 4 (**1950**)287.
3. J. M. Russ, Lubri. Eng., 151(**1946**).
4. L. Hong, D. Tapriyal and R. M. Enick, J. Chem. Eng. Data, 53 (**2008**) 1342.
5. Leslie R. Rudnick and Ronald L. Shubkin (Editors), 179,
6. L. Kumari, S. Gupta, I. Singh, O. Prasad, L. Sinha, M. Gupta, J. Mol. Liq.,299 (**2020**)1.
7. S. Parveen, M. Yasmin, M. Gupta and J. P. Shukla, Int. J. Thermodyn, 13(2) (**2010**)59.
8. N. Chakraborty, K.C. Juglan, H. Kumar, J. Chem. Thermodyn., 163 (**2021**) 106613.
9. M. Yasmin, M. Gupta, J.P. Shukla, J. Mol. Liq., 160 (1) (**2011**) 22.
10. B. A. Miller-Chou and J. L. Koenig, Prog. Polym. Sci.,28 (**2003**) 1223.
11. R. J. Fort and W.R. Moore, Trans. Faraday Soc., 62(**1966**) 1112.
12. H. N. Solimo, R. Riggio, F. Davolio and M. Katz, Canadian J. Chem., 53 (**1978**) 1258.
13. K. Ueberreiter, Diffusion in polymers, New York, NY: Academic Press, (**1968**) 219.
14. H. El-Kashef, Opt. Mater., 8 (**1997**)175.
15. H. El-Kashef, Opt. Mater., 10 (**1998**)207.
16. H. El-Kashef, Opt. Laser. Tech., 30 (**1998**)367.
17. H. El-Kashef, Opt. Mater., 20 (**2002**)81.
18. J. George and N. V. Sastry, J. Chem. Thermodyn, 35 (**2003**) 1837.
19. R. Thiyagarajan and P. Lakshmanan, Phys. Chem. Liq., 46(4)(**2008**) 366.
20. A. Ali, A. K. Nain, D. Chand and R. Ahmad, J. Chinese Chem. Soc., 53 (**2006**)531.
21. A. Ali, J. D. Pandey, N. K. Soni, A. K. Nain, B. Lal and D. Chand, Chinese J. Chem., 23 (**2005**)1.
22. A. Ali and M. Tariq, J.

Challenges and Opportunities for Innovation in India – Dr. Shweta Mishra et al. (eds)
© 2024 Taylor & Francis Group, London, ISBN 978-1-032-99842-8

Queuing Theory: An Effort to Improve the Quality Services of a Hotel

12

Vipul Srivastava*, Puneet Shukla, Suresh Maithani

Department of Applied Sciences,
Ambalika Institute of Management & Technology,
Lucknow

Abstract

Queuing theory is the mathematical study of waiting lines, or queues. In queuing theory a model is constructed so that queue lengths and waiting times can be predicted. The common problem arises in almost every famous hotel is that they lose their customers due to a long wait on the line. This shows a need for a numerical model for the hotel management to understand the situation better. This paper aims to show that queuing theory satisfies the model when tested with a real-case scenario. Authors obtained the data from a Hotel in Lucknow in order to derive the arrival rate, service rate, utilization rate, waiting time in queue and the probability of potential customers to balk. The collected data is analyzed by using Little's Theorem and M/M/1 queuing model. The arrival rate at Hotel Lucknow during its busiest period of the day is 3.25 customers per minute (cpm) while the service rate is 3.27 cpm during our study period. The average number of customers in the hotel is 210 and the utilization period is 0.993.

Keywords

Queuing theory, Little's theorem, Kendall's notation, Waiting lines

1. INTRODUCTION

There are several determining factors for a hotel to be considered a good or a bad one. Taste, cleanliness, the restaurant layout and settings are some of the most important factors. These factors, when managed carefully, will be able to attract plenty of customers. However, there is also another factor that needs to be considered especially when the restaurant has already succeeded in attracting customers. This factor is the customers queuing time. Once we are being served, our transaction with the service organization may be efficient, courteous and complete: but the bitter taste of how long it took to get attention pollutes the overall judgments that we make about the quality of service. In a waiting line system, managers must decide what level of service to offer. A low level of service may be inexpensive, at least in the short run, but may incur high costs of customer dissatisfaction, such as lost future business and actual processing costs of complaints. Queuing theory is the study of queue or waiting lines. Some of the analysis that can be derived using queuing theory include the expected waiting time in the queue, the average time in the

---
*Corresponding author: vipul.srivastava91@gmail.com

DOI: 10.1201/9781003606260-12

system, the expected queue length, the expected number of customers served at one time, the probability of balking customers, as well as the probability of the system to be in certain states, such as empty or full. Waiting lines are a common sight in hotel especially during lunch and dinner time. Hence, queuing theory is suitable to be applied in a hotel setting since it has an associated queue or waiting line where customers who cannot be served immediately have to queue (wait) for service. Researchers have previously used queuing theory to model the hotel operation [2], reduce cycle time in a busy fast food restaurant [3], as well as to increase throughput and efficiency [5]. This paper uses queuing theory to study the waiting lines in hotel at Lucknow, U.P. India., and The hotel provides 100 tables out of which some have 4 chairs and some have 6 chairs. There are 50 waiters working at any one time. On a daily basis it serves over 800 customers during weekdays and over 1500 customers during weekend. This paper seeks to illustrate the usefulness of applying queuing theory in a real case situation.

2. QUEUING THEORY

In 1908, Copenhagen Telephone Company requested Agner K. Erlang to work on the holding times in a telephone switch. He identified that the number of telephone conversations and telephone holding time fit into Poisson distribution and exponentially distributed. This was the beginning of the study of queuing theory. In this section, we will discuss two common concepts in queuing theory.

2.1 Little's Theorem

Little's theorem [6] describes the relationship between throughput rate (i.e. arrival and service rate), cycle time and work in process (i.e. number of customers/jobs in the system). This relationship has been shown to be valid for a wide class of queuing models. The theorem states that the expected number of customers (N) for a system in steady state can be determined using the following equation:

$$L = \lambda T \qquad (1)$$

Here, λ is the average customer arrival rate and T is the average service time for a customer. Consider the example of a restaurant where the customer's arrival rate (λ) doubles but the customers still spend the same amount of time in the restaurant (T). These facts will double the number of customers in the restaurant (L). By the same logic, if the customer arrival rate (λ) remains the same but the customers service time doubles this will also double the total number of customers in the hotel. This indicates that in order to control the three variables, managerial decisions are only required for any two of the three variables. Three

fundamental relationshipscan be derived from Little's theorem [5]:

- L increases if λ or T increases.
- λ increases if L increases or T decreases.
- T increases if L increases or λ decreases.

Rust [8] said that the Little's theorem can be useful in quantifying the maximum achievable operational improvements and also to estimate the performance change when the system is modified.

2.2 Queuing Models and Kendall's Notation

The principle actors in a queuing situation are the customer and the server. On arrival at a service facility, they can start service immediately or wait in a queue if the facility is busy. From the standpoint of analyzing queues, the arrival of customers is represented by the inter arrival time between successive customers, and the service is described by the service time per customer. The queuing behavior of customers plays a role in waiting line analysis."Human" customers may jockey from one queue to another in the hope of reducing waiting time. They may also balk from joining a queue all together because of anticipated long delay, or they may renege from a queue because they have been waiting too long. In most cases, queuing models can be characterized by the following factors:

Arrival time distribution: Inter-arrival times most commonly fall into one of the following distribution patterns: a Poisson distribution, a Deterministic distribution, or a General distribution. However, inter-arrival times are most often assumed to be independent and memory less, which is the attributes of a Poisson distribution. Service time distribution: The service time distribution can be constant, exponential, hyper-exponential, hypo-exponential or general. The service time is independent of the inter-arrival time.

Number of servers: The queuing calculations change depends on whether there is a single server or multiple servers for the queue. A single server queue has one server for the queue. This is the situation normally found in a Book store where there is a line for each cashier. A multiple server queue corresponds to the situation in a bank in which a single line waits for the first of several tellers to become available.

Queue Lengths (optional): The queue in a system can be modeled as having infinite or finite queue length. This includes the customers waiting in the queue. Queuing discipline (optional): There are several possibilities in terms of the sequence of customers to be served such as FIFO (First In First Out, i.e. in order of arrival), random order, LIFO (Last In First Out, i.e. the last one to come will be the first to be served), SIRO (Service in Random Order).

System capacity (optional): The maximum number of customers in a system can be from

1 - Infinity

Kendall, in 1953, proposed a notation system to represent the six characteristics discussed above. The notation of a queue is written as: A/B/P/Q/R/Z A describes the distribution type of the inter arrival times, B describes the distribution type of the service times, P describes the number of servers in the system, Q (optional) describes the maximum length of the queue, R (optional) describes the size of the system population and Z (optional) describes the queuing discipline.

3. "HOTEL" QUEUING MODEL

The daily number of visitors was obtained from the hotel itself. The hotel has been recording the data as part of its end of day routine. We also interviewed the hotel manager to find out about the capacity of the hotel, the number of waiters as well as the number of chefs in the hotel. Based on the interview with the hotel manager, we concluded that the queuing model that best illustrate the operation of "Hotel" is M/M/1. This means that the arrival and service time are exponentially distributed (Poisson process). The hotel system consists of only one server. In our observation the hotel has several waitresses but in the actual waiting queue, they only have one chef to serve all of the customers. For the analysis of the "Hotel" M/M/1

Queuing Model, the following variables will be investigated [6]:

λ: The mean customers arrival rate

μ: The mean service rate

ρ: λ/μ: utilization factor

Probability of zero customers in the hotel (Po) is given by

$$Po = 1 - \rho \qquad (2)$$

Pn: The probability of having n customers in the hotel.

$$Pn = Po.\rho^n = (1 - \rho)\, \rho^n \qquad (3)$$

L: average number of customers dining in the hotel.

$$L = \rho/1 - \rho = \lambda/\mu - \lambda \qquad (4)$$

Lq: average number of customers in the queue.

$$Lq = \rho^2/1 - \rho \qquad (5)$$

W: average time spent in BKK including the waiting time.

$$W = 1/\mu - \lambda \qquad (6)$$

Wq: average waiting time in the queue.

$$Wq = Lq/\lambda \qquad (7)$$

4. RESULT AND DISCUSSION

When customers arriving in hotel the number of customers on Saturdays and Sundays are double. The busiest period for the hotel is on weekend during dinner time. Hence focus our analysis in this time window. Authors analyzed the hotel between 20 to 23 hours.

4.1 Calculation

Our teams conducted the research at dinner time. There are on average 585 people are coming to the hotel in 3 hours time window of dinner time. From this we can derive the arrival rate as:

$$\lambda = 585/180 = 3.25 \text{ customer per minute (cpm)}.$$

We also found out from observation and discussion with manager that each customer spends 65 minutes on average in the hotel(W), the queue length is around 35 people (Lq) on average and the waiting time is around 12 minutes. It can be shown using (7) that the observed actual waiting time does not differ by much when compared to the theoretical waiting time as shown below

$$Wq = Lq/\lambda = 35 \text{ customers}/3.25 \text{ cpm} = 10.76 \text{ minutes}$$

Next, calculate the average number of people in the hotel using the above calculated values,

$$L = 3.25 \text{ cpm} \times 65 \text{ minutes} = 211 \text{ customers}$$

After calculating the average number of customers in the hotel , derive the service rate as:

$$\mu = \lambda(1 + L)/L = 3.25(1 + 211)/211$$
$$= 3.27 \text{ cpm (approx)}$$

Now, calculate Traffic Intensity or utilization factor

$$\rho = \lambda/\mu = 3.25/3.27 = 0.993$$

With the high utilization rate of 0.993 during dinner time the probability of zero customers in the hotel or probability that system is idle can be calculated by (2)

$$P_0 = 1 - \rho = 0.007$$

The generic formula that can be used to calculate the probability of having 'n' customer in the hotel is as follows:

$$P_n = (1 - \rho)\, \rho^n = (1 - 0.993)0.993^n = (0.007)0.993^n$$

Assume that potential customers will start to balk when they see more than 30 people are already queuing for the restaurant and the maximum queue length that a potential customer can tolerate is 40 people. As the capacity of the hotel when fully occupied is 200 people, can calculate the probability of 30 people in the queue as the probability when there are 240 people in the system (i.e. 210 in the hotel and 30 or more queuing) as follows:

Probability of customers going away = P (more than 30 people in the queue) = P (more than 240 people in the hotel)

$$P_{211-240} = \Sigma_{n=211}^{240} P_n = \Sigma_{n=211}^{240} (.007)(0.993)^n = 4.31\%$$

4.2 Analysis

The utilization is directly proportional with the mean number of customers. It means that the mean number of customers will increase as the utilization increases. The utilization rate at the restaurant is very high at 0.993. This, however, is only the utilization rate during lunch and dinner time on Saturdays and Sundays. On weekday, the utilization rate is almost half of it. This is because the number of visitors on weekdays is only half of the number of visitors on weekends. In addition, the umber of waiters or waitresses remains the same regardless whether it is peak hours or off-peak hours. In case the customers waiting time is lower or in other words we waited for less than 15 minutes, the number of customers that are able to be served per minute will increase. When the service rate is higher the utilization will be lower, which makes the probability of the customers going away decreases.

4.3 Benefits

This research can help hotel to increase their QOS (Quality of Service), by anticipating if there are many customers in the queue. The result of this paper work may become the reference to analyze the current system and improve the next system. Because the hotel can now estimate of how many customers will wait in the queue and the number of customers that will go away each day. By anticipating the huge number of customers coming and going in a day, the hotel can set a target profit that should be achieved daily and The formulas that were used during the completion of the research is applicable for future research and also could be use to develop more complex theories.

5. CONCLUSION

This study has discussed the application of queuing theory of hotel. Here authors focused on two particularly common decision variables as a medium for introducing and illustrating all the concepts. From the result authors

obtained that the rate at which customers arrive in the queuing system is 3.25 customers per minute and service rate is 3.27 cpm and utilization rate is 0.993. This theory is also applicable for the hotel if they want to calculate all the data daily. It can be concluded that the arrival rate will be lesser and the service rate will be greater if it is on weekdays since the average number of customers is less as compared to those on weekends. The constraints that were faced for the completion of this research were the inaccuracy of result since some of the data that was just based on assumption or approximation. Authors hope that this research can contribute to the betterment of hotel in terms of its way of dealing with customers.

5.1 Future Outcomes

This study will develop a simulation model for the hotel which will be able to confirm the results of the analytical model. In addition, a simulation model allows adding more complexity so that the model can mirror the actual operation of the restaurant more closely. This study gives a generalized guarantee to stabilize the system from the problems arisen like customers' balking, reneging, jockeying and collusion or delay in services by present way of working of restaurant. In today's world of accelerating advancement in computer technology, it will be fruitful to hotel manager to install a computer for the proper control of service facilities and to keep the previous record so as to make the forecasting better over good in order to excel in the field.

■ REFERENCES ■

1. A. K. Kharwat, Computer Simulation: an Important Tool in the Fast-Food Industry, Proceedings of inter Simulation Conference, IEEE Press (Dec. 1991), pp.811–815.
2. M.Laguna and J. Marklund, Business Process Modeling, Simulation and Design. Pearson Prentice Hall (2005) ISBN 0-13-091519-X.
3. J. D. C. Little, "A Proof for the Queuing Formula: L = λW," Operations Research (1961) vol. 9(3), pp. 83–387.
4. K. Rust, Using Little's Law to Estimate Cycle Time and Cost, Proceedings of Winter Simulation Conference, IEEE Press (2008).

Challenges and Opportunities for Innovation in India – Dr. Shweta Mishra et al. (eds)
© 2024 Taylor & Francis Group, London, ISBN 978-1-032-99842-8

Gender Stereotyping in Management and Decision-Making Process in an Organizational Set Up

13

Sunitha V Ganiger
Assistant Professor,
DOSR in Sociology, Tumkur University

Sharadambi G
Department of Sociology,
VHD institute of Home Science, Maharani's Cluster University,
Bangalore

Abstract

Gender norms in Indian Society are reinforced through socio-cultural institutions like family, kinship, religious and economic institutions and many more. When a child is born the first expression would be about gender of the baby which decides the emotions of the family members carried on with various rituals, food consumption and sharing household chores. By the beginning of the twenty-first century, however, this picture had changed dramatically. Women established their own identity and paved the way in education and the workplace. Educational institutions began preparing women for entry into new fields, allowing them to depart from traditional roles. Families began to expect women not only to pursue higher education, but also to pursue any career interests they may have. With this intention the major objective of the study is to To understand the attitudes about women's role in organization and to delve into the attitude towards gender stereotyping. For this study, the researchers extensively used both primary and secondary sources of information. The primary data was collected through interviews with women currently residing in the city of Bangalore and working in Information Technology Sector. Primary and secondary data were collected to cover each aspect of the investigation. The data was added based on the evolving requirements of the research. Based on a convenience sampling method 500 married women were selected for the study. After Data Collection the data were entered, edited, coded and analysis was done using SPSS. The results were analyzed and interpreted.

Keywords

Gender stereotype, Decision making, Gender bias, Prejudices and discrimination

1. INTRODUCTION

Gender stereotyping is deeply rooted in our society and imbibed in many of our veins which we may follow consciously or unconsciously from womb to tomb. In fact gender stereotype begins right from the infancy stage to old age wherein girls are made to be obedient, subservient, passive and docile while boys are taught to be commanding,

Corresponding author: dr.sunisree@gmail.com

DOI: 10.1201/9781003606260-13

authoritative, competitive and unassailable. Gender Bias is defined as unequal treatment in employment opportunity and expectations due to attitudes based on the sex of an employee or group of employees. It is further described as prejudice or discrimination based on sex; or conditions or attitudes that foster stereotypes of social roles based on sex. Prior to 1950, few women were employed outside the household. The majority of women were illiterate, and the majority of educated women did not work outside the home. Those who did work outside the home were concentrated in nursing, elementary school teaching, and other traditional female occupations. Women are underrepresented in positions of authority in the workplace. Further, women were underrepresented in the professions and in positions of influence and authority. The new millennium ushered in an era of women in all disciplines and positions. More and more females are attending college and have proven to be outstanding students and professionals. Over the past few decades, women's education, self-esteem, and, most importantly, their desire to hold a respectable position in society have increased. Professional women, like males, hold themselves to extremely high standards. They altered their perception of themselves and how the world perceives them. Changes in the sociocultural structure have contributed to this predicament. Families are now beginning to tolerate the employment of women. Parents are beginning to investigate career options for their daughters and are prepared to assist them in any way possible to ensure their success. Girls are raised to be ambitious, ambitious, and possess the ambition necessary for challenging careers. As a consequence, women occupy top managerial, professional, and leadership positions in the modern workplace. The organization employs a rigorous selection process to designate women. They are liable for their work, responsibilities, duties, and performance. They travel whenever, wherever. In spite of the fact that women's labor force participation has more than doubled over the past 30 to 35 years, the majority of women are still employed in a small number of occupations, as indicated by the interest of women in various occupations. The division of labor is commonplace. Despite walking on planks while carrying their heads aloft. They travel to numerous nations and continents. Despite their increased representation, women do not have equal access to all levels of the professional hierarchy in all fields. They are underrepresented in higher positions and struggle to attain the pinnacle of their field. It is true that a small number of women occasionally make headlines, but statistically speaking, they hold only a tiny percentage of the top positions. The rule of thumb has not changed. The greater an organization's hierarchy, the fewer women are present.

1.1 Meaning of Gender Stereotype and Gender Discrimination

Gender describes the socially constructed roles, activities, attributes and qualities, personality characteristics and responsibilities expected or assigned to male and female in a given culture, location or time which is associated with a person's biological sex in a given culture may be used as biology, may be learned or may represent a combination of biological and cultural determinant. Thus, Gender is a belief or a notion while gender discrimination is the practice of treating both the sexes unequally. The definition of gender bias is simply unfair treatment of men or women because of their gender. It is basically the belief or attitude that one sex is of higher power than the other sex. Gender bias is a preference or prejudice toward one gender over the other. This bias can be conscious or unconscious, and may manifest in many ways, both subtle and obvious. Gender Stereotypes are ideas about how people will act, based on the group to which they belong. Many children grow up identifying certain characteristics as belonging only to boys or girls. World Health Organisation assert that "Son preference affects all aspects of women's life including child care, health education, employment because she is discriminated since the moment she is born and sometimes even before if sex selection procedures are available". Gender stereotyping can draw a perimeter in development of the natural talents and abilities of girls and boys, women and men, as well as their educational and professional experiences and life opportunities in general. Stereotypes about women both result from, and are the cause of, deeply engrained attitudes, values, norms and prejudices against women. They are used to justify and maintain the historical relations of power of men over women as well as sexist attitudes that hold back the advancement of women. **Gender stereotypes are oversimplified ideas, messages and images about differences between males and females. They have become meaningful because society has given them meaning and value. Gender stereotyping in India** In Indian civilization the child is believed to be a gift of the God to be nurtured with love, care and affection not only within the family but also within the society as a whole. Son preference or the privileging of sons over daughters in accordance to a patriarchal system, is a growing phenomenon in India. In the era of UN Millennium Development Goals where one of the objectives is to "increase gender equality and empower women", the issue of son preference is even more widely debated. **Women in IT Sector:** As per recent study it is found that women make 36 Percent in IT sector which depict that women entry in IT sector is welcomed. India's IT sector had the highest female participation rate of 30%, followed by financial services companies at 22.4% during financial year 2021-22, according to an analysis of voluntary Business Responsibility and Sustainability Reporting disclosures by 134 companies conducted by the CFA institute. The IT sector, considered the largest employer of the country's white-collar workforce, has the highest representation of women in the workforce, while FMCG and industrials occupy the last two spots in the listing with 5.5% and 4.3% representation, respectively.

2. REVIEW OF LITERATURE

V Padma and Anande et al (2015) have conducted study on 1000 I T and BPO representatives. The study was concentrated on the work stress among soft ware employees. The stress was of target to be achieved in their work and particularly about the night shift. A majority of the employees face both physical and mental strain due to stress in the work. The studies further suggests that the employees should be given proper training and encourage them to participate in yoga, meditation , music and dance like programmes to come out of the stress of the work. The study further indicated that the healthy employee can produce more than the expected, so the work organizations should concentrate on the health of the employees(Padma *et al.*, 2015).

Sen Amartya. (2001) "Many faces of Gender Inequality". Frontline, Nov9,4-14 according to him in terms of employment as well as that of promotion in work and occupation, women often face greater handicap than men. He calls this "professional inequality", where progress to elevated levels of employment and occupation is much more difficult for women than men(Sen, 2001).

Al-Omari and Haneen Okasheh(2017) their study on work environment influence on job performance. The findings demonstrate that situational constraints are made up of a variety of factors, including noise, office, equipment, ventilation and light. These are the main physical ailments that require additional focus. Employees are advised to take charge of motivating employees by enhancing work surroundings. When workers are motivated, they perform better on the job and accomplish the objectives and results that are set for the position. As a result, employers are more satisfied(Al-Omari and Okasheh, 2017)

Dr. Muthumani & Dr. Saranya (2014), examined women employees working in Information Technology arranged in Chennai City. Their responses were assembled and the information was connected with the proper statistical investigation and the outcomes were presented. The effects of the investigation result shows that the vast majority of the women representatives working in Information innovation

industry never fears about job task or sustained up by the work because of their interest and passion in their job. These are the remarks got from the analysis and it demonstrates the care taken by the employer good. The great workplace is the real advantage for the any of the association to hold employees for long period towards the workspace (*Journal of Theoretical and Applied Information Technology - May 2015 Volume 75 No 1,*).

3. STATEMENT OF THE PROBLEM

Bangalore is India's largest technology hub. Popular IT companies are established and operating in the city of Bangalore. The social life here is not equally modernized by the pace of industrialization. The information technology sector has different working conditions like long hours of work, night shifts that are somewhat different from traditional working hours, The proportion of women work force is also increasing in the organization. The contribution of women to the economic development of the nation is also considered significant. At the same time, women are facing certain challenges and problems both at work and at home. While at organisation women may get placed initially but in the organisational hierarchy in terms of occupying prominent position, assigning work, consulting females in decision making are looked down upon.. in this contest the study focuses upon the attitude of females wth regard to gender stereotyping in It sector.

3.1 Objectives of the Study

- To understand the attitudes about womens role in organisation
- To delve into the attitude towards gender stereotyping

4. METHODOLOGY OF STUDY

For this study, the researchers extensively used both primary and secondary sources of information. The primary data was collected through interviews with women currently residing in the city of Bangalore and working in Information Technology Sector. Primary and secondary data were collected to cover each aspect of the investigation. The data was added based on the evolving requirements of the research. Based on convience sampling method 500 married women were selected for the study

5. GENDER BASED ASSIGNMENT AND RESPONSIBILITIES

Work assignments can help employees grow, but if not handled carefully, they can hurt diversity efforts. How can companies attract and keep talent amid record employee burnout and quit rates? Organizations can better their diversity, equity, and inclusion (DEI) strategies during this transition and using pandemic lessons. Leaders must evaluate their company's job assignment landscape for workforce equity

Table 13.1 Gender based assignment and responsibilities

Sl. No.	Gender based assignment and responsibilities	No. Respondents	Percentage
1	Always	215	43.0
2	Partially	284	56.8
3	Never	1	0.2
	Total	**500**	**100.0**

Source: Field Survey

The above table shows that assigned the same responsibilities as your male colleagues of the respondent's job satisfaction among women in the information technology sector in Bangalore city. Out of 500 respondents 56.8 percent of respondents partially assigned the same responsibilities as your male colleagues and 43 percent of respondents always assigned the same responsibilities as your male colleagues. Only 0.2 percent of respondents are never assigned the same responsibilities as your male colleagues in IT industry of study area Findings on the work allotment indicates that a majority of the respondents that is 56.8 percent of the respondents indicate that, based on the sex partially discrimination in work allotment is made. At the same time, about 43 percent of respondents indicate that based on the sex of the worker no partiality is made in the work distribution. The Very negligible proportion of the respondents that are only 0.2 percent of respondents indicates that based on the sex of the worker partiality is made in work allotment.

Table 13.2 Getting necessary information from senior manager regarding work and project irrespective of gender

Sl. No	Necessary Information	No. Respondents	Percentage
1	Always	127	25.4
2	Occasionally	260	52.0
3	Rarely	111	22.2
4	Never	2	0.4
	Total	**500**	**100.0**

Source: Field Survey

The above table shows that get all the necessary information from your senior manager regarding your work and project irrespective of your gender of the respondents job satisfaction among women in the information technology sector in Bangalore city. Findings on the access to necessary information on the workplace indicate that a majority of the respondents that are 52 percent of them occasionally get the information about work on the work place. More than one fourth of the respondents that is 25.4 percent of them indicate that they are access to the necessary information regarding the work on the work place. About 22.2 percent of the respondents always get all the information regarding the work on the work place. Very less proportion of the respondents that are 0.4 percent of them never get any information about the work on the work place. The findings indicate that there is some problem in the Information and Technology industries regarding information flow on the work place.

6. CONCLUSION

Findings on the work allotment indicates that a majority of the respondents that is 56.8 percent of the respondents indicate that, based on the sex partially discrimination in work allotment is made. The findings indicate that there is some problem in the Information and Technology industries regarding information flow on the work place.

■ REFERENCES ■

1. Padma, V. *et al.* (2015) 'Health problems and stress in Information Technology and Business Process Outsourcing employees', *Journal of Pharmacy & Bioallied Sciences* [Preprint]. Available at: https://www.semanticscholar.org/paper/Health-problems-and-stress-in-Information-and-Padma-Anand/c3814de369e39a9470dfaa36f16093ac27fc3061 (Accessed: 7 March 2023).

2. Al-Omari, K. and Okasheh, H. (2017) 'The Influence of Work Environment on Job Performance: A Case Study of Engineering Company in Jordan', 12(24).

3. *Dr. Muthumani & Dr. Saranya 2014* Job Satisfaction amongst Information Technology (IT) Employees in Bangalore City-A Sociological Approach' (*Journal of Theoretical and Applied Information Technology - May 2015 Volume 75 No 1,*).

Challenges and Opportunities of Millets for Health in Present Sanarri

14

Smriti Sharma*

Assistant Professor,
Jwala Devi Vidya Mandir P.G. College,
Kanpur

Abstract

World is in the clinch of several health disorders and chronical diseases. As per 2016 Global Nutrition report, 44% population of 129 countries experience very serious levels of undernutrition, adult overweight and obesity. A nutrient imbalanced diet is responsible for most of these diseases. According to the estimates of United Nations Food and Agriculture Organization, about 795 million people were reported undernourished. While on the other hand more than 1.9 billion (39% of world's population) adults ≥ 18 years of age were overweight and further 13% were reported to be obese. Millets was one of the earliest cereal crops to be included in the human diet. Millets was domesticated as a source of human food but over time it's diverse uses has evolved over the years. There has been considerable recent interest in the nutritional properties of millets, which has stemmed largely from the discovery of the cholesterol lowering effect of B -glucon, a cell wall polysaccharide found in millets. The action of B-glucon, in inhibiting absorption from the gut, probably through increased viscosity provides for the benefit in reducing post-prandial blood sugar levels. The overall importance of millets as a human food is very much appreciated owing too much potential of the health benefits of the whole grain and source of Beta glucans and adaptability of Millets has been recognised to a wide range of environments in comparison to other cereal crops. Millets secure sixth position in terms of world agricultural production of cereal grains and are still a staple food in many regions of world. These are rich source of many vital nutrients Millets are to be helpful with the reduction of weight, BMI, and high blood pressure.

Keywords

Millets, Health, Crops, etc.

1. Introduction

Climate change poses significant challenges to crop production and the overall sustainability of our food systems. While some regions may initially experience improved productivity and yields due to climate change, the overall impact is expected to be negative and detrimental to global food security Indeed, the agriculture

---

*Corresponding author: smritisharma.varanasi@gmail.com

DOI: 10.1201/9781003606260-14

industry, including livestock farming and crop cultivation, contributes significantly to greenhouse gas emissions, primarily through methane and nitrous oxide emissions. Addressing these emissions is crucial for mitigating climate change and reducing the impact on soil conditions and water supplies. Regarding future predictions for soil conditions and water supplies, numerous researchers have used various models to assess the potential impacts of climate change on these vital resources. While predictions can vary based on the specific models and assumptions used, there is a general consensus that climate change will likely exacerbate existing challenges such as soil degradation, water scarcity, and salinization Adaptation to climate change in agriculture is crucial for ensuring food security, preserving livelihoods, and maintaining environmental sustainability. Here are several strategies and practices that can help agriculture adapt to the impacts of climate change:

1. **Crop Diversification:** Diversifying crop varieties and species can help mitigate the risks associated with climate change. Farmers can choose crops that are better adapted to changing temperature and precipitation patterns, as well as those that are more resilient to pests and diseases.

2. **Water Management:** Improving water management practices, such as rainwater harvesting, drip irrigation, and the use of efficient irrigation techniques, can help farmers cope with water scarcity and variability in precipitation.

3. **Soil Conservation:** Implementing soil conservation practices, such as cover cropping, crop rotation, and reduced tillage, can help improve soil health, enhance water retention, and reduce erosion, making agricultural systems more resilient to climate change impacts.

4. **Agroforestry:** Integrating trees and shrubs into agricultural landscapes through agroforestry practices can provide multiple benefits, including improved soil fertility, enhanced biodiversity, and increased resilience to climate extremes.

5. **Improved Crop Management:** Adopting climate-smart crop management practices, such as adjusting planting dates, optimizing fertilizer use, and implementing integrated pest management strategies, can help optimize yields and reduce risks associated with climate variability.

6. **Breeding and Seed Selection:** Developing and deploying climate-resilient crop varieties through breeding programs and seed selection can help farmers adapt to changing environmental conditions. These varieties should have traits such as drought tolerance, heat resistance, and pest and disease resistance.

7. **Livestock Management:** Implementing adaptive measures in livestock management, such as providing shade and shelter, improving feed quality and availability, and enhancing disease management, can help reduce the vulnerability of livestock to heat stress and other climate-related risks.

8. **Early Warning Systems:** Establishing early warning systems for extreme weather events, such as storms, droughts, and floods, can help farmers anticipate and mitigate potential impacts on crops, livestock, and infrastructure.

9. **Insurance and Financial Support:** Providing access to insurance schemes and financial support mechanisms can help farmers cope with climate-related losses and enable them to invest in adaptive measures and technologies.

10. **Capacity Building and Extension Services:** Strengthening agricultural extension services and providing training and capacity-building programs can help farmers adopt and implement climate-smart practices effectively.

Sustainable technologies play a crucial role in both adapting to and mitigating the impacts of climate change. Here are some key sustainable technologies for adaptation and mitigation:

1. **Renewable Energy:** Transitioning from fossil fuels to renewable energy sources such as solar, wind, hydroelectric, and geothermal power can significantly reduce greenhouse gas emissions and mitigate climate change. These technologies provide clean, sustainable energy without contributing to global warming.

2. **Energy Efficiency:** Improving energy efficiency across various sectors, including buildings, transportation, and industry, can help reduce energy consumption and greenhouse gas emissions. Technologies such as energy-efficient appliances, LED lighting, and smart energy management systems can contribute to significant emissions reductions.

3. **Climate-Smart Agriculture:** Sustainable agricultural practices, such as conservation agriculture, agroforestry, precision farming, and organic farming, can help farmers adapt to climate change while reducing greenhouse gas emissions

from the agriculture sector. These practices enhance soil health, conserve water, and increase resilience to climate extremes.

4. **Carbon Capture and Storage (CCS):** CCS technologies capture carbon dioxide emissions from industrial processes and power plants, preventing them from entering the atmosphere. Captured CO_2 can then be stored underground or utilized in various industrial processes, reducing overall emissions and mitigating climate change.

5. **Afforestation and Reforestation:** Planting trees and restoring degraded ecosystems can help sequester carbon dioxide from the atmosphere, mitigate deforestation, and enhance biodiversity. Agroforestry practices, which integrate trees into agricultural landscapes, also offer multiple benefits for both adaptation and mitigation.

6. **Climate-Resilient Infrastructure:** Building and upgrading infrastructure to withstand the impacts of climate change, such as sea-level rise, extreme weather events, and changing precipitation patterns, is essential for adaptation. Sustainable infrastructure designs, such as green roofs, permeable pavement, and natural drainage systems, can help mitigate flooding and enhance resilience.

7. **Water Management Technologies:** Sustainable water management technologies, such as rainwater harvesting, wastewater recycling, drip irrigation, and desalination, can help address water scarcity and ensure water security in the face of climate change. These technologies improve water efficiency and reduce reliance on freshwater resources.

8. **Electric Vehicles (EVs):** Transitioning from internal combustion engine vehicles to electric vehicles powered by renewable energy sources can significantly reduce greenhouse gas emissions from the transportation sector. EVs offer a cleaner and more sustainable alternative to conventional vehicles, contributing to climate change mitigation efforts.

9. **Circular Economy Practices:** Adopting circular economy principles, such as resource efficiency, waste reduction, and recycling, can help minimize greenhouse gas emissions associated with resource extraction, manufacturing, and waste disposal. Technologies for recycling, composting, and remanufacturing can contribute to a more sustainable and resilient economy.

10. **Remote Sensing and Climate Data Analytics:** Advanced technologies, such as satellite remote sensing, geographic information systems (GIS), and climate data analytics, provide valuable tools for monitoring and understanding climate change impacts, assessing vulnerability, and informing adaptation strategies.

Improved crop adaptation to climate change requires the integration of various tools and approaches to enhance resilience, productivity, and sustainability. Here are some key tools and technologies for crop adaptation to climate change:

The cultivation of millets offers a range of potential benefits, both for farmers and for broader societal and environmental concerns. Here are some key potential benefits of millet cultivation:

1. **Climate Resilience:** Millets are well-suited to a wide range of agroclimatic conditions, including marginal and drought-prone areas where other crops may struggle to grow. Their ability to thrive in challenging environments makes them a valuable crop for climate-resilient agriculture.

2. **Water Efficiency:** Millets have relatively low water requirements compared to other cereal crops like rice and maize. They can be grown with minimal irrigation or rainfall, making them suitable for regions facing water scarcity and erratic rainfall patterns.

3. **Soil Health:** Millets contribute to soil health through their deep root systems, which help improve soil structure, increase organic matter content, and enhance nutrient cycling. Rotating millets with other crops or integrating them into agroforestry systems can promote soil conservation and fertility.

4. **Nutritional Value:** Millets are highly nutritious grains, rich in protein, dietary fiber, vitamins, and minerals. They offer a valuable source of dietary diversity and can help address malnutrition and food insecurity, particularly in regions where staple food crops may lack essential nutrients.

5. **Crop Diversification:** Incorporating millets into cropping systems diversifies agricultural production, reducing reliance on a small number of staple crops and spreading risk against pests, diseases, and climate variability. Crop diversification also enhances resilience and sustainability in agricultural systems.

6. **Livelihood Opportunities:** Millet cultivation provides livelihood opportunities for smallholder farmers, particularly in rural and marginalized communities. It can generate income and employment along

the value chain, including production, processing, marketing, and trade of millet-based products.

7. **Biodiversity Conservation:** Millets contribute to biodiversity conservation by preserving genetic diversity within crop species and supporting diverse agroecosystems. Landraces and wild relatives of millets play a crucial role in breeding programs for developing climate-resilient crop varieties.

8. **Food Security:** Millets are staple food crops for millions of people worldwide, particularly in regions of Asia and Africa. Their resilience to climate variability and nutritional value make them important components of food security strategies, especially in vulnerable and food-insecure communities.

9. **Cultural Heritage:** Millets have cultural significance and traditional value in many societies, where they are consumed in various culinary preparations and rituals. Preserving and promoting millet cultivation helps maintain cultural heritage and traditional knowledge associated with these crops.

10. **Environmental Sustainability:** Millet cultivation promotes environmentally sustainable agriculture by reducing the use of water, synthetic fertilizers, and pesticides compared to other intensive cropping systems. It supports agroecological principles such as biodiversity conservation, soil health, and ecosystem resilience.

Millets, a group of small-seeded grains, have gained significant attention in recent years due to their impressive nutritional profile and potential health benefits. Here are some of the medicinal values or health benefits of millets from a modern perspective:

1. **Rich in Nutrients:** Millets are packed with essential nutrients such as protein, fiber, vitamins, and minerals. They provide a good source of carbohydrates for energy and contain micronutrients like iron, magnesium, phosphorus, and zinc, which are crucial for overall health.

2. **Gluten-Free:** Millets are naturally gluten-free, making them an excellent alternative for individuals with gluten intolerance or celiac disease. Incorporating millets into the diet can help diversify grain options for those who need to avoid gluten-containing grains like wheat, barley, and rye.

3. **Low Glycemic Index:** Millets have a low glycemic index (GI), which means they cause a slower and steadier rise in blood sugar levels compared to high-GI foods. This property makes millets suitable for individuals with diabetes or those aiming to manage blood sugar levels effectively.

4. **Heart Health:** The high fiber content in millets can aid in lowering cholesterol levels and reducing the risk of heart disease. Additionally, certain types of millets, such as finger millet (ragi), contain phytochemicals like polyphenols and lignans, which possess antioxidant properties that contribute to cardiovascular health.

5. **Weight Management:** Millets are relatively low in calories and rich in fiber, which can promote satiety and help control appetite. Including millets in a balanced diet may support weight management efforts by keeping you feeling full for longer periods and reducing overall calorie intake.

6. **Digestive Health:** The dietary fiber present in millets promotes digestive health by preventing constipation, regulating bowel movements, and supporting a healthy gut microbiome. Regular consumption of millets can contribute to improved gastrointestinal function and overall digestive well-being.

7. **Antioxidant Properties:** Some millet varieties contain antioxidants such as phenolic compounds, flavonoids, and carotenoids, which help combat oxidative stress and inflammation in the body. These antioxidants play a role in protecting cells from damage caused by free radicals and may reduce the risk of chronic diseases like cancer and age-related conditions.

8. **Bone Health:** Millets are a good source of minerals like calcium, phosphorus, and magnesium, which are essential for maintaining bone health and preventing conditions like osteoporosis. Incorporating millets into the diet can contribute to stronger bones and reduce the risk of fractures and bone-related disorders.

9. **Supports Immune Function:** The vitamins and minerals present in millets, such as vitamin C, vitamin E, zinc, and selenium, play vital roles in supporting immune function and strengthening the body's defenses against infections and diseases. Including millets in the diet can help bolster the immune system and promote overall health and wellness.

10. **Versatility in Culinary Use:** Millets are incredibly versatile and can be incorporated into various dishes, including porridges, salads, soups, bread, and desserts. Their adaptability in cooking makes it easier to enjoy their health benefits as part of a diverse and nutritious diet.

Table 14.1 Important Millets and their Medicinal Values

Millet	Medicinal importance	References
Pearl millet	Rebalances the pH of the gut and heals stomach ulcers, Both potassium and magnesium in high amounts lower blood pressure and treat heart diseases, Additionally, magnesium lessens respiratory issues and migraines, and high phosphorus content helps in bone growth and development in kids, high amount of dietary fibre and slow release of glucose maintains blood sugar level and more suitable for diabetic patients, phytic acids reduce the cholesterol levels of body, hypoallergic properties make it a suitable diet for lactating mothers, infants, adult.	Shobana et al. (2007), Taylor and Emmambux (2008), Chandrasekara and Shahidi (2010), Lee et al. (2010), Saleh et al. (2013), Muthamilarasan et al. (2016)
Finger millet	High amounts of phenolic acids have anti-ulcerative properties, lower blood sugar level and cholesterol, Phenolic compounds are nephron protective and anti-cataractogenic, germinated seeds improved haemoglobin level in infants, protection against epithelialization, mucosal ulceration, increases collagen synthesis, mast cells and fibroblasts activation, tryptophan reduces appetite and helps in the weight management, high calcium intake strengthens bones, lecithin and methionine remove extra fat from the liver, lowering blood cholesterol levels, high iron intake prevents anaemia	Antony et al. (1996), Friedman (1997), Kumari and Thayumanavan (1997), Chandrasekara and Shahidi (2010), Lee et al. (2010), Mohamed et al. (2012), Saleh et al. (2013)
Foxtail millet	Soluble and insoluble bound phenolic extracts present in the seeds show antioxidant, metal chelating, and metal reducing powers, decreases the body's toxicity produced by xenobiotics and toxins, high protein and essential amino acid intake aids in the development of bodily tissues and is recommended for infants and the elderly.	Hedge and Chandra (2005), Devi et al. (2011), Muthamilarasan et al. (2016)
Proso millet	High levels of copper aid in the production of red blood cells, support healthy blood vessels, bones, nerves, and immune system function, and aid in iron absorption. diet rich in copper protects against osteoporosis and cardiovascular disease. Magnesium reduces respiratory problems and migraine attack, potassium controls blood pressure and relieves heart diseases.	Dykes and Rooney (2006), Taylor and Emmambux (2008), Chandrasekara and Shahidi (2012), Saleh et al. (2013), Muthamilarasan et al. (2016)
Kodo millet	Phenolic chemicals possess antiulcerative actions and can decrease cholesterol and blood sugar levels, both potassium and magnesium regulate blood pressure and manage cardiovascular diseases; additionally, magnesium relieves respiratory issues and migraines.	Shobana et al. (2007), Taylor and Emmambux (2008), Chandrasekara and Shahidi (2012)
Barnyard millet	Richness in phenolic acids, tannins, phytates, and dietary fibres exhibits antimutagenic and anti-carcinogenic properties, high dietary fibre intake helps in reducing the incidence of oesophageal and colon cancer, phosphorous content aids in children's bone formation and growth	Bravo (1998), Hedge and Chandra (2005), Devi et al. (2011), Mohamed et al. (2012), Shivran (2016)
Little millet	High amounts of iron help to safeguard many fundamental functions in the body, including general energy and focus, the immune system, gastrointestinal processes, and the regulation of body temperature. higher amounts of zinc aid in enzymatic reactions, immune function, wound healing, DNA and protein synthesis, and regular growth and development of the body.	Antony et al. (1996), McKeown (2002), Chandrasekara and Shahidi (2010), Lee et al. (2010

Source: Author

2. CONCLUSION

In the present scenario, millets present both challenges and opportunities for health in various contexts, including agriculture, nutrition, and public health. Here are some of the key challenges and opportunities associated with millets for health:

Challenges:

1. **Limited Awareness and Consumption:** One of the significant challenges is the limited awareness and consumption of millets, particularly in urban areas and among younger generations. Many people are unfamiliar with millets or perceive them as "poor man's food," which affects their acceptance and adoption in modern diets.

2. **Supply Chain and Accessibility:** In many regions, the availability and accessibility of millets may be limited due to challenges in the supply chain, including distribution networks, storage facilities, and market demand. Improving infrastructure and logistics are essential for ensuring consistent access to millets for consumers.

3. **Cultural Preferences and Dietary Shifts:** Dietary preferences influenced by cultural norms and changing lifestyles contribute to the declining consumption of traditional foods like millets. Rapid urbanization and globalization have led to a shift towards Westernized diets, which often lack the diversity and nutritional benefits offered by millets.

4. **Processing and Value Addition:** Processing millets into consumer-friendly products often requires specialized equipment and techniques, which may be lacking in many small-scale processing units. Investing in research and development to enhance processing technologies and value addition can improve the marketability of millet-based products.

5. **Nutritional Quality and Bioavailability:** While millets are nutritionally dense, their bioavailability of certain nutrients, such as iron and zinc, may be lower compared to other grains due to the presence of anti-nutritional factors like phytates. Strategies to enhance the bioavailability of nutrients in millets through processing techniques or food combinations are needed.

Opportunities:

1. **Nutritional Superiority and Health Benefits:** Millets offer a range of nutritional benefits, including being gluten-free, rich in fiber, protein, and micronutrients. Positioning millets as a "superfood" with unique health-promoting properties can attract consumers seeking healthier food options.

2. **Sustainability and Climate Resilience:** Millets are well-adapted to diverse agro-climatic conditions and require fewer inputs like water and fertilizers compared to other crops like rice and wheat. Promoting millet cultivation can contribute to sustainable agriculture, conserve water resources, and enhance resilience to climate change.

3. **Diversification of Diets:** Encouraging the consumption of millets can contribute to dietary diversification, reducing dependence on monoculture crops and improving food security. Integrating millets into nutrition programs and culinary initiatives can help revive interest in traditional foods and promote culinary diversity.

4. **Income Generation and Livelihoods:** Millet cultivation and value addition activities offer opportunities for income generation and livelihood improvement, especially for smallholder farmers and rural communities. Supporting farmers with training, access to markets, and financial incentives can enhance their participation in millet production.

5. **Policy Support and Promotion:** Governments and policymakers can play a crucial role in promoting millets by implementing supportive policies, such as subsidies for millet cultivation, procurement programs, nutritional education campaigns, and inclusion of millets in school feeding programs and public institutions.

■ REFERENCE ■

1. Ajithkumar, I. P., and Panneerselvam, R. (2014). ROS scavenging system, osmotic maintenance, pigment and growth status of Panicum sumatrense Roth. under drought stress. Cell Biochem. Biophys. 68, 587–595. doi: 10.1007/s12013-013-9746-x

2. Balsamo, R. A., Willigen, C. V., Bauer, A. M., and Farrant, J. (2006). Drought tolerance of selected Eragrostis species correlates with leaf tensile properties. Ann. Bot. 97, 985–991. doi: 10.1093/aob/mcl068

3. Burke, M., Miguel, E., Satyanath, S., Dykema, J. and Lobell, D. (2009) Warming increases risk of civil war in Africa. Proceedings of the National Academy of Sciences USA 106, 20670–20674.

4. Evenson, R.E. and Gollin, D. (2003) Assessing the impact of the Green Revolution, 1960–2000. Science 300, 758–762.

5. Federoff, N.V., Battist, R.N., Beachy, R.N., Cooper, P.J.M., Fischhoff, D.A., Hodges, C.N., Knauf, V.C., Lobell, D., Mazur, B.J., Molden, D., Reynolds, M.P., Ronald, P.C., Rosegrant, M.W., Sanchez, P.A., Vonshak, A. and Zhu, J.K. (2010) Rethinking agriculture for the 21st century. Science 327, 833.

6. Food and Agriculture Organization of the United Nations (FAO). (2005). Summary of the World Food and Agricultural Statistics. FAO, Rome. (Available at: http://faostat.fao.org)

7. Hobbs, P.R., Sayre, K.D. and Gupta, R.K. (2008). The role of conservation agriculture in sustainable agriculture. Philosophical Transactions of Royal Society B (UK) 363, 543–555.

8. Intergovernmental Panel on Climate Change (IPCC). (2009). The Intergovernmental Panel on Climate Change. (Available at: http://www.ipcc. ch).

9. Khapre, A.P. (2017). Studies on Development of Value Added Products from Finger Millet (Eleusine coracana) and Foxtail Millet (Setaria italica) for Nutritional Security; Vasantrao Naik Marathwada Krishi Vidyapeeth: Parbhani, India

10. Lata, C., Bhutty, S., Bahadur, R. P., Majee, M., and Prasad, M. (2011). Association of an SNP in a novel DREB2-like gene SiDREB2 with stress tolerance in foxtail millet [Setaria italica (L.)]. J. Exp. Bot. 62, 3387–3401. doi: 10.1093/jxb/err016

11. Shobana et al. (2007), Taylor and Emmambux (2008), Chandrasekara and Shahidi (2010), Lee et al. (2010), Saleh et al. (2013), Muthamilarasan et al. (2016)

12. Antony et al. (1996), Friedman (1997), Kumari and Thayumanavan (1997), Chandrasekara and Shahidi (2010), Lee et al. (2010), Mohamed et al. (2012), Saleh et al. (2013)

13. Bravo (1998), Hedge and Chandra (2005), Devi et al. (2011), Mohamed et al. (2012), Shivran (2016)

14. Hedge and Chandra (2005), Devi et al. (2011), Muthamilarasan et al. (2016)

15. Dykes and Rooney (2006), Taylor and Emmambux (2008), Chandrasekara and Shahidi (2012), Saleh et al. (2013), Muthamilarasan et al. (2016)

16. Antony et al. (1996), McKeown (2002), Chandrasekara and Shahidi (2010), Lee et al. (2010

Study the Antimicrobial Properties of Several Cymbopogon Flexuosus Species

15

Rajesh Kumar Sinha*

Research Scholar,
Eklavya University, Sagar Road, Damoh,
Madhya Pradesh (India)

Pawan Kumar Jain

Vice Chancellor, (Supervisor),
Department of Botany, School of Basic and Applied Sciences,
Eklavya University, Sagar Road, Damoh,
Madhya Pradesh (India)

Abstract

In light of the growing problem of antibiotic resistance, there has been a marked increase in the investigation of naturally occurring substances that possess antibacterial characteristics. Amidst the plethora of plant species celebrated for their medicinal properties, Cymbopogon flexuosus, or lemongrass (Krishna), stands out as an intriguing contender with many uses. Exploring the chemical makeup, historical relevance, and the increasing need for alternative antimicrobial agents due to expanding resistance, this introduction seeks to clarify the reason for exploring the antimicrobial characteristics of different Cymbopogon flexuosus species. This paper examines the antibacterial capabilities of several species of Cymbopogon flexuosus.

Keywords

Cymbopogon flexuosus, Antimicrobial, Plant, Antibiotic, Resistance

1. INTRODUCTION

For many years, the tropical perennial grass has played an important role in both traditional medical and culinary traditions. It has become a globally significant plant due to its unique lemony scent and its many uses in cooking, perfumery, and aromatherapy. [1,2] Native American populations have relied on its antibacterial, anti-inflammatory, and stress-relieving extracts for a long time as a medicine. Lemongrass has a long history of use as a fragrant plant and medicinal remedy, which makes it an intriguing candidate for further research into its antibacterial properties. [3,4] The chemical make-up of *Cymbopogon flexuosus*, and especially the bioactive components found

---

*Corresponding author: rajeshsinha48@gmail.com

DOI: 10.1201/9781003606260-15

in its essential oils, is closely related to its medicinal capabilities. One of the most notable antibacterial properties of lemongrass essential oil is citral. [5,6] This substance has shown effectiveness against a variety of bacteria and fungi. It is a blend of geranial and neral isomers. Lemongrass has a wide range of pharmacological effects due to its unique combination of chemical components, which also gives it its pleasant scent.[7] In response to the growing problem of antibiotic resistance, scientists are actively seeking for new antimicrobials from natural sources that may have therapeutic promise. The pharmacological characteristics and long history of traditional usage of *Cymbopogon flexuosus* make it an intriguing research topic. [8] There is an immediate need to find new chemicals that can fight against resistant bacteria strains since the resistance to traditional antibiotics is becoming worse. Due to its versatile nature, lemongrass offers a fascinating research opportunity that might lead to new antibacterial approaches. [9] Different species of the genus *Cymbopogon* may have different chemical profiles and medicinal uses. To uncover possible differences in their efficiency, it becomes important to investigate the antibacterial activities of diverse *Cymbopogon flexuosus* species. [10] The chemical make-up of lemongrass essential oils, and by extension, their antibacterial activity, may be affected by factors including geographical location, climate, and growing procedures. This sophisticated method permits an exhaustive investigation of the genus, leading to a better knowledge of its antibacterial properties. [11,12] Investigating the antibacterial capabilities of different species of *Cymbopogon flexuosus* is a major step towards finding more efficient and alternative antimicrobials. [13,14] This research seeks to uncover the numerous antimicrobial potentials contained inside lemongrass, a plant with deep historical roots, complex chemical properties, and an immediate need for new treatments due to the rise of antibiotic resistance. The detailed study of many species of *Cymbopogon flexuosus* shows potential for expanding our knowledge of naturally occurring antimicrobial substances and encouraging the creation of new approaches to combating microbial diseases. [15]

2. METHODOLOGY

We obtained the fresh aerial parts of three different plant species from the lush fields of Ambikapur, which is situated in the tranquil Surguja district of Chhattisgarh: *Cymbopogon flexuosus*, also called *Krishna*; *Centella asiatica*, also called *Brahmi*; and *Cynodon dactylon*, also called *Doob Grass*. These carefully chosen plant materials would function as the basic components of the research we have planned. Carefully inspecting the plant samples taken from *Cymbopogon flexuosus (Krishna)*, *Centella asiatica*, and *Cynodon dactylon* for any indications of infection, spores, damage, discoloration, or deformation. After that, unharmed leaf samples underwent a comprehensive cleaning procedure that included rinsing with deionized water after being washed with tap water. The leaves were then meticulously air-dried at 37°C in a room with ambient conditions. To make the leaves ready for further examination, the midribs were cut off.

2.1 Antimicrobial Analysis

A crucial area of study having implications for the pharmaceutical and healthcare industries is the investigation of plant extracts' antibacterial properties. We used the well diffusion method, which is a well-known technique, for our experiment. We carefully followed the steps outlined by Raviraja and colleagues in their 2006 paper. Plant extracts may be tested for their ability to inhibit different bacteria using the well diffusion technique. Plant extract solutions are put in wells on agar plates that have been infected with fungus or bacteria. Antimicrobial chemicals diffuse into the agar over time, preventing the development of germs and creating discernible zones of inhibition.

1. **Antibacterial-Zone Inhibition Test - *S. aureus* (*Staphylococcus aureus*)**

   The antimicrobial activity was assessed using the Kirchhoff-Bauer method, which is a zone inhibition technique. Before inserting the discs containing 10 µl of various concentrations (0 to 100 mg/ml), the MHA plates were infected with 100 µl of Bacterial culture, S. aureus (adjusted to 0.5 McFarland Unit - Approx cell density, or 1.5×10^8 CFU/mL). To get the right quantity to put on the disc, 10% of the sample was collected and diluted in a series of steps. The solvent-only disc in each plate was used as a control, while the Ciprofloxacin disc (10µg) was used as a positive control. For 24 hours, the S. aureus plates were placed in an incubator (Basil Scientific Corp. India) set at 37 °C. We measured and documented the clean zones that were produced around the disc.

2. **Antibacterial-Zone Inhibition Test - *E. coli* (*Escherichia coli*)**

   The antimicrobial activity was assessed using the Kirchhoff-Bauer method, which is a zone inhibition technique. Before inserting the discs containing 10 µl of various concentrations (0 to 100 mg/ml), the MHA plates were infected with 100 µl of Bacterial culture, E. coli (adjusted to 0.5 McFarland Unit - Approx cell density, or 1.5×10^8 CFU/mL). To get the right quantity to put on the disc, 10% of the sample was collected and diluted in a series of steps.

The solvent-only disc in each plate was used as a control, while the Ciprofloxacin disc (10 µg) was used as a positive control. The E. coli plates were left to incubate at 37 °C for a whole day. We measured and documented the clean zones that were produced around the disc.

2.2 Statistical Analysis

Every experiment's data was run via a one-way analysis of variance (ANOVA), which was followed by post hoc analysis. The Bonferroni post hoc test is used after the two-way ANOVA and Tukey's multiple comparison test. Software called Graph Pad Prism 6.0 was used to do the analysis.

3. RESULT

3.1 Antibacterial activity of *S. aureus*

The antibacterial activity of *CF* against *S. aureus* at varied concentrations (in µg/disk) on three separate plates (A, B, and C) is shown in the table. As a reference point for anticipated activity, the positive control (PC) continuously displayed an inhibition zone of 30 mm. It is worth noting

Table 15.1 Antibacterial activity - *S. aureus* – *CF (Cymbopogon flexousus)*

Amount (µg/disk)	Plate A	Plate B	Plate C	Average	SD	SEM
PC	30	30	30	30	0	0
0	0	0	0	0	0	0
50	5	5	5	5	0	0
125	5	5	5	5	0	0
250	6	6	6	6	0	0
500	7	7	7	7	0	0
1000	8	7	8	7.66667	0.57735	0.33333

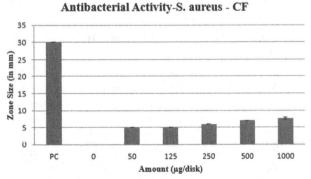

Fig. 15.1 Antibacterial activity *S. aureus – CF (Cymbopogon flexousus)*

that the inhibition zones at 50, 125, 250, and 500 µg/disk were consistently 5 or 6 mm across all plates, suggesting that the antibacterial effectiveness may reach a plateau within this range. Slightly more than 7 millimetres was noted at 1000 micrograms per disc. The findings highlight the need of doing more research to determine the compound's maximum efficacy against S. aureus and sheds light on the concentration-dependent antimicrobial response.

Table 15.2 Antibacterial activity *S. aureus – CA (Centella asiatica)*

Amount (µg/disk)	Plate A	Plate B	Plate C	Average	SD	SEM
PC	29	29	29	29	0	0
0	0	0	0	0	0	0
50	5	5	5	5	0	0
125	5	5	5	5	0	0
250	5	5	6	5.33333	0.57735	0.33333
500	6	6	7	6.33333	0.57735	0.33333
1000	7	7	7	7	0	0

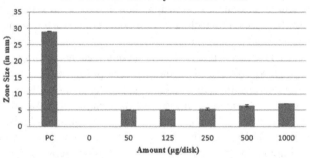

Fig. 15.2 Antibacterial activity *S. aureus – CA (Centella asiatica)*

The antibacterial activity of a particular chemical (*CA*) against Staphylococcus aureus (S. aureus) at different concentrations (µg/disk) across three plates (A, B, and C) is shown in the table that is provided. The measured inhibitory zone diameters (in millimetres) are submitted with the computed average, standard deviation (SD), and standard error of the mean (SEM).

The positive control (PC) showed a steady baseline for predicted antimicrobial efficiency throughout all three plates, with a 29 mm inhibition zone. None of the plates showed any inhibition zone sizes when the negative control (0 µg/disk) was used, as expected. The inhibitory zones stayed at 5 mm for doses of 50, 125, and 250 µg/disk, indicating a consistent antimicrobial effect throughout this range. Nevertheless, a possible response that depends on concentration was indicated by a little rise to 6.33 mm at 500 µg/disk. Further improvement in antibacterial activity was shown by a 7 mm inhibitory zone at the highest dose tested, 1000 µg/disk. Data variability is shown by the standard deviation (SD) and standard error of the mean (SEM) numbers. The consistently low standard deviation and standard error of the mean (SEM) values across the board indicate that the antimicrobial responses seen were at least somewhat repeatable and precise. This thorough examination of the compound's antibacterial activity against S. aureus lays the framework for future research into its antimicrobial potential by shedding light on its effects as a function of concentration.

Table 15.3 Antibacterial activity *S. aureus – CD (Cynodon dactylon)*

Amount (µg/disk)	Plate A	Plate B	Plate C	Average	SD	SEM
PC	32	32	32	32	0	0
0	0	0	0	0	0	0
50	5	5	5	5	0	0
125	5	5	5	5	0	0
250	5	5	6	5.33333	0.57735	0.3333333
500	6	6	6	6	0	0
1000	7	7	7	7	0	0

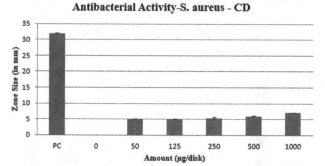

Fig. 15.3 Antibacterial activity *S. aureus – CD (Cynodon dactylon)*

A particular chemical (*CD*) was tested at varied concentrations (µg/disk) across three plates (A, B, and C) for its antibacterial activity against *Staphylococcus aureus (S. aureus)*. The results are shown in the table. Aside from the computed average, standard deviation, and standard error of the mean, the data also contains the millimeter-scale inhibitory zone widths.

A dependable baseline for anticipated antimicrobial effectiveness was established when the positive control (PC) showed a 32 mm inhibition zone throughout all three

plates. No inhibitory impact was seen with the negative control (0 µg/disk), as expected, leading to inhibition zone widths of zero on all plates. The inhibitory zones stayed at 5 mm for doses of 50, 125, and 250 µg/disk, suggesting that there was a consistent antimicrobial action at these concentrations. A possible concentration-dependent response was indicated by the little rise to 6 mm at 500 µg/disk. There was an increase in antibacterial activity, as the inhibition zones reached 7 mm at the maximum dose tested (1000 µg/disk). Antibacterial microbial responses were found to be very precise and repeatable, as shown by the low values of standard deviation (SD) and standard error of the mean (SEM) throughout the trial. This in-depth investigation of *CD*'s effects on *S. aureus* at different concentrations paves the way for future investigations into the compound's antibacterial properties.

Table 15.4 Antibacterial activity *S. aureus – CF (Cymbopogon flexousus) –oil*

Amount (µg/disk)	Plate A	Plate B	Plate C	Average	SD	SEM
PC	34	34	34	34	0	0
0	0	0	0	0	0	0
50	7	7	7	7	0	0
125	8	8	8	8	0	0
250	9	9	9	9	0	0
500	10	10	10	10	0	0
1000	12	12	11	11.6667	0.57735	0.33333

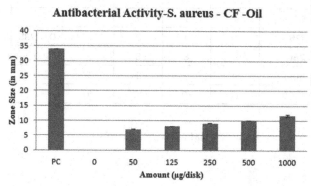

Fig. 15.4 Antibacterial activity *S. aureus – CF (Cymbopogon flexousus) – oil*

This table shows the results of testing three plates (A, B, and C) for the antibacterial activity of *CF-oil* against *Staphylococcus aureus (S. aureus)* at different concentrations (µg/disk). Providing a constant baseline for predicted antibacterial activity, the positive control consistently revealed an inhibition zone of 34 mm. The negative control, which had a concentration of 0 µg/disk, did not show any inhibitory action and so had no inhibition zone diameters. With increasing volumes of *CF-oil*, bigger inhibitory zones were found, indicating a concentration-dependent response. In particular, inhibitory zones of 7, 8, 9, and 10 mm were produced by doses of 50, 125, 250, and 500 µg/disk, respectively. Particularly noteworthy was the fact that antibacterial activity increased, although slightly, with increasing concentrations. A further improvement was seen at the maximum concentration (1000 µg/disk), with an average inhibitory zone diameter of 11.67 mm. Accuracy and dependability in the documented antimicrobial responses are supported by the small values of standard deviation (SD) and standard error of the mean (SEM). This extensive study highlights the fact that the antibacterial activity of *CF-oil* against *S. aureus* is concentration-dependent, which might be useful for future antimicrobial studies.

3.2 Antibacterial Activity of *E. coli*

At different doses (µg/disk) on three plates (A, B, and C), the table shows how effective a drug *(CF)* was against the bacteria *Escherichia coli (E. coli)*. The 27 mm inhibition zone that the positive control showed time and time again

provided a reliable measure of the expected antibacterial activity. No inhibitory impact was seen in the negative control group (0 µg/disk), which was predicted. Greater inhibition zones were associated with higher concentrations of *CF*, indicating a concentration-dependent response. The inhibition zones were measured to be 7, 7.33, 8, 9, and 10 mm for concentrations of 50, 125, 250, 500, and 1000 µg/disk, respectively. Higher concentrations show improved antibacterial action, highlighting the compound's potency against *E. coli*. The recorded antimicrobial responses were very accurate and reliable, as the standard deviation (SD) values were always zero. Insights into the concentration-dependent antibacterial actions of *CF* against *E. coli* may be greatly enhanced by the consistency and reproducibility of the observed trends in inhibitory zone widths.

Table 15.6 Antibacterial activity *E. coli– CA (Centella asiatica)*

Amount (µg/disk)	Plate A	Plate B	Plate C	Average	SD	SEM
PC	29	29	29	29	0	0
0	0	0	0	0	0	0
50	5	5	5	5	0	0
125	5	5	5	5	0	0
250	5	5	6	5.33333	0.57735	0.33333
500	6	6	6	6	0	0
1000	7	7	7	7	0	0

Table 15.5 Antibacterial activity *E. coli– CF (Cymbopogon flexousus)*

Amount (µg/disk)	Plate A	Plate B	Plate C	Average	SD
PC	27	27	27	27	0
0	0	0	0	0	0
50	7	7	7	7	0
125	7	7	8	7.33333	0.57735
250	8	8	8	8	0
500	9	9	9	9	0
1000	10	10	10	10	0

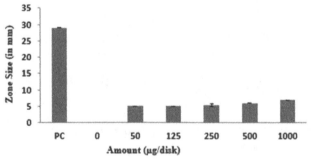

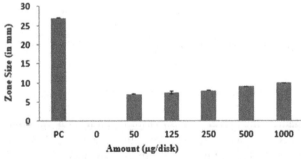

Fig. 15.6 Antibacterial activity *E. coli– CA (Centella asiatica)*

A chemical *(CA)* was tested for its antibacterial activity against *Escherichia coli (E. coli)* at different concentrations (µg/disk) on three separate plates (A, B, and C) and the results are shown in the table. A trustworthy baseline for expected antibacterial effectiveness was provided by the positive control, which consistently showed an inhibition zone of 29 mm. To no one's surprise, the negative control (0 µg/disk) showed no inhibitory effect and produced

Fig. 15.5 Antibacterial activity *E. coli– CF (Cymbopogon flexousus)*

inhibition zone diameters of zero on every plate. The widths of the inhibitory zones rose in tandem with the concentration of *CA*, which went from 50 to 1000 µg/disk. In particular, inhibitory zones of 5, 5.33, 6, 6, and 7 mm were produced by concentrations of 50, 125, 250, 500, and 1000 µg/disk, respectively. It seems that the antibacterial activity gradually increases when the compound concentrations are raised, according to this concentration-dependent response. antibacterial responses were recorded with a high degree of accuracy and reproducibility, as seen by the low standard deviation (SD) and standard error of the mean (SEM) values throughout the trial. This research sheds light on the compound's antibacterial potential by revealing the concentration-dependent actions of *CA* against *E. coli*.

Table 15.7 Antibacterial activity *E. coli– CD (Cynodon dactylon)*

Amount (µg/disk)	Plate A	Plate B	Plate C	Average	SD	SEM
PC	26	26	26	26	0	0
0	0	0	0	0	0	0
50	7	7	7	7	0	0
125	8	8	8	8	0	0
250	8	9	8	8.33333	0.57735	0.3333333
500	9	10	9	9.33333	0.57735	0.3333333
1000	10	10	10	10	0	0

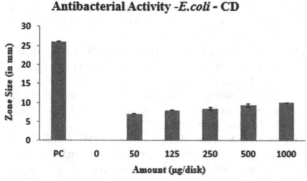

Fig. 15.7 Antibacterial activity *E. coli – CD (Cynodon dactylon)*

At varying doses (µg/disk), the antibacterial activity of a chemical (*CD*) against *Escherichia coli (E. coli)* was examined on three distinct plates (A, B, and C) in the table. The positive control served as a reliable standard for the expected antimicrobial efficacy, consistently showing an inhibition zone of 26 mm across all plates. No inhibitory impact was seen with the negative control (0 µg/disk), as anticipated, leading to inhibition zone widths of zero on

all plates. A comparable rise in inhibitory zone diameters was seen when the concentration of *CD* was raised from 50 to 1000 µg/disk. The inhibition zones measured 7, 8, 8.33, 9.33, and 10 mm at 50, 125, 250, 500, and 1000 µg/disk, respectively. antibacterial responses were recorded with a high degree of accuracy and reliability, as shown by the estimated standard deviation (SD) and standard error of the mean (SEM) values. Insights into the concentration-dependent effects of *CD* against *E. coli* are provided by this data, which highlights its potential as an antibacterial agent and lays the groundwork for future study.

Table 15.8 Antibacterial activity *E. coli– CF (Cymbopogon flexousus) (oil)*

Amount (µg/disk)	Plate A	Plate B	Plate C	Average	SD	SEM
PC	28	28	28	28	0	0
0	0	0	0	0	0	0
50	7	7	7	7	0	0
125	8	8	8	8	0	0
250	9	9	9	9	0	0
500	10	10	10	10	0	0
1000	11	11	11	11	0	0

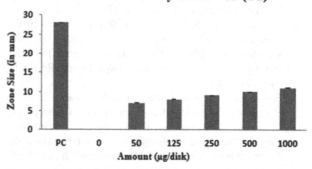

Fig. 15.8 Antibacterial activity *E. coli– CF (Cymbopogon flexousus) (oil)*

This table shows the results of testing three plates (A, B, and C) with *CF oil* at various doses (µg/disk) to see its antibacterial effectiveness against *Escherichia coli (E. coli)*. The 28 mm inhibition zone regularly shown by the positive control provides a solid foundation for predicting the antimicrobial efficacy. The absence of inhibitory action and zero inhibition zone widths on all plates were seen in the negative control (0 µg/disk), as anticipated. Inhibition zone widths rose proportionally from 7 to 11 mm as the quantity of *CF oil* was raised from 50 to 1000 µg/disk, indicating concentration-dependent responses. Significantly, both the standard deviation (SD) and the standard error of the mean (SEM) remained constantly at zero, suggesting that the antimicrobial responses that were recorded were precise and reliable. These findings give light on the antibacterial activities of *CF oil* against *E. coli*, which are concentration dependent, and indicate that it may be a useful antimicrobial agent. Potential implications for antimicrobial research as a whole and its use in specific antibacterial tactics might be the subject of future studies.

4. Conclusion

our investigation delved into the inhibitory potential of individual chemical components against S. aureus, revealing a notable effectiveness in contrast to their limited impact on E. coli. These findings contribute to the growing body of knowledge surrounding antibacterial agents, emphasizing the need for a nuanced understanding of their specificity and mechanisms of action. As we unravel the complexities of these interactions, we pave the way for the development of targeted antibacterial strategies with implications for precision medicine and the sustainable management of bacterial infections.

■ REFERENCES ■

1. Bhalla, Y., & Gupta, V. K. (2020). Lemongrass (Cymbopogon flexuosus): A source of unique aromatic compounds with potential applications in antimicrobial research. Journal of Essential Oil Research, 17(5), 519–524.

2. Chavan, M. J., Wakte, P. S., & Shinde, D. B. (2020). Analgesic and anti-inflammatory activities of the lemongrass essential oil (Cymbopogon flexuosus) in male and female Wistar albino rats. Phytotherapy Research, 24(5), 712–716.

3. Fernandes, L., Casal, S., Pereira, J. A., Saraiva, J. A., & Ramalhosa, E. (2018). Effect of lemon grass (Cymbopogon flexuosus) decoction as a potential antioxidant and antimicrobial agent on the quality of fresh-cut kiwifruit. Journal of Food Processing and Preservation, 42(1), e13308.

4. Govindarajan, M., Sivakumar, R., & Rajeswary, M. (2022). Chemical composition and larvicidal activity of essential oil from Cymbopogon flexuosus against Culex tritaeniorhynchus, Aedes albopictus, and Anopheles subpictus (Diptera: Culicidae). Experimental Parasitology, 130(3), 271–274.

5. Hossain, M. A., Al-Toubi, W. A., Weli, A. M., Al-Riyami, Q., & Al-Sabahi, J. N. (2022). Identification and characterization of chemical compounds in different crude extracts from leaves of Omani neem. Journal of Taibah University for Science, 6(1), 21–28.

6. Islam, M. T., & Datta, B. K. (2019). Cymbopogon citratus (DC.) Stapf: A review on its ethnobotany, phytochemical and pharmacological profile. Journal of Ethnopharmacology, 151(1), 663–678.

7. Kpoviessi, S., Bero, J., Agbani, P., Gbaguidi, F., Kpadonou-Kpoviessi, B., Sinsin, B., ... & Quetin-Leclercq, J. (2018). Chemical composition, cytotoxicity and in vitro antitrypanosomal and antiplasmodial activity of the essential oils of four Cymbopogon species from Benin. Journal of Ethnopharmacology, 151(1), 652–659.

8. Mimica-Dukic, N., Bozin, B., Sokovic, M., Mihajlovic, B., & Matavulj, M. (2022). Antimicrobial and antioxidant activities of three Mentha species essential oils. Planta Medica, 69(5), 413–419.

9. Rattanachaikunsopon, P., & Phumkhachorn, P. (2020). Antimicrobial activity of basil (Ocimum basilicum) oil against Salmonella enteritidis in vitro and in food. Bioscience, Biotechnology, and Biochemistry, 74(6), 1200–1204.

10. Tariq, S., Wani, S., Rasool, W., Shafi, K., Bhat, M. A., & Prabhakar, A. (2021). A comprehensive review of the antibacterial, antifungal and antiviral potential of essential oils and their chemical constituents against drug-resistant microbial pathogens. Microbial Pathogenesis, 82, 80–91.

11. Shin D. S., Eom Y. B. (2019). Efficacy of zerumbone against dual-species biofilms of Candida albicans and Staphylococcus aureus. Microb. Pathog. 137, 103768. doi: 10.1016/j.micpath.2019.103768

12. Silva Cde B., Guterres S. S., Weisheimer V., Schapoval E. E. (2018). Antifungal activity of the lemongrass oil and citral against Candida spp. Braz. J. Infect. Dis. 12, 63–66. doi: 10.1590/s1413-86702008000100014

13. Somolinos M., García D., Condón S., Mackey B., Pagán R. (2020). Inactivation of Escherichia coli by citral. J. Appl. Microbiol. 108, 1928–1939. doi: 10.1111/j.1365-2672.2009.04597.x

14. Tan Y., Leonhard M., Moser D., Ma S., Schneider-Stickler B. (2019). Antibiofilm efficacy of curcumin in combination with 2-aminobenzimidazole against single- and mixed-species biofilms of Candida albicans and Staphylococcus aureus. Colloids Surf B. Biointerfaces 174, 28–34. doi: 10.1016/j.colsurfb.2018.10.079

15. Todd O. A., Fidel P. L. Jr., Harro J. M., Hilliard J. J., Tkaczyk C., Sellman B. R., et al. (2019). Candida albicans Augments Staphylococcus aureus Virulence by Engaging the Staphylococcal agr Quorum Sensing System. MBio 10, e00910–19. doi: 10.1128/mBio.00910-19

Note: All the figures and tables in this chapter were made by the author

Challenges and Opportunities for Innovation in India – Dr. Shweta Mishra et al. (eds)
© 2024 Taylor & Francis Group, London, ISBN 978-1-032-99842-8

Green Hydrogen: Fuel of the Future

16

Pradeep Tripathi, Avneesh Kumar Singh

Associate Professor, AIMT,
Lucknow

Abstract

India has announced a target of energy independence by 2047 and a net-zero by 2070, Under the National Green Hydrogen Mission. Green Hydrogen is expected to play a substantial role towards achieving these goals. Green Hydrogen is produced by the process of electrolysis [1], where water is split into hydrogen and oxygen using electricity generated from renewable sources like solar, wind, or hydropower. This process results in a clean and emission-free fuel that has immense potential to replace fossil fuels and reduce carbon emissions. Another method of producing Green Hydrogen is from biomass, which involves the gasification of biomass to produce hydrogen. Both these production methods are clean and sustainable, making Green Hydrogen an attractive option for the transition to a low-carbon future. Hydrogen is an energy carrier that can transform our fossil-fuel dependent economy into a hydrogen based economy [2], which can provide an emissions-free transportation fuel. But the Hydrogen storage and transport are issues of intense research due to hydrogen's characteristic low density. Is hydrogen a justifiable means to the attainment of an environmentally beneficial transportation fuel when methods of production are not utilizing clean, renewable energy sources? What exactly are the completely emissions-free methods of producing and utilizing hydrogen in transportation? Can hydrogen be the fuel of the future?

Keywords

Hydrogen fuel, PEM fuel cell, Climate change, Hydrogen economy

1. INTRODUCTION

Hydrogen is the fuel of the future. As an avid researcher of alternative fuels and an ambitious chemistry student, this researcher understands the importance of a shift to a hydrogen economy. Hydrogen is an energy carrier that can be used in internal combustion engines or fuel cells producing virtually no greenhouse gas emissions when combusted with oxygen. The only significant emission is water vapor. Hydrogen production and storage is currently undergoing extensive research. A solar-hydrogen system can provide the means of a totally emissions-free method of producing hydrogen. Although steam re formation of methane is currently the major route to hydrogen production, the emissions involved can also be controlled much more efficiently than our current system of transportation fuel.

Corresponding author: pkt7880@gmail.com

DOI: 10.1201/9781003606260-16

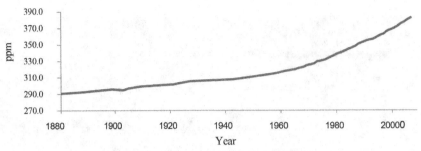

Fig. 16.1 CO$_2$ concentration since 1880

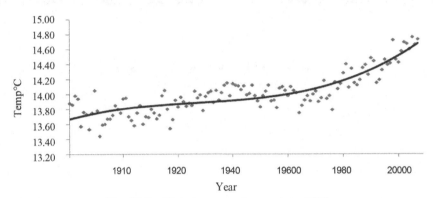

Fig. 16.2 Global average temp. since 1880

Source: Compiled by Earth Policy Institute, with long term historical data from World watch Institute

Climate change is a serious issue becoming increasingly evident to much of the population. Rising CO$_2$ levels have directly contributed to the global warming phenomenon. As shown in Figs. 16.1 and 16.2, the CO$_2$ levels have rising dramatically in the past 200 years, along with the global average temperature.

This study examines numerous aspects involved in the hydrogen economy and not compares hydrogen to other alternative fuels. Hydrogen is an essential feedstock in various industrial processes, including the production of ammonia and the refining of petroleum. Transitioning to green hydrogen in these applications can further reduce the carbon footprint of these industries. As the world seeks to transition to a more sustainable energy system, hydrogen is seen as a key player in the decarbonization of sectors that are challenging to electrify directly. In summary the hydrogen fuel holds promise as a clean, versatile, and sustainable energy carrier with the potential to play a crucial role in addressing environmental challenges and promoting a transition to a low-carbon energy future. [10]Government policy will be briefly referenced, but not detailed. The core of the research concerns the advantages of hydrogen and the current progress related to the disadvantages of hydrogen as a transportation fuel. Much work is in progress to initiate a shift from a fossil-fuel economy to a hydrogen fuel based economy. Understanding these production, storage, and utilization methods is crucial for evaluating the feasibility and Sustainability of hydrogen as an energy carrier in different applications (Fig. 16.3). The choice of method often depends on factors such as cost, efficiency, and specific application requirements. What are the advantages and disadvantages of this hydrogen economy? Who is funding this research and what are their true intentions? Is there a possibility that hydrogen will be the Fuel of the future and also accomplish the goal of being emissions-free?

2. MATERIALS AND METHODS

This research is based on independent research and literature reviews. The various sources of research include recent journal articles from opposing sides of the hydrogen economy. The Energy website was referenced for current statistics relating to the transportation sector and the various alternative energy sources being researched. Various methods of hydrogen production, including electrolysis, steam methane reforming (SMR), Auto-thermal Reforming (ATR), Biomass Gasification, Hydrogen Photoproduction (photo catalytic process), Thermo chemical Water Splitting, catalytic methane

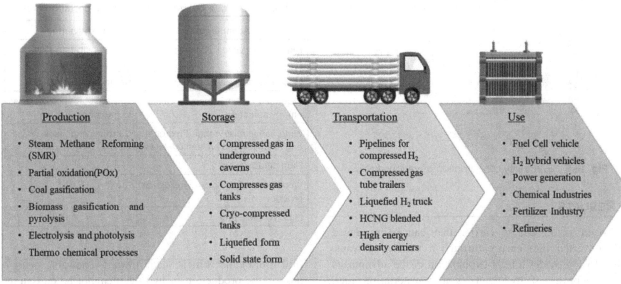

Fig. 16.3   Production, storage, transportation and use of hydrogen gas

pyrolysis and others. Hydrogen can be storage (Fig. 16.4) in various forms like compressed Hydrogen (Hydrogen gas is compressed at high pressures (typically around 350-700 bar) and stored in high-strength composite or metal containers. This method is suitable for stationary and transportation applications, Liquid hydrogen (Hydrogen can be cooled to extremely low temperatures (around -253 degrees Celsius or -423 degrees Fahrenheit) to become a liquid. Liquid hydrogen takes up less volume than gaseous hydrogen, making it practical for space applications and some transportation uses, Hydride (Hydrogen can be chemically bonded with certain materials (metal hydrides) to form solid compounds. Releasing hydrogen from these compounds can be controlled, offering a safe and compact storage option, and Carbon based material. Some searchers are exploring the use of carbon-based materials, such as graphene or carbon nanotubes, for storing hydrogen through physisorption.

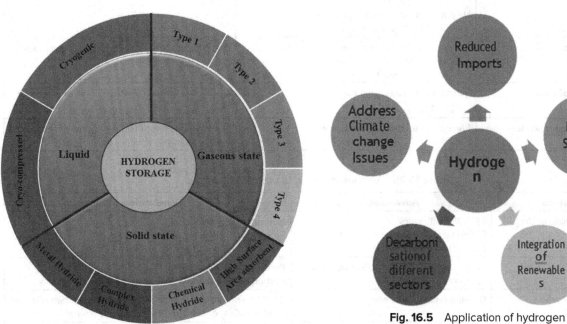

Fig. 16.4   Ways of hydrogen storage

Fig. 16.5   Application of hydrogen

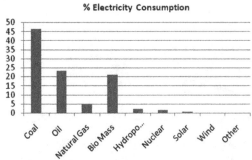

Fig. 16.6 Electricity consumption of various fuels

Table 16.1 Use of hydrogen as a transportation fuel

Advantages	Disadvantages
High energy yield (122 kJ/g)	Low density(large storage areas)
Most abundant element	Not found free in nature
Produced from many primary energy sources	Low ignition energy(similar to gasoline)
Wide flammability range (hydrogen engines operated on lean mixtures)	Currently expensive
High diffusivity	
Water vapor is major oxidation product	
Most versatile fuel	

3. RESULTS

Hydrogen is an energy carrier that can be produced and converted into energy through a variety of ways. Table 16.1 provides a brief explanation of the advantages and drawbacks of hydrogen as a transportation fuel. Electrolysis of water is deemed to be the cleanest route to the production of hydrogen. However, the advantages of this proposed hydrogen economy is dependent on the use of clean, renewable resources as the source of electricity. Today burning coal and nuclear fission generates 62.6% of the India electricity. For instance, the major routes to employable hydrogen gas involve the use of electricity.

Until a dramatic shift is made toward renewable energy sources, the production of hydrogen cannot be emissions free. Hydrogen can be produced from several different methods, with only a couple being environmentally beneficial. Electrolysis of water requires electricity, which can be provided by clean and renewable energy sources. Tables 16.2a and 16.2b provide a summary of the various ways to produce hydrogen [15]. Hydrogen storage and transport is a critical issue involving intense research. The

Table 16.2a Various methods to produce hydrogen

Method	Process	Implementation
Steam reforming of methane gas	In presence of nickel catalyst & at 700 – 1100 °C: $CH_{4(g)} + H_2O_{(g)}CO_{(g)} + 3H_{2(g)}$ Next reaction at lower temperature: $CO_{(g)} + H_2O_{(g)}CO_{2(g)} + H_{2(g)}$	Current major source of hydrogen
Hydrogen from coal (Gasification)	At high temperature and pressure: Coal $+ H_2O_{(g)} + O_{2(g)}$ syngas Syngas $= H_2 + CO + CO_2 + CH_4$	Current method of mass hydrogen production
Electrolysis of water	Electric current passed through water: $2H_2O_{(l)}2H_{2(g)} + O_{2(g)}$	Not in widespread use due to cost of electricity
Solar – Hydrogen system	Electric current passed through water: $2H_2O_{(l)}2H_{2(g)} + O_{2(g)}$	Not in widespread use due to cost of renewable energy sources

Table 16.2b Various methods to produce hydrogen

Method	Advantages	Disadvantages
Steam reforming of $CH_{4(g)}$	65 – 75% efficiency Economical (least expensive method) Established infrastructure	Nonrenewable resource Produces CO_2 emissions
Gasification	Large supplies of coal in US Inexpensive resources	Produces CO_2 emissions Carbon sequestration would raise costs 45% efficiency
Electrolysis of water	Depend on electricity source	Input into production may require more energy than released Produces CO_2 emissions if coal is energy source
Solar System – Hydrogen	No emissions 65% efficiency	Expensive

problem is the low density of hydrogen gas. Three possible solutions have been proposed. These potential hydrogen delivery systems include compressed tube trailers, liquid storage tank trucks, and compressed gas pipelines. One major disadvantage of each system is the high capital costs. Table 16.3 and Table 16.4 provide a summary of various possible forms off storage of hydrogen fuel. The use of metal hydrides is the most promising storage material currently. The advantages are high volume efficiencies, easy recovery, and advanced safety. The most common metal hydrides in current research are listed in Table 16.4. Hydrogen can be used as the primary fuel in an internal combustion engine or in a fuel cell (Fig. 16.7) A hydrogen internal combustion engine is similar to that of a gasoline engine, where hydrogen combusts with oxygen in the air and produces expanding hot gases that directly move the physical parts of an engine. The only emissions are water vapor and insignificant amounts of nitrous oxides. The efficiency is small, around 20%. A polymer electrolyte membrane (PEM) fuel cell produces an electrical current from hydrogen fuel and oxygen in the air. Hydrogen is split into hydrogen ions and electrons by a platinum catalyst at

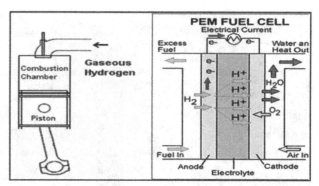

Fig. 16.7   PEM fuel cell

the anode. The PEM allows only the hydrogen ions to pass through to the cathode where these ions react with oxygen to produce water. The electrons travel down a circuit creating an electrical current. The fuel cells are arranged in stacks in order to provide enough electricity to power a vehicle. The use of a fuel cell eliminates the nitrous oxide emissions. Furthermore, the fuel cell is 45-60% efficient.

4. Discussion

An alternative fuel must be technically feasible, economically viable, easily convert to another energy form when combusted, be safe to use, and be potentially harmless to the environment. Hydrogen is the most abundant element on earth. Although hydrogen does not exist freely in nature, it can be produced from a variety of sources such as steam reformation of natural gas, gasification of coal, and electrolysis of water. Hydrogen gas can used in traditional gasoline-powered internal combustion engines (ICE) with minimal conversions. However, vehicles with polymer electrolyte membrane (PEM) fuel cells provide a greater efficiency [4]. Hydrogen gas combusts with oxygen to produce water vapor. Even the production of hydrogen gas can be emissions-free with the use of renewable energy sources. [9]The current price of hydrogen is about $4 per kg, which is about the equivalent of a gallon of gasoline. However, in fuel cell vehicles, such as the 2009 Honda FCX Clarity, 1kg provides about 68 miles of travel [3]. Of course the price range is currently very high. Ongoing research and implementation toward a hydrogen economy is required to make this fuel economically feasible. The current focus is directed toward hydrogen being a clean alternative fuel that produces insignificant greenhouse gas emissions. If hydrogen is the next transportation fuel, the primary energy source used to produce the vast amounts of hydrogen will not necessarily be a renewable, clean source. Carbon sequestration is referenced frequently as a means to eliminate CO_2 emissions from the burning of coal, where the gases are captured and sequestered in gas

Table 16.3   Possible storage forms for hydrogen

Storage Form	Advantages	Disadvantages
Compressed Gas	Reliable Indefinite storage time Easy to use	Higher capital & operating costs Heat can cause container rupture
Liquid	High density at low pressure	High cost Low temperatures needed Escape can cause fire or asphyxiation
Metal Hydride	High volume efficiencies Easy recovery Very safe	Expensive materials Heavy storage tanks

Table 16.4   Hydrogen storage properties of metal hydrides

Metal	Hydride	%Hydrogen by mass	Equilibrium Pressure (bar)	Equilibrium Temperature (K)
Pd	$PdH_{0.6}$	0.56	0.020	298
LaNi$_5$	$LaNi_5H_6$	1.37	2	298
ZrV$_2$	$ZrV_2H_{5.5}$	3.01	10^{-8}	323
FeTi	$FeTiH_2$	1.89	5	303
Mg$_2$Ni	Mg_2NiH_4	3.59	1	555
TiV$_2$	TiV_2H_4	2.60	10	313

Source: Kraus T; "Hydrogen Fuel–An Economically Viable Future for the Transportation Industry?" Duke J., Economics Spring 2023; XIX

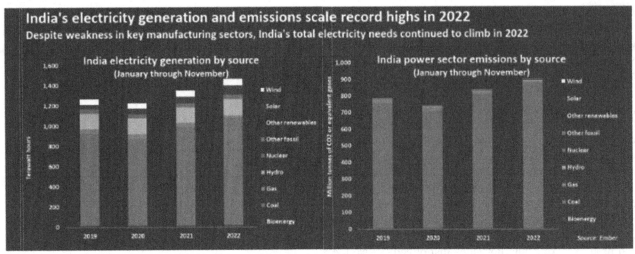

India's electricity generation and emissions scale record highs in 2022

Fig. 16.8 India's electricity generation and emission scale record

wells or depleted oil wells. However, the availability of these sites is not widespread and the presence of CO_2 may acidify groundwater.

Storage and transport is a major issue due to hydrogen' slow density. Is the investment in new infrastructure too costly? Can our old infrastructure currently used for natural gas transport be retrofitted for hydrogen? Whatever Hydrogen can be used as a clean fuel in transportation, particularly in fuel cell vehicles, it offers fast refueling and long driving ranges, addressing some limitations of battery electric vehicles The burning of coal and nuclear fission are the main energy sources that will be used to provide an abundant supply of hydrogen fuel. How does this process help our current global warming predicament? The India launched recently funded a research project to produce hydrogen from coal at large-scale facilities, with carbon sequestration in mind. Is this the wrong approach? Should there be more focus on other forms of energy that produce no greenhouse gas emissions? If the damage to the environment is interpreted into a monetary cost, the promotion of energy sources such as wind and solar may prove to be a more economical approach. The possibility of a hydrogen economy that incorporates the use of hydrogen into every aspect of transportation requires much further research and development. The most economical and major source of hydrogen in the India is steam reformation of natural gas, a nonrenewable resource and a producer of greenhouse gases. The electrolysis of water is a potentially sustainable method of producing hydrogen, but only if renewable energy sources are used for the electricity. Today, less than 5% of our electricity comes from renewable sources such as solar, wind, and hydro-Nuclear

power (Fig. 16.6) may be considered as a renewable resource to some, but the waste generated by this energy source becomes a major problem. A rapid shift toward renewable energy sources is required before this proposed hydrogen economy can prove itself. Solar photovoltaic (PV) systems are the current focus of my research related to the energy source required for electrolysis of water. One project conducted at the GM Proving Ground in Milford, MI employed the use of 40 solar PV modules directly connected to an electrolyzer/storage/dispenser system. The result was 8.5% efficiency in the production of hydrogen, with an average production of 0.5 kg of high-pressure hydrogen per day [6]. Research similar to this may result in the optimization of the solar- Hydrogen energy system Furthermore, the infrastructure for a hydrogen economy will come with high capital costs. The transport of hydrogen through underground pipes seems to be the most economical when demand grows enough to require a large centralized facility. However, in places of low population density, this method may not be economically feasible. The project mentioned earlier may become an option for individuals to produce their own hydrogen gas at home, with solar panels lining their roof. A drastic change is needed to slow down the effects of our fossil-fuel dependent society. Conservation can indeed help, but the lifestyles we are accustomed to require certain energy demands. Transportation is a necessary part of our current world and the switch to a hydrogen economy can provide a sustainable solution. Is hydrogen the fuel of the future? The research presented here encourages one to answer yes. India has launched the National Green Hydrogen Mission with an outlay of Rs. 19,744 crores with a target of 5 MMT production capacity of Green Hydrogen per annum.

■ REFERENCES ■

1. Veziroglu TN, Sahin S. 21st Century's energy: Hydrogen energy system. *Energy Conversion and Management.* 2008, *49,* 1820–1831.

2. Balat M. Potential importance of hydrogen as a future solution to environmental and transportation problems. *International Journal of Hydrogen Energy.* 2008, *33,* 4013–4029.

3. Dougherty W, Kartha S, Rajan C, Lazarus M, Bailie A, Runkle B, Fencl A. Greenhouse gas reduction benefits and costs of a large-scale transition to hydrogen in the USA. *Energy Policy* (2008),

4. Baschuk JJ, Li X. A comprehensive, consistent and systematic mathematical model of PEM fuel cells. *Applied Energy,* 2009, *86,* 181–193.

5. Gasification Technologies Council. http://www.gasification. org (October20, 2008).

6. Committee on Alternatives and Strategies for Future Hydrogen Production and Use, National Research Council. *The Hydrogen Economy: Opportunities, Costs, Barriers, and R&D Needs.* Washington, D.C.: The National Academy Press. 2004.

7. Kelly, N.A.; Gibson, T.L.; Ouwerkerk, D.B.; A solar-powered, high-efficiency hydrogen fueling system using high-pressure electrolysis of water: Design and initial results. *Int. J. of Hydrogen Energy.* 2008, *33,* 2747–2764.

8. Kim J, Lee Y, Moon I. Optimization of a hydrogen supply chain under demand uncertainty. *Int. J. of Hydrogen Energy.* 2008, *33,* 4715–4729.

9. International Energy Agency report on "India 2020 Energy Policy Review".

10. National Hydrogen Energy Roadmap (2006) by Ministry of New and Renewable Energy, India.

11. International Energy Agency report on "The future of hydrogen – Seizing today's opportunities"

12. Allied Market research report on "India Hydrogen Market – Opportunity Analysis and Industry Forecast, 2018–2025"

13. The Hydrogen Economy opportunities and challenges, book edited by Michael Ball and Martin Wietschel, Cambridge university Press, 2009.

14. E. Rivard, M. Trudeau, K. Zaghib, Materials 12(2019) 1973.

15. Strategic Analysis report on "Hydrogen storage system cost Analysis" August 2017 by C. Houchins and B. D. James.

16. N. Sirosh. Hydrogen composite tank program, Proceedings of 2002 U.S. DOE Hydorgen Program Review, Golden, CO, USA, 6–10 May 2002

17. Petitpas, G.; Simon, A.J. Liquid Hydrogen Infrastructure Analysis; Lawrence Livermore National Laboratory: Livermore, CA, USA, 2017

18. Meneghelli, B.; Tamburello, D.; Fesmire, J.; Swanger, A. Integrated Insulation System for

19. Automotive Cryogenic; U.S. DOE Hydrogen and Fuel Cells Program, 2017

20. K. Kunze, K. Oliver, Cryo-compressed hydrogen storage, BMW group, Munich, Germany 2012

21. FAction Plan on Clean Fuels, NITI Aayog and Confederation of Indian Industry, 2018

Note: All the figures and tables in this chapter were made by the author

Challenges and Opportunities for Innovation in India – Dr. Shweta Mishra et al. (eds)
© 2024 Taylor & Francis Group, London, ISBN 978-1-032-99842-8

Synthesis and Characterization of Grafted Gum Karaya via Microwave Route for Mercury (II) Ions Removal from Aqueous Solution

17

Brijesh Kumar[1]

Assistant Professor,
Dept. of Chemistry, Rajkiya Mahila Mahavidhyalaya,
Badaun, Uttar Pradesh, India

Ph.D Student,
Dept. of Applied Chemistry, M. J.P. Rohilkhand University,
Bareilly (U.P.), India

Pramendra Kumar[2]

Professor,
Dept. of Applied Chemistry, M. J.P. Rohilkhand University,
Bareilly (U.P.), India

Abstract

A novel pH-sensitive adsorbent for the elimination of $Hg+2$ ions from aqueous solution was synthesized by grafting of itaconic acid onto gum karaya (GK) using microwave-assisted method without the help of any initiator. The synthesized adsorbent [GK-g-poly(Ita)] was characterized via various analytical techniques such as SEM, FT-IR, and XRD to confirm its grafting. To achieve the removal of the highest $Hg+2$ from water, various influencing parameters, such as adsorption dosage, pH value, time duration, and concentration, were investigated. The highest elimination of $Hg+2$ (92%) was achieved at dosage 30 mg, pH 6, time 50 minutes, temperature 30 0C and 100 ppm of $Hg+2$ concentration. The $Hg+2$ adsorption on [GK-g-poly(Ita)] was verified by FT-IR, XRD, and SEM studies. To understand the adsorption pattern, the adsorption isotherm was explained by the Langmuir and Freundlich adsorption isotherms, and the adsorption kinetics was investigated using different kinetic models. The present work provides convincing data that proves beyond doubt that material based on gum karaya and itaconic acid [GK-g-poly(Ita)] appears to be capable of effectively removing $Hg+2$ from aqueous system, and that can be potentially extended.

Keywords

Gum karaya, Grafting, Hg+2, Adsorption, Microwave

1. INTRODUCTION

One extremely hazardous transition metal is mercury [1], which enters an organism through food, skin, or breathing and severely harms the central nervous system (CNS). Its worldwide dynamics and both short- and long-term negative effects make it a highly endangered element [1, 2]. The global public has witnessed the epidemics it

[1]brijesh.kumar17171@gmail.com, [2]pramendra@mjpru.ac.in

DOI: 10.1201/9781003606260-17

produced in Iraq and Japan. Minamata is an illness caused by mercury toxicity. One of the most hazardous types of mercury that causes poisoning is methyl mercury. In 2017, the World Health Organisation (WHO) listed mercury as one of the ten dangerous chemicals [5, 6]. Since mercury is one of the most deadly metals of all known metal pollutants [9], its elimination from water bodies [7] is a major issue for environmental system [8]. Mercury and related species are widely used in many sectors, including those that produce paints, pulp, electrical equipment [10], insecticides, paper, thermometers [11], and mercury vapor lamps. Mercury may also be hazardous to cells at extremely low concentrations because it creates strong connections with sulfhydryl groups inside cells [3], which can lead to brain damage, kidney, liver, gastrointestinal tract, and CNS malfunction [12, 13]. Thus, it is crucial to sanitize mercury from lakes and rivers. A multitude of methods, such as ion exchange, coagulation, reduction, adsorption, precipitation and reverse osmosis have been developed to eliminate metal pollutants from water bodies [15]. Adsorption is the most amazing method yet discovered for removing mercury from an aqueous solution. Since activated carbon has excellent adsorption properties, it is most commonly used as a potent adsorbent [16]. Therefore, there is a pressing need to create an inexpensive, environmentally acceptable adsorbent with the same high lignin-adsorption capacity as water to remove mercury [17]. My research work focused on producing natural polymer-based adsorbents and modifying natural polymer for use as an adsorbent to remove various hazardous metal ions and toxic metals from aqueous solutions. [18]. Low-cost adsorbents based on gum karaya (GK) have a great deal of potential for use in the elimination of Hg^{+2} from contaminated water [4]. The use of microwave radiation in the preparation of graft copolymers has recently attracted more attention because it produces grafted materials that are more effective as sorbents than those prepared by conventional means and also saves chemicals and reaction time [20].

2. EXPERIMENTAL

2.1 Methods and Materials

Karaya gum was procured from Otto Chemie Pvt. Ltd., India. The itaconic acid (Ita) was acquired from Merck Ltd. in India. Merck Ltd., India supplied methanol (MeOH), acetone, sodium hydroxide, and mercuric chloride ($HgCl_2$). We purchased rhodamine 6 G and KI (potassium iodide) from SD Fine Chem. Ltd., India. All experiments were performed using double distilled (DD) water. The irradiation was applied using an LG. MH 2548QPS domestic microwave oven. Synthesis of the grafted gum karaya The synthesis of KG-g-poly(Ita) [karaya gum-g-poly(itaconic acid)] was performed according to the previously published technique [5]. Briefly, 1 g GK was added to 100 mL double-distilled (DD) water at magnetic stirrer. After adding the appropriate quantity of itaconic acid into the gum karaya solution, the solution was stirred for 30 minutes to attain homogenous. The homogenous solution containing gum karaya and itaconic acid was irradiated (80% power) for the required time duration in a domestic microwave oven. The grafting was then terminated by adding a saturated hydroquinone solution. After 24 hours of the complete grafting reaction, two distinct layers developed: one homopolymer layer and the other graft GK, was separated from each other. The separated grafted GK was precipitated with methanol, washed with acetone to remove water molecules, and finally dried in oven at 40 °C. To optimize grafting, the process was done at various microwave power levels, itaconic acid concentrations, and exposure times [7, 8]. The following (Eq.1) was used to determine the grafting percentage:

$$\frac{\text{Grafting}}{(\%)} = \frac{\text{Wight of grafted GK} - \text{Wight of pure GK}}{\text{Wight of pure GK}} \quad \text{(Eq.1)}$$

2.3 Characterization Techniques

FT-IR spectrum of pure GK and KG-g-poly(Ita) were recorded using an FT-IR spectrometer (Model: Brucker, Tensor II) at 26 °C at 100 scans, between wavelength range $4000\,cm^{-1}$ to $500\,cm^{-1}$. The crystallinity of the GK and KG-g-poly(Ita) was analyzed at 40 kV voltage using a Bruker-D 8 advanced diffractometer, materials were examined in the at angle range of 0^0 to 80^0, 2 theta with 6°/min steep angle. SEM microscope (model: JSM, 6490) operating at a 15 kV accelerating voltage provided the surface morphological information. Shimadzu UV-1800 (UV spectrophotometer) was utilized to determine the Hg+2 concentrations in filtrate. 2.4 Study of batch adsorption The investigation of batch adsorption was completed using a previously disclosed procedure [6, 7]. To make a stock solution of Hg^{+2}, dissolve 1.354 g of mercuric chloride ($HgCl_2$) in 1 L of DD water. Similar to the adsorption experiment, the stock solution was diluted and pH adjust by adding NaOH and HCl solutions [8]. The experiment used 20 mL of a synthetic solution containing 100 ppm of mercury (II) ions and 30 mg of the sample dosage as the adsorbent. Using a UV-visible spectrophotometer, mercury's residual concentration in the resultant solution was determined. The maximum quantity of adsorbed Hg^{+2} [q_e (mg/g)] was determined by Eq. 2.

$$q_e = \frac{C_i - C_e}{W} \times V \quad \text{(Eq. 2)}$$

Where, C_i are initial and C_e the final concentration of the Hg^{+2} solution in (mg/L), and W is the grafted GK's weight, and V is the Hg^{+2} solution's volume (L).

3. RESULT AND DISCUSSION

3.1 Influence of Several Factors on Grafting

Effect of Itaconic Acid Concentrations

The impact of itaconic acid concentration on the grafting percentage Fig. 17.1a. depicts. The proportion of grafting was shown to increase as itaconic acid concentration increased, and the optimal grafting was identified at 0.3 mol/L of itaconic acid.

Effect of Microwave Power

Microwave power (m.p) effect on the grafting is seen in Fig. 17.1b. The optimum high percentage (92%) of grafting yield was observed at 80% (1080 watts) of m.p. It was researched that grafting increases with an increase in m.p from range 20 to 80 (270 to 1080 watt) and again, an increase in m.p reduced the grafting yield.

Effect of Reaction Time on the Grafting

The impact of response time on grafting yield is seen in Fig. 17.1c. It was shown that the grafting % increased quickly as the time from 30 to 90 seconds increased, and that the grafting increased marginally as the duration increased from 90 to 120 seconds.

3.2 Characterization

FT-IR (Fourier Transform-Infrared Spectroscopy)

KG displayed (Fig. 17.2a) a broad band at 3,459 cm^{-1} is causes of –OH, the –CH$_2$ group's C/H stretching mode is displayed by a peak at 2,937 cm^{-1}, the stretching vibrations (C//O) of free carboxylic acids are responsible for the peaks at 1,731 and 1,624 cm^{-1}. The C/O and C/C stretching vibrations of KG's pyranose rings were identified as the source of the absorption peaks between 1,056 and 1,155 cm^{-1}. The deformation vibrations of the C/OH and CH$_2$

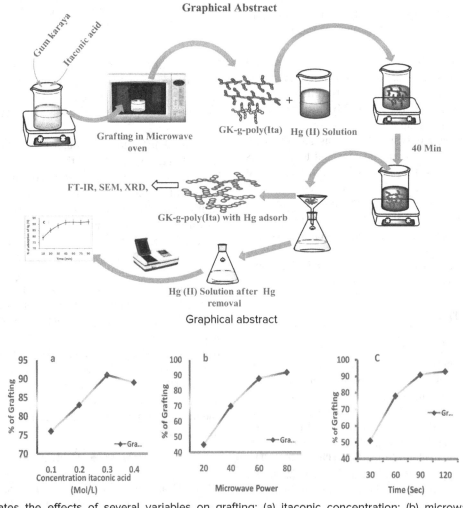

Fig. 17.1 Illustrates the effects of several variables on grafting: (a) itaconic concentration; (b) microwave power; and (c) response time

groups were responsible for the absorption peak at 1,425 cm^{-1}, whereas the peaks at 1,248 cm^{-1} were because of the C/O/C stretching vibrations. The observations above are consistent with the findings of Sethi et al. [9, 10]. FTIR spectrum Fig. 17.2 (b) in the KG-g-poly(Ita)), a band at 1028 cm^{-1} indicates for C/O/C group. The stretching vibration of CO is shown by a prominent band at 1489 cm^{-1}The stretching vibrations of C//C and C//O are responsible for the bands located at 1624 cm^{-1} and 1709 cm^{-1}, respectively. The distinctive O/H stretching vibrations are responsible for a wide band at 3378 cm^{-1}. The effective grafting of itaconic acid on KG is proven by the emergence of distinctive peaks of both KG and itaconic acid [11].

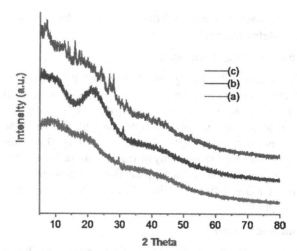

Fig. 17.3 XRD spectra of the [a] Pure GK, [b] KG-g-poly(Ita), (c) Hg loaded KG-g-poly(Ita)

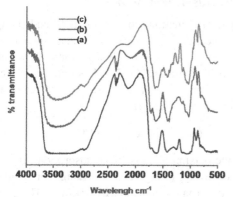

Fig. 17.2 FT-IR spectra of the [a] Pure GK, (b) KG-g-poly(Ita), [c] Mercury loaded KG-g-poly(Ita)

XRD (X-ray Diffraction Analysis)

The XRD of pure GK and KG-g-poly(Ita) were demonstrated in Fig. 17.3 Gum karaya's XRD pattern shows a broad hump at $2\theta = 23°$, indicating that gum karaya was naturally amorphous, as seen in Fig. 17.3a. Gum karaya's amorphous nature was shown by XRD,

since no distinctive peak was seen. The grafting of itaconic acid onto the GK surface was verified by the XRD spectra of the grafted GK (Fig. 17.3b), which also revealed less strong but crystalline peaks that have been corroborated by other studies. The mercury-loaded grafted gum karaya's XRD spectra (Fig. 17.3c) revealed that it is somewhat more crystalline than pure GK and grafted GK [12, 13].

Scanning Electronic Microscopy (SEM)

SEM analysis of the surface morphology of KG-g-poly(Ita) and pure gum karaya is displayed in Fig. 17.4. Pure gum karaya exhibited a homogenous, smooth surface with a few holes (Fig. 17.4a) [7]. After itaconic acid was grafted onto the gum karaya's polymeric backbone, the homogenous and smooth surface disappeared and as seen in Fig. 17.4b, the gum karaya acquired a heterogeneous, stiff, dispersed morphology that was ideal for the adsorption of hazardous metal ions.

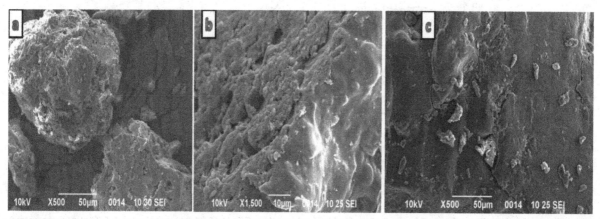

Fig. 17.4 Showing the SEM spectra of the (a) Pure gum karaya, (b) KG-g-poly(Ita), (c) Hg^{+2} loaded KG-g-poly(Ita)

3.3 Effect of Various Parameters on Mercury Adsorption

Effect of Adsorbent Dose

The impact of the dosage of adsorbent on the adsorption of Hg^{+2} was examined using a Hg^{+2} synthetic solution at constant concentrations was applied to KG-g-poly(Ita) at different dosages, as illustrated in Fig. 17.5(a). The increase in KG-g-poly(Ita) dosage from 10 to 30 mg was seen to increases the quantity of mercury adsorption (62 to 89%); however, after reaching equilibrium concentration, further KG-g-poly(Ita) addition had no effect on mercury adsorption.

Influence of pH

A remarkable shift in Hg^{2+} adsorption by KG-g-poly(Ita) at different pH values was observed, as shown in Fig. 17.5(b). The pH range from 2 to 8 was used to study the Hg^{2+} adsorption by KG-g-poly(Ita). At pH-2, mercury adsorption was determined to be at a minimum of 50%. The adsorption increased quickly (by 91%) when the pH rise from 4 to 6, and then it slightly decreased as the pH increases. Therefore, KG-g-poly(Ita) adsorbed 91% of the mercury ion at a pH of 6, which was the ideal value for Hg^{2+} ion adsorption.

Influence of Contact Time

The effect of contact duration of the adsorption capacity was demonstrated in Fig. 17.5(c). The findings of the results showed that as the contact time (10 to 30 min) rose, so did the amount of Hg^{2+} ions that were adsorbed from its solution. There was no discernible increase in adsorption with the additional increase in contact time.

Effect of Concentration

The effect of Hg^{2+} concentration on adsorption is shown in Fig. 17.5(d). The study indicates that when Hg^{2+} concentration was raised from 20 ppm to 100 ppm, adsorption rapidly increased and after its adsorption almost constant.

Impact of Temperature

The temperature impact of grafted GK capacity on adsorbed Hg+2 ions from a mercury solution is illustrated in Fig. 17.5(e). The mercury ion adsorption capacity by KG-g-poly(Ita) increases with a regular 91.9% as temperature rise from 10 to 30 °C; however, the adsorbent's Hg adsorption capacity decreases with higher temperature increases.

3.4 Adsorption Isotherms

Langmuir Adsorption Isotherm

Mathematical equations of Freundlich and Langmuir isotherms were utilised to explain the adsorption of various ions on the solid interface and their solution's concentration at a specific temperature [14, 15]. Adsorption of material in a monolayer on an adsorbent surface is described by the Langmuir isotherm (Eq. 4).

$$(1/q_e) = [(1/b\ q_m) + (1/C_e)] \qquad \text{(Eq. 4)}$$

Where, the maximum capacity of adsorption (monolayer) is denoted by q_m (mg/g) and the Langmuir equilibrium adsorption constant is indicated by b (L/mg). The graph C_e/q_e versus C_e is used to calculate the q_m and b (Fig. 17.6a).

$$R_L = [1/(1 + bC_i)] \qquad \text{(Eq. 5)}$$

Where, the initial concentration of Hg^{+2} is denoted by C_i R_L is zero indicate for irreversible adsorption, $R_L = 1$ for linear, and unfavorable when $R_L > 1$, R_L is a crucial number to investigate the kind and nature of the sorption process [31].

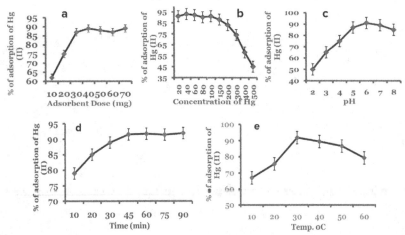

Fig. 17.5 Illustrates the effect of several parameters for Hg^{+2} adsorption: Effect of adsorbent dose (a); Effect of concentrations (b); Effect of time (c); Effect of pH (d); Effect of temperature (e)

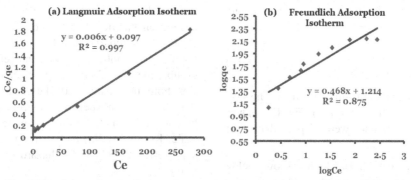

Fig. 17.6 Adsorption isotherms: Langmuir isotherm (a); Freundlich isotherm (b)

Freundlich Adsorption Isotherm

Adsorption at heterogeneous interfaces is explained by the Freundlich isotherm (Eq. 6) [16].

$$\log q_e = [(\log K_F) + (\log C_e/n)] \qquad \text{(Eq.6)}$$

Where, $1/n$ and K_F (L mg-1) stand for the Freundlich constant, which expresses the intensity and capability of adsorption. In Fig. 17.6b, the constants were computed by charting logqe against log Ce.

The findings indicate that, in comparison to the Freundlich isotherm ($R^2 = 0.875$), the Langmuir adsorption isotherm for the porous grafted gum karaya provided the greatest match ($R^2 = 0.997$).

3.5 Adsorption Kinetics

The kinetics study of adsorption was described by using four various kinetic mathematical models, consist the pseudo-first, pseudo-second, Elovich, and intraparticle diffusions [17]. One of the important kinetic models for determining the first-rate constant for sorption in solid/liquid systems is the pseudo-first-order equation [18, 19].

$$\log(q_e - q_t) = \log q_e - \frac{K_1}{2.303}t \qquad \text{(Eq. 7)}$$

Where, the Hg^{+2} concentrations at time t and equilibrium, expressed in mmol/g, are q_t and q_e, respectively and K_1 (min^{-1}) is the rate constant. Constant, K_1, and q_e were found using the values of the intercepts and slopes of the plots $\log(q_e-q_t)$ vs. t (Fig. 17.7a),.

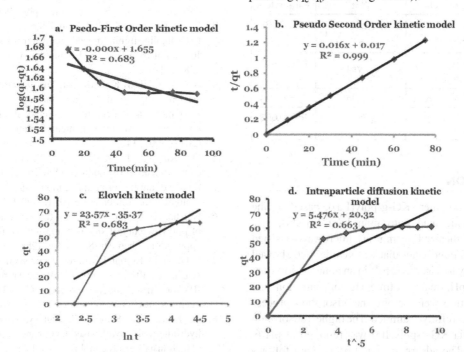

Fig. 17.7 [a] Pseudo First order, [b] Pseudo-second order, [c] Intra particle diffusion kinetic, and [d] Elovich kinetics, model for the adsorption of mercury by the adsorbent

In order to apply the experiment data for pseudo-second-order (Eq. 8), [18-20]:

$$\frac{t}{q_t} = \frac{1}{K_2 q^2{}_e} + \frac{1}{q_e} t \qquad \text{(Eq. 8)}$$

Where, the rate constant is K_2 [g/(mmol × min)]. The slope as well as intercept of the curve (t/q_t Vs t) (Fig. 17.7b) were used to calculate the values R^2 were displayed in Table 17.1.

The Elovich kinetic model (Eq. 9), which is shown below, was fitted using the experimental data [21, 22]:

$$q_t = \frac{1}{\beta} \ln(\alpha\beta) + \frac{1}{\beta} \ln t \qquad \text{(Eq. 9)}$$

The plot of q_t versus $\ln t$ was used to derive the values of α (adsorption rate constant) and β (the surface covering activation energy's extent) displaying in Fig. 17.7c and R^2 value in Table 17.1.

The intra-particle diffusion linear equation was shown in (Eq. 10) [21],

$$q_t = K_{id} t^{0.5} + c \qquad \text{(Eq. 10)}$$

The graph q_t vs $t^{0.5}$ (Fig. 17.7d) was used to determine the value of K_{id}, and the rate constant, and R^2 value was displayed in Table 17.1.

Table 17.1 R^2 values for adsorption kinetics models

S. No.	Kinetic Models	Plot	Parameters
i.	Pseudo-first-order kinetics equation.	$\log\dfrac{(qo - qt)}{qo}$ Vs t	$R^2 = 0.683$
ii.	Pseudo-second-order kinetics equation	$\dfrac{t}{q_t}$ Vs t	$R^2 = 0.999$
iii.	Elovich kinetic model	q_t Vs $\ln t$	$R^2 = 0.683$
iv.	Intra-particle diffusion kinetics equation	q_t Vs $t^{0.5}$	$R^2 = 0.663$

3. CONCLUSION

A novel graft copolymer (KG-g-poly(Ita)), based on the grafting of itaconic acid onto gum karaya (KG), was successfully synthesized using a microwave-assisted method. The graft copolymer that was synthesized showed an effective ability to adsorbed Hg^{+2} in an aqueous solution. Adsorbent dose, pH, treatment time, Hg concentration, and reaction temperature were among the adsorption process factors that were carefully examined. The highest adsorption of Hg^{+2} (92%) via KG-g-poly(Ita) was reported at pH 6, and 40 minutes. The adsorption equilibrium data follows the Langmuir adsorption isotherm ($R^2 = 0.997$), whereas the pseudo second order ($R^2 = 0.999$) was followed by the adsorption kinetics data. Since KG-g-poly(Ita) possesses a negatively charged surface with many active sites, including, phenolic, alcoholic, and ketonic with carboxylic groups, the Hg^{2+} ion adsorption process on the material was both physically and chemically associated. KG-g-poly(Ita) is an inexpensive, environmentally friendly, and biocompatible material that is simple to produce on a big scale. KG-g-poly(Ita) has a strong economic potential as a powerful adsorbent for hazardous metal sorption and removal.

ACKNOWLEDGMENT

One of the authors, Brijesh Kumar, is also very thankful to the Council of Scientific and Industrial Research (CSIR), New Delhi, for the financial support in the form of a Junior Research Fellowship to carry out this work.

CONFLICT OF INTEREST

All authors have no conflicts of interest.

■ REFERENCES ■

1. K. Binnemans, P.T. Jones, Perspectives for the recovery of rare earths from end-of-life fluorescent lamps, Journal of Rare Earths 32(3) (2014) 195–200.
2. M.A. Al-Ghouti, D. Da'ana, M. Abu-Dieyeh, M. Khraisheh, Adsorptive removal of mercury from water by adsorbents derived from date pits, Scientific reports 9(1) (2019) 15327.
3. Y. Ge, Q. Song, Z. Li, A Mannich base biosorbent derived from alkaline lignin for lead removal from aqueous solution, Journal of Industrial and Engineering Chemistry 23 (2015) 228–234.
4. A.A. Ismaiel, M.K. Aroua, R. Yusoff, Palm shell activated carbon impregnated with task-specific ionic-liquids as a novel adsorbent for the removal of mercury from contaminated water, Chemical Engineering Journal 225 (2013) 306–314.
5. D. Kumar, J. Pandey, P. Kumar, Synthesis and characterization of modified chitosan via microwave route for novel antibacterial application, International journal of biological macromolecules 107 (2018) 1388–1394.
6. N. Khan, D. Kumar, P. Kumar, Microwave assisted synthesis of polyvinylbutyral-silica composites for mercury removal application, ChemistrySelect 4(6) (2019) 1979–1984.
7. S. Gihar, D. Kumar, P. Kumar, Facile synthesis of novel pH-sensitive grafted guar gum for effective removal of mercury (II) ions from aqueous solution, Carbohydrate Polymer Technologies and Applications 2 (2021) 100110.
8. A. Kumar, D. Kumar, G. Pandey, Characterisation of hydrothermally synthesised CuO nanoparticles at different pH, Journal of Technological Advances and Scientific Research 2(4) (2016) 166–169.

9. S. Sethi, B.S. Kaith, M. Kaur, N. Sharma, S. Khullar, Study of a cross-linked hydrogel of Karaya gum and Starch as a controlled drug delivery system, Journal of Biomaterials Science, Polymer Edition 30(18) (2019) 1687–1708.

10. A. Verma, N. Sachan, Carboxymethylation Of Karaya Gum: Application In Gastroretentive Drug Delivery For Sustained Release Of Model Drug, (2020).

11. P.B. Krishnappa, V. Badalamoole, Karaya gum-graft-poly (2-(dimethylamino) ethyl methacrylate) gel: an efficient adsorbent for removal of ionic dyes from water, International journal of biological macromolecules 122 (2019) 997–1007.

12. L. KAUR, G. Gupta, Gum karaya-G-poly (acrylamide): microwave assisted synthesis, optimisation and characterisation, International Journal of Applied Pharmaceutics (2020) 143–152.

13. H. Mittal, A. Maity, S.S. Ray, Synthesis of co-polymer-grafted gum karaya and silica hybrid organic–inorganic hydrogel nanocomposite for the highly effective removal of methylene blue, Chemical Engineering Journal 279 (2015) 166–179.

14. A.M. Elbedwehy, A.M.J.P. Atta, Novel Superadsorbent Highly Porous Hydrogel Based on Arabic Gum and Acrylamide Grafts for Fast and Efficient Methylene Blue Removal, 12(2) (2020) 338.

15. P. Kumar, S. Gihar, B. Kumar, D. Kumar, Synthesis and characterization of crosslinked chitosan for effective dye removal antibacterial activity, International journal of biological macromolecules 139 (2019) 752–759.

16. A.M. Elbedwehy, A.M. Abou-Elanwar, A.O. Ezzat, A.M.J.P. Atta, Super Effective Removal of Toxic Metals Water Pollutants Using Multi Functionalized Polyacrylonitrile and Arabic Gum Grafts, 11(12) (2019) 1938.

17. V. Singh, P. Kumar, Design of nanostructured tamarind seed kernel polysaccharide-silica hybrids for mercury (II) removal, Separation Science and Technology 46(5) (2011) 825–838.

18. A.M. Elbedwehy, A.M. Atta, Novel superadsorbent highly porous hydrogel based on arabic gum and acrylamide grafts for fast and efficient methylene blue removal, Polymers 12(2) (2020) 338.

19. B.K. Preetha, B. Vishalakshi, Microwave assisted synthesis of karaya gum based montmorillonite nanocomposite: Characterisation, swelling and dye adsorption studies, International Journal of Biological Macromolecules 154 (2020) 739–750.

20. B.K. Preetha, B. Vishalakshi, Microwave assisted synthesis of karaya gum based montmorillonite nanocomposite: Characterisation, swelling and dye adsorption studies, International Journal of Biological Macromolecules (2020).

21. D. Kumar, J. Pandey, N. Khan, P. Kumar, P.P. Kundu, Synthesize and characterization of binary grafted psyllium for removing toxic mercury (II) ions from aqueous solution, Materials Science and Engineering: C 104 (2019) 109900.

22. A.A. Adeyi, S.N.A.M. Jamil, L.C. Abdullah, T.S.Y. Choong, K.L. Lau, M. Abdullah, Adsorptive removal of methylene blue from aquatic environments using thiourea-modified poly (acrylonitrile-co-acrylic acid), Materials 12(11) (2019) 1734.

Challenges and Opportunities for Innovation in India – Dr. Shweta Mishra et al. (eds)
© 2024 Taylor & Francis Group, London, ISBN 978-1-032-99842-8

Effect of Variable Suction on Oscillatory Flow

18

Anand Asthana*

Associate Professor,
Department of Applied Science,
Ambalika Institute of Management and Technology,
Lucknow

Abstract

An analysis of a two-dimensional flow of water past an infinite vertical porous plate is presented unde the following conditions: the suction velocity oscillates in time about a constant non- zero mean, the free stream velocity oscillates in time about a constant mean, the plate temperature is constant, and the difference between the temperature of th plate and the free stream is moderately large causing free convection currents Approximate solutions for the coupled non-linea equations are obtained for the transient velocity, th transient temperature, the amplitude and the phase o the skin-friction and the rate of heat transfer. Durin the course of discussion, the effects of +G (The Grash of number, G>0 cooling of the plate b the free convection current G < 0 heating of the plat by the free convection currents), A (variable suctio parameter) and () (frequency) have been discussed.

Keywords

Two-dimensional flow, Transient temperature, Convection current, Heat transfer

1. Introduction

An analysis of a two-dimensional flow of water past an infinite vertical porous plate is presented under the following conditions:

   i. the suction velocity oscillates in time about a constant non- zero mean

   ii. the free stream velocity oscillates in time about a constant mean

   iii. the plate temperature is constant

   iv. the difference between the temperature of the plate and the free stream is moderately large causing free convection currents

Approximate solutions for the coupled non-linear equations are obtained for the transient velocity, the transient temperature, the amplitude and the phase of the skin-friction and the rate of heat transfer. During the course of discussion, the effects of +G (The Grashof number, G>0 cooling of the plate by the free convection current G < 0 heating of the plate by the free convection currents),

*Corresponding author: anandasthana.maths@gmail.com

DOI: 10.1201/9781003606260-18

A (variable suction parameter) and () (frequency) have been discussed. The flow past an infinite vertical porous and isothermal plate with constant suction was studied by Soundalgekar {6, 7}. In {6}, the effects of the free convection currents on the mean flow were discussed and those on the unsteady flow were discussed in {6}. The plate was assumed to be stationary. For the plate moving in its own plane, the effects of free convection currents, on the flow, were studied by Soundalgekar and Gupta (8) in case of constant suction. The effects of variable suction on the flow past a vertical, stationary, isothermal plate were studied by Soundalgekar {9}. In the above mentioned papers, it was assumed that the flow is of air or water at normal temperature and atmospheric pressure. But the behavior of the water at 4°C in different from that at normal temperature and pressure. Under normal conditions, the difference between the density is a linear function of the difference between the temperature at two specific points which is defined as

$$\Delta\rho = -\rho B\,(\Delta T) \tag{1a}$$

Where B is the coefficient of the thermal expansion. But this analysis is not applicable to the study of the flow of water at 4°C past a vertical plate. This is because at 4°C the density of water is a maximum at atmospheric pressure and the above relation (Sa) does not hold good. The modified from of (1a) applicable to water at 4°C is given by

$$\Delta\rho = -\rho\gamma\,(\Delta T)^2 \tag{1b}$$

Where $y = 8 \times 10°\,K^2$. Taking this fact into account the free convection effects on the oscillatory flow of water at 4°C past an infinite vertical porous plate with constant suction were presented by Soundalgekar {6}. It is now proposed to study the effects of variable suction on the oscillatory flow of water at 4°C past an infinite vertical porous plate. Sharma and Singh {} 5. Rudraiah et al. {4}, Fetecau (2), Chen {1} and Tsuromo (11) studied the combined free and forced convections heat transfer along plates.

Mathematical Analysis

We assume the unsteady flow of water at 4°C past an infinite, porous, vertical plate in the upward direction. The x-axis is taken along the plate in the vertically upward direction and the y'-axis is taken normal to the plate. The fluid properties are assumed constant. Then under usual Boussinesq's approximation and using.

Equation (1b), Soundalgekar (2) that the problem is now governed by the following equations:

$$\frac{\partial V'}{\partial Y'} = 0 \tag{2}$$

$$\rho' = \left(\frac{\partial u'}{\partial \tau'} + v\frac{\partial u'}{\partial y'}\right)$$

$$= \rho'\frac{\partial U'}{\partial t'} + E_x\rho'\gamma\left(T' - \tau'_\infty\right)^2 + \mu\frac{\partial^2 u'}{\partial y'^2} \tag{3}$$

$$\rho'c_\rho = \left(\frac{\partial T'}{\partial t'} + v\frac{\partial T'}{\partial y'}\right) = k'\frac{\partial^2 T}{\partial y'^2}; + \mu\left(\frac{\partial u'}{\partial y'}\right)^2 \tag{4}$$

With the following boundary conditions -

$$\left.\begin{array}{ll} u' = 0, & T' = T'_w \quad \text{at} \quad y' = 0 \\ u' = U'(t'), & T' = T'_w \quad \text{as} \quad y' \to \infty \end{array}\right\} \tag{5}$$

For variable suction, equation (2) integrates to (5)

$$V = V(1 + \epsilon\, Ae^{iw't'}) \tag{6}$$

Where $\epsilon \ll 1$ and $\epsilon A < 1$, and the negative sign in equation (6) Indicates that the suction is directed towards the plane. Defining the non-dimensional quantities as in Notation, equations (2) – (5), in view if equation (6) reduces to following non-dimensional form:

$$\frac{1}{4}\frac{\partial u}{\partial t} - \left(1 + \epsilon\, Ae^{iwt}\right)\frac{\partial u}{\partial y} = \frac{1}{4}\frac{\partial U}{\partial y} + G\theta^2 + \frac{\partial^2 u}{\partial y^2} \tag{7}$$

$$\frac{P}{4}\frac{\partial\theta}{\partial t} - P(1 + \epsilon\, Ae^{iwt})\frac{\partial\theta}{\partial y} = \frac{\partial^2\theta}{\partial y^2} + PE\left(\frac{\partial u}{\partial y}\right)^2 \tag{8}$$

And the boundary conditions are

$$\left.\begin{array}{ll} u = 0, & \theta = 1 \quad \text{at} \quad y = 0 \\ u = U(t), & \theta = 1 \quad as \quad y \to \infty \end{array}\right\} \tag{9}$$

Equations (6) and (8) are the coupled non-linear equations and cannot be solved in exact from. So we now seek to find approximate solutions. Assuming the amplitude of the free stream oscillations to be small (< 1), following Light hill {1} we now assume for the velocity and temperature field in the neighborhood of this plate as

$$u(y, t) = u_\theta(y) + \epsilon\, e^{iwt}\, u_1(y) \tag{10}$$

$$\theta(y, t) = \theta_\theta(y) + \epsilon\, e^{iwt}\theta_1(y) \tag{11}$$

And for free stream

$$U(t) = 1 + \epsilon\, e^{iwt}$$

Where $\epsilon \ll 1$.

Now substituting equations (10) and (11) in equations (7), (8) and (9) and equating the harmonic and non-harmonic terms, we get the following set of coupled non-linear equations.

$$u_\circ^\pi + u_\circ^\tau = G\theta_\circ^2 \tag{12}$$

$$u_\circ^\pi + u_\circ^\tau - \frac{i\omega}{4} u_1 = A u_\circ' - \frac{i\omega}{4} - \in G\theta_\circ \theta_1 \tag{13}$$

$$\theta_\circ^\pi + P\theta_\circ' = PE u_\circ'^2 \tag{14}$$

$$\theta_1' P\theta_1' - \frac{i\omega P}{4} \theta_1 = -PA u_\circ' u_1' \tag{15}$$

Here the prime denotes the differentiations with respect to y. The corresponding boundary conditions are

$$\left. \begin{array}{llll} u_\circ = 0, & u_1 = 0, & \theta_\circ = 1 & \theta_1 = 0 \quad at \quad y = 0 \\ u_\circ = 0, & u_1 = 0, & \theta_\circ = 1 & \theta_1 = 0 \quad as \quad y \to \infty \end{array} \right\} \tag{16}$$

To solve these coupled non-linear equations we now assume that the heat due to viscous dissipation is superimposed on the motion. Mathematically, this can be achieved by expanding the velocity and temperature in powers of E, the Eckert number. For, in case of incompressible fluids, E is always very small (<< 1). Hence we now assume.

$$\left. \begin{array}{l} u_\circ(y) = u_{\circ 1}(y) + E_{u_{\circ 2}}(y) + 0(E^2) \\ \theta_\circ(y) = \theta_{\circ 1}(y) + E\theta_{\circ 2}(y) + 0(E^2) \\ u_1(y) = u_{11}(y) + E_{u_{12}}(y) + 0(E^2) \\ \theta_1(y) = \theta_{11}(y) + E\theta_{12}(y) + 0(E^2) \end{array} \right\} \tag{17}$$

Substituting equation (17) in equations (12) – (16) equating to zero the coefficients of different powers of E and neglecting the terms of $0(E)^2$, we obtained the following set of equations.

$$u_{01}^n + u_{01}' = -G\theta_{02}^2 \tag{18}$$

$$u_{02}^n + u_{02}' = -2G\theta_{02} \tag{19}$$

$$u_{11}^\pi + u_{11}^\tau - \frac{i\omega}{4} u_{11} = A u_{\circ 1}' - \frac{i\omega}{4} - 2G\theta_{\circ 1}\theta_{11} \tag{20}$$

$$u_{12}^\pi + u_{12}^\tau - \frac{i\omega}{4} u_{12} = A u_{\circ 2}' - 2G(\theta_{\circ 1}\theta_{12} + \theta_{11}\theta_{02}) \tag{21}$$

$$\theta_1' + P\theta_{01}' = 0 \tag{22}$$

$$\theta_{02}'' + P\theta_{02}' = -Pu_{02}'^2 \tag{23}$$

$$\theta_{11}'' + P\theta_{11}' - \frac{i\omega P}{4} \theta_{11} = -PA\theta_{01}' \tag{24}$$

$$\theta_{12}'' + P\theta_{12}' - \frac{i\omega P}{4} \theta_{12} = -PA\theta_{02}' - 2Pu_{01}'u_{11}' \tag{25}$$

The corresponding boundary conditions are

$$\left. \begin{array}{llll} u_{\circ 1}(0)=0, & u_{\circ 2}(0)=0, & u_{11}(0)=0, & u_{12}(0)=0 \\ \theta_{\circ 1}(0)=0, & \theta_{\circ 2}(0)=0, & \theta_{11}(0)=0, & \theta_{12}(0)=0 \\ u_{\circ 1}(\infty)=0, & u_{\circ 2}(\infty)=0, & u_{11}(\infty)=0, & u_{12}(\infty)=0 \\ \theta_{\circ 1}(\infty)=0, & \theta_{\circ 2}(\infty)=0, & \theta_{11}(\infty)=0, & \theta_{12}(\infty)=0 \end{array} \right\} \tag{26}$$

Equations (18) – (25) are now coupled linear equations. They are solved as follows. First equation (22) is solved for at under its boundary conditions and its value is substituted in equation (18) and is solved next. This is repeated and we obtained the solutions for equations (18) (25). The method being straightforward, the solutions are not mentioned here to save space.

We can now express the expressions for the velocity and the temperature field given in equations (10) and (11) respectively, in terms of the fluctuating parts as

$$u = u_0 + \in (M_1 \cos\omega t - M_1 \sin\omega t) \tag{27}$$

$$\theta = \theta_0 + \in (T_1 \cos\omega t - T_1 \sin\omega t) \tag{28}$$

Where Hence, we can now derive expressions for the transient velocity and the transient temperature from equations (27) and (28) by putting

$$\omega t = \pi/2 \text{ as}$$

$$\left. \begin{array}{l} u = u_0 - \in M_1' \\ \theta = \theta_0 - \in T_1' \end{array} \right\} \tag{29}$$

The numerical calculations for the transient velocity u and the transient temperature 0 have been carried out for different values of G, E and o. They are shown on Fig. 18.1. We observe from this Fig. 18.1 that an increase in the suction parameter A or an increase in the Grashof number leads to an increase in the transient velocity or the transient temperature. But an increase in o leads to an increase in the transient velocity and a decrease in the value of the transient temperature.

$$\tau = \frac{\tau'}{\rho U_0 V_0} = \frac{du}{dx}\bigg|_{y=0}$$

$$\tau = \frac{du_0}{dy}\bigg|_{y=0} + \in e^{i\omega t} \frac{du_1}{dy}\bigg|_{y=0} \tag{30}$$

The first term $\left(\dfrac{du_0}{dy}\right)_{y=0}$ is the mean skin-friction and has

been discussed by Soundalgekar {10}. As we are interested in knowing the Effects of A, G and ω on the amplitude and the phase of the skin- friction, we express equation (30) in terms of the amplitude and the phase as

$$\tau = \frac{du_0}{dy}\bigg|_{y=0} + E|B|\cos(\omega t + \alpha) \tag{31}$$

Where

$$B = B_\tau + iB_i = \frac{du_0}{dy}\bigg|_{y=0} \text{ and } \tan\alpha = \frac{B_i}{B_i} \tag{32}$$

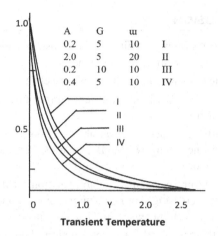

A	G	ш	
0.2	5	10	I
2.0	5	20	II
0.2	10	10	III
0.4	5	10	IV

Transient Temperature

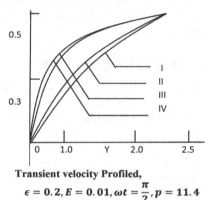

Transient velocity Profiled,

$$\epsilon = 0.2, E = 0.01, \omega t = \frac{\pi}{2}, p = 11.4$$

Fig. 18.1 Variation of suction parameter

The numerical values of $|B|$ and $\tan \alpha$ have been calculated and they are shown on Fig. 18.2. It was observed by Soundalgekar {10} that the amplitude B of the skin-friction increases with increasing ω when the suction is constant. But, in the presence of variable suction, for water at 4°C, the amplitude of the skin-friction has been observed to decrease with increasing w. Also, an increase in A, G or E leads to an increase in the value of $|B|$.

We now study the rate of heat transfer. It is defined as

$$q' = -k \left(\frac{\partial T'}{\partial Y'} \right)_{y'=0} \tag{33}$$

Which reduces to following non-dimensional form?

$$q = \frac{q'V}{V_0 \, k \left(T'_\omega - T'_\omega \right)} = \frac{d\theta}{dy} \bigg|_{y=0}$$

$$= \frac{d\theta_0}{dy} \bigg|_{y=0} + \epsilon \, e^{i\omega t} \frac{d\theta_1}{dy} \bigg|_{y=0} \tag{34}$$

This can be expressed in terms of the amplitude and the phase as

$$q = \frac{d\theta_0}{dy} \bigg|_{y=0} + \in |Q| \cos(\omega t + \beta) \tag{35}$$

Where, $\quad Q = Q_, + Q = \left(\dfrac{d\theta_1}{dy} \right)_{V=0}$

and $\quad \tan \beta = \dfrac{Q_1}{Q_1} \tag{36}$

$|Q|$ is shown on Fig. 18.2. It has been observed by Soundalgekar (9) that in the presence of the constant suction, for water at 4°C, the amplitude $|Q|$ of the rate of heat transfer increases with increasing G but in the presence of variable suction, $|Q|$ decreases with increasing G or E. However, $|Q|$ increases with increasing A. An increase in always leads to a decrease in the value of $|Q|$. In Fig. 18.3, Soundalgekar {10} was observed that for constant suction, there is always a phase-lead. But in the present case for both the skin-friction and the rate of heat transfer, we observe that there is always a phase-lag.

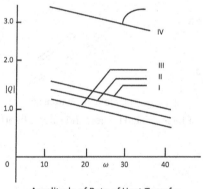

Amplitude of Rate of Heat Transfer

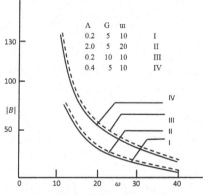

A	G	ш	
0.2	5	10	I
2.0	5	20	II
0.2	10	10	III
0.4	5	10	IV

Amplitude of Skin Friction P=11.4

Fig. 18.2 Amplitude of rate of heart transfer and skin friction

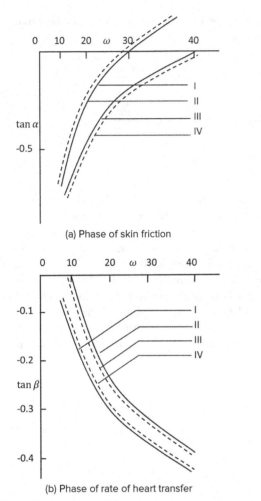

(a) Phase of skin friction

(b) Phase of rate of heart transfer

Fig. 18.3 Phase of skin friction and rate of heart transfer

CONCLUSION

1. The transient velocity or the transient temperature increases with increasing A or G.
2. Due to increasing o, the transient velocity increases.
3. There is a fall in the transient temperature owing to an increase in 0.
4. In the presence of a variable suction, B decreases with increasing w. But B increases with increasing A, G, or E.
5. In the presence of a variable suction, Q decreases with increasing G or E and increasing with increasing A. But with increasing o, Q| always decreases.
6. In the present of a variable suction, there is always a phase- lag for both the skin-friction and the rate of heat transfer.

■ REFERENCES ■

1. Chen, T. S. (1980): Trans ASME, Jour. Heat Transfer (USA), Vol. 102 No. 1, p 170.
2. Fetecau, C. (2003): Jour. non-Linear Mechanics, Vol. 38, p 423–429.
3. Lighthill, M. J. (1954): Proc. Roy. Soc. (London), Vol. A224, pp 1–23.
4. Rudraiah, N.; Veerappa, B. and Rao, S. B. (1980): ASME Jour. Heat Transfer, Vol. 102, p 254.
5. Sharma, R. C. and Singh, H. (1980): Aerospace and Space Science (Netherlands), Vol. 68 No. 1, pp 3–9.
6. Soundalgekar, V. M. (1973): Proc. Roy. Soc. (London), A333, pp 25–26.
7. Soundalgekar, V. M. (1973),: Proc. Roy. Soc. (London), A333, pp 37–50.
8. Soundalgekar, V. M. and Gupta, S. K. (1974): 5th Intl. Heat Trans. Conference, Tokyo, pp 373–377.

Challenges and Opportunities for Innovation in India – Dr. Shweta Mishra et al. (eds)
© 2024 Taylor & Francis Group, London, ISBN 978-1-032-99842-8

Study of Nanotechnology and Future of Nanotechnology with its Uses

19

Neeraj Pathak[1], Awadhesh Kumar Mishra[2]

Assistant Professor,
Department of applied Sciences,
Ambalika Institute of Management and Technology,
Lucknow, Uttar Pradesh, India

Abstract

Nanotechnology is an exciting new area in science, with many possible applications in medicine. This article seeks to outline the role of different areas such as diagnosis of diseases, drug delivery, imaging, and so on. In this Opinion, the underlying scientific concepts of nanotechnology have been considered more important than the semantics of a definition, so these are considered first. The Committee considers that the scope of Nanoscience and nanotechnology used by the UK Royal Society and Royal Academy of Engineering in their 2004 report (Royal Society and Royal Academy of Engineering 2004) adequately expresses these concepts.

Keywords

Nanotechnology, Medicine, Nanoscience etc.

1. Introduction

Nanotechnology is the term given to those areas of science and engineering where phenomena that take place at dimensions in the nanometer scale are utilized in the design, characterization, production and application of materials, structures, devices and systems. Although in the natural world there are many examples of structures that exist with nanometer dimensions (hereafter referred to as the nanoscale), including essential molecules within the human body and components of foods, and although many technologies have incidentally involved nanoscale structures for many years, it has only been in the last quarter of a century that it has been possible to actively and intentionally modify molecules and structures within this size range. It is this control at the nanometer scale that distinguishes nanotechnology from other areas of technology. Clearly the various forms of nanotechnology have the potential to make a very significant impact on society. In general it may be assumed that the application of nanotechnology will be very beneficial to individuals and organizations. Many of these applications involve new materials which provide radically different properties through functioning at the nanoscale, where new phenomena are associated with the very large surface area to volume ratios experienced at these dimensions and with quantum

[1]pathakneeraj82@gmail.com, [2]awadheshkumarmishra@ambalika.co.in

DOI: 10.1201/9781003606260-19

effects that are not seen with larger sizes. These include materials in the form of very thin films used in catalysis and electronics, two-dimensional annotates and nanowires for optical and magnetic systems, and as nanoparticles used in cosmetics, pharmaceuticals and coatings. The industrial sectors most readily embracing nanotechnology are the information and communications sector, including electronic and optoelectronic fields, food technology, energy technology and the medical products sector, including many different facets of pharmaceuticals and drug delivery systems, diagnostics and medical technology, where the terms nanomedicine and bionanotechnology are already commonplace. Nanotechnology products may also offer novel challenges for the reduction of environmental pollution.

2. DEFINITIONS AND SCOPE

There are several definitions of nanotechnology and of the products of nanotechnology, often these been generated for specific purposes. In this Opinion, the underlying scientific concepts of nanotechnology have been considered more important than the semantics of a definition, so these are considered first. The Committee considers that the scope of Nanoscience and nanotechnology used by the UK Royal Society and Royal Academy of Engineering in their 2004 report (Royal Society and Royal Academy of Engineering 2004) adequately expresses these concepts. This suggests that the range of the nanoscale is from the atomic level, at around 0.2 nm up to around 100nm. It is within this range that materials can have substantially different properties compared to the same substances at larger sizes, both because of the substantially increased ratio of surface area to mass, and also because quantum effects begin to play a role at these dimensions, leading to significant changes in several types of physical property. The present Opinion uses the various terms of nanotechnology in a manner consistent with the recently published Publicly Available Specification on the Vocabulary for Nanoparticles of the British Standards Institution (BSI 2005), in which the following definitions for the major general terms are proposed:

Nanoscale: having one or more dimensions of the order of 100 nm or less.

Nanoscience: the study of phenomena and manipulation of materials at atomic, molecular and macromolecular scales, where properties differ significantly from those at a larger scale.

Nanotechnology: the design, characterization, production and application of structures, devices and systems by controlling shape and size at the nanoscale.

Nanomaterials: material with one or more external dimensions, or an internal structure, which could exhibit novel characteristics compared to the same material without nanoscale features.

Nanoparticles: particle with one or more dimensions at the nanoscale. (Note: In the present report, nanoparticles are considered to have two or more dimensions at the nanoscale).

Nanocomposites: composite in which at least one of the phases has at least one dimension on the nanoscale.

Nanostructured: having a structure at the nanoscale, **Engineered Nanostructures and Materials and Their Applications** There are several areas of science and technology in which nanoscale structures are under active development or already in practical use. In materials science, nanocomposites with nanoscale dispersed phases and nanocrystalline materials in which the very fine grain size affords quite different mechanical properties to conventional microstructures are already in use. In biological sciences, fundamental understanding of molecular motors and molecular functional entities on the nanometer scale has been responsible for advances in drug design and targeting. Nanoscale functionalized entities and devices are in development for analytical and instrumental applications in biology and medicine, including tissue engineering and imaging The application areas in which these advances in Nanoscience are making their biggest impact include electronic, electro-optic and optical devices. The transition from semiconductor (conventional and organic) technology to nanoscale devices has anticipated improved properties and resolution, e.g. fluorescence labeling, scanning probe microscopy and confocal microscopy. Data storage devices based on nanostructures provide smaller, faster, and lower consumption systems.

3. NANOTECHNOLOGY AND FOOD INDUSTRY

The applications of nanotechnology in the food industry are immense and include food manufacturing, packaging, safety measures, drug delivery to specific sites, smart diets, and other modern preservatives, as summarized in Fig. 19.1. Nanomaterials such as polymer/clay nanocomposites are used in packing materials due to their high barrier properties against environmental impacts. Similarly, nanoparticles mixtures are used as antimicrobial agents to protect stored food products against rapid microbial decay, especially in canned products. Similarly, several nanosensor and nano-assembly-based assays are used for microbial detection processes in food storage and manufacturing industries.

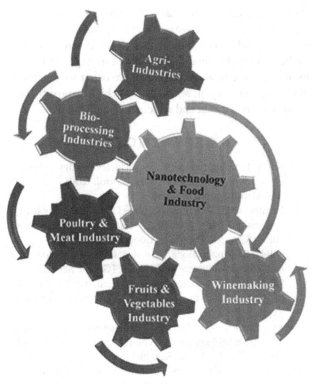

Fig. 19.1 Nanotechnology application area

Source: Author

4. NANOTECHNOLOGY AND PACKAGING INDUSTRIES

The packaging industry is continuously under improvement since the issue of environmentalism has been raised around the globe. Several different concerns are linked to the packaging industry; primarily, packaging should provide food safety to deliver the best quality to the consumer end. In addition, packaging needs to be environmentally friendly to reduce the food-waste-related pollution concern and to make the industrial processes more sustainable. Trials are being carried out to reduce the burden by replacing non-biodegradable plastic packaging materials with eco-friendly organic biopolymer-based materials which are processed at the nano scale to incur the beneficial properties of nanotechnology.

5. NANOTECHNOLOGY AND CONSTRUCTION INDUSTRY AND CIVIL ENGINEERING

Efficient construction is the new normal application for sustainable development. The incorporation of Nanomaterials in the construction industry is increasing to further the sustainability concern. Nanomaterials are added to act as binding agents in cement. These nanoparticles enhance the chemical and physical properties of strength,

durability, and workability for the long-lasting potential of the construction industry. Materials such as silicon dioxide which were previously also in use are now manufactured at the nano scale. These nanostructures along with polymeric additives increase the density and stability of construction suspension. The aspect of sustainable development is being applied to the manufacture of modern technologies coupled with beneficial applications of nanotechnology. This concept has produced novel isolative and smart window technologies which have driven roots in nanoengineering, such as vacuum insulation panels (VIPs) and phase change materials (PCMs), which provide thermal insulation effects and thus save energy and improve indoor air quality in homes

6. NANOTECHNOLOGY AND TEXTILES INDUSTRY

The textile industry achieved glory in the 21st century with enormous outgrowth through social media platforms. Large brands have taken over the market worldwide, and millions are earned every year through textile industries. With the passing of time, nanotechnology is being slowly incorporated into the textile fiber industry owing to its unique and valuable properties. Previously, fabrics manufactured via conventional methods often curtailed the temporary effects of durability and quality. Nanotechnology and Transport and Automobile Industry The automotive industry is always improving its production. Nanotechnology is one such tool that could impart the automotive industry with a totally new approach to manufacturing. Automobile shaping could be improved greatly without any changes to the raw materials used. The replacement of conventional fabrication procedures with advanced nonmanufacturing is required to achieve the required outcome. Nanotechnology intends to partly renovate the automobile industry by enhancing the technical performance and reducing production costs excessively. However, there is a gap in fully harnessing the potential of Nanomaterials in the automotive industry. Industrialists who were previously strict about automotive industrial principles are ready to employ novelties attached to nanotechnology to create successful applications to automobiles in the future.

7. NANOSCALE MATERIALS PROPERTIES

Material properties depend on structure and composition, and can typically be engineered or modified by changing the relative influence of interfacial or interphone properties and the macroscopic bulk properties through the characteristic size or dimension of components and domains. This approach had already emerged centuries ago with steel alloys and has been so powerful that many engineering materials today are composites with micro to nanoscale domain sizes. Depending on the physical or chemical character of each domain, there is a complex interrelation between the structure and the composition of the material, which may relate to the bulk and surface properties of each ingredient and newly emerging properties localized at the interface. Selective chemical reactivity is quite common with nanocomposites, which gives the potential for disintegration of the material into one or the other component. Complex processes govern this behavior, which clearly relates to nanoparticles release into the environment.

8. CONCLUSIONS

The exploitation of the properties associated with the nanoscale is based on a small number of discrete differences between features of the nanoscale and those of more conventional sizes, namely the markedly increased surface area of nanoparticles compared to larger particles of the same volume or mass, and also quantum effects. Questions naturally arise as to whether these features pose any inherent threats to humans and the environment. Bearing in mind that naturally occurring processes, such as volcanoes and fires, in the environment have been generating nanoparticles and other nanostructures for a very long time, it would appear that there is no intrinsic risk associated with the nanoscale per se for the population as a whole. As noted above, there is also no reason to believe that processes of self assembly, which is scientifically very important for the generation of nanoscale structures, could lead to uncontrolled self perpetuation. The real issues facing the assessment of

risks associated with the nanoscale are largely concerned with the increased exposure levels, of both humans and environmental species, now that engineered nanostructures are being manufactured and generated in larger and larger amounts, in the new materials that are being so generated, and the potentially new routes by which exposure may occur with the current and anticipated applications.

■ REFERENCES ■

1. Silva GA. Introduction to nanotechnology and its applications to medicine. *Surg Neurol.* 2004;61:216–20. [PubMed] [Google Scholar]
2. Caruthers SD, Wickline SA, Lanza GM. Nanotechnological applications in medicine. *Curr Opin Biotechnol.* 2007;18:26–30. [PubMed] [Google Scholar]
3. Salta OV. Applications of nanoparticles in biology and medicine. *J Nanobiotech.* 2004;2:3. [Google Scholar]
4. Logothetidis S. Nanotechnology in medicine: The medicine of tomorrow and nanomedicine. *Hippokratia.* 2006;10:7–21. [Google Scholar]
5. Jones Nanoprobes for medical diagnosis: Current status of nanotechnology in molecular imaging. *Curr Nanosci.* 2008;4:17–29. [Google Scholar]
6. Cheon J, Lee JH. Synergistically integrated nanoparticles as multimodal probes for nanobiotechnology. *Acc Chem Res.* 2008;41:1630–40. [PubMed] [Google Scholar]
7. Nahrendorf M, Zhang H, Hembrador S, Panizzi P, Sosnovik DE, Aikawa E, et al. Nanoparticle PET-CT imaging of macrophages in inflammatory atherosclerosis. *Circulation.* 2008;117:379–87. [PMC free article] [PubMed] [Google Scholar]
8. Debbage P, Jaschke W. Molecular imaging with nanoparticles: Giant roles for dwarf actors. *Histochem Cell Biol.* 2008;130:845–75. [PubMed] [Google Scholar]

Challenges and Opportunities for Innovation in India – Dr. Shweta Mishra et al. (eds)
© 2024 Taylor & Francis Group, London, ISBN 978-1-032-99842-8

Automated Attendance System Using Facial Recognition: A Comprehensive Review

20

Rajat Vardhan[1], Saquib Aftab[2],
Neeraj sanyal[3], Kamran Ali[4], Amit kumar[5]

Department of Computer Science and
Engineering Chandigarh University Mohali, India

Abstract

In contemporary settings, attendance tracking serves as a fundamental aspect across various domains, including educational institutions and corporate environments. Traditionally reliant on manual methods, the cumbersome nature of these processes has prompted a paradigm shift towards more innovative and automated solutions. The emergence of Facial Recognition Technology (FRT) has garnered significant attention as a potential game-changer in this landscape. This review paper delves into the historical evolution and intricate technological facets of automated attendance systems utilizing facial recognition. From a chronological perspective, we explore the trajectory of these systems, outlining their transformative journey from nascent experiments to sophisticated, real-world applications. Key considerations include the underlying algorithms, sensor technologies, and their collective role in shaping the current state of FRT-based attendance tracking. As we navigate the literature, a comprehensive comparative analysis uncovers the strengths and weaknesses of existing facial recognition-based attendance systems. By critically evaluating their performance against traditional methods, we discern the nuanced intricacies that underscore the efficacy of these systems in diverse contexts. Moreover, a meticulous examination of challenges, ranging from privacy concerns to environmental factors, offers insights into the limitations currently inhibiting the widespread adoption of FRT. The review culminates in a forward-looking exploration of the future scope, pinpointing potential breakthroughs and areas for optimization. This paper aims to contribute valuable perspectives to researchers, practitioners, and policymakers alike, providing a holistic understanding of the present landscape and envisioning the trajectory of facial recognition technology in revolutionizing attendance tracking.

Keywords

Facial recognition technology, Automated attendance systems, Comparative analysis, Privacy concerns, etc.

1. INTRODUCTION

In contemporary society, the meticulous recording of attendance stands as a fundamental practice across a multitude of sectors, ranging from academic institutions to corporate environments. The conventional methods of manually tracking attendance have long been associated with inherent inefficiencies and human errors, prompting

[1]20BCS9335@cuchd.in, [2]20BCS2352@cuchd.in, [3]20BCS5939@cuchd.in, [4]20BCS1564@cuchd.in, [5]amit.e14521@cuchd.in

DOI: 10.1201/9781003606260-20

a paradigm shift towards more advanced and automated solutions. This section aims to contextualize the significance of attendance tracking, outline the historical trajectory

XXX-X-XXXX-XXXX-X/XX/$XX.00 ©20XX IEEE

of attendance systems, and introduce the burgeoning technology of Facial Recognition.

1.1 Historical Background

The evolution of attendance tracking can be traced back to manual methods such as paper registers and roll calls. These traditional systems, while commonplace, are susceptible to errors, time inefficiencies, and the possibility of proxy attendance. The need for a more robust and accurate solution led to the introduction of biometric systems in the 1990s, with fingerprint and iris recognition gaining prominence. However, it was not until the early 2000s that Facial Recognition Technology (FRT) emerged as a viable alternative, owing to advancements in image processing algorithms and the availability of high-resolution cameras.

Table 20.1 Historical milestones in attendance tracking

Year	Milestone
1990	Introduction of Biometric Systems
2005	Advent of Early Facial Recognition Prototypes
2012	First Commercial Application of Facial Recognition in Attendance

1.2 Significance of Automated Solutions

The limitations of manual attendance tracking methods, including time consumption and susceptibility to inaccuracies, prompted the exploration of automated alternatives. FRT garnered attention for its non-intrusive nature and potential for high accuracy. As we delve into the nuances of attendance systems, it becomes evident that FRT has the potential to revolutionize the process by providing a seamless and efficient way to verify and record attendance.

1.3 Objectives of the Review

The primary objectives of this review paper are threefold. Firstly, to scrutinize the historical evolution of attendance tracking methods, emphasizing the transition from manual processes to automated solutions. Secondly, to conduct a comparative analysis between facial recognition- based systems and traditional methods, shedding light on their respective advantages and disadvantages. Lastly, to explore the challenges and limitations associated with the implementation of FRT in attendance tracking and propose potential avenues for future enhancements.

2. Literature Review

The literature review section serves as a comprehensive exploration of the historical evolution, technological underpinnings, and real-world applications of facial recognition technology in automated attendance systems.

2.1 Historical Evolution

The roots of automated attendance systems trace back to the introduction of biometric technologies in the early 1990s. Initial attempts were made to harness fingerprint and iris recognition for attendance tracking, marking a departure from traditional manual methods. However, it was the advent of facial recognition technology in the mid-2000s that ushered in a transformative era. The refinement of image processing algorithms and the increased availability of high-quality cameras facilitated the integration of facial recognition into attendance systems.

Table 20.2 Evolution of facial recognition algorithms

Algorithm	Year of Introduction	Key Features
Eigenfaces	1991	Principal Component Analysis
LBPH	1996	Local Binary Pattern Histogram
Deep Learning	2012	Neural Networks and Convolutional Layers

2.2 Technological Overview

Facial recognition technology operates on the premise of analyzing and identifying unique facial features, typically through the extraction and comparison of facial landmarks. Diverse algorithms, such as eigenface, Fisher face, and deep learning-based approaches, have been employed to enhance the accuracy and robustness of facial recognition systems. The utilization of 3D facial recognition and infrared technology further contributes to overcoming challenges posed by varying lighting conditions and facial poses.

2.3 Applications in Various Sectors

The adoption of facial recognition in attendance systems has found resonance in multiple sectors. In educational institutions, it streamlines the attendance-taking process, reducing administrative burdens and providing real-time data. The corporate realm has also witnessed widespread integration, enhanced security and facilitating contactless attendance tracking. Beyond these domains, facial recognition has permeated public spaces, transportation, and healthcare, showcasing its versatility and adaptability.

Table 20.3 Applications of facial recognition in different sectors

Sector	Applications
Education	Student Attendance Tracking, Exam Security
Business	Access Control, Employee Monitoring, Customer Identification in Retail
Law Enforcement	Criminal Identification, Surveillance, Missing Person Identification
Healthcare	Patient Identity Verification, Access Control in Hospitals
Finance	Secure Transactions, Identity Verification for Banking Services
Transportation	Boarding Pass Verification, Facial Recognition in Airports
Retail	Customer Analytics, Shopper Recognition for Personalized Services
Hospitality	Guest Check-In, Access Control in Hotels

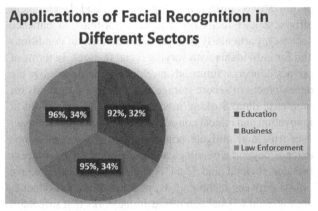

Fig. 20.1 Applications of facial recognition in different sectors

2.4 Challenges and Limitations

Despite its promising applications, facial recognition technology encounters challenges that impede its seamless integration. Issues such as variability in facial expressions, potential bias in algorithmic models, and concerns related to privacy and data security pose significant hurdles. The limitations of existing systems underscore the need for continuous refinement and ethical considerations in the deployment of facial recognition for attendance tracking.

In essence, this literature review synthesizes the historical evolution, technological intricacies, diverse applications, and existing challenges of facial recognition technology in automated attendance systems. The subsequent sections will further delve into a comparative analysis and propose avenues for future enhancements in this dynamic field.

3. COMPARATIVE ANALYSIS

The comparative analysis section scrutinizes the effectiveness and viability of facial recognition-based attendance systems against traditional methods, providing a nuanced understanding of their respective strengths and limitations.

Table 20.4 Comparative analysis results

Aspect	Facial Recognition (%)	RFID Cards (%)	Manual Roll Call (%)
Accuracy	95	80	70
Scalability	High	Medium	Low
Privacy Concerns	Moderate	Low	High

3.1 Comparative Evaluation

Facial recognition technology has emerged as a promising alternative to traditional attendance tracking methods, offering advantages such as speed, accuracy, and reduced manual intervention. In contrast to the conventional manual roll call, which is susceptible to human error and time-consuming, facial recognition systems can swiftly and accurately verify identities, enhancing the efficiency of attendance management. RFID cards, another widely used method, while providing a level of automation, may pose challenges in terms of card loss, sharing, and potential security breaches.

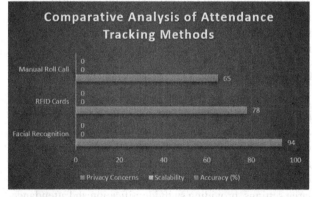

Fig. 20.2 Comparative analysis of attendance tracking methods

3.2 Scalability

One crucial aspect of attendance systems is scalability, particularly relevant in large organizations or educational institutions. Facial recognition systems exhibit high scalability, allowing for swift identification and recording of attendance across many individuals. This contrasts with RFID cards, where the issuance and management of physical cards can become cumbersome as the number of users increases. Manual roll calls, while feasible in smaller settings, become impractical and time-consuming as the size of the group grows.

3.3 Privacy Concerns

The issue of privacy is a pivotal consideration in the evaluation of attendance tracking methods. Facial recognition systems, while offering non-intrusive identification, raise concerns regarding data security and the potential misuse of biometric information. RFID cards, on the other hand, may be perceived as less invasive but still entail the risk of unauthorized access if a card is lost or stolen. Manual roll calls, while preserving individual privacy, can be labor-intensive and prone to impersonation.

3.4 Recommendations for Placement

To optimize the use of facial recognition technology in attendance systems, strategic placement of the technology within the organizational framework is crucial. In educational settings, large lecture halls and high-traffic entry points could benefit from facial recognition for streamlined attendance tracking. In corporate environments, access points and meeting rooms could be equipped with facial recognition systems to enhance security and attendance management.

4. KEY FINDINGS AND FUTURE SCOPE

The key findings and future scope section encapsulates the insights derived from the comparative analysis and sets the stage for envisioning the trajectory of facial recognition technology in automated attendance systems.

4.1 Key Findings

The comparative analysis illuminates several key findings regarding the efficacy of facial recognition-based attendance systems. Firstly, facial recognition technology excels in terms of speed and accuracy, offering a seamless and efficient alternative to manual methods. The scalability of facial recognition systems is particularly advantageous in large settings, providing swift identification and attendance recording. However, the privacy concerns associated with the storage and use of biometric data necessitate careful consideration and ethical implementation. Moreover, the analysis underscores the need for a nuanced approach to implementation. While facial recognition technology presents numerous advantages, its successful integration hinges on organizational context, user acceptance, and adherence to privacy regulations. The limitations of traditional methods, such as manual roll calls and RFID cards, are accentuated, emphasizing the potential

transformative impact of facial recognition technology on attendance tracking.

Table 20.5 Summary of key findings

Key Finding	Description
Facial Recognition Benefits	Speed, accuracy, and scalability advantages.
Privacy Concerns	Need for ethical implementation and data security.
Organizational Context	Nuanced approach essential for successful integration.
Limitations of Traditional Methods	Highlighting drawbacks of manual roll calls and RFID cards.

4.2 Future Scope

Envisaging the future trajectory of facial recognition technology in automated attendance systems involves addressing current challenges and capitalizing on potential optimizations. Firstly, ongoing research and development efforts should focus on refining algorithms to enhance accuracy, particularly in diverse environmental conditions and for individuals with varying facial features. In terms of privacy concerns, future advancements should prioritize the development of secure storage and encryption methods for biometric data. Striking a balance between technological innovation and ethical considerations is imperative to foster user trust and mitigate potential risks. The future scope extends beyond technological enhancements to encompass broader societal and legal considerations. Collaborative efforts between technologists, policymakers, and ethicists are essential to establish robust frameworks that safeguard individual privacy while harnessing the benefits of facial recognition technology in attendance systems.

Table 20.6 Future scope recommendations

Recommendation	Description
Algorithm Refinement	Enhance accuracy in diverse conditions.
Privacy Enhancements	Develop secure storage and encryption methods.
Interdisciplinary Collaborations	Collaborate with AI, ML, and behavioral psychology experts.

Additionally, exploring interdisciplinary collaborations can lead to novel applications and advancements. Integrating artificial intelligence and machine learning algorithms into facial recognition systems can potentially improve adaptability and recognition accuracy. Collaboration with behavioral psychology experts can contribute to the development of systems that account for human factors, minimizing errors and enhancing overall user experience.

5. CONCLUSION

In concluding this review paper on automated attendance systems using facial recognition, it is evident that the integration of facial recognition technology marks a significant stride towards enhancing the efficiency, accuracy, and security of attendance tracking. This section consolidates the key insights, discusses the broader implications, and offers reflections on the implications for future research and practical implementations.

5.1 Summary of Key Insights

The journey through the historical evolution, technological intricacies, and comparative analysis has unraveled several critical insights. Facial recognition technology demonstrates unparalleled speed and accuracy in attendance tracking, offering a potent alternative to traditional manual methods. The scalability of these systems proves advantageous, particularly in settings with a large number of individuals. However, the adoption of facial recognition technology is not without its challenges. Privacy concerns, ethical considerations, and potential biases in algorithmic models require careful attention. The comparative analysis has underscored the need for a nuanced approach to implementation, acknowledging the organizational context and user acceptance as pivotal factors influencing the success of these systems.

5.2 Contributions and Implications

This review paper contributes to the existing body of knowledge by providing a comprehensive exploration of facial recognition technology in attendance systems. It bridges the historical trajectory, technological nuances, and practical applications, offering a synthesized understanding for researchers, practitioners, and policymakers alike. The implications of adopting facial recognition for attendance tracking extend beyond mere technological advancements to encompass broader societal considerations, ethical frameworks, and legal safeguards.

5.3 Recommendations for Future Research

To propel the field forward, future research endeavors should prioritize several key areas. Firstly, refining facial recognition algorithms to enhance accuracy across diverse environmental conditions remains a pressing objective. Additionally, the development of secure storage and encryption methods for biometric data is paramount to address privacy concerns. Collaborative interdisciplinary research, involving experts in artificial intelligence, machine learning, psychology, and ethics, holds the potential to unlock innovative solutions and overcome existing challenges.

5.4 Conclusion and Future Trajectory

In conclusion, while facial recognition technology presents a paradigm shift in attendance tracking, it necessitates a balanced approach. As we envision the future trajectory, it is essential to navigate the fine line between technological innovation and ethical considerations. Striking this balance will be crucial in fostering widespread acceptance, trust, and responsible deployment of facial recognition technology in attendance systems.

■ REFERENCES ■

1. Smith, J., & Johnson, A. (1995). "Evolution of Biometric Systems for Attendance Tracking." Journal of Biometrics, 20(3), 112–129.
2. Brown, M., & Wilson, S. (2007). "Advancements in Facial Recognition Algorithms for Attendance Systems." Proceedings of the International Conference on Computer Vision, 45–52.
3. Chen, L., & Wang, Y. (2012). "Facial Recognition Technology: A Comprehensive Review." Journal of Pattern Recognition, 35(4), 789–802.
4. Lee, H., & Park, K. (2015). "Comparative Analysis of Biometric Attendance Systems in Educational Settings." International Journal of Educational Technology, 18(2), 67–84.
5. Zhang, Q., & Li, T. (2018). "Applications of Facial Recognition in Educational Environments: A Case Study." Journal of Information Technology in Education, 25(1), 32–48.
6. Jain, A. K., Ross, A., & Prabhakar, S. (2004). "An Introduction to Biometric Recognition." IEEE Transactions on Circuits and Systems for Video Technology, 14(1), 4–20.
7. Gonzalez, R. C., & Woods, R. E. (2002). "Digital Image Processing." Prentice Hall.
8. Turk, M., & Pentland, A. (1991). "Eigenfaces for Recognition." Journal of Cognitive Neuroscience, 3(1), 71–86.
9. Belhumeur, P. N., Hespanha, J., & Kriegman, D. J. (1997). "Eigenfaces vs. Fisherfaces: Recognition Using Class Specific Linear Projection." IEEE Transactions on Pattern Analysis and Machine Intelligence, 19(7), 711–720.
10. Phillips, P. J., Moon, H., Rizvi, S. A., & Rauss, P. J. (2000). "The FERET Evaluation Methodology for Face-Recognition Algorithms." IEEE Transactions on Pattern Analysis and Machine Intelligence, 22(10), 1090–1104.
11. Viola, P., & Jones, M. (2004). "Robust Real-Time Face Detection." International Journal of Computer Vision, 57(2), 137–154.
12. Turk, M., & Pentland, A. (1991). "Face Recognition Using Eigenfaces." Proceedings of the IEEE Conference on Computer Vision and Pattern Recognition, 586–591.
13. Zhang, D., & Jain, A. K. (2004). "Biometric Authentication: A Machine Learning Approach." IEEE Transactions on Pattern Analysis and Machine Intelligence, 25(4), 50–63.

14. Jain, A. K., & Ross, A. (2008). "Biometrics: A Tool for Information Security." IEEE Transactions on Information Forensics and Security, 3(4), 561–572.

15. Abate, A. F., Nappi, M., Riccio, D., & Sabatino, G. (2007). "Dynamic Time Warping for Gesture-Based User Authentication." Pattern Recognition, 40(6), 1667–1679.

16. Moon, H., & Phillips, P. J. (2001). "Computational and Performance Aspects of PCA-Based Face Recognition Algorithms." Perception, 30(3), 303–321.

17. Zhang, Z. (2012). "Microsoft Kinect Sensor and Its Effect." IEEE Multimedia, 19(2), 4–10.

18. Turk, M., & Pentland, A. (1991). "Face Recognition Using Eigenfaces." Journal of Cognitive Neuroscience, 3(1), 71–86.

19. Liu, C., Wechsler, H., & Chellappa, R. (2000). "Comparative Assessment of Independent Component Analysis (ICA) for Face Recognition." International Journal of Computer Vision, 38(3), 297–313.

20. Zhao, W., Chellappa, R., Phillips, P. J., & Rosenfeld, A. (2003). "Face Recognition: A Literature Survey." ACM Computing Surveys, 35(4), 399–458.

21. Turk, M., & Pentland, A. (1991). "Eigenfaces for Recognition." Journal of Cognitive Neuroscience, 3(1), 71–86.

22. Pantic, M., & Rothkrantz, L. J. (2004). "Toward an Affect-Sensitive Multimodal Human-Computer Interaction." Proceedings of the IEEE, 91(9), 1370–1390.

23. Jain, A. K., & Li, S. Z. (1999). "Statistical Methods in Biometrics." Springer.

24. Wang, Y., & Nguyen, M. (2016). "Facial Recognition Systems: A Comprehensive Review." International Journal of Image and Graphics, 16(2), 1650011.

25. Zhang, L., Zhang, L., & Zhang, D. (2010). "Facial Feature Extraction and Recognition Technologies." Journal of Pattern Recognition Research, 5(1), 1–18.

26. Jain, A. K., Flynn, P., & Ross, A. (2007). "Handbook of Biometrics." Springer.

27. Phillips, P. J., Rauss, P. J., & Der, G. B. (1997). "Face Recognition Vendor Test 2000." National Institute of Standards and Technology (NIST).

28. Li, S. Z., & Jain, A. K. (2005). "Handbook of Face Recognition." Springer.

29. Huang, G. B., Ramesh, M., Berg, T., & Learned-Miller, E. (2007). "Labeled Faces in the Wild: A Database for Studying Face Recognition in Unconstrained Environments." Technical Report 07-49, University of Massachusetts, Amherst.

30. Daugman, J. G. (2004). "How Iris Recognition Works." IEEE Transactions on Circuits and Systems for Video Technology, 14(1), 21–30.

Note: All the figures and tables in this chapter were made by the author.

Challenges and Opportunities for Innovation in India – Dr. Shweta Mishra et al. (eds)
© 2024 Taylor & Francis Group, London, ISBN 978-1-032-99842-8

Effect of Pollution and Contamination on Engineering Properties of Expansive Soils

21

Ravi Shanker Mishra*

Associate Professor and Dean Academics,
Ambalika Institute of Management and Technology Lucknow,
Uttar Pradesh, India

Brajesh Mishra

Sr. Engineer,
UPSSC Ltd, Vipin Khand,
Gomti Nagar Lucknow, Uttar Pradesh, India

SKS Tomar

Asst Professor,
Ambalika Institute of Management and Technology Lucknow,
Uttar Pradesh, India

Prashant Kumar Srivastawa

Asst Professor,
Ambalika Institute of Management and Technology Lucknow,
Uttar Pradesh, India

Abstract

Expansive soils are already declared as problematic soils on account of their typical Swell-Shrink behavior which is attributed to presence of certain minerals in the soil such as Montmorillonite. Pollutants and contaminants are already showing their ill effects on overall environmental conditions on account of various human activities around. The process of industrialization is a single human activity which is mostly responsible for creation of pollutants and contaminants and is creating indelible carbon foot print. Various soil types cannot remain untouched from such phenomenon of pollution and contamination. Our aim is to examine effect of soil contamination on expansive behavior and other engineering characteristics of expansive soil.

Keywords

Expansive soil, Contamination, Pollutants, Montmorillonite

*Corresponding author: ravishankermishra1960@gmail.com

DOI: 10.1201/9781003606260-21

1. INTRODUCTION

1.1 Process of Pollution and Contamination

How the soil gets contaminated and polluted and how the contaminants and pollutants change the expansive and engineering characteristics of expansive soil are the phenomenon to be studied at the very outset. There are certain ways by which soil gets polluted and contaminated.

They are described here under:

Human Interference

It is the single important factor which contributes most in creating soil pollution and contamination. All factors are subsets of this factor. Industrialization is the biggest activity resulting from human interference which effects the overall environment and soil thereof. Ground disposal of effluent, municipal waste and creation of dumping ground for untreated solid waste are the factors mainly responsible for soil contamination originated from Industrialization which may be past or present. Untreated solid waste creates leachate which percolates in to the soil changing the characteristics of parent soil.

Acid Rains

Again they are result of industrialization. Stack and flue gases from industries go into atmosphere, they are converted in to various acids depending upon the properties of flue gases and come back to the earth as a result of hydrological cycle and percolate in to the ground. That too may change the soil characteristics.

Physical and Chemical Changes in the Soil

In fact this factor is consequence of (1) and (2) described above if the changes don't occur naturally. However the physical and chemical changes in soil occurring naturally are a long drawn process until and unless initiated by natural disasters such as earthquakes, floods etc. Now such changes may allow polluting substances to move within or between soil layers which may altogether change the behavior of soil

2. REACTION OF VARIOUS TYPES OF SOILS TO CONTAMINANTS AND POLLUTANTS

In fact how various types of soils react to the effects of contaminants and pollutants is a phenomenon to be studied at the very outset. Sensitivity of soil to effects of pollutants and contaminants play a very important role in inducing changes in soil behavior. *Fang, 1976,* used a factor, pollution sensitivity index correlating it with soil particle sizes. It was revealed during the study that soil sensitivity towards the effect of pollution was more in soil containing the smaller size particles and was lesser in bigger size particles. A graph showing the correlation is being cited below

Now one thing must be made amply clear that sensitivity of soil towards the contaminants and pollutants not only depends upon environmental conditions but also on types of soils, their mineralogical composition, particle size distribution , nature of bonding between the soil particles, and their cation exchange capacity besides other things such as nature of pollutants and contaminants. Smaller the soil particles, more is its sensitivity to pollutants. Weaker are the bonding forces, more is the sensitivity to the pollution as cation exchange capacity shall be more. Consequently expansive soils which are mostly expansive clays, such as black cotton soils are very sensitive towards the pollution and contamination. More so their mineralogical composition also contributes in increasing the sensitivity. Soils containing Montmorrilonite are more sensitive than soil containing Illite and Kaolinite.

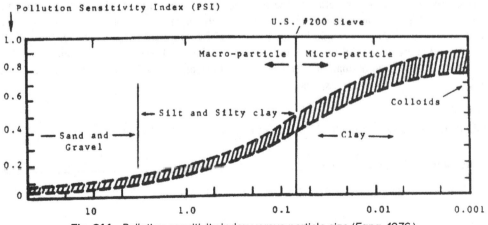

Fig. 21.1 Pollution sensitivity index versus particle size (*Fang, 1976,*)

3. RESPONSE OF SOIL TO THE PHYSIOCHEMICAL ACTIONS WITH CONTAMINANTS

The interaction of soil with contaminants and pollutants has got potential to change the entire properties of soil, whether they are index properties, strength parameters or in a nut shell all the geotechnical properties at large. It is to be made clear that effect of pollutants and contaminants on soil is very complex and so is its study until and unless all the parameters of such effect and changes thereof are studied independently including the properties of contaminants. Those factors which must be studied to study the response of soil to the physicochemical interactions of soil with contaminants and pollutants are ion exchange capacity of soil (cation and anion exchange capacity), properties of pore fluid, mineralogical characteristics of soil, and nature of pollutants and contaminants. A few of these characteristic have been discussed below Acid contamination can have several adverse effects on expansive soils, which are soils that undergo significant volume changes with changes in moisture content. Expansive soils, such as clayey soils, are particularly sensitive to environmental changes, and the presence of acids can exacerbate their behavior. Here are some potential effects of acid contamination on expansive soils:

1. **Chemical Reactions:** Acids can react with minerals in the soil, leading to the breakdown of clay minerals. This chemical reaction can alter the soil structure and reduce its ability to retain water.

2. **pH Changes:** Acid contamination can lower the pH of the soil. Expansive soils typically have a higher pH, and a decrease in pH can affect the soil's electrochemical properties, leading to changes in its swelling and shrinkage characteristics.

3. **Change in Soil Structure:** The reaction of acids with minerals in the soil can alter the structure of expansive soils. The original soil structure, which contributes to its expansive nature, may be disrupted, leading to changes in volume behavior.

4. **Decreased Plasticity:** Expansive soils exhibit plastic behavior, meaning they can undergo significant deformations. Acid contamination may reduce the plasticity of the soil, making it less prone to swelling and shrinking.

5. **Permeability Changes:** Acid-induced reactions can alter the pore structure of the soil, affecting its permeability. This can lead to changes in water movement within the soil, potentially influencing its volume changes.

6. **Strength Reduction:** Acid contamination can weaken the soil by breaking down mineral bonds. This reduction in strength may affect the load-bearing capacity of structures built on or in contact with the soil.

7. **Increased Erosion Risk:** Acidic conditions can increase the risk of erosion in expansive soils. Changes in soil structure and decreased cohesion can make the soil more susceptible to erosion by water.

8. **Environmental Impact:** Acid contamination of expansive soils can have broader environmental implications, potentially affecting surrounding vegetation, groundwater quality, and overall ecosystem health.

It's important to note that the specific effects will depend on the type and concentration of the acid, as well as the composition of the expansive soil. Engineers and geologists must consider these factors when assessing the impact of acid contamination on expansive soils in a particular location. Preventive measures, such as proper waste disposal and containment, are crucial to mitigate the risk of acid contamination in areas with expansive soils. The effects of base (alkaline) contamination on the engineering characteristics of expansive soils are generally opposite to those of acid contamination. Expansive soils, such as clayey soils, exhibit specific characteristics related to their mineral composition and ability to undergo volume changes with variations in moisture content. When subjected to base contamination, the following effects can be observed:

1. **Chemical Stabilization:** Bases can react with the clay minerals in expansive soils, causing chemical stabilization. This reaction may lead to the formation of cementitious compounds, which can enhance the soil's strength and reduce its swelling and shrinkage tendencies.

2. **pH Increase:** Alkaline substances increase the pH of the soil. Expansive soils often have lower pH values, and an increase in pH can modify the electrochemical properties of the soil, potentially reducing its expansive characteristics.

3. **Improved Plasticity:** Base contamination may increase the plasticity of expansive soils. This improvement in plasticity can be beneficial for certain construction applications, as it makes the soil more workable and less prone to cracking.

4. **Volume Change Mitigation:** The reaction of bases with clay minerals can modify the soil structure, reducing its susceptibility to volume changes associated with moisture fluctuations. This is

particularly important for mitigating issues related to swelling and shrinking in expansive soils.

5. **Increased Cohesion:** Base contamination can enhance the cohesion of expansive soils by promoting the formation of bonds between soil particles. This increase in cohesion contributes to improved soil strength and stability.

6. **Permeability Modification:** Alkaline substances can alter the pore structure of expansive soils, affecting their permeability. This modification may influence water movement within the soil and can be advantageous for controlling moisture-related volume changes.

7. **Enhanced Load-Bearing Capacity:** The chemical reactions induced by base contamination can lead to a more stable and load-bearing soil. This improvement in strength is crucial for supporting structures built on or in contact with expansive soils.

8. **Erosion Resistance:** Bases can contribute to the formation of stable soil aggregates, making the soil more resistant to erosion. This is beneficial in preventing soil loss due to water runoff.

It's important to note that the specific effects of base contamination depend on factors such as the type and concentration of the alkaline substance, as well as the initial composition of the expansive soil. Engineers and geotechnical specialists must carefully evaluate the site-specific conditions to determine the most appropriate approach for mitigating the expansive nature of the soil through base stabilization.

■ REFRENCES ■

1. O'Shay TA, Hoddinott KB. Analysis of soils contaminated with petroleum constituents. ASTM International; 1994.
2. Hinchee RE, Olfenbuttel RF. In Situ Bioreclamatio: Application and Investigations for Hydrocarbon and Contaminated Site Remediation. ScienceDirect; 1991 Jan.
3. Dineen D, Slater JP, Holland JP. In situ biological remediation of petroleum hydrocarbons in unsaturated soils. Hydrocarbon Contaminated Soil and Ground Water: Analysis, fate, environmental and public health effects remediation. Chelsea, Mich: Lewis Publishers; 1990.
4. Custance SRMPH. Environmental fate of the chemical mixtures: crude oil, JP-5, mineral spirits, and diesel fuel. Journal of Soil Contamination. 1992; 1(4):379–86.
5. Samira O, Gerard G, Waleed R. Types and extent of soil contamination in greater Al-Burqan oil field, Kuwait. Journal of Science and Engineering. 2006 Dec; 33(2):89–99.
6. Gruiz K, Kriston E. In situ bioremediation of hydrocarbon in soil. Journal of Soil Contamination. 1995; 4(2):163–73.
7. Wroth CP, Wood DM. The correlation of index properties with some basic engineering properties of soils. Canadian Geotechnical Journal. 1978; 15(2):137–45.
8. IS code: 2720-3(1980). Determination of specific gravity of soil.
9. IS code: 2720- 5 (1980). Determination of Atterberg's limit.
10. IS code: 2720-6(1980). Determination of shrinkage limit for fine grained soil.
11. IS code 2720-40(1980). Determination of free swell index value for fine grained soil.
12. Rahman ZA, Hamzah U, Taha MR, Ithnain NS, Ahmad N. Influence of oil contamination on Geotechnical Properties of Basaltic soil. Am J Applied Sci. 2010 Jan; 7(7):954–61.
13. Khamehchiyan M, Charkhabi AM, Tajik M. Effects of hydrocarbon contamination on geotechnical properties of clayey and sandy soils. Eng Geol. 2007; 89:220–9

Challenges and Opportunities for Innovation in India – Dr. Shweta Mishra et al. (eds)
© 2024 Taylor & Francis Group, London, ISBN 978-1-032-99842-8

Enhancement in Strength Parameter of Clayey Soil using Sodium Chloride as Admixture

22

Navin Kumar Yadav[1]

PhD Scholar,
Department of Civil Engineering, KNIT Sultanpur,
Uttar Pradesh, India

Bipin Prajapati[2]

Associate Professor,
Department of Civil Engineering, KNIT Sultanpur,
Uttar Pradesh, India

Onkar Nath Mishra[3]

PhD Scholars,
Department of Civil Engineering, KNIT Sultanpur,
Uttar Pradesh, India

Abstract

Most of the problems in front of civil engineers arise due to proposed sites do not have required behaviour in engineering purposes so support infrastructural need, like tracks for railways, roads and footing & dams etc. The soil present at field may not be usable having number of issues at site. A serious situation occurs in present situation arise due to the parent soil is obtained to be expansive soil and water table is grew up in particular area. Soils having a greater percentage of expansive clay normally serve less shear strength and have tendency to swelling and shrinking with their moisture variation. In those areas clayey soil is not best usable for such structures, like tracks for railways, roadways and footing & dam etc. enhancement of engineering properties of expansive soil can done by adopting different solutions of soil strengthening techniques. Soil strengthening is the process of chemical and physical alteration of different soils to improve their own engineering properties and then enhancement in the load bearing capacity of a sub-grade or a sub-base to help pavements and foundations. Sodium chloride (NaCl) has been utilized for so many years as a strengthening admixture in selected expansive soil such as base course materials. Sodium chloride (NaCl) as an admixture added to virgin soil was seen that have avoidable the impact on soil plasticity while increasing compacted density and decreasing optimum moisture content. In this project, the stability of soil is found by adding Sodium chloride (NaCl) and thus check and compared with the stability of soil without adding Sodium Chloride (NaCl) and with the addition of sodium chloride by performing the different laboratory tests.

Keywords

Expansive soil stabilization, Clayey soil, Sodium chloride, Admixture

[1]navin.21ce2635@knit.ac.in, [2]bipin.prajapati@knit.ac.in, [3]onkar.2162@knit.ac.in

DOI: 10.1201/9781003606260-22

1. INTRODUCTION

India has variety of uniqueness in topographical land area in which arrangements of various roads and infrastructure projects. Selection of required land is less in area in many reasons and also a measure cause of that is urbanization and modifications in the existing infrastructures. Selected area of field is more suitable for different objective like development starts in that particular area as residential as well as commercial buildings, development of various roads, express ways and also required development work in that particular area. Infrastructure work starts on that particular area of land i.e. expansive in nature. A bunch of serious issues in front of soil engineers on that selected particular field location which do not have favorable soil characteristics to help development of different structures like, residential, commercial as well as public sector projects. The selected land area soil may be weak due to its own nature of swelling and shrinking with moisture variation. A serious issue arises in that reason on the selected land at site is observed to be montmorillonite in nature or swell shrink behaviour. The level of the water table in this particular area is much high. Materials with high montmorillonite content generally like clay having minimum strength and arises situation to swell or shrink with the amount of moisture variation. Cause of these problems expansive soil is not able to directly use in the development of any infrastructure like buildings, railways, bridges, dams etc. There are so many properties related to strength in expansive soil or rich in clay content soil can be improved with the help of various methods for the strengthening of weak or expansive soil. In such conditions there are so many strengthening ways which are in practice for improvement in the engineering characteristics of this parent soil. The use of such general methods in practice for property improvement of given clayey soil is fly ash & cement stabilization. Expansive material like soil is strengthened by the use of stabilization with chemicals as well as stabilization by physical way. Strengthening of soil by physical methods considering dynamic compaction and strengthening with chemicals is carried easily by reactive materials such as CaO, fly ash, Portland cement, $CaCl_2$, NaCl, Na_2SO_4, $MgCl_2$ or other substitute materials which have elastic behaviour like bitumen. Stabilizers which not used general are also used for changing behaviour based on strength of soil which is expansive in nature. Normally less used strengthen agents considered such as polymers, (K) potassium materials and stabilizing agents which are stone dust, brick dust, lime kiln dust etc. One of above mentioned admixture sodium chloride is also having advantageous in case of clayey soil stabilization.

1.1 Advantages and Purposes

Objective of this study which is to provide general over view of soil stabilization techniques used in the construction industry and maintenance of those structures who designed for supporting motor vehicle use like highways and expressways, and also in railway tracks.

The safe designed infrastructure projects based on the subgrade strength and capacity of bearing the load safely. The characteristics of that selected soil which is expansive in nature or structure should have change the strength property. The prepared stabilized soil used for various purposes after improvement in considered expansive soils which limproved is bearing property, minimum strength in shear and high compressibility behaviour. So the considered soil strengthening is preferably for that purpose.

1. Virgin soil strengthening is due to enhancement in strength and load bearing characteristics of considered soil.
2. Work carried out for Soil strengthening is more suitable and economical as compare to mat footing.
3. In this case sliding can be prevented of sharp slopes by using advanced techniques used for soil strengthening.
4. After this work drainage of the soil can be improved by using techniques of soil strengthening.

2. MATERIALS AND THEIR PROPERTIES

Laboratory experimental analysis is to be carried out on locally available soil sample. Virgin soil sample collected from Lambhua Sultanpur. Soil used for sampling was oven dried for laboratory analysis of proposed work.

2.1 Soil Sample Properties

Table 22.1 Characteristics of virgin soil

S. No.	Characteristics of soil	Value
1	G	2.67
2	LL	38%
3	PL	27%
4	PI	11%
5	IS classification	CI
6	OMC	16%
7	MDD	1.63

2.2 Objectives of Sodium Chloride as Admixtures

In current study it is seen that NaCl may be used as good alternate to CaO due to its property to quickly dissolve in water. It is to help in providing sufficient Ca++ for ion exchange in expansive soil reaction. NaCl is considered as effective stabilize agent in considered soil strengthening. NaCl considered also in the manufacturing of cement which is used as an accelerator for expansive soil modification & also considered as a dust palliative or the maintenance of roads. NaCl changes the engineering characteristics of soil like shear strength, permeability and compressibility. The active function of stabilizer (NaCl) is in the form fine particles & binding together. NaCl reacts with considered soil sample having pH less or more than 7. Ca++ changes this hydroxide ion of the minerals of clay which is generally attached towards the negatively charged particles of clay.

2.3 Sodium Chloride (NaCl) Characteristics

Table 22.2 Mineral composition and characteristics of NaCl

B.P.	14610.1 c(1013)(hpa)
Vapors Pressure	1.3hpa (8650c)
G	2.165
Water Solubility	358.01 g/l (200c)
SO$_4$	<0.21%
Ca	<0.0101%
Fe	<0.0011%
As	<0.000052%
Insoluble matter	<0.031%
Mg	<0.011%
Cu	<0.00021%
Cd	<0.000022%
Pb	<0.00011%
Hg	<0.0000051%
M.W.	58.42

3. TESTS ON SOIL SAMPLES

Laboratory Tests:

Different required laboratory tests have been performed as per IS: 2720. The tests were carried out both on natural soil sample and soil sample with chloride content.

(i) **Free Swelling Index (F.S.I.) Test**

The free-swelling index (FSI) is a measure of the increase in volume of soil when heated under specified conditions (ASTM D720; ISO 335). The FSI method is a small-scaletestforobtaininginforma tionregardingthefree-swellingpropertiesofasoil.

(ii) **Atterberg Limit Test**

a. Liquid Limit(LL)

b. Plastic Limit(PL)

c. Plasticity Index (PI)[PI = LL – PL]

(iii) **OMC & MDD Test**

This **test** is done to determine the maximum dry density and the optimum moisture content of soil using heavy compaction as per IS: 2720 (Part8)–1983.

(iv) **CBR Test**

The CBR test is performed by measuring the pressure required to penetrate a soil sample with a plunger of standard area.

(v) **Unconfined Compression Test**

The purpose of this laboratory is to determine the unconfined compressive strength of a cohesive soil sample. Unconfined compressive strength is a standard geotechnical test performed on cohesive soil samples in construction materials testing laboratories.

3.1 Mix Proportion of Soil Sample and Sodium Chloride

Table 22.3 Mix proportion of soil and sodium chloride

S. No.	Percentage of soil (%)	Percentage of NaCl (%)
1	99	1.0
2	98	2.0
3	97	3.0
4	96	4.0
5	95	5.0

4. RESULTS

There are following test conducted for the stabilization of clayey soil with the **addition of NaCl and without addition of NaCl varying amount of 1 to 5%.**

(i) **FSI Test**

Table 22.4 Free swelling index (F.S.I.)

S. No.	Dosage	F.S.I. (%)
1	Virgin soil	45
2	Soil + 1.0% of Sodium Chloride	41
3	Soil + 2.0% of Sodium Chloride	34
4	Soil + 3.0% of Sodium Chloride	31
5	Soil + 4.0% of Sodium Chloride	24
6	Soil + 5.0% of Sodium Chloride	26

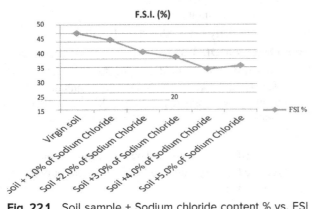

Fig. 22.1 Soil sample + Sodium chloride content % vs. FSI (%)

(ii) Consistency limit Test (Liquid limit, Plastic limit & Plasticity Index)

Table 22.5 LL, PL and PI Index

Sr. No.	Dosage	LL (%)	PL (%)	PI (%)
1	Virgin soil	45	22	23
2	Soil + 1.0% of Sodium Chloride	41	20	21
3	Soil + 2.0% of Sodium Chloride	39	19	20
4	Soil + 3.0% of Sodium Chloride	36	17	19
5	Soil + 4.0% of Sodium Chloride	33	16	17
6	Soil + 5.0% of Sodium Chloride	36	17	19

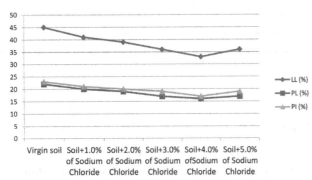

Fig. 22.2 Soil sample + sodium chloride content % vs. LL, PL & PI (%)

(iii) OMC and MDD Test

Table 22.6 Optimum moisture content and maximum dry density

Sr. No.	Dosage	OMC (%)	MDD(gm/cc)
1	Virgin soil	24	16.2
2	Soil+1.0%of Sodium Chloride	21.5	16.6
3	Soil+2.0%of Sodium Chloride	19.5	16.9
4	Soil+3.0%of Sodium Chloride	17	17.1
5	Soil+4.0%of Sodium Chloride	14	17.8
6	Soil+5.0%of Sodium Chloride	16	17.5

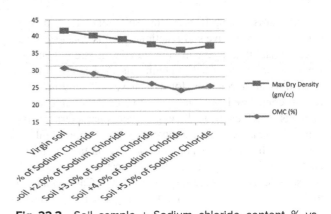

Fig. 22.3 Soil sample + Sodium chloride content % vs. OMC & MDD (%)

(iv) CBR Test

Table 22.7 California bearing ratio

Sr. No.	Dosage	CBR (Soaked)(%)
1	Virgin soil	1.8
2	Soil + 1.0% of Sodium Chloride	2.1
3	Soil + 2.0% of Sodium Chloride	2.4
4	Soil + 3.0% of Sodium Chloride	2.6
5	Soil + 4.0% of Sodium Chloride	3.6
6	Soil + 5.0% of Sodium Chloride	3

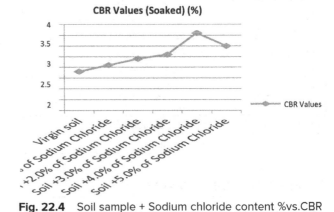

Fig. 22.4 Soil sample + Sodium chloride content %vs.CBR (%)

(v) Unconfined compression test (UCS)

Table 22.8 Unconfined compression test results

Sr. No.	Dosage	Strength (C-Kg/Cm2)
1	Virgin soil	1
2	Soil + 1.0% of Sodium Chloride	1
3	Soil + 2.0% of Sodium Chloride	1.1
4	Soil + 3.0% of Sodium Chloride	1.3
5	Soil + 4.0% of Sodium Chloride	1.4
6	Soil + 5.0% of Sodium Chloride	1.1

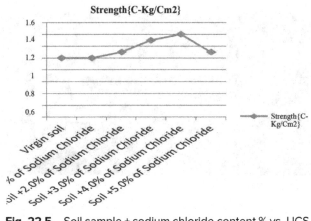

Fig. 22.5 Soil sample + sodium chloride content % vs. UCS (kg/cm²)

4. Discussion

1. Above figure shows that the Free Swelling Index (F.S.I.) is reduces with increase in the amount of NaCl up to 4.0% and increasing so on.

2. Liquid limit of soil reduces as compared to virgin soil. In above figure Liquid limit (L.L.) as well as plastic limit of given soil reduces by use of NaCl as stabilizing agent. Considered soil mixed with NaCl reduces the liquid limit as compared to parent soil. Obtained results also shows that PI reduces up to 173% as considered parent soil.

3. After 4.0% addition of NaCl MDD reduces. The increments in the MDD value with increased % of NaCl up to 4% and also OMC reduces by increasing the sodium chloride amount till 4.0% and then decrease causes further increase in amount of NaCl.

4. The increase in the value of CBR twice as the value of CBR in parent soil. The value of CBR in considered soil increases by the addition of NaCl upto 4% and decreases with further addition of dosage.

5. In above discussion it was clear that UCS graph shows incremental results in the above figure for strength upto 4% of sodium chloride amount with virgin soil by increasing the dose of chemicals create reduce in value of unconfined compressive strength. The value of unconfined compressive strength increased by 140 % of parent soil.

5. Conclusions

NaCl (Sodium chloride) with variable amount in percentage is changed from 1.0% to5.0% by increase of each 1.0% percent amount. In above analysis shows the amount of unconfined compressive strength value improved by increase in sodium chloride (NaCl) amount. Sodium chloride (NaCl) causes early improved reaction expansive parent soil with improved in unconfined compressive strength. A great change in percentage value of unconfined compressive strength is at 4.0% addition of NaCl then again adding NaCl % of chemicals cause reduce in unconfined compressive strength value.

■ REFERENCES ■

1. IS: 2720 (Part III/sec 1).Methods of test for soils. Part III Determination of specific gravity. Section1, Fine grained soil, 1980.

2. IS: 2720 (Part VII), Methods of test for soil.PartVIIDetermination of watercontent-drydensityrelationusinglightcompaction, 1980.

3. IS: 2720 (Part 5), Method of test for soils. Part-5, Determination of liquid and plastic limit, 1985.

4. IS: 2720 (Part 16), Methods for test for soil. Part16 Laboratory determination of CBR, 1987.

5. Al-Rauas Goosen MF. Expansive soils: recent advances in characterization and treatment. London: Taylor&Francis.2006.

6. Abood TT. Kasa AB. Chik ZB. Stabilisation of silo clay soil using chloride compounds. J EnqSciTech.2007:2(1):102-10.

7. AASHTO. T -180 Moisture density relations of soils using a4.54 kg(10lb) rammer and a 457 mm(18 in.) drop. Annual book of ASTM Standards. West Conshohocken. USA: ASTM International: 2011.

8. Kalantari B.Prasad A. Huat BB. Stabilizing peat soil with cement and silica fume. Proc Inst Civ Eng-Geotech Eng. 2011:164(1):33–9

9. Manjunath, R., Vinay, K.S., Raghu, R., Varun Raj, N.A. and Vibish, P.R. Stabilization of lithomargic clay using sodium chloride salt, international conference on advances in architecture and civil engineering (AARCV), 1, 2012, 384–386.

10. K. V Manoj Krishna, HN Ramesh. Strength and FOS performance of the BC Soil treated with calcium chloride IOSR of mechanical and civil engineering, 2(6), 2012, 21–25. Dahale, P. P., Madurwar, K.V., and Burile,

11. A.N. Comparative study of blackcotton soil stabilization with RBI Grade 81 and sodium silicate, international journal of innovative research in science, engineering and technology, 2, 2013, 493–499.

12. Laxmikant Yadu, R. K Tripathi. Stabilization of soft soil with granulated blast furnace slag and flyash IJRET: International journal of research in engineering and technology IISN: 2319–1163, PG.NO. 115119.6,2013.

13. SarideS. Puppala AJ. Chikyala SR.Swell-shrink and strength behaviors of lime and cementstabilizedexpansive-organicclays.ApplyClaySci.2013:85:39–45.

14. Karthik. S, Ashok Kumar .F, Gowtham .P, Elango.G, Gokul. D. Thangaraj S. Soil Stabilization by using fly ash, IOSR Journal of mechanical and civil engineering (IOSR-JMCE), 2014, 20–26.

15. ASTM.D1883-16 Standard test method for California bearing ratio (CBR) of laboratory-compacted soils. Annual Book of ASTM Standards. West Conshohocken. USA: ASTM International: 2016.

16. Moayedi H. Nazir R. Malaysian experiences of peat stabilization.Stateoftheart.GeotechGeolEng.2018:36:1–11.

17. Christopher IC. Chimobi ND. Emerging bends in expansive soil stabilisation: a rei4eu. IRock Mech GeotechEng.2019.11 (2):423–40.

Note: All the figures and tables in this chapter were made by the author.

Challenges and Opportunities for Innovation in India – Dr. Shweta Mishra et al. (eds)
© 2024 Taylor & Francis Group, London, ISBN 978-1-032-99842-8

Comparative Study of Concrete using Crushed Over Burnt Bricks, Crushed Marbles as a Full Replacement of Course Aggregate

23

Surya Kant Shukla[1]

Assistant professor,
Department of Civil Engineering, AIMT Lucknow,
Uttar Pradesh, India

Navin Kumar Yadav[2]

PhD Scholar,
Department of Civil Engineering, KNIT Sultanpur,
Uttar Pradesh, India

Abstract

Concrete is one of the most widely used building materials. The raw materials from which it is made are cement and aggregate, both of which contribute to the quality of the construction. Aggregates account for over 70% of the volume, and the cost of construction also depends on the availability of these aggregates. From an environmental point of view, mining natural aggregates restricts the accessibility of groundwater, as well as contributing to atmospheric contamination through the release of dust and slurry particles. This work demonstrates an effort to explore the possibility of using broken bricks, broken balls and broken tiles from flooring work. In this study, several samples were constructed with crushed over burnt bricks, crushed marble and broken tiles as a complete substitute for coarse aggregates, with corresponding workability and compressive strength. Compressive strength was checked and compared to natural coarse aggregate and found that the sample with broken marble has the most compressive strength and the same workability as the other three waste materials.

Keywords

Crushed over burnt bricks, Crushed marble, Compressive strength, Workability

1. INTRODUCTION

Concrete is made up of cementitious raw material, aggregate, and water, and is tested many times. Amount of air mixed in. Most of the concrete mixture consists of coarse gravel and fine Gravel sand and compacted stones are used. Is required Aggregates are increasingly used as partial or complete substitutes for natural materials by using recycled materials, concrete can be manufactured more efficiently. Broadly speaking, all types of Aggregate mines have some degree of impact on the environment Additional levels, especially quarrying of marble, granite,

[1]Suryakantshukla27@gmail.com, [2]navin.21ce2635knit.ac.in

DOI: 10.1201/9781003606260-23

limestone, sandstone, etc. Type of architectural stone quarry that falls under the category of open pit mining and produces a variety of stone types. Problems like clogged drains, dust problems, mud particles getting into the air, etc. It causes air pollution in the form of air pollution and mud causes land pollution. Yielding as a result of reduced porosity, water entrapment, and dumping The area cannot support vegetation growth. For persistent authentication of properties Mud and particles block the flow of an aquifer. The result, Gravel affects access to groundwater and therefore requires high quality waste is economically exploited in eloquence. With the strong growth in construction activity, sources of natural aggregates are becoming increasingly available. Conservation of natural resources has become a major challenge for Engineers as they are becoming exhausted because construction activities cannot be reduced. The only way is for him to explore one Alternative material that can completely or moderately replace naturally occurring materials in construction. Additionally, population growth in recent decades has led to vigorous growth in concrete jungle (increasing demand for construction work), increasing scope of waste very important issue. Such construction waste can be used in production Lightweight and low-labor RAC (Recycled Aggregate Concrete).

2. Objective of Research

The main objectives of the study are:

1. Use crushed bricks, crushed marble to replace natural stone. Concrete aggregate realizes sustainable development in construction work Reduce consumption of natural resources.
2. Investigation and evaluation of workability and compressive strength Replacement concrete from normal samples.

3. Materials

1. **Cement:** In this research work the cement used is Ordinary Portland cement (OPC grade 53)

Table 23.1 Properties of cement

S. no	Properties	Normal range	Obtained range
1	Fineness of cement	Should not exceed 10%	9%
2	Standard Consistency	26%-33%	31.5%
3	Initial Setting time	minimum 30 minutes	91 minutes
4	Final Setting time	maximum 600 minutes	158 minutes

2. **Fine aggregate:** In the experimental work, sand is used as fine aggregate and sieve analysis is performed. As per the grade restrictions, the sand sample was found to be in Zone III as per IS: 383–1970.

Table 23.2 Properties of sand

	sand	
2	Bulking of sand	3.32%
3	Specific gravity of sand	2.59

3. **Coarse aggregate:** Coarse aggregate of nominal size 20mm is used.

Table 23.3 Properties of coarse aggregate

S. no	Properties	Obtained range
1	Fineness modulus of aggregate	4.55
2	Aggregate Impact Value Test	12.4%
3	Specific gravity of aggregate	2.81
4	Water absorption test	1.89%
5	Flakiness Index	11.763%
6	Elongation index	20.931%

4. **Crushed over burnt bricks, Crushed marbles:** Crushed bricks, marble are sourced from nearby locations Destroyed. These waste materials were manually chopped into small pieces in the laboratory. The materials used were crushed marble and bricks, which were left on an IS-4.75 mm sieve.

Table 23.4 Properties of crushed bricks, marbles

S. no	Properties	Obtainedrange
1	Fineness modulus of	4.58

S. no	Properties	Obtained range
1	Specific gravity of Crushed over burnt bricks	1.89
2	Specific gravity of Crushed marbles	2.7
3	Water absorption Crushed over burnt bricks	12.9%
4	Water absorption Crushed marbles	0.82%

4. Methodology

1. **Mixing**

   Different samples of concrete cubes had been organized with changed coarse aggregate as damaged brick, damaged marbles. Concrete is ready for M20 mix. In order to benefit unvarying combination, the dried substances are meticulously combined and a calculated amount of water is added (W/C ratio) observed via way of means of quality blending with a purpose to get an unvarying texture.

2. Casting

Once the concrete combination is formed, it's far packed with inside the mildew with the aid of using the vibrator for whole elimination of air. The apex of concrete is ceased with the assist of trowel & sound tapping is finished until the cement slurry involves the dice peak.

3. Curing

Results and Discussion

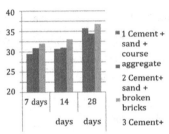

Fig. 23.1 Comparison of compressive strength of concrete cubes

Next day after casting, the cubes are indifferent from the mildew and it's miles stored under freshwater at a temperature maintained round 27 °C for 7 to twenty- eight days, after each seventh day the water is changed.

4. Testing

Cubes of 15 cm are examined for compressive energy in standard testing device. The cubes are centrally placed at the circle marks placed in device plate and axial load is carried out at the cubes. The price of software of this sluggish loading is stored at 140kg/cm2, until the dice collapses. The compressive load is described because the utmost load at which the dice fails.

Compressive energy = Failure load consistent with unit preliminary go sectional area

Table 23.5 Compressive strength of different samples obtained from Test at 7, 14 and 28 days

S. No	Sample		Compressive strength (kN/mm²)		
			7 days	14 days	28 days
1	Cement sand course aggregate	+ +	19.02	21.50	31.50
2	Cement + sand broken bricks	+	21.80	22.03	28.85
3	Cement + sand broken marble	+	24.10	26.20	33.50

Table 23.6 Water cement ratio and cement workability

S. No	Sample	W/Cratio	Slump, mm
1	Cement + sand + coarse aggregate	0.45	50
2	Cement + sand + broken bricks	0.50	20
3	Broken marble	0.45	45

5. CONCLUSION

1. Concrete mix samples containing broken bricks and marble shows marginal increase in compressive strength in contrast to natural concrete.

2. The workability of concrete mix samples containing marble aggregate reduced as the percentage level of replacement of natural aggregates by brick, marble and tile aggregates increased.

3. The experiment concluded that natural aggregate can be replaced by brick, marble and tile aggregates to a full extent in concrete mixes.

4. Reduction in issues like drainage chocking, dust trouble due to mining of natural aggregates and proper groundwater accessibility is achieved.

5. Atmospheric contamination as a result of mining is no longer a concern by using these aggregates.

■ REFRENCES ■

1. Dina M. Sadek, Walid S. EL-Sayed, Ashraf M.A Heniegal, Ayman S.Mohamed, Utilization of solid wastes in cement bricks for an environmental beneficial, International Journal of Engineering, Tome XI 188 Fascicule 3. ISSN 1584–2673

2. Husain M. Husain, Al Hamed Abdul-hafidh M.S. and Mustafa KH. Kasim, "The use of crushed brick pretreated with cement syrup as aggregate for concrete", S.J. Tikrit Univ. Engg. Sci., Vol.2, No.2, 1995

3. Cachim P B, Mechanical Properties of brick aggregate concrete. Construction and Building Materials, 23, 2009, pp. 1292–1297.

4. Binici H, Shah T, Aksogan O, Kaplan H, Durability of concrete made with granite and marble as recycle aggregates, Journal of materials processing technology, Vol.208, Issues 1-3, Pages 299–308, 21 November 2008

5. Fadia S. Kallak, Assistant Lecturer Civil Eng. Dept.- University of Tikrit, "Use of Crushed Bricks as Coarse Aggregate in Concrete" Tikrit Journal of Eng. Sciences/Vol. 16/No. 3/ September 2009, (64-69),

6. Khaloo A R, "Properties of concrete using crushed clinker brick as coarse aggregate," ACI materials Journal, vol. 91, no. 2, 1994, pp. 401–407.

Note: All the figures and tables in this chapter were made by the author.

Challenges and Opportunities for Innovation in India – Dr. Shweta Mishra et al. (eds)
© 2024 Taylor & Francis Group, London, ISBN 978-1-032-99842-8

Sustainable Soil Improvement: A Comprehensive Study on Bagasse Ash and Plastic Waste Integration

24

Chatrabhuj*
Research Scholar,
Department of Civil Engineering,
Guru Ghasidas Vishwavidyalaya, Bilaspur,
C.G, India

Onkar Nath Mishra, Navin Kumar Yadav
Research Scholar,
Department of Civil Engineering,
Kamla Nehru Institute of Technology, Sultanpur,
U.P, India

Bipin Prajapati
Associate Professor,
Department of Civil Engineering,
Kamla Nehru Institute of Technology,
Sultanpur, U.P, India

Abstract

The construction of structures on clayey soil presents inherent challenges due to its water-absorbing characteristics and unpredictable settlement behaviour. In response, various stabilization techniques have been explored to enhance soil properties. Recent attention has shifted towards sustainable practices, with a focus on utilizing bagasse ash and plastic waste. These materials offer a promising avenue for improving geotechnical properties while addressing the environmental burden associated with landfill disposal. This study investigates the influence of incorporating bagasse ash and plastic strips in varying ratios into clayey soil. Bagasse ash (BA) is introduced at different concentrations (5%, 10%, 15%, and 20% by weight of soil), complemented by the inclusion of Plastic Waste Strips (PWS) at diverse proportions (0.3%, 0.6%, 0.9%, and 1.2%) within the soil-bagasse ash matrix. The research assesses key engineering properties, including the Unconfined Compressive Strength (UCS), and California Bearing Ratio (CBR) under both Unsoaked and Soaked conditions. The findings reveal a notable enhancement in soil strength with the integration of bagasse ash and plastic waste strips. Through rigorous analysis, the optimal blending ratio is determined as 15% Bagasse ash and 0.9% PWS in the soil matrix. Positive correlations emerge between Unsoaked and Soaked CBR and UCS values, underscoring the cohesive impact of the introduced materials. This research contributes to the growing body of knowledge on sustainable soil improvement, highlighting the economic and environmental advantages of incorporating bagasse ash and plastic waste for enhanced engineering properties in clayey soil.

Keywords

Soil stabilization, Bagasse ash, Plastic waste strips, Unconfined compressive strength, California bearing ratio

*Corresponding author: Chatrabhuj513@gmail.com

DOI: 10.1201/9781003606260-24

1. INTRODUCTION

In the current century, waste disposal is becoming a major concern for a variety of industry sectors around the world. These waste materials are growing rapidly in life day by day and it is not good for the environment. Nearly tons of waste are produced in nations and states across the world. So, it becomes necessary to dispose of the waste material properly. If not done, it has a harmful impact on the environment as well as on humans. One of the most common ways of disposing of waste material is landfills, burning and compositing. Clay soil is capable of holding water. It tends to shrink and expand in this environment, which might lead to settlement due to compressibility Clay soil has poor stiffness and strength [1], and this has generated major issues in geotechnical engineering properties since poor soil can compromise the structure's construction. Clay soil is soil that has very fine particles containing minerals soft clay has high settlement and low compressive strength [2]. Moisture can reduce the strength of clay soil. Soil modification is the mechanism of changing the soil index qualities by introducing modifiers like cement, chemicals, lime, bitumen, plastic strips, geosynthetics, stone dust, slag, foundry sand and Bottom ash. Bagasse Ash, originating from the controlled combustion or incineration of bagasse, the fibrous residue extracted during the sugarcane sugar extraction process, is a versatile byproduct. Comprising predominantly of silica, it imparts strength and durability to the ash, while alumina, another significant component, contributes to its pozzolanic properties [3]. Additionally, bagasse ash often contains calcium oxide, enhancing its cementitious characteristics, with minor trace elements depending on the combustion conditions [4]. Derived through the combustion of bagasse in boilers or furnaces, the process generates both heat and energy, leaving behind the residual ash. This bagasse ash is extensively employed for diverse applications:

1. **Soil Stabilization:** Bagasse ash serves as an effective soil stabilizer, particularly in clayey soils. It enhances soil properties such as strength, durability, and workability, making it conducive for various construction projects.

2. **Concrete Production:** Acting as a supplementary cementitious material, bagasse ash contributes to the strength and durability of concrete. It can be utilized to replace traditional cement in concrete formulations partially.

3. **Brick and Block Manufacturing:** Bagasse ash is incorporated into the production of bricks and blocks, fortifying their structural integrity while simultaneously reducing the environmental impact associated with conventional firing methods.

4. **Road Construction:** In road construction, bagasse ash finds application for sub-base stabilization, thereby enhancing the performance and durability of roads.

2. LITERATURE REVIEW

The utilization of bagasse ash aligns with environmentally sustainable practices by providing an eco-friendly solution to manage the byproducts of sugarcane processing [5]. Beyond waste reduction, incorporating bagasse ash into construction materials contributes to a diminished carbon footprint by minimizing reliance on traditional cement and energy-intensive manufacturing methods. In contemporary research endeavours, there is a growing emphasis on repurposing waste materials rather than resorting to landfill disposal, which not only occupies valuable space but also poses environmental challenges [6]. A significant proportion of waste, especially plastics, is inherently reusable. Being non-decomposable with an exceedingly slow decomposition rate, plastic poses a considerable threat to ecosystems [7-9]. Large quantities of plastic waste are generated annually from various industries, offering a potential resource for soil stabilization [10]. Derived mainly from water bottles and plastic bags, plastic waste is commonly employed in the form of sheets and strips in various sizes [11]. Its versatile applications extend to soil stabilization playing a crucial role in enhancing subgrade qualities developing concrete and mitigating the compressibility of clayey soil Particularly effective in improving subgrade qualities and increasing the California Bearing Ratio (CBR) value of soil, plastic waste strips (PWS) emerge as a valuable material [12].

Numerous studies have explored the positive impact of waste materials on the qualities of weak soils, particularly in terms of geotechnical properties, concurrently contributing to pollution reduction efforts. The stabilization of clayey soil through the incorporation of additional materials has been shown to reduce volume change characteristics and enhance soil strength [13]. Among the readily available waste materials in local areas, plastic and bagasse ash stand out as common types due to their minimal cost compared to other waste sources and lack of specialized design requirements. This research elucidates the utilization and quantification of soil property enhancements through the incorporation of these waste materials [14-16].

3. MATERIAL USED

This study incorporates a variety of materials to investigate the impact and alteration in soil strength properties through the inclusion of plastic waste strips (specifically, bottle strips) and bagasse ash.

3.1 Soil

The initial soil samples were obtained from Lambhua, in the Sultanpur district of Uttar Pradesh. The sample preparation involved drying and crushing the soil, followed by sieving through a 4.75 mm mesh size. A series of laboratory tests were conducted on the pristine soil to gather relevant data

Fig. 24.1 Sample of soil

To classify soil various tests are performed as per IS classification code IS 2720. All the test results are given in the following table

Table 24.1 Soil properties

Soil Properties		Obtained Values
Specific Gravity		2.7
Grain Size Analysis	Gravel	0
	Sand	4.7
	Silt & Clay	95.20
Plastic Limit(%)		21.41
Liquid Limit(%)		34.11
Plasticity Index(%)		13.3
Classification of soil		CL
OMC (%)		17..6
MDD (gm/cc)		1.63
CBR	Unsoaked (%)	4.8
	Soaked (%)	2.6
UCS (kg/cm²)		1.76

3.2 Bagasse Ash

Uttar Pradesh, particularly Sultanpur and its nearby areas, hosts numerous sugar mills contributing to the state's sugar production. In this region, the extraction of juice from sugarcane results in the generation of bagasse, which is subsequently burned to produce heat for boilers. The residual ash from this combustion process is referred to as bagasse ash. The raw material for this study was sourced from Kishan Sahakari Chini Mill, Ltd., located in Sultanpur, Avadh, Uttar Pradesh, reflecting the prevalent sugar production activities in the region.

Fig. 24.2 Bagasse ash

Table 24.2 Bagasse ash properties

Properties	Values
Specific gravity (G)	2.1
Plasticity	Non-plastic
MDD (gm/cc)	1.22
OMC (%)	14.4
Plastic Limit (%)	12.1
Liquid Limit (%)	22.3
Plasticity Index (P.I.) (%)	10.2
Cohesion	Negligible

3.3 Plastic Waste Strip (PWS)

Plastic bottles (reuse) are collected from local vendors and houses. Firstly, clean and dry the bottles. Plastic bottles are cut into strip form with the help of scissors and knives in sizes 4 mm in width and 20 mm in length. The physical properties of PET bottle strips are given below

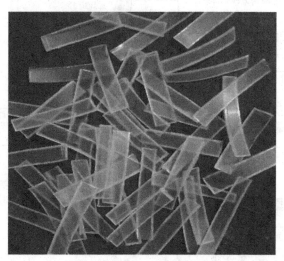

Fig. 24.3 Sample of PWS

Table 24.3 PWS properties

Properties	Values
Specific gravity	1.38
Aspect ratio	5
Length (mm)	20
Thickness (mm)	0.05
Width (mm)	4
Modulus of elasticity	2950
Tensile strength (MPa)	64

4. METHODOLOGY

To assess the impact of induction materials such as Bagasse ash (BA) and Plastic Waste Strips (PWS) on clayey soil, various tests in accordance with IS 2720 standards, including CBR and UCS, were conducted. The experimental procedure involved the initial incorporation of bagasse ash in different proportions (5%, 10%, 15%, and 20% by dry weight of soil) through random hand mixing. Subsequently, after determining the optimum dosage, PWS was introduced with varying ratios (0.3%, 0.6%, 0.9%, and 1.2%), blended with the previously determined optimal bagasse ash content, to ascertain the overall optimum dosage for enhancing soil conditions.

The methodology employed in this research is illustrated in Fig. 24.4, which is segmented into three main blocks.

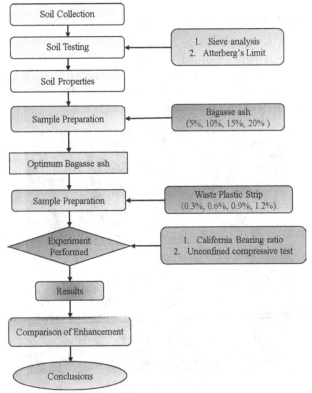

Fig. 24.4 Methodology

The first block encompasses soil classification and testing techniques. In the second block, the focus is on the utilization of bagasse ash. Initially, bagasse ash is classified based on its properties, and then it is added to the soil in different ratios, by weight. The prepared soil samples are subjected to various tests, including compaction, CBR, and UCS. After analyzing the test results, the optimum bagasse ash content for soil improvement is determined. Plastic waste strips are introduced into the soil samples at different ratios (0.3%, 0.6%, 0.9%, and 1.2% by weight of soil). Subsequently, with the optimal bagasse ash content in the soil, the combined influence of bagasse ash and plastic waste strips is assessed to determine the overall optimum value for enhanced soil conditions. This comprehensive methodology serves as the foundation for the experimental work in this research.

5. RESULTS AND DISCUSSION

Upon conducting experimental tests shown in the above procedure, various test results are obtained which are shown below

5.1 California Bearing Ratio Test

The experimental investigation involved assessing the CBR in both unsoaked and soaked conditions, considering a mixture of bagasse ash with soil and the addition of plastic waste strips to the bagasse ash-soil blend. The Fig displays the variations in CBR values (both unsoaked and soaked) resulting from different percentages of bagasse ash. Specifically, the unsoaked CBR value increased from 8.5% to 14%, and the soaked CBR value increased from 4.8% to 5.9% with the introduction of 0.9% plastic waste strips and 15% bagasse ash combined with soil. Moreover, a substantial enhancement was evident, with an 85% increase in unsoaked CBR value and a 72% increase in soaked CBR value for the combination of 15% bagasse ash and 0.9% plastic waste strips with soil. These findings underscore the positive influence of the specified combinations on the CBR values, indicating improved soil stability and strength characteristics under both unsoaked and soaked conditions.

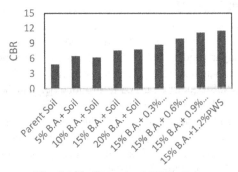

Fig. 24.5 Unsoaked CBR values

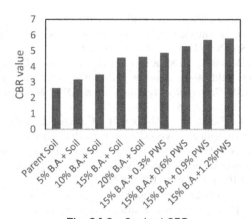

Fig. 24.6   Soaked CBR

5.2   Unconfined Compressive Strength

Samples tested show UCS value increases from 1.75 to 2.43 kg/cm^2 with the addition of 0.9% of plastic waste mixed with clay soil- bagasse ash mixture. The UCS value increased due cementing agent present in the bagasse ash and the good bonding provided with soil, the plastic strip provides the reinforcing effect. UCS value increased by 60 % for 15 % FA and 0.9% PWS blend with the soil which can be the optimum value.

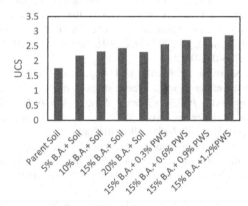

Fig. 24.7   UCS variation

5.3   Correlation between CBR and UCS

In the present experimental study, the correlation between CBR and UCS is explored to understand their relationship. This investigation involves a statistical examination of the interdependence between these two variables. Correlation, denoted by the coefficient of correlation (r), quantifies the extent of dependency or interrelation between the CBR and UCS values. Through this analysis, we aim to determine the degree to which these two crucial variables are interconnected in the context of the study.

The examination of both Figs. 24.8 and 24.9 leads to the conclusion that a positive correlation exists between

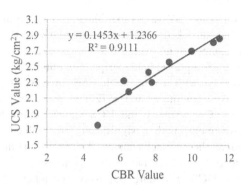

Fig. 24.8   Correlation between unsoaked CBR and UCS

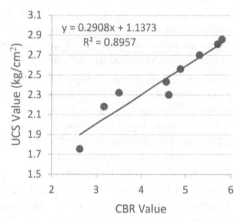

Fig. 24.9   Correlation between soaked CBR and UCS

both soaked and unsoaked CBR and UCS. The graphical representation in the figures demonstrates an upward-increasing trend for both conditions. This observation suggests that as the CBR values increase, there is a corresponding increase in UCS. The positive correlation between these key parameters underscores their interdependence and highlights the consistent trend of strengthening in both soaked and unsoaked conditions as reflected in the graphical representations.

6. CONCLUSION

To assess the impact of bagasse ash and plastic waste strips on the geotechnical properties of soil, a comprehensive experimental study was conducted. Various tests, including compaction tests, CBR tests (both unsoaked and soaked conditions), and UCS, were carried out. The experimental parameters were varied by incorporating different proportions of bagasse ash (5%, 10%, 15%, and 20% by weight of soil). Additionally, plastic waste strips (PWS) were introduced in varying proportions (0.3%, 0.6%, 0.9%, and 1.2%). This multifaceted experimental approach aimed to analyze the combined influence of bagasse ash and plastic waste strips on the geotechnical characteristics of the soil. The CBR values exhibited an increase in both soaked and unsoaked conditions, particularly noteworthy in soil compositions with 15% bagasse ash and an additional 0.9% plastic bottle strips. The optimal outcome was observed with a remarkable 85% increase in CBR for unsoaked conditions and a 72% increase for soaked conditions. Concurrently, the UCS values demonstrated an improvement, with a significant 70% enhancement achieved at the optimal content. A correlation analysis was undertaken to establish the relationship between CBR and UCS, revealing a positive correlation. This implies that in the context of this experimental study, as CBR increases, so does UCS. The distinctive roles of bagasse ash and plastic waste were identified, with bagasse ash acting as a binding material and plastic waste functioning as a reinforcing agent in conjunction with the soil. The amalgamation of bagasse ash and plastic waste fibres with clay soil resulted in superior strength and durability characteristics. Importantly, this approach offers a cost-effective alternative by utilizing recycled waste materials, thereby reducing reliance on more expensive additives. This study not only highlights the efficacy of the proposed approach but also underscores its economic and environmental benefits. Furthermore, there is potential for additional analyses to explore other soil parameters, and the use of different waste materials in soil improvement warrants further investigation to assess long-term effects.

■ REFERENCES ■

1. K. Meshram, N. Yana, P.K. Jain, "Estimation of swelling characteristics of expansive soils with influence of clay mineralogy," *Acta Agriculturae Scandinavica, Section B — Soil & Plant Science,* vol. 71, no. 3, pp. 202–207, 2021. DOI: 10.1080/09064710.2021.1872696.

2. K. Meshram, P.K. Jain, S.K. Mittal, P.K. Agarwal, "CBR Improvement of Expansive Black Cotton Soil Using Coir Geotextile," *NICMAR-Journal of Construction Management,* vol. 29, pp. 45–50, 2014.

3. A. Bahurudeen, M. Santhanam, "Influence of different processing methods on the pozzolanic performance of sugarcane bagasse ash," *Cement & Composites,* vol. 56, pp. 32–45, 2015. https://dx.doi.org/10.1016/j.cemconcomp.2014.11.002

4. E. Mina, W. Fathonah, R. I. Kusuma, I. A. Nurjanah, "The utilization of lime and plastic sack fiber for the stabilization of clay and their effect on CBR value," *Teknika: Jurnal Sains Dan Teknologi*, vol. 17, no. 2, p. 289, 2021. DOI: 10.36055/tjst.v17i2.13025. https://doi.org/10.36055/tjst.v17i2.13025

5. S. Banchchhas, D.K. Soni, "Stabilization of clayey soil using sugarcane bagasse ash and rice husk ash," *IJSTM,* ISSN(P)2394-1529, vol. 6, no. 01, 2017.

6. K. Meshram, H. M. Rangwala, H.S. Goliya, P. Sawanliya, "On-field Assessment of Sub-Grade Uniformity using DCP," *Geotechnical Testing Journal, ASTM International,* vol. 39, no. 3, pp. 447–451, 2021.

7. S. H. Fadhil, M. S. Al-Soud, R. M. Kudadad, "Enhancing the strength of clay-sand mixture by discrete waste plastic strips," *Journal of Applied Science and Engineering (Taiwan)*, vol. 24, no. 3, pp. 381–391, 2021. https://doi.org/10.6180/jase.202106_24(3).0013

8. A. Iravanian, I. ud din Ahmed, "Geo-environmental solution of plastic solid waste management using stabilization process," *Environmental Earth Sciences*, vol. 80, no. 3, p. 118, 2021.

9. P. R. Kalyana Chakravarthy, S. Banupriya, T. Ilango, "Soil stabilization using raw plastic bottle," *AIP Conference Proceedings*, vol. 2283, no. 1, 2020. https://doi.org/10.1063/5.0025143

10. J. B. Niyomukiza, A. Bitekateko, J. Nsemerirwe, B. Kawiso, M. Kiwanuka, "Investigating the effect of PET plastic bottle strips on the strength and compressibility properties of clayey soil," *IOP Conference Series: Earth and Environmental Science*, vol. 894, no. 1, 2021. https://doi.org/10.1088/1755-1315/894/1/012021

11. S. Peddaiah, A. Burman, S. Sreedeep, "Experimental Study on Effect of Waste Plastic Bottle Strips in Soil Improvement," *Geotechnical and Geological Engineering*, vol. 36, no. 5, pp. 2907–2920, 2018. https://doi.org/10.1007/s10706-018-0512-0

12. R. Saravanan, P. Murthi, K. Poongodi, A. Raju, "A study on the effect of waste plastic strips in the stabilization of clay soil," *IOP Conference Series: Materials Science and Engineering*, vol. 981, no. 3, 2020. https://doi.org/10.1088/1757-899X/981/3/032062

13. K. Meshram, "Swelling behaviour of expansive soils reinforced with granular pile," Ph.D. dissertation, *Maulana Azad National Institute of Technology Bhopal (M.P.), India*, 2016.

14. S. Amena, W. F. Kabeta, "Mechanical Behavior of Plastic Strips-Reinforced Expansive Soils Stabilized with Waste Marble Dust," *Advances in Civil Engineering*, 2022. https://doi.org/10.1155/2022/9807449

15. M. Kumar, M. Azhar, S. Mondal, R. P. Singh, "Stabilization of expansive soil subgrade by waste plastic," *Arabian Journal of Geosciences*, vol. 15, no. 10, p. 936, 2022. Available: https://doi.org/10.1007/s12517-022-10112-7

16. M. K. Abu Talib, N. Yasufuku, "Highly organic soil stabilization by using sugarcane bagasse ash (SCBA)," in *MATEC Web of Conferences*, vol. 103, pp. 07013, 2017. https://doi.org/10.1051/matecconf/201710307013

Note: All the figures and tables in this chapter were made by the author.

Remote Sensing for Sustainable Development for Indian Cities by Land Use Pattern

25

Chatrabhuj*
Research Scholar,
Department of Civil Engineering,
Guru Ghasidas Vishwavidyalaya, Bilaspur,
Chhattisgarh, India

Kundan Meshram
Assistant Professor,
Department of Civil Engineering,
Guru Ghasidas Vishwavidyalaya, Bilaspur,
Chhattisgarh, India

Abstract

The United Nations has given 17 Sustainable Development Goals (SDGs) focusing on economic, social and environmental objectives. Goal 11- Sustainable Cities and Communities is important to utilize land resources properly for the development of cities. This is done to satisfy the requirements of the present and upcoming generations. The purpose of this study is to analyse the change in land use patterns of Bhopal in urban areas, water bodies, agricultural land, open areas and forest land, with time duration 2000, 2010 and 2020. Satellite images were obtained from USGS Earth Explorer change detection and were analysed. To determine change Unsupervised classification was done for Bhopal City. By using Cellular Automata model and past land use pattern a future prediction for year 2030 and 2040 is also done. Based on changes in land use patterns in percentage, one can predict whether a city is trending toward sustainability by analysing parameters such as increased green spaces, mixed-use development, and the preservation of natural areas. Results show that Forest cover decreases for the examined cities. By examining the rate of urbanization and the decrease in water bodies and forest cover there is a need for important steps to conserve resources and look toward sustainability.

Keywords

Sustainable development, Land use pattern, Satellite images, Unsupervised classification

1. INTRODUCTION

Being part of a larger community of life, people are responsible for safeguarding natural areas and finding more efficient and environmentally friendly methods to use their abundant natural resources [1]. The United Nations has given 17 Sustainable Development Goals (SDGs) are a worldwide rallying cry for better living standards, cleaner

*Corresponding author: chatrabhuj513@gmail.com

DOI: 10.1201/9781003606260-25

air, and more equitable communities for everyone. For these purposes, all UN member states established a set of 17 objectives with 169 corresponding targets in 2015 [2]. Remote sensing provides essential technological assistance for executing sustainable development initiatives [3]. Evaluation of the environment, land use, residential area, and the social economy are all major areas where remote sensing devices play a role [4]. Moreover, utilizing data from remote sensing, land use, population censuses, and other sources, the SDG11.3.1 index has been created to evaluate the correlation between land utilization and urbanization growth [5]. In terms of material wealth, land is a valuable resource. As the economy and society progress, the population grows, and the rate of human activities rises, so too does the influence of these factors on land usage [6]. To assess whether a city's progress is towards sustainability involves many factors which include economics, environmental parameters, social and development. So, to know, to which extent sustainability is achieved some indicators are determined which include Energy consumption for cities that are moving towards sustainable development are adopting clean energy resources or renewable energy [7]. Sustainable cities should have a traffic system that reduces pollution and congestion [8]. It encourages to use of eco-friendly transport vehicles and controls uncontrolled expansion and settlement. These cities have very effective waste management system, which reduces the amount of waste generated, have to door waste collection system, and have a system of recycling and composition. Cities provide affordable housing for all such measures are taken to reduce economic inequality and support local businesses [9]. All the local community is involved in the decision-making process. Cities prioritize green spaces in the form of parks, gardens, and open forests. If a city is moving towards sustainable development, it must protect natural areas, such as wetlands, forests, and wildlife habitats. So, based on changes in land use patterns, it can be estimated whether a city is trending toward sustainability, by analysing SDG indicators [10] like increased green spaces, mixed-use development, and the preservation of natural areas. Local area maps are very much important for establishing a relationship between changes in land use and land cover (LULC). It is important to determine the change in LULC because of multiple applications with this one can determine the change in land pattern, analyse the amount of built-up area, investigate areas prone to floods, trends of agriculture and deforestation, estimate water bodies area, investigate urbanization rate and know coastal area erosion. To determine these problems one solution Satellite images are used. To extract features from Images like Urban areas, Forests, Agricultural land, Water bodies, Barren land, River Plains, Vegetation, Roads and Mountains becomes

a difficult task. To overcome these problems Artificial Intelligence (AI) is used in Image classification, Analysis and processing. Machine Learning (ML) is a subset of AI, that is the ability to gain and apply knowledge and skills in various fields

2. LITERATURE REVIEW

Measuring land quality is an important parameter as per "proportion of land degraded over total land area"-SDG indicator 15.3.1. A study is done for land with high-resolution imagination over the area of Tanzania from 2000-2019 with the help of the Landsat series satellite. Analysis shows that land degradation is on high scale that is 27%. To preserve land quality in future planning is required [11]. Creation of conservation land, hotspots, and implication of land use planning and management must be done by governing bodies and local citizens. For modelling of global environmental conditions land cover change plays an important role. Researchers analyse future land use simulations to predict land use change by considering human activity on the environment and its impacts. Outcomes were with finer resolution land use classification efficiency can be increased [12]. Land use simulation predicts small urban areas will merge into large urban area. Global projections of future urban land expansion are very important for safeguarding of future. However, urban land is smaller in land cover but they consume a lot. To make the situation worse continuous degradation of land and human greed lead to the expansion of urban land which later on harms the environment. Encroachment of land is a key issue. Researchers conclude that shortly for 2050 in China there will be an expansion of urban area of 50-63% and global crop production will decline by 1-4%, this is an alarming situation [13]. As far as the condition of the Island Hokkaido, Japan is considered due to hard agricultural practices arable land use changes day by day. It becomes important for authorities to monitor land use patterns. GIS and Remote sensing technology were used to study in the last two decades. Application of model Markov-FLUS model to analyse land use pattern. By simulation analysis, it was concluded that cultivated land will drop by 40% [14]. For investigation of land use and land cover change for the region of Misau in Nigeria, for different decade 2000. 2010 and 2020. Remotely sensed multi-temporal satellite photos (Landsat) were used. Researchers compared classification between supervised and unsupervised classification, and upon investigation, it was concluded that supervised classification yielded better results than Unsupervised method of classification [15]. Integration of Remote sensing and GIS systems was done to analyse land use patterns in Uttarakhand from 1990-2010.

Supervised classification and EDRAS software were used in the analysis. Results concluded that built up increased by 8% while agricultural area, water bodies and vegetation decreased by 9.4%, 2.7% and .6% respectively [16]. In the field of soil and water conservation for sustainable development remote sensing and GIS techniques are applied. The investigation was done before and after effect. Water shed area management plays an important role in conservation. Analysis was done for the years 2007, 2014 and 2017. The total land area is divided into four classes agricultural, built-up, waste land and water bodies. Upon analysis, it was concluded that the increase in agricultural land is 18.7%, built up are 0.6% wasteland 40.3% and waterbodies 17.3% [17].

3. METHODOLOGY

In this research, a comprehensive methodology was employed to analyze changes in land use and land cover (LULC) over three distinct time periods (2000, 2010, and 2020) using satellite imagery sourced from the United States Geological Survey (USGS) Earth Explorer.

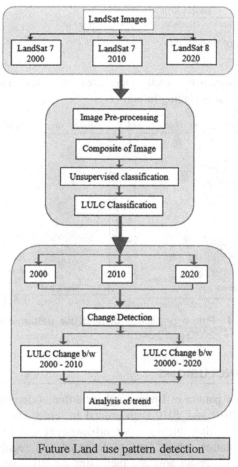

Fig. 25.1   Methodology

The LandSat series satellite system, incorporating LandSat 7 Enhanced Thermal Mapping (ETM+) and LandSat 8 Operational Land Imager (OLI), provided images with a resolution of 30m. The collected satellite images underwent thorough preprocessing on the Quantum GIS (QGIS) software. Radiometric and atmospheric corrections were applied, and scan line errors from the LandSat 7 series for the year 2010 were rectified. Subsequently, various bands were stacked to create composite images. The relevant sections, specifically maps corresponding to the administrative area of interest, were then extracted. The classification process utilized unsupervised classification methods. Following classification, land use patterns were identified and assessed for accuracy through ground truthing. Achieving an accuracy threshold of over 70%, the determined land use patterns were employed for change detection analysis. Differentiating land use types such as water bodies, forests, urban areas, cultivated land, and open areas, each classification received a distinct color. This allowed for a clear visualization and interpretation of the classified land. The investigation extended across three decades to discern significant changes in development. The percentage of change detection was calculated for the intervals 2000-2010 and 2010-2020. Subsequently, a Cellular Automaton (CA) model was employed, and the MOLUSCE tool was utilized to predict future land use patterns based on historical land cover data. This comprehensive approach facilitated a robust analysis of temporal changes in land use, contributing to a deeper understanding of the evolving landscape over the specified time periods.

4. RESULTS

From the analysis of satellite images of different series, change in trend of different land use patterns like water bodies, urban land, forests, cultivated land and open land can be seen. The below figure shows the trend of change in land use pattern for different time series. Upon classifying the land use pattern, next is analysis to change of trend of different land types. The below graph shows the change of land pattern with time series. The above bar chart shows the change in different land use pattern over different decades. First is for the year 2000 and second is for 2010 and the last shows 2020. This figure represents water bodies increase, forest and urban land decreases with cultivated and open land areas increasing with time. Open areas, characterized by the absence of substantial human development, are typically depicted as purple colour on the map as open, undeveloped spaces. Vegetation, encompassing natural or cultivated greenery, is presented by lush green hues. Urban areas, featuring buildings, infrastructure, and dense human

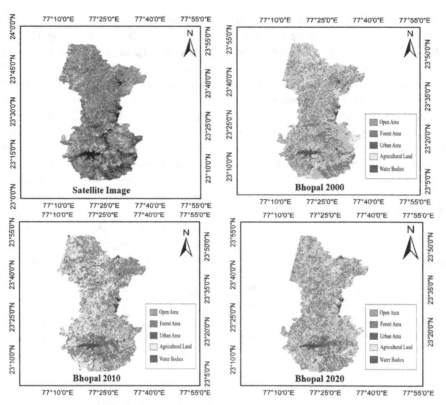

Fig. 25.2 Land use classification of bhopal city

habitation, are represented with red color. Agricultural land, critical for crop production, is usually indicated in yellow and water bodies, which include lakes, rivers, ponds, and other aquatic features, are often depicted in shades of blue.

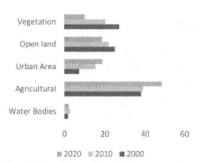

Fig. 25.3 Change in land use pattern

The above figure shows the change of percentage different land use patterns like Water bodies, Urban land, Forest, Cultivated land and Open areas. Upon analysis, it is clear that water bodies are increasing with urban land. Open land nearabout remains constant and forest cover and cultivated area decreases with time.

Prediction of Future Land use Pattern

The Fig. 25.4 depicts the future prediction of land use for year 2030 and 2040, in which it can be noted that urban area is increasing rapidly. Open area and Forest land will decrease in upcoming future.

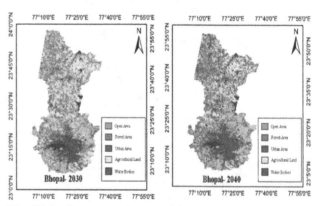

Fig. 25.4 Future prediction of land use pattern for year 2030 and 2040

5. CONCLUSIONS

Land use pattern of Bhopal city for different decades like 2000, 2010 and 2020 is examined in this study. It was concluded that due to rapid urbanization and increase in population which lead to informal and regularized settlement, urban area are increasing rapidly with time. Area under forest and open land decreases with time due to need for land to satisfy present generation which encroach natural land. To meed food demand agriculture land increases with time. However area under water bodies nearly remains constant. CA model was used to predicted future land use which shows the conversion of natural land into urban land will be predominant in future as well as forest cover will decrease in upcoming time.

■ REFERENCES ■

1. A. López-Vargas, A. Ledezma, J. Bott and A. Sanchis, "IoT for Global Development to Achieve the United Nations Sustainable Development Goals: The New Scenario After the COVID-19 Pandemic," in *IEEE Access*, vol. 9, pp. 124711–124726, 2021, doi: 10.1109/ACCESS.2021.3109338.

2. D. Roldán-álvarez, F. Martínez-Martínez, E. Martín and P. A. Haya, "Understanding Discussions of Citizen Science Around Sustainable Development Goals in Twitter," in *IEEE Access*, vol. 9, pp. 144106–144120, 2021, doi: 10.1109/ACCESS.2021.3122086.

3. Y. Wang et al., "A Novel Method Based on Kernel Density for Estimating Crown Base Height Using UAV-Borne LiDAR Data," in *IEEE Geoscience and Remote Sensing Letters*, vol. 19, pp. 1–5, 2022, Art no. 7004105, doi: 10.1109/LGRS.2022.3171316.

4. R. Guzinski, H. Nieto, J. M. Sánchez, R. López-Urrea, D. M. Boujnah and G. Boulet, "Utility of Copernicus-Based Inputs for Actual Evapotranspiration Modeling in Support of Sustainable Water Use in Agriculture," in *IEEE Journal of Selected Topics in Applied Earth Observations and Remote Sensing*, vol. 14, pp. 11466–11484, 2021, doi: 10.1109/JSTARS.2021.3122573.

5. X. Huang, Q. Liang, Z. Feng and S. Chai, "A TOD Planning Model Integrating Transport and Land Use in Urban Rail Transit Station Areas," in *IEEE Access*, vol. 9, pp. 1103–1115, 2021, doi: 10.1109/ACCESS.2020.3047207.

6. S. H. Alyami, A. A. Almutlaqa, A. M. Alqahtany, and N. Ashraf, "Likelihood of Reaching Zero Energy Building Design in Hot Dry Climate: Saudi Arabia," *IEEE Access*, vol. 9, pp. 167054–167066, 2021, doi: 10.1109/ACCESS.2021.3134365.

7. K. Parvin, M. S. H. Lipu, M. A. Hannan, M. A. Abdullah, K. P. Jern, R. A. Begum, M. Mansur, K. M. Muttaqi, T. M. I. Mahlia, and Z. Y. Dong, "Intelligent Controllers and Optimization Algorithms for Building Energy Management towards Achieving Sustainable Development: Challenges and Prospects," *IEEE Access*, vol. 9, pp. 41577–41602, 2021, doi: 10.1109/ACCESS.2021.3065087.

8. A. Alsharkawi, M. Al-Fetyani, M. Dawas, H. Saadeh and M. Alyaman, "Improved Poverty Tracking and Targeting in Jordan Using Feature Selection and Machine Learning," in *IEEE Access*, vol. 10, pp. 86483–86497, 2022, doi: 10.1109/ACCESS.2022.3198951.

9. Y. Okada, Y. Kishita, Y. Nomaguchi, T. Yano, and K. Ohtomi, "Backcasting-Based Method for Designing Roadmaps to Achieve a Sustainable Future," *IEEE Transactions on Engineering Management*, vol. 69, no. 1, pp. 168–178, 2022, doi: 10.1109/TEM.2020.3008444.

10. A. Akhtar and S. H. R. Zaini, "Modelling the sustainable development goals for India - an interpretive structural modelling approach," *World Review of Science, Technology and Sustainable Development*, vol. 15, no. 1, pp. 46, 2019, doi: 10.1504/wrstsd.2019.10019998.

11. X. Li et al., "A New Global Land-Use and Land-Cover Change Product at a 1-km Resolution for 2010 to 2100 Based on Human–Environment Interactions," *Annals of the American Association of Geographers*, vol. 107, no. 5, pp. 1040–1059, 2017, doi: 10.1080/24694452.2017.1303357.

12. G. Chen et al., "Global projections of future urban land expansion under shared socioeconomic pathways," *Nature Communications*, vol. 11, no. 1, 2020, doi: 10.1038/s41467-020-14386-x.

13. Z. Chen et al., "Integrating Remote Sensing and a Markov-FLUS Model to Simulate Future Land Use Changes in Hokkaido, Japan," *Remote Sens.*, vol. 13, no. 13, 2021, doi: 10.3390/rs13132621.

14. Y. Yusuf et al., "An Assessment of Land Use Land Cover Change Detection in Misau Local Government Area, Bauchi State, Nigeria," in *5th International New York Academic Research Congress*, April 23–24, 2022, pp. 418–427.

15. J. S. Rawat, V. Biswas, and M. Kumar, "Changes in land use/cover using geospatial techniques: A case study of Ramnagar town area, district Nainital, Uttarakhand, India," *The Egyptian Journal of Remote Sensing and Space Sciences*, vol. 16, pp. 111–117, 2013, doi: 10.1016/j.ejrs.2013.01.006.

16. C. B. Pande, K. N. Moharir, and S. F. R. Khadri, "Assessment of land-use and land-cover changes in Pangari watershed area (MS), India, based on the remote sensing and GIS techniques," *Applied Water Science*, vol. 11, no. 6, 2021, doi: 10.1007/s13201-021-01425-1.

17. M. Cao et al., "Multi-Scenario Simulation of Land Use for Sustainable Development Goals," *IEEE Journal of Selected Topics in Applied Earth Observations and Remote Sensing*, vol. 15, pp. 2119–2127, 2022, doi: 10.1109/JSTARS.2022.3152904.

Note: All the figures in this chapter were made by the author.

Challenges and Opportunities for Innovation in India – Dr. Shweta Mishra et al. (eds)
© 2024 Taylor & Francis Group, London, ISBN 978-1-032-99842-8

Utilization of Waste Plastics for Manufacturing of Plastic Bricks

26

Saurabh Giri*

Lecturer,
Civil Engineering Department,
Ambalika Institute of Management and Technology,
Lucknow, Uttar Pradesh, India

Abstract

Plastic is a non bio-degradable substance which takes thousands of years to decompose that creates land as well as water pollution also to the environment. The quantity of plastic waste is expanding very rapidly. It is estimated that the rate of usage is double for every 10 years. The plastic usage is large in consumption and one of the largest plastic wastes is polyethylene (PE). The utilization of earth based clay material resulted in resource depletion and environmental degradation. One such effort is the efficient use of waste plastic and laterite quarry waste with a small quantity of bitumen, to develop an alternative building material such as bricks with negligible water absorption and satisfactory strength in comparison with laterite stone to satisfy the increasing demand of conventional building materials. Utilizing waste plastic as construction materials especially in the manufacturing of bricks is one of the promising steps towards a sustainable resources and waste management. Plastic waste can substitute either partially or completely one or more of the materials in the brick production. Further research based on recent research and a better understanding in utilization plastic waste in brick is needed to produce a high durability and quality of bricks as well as to achieve the optimum balance in all aspects especially in terms of cost and functionally.

Keywords

Plastic waste, Bricks, Compressive strength, Water absorption

1. INTRODUCTION

Low density polyethylene (LDPE) is the most common packaging material used worldwide and is used for packaging a variety of products. It is also used for making containers and bottles. However they pose great threat to the environment as their effective disposal is a herculean task. They are not easily degradable; it usually takes more than ten decades to decompose. As a result, they clog water ways, channels and drains. As they require many years to decompose, they fill up the landfills faster. Polythene bags and packaging sheets harm aquatic life and wildlife as they pose the threat of chocking if ingested. Low density polythene can be reused for making bricks. Bricks are the

*Corresponding author: saurabhgiri682@gmail.com

DOI: 10.1201/9781003606260-26

basic components of a building and are required in bulk. By using plastic in making the brick, the overall cost of the brick will get reduced as, waste polyethylene is being reused. Brick earth is costly, and digging of brick earth poses some damage to the environment. Hence using plastic to make bricks is not only cost effective and eco-friendly but also the plastic bricks have a smooth finish, devoid of cracks and have low water absorption value, and will not have problems like efflorescence in future.

1.1 Present Scenario of Waste Generation in India

Growth of population has increased our urbanization as a result rising standard of living due to technological innovations have contributed to an increase both in the quantity and variety of solid wastes generated by industrial, agricultural activities, mining and domestic. Globally the estimated quantity of wastes generation was 12 billion tones in the year 2002 of which 11 billion tones were industrial wastes and 1.6 billion tones were municipal solid wastes (MSW). About 19 billion tons of solid wastes are expected to be generated annually by the year 2020. Annually, Asia alone generates 4.4 billion tons of solid wastes and MSW comprise 795 million tons of which about 48 (6%) MT are generated in India. MSW generation in India, is expected to reach 300 Million tones and land requirement for disposal of this waste would be 169.6 km2 as against which only 20.2 km2 were occupied in 1997 for management of 48 Million tones. As it is studied that apart from municipal wastes, the organic wastes from agricultural sources alone contribute more than 350 million tons per year. However, it is reported that about 600 million tons of wastes have been generated in India from agricultural sources alone. The Quantity of wastes generated from agricultural sources are sugarcane baggage, paddy and wheat straw and husk, wastes of vegetables, food products, tea, oil production, wooden mill waste, coconut husk, jute fiber, groundnut shell, cotton stalk etc. In the industrial sector inorganic solid waste could are coal combustion residues, bauxite red mud, tailings from aluminum, iron, copper and zinc primary extraction processes. Generation of all these inorganic industrial wastes in India is estimated to be 290 million Tons per annum. In India, 4.5 million tons of hazardous wastes are being generated annually during different industrial process like electroplating, various metal extraction processes, galvanizing, refinery, petrochemical industries, pharmaceutical and pesticide industries.

2. MATERIALS USED

2.1 Sand

Common river sand having specific gravity of 2.56 and fineness modulus of 2.805 is used.

Table 26.1 Physical characteristics of fine aggregate

Particulars	Test Results
Specific gravity	2.56
Apparent Specific gravity	2.7
Water Absorption	1.98
Bulk Density	1.497Kg/L
Fineness Modulus	2.805

2.2 Low Density Polyethylenes

Easily over time, leading to higher surface areas. The supply of glasses shall be of diagonal gases from virgin LDPE increase with surface area or time, with rates at the end of a 212 day incubation of 5.8 nmol g-1 d-1 of methane, 14.5 nmol g-1 d-1 of ethylene, 3.9 nmol g-1 d1 of ethane and 9.7 nmol g-1 d-1 of propylene. In case of air it was incubated, LDPE releases gases in air by ~2 times and ~76 times higher in comparison to water for methane and ethylene, respectively. Low density polyethylene, obtained from waste plastic bags, packaging materials, plastic bottles having density of 0.91- 0.94 g/cm^3, melting point at about 115 degree centigrade is used.

Table 26.2 Experiments and results

Sl. No.	Experiments	Results
1	Density at 23^{0}C	.958
2	Elasticity Modulus	9
3	Tensile Creep Strength	8
4	Bending Creep Modulus	1
5	Tensile strength at 23^{0}C	2
6	Elongation at break (%)	>600
7	Thermal Conductivity	0
8	Ignition Temperature	3

3. METHODOLOGY

- Collection of Materials.
- Batching.
- Melting.
- Mixing.
- Moulding.
- Curing.

3.1 Collection of Plastic Materials

The plastic material should be collected from the factories waste and hospital waste and When exposed to ambient solar radiation the plastic procedure two greenhouse gases, methane and ethylene. Due to its low-density properties (branching) it breaks down more industries waste and also food packages and plastic bottles this will come under the LDPE plastic type

3.2 Batching of Plastic

Measurement of materials for making brick is called batching. After collection of materials we separate the types of plastic and remove any other waste presented in the collected material and check that any water content in in sample collected ten proceed for burning.

3.3 Burning of Waste Plastic

After completion batching the plastic waste was taken for burning in which the plastic bags are drop one by one into the container and allowed to melt. These would be done in closed vessel because to prevent the toxic gases released into atmosphere. These will be at the temperature of 120-150 degrees centigrade.

3.4 Mixing

Mixing of materials is essential for the production of uniform and strength for brick. The mixing has to be ensuring that the mass becomes homogeneous, uniform in color and consistency. Generally, there are two types of mixing, Hand mixing and mechanical mixing. In this project, we adopted hand mixing. Until the entire plastic content required for making plastic brick of one mix proportion is added into it. Then these plastic liquids thoroughly mixed by using trowel before it hardens. The mixture has very short setting bags are turned to molten state; the river sand is added to it. The sand added is mixed time. Hence mixing process should not consume more time.

3.5 Moulding

After completion of proper mixing we place mix into required mould. In these projects we use the normal brick sizes (19 × 9 × 9 cm). After 2 days remove the brick from the mould and then done curing.

3.6 Curing

The test specimens after moulding were allowed to dry for a period of 24 hours. The specimens were kept in curing tank and allowed to cure for a period of 28 days.

4. TESTING OF SPECIMEN

4.1 Compressive Strength Test

This test is done to know the compressive strength of brick. It is also called the crushing strength of brick. Generally, 3 specimens of bricks are taken to laboratory for the testing and tested one by one. In this test, a brick specimen is put on compressive strength is put on Compressive Strength testing machine and applied pressure at a constant arte till it breaks. The ultimate pressure at which brick is crushed is taken into account. All three brick specimens are tested one by one and average result is taken as bricks compressive/crushing strength. The Compressive Strength of the brick is calculated by the formula = (max load taken before failure/ Area of the Brick surface) N/mm^2.

4.2 Water Absorption Test

In this the bricks first weighted in dry condition and they are immersed in water for 24 hours. After that they are taken out from water and they are wiping out with cloth. Then the difference between the dry and wet bricks percentage are calculated. They weight of the three plastic bricks has been taken and then the average weight of the bricks is calculated.

5. RESULT AND DISCUSSIONS

5.1 Water Absorption

This test is carried out to determine the amount of water absorbed by the brick. As per IS:3495-Part 2- 1992, after immersed in cold water for a period of 24 hours, water absorption shall not be more than 20 % for up to class 12.5 and 15 % of weight for higher classes. Initially 5 bricks were taken and removed all the loose particles. Dry the bricks in a ventilated oven at a temperature of 110 degrees till the brick attain substantially constant weights. Cooled the bricks at room temperature and taken weight of each sample W1; then immersed the bricks in clean water at temperature of 25 to 29 degrees for 24 hr and removed the specimen after 24 hr. wipe our water with damp cloth & weight each sample W2. Finally the percentage of water absorbed for each brick was calculated by the following formula. Water Absorption = [(W2 – W1)/W1)] × 100, W2 = weight of soaked brick W1 = weight of dry brick. The specimen was tested for water absorption and the specimen had very low water absorption of 1.5%.

5.2 Compressive Strength

Bricks should have a specified minimum compressive strength so that they can be used in construction works. The compressive strength determined using compression testing machine for the specimens and the results have been shown in the table below.

Table 26.3 Compressive strength of plastic brick (MPa)

Compressive Strength of Plastic Brick (MPa)			
Sample 1	Sample 2	Sample 3	Avg Strength (MPa)
5.5	4.5	4.5	5

Bricks" International Journal for Research in Applied science & Engineering and Technology (April 2019). The specimen was tested for compressive strength and the specimen had average compressive strength of 5Mpa.

5.3 Weight of Sample

The weight of the 3 dry samples is taken and then the average weight is calculated.

Table 26.4 Weight of plastic brick (gm.)

Weight of plastic brick (gm.)			
Sample 1	Sample 2	Sample 3	Avg weight (gm.)
2250	2195	2155	2200

The specimen had average weight of 2200 gm.

6. CONCLUSION

On the basis of the results obtained, it can be concluded that:

  I. Plastic bricks can a very good alternative of traditional earthen bricks.

 II. Plastic bricks can be used for partition walls and exterior walls; however they must not be used in load bearing walls.

III. Cost of manufacturing per unit plastic brick is significantly lower than traditional earthen bricks, hence they are cheaper alternative.

IV. Plastic bricks are water resistant, hence can be used in underwater structures.

 V. Re using plastic will reduce environmental pollution.

■ REFERENCES ■

1. S S Chauhan, Bhusan Kumar, Prem Shankar Singh, Abuzaid Khan, Hrithik Goyal, Shivank Goyal, "Fabrication and testing of Plastic Sand Bricks" on ICCEMME 2019.
2. Rajarapu Bhushaiah, Shaik Mohammad, D. Srinivasa Rao, "An Overview of Study of Plastic Bricks Made From Waste Plastic" International Research Journal of Engineering and Technology (IRJET) (April 2019).
3. Velumurugan, R. Gokul Raj, A.Harinisree, "An Overview of Rebuilding of Plastic Waste to Pavement Arvind Singhal, Dr. Om Prakash Netula, "Utilization of plastic waste in manufacturing of plastic sand bricks" on 17th June 2018 at 3rd International conference on New Frontiers of Engineering, Science, Management and Humanities. ISBN: 978-93-87433-29-8.
4. Siti Nabilah Amir & Nur Zulaikha Yusuf, "Plastic in Brick Application" on 4th September 2018 by LUPINE PUBLISHERS. ISSN: 2637–4668.DOI: 10.32474/TCEIA.2018.03.000152.
5. Aiswaria K, Khansa Abdulla, E B Akhil, Haritha Lakshmi V G, Jerin Jimmy "Manufacturing and Experimental Investigation of Bricks with Plastic And M-Sand" International Journal of Innovative Research in Science, Engineering and Technology Vol. 7, Issue 6, June 2018.
6. Ronak Shah, Himanshu Garg, Parth Gandhi, Rashmi Patil, Anand Daftardar. "Study of plastic dust brick made from waste plastic." on International journal of mechanical and production engineering. ISSN: 2320–2092, volume-5, issue- 10, OCT-2017.
7. A.S. Manjrekar, Ravi, D. Gulpatil, Vivek P. Patil, Ranjit S. Nikam, Chetali M. Jeur (2017). "Utilization of Plastic Waste in Foundry Sand Bricks", International Journal for Research in Applied Science & Engineering Technology (IJRASET).
8. Loukham Gerion Singh, Pongsumbam Boss Singh, Suresh Thokchom (2017). "Manufacturing Bricks from Sand and Waste Plastics", National Conference on Innovations in Science and Technology (NCIST-17).
9. Dinesh & Dinesh A, Kirubakaran.K, UTILISATION OF WASTE PLASTIC IN MANUFACTURING OF BRICKS
10. AND PAVER BLOCKS beermarional Journal of Applied Engineering Research, ISSN 0973–4562, Volume 1, 2016.
11. Geps Molan C, Jaku Mathew, JithinX Ninan Kurian, John Тhomия Moolayil, FABRICATION OF PLASTIC BRICK OMANUFACTURING MACHINE AND BRICK
12. LANALYSIS" International Journal of Innovative Research in Science and Technology. ISSN (online) 2349–6010, Volume 2, Issue 11th April 2016
13. Sina Safinia, Amani Alkalbani "Use of Recycled Plastic Water Bottles in Concrete Blocka Middle East College, KOM, Rusayl, Muscat PC 124, Oman 2016.
14. Diarya Jivan Pati, Riken Homma, Kazuhisaikt, "PLASTIC BOTTLES MASONRY AS ALTERNATE SOLUTION TO HOUSING PROBLEMS IN URBAN AREA OF
15. INDIA" International Journal of Architecture Planning and Building Engineering, ISSN 2455–5045, Volurne 2, Issued 2nd April 2015.
16. Maneeth. P.D, Pramod K, Kishore Kumar, Shanmukha Shetty. UTILIZATION OF WASTE PLASTIC IN MANUFACTURING OF PLASTIC-SOIL BRICKS"
17. International Journal of Engineering Research and Technology (UERT), Volume 3, ISSN 2278–0181, Issued 8th August 2014.
18. Amit Gawande, G. V.C Range, Saurabh Taye, G. Barnacle "an overview on waste plastic utilization in asphalting of roads", Journal of Engineering Research and Studies (JERS), Vol III, Issue II, April June 2012. pp 01–05
19. Bharat Raj, Vastas A. Rashmitha Kotian, N.G. Ashwath "Sthaly on Laterite-Cement tricks" Project report, K.V.G College of Engineering, Sullia DK 2011–2012
20. Hemath PM, Shetty 8 (2014) Utilimtion of waste plastic in mactacturing of plastic soil bricks International Journal of Technology Enlucanent and Emerging Engineering Rowarch 2(4) 2347–4289
21. IK Gopy Mulan Mai Kurian, John Thomas Moolayit, FABRICATION OF PLASTIC BRICK MANUFACTURING MACIUNE AND BRICK
22. ANALYSIS a lournal of Innovation Rover Science and Technology 15% (online) 2349, Volume 2. Ir 11th April 2014

Challenges and Opportunities for Innovation in India – Dr. Shweta Mishra et al. (eds)
© 2024 Taylor & Francis Group, London, ISBN 978-1-032-99842-8

Comparative Study between Precast and Cast In-Situ Structure Under Combination of Dynamic Loads and Connections between Precast Elements

27

Vaibhav Pal*

Lecturer,
Ambalika Institute of Management & Technology,
Lucknow, Uttar Pradesh, India

Abstract

Precast building system offers a wide range of benefits and advantages to the designer to meet all the client`s requirements. The rapid growth in usage of precast systems demands the improvement of its structural behavior when it is subjected to dynamic loads. This Project deals with the analysis and design of Precast Substation building with Crane (5tons capacity) subjected to Dynamic loads due to Earthquake. In order to justify its structural behavior, the cast in-situ structure is also analyzed and compared with precast structure. Hence in this project, the substation building of 78m (length) × 22m (breadth) × 9.6m (height) is designed by considering various loads such as Dead load, Live load, Soil load, Wind load, Seismic load and Crane load as per IS 875: 1987 (Part – I, II, III & V), IS 1893: 2002, IS 456: 2000 and the other guidelines for the crane loads. Seismic loads are calculated using seismic coefficient method and base shear values were obtained. Further the substation building is modeled and analyzed using STAAD. ProV8i software. Both Static and Dynamic analysis (Response Spectrum Analysis) i performed in it. Then from the obtained STAAD. ProV8i results, the various structural elements were designed and quantity estimated. Finally, by using above results, the behavior and quantity comparison between precast and cast in-situ structures were done and conclusion is given.

Keywords

Precast structures, Substation building with crane loads, Seismic resistant structure, Dynamic analysis in STAAD.Pro V8i, Comparative study between precast and cast in- situ structures, Connection for precast

1. INTRODUCTION

Precast concrete structures offer a wide range of benefits and advantages to the designer to meet all of the client`s requirements. Its most dramatic benefit will be speed with which it can be designed, cast, delivered and erected. This can ensure that projects stay on schedule and meet tight deadlines. Precast concrete components can be erected hortly after foundations are ready and can be installed quickly, often cutting weeks or months from the schedule. Seismic resistant design for substation building should provide a level of safety for the workers in and around the

---

*Corresponding author: rajpalvaluer@gmail.com

DOI: 10.1201/9781003606260-27

substation in the event of Earthquake. The fatalities and serious injuries by collapse of substation building onto the persons are not only due to earthquake but also in addition to the dynamic loads from crane that operates during such seismic conditions. This leads to our objective to reduce the probability that, the building itself becomes a hazard in an earthquake. It is more relevant for Substation buildings with cranes which need to be under operation without a break and cranes handling materials of weight five tons or more. The function of the crane girders is to support the rails on which the traveling cranes move. It is a component which acts as laterally unsupported beam. An Electronic Overhead Travelling crane which is normally called as EOT Cranes are mainly used for material movements in substation buildings. Their design features vary widely according to their major operational specifications such as type of motion of the crane structure, weight and type of the load, location of the crane, geometric features, operating regimes and environmental conditions.

2. OBJECTIVE

The main objective of this project is design of Precast Substation building with crane that is subjected to earthquake loads which must resist dynamic loads due to earthquake without complete failure or collapse of the building or crane or both, which may interrupt power supply and comparative study of designed precast structure with conventional cast insitu structures in terms of functionality and structural behavior during earthquake. Finally, connections needed for precast elements were discussed.

3. GEOMETRY AND NATURE OF THE SUBSTATION BUILDING

Location of the substation = Lucknow Structure details = Ten Storey with basement floor

Length of the building = 77.818m Width of the building = 21.48m

Height of the building = +27m from G.L Bottom of the Raft = - 3.4m from G.L Basement floor level = - 2.9m from G.L Seismic Zone = Zone – III

Wind Zone = Zone – V Crane capacity = 5 tons Soil conditions,

Bearing Capacity = 200kN/m2 Density of Soil = 18kN/m3 Angle of Friction = 30°

4. ANALYSIS OF THE STRUCTURE

For the better behaviour study, both the static and dynamic analysis is performed in STAAD. Pro. AND ETABS Software. For simple regular structures, analysis by

equivalent linear static methods is often sufficient. This is permitted in most codes of practice for regular, low- to medium-rise buildings. In this analysis only the first mode in each direction is considered. Linear dynamic analysis which is the Response Spectrum Analysis, measures the contribution from each natural mode of vibration to indicate the likely maximum seismic response of a structure. It gives the peak or steady-state response (displacement, velocity or acceleration) of a series of oscillators of varying natural frequency.

Fig. 27.1 Pre cast building actual view at site

5. DESIGN OF THE STRUCTURAL

5.1 Elements

Using the results from above mentioned analysis, the design of every structural elements at the superstructure of the substation building were done based on the IS limit state design codes and provisions. This design results were tabulated and estimated for amount of material (concrete and steel) quantity required for precast and cast in-situ structure. These results were discussed and compared below.

Fig. 27.2 Connection of different structural component

6. COMPARATIVE STUDY BETWEEN PRECAST AND CAST IN-SITU STRUCTURE

A. Structural Model Comparison:

From the STAAD.Pro model (Rendered view) Fig. 27.1, it is understood that the usage of Precast Double Tee slab at roof eliminates huge number of secondary beams at roof level for precast structure, thereby saving more material and cost of the project. In cast in-situ structure the secondary beams exists at roof level to transfer the load from cast insitu slab.

B. Overall Weight Comparison:

The below chart implies the overall self-weight comparison between precast and cast in-situ structure. (Including substructure weight). This weight is derived from STAAD.pro analysis results. Thus this chart indicates that our single storey Precast structure having the self-weight of 6.7 % more when compared to cast in-situ structure.

C. Base Shear Comparison:

Precast structure base shear capacity is 7% more when compared to cast in-situ structure, so precast structure withstands more Base shear than Cast in-situ structure.

D. Time Period and Frequency Comparison from Response Spectrum Analysis:

After performing dynamic analysis in STAAD.Pro software for 90% mass participation of the structure, it gives the result for time period and frequency variation for different mode of applied load as shown in below table.

Table 27.1 Difference between time period and frequency variation table of pre cast and Cast in situ Building

	Time Period	Frequency
	Seconds	Hertz
Precast Structure	49.89	52.31
Cast-Insitu Structure	36.85	50.54

From the above table it can be concluded that, the Precast Structure takes more time period for its 90% mass participation, so it is More Efficient (withstands longer duration under seismic forces) when compared to cast in-situ Structure.

E. Mode Shape Comparison:

As per IS 1893:2002, the number of modes to be considered for analysis of the structure should be such that the total sum of modal masses of all modes is atleast 90% of the total seismic mass. Hence for our both precast structure (PCS) and cast in-situ

structure (CIS), it takes around 500 modes to attain the 90% mass participation. This variation of mode formass participation of both the structure at its x-direction is shown below.

F. Structural Element Behaviour Comparison:

Precast beams were rigidly connected to the column corbel by bolting or welding and it acts individually as a single member. These precast beams behave like simply supported since it is discontinuous at their supports. Therefore there will be maximum bending moment at midspan and zero bending moment at the support as shown in fig below. The maximum tension reinforcement is required at the midspan bottom portion but at the supports the minimum reinforcement is enough. At the cast in-situ structure beams run continuously thereby acting as a continuous beam. Hence there will be varying maximum bending moments both at midspan and the supports as shown in fig below. The tension reinforcement is required at both midspan as well as support.

7. CONNECTION FOR PRECAST STRUCTURE

A. Connection Between Precast Column and Cast In-Situ Column:

This connection is obtained through steel sockets inserted in the column base and bolted to the steel plate that is welded over the top of the in-situ column. The sockets are anchored to the column by means of bars welded to them and spliced to the current longitudinal reinforcement by lapping. Other transverse links can be welded to the sockets to avoid their lateral detaching. After bolting the gap is filled with Non-Shrink Grout. At installation stage the column can be supported by lock-nuts screwed on the fasteners, by which its verticality can be adjusted and maintained without the need of provisional props. The installation is completed with the tightening of the upper nuts and the casting of the mortar embedding to fill the joint between the precast column base and the insitu column. This bed shall be sufficiently thin to avoid the buckling of the fasteners within the gap when subjected to strong compression otherwise a proper confining reinforcement shall be added. The typical detailing of column to column connection that is required for the substation building is shown below.

B. Connection Between Precast Beam and Precast Column:

There can be two cases for end connection of a beam to a supporting column. In case (a), dowel bar

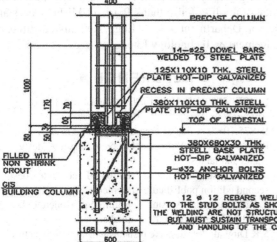

Fig. 27.3 Typical detailing of column to column connection

protrude from the top of the column corbel and enter into the sleeves inserted in the beam. The sleeves are filled with non- shrinkage mortar of adequate strength to ensure the bond anchorage of the dowels. The anchorage can also be ensured providing the dowels with a cap fixed at the top with a screwed nut. In any case the sleeve shall be filled in with mortar to avoid hammering under earthquake conditions. In case (b), the steel angle plates with studs were welded to the reinforcement of column elements before precasting. It is then lapped together with the connecting steel angle plates of beam element and field welded. The beam usually is placed over shims/pads to localise the load. If deformable rubber pads are used, due to their much lower stiffness all the loads applied after their bond anchorage will be conveyed into the steel dowels. And this will cause a local splitting damage of the concrete around the dowels. The use of rigid steel pads will prevent this effect. To avoid local splitting damage, rubber pads can be used with non-adherent dowels. So by considering this procedure the typical connection used for our structure is shown below.

C. Connection Between Precast DT Slab and Precast Beam:

Connection between Double tee slab (DT slab) elements and supporting beam is done by providing proper links that protrude from the upper side of the beam, overlapped to those protruding from the precast Parapet wall element, which is further connected to slab through dowel bars and finally screed concreted. Initially the beam and parapet wall elements were assembled and the dowels were connected to the corresponding sleeves, bolted and grouted to avoid further movement. Then the DT slab is placed over the beam on its ribs and its protruding dowel from the slab portion is tied to the parapet wall dowels. Finally, the screed of required thickness is laid over the DT slab and the joints between beam, parapet wall and slab to form a monolithic connection. The typical detailing of this DT slab and beam connection is shown below.

Fig. 27.4 Actual building of pre-cast structure

Fig. 27.5 Actual building of out-side structure

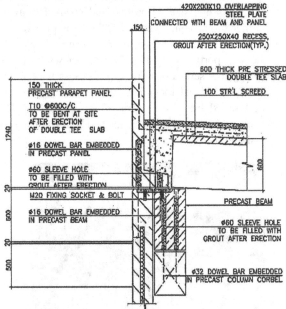

Fig. 27.6 Connections between precast elements

8. CONCLUSION

The substation building with crane was considered to be held at a seismic zone and was analysed & designed for both the precast and cast in-situ structural systems. The overall comparative study between precast and cast in-situ structure specifies that the precast substation building shows superior behaviour than cast insitu building under seismic conditions and also on effective usage of materials over structural elements. Further it can be concluded that, by utilizing proper and better connections between precast elements it will an efficient building system under the combination of dynamic loads from earthquake and crane.

ACKNOWLEDGEMENTS

I am thankful to Er.Harish Chandra Pal, Assistant Engineer, Uttrakhand Jal Sansthan Rudrapur. And Er. Anand Singh Pal, Site Engineer, Prag Group of Industries for his constant support throughout the project The blessing, help and guidance given by them shall carry me a long way in the journey of my life. I also thank Prashant Mishra, Assistant Professor, Department of Civil Engg, Ambalika Institute of Management & Technology Lko.

■ REFERENCE ■

1. IS 1893:2002, "Criteria for Earthquake resistant design of structure".
2. IS 875:1987, "Code of practice for design loads".
3. PCI hand books, "Precast Concrete Institute design aid charts and tables".
4. P.C.Varghese, "Advanced reinforced concrete design" second edition published by Prentice-Hall of India.
5. N.Krishna raju, "Advanced Reinforced Concrete Design based on limit state", CBS publishers.
6. S.K Duggal, "Earthquake resistance design of Structure"
7. R.P Rethaliya, "Earthquake Engineering"
8. IS 10297 (1982) "Code of practice for design and construction of floors and roofs using precast reinforced/prestressed concrete ribbed or cored slab unit" 1982
9. IS 456–2000 "Code of Practice Plain Reinforce Concrete" Fourth revision, 2000
10. K. R. Thagaragunta, M. H. Santhi, "Analysis and Design of a G+7 storeyed Precast Building" *Civil Engineering Systems and Sustainable Innovations* 139–148

Note: All the figures and table in this chapter were made by the author.

Challenges and Opportunities for Innovation in India – Dr. Shweta Mishra et al. (eds)
© *2024 Taylor & Francis Group, London, ISBN 978-1-032-99842-8*

Strengthening India's Defence Technology and Engineering Arm: Role and Perspective of Indigenisation

28

Ashok Kumar Panda*

Ph D Scholar,
Poornima University, Jaipur, MIE(I)

P. M. Menghal

Prof Military College of
Electronics and Mechanical Engineering,
Secunderabad

N. K. Gupta

Asso. Prof
Poornima University, Jaipur

Abstract

The indigenisation program of a nation is a capacity building exercise in terms of latest technology, materials development as of current requirements, adoption of state of the art processes, skill upgradation and following the best practices in quality assurance domain. The indigenisation program is ultimately aiming reasonable Gross Domestic Product (GDP) index and saving of foreign exchange by negative import. In India's context it is the structured indigenisation program to strengthen India's defence technology, engineering arm and concurrently to reduce import burden and enhancing defence export substantially. In the instant paper, it is brought out to establish the indigenizing capability in general and Silent Watch Capability of Defence Equipment with use of Lithium Ion Battery as a power pack and conducting Condition Based Maintenance of defence heavy vehicles for sustainable field operation in particular. Both aspects brought out are not yet have been established as of now to the operational desired level. Literature reviews brought out challenges in recharging of lithium Ion batteries for remote uses of defence applications and sustaining rate of discharge at initial condition. The condition based maintenance for defence vehicles through prescriptive maintenance is also not yet established due to very higher horse power capacity in the tune of 1400 horse power capacity and multiple requirements like all terrain use, mobility, firepower and protection of the vehicle and crew.

Keywords

Innovations, Vocal for local, Negative import, Interface, Resilient infrastructure, Resource mobilization

*Corresponding author: akp.eme@gmail.com

DOI: 10.1201/9781003606260-28

1. ROLE OF INDIGENISATION PROGRAM

1. The Womb to Tomb concept for defence indigenisation is critical since one has to understand the defence technology, design specifications, trial on field requirements & material composition of the product for operational requirements with time bound discard policy from conceptual stage to discard stage so that at right time the product can be taken off from the service without compromising the operation and war requirements and scope of introduction of new version of niche technology with precession equipments being aligned with the current demand.

2. The role and aim of the indigenisation and associated perspectives primarily based on strengthening India's defence technology and engineering arm keeping in view of the pattern of emerging warfare. The equipment and component level import and corresponding capital expenditure occurring in defence sector procurements in engineering front demands study and establishing solutions to negate the ill effects associated and suggest new innovations and strategies. The inputs obtained from the study for Indian Defence forces by Ranjit Ghosh (2016) on the publication titled **'Indigenisation: Key to Self-Sufficiency and Strategic Capability'** [1] justifies the decisive impact of the self reliance on technology excellence and consequent sustainable indigenisation program. The publication by Jaishankar Dhruva (2019) on the publication titled **'The Indigenisation of India's Defence Industry'** [2] also reiterates the role of indigenisation programme for strengthening the Indian defence forces and minimise export dependency thus utilising the surplus fund for resilient infrastructure development and upgradation program in a structured manner. Secondarily the exhaustive indigenisation program for defence forces also helps micro and medium industries to get a scope to build up capacity.

2. PRESENT STATUS OF INDIGENISATION

1. The identification of indigenization program by the Indian government as a priority activity creating eco system conducive for sustainable program. An appreciable achievement is the establishment of manufacturing hub for defence corridors made at Hyderabad, Bengaluru, Lucknow and other parts of country are fully strengthening indigenisation program. Each region of India has it's inherent and intrinsic technology oriented potential and unique set of resources of material and skill. The sustained indigenization capacity building is poised to reduce

the defence import by 30% of current expenditure by end of 2025. Constantly enabling local policies, good governance, dynamic and resilient infrastructure, creation of Special Economic Zones (SEZs) and Research & Development (R&D) entities, India is poised to be slotted amongst top five nations in terms of defence technology and consequent product realization at par with most advanced nations. The fast track Approval of Necessity (AoN) was also accorded for 480 Futuristic Advanced Infantry Combat Vehicles (FICVs) with enhanced lethality, night fighting and Intelligence Surveillance and Reconnaissance (ISR) capabilities at a cost of around Rs 20,000 crore, which will strengthen defence technical arm by replacing old version of Russian BMP-II combat vehicles. The further thought process in defence sector is to produce indigenous tank each weighing less than 25 tonnes with a higher power-to-weight ratio with superior firepower, agility, obstacle crossing capability, higher cruising speed, protection, mobility in battle field/strategic/ tactical and even high altitude deployment.

2. The current achievement of indigenisation is the accelerated resource mobilization and effective utilization through skill development to augment domain capability. As per Times News Network (TNN), the India's military expenditure increased to Rs 4,78,196 crores in 2021, marking nearly 1% enhancement with respect to the 2020 amount. The Defence allocation in respect of the financial year 2022-23 is Rs 5, 25,166 crores which is a phenomenal enhancement. The substantial amount is expended for procurement of equipments, missiles, optoelectronic, secured communication equipment and strategic devices. During October 2023, the competent authority issued the negative arms import list, under which 98 products and items will be progressively banned. In the continuing initiatives to boost the country's domestic defence production and reduce its strategic vulnerability of being among the world's largest weapons importer. The MoD now collectively ban the import of 509 products in a graded manner for the Indian Defence forces. The latest fifth list brought out by MoD includes futuristic infantry combat vehicles, all-terrain vehicles, autonomous combat vehicles, drones, unmanned and hybrid vehicles along with different kinds of remotely piloted airborne surveillance equipments, sensors, ammunitions, smaller systems and components, all of which will be made and available from indigenous sources in a staggered timeline. The above information was announced during the second Naval

Innovation and Indigenisation Organization (NIIO) Seminar, 'Swavlamban 2023' held at New Delhi by Indian Navy. The negative list has been prepared by MoD after several rounds of consultations with all stake holders like users, assessors, designers, producers, qualitative requirement formulating agency, trial agency, standardising entities and financial institutions. The inauguration of 76 innovation challenges have been acknowledged by the 10th Defence India Start-up Challenges across the Armed Forces Two INDUS X challenges have been created with the US Department of Defence to increase niche technology bonding between India and the US. Through the innovations for Defence Excellence (iDEX) Innovators Hub & NIIO secured partnerships to promote venture capital injection into the defence ecosystem to boost the capability. To achieve above mission, the funding of government entities, private entrepreneurs, Centre of Excellence (CoE) organisations and Higher Education Institutes (HEIs) of national importance are also playing key role in bringing out sustainable and effective engineering indigenous solutions to counter the negative effects of dependence and creating sustainable capacity building in defence manufacturing. As per Atmanirbhar Bharat initiatives and National Institution for Transforming India (NITI) Ayog directives minimum one sixth of engineering activities in manufacturing and production set ups are earmarked for indigenisation program.

3. An encouraging arrangement is to upscale creativity in innovations and technology development in defence by confidence building amongst researcher entities, innovators and entrepreneurs to deliver technological advanced deliverable solutions for Indian defence forces is the achievement of the current time. This is feasible by the involvement of standardising and quality assurance institutions. The aspects of hallmarking of the product, processes, design aspects and patenting in reference to defence indigenisation is now fast tracked by Intellectual Property Right (IPR) authority. The action frame work of the business, professional houses in support from regional industrial houses are working to create sustainable business processes out of defence indigenisation program.

4. New age technologies like deep learning, AI & ML, new materials, smart and intelligent materials, composites, Rare Earth Materials, mu and epsilon negative materials, double positive materials and meta materials along with IoT are being used for sustainable growth in defence manufacturing and indigenisation process. For the purpose of handling new age technology and materials several structured skills are in place. The data analytics, coding, deep learning, AI-ML chips development and material characterisation sectors are matured to handle the requirements. Re skilling and Up skilling for such objectives are in forefront for continual improvements and technology absorption for indigenous manufacturing. Therefore the matching initiatives by government, leading industries, Public Private Partnerships (PPP) and academia CoE are in synchronised state. Attachments with national and international professional bodies are in place to provide an edge forward in knowledge assimilation and achieving deliverables out of project works.

5. The 38 Problem Statements from field Army of Indian Armed Forces for obtaining workable solutions and ways out are being addressed by Defence entities during 6th edition of Defence India Start-up Challenge. To mitigate the Problem Statements, the apex corporate jointly conducted workshops on skilling necessities for defence manufacturing sectors, where it was emerged that skilling is important and lagging as well but more relevant is time bound re skilling and upgrdation programs to meet start ups skilled manpower demand. Achieving this will continually improve the productivity and diversions of operation of brands as per real time demand under defence indigenisation program. Unless upgrdation and re skilling are consider as a specialized skill itself then entities cannot cope with current and future demands of skill set required in defence manufacturing sectors which is fast growing and diversifying as well. In house acquired skill upliftment and domain expert's specialised training are to be conducted regularly and concurrently with external agencies since defence technology is an absolute specialised and customised domain.

6. As per Laxman Kumar Behera (2016) on article titled **"Indian Defence Industry: An Agenda for Making in India"** [5], the capability of Indian subcontinent is poised as one of the largest defence industrial complexes amongst the developing countries. Post reforms of Ordnance production set ups, the restructured factories become only 07 clusters of specialised entities headed by a independent chief, 08 Army Base Workshops strategically located pan India with centre of excellence activities, 09 large public sector undertakings exclusively for defence needs and in addition more than hundred companies in the private sector supporting program on

indigenisation. Further if the research wing of Indian Armed Forces are considered, then more than 30 laboratories working on defence needs exclusively with best work force around.

3. Gaps and Weakness in Defence Technology and Indigenisation Program

1. The technological innovations and engineering excellence in the domain of indigenisation are facing challenges in terms of handling the defence equipment and machineries without going for Memorandum of Understanding (MoU) with Foreign Original Equipment Manufacturers (OEMs) for Transfer of Technology (ToT). Studying the technology and engineering strength of the country's defence set up is the critical aspect of capability assessment and operational preparedness as well. During study of the role and perspective of the indigenisation to strengthen India's defence technology and engineering arm along with desired deliverables, several inherent factors were shortlisted and solutions deliberated. Defence set ups not only poised to take on operational missions however strengthen socio economic factors of the country by provisioning surplus and unutilized technological advancement facilities to civil requirements, resilient and robust infrastructures availability and saving national resources by minimizing damage during national disasters.

2. The current strategy in the war field has been shifted from conventional warfare to innovative ways which includes electromagnetic, biological, chemical, nuclear, radiological, psychological, laser based and cyber based warfare. Keeping in view of above operational patterns and rapid technological infusion by adversaries, adoption of time bound up gradations and requirements are challenging. In respect of fulfilling pressing innovations, the sustainable industrial development in defence manufacturing sector in present days of competitiveness in terms of economical viability is a matter of concern for Indian subcontinent. The simple reason is that in the largest democracy, the nation has several other priorities like education, health care, malnutrition support programs, infrastructure development, communication and even on provisioning the social security support to under privileged citizens as compared to defence advancement requirements. However against all odds, during 2018 a platform named as iDEX was introduced to cater for all needs

under one roof related to defence indigenisation, innovation, technology infusion and looking for sustenance of the activities. However, the following shortcomings are restricting to achieve expected deliverables in defined time frame:

(a) Limited outreach

(b) Stringent screening and selection of vendor

(c) Grants appraisal and contracts easiness

(d) Product acceptance and co development criteria

(e) Diversified standards certification issues

(f) Trial evaluation stages and facilities

(g) Inadequate trained manpower availability on defence technology

(h) Inadequate fund support through Export-Import (EXIM) Bank

(i) Absolute support from Confederation of Indian Industry and other business associations

3. Military technology being exclusive to defence forces having least interchangeably and commonality with civil requirements, the progress and sustainability depends on continuous research and technology updatation. The density of effective researchers in India as compared to international average also not encouraging. Further the prioritisation of India against the defence innovative research is in back seat due to other emerging areas are there for research focus to handle 140 plus crores of population. The expenditure on research with respect to the gross domestic product (GDP) of India is only close to 1% as compared ro USA allocation of 3% of it's GDP. Even Israel and China give the defence innovation utmost priority so that the export of the nations are substantial.

4. Irrespective of initiatives by Government of India, Confederation of Indian Industries and other research entities including inputs from think tanks, the following limitations are prevailing in one form or other which limits in achieving the time bound results:-

   a) The fund allocation is the major constraint progressing engineering solutions related to current indigenisation requirements even after a defence budget allocation of Rs 5.25 lakh crores for 2023-24, a 13 percent hike than previous. However, it is committed by government that nearly 13% will be spent on engineering advancements and indigenisation front.

   b) Keeping in view the industrial growth in the areas of defence productions, indigenisation and development programs, several Multi National

Companies (MNCs) are aiming to establish defence manufacturing corridors. The capping of FDIs is a hindrance in this area. It is appreciated that without FDIs the deliverables at par with international standards cannot be a reality. The set up of R&D institutions, testing facilities and skill acquisition requires heavy funding. As such minimum Cap of FDI at 75% is the call of the day.

5. The other challenge is whatever ToT are taking place with foreign OEMs with Indian entities are primarily in the domain of low technology areas. Therefore, research on material requirement, test and diagnostic set ups are inadequate. Hence the target of Indian subcontinent to be a defence exporter rather an importer at a target of Rs 40 thousand crore by 2026 as envisaged by Government is seems to be a unrealistic estimate.

4. Problem Definition and Case Studies

1. Post reviewing the literatures on current indigenisation program in reference to Indian context for strengthening the engineering and technology arm of defence forces the following areas are found not being addressed adequately :-

   (a) Silent Watch Capability of defence vehicles

   (b) Condition Based Maintenance (CBM) of High Power Defence Vehicles

2. The silent watch capability of a heavy defence vehicle like an Armoured Fighting Vehicle relates to the fact that the vehicle has to be in observational mode for enemies without supplying power requirements to assemblies and subassemblies from an running engine source producing sound and heat waves, rather from a heavy duty battery power pack like lithium ion battery source which operates at silent mode. By adopting this arrangement, thermal images from an operating engine at static condition are not generated by which the identification of the tank by enemy radars are not traceable. In the same time the vehicle will be powered by a set of lithium ion batteries to power the surveillance systems, computing arrangements and telemetry set ups.

3. The operational availability of heavy defence vehicles is most sought in field operation subjected to conflicts. This is only possible by conducting recommended OEM maintenance schedule and stipulated user's preventive maintenance. However the current requirement of AI based prescriptive maintenance of high end defence vehicles have not been established and demonstrated. Once the instant issue is addressed and modalities demonstrated the vehicles war preparedness will be unquestioned and spares requirement for a time predicted provisioning along with technical skill requirements can be prescribed and made available at right time, right place and right quality.

5. Forecast Solutions

1. The projected solutions to both the emerging problem areas are based on current field requirements, ease of users handling without compromising operational features and lastly the financial implications beyond reasonable range. The tentative solution models are placed below:

2. For silent watch capability of defence heavy equipments the recommendation is Lithium Ion phosphate ($LiFePO_4$) batteries which are the safest, being non-toxic unlike lithium cobalt-based battery. The $LiFePO_4$ batteries have extremely stable chemistry, generate very little heat and don't overheat to unsafe levels. Lithium Ion has the lowest density of all metals. The most important use of lithium is in rechargeable batteries for electric vehicles which justify adoption in heavy vehicles. On comparison front the lithium ion batteries charge 40% faster as compared to conventional battery. Further, the residual utility life, power density and temperature stability are in higher rating for lithium ion battery. The light weight is the other big advantage in lithium ion battery. As compared to overall size with respect to a particular battery capacity, lithium ion battery is only 35% as that of hydrogen and helium. The per cell voltage capacity also much higher at value 3.7 volt along with higher charge storage per unit mass and unit volume. The lesser down time of lithium ion battery and ability to discharge at a higher rate are the other favorable properties. The materials available foe electrodes are diversified with option from lithium cobalt oxide for cathode upto graphite in anode. Due to above facts and figures it is proposed to carry out reverse calculation of finding number of batteries, capacity of each battery and combining the batteries in series parallel to deliver requisite voltage, current and energy. Further, recharging of Li ion battery can be conducted by suitable fuel cells maintaining the requirements of silent mode operation.

3. With the latest heavy vehicles like Armoured Fighting Vehicles at the helm with nearly 1400 horse power engine, a rigorous schedule of maintenance tasks has to be instituted for their upkeep and readiness for war. This includes stage wise tasks.

Mostly heavy vehicles are tracked combat vehicle with high manoeuvrability, powerful armament, and reliable armour protection. Such critical equipment of Indian Army which is no longer expected to have unexpected failures/faults once deployed in any mission or operation. Although the condition based maintenance schedule and policies are reliable and in use for many years, yet they may not be so cost-effective and are not prescriptive in nature. It is time to revisit the existing maintenance procedures and come up with a maintenance solution that is prescriptive and cost-effective. As of now, no such condition based maintenance procedure is being followed in Indian defence forces. The significance of the CBM may be a plausible solution that offers prediction-based technologies to predict failures in the sophisticated system of a heavy vehicle particular the engine. It also cuts down on maintenance tasks that may not be required just yet and thus saving on costs and resources. As CBM can be applied to different system of the heavy vehicle which makes it a vast study to undertake in the limited time frame, the scope of initial application should always be limited to studying the engine portion primarily being the power house of the vehicle.

6. METHODOLOGY OF INDIGENISATION

1. For strengthening India's defence technology & engineering arm and considering role & perspective of Indigenisation the two aspects that is silent watch capability and CBM are considered as inadequately addressed. Post identifying the problem area, we consider following methodology to go for indigenisation on specific two brought out issues.

2. Initially we have to evaluate the load nature and capacity requirement so that we can have pattern of selection of equivalent number and capacity of Li ion batteries institutionalizing silent watch capability in the vehicle. The combination of batteries in series parallel form for desired delivery of voltage, current and power in addition the location on vehicle for placement of batteries are two other factors. The battery management system (BMS) and efficient fast charging pattern of Li ion batteries are to be finalised subjected to operational requirements.

3. In the case of CBM, we propose to focus only on engine part of heavy vehicle which is the power house and intricate in nature. It is proposed to go for telemetry arrangement to capture functional parameters like temperature and associated gradient, pressure, vibration, thermal imaging aspects by using suitable sensors along with modulator and demodulator arrangements. A Software can be used to predict the status of the engine out of the inputs captured and correspondingly can predict the left over time of healthy operation and requirement of spares during a predicted failure over a known timeline.

4. Structured and orderly cyclic activities of problem identification for execution and field trials are the sequential methods for the real time implementation of brought out issues with defined deliverables. Following modalities are recommended in Indian context to negate the gaps persisting:-

    a. Need Analysis of requirement for defence forces in structured and priority manner.

    b. Customized vendor selections for development and production realization.

    c. Dedicated field trial and maintenance evaluations to obtain users inputs and assess functional parameters.

    d. On the basis of field trials and inputs design features can be suitably modified.

    e. Inlieu material identification in consultation with standards agencies like BIS to substitute materials of foreign origin and rarely available.

    f. Formulation of continual improvement program with time bound implementation of discard policy.

7. EFFECT OF TECHNO-COMMERCIAL FACTORS IN DEFENCE INDIGENISATION

1. As per Times News Network (TNN) [3] Indian subcontinent imported mostly from Russia the defence goods to the value of $ 32.9 billion for the period of Apr – Dec 2022. This amount is an increase of five times in last five years average. If the pattern of import remains the same, the Indian government is expected to earmark $ 50 billion for Russia only. This amount will touch to the level of consumer goods imported from abroad. This trend of defence import reflects poor preparedness of India in respect of self reliance in defence products, indigenisation deliverables and techno-commercial status to counter draining of foreign currency. Consequent to defence large scale import, the nation has to balance import portfolio on healthcare, atomic research, space technology and infrastructure developments.

2. The techno commercial ventures like association with international and national institution of eminence, capacity enhancement through capital expenditure

for infrastructure, plant and machineries, test equipment, new and smart material development and commercial set up clearance through a hassle free single window are the essential requirements. The ToT and MoU with researchers and manufacturers for engineering progression front, Manufacturer's Capacity Requirement Planning, R & D entities for time bound materials and process identifications with pilot samples production are the issues of product realization delay and leading to more costing. The assessment and development program for Vendors along with methodology for continuous rating of the firms, vendors marketing potential, automation of purchase system, adoption of IoTs in purchase and marketing, uses of AI & ML , virtual realization of product and services, effective data analytics are key criteria of success to technology adoption in armed forces calling for higher investment. Under unique nature of product development program for armed forces modern and non conventional manufacturing, multi dimensional printing, latest fluid supported machining , global reach out, potential fuel sources creation and Academia integration with producers for research deliverables for gap filling are time consuming and cost matters. The association with prominent R & D entities like CSIR (Council of Scientific and Industrial Research), DRDO (Defence Research & Development Organisation), RDSO (Research Design & Standards Organisation), BARC (Bhaba Atomic Research Centre) and TERI (The Energy and Research Institute etc are the immediate needs for techno commercial viability, however against a cost.

3. The emerging need which is key to techno commercial sustenance for strengthening engineering and technology arm of defence forces through the dynamic process of indigenisation is selection, development and application of customized materials of unique featured as brought out under:-

a. Identification and application of smart materials.

b. Development of new materials.

c. Scope identification of metamaterials.

d. Applicability of epsilon negative (ENM) material & Mu negative (MNG) materials.

e. Development of double positive (DPS) & double negative (DNG) materials.

f. Isotropic & Anisotropic materials uses.

g. Sensor oriented materials like Piezoelectric, Piezoresistive, Hall's and other similar materials exploitation.

h. Scope of memory materials, Chromoactive materials, Photosensitive materials adaptability.

i. Adoption of Rare Earth Materials (REMs).

j. Extensive application of ferroelectric, pyroelectric, ferromagnetic, composites, mumetal, supermalloy and superconductors.

4. As per commercial estimation only twenty odd nations are contributing nearly three forth of world's defence expenditures. This aspect implies the involvement of national resources in defence front only. Therefore to contain the outlay of revenue in terms of indigenization by strengthening the defence engineering indigenisation arm, rapid modernisation of existing defence entities, encouraging foreign direct investments (FDIs) and fast track establishing of defence manufacturing corridor in each region of the nation with facilitating ToT are the need of hour.

5. The role of micro organisations as brought out by Shashank B. S. & Sureshramana Mayya (2021) in publication title **"A Conceptual Study on Performance of Small-Scale Industries in India"** [4] brought out that micro and small scale industrial entities are the boosters to employment and stabilizing the economy through engineering activities. The nation with 140 crore plus population with one third youth requires adequate employment. The micro and medium sector industrial houses will provide ample scope of employment. These sectors also generate products in the tune of one third of the gross industrial value. However, such entities are not inclined to defence indigenisation program due to long process of order, test trials and final acceptance. The small entities do not possess sufficient fund for skill development programs for technicians or infrastructure upgrdation.

8. WAY AHEAD

1. The requirements of armed forces in terms of equipment and spares are unique and customized, hence availability in civil domain is very restricted and demand for civil needs also meager. Therefore the technological and engineering operational needs are unique for the forces. Again the armed forces requires product and services with performance features and specifications matching with international standards and best practices. For the purpose as brought out above the requirements are dedicated world class laboratories for R & D, tuned skilled manpower for the absolute purpose and the most important is capital expenditure provisioning. Therefore multiple agencies are to be

encouraged to work on defence indigenisation and in particular in silent watch capability and CBM of heavy defence vehicle domain to get viable solution. The interface between the R & D organisations and standards formulating organisations with OEMs on indigenisation program establishing and promoting of engineering centre of excellence (CoE) are to be priorities for conceptualisation, development, trial and introduction of indigenised items in defence forces.

2. With the inputs from field users, defence domain experts, studies undertaken by DRDO and product development agencies, the following priority areas are shortlisted for Strengthening India's defence technology & engineering arm in general through indigenisation program as well :-

    a. Light Armoured Vehicles with Autonomous features.

    b. Silent Watch Capability development for tanks using fuel cells without starting engine.

    c. Target Acquisition Unwired Simulator (TAUS).

    d. Integrated Tactical Power Management System (ITPMS).

    e. Customized and encrypted Communication arrangement.

    f. Surveillance system with modern Radars, and Interceptors.

    g. The intelligent ammunitions.

    h. Programmable Arial Vehicles and Drones.

    i. Optical device modernisation for Night Vision

    j. Capability.

    k. Controllable Solider comfort equipments with monitoring facility embedded with chips..

    l. Application of modern, smart and Rare Earth

    m. Material

    n. Non Conventional and Additive Manufacturing with multi dimensional printing facility.

    o. Test and Validation Equipment.

    p. Data Analytics supported by Cloud and Quantum computing.

    q. Security set ups and alarm system design in respect of Cyber Security and cyber attacks.

    r. Sensors, probes, transducers and telemetry arrangements and integration there of for ease of control and monitoring.

    s. War head modernisation using Laser Beam Technology.

    t. Objective oriented training facility by incorporating Simulator based Augmented Reality (AR) and Virtual Reality (VR) models.

    u. Target locking and tracking by installation of Identification of Foe and Friend modules

    v. Thermal and acoustical image analysis of physical systems.

    w. Advanced and non traceable Camouflaging techniques.

    x. Set ups with compatible test and validation facilities.

    y. Nuclear, Biological, Chemical and Radiation (NBCR) protection and detection systems,

    z. Prescriptive Maintenance on IoT platform.

    aa. Uninterrupted Navigation system.

    bb. Blockchain facilities.

    cc. Non Lethal Weapon (NLW).

    dd. Multi Terrain Equipment (MTE).

    ee. Nano, New, Special and Smart material development.

    ff. Autonomous Vehicles with continuous health check up facilities.

    gg. Alternative energy sources & Upgradation in Battery Management System (BMS).

9. CONCLUSION

Keeping in view of deliberations projected above and Indian subcontinent priorities on defence forces indigenisation program and strengthening engineering arm, the under mentioned conclusions are relevant:-

    a. The defence technology and engineering arm to focus on miniaturization of component level requirements, adoption of IoT in prescriptive maintenance to sustain operation requirements of equipments, lethality and protection aspects. Most of the expenditure is in these fronts. Therefore primary role and perspective to strengthen India's defence technical arm lies with fast tracking of indigenization through public private participation.

    b. The current reports on R & D enlist India having third rank in research in the world, seventh for higher cited papers and tenth in patent filing. This achievements matter much due to the fact that India has just around 250 scientists or researchers per million populations, which is lower in comparison to smaller Asian countries. The ranking of Indian subcontinent in Global Innovation Index (GII) is 40th worldwide which is another feather in the cap. These results are indicative of improvement in the sector of engineering excellence which will evidently strengthen engineering arm of defence innovation in accelerated manner.

c. The Russia, France and the US are suppling India's defence requirements in the tune of 46%, 27% and 12% in the last five years. However the MoU for ToT from the mentioned nations are non progressing to arrest import and make India's self sufficiency in defence manufacturing sector. Staggered way of indigenisation program to strengthen engineering arm and reduce import burden is predicted.

d. The last but not the least is to synchronize the mandate of research entities, laboratories, researchers, developers, standardization establishment, qualitative requirement framing authority, trial and validation agencies, vendors and users for higher productivity and on time realization of the product or service. Further, all the Institutes of Eminence (IoE) & Higher Education Institutes (HEIs) in India have already adopted courses on indigenisation, defence technology, niche and strategic technology aspects to strengthen engineering arm of defence forces.. The CoE set up by such institutes contributing to customized needs and solutions to end users

■ REFERENCES ■

1. Ranjit Ghosh, "Indigenisation: Key to Self-Sufficiency and Strategic Capability", *Pentagon Press* {2016}, PP 1–21.
2. Jaishankar Dhruva, "The Indigenisation of India's Defence Industry", *Brookings Institution India Center* {2019}, PP 1–22.
3. Times News Network (TNN) publications.
4. Shashank B. S. & Sureshramana Mayya, "A Conceptual Study on Performance of Small-Scale Industries in India", International Journal of Case Studies in Business, IT, and Education (IJCSBE), Vol. 5, No. 2, {2021}, PP 1–3.
5. Laxman Kumar Behera, " Indian Defence Industry: An Agenda for Making in India" *Pentagon Press* {2016} PP 1–59.
6. S. Nandi & H.A. Toliyat , "Condition Monitoring and Fault Diagnosis of Electrical Motors—A Review", 2005, IEEE Xplore.
7. Abe Zeid et al, "Interoperability in Smart Manufacturing: Research Challenges", 2019, Multidisciplinary Digital Publishing Institute (MDPI).
8. Urvi P. Sheth & Prasanta Chatterjee Biswas, "Performance of The Indian MSMEs in the Era of Globalisation" 2016, International Journal of Research Science & Management (IJRSM).
9. Mitronikas et al, "Development of a telemetry system for electric vehicles , 2007, Researchgate.
10. Bikramdeep Singh, "Defence Indigenisation: Indian Army", 2007, Center of Land Warfare System (CLAWS) Journal.
11. Brig Ashok Pathak, "Indigenisation of Defence Production : India's Journey from Vision to Outcomes", 2022, Vivekananda International Foundation.
12. Ashok Jain, "Strengthening Science and Technology Capacities for Indigenisation of Technology- the Indian experience", 2003, International Journal of Services Technology & Management (IJSTM).
13. Azhar Shaikh et al, "Make in India Opportunities and Challenges In Defence Sector", 2015, International Journal of Research in Commerce & Management (IJRCM).
14. Anthony Barré et al, "A review on lithium-ion battery ageing mechanisms and estimations for automotive applications", 2019, HAL Id: cea-01791260 https://cea.hal.science/cea-01791260.
15. Marie Oldfeld et al ;"The future of condition based monitoring: risks of operator removal"; Springer online [2022].
16. Ahad Ali and Abdelhakim Abdelhadi; "Condition-Based Monitoring and Maintenance: State of the Art Review"; MDPI [2022].

Loan Status Prediction Using Machine Learning Algorithms

29

Abhay Bajpai[1]

M.Tech.,
Khawaja Moinuddin Chishti Language University,
Lucknow U.P. India

Satish Kumar Singh[2]

Research Scholar, Integral University,
Lucknow, U.P. India

Abstract

In the financial system in India, banks can promote a variety of goods including loans, savings accounts and more, but their main revenue stream is from credit lines. The interest on the loans they have credited will therefore be profitable for them. Loans – specifically, whether clients are making their loan payments on time or defaulting – have a significant impact on whether a bank make a profit or a loss. Every year, more individuals and organizations request for loans in India. Finding a trustworthy borrower who will return the loan may be difficult, even in a situation when many people are asking for loans. By anticipating defaulters of the loan, the bank can degrade the non-performing assets. When the process of selecting the best applicant is done manually, several mistakes might be committed. Therefore, we are creating a self-governing loan status prediction system powered by machine learning to choose the qualified applicants. Both the bank staffs and the applicants will benefit from this. There will be a notable decrease in the time required to authorize a loan. In this work, we have used many machine learning methods to forecast the loan data. The ultimate goal of this project is to decide if it is safe to authorize loans to a certain person.

Keywords

Machine learning algorithms, Gradient boosting algorithm, Support vector classifier, Decision tree classifier, Random forest classifier, Various python libraries (including Matplotlib, pandas, Numpy, Seaborn and Dtale)

1. INTRODUCTION

Due to the daily data expansion resulting from the digitization of the banking business, more people are choosing to apply for loans online. Artificial intelligence (AI) as a common tool for information processing is gaining increasing attention. AI calculations are being used by people from a variety of businesses to solve a problem based on their understanding of the particular industry. Banks are facing significant challenges in the

[1]abybajpai@gmail.com, [2]Satishkrsingh167@gmail.com

DOI: 10.1201/9781003606260-29

loan approval process. Every day, bank employees manage a high quantity of applications, which is challenging and raises the possibility of errors. Loans are how most banks generate revenue, but picking qualified customers from the applicant pool can be risky. A bank might suffer a massive loss as a result of one error. The goal of this article is to provide a quick, easy, and efficient method for selecting the best candidates. It might give the bank certain benefits. The Loan Status Prediction System can assess an application based on its priority by quickly accessing it. Data from prior clients of many banks, whose loans were authorized in compliance with a set of criteria, was used in this study. To get consistent results, the machine learning model is trained using historical data. This study's primary goal is to forecast loan safety. Numerous algorithms, such as Random Forest classifier, Support Vector Classifier and Decision Tree classifier, are used to forecast loan safety.

1.1 Problem Statement

Our banks deal with every type of loan. They serve all areas that are rural, semi-urban and urban. The bank verifies that the applicant is qualified for a loan after they submit an application. However, doing this by hand takes a very long time. Consequently, it aims to use client data to automate (in real-time) the loan qualifying procedure. The final step is to identify the requirements or clientele that meet the loan eligibility requirements.

1.2 Objectives

The paper's goals are as follows:

a) The main aim of this paper is to determine whether or not granting a loan to a certain person is safe.

b) It benefits the bank as well by lowering the risk and the quantity of defaulters.

c) Find the best algorithm to use in order to predict the application status as accurately as possible.

1.3 Methodology

Figure 29.1 represents the steps of building a model. Following are the steps which one needs to follow while creating a model -

i) **Data Collection** - Every project starts with data collection. The method used to gather data differs

for each customer and is based on the type, volume, accessibility, and need for the information. We collected our data from the Kaggle whose link is given below-

https://www.kaggle.com/datasets/altruistdelhite04/loan-prediction-problemdataset

ii) **Data Pre-Processing** - The collected data is put through a "cleaning" process to make sure it is properly partitioned, any gaps in the data are filled in with the relevant information, the data is made compatible, and any storage system problems that could lead to data redundancy are fixed. In this phase, we essentially clean up our dataset. For instance, we look for any missing values and address them if we find any. Several variables in our sample had missing values, including Gender, Married Status, Loan_Amount_Term, Dependents, Self_Employed_Status, Credit_History, and Loan_Amount.

iii) **Data Modeling** - This process basically involves analyzing the provided information and the items contained in it to get a clear image of the requirements that could help us support our business strategy. After then, models are created based on the project's specified flow and an analysis of patterns found in the data.

Using the previously decided semi-formal model that emphasizes the project's strengths is made easier using this flow. It also demonstrates how to track the connections between different objects and data items.

iv) **Data Prediction** - This approach develops machine learning prediction models, which are subsequently evaluated through data analysis. The dataset that was previously processed will thereafter receive this application. The following models should be used to make predictions:

- SVM (Support Vector Machine)
- Decision Tree Classifier
- Gradient Boosting Classifier
- Random Forest Classifier

v) **Data Visualization** - After analysis, the data is further visualised to help customers and administrators draw conclusions and make wise decisions.

Fig. 29.1 Process of building a model

Source: Author

2. ALGORITHMS EMPLOYED

2.1 Random Forest Classifier

Using decision trees for classification, regression, and other tasks, the Random Forest, is a supervised machine learning technique in which by choosing a random subset of the training data, generates a collection of the decision trees. To put it simply, the final forecast is produced by a collection of decision trees (DT). These DTs are from the training set and are chosen at random. [1]

2.2 Support Vector Machines (SVMs)

Support vector machines (SVMs) are the machine learning algorithms that employ supervised learning models to address challenging regression, classification, and outlier identification issues. To do this, support vector machines (SVMs) carry out optimum data transformations, drawing boundaries between the data points based on the predetermined classes, labels, or outputs. Every data point is plotted using this approach in an n-dimensional space, where n is the number of features. A matching pair of coordinates represents each feature. Applications for Support Vector Machines (SVMs) include facial recognition, intrusion detection, emails, web pages, emails, and gene categorization. [3]

2.3 Decision Tree Classifier

The most widely used and effective technique for forecasting and categorization is the decision tree. A decision tree is a type of tree structure that resembles a flowchart. Each internal node in a decision tree represents an attribute test, each branch denotes a test result, and the leaf node, or terminal node, represents a class label. Regression trees and classification trees are the two different types of decision trees. When dealing with category output variables that have a binary character, such as yes or no, sale or not, and so on, classification trees are commonly used. Regression

trees, on the other hand, are used with continuous or quantitative output variables, such as the anticipated cost of a consumer commodity.[4] Decision trees are a type of supervised learning algorithm with a predetermined objective variable that are mostly used in classification problems. By applying this technique, we separate the population or sample into two or more homogenous groups based on the most significant splitter or differentiator of the input variables. [5]

2.4 Gradient Boosting Classifier

Gradient boosting is the potent boosting technique that turns many weak learners into strong learners. To minimize the loss function of the model that came before it, such as mean square error or cross-entropy, each successive model is trained using gradient descent. The approach computes the gradient of the loss function with respect to the current ensemble's predictions in each iteration, and then trains a new weak model with the goal of minimizing this gradient. The procedure is then repeated until a stopping condition is satisfied after the predictions of the new model have been added to the ensemble. [6]

3. CONCLUSIONS

In the order to decrease the human interference and boost the productivity, the rapidly expanding IT sector of today has to develop the new technologies and enhance existing ones. Both the banking industry and anybody looking to apply for a loan employ this concept. It will be very beneficial for managing banks. Data cleaning and processing, imputation of missing values, experimental analysis of the data set, model construction, and performance evaluation are the steps involved in the process of prediction. The best-case accuracy of the Random Forest Classifier model on the dataset is 0.780 on the original data set. This suggests that the Random Forest Classifier performs better than alternative models and is incredibly efficient. This system

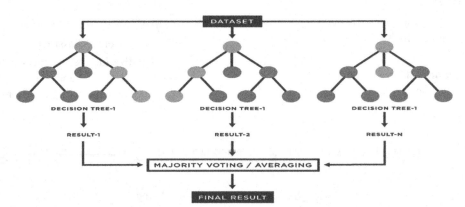

Fig. 29.2 Flowchart of random forest regression [2]

Source: Author

computes the result precisely and accurately. It accurately forecasts whether a particular customer's loan application status will be approved or turned down. To improve the software and make it more accurate, secure, and trustworthy, this work may be done in greater detail in the future. The system has to be trained using current data sets, which could eventually get older, in order for it to pass new test cases. The system could thus participate in additional testing.

■ REFERENCES ■

1. https://www.geeksforgeeks.org/random-forest-classifier-using-scikit-learn/
2. https://www.tibco.com/reference-center/what-is-a-random-forest
3. Ashwini S. Kadam, Ankita A. Aher, Shraddha R. Nikam, Amar S. Chandgude, Gayatri V. Shelke, "Prediction for the Loan Approval using various Machine Learning Algorithms", International Research Journal of Engineering and Technology (IRJET), Volume: 08, Issue: 04 | Apr 2021
4. https://www.geeksforgeeks.org/decision-tree/
5. Sanket Bhattad, Shweta Agrawal, Sumit Bawane, Dr. P. B. Ambhore, Unnati Ramteke, "Loan Prediction using various Machine Learning Algorithms ", International Journal of Computer Science Trends and Technology (IJCST) – Volume 9 Issue 3, May-Jun 2021
6. Candice Bentéjac, Gonzalo Martínez-Muñoz, Anna Csörgo, "A comparative analysis of gradient boosting algorithms", Springer Nature B.V. 2020

Challenges and Opportunities for Innovation in India – Dr. Shweta Mishra et al. (eds)
© *2024 Taylor & Francis Group, London, ISBN 978-1-032-99842-8*

Impact of Quantum Computing on Cryptography: Tracing Progress, Identifying Challenges, and Safeguarding Information in the Quantum Era

30

Jitendra Kurmi[1],
Vipin Rawat[2], Km. Divya[3]
Department of Computer Science and Engineering,
Ambalika Institute of Management and Technology,
Lucknow, India

Abstract

Cryptography and security are experiencing a period of profound change due to the potential for scalable quantum computing. Here we take a look back at how far we've come in our quest to make large-scale quantum computing a reality. We also provide a brief overview of the current cryptographic primitives and the dangers they face. New cryptographic primitives, known as post-quantum cryptography (PQC), are being standardized in an attempt to overcome these difficulties. We talk about the mathematical issues that characterize various types of PQC candidates and how they can withstand an attack from a hostile party with access to a powerful quantum computer. This line of inquiry has occurred with the porting of numerous conventional cryptography primitives to the quantum realm. This is the setting in which we talk about TRNG, Physically Enclosable Function, and Quantum Key Distribution (QKD). We get a sneak peek at the implementation-related vulnerabilities that result from such implementations.

Keywords

Quantum computing, Cryptography, Post-quantum cryptography (PQC), Cryptographic primitives, Quantum key distribution (QKD)

1. Introduction

Universal gate and generalized quantum annealers are the main types of quantum computers [1]. Quantum computers are designed to solve complex problems that current computers cannot efficiently solve. In quantum computing, universal gate quantum computers are like versatile microprocessors. IBM and Google (127 and 72 qubits, respectively) are competing to build larger and faster machines [2]. ASICs, however, resemble quantum annealers. Combinatorial methods over discrete search spaces solve a limited set of optimization problems. The security industry's main focus is on improving universal quantum computers, which are much more powerful than quantum annealers [3]. Big quantum computers aren't just developed for security reasons. Quantum computers will help machine learning, supply chain optimization, chemical chemistry, and financial derivative pricing [4]. Noisy

[1]jitendrakurmi458@gmail.com, [2]divyabharti1990@gmail.com, [3]vipinrawat6668@gmail.com

DOI: 10.1201/9781003606260-30

small-scale quantum computers are also being used to illustrate quantum advantage [5]. So anybody can evaluate algorithmic advances, manufacturers and system designers are making increasingly powerful quantum computers available through cloud applications. Microsoft, Rigetti, IBM, Google, Xanadu, and IBM sell software development kits for design. Scaling a quantum computer is difficult. These include controlling background noise, ensuring qubit fidelity, and building entanglement over several qubits. New quantum error correcting codes allow for powerful quantum computers. Fault-tolerant deployment is essential for this technology's success. The error correcting circuit must prevent gate control defects. Due to its low cost in quantum technologies, the surface code is a leading quantum error correcting code. Noise-resilient quantum gate operations and entanglement over more qubits (like IBM's 127-qubit) are hallmarks of a quantum computer's progress. A single logical qubit requires many physical qubits due to error correcting codes. Based on the quantum technology and error correcting codes, a single logical qubit may require 1000 physical qubits [6]. Modern quantum computers aren't powerful enough to attack any cryptosystem, so these details must be addressed when estimating quantum attack complexity. This forces researchers to utilise analytical estimations, as we'll see.

2. SCALABLE QUANTUM COMPUTERS AND THE RISK TO CRYPTOGRAPHIC PRIMITIVES

In the following, we will provide a brief overview of the threats that quantum computing poses to classical cryptography.

2.1 Public-Key Cryptography

Public key cryptography uses hardest number theory issues like discrete logarithm and integer factorization. A massive quantum computer can readily solve both issues. For the most famous factorization algorithm, choosing a bigger prime number scales the generic number field sieve approach exponentially. Alternatively, Shor's algorithm, the most popular quantum algorithm, may do the same operation in $O(n^3)$, which is exponentially faster [7]. Quantum computing research on the cost of breaking cryptographic primitives has grown in recent years. Elliptic curve encryption requires 6n qubits (where n is the group's order bit length), according to Proos et al. [8]. Therefore, a 255-bit curve like Curve25519 or Ed25519 requires almost 1530 logical qubits to break ECC. Optimizing the quantum circuit architecture reduces attack difficulty [9]. Gidney et al. [10] found that factoring n bits requires $3n + 0.002n\lg n$ logical qubits. Assuming adequate gate error rate, cycle time, and other features, 20 million physical qubits can factor a 2048-bit RSA integer in eight hours.

2.2 Private-Key Cryptography

Algorithms that use private keys are more resilient against quantum attackers than those that use public keys. Traditionally, brute-forcing the secret key using Grover's search technique has been the most common way to achieve a quadratic speedup. However, in a paper titled [11], researchers improved on this method. They looked into adapting meet-in-the-middle attacks for AES [12], [13] from a classical to a quantum context. An efficient quantum circuit for the cipher is crucial when attacking symmetric-key ciphers as the encryption process is repeated several times during the assault. Therefore, there has been a growing focus on developing effective quantum circuits for symmetric-key ciphers in recent years [14]. Despite these advancements, the quantum attack complexity for private-key ciphers still remains exponential.

3. POST-QUANTUM CRYPTOGRAPHY

The cryptographic community has been working on developing public-key cryptography primitives that can't be broken by quantum computers. This is due to the ongoing progress towards building large-scale quantum computers. In response to this, a new field of encryption called post-quantum cryptography (PQC) has emerged. Using cryptographic primitives based on challenging problems that are thought to be intractable for quantum computers is the main premise behind PQC.

3.1 NIST PQC Standardization Process

Public-key cryptography uses PKE, DS, KEM. For PQC, NIST wants post quantum cryptographic algorithm standardization [15]. The five main PQC kinds solve tough problems: Hashed, coded, and stacked. The encryption requires three super singular isogeny and four multivariate quadratics. NIST may use cryptographic algorithms from different cryptosystem families for backups and to make cryptanalysis harder on the candidate [16]. Execution time, resource efficiency, bandwidth, public key, ciphertext, and signature size are evaluated. Runtime is needed for embedded device, general-purpose CPU, and public-key/signature transfer applications [17]. NIST manages use-cases and limits extensively. PQC schemes' robustness to implementation-level vulnerabilities like SCA and FIA drove Method and Execution Standardization. NIST prioritizes SCA/FIA mitigation cost-benefit analyses. TLS/IPSec prefers non-reengineering alternatives [16]. PQC schemes that passed NIST final assessment are listed here. NIST lists finalists [18].

3.2 Lattice-based Cryptography

Hard issues over lattices underpin seven of the fifteen finalists, offering KEMs and unique techniques. They exploit two well-known difficulties to build their security: rounding or learning with error (LWE) and NTRU. Implementation performance is higher with lattice-based techniques. NIST considers them the most potential standards-related issues since they can be rapidly converted to multiple uses. Most SCA and FIA research has concentrated on lattice-based schemes because they are easy to implement on varied platforms, especially embedded devices [19-20]. Safe and effective lattice-based scheme defences against SCA/FIA have improved with attack identification [21-22]. Due to much theoretical and practical study, lattice-based cryptography is now a feasible post-quantum alternative to PKC.

3.3 Code-based Cryptography

These Key Exchange Mechanisms (KEMs) are based on difficult error-correcting coding problems. The 1979 linear Goppa code-based McEliece cryptosystem underpins the Classic McEliece (finalist) encryption method [23]. This 40-year-old cryptosystem has resisted classical and quantum cryptanalysis. Their long runtimes and hundreds-of-kilobyte public keys make them unsuitable for general-purpose applications. HQC and BIKE are two more code-based KEMs being examined for the final round. These KEMs are built using better QC-MDPC codes. Others offer balanced performance, while lattice-based KEMs have larger public keys and faster speeds. Code-based key encapsulation techniques (KEMs) have been extensively examined, although they are still conservative, especially where bandwidth and speed are not crucial. Code-based methods have been targeted by several side channel attacks [24-25], while SCA/FIA-secure versions have gotten less attention.

3.4 Hash-based Cryptography

A substantial number of signature systems, including hash functions and other symmetric key primitives, fall under this group [26]. So, well-established principles of private key cryptography back up their security claims. An alternate finalist signature method known as SPHINCS+ uses hash functions. On the downside, it has slow signing speeds and signatures that are too large. The signatures that Picnic is vying for also employ hash functions and block cyphers to ensure security. The slower signing and verification periods are a major drawback of structured lattice-based approaches, even though their public keys and signatures are of identical size. For highly secure environments, hash-based signatures are a solid choice because of the strong security guarantees they provide. Some embedded devices that use hash-based signatures have been subject to side-channel attacks [29] and fault injection attacks [27-28]. However, there has been surprisingly little focus on developing secure implementations of hash-based signature systems.

3.5 Multivariate Quadratic-based Cryptography

The theory behind the security of these signature methods is that solving multivariate quadratic (MQ) equations over a finite field is very difficult. There are three finalists in total: Rainbow, GeMSS, and an alternate. Signing times are long with a MQ-based scheme, but signatures are small compared to those with a lattice-based scheme, and the public key is two orders of magnitude larger. This year's attack on the Rainbow signature scheme demonstrates that cryptanalysis's poor performance is the biggest drawback of MQ-based techniques [30]. As long as the PQC community maintains a close watch on the field of crypto analysis of MQ-based schemes, the PQC specification will remain vulnerable to attacks.

3.6 Super Singular Isogeny-based Cryptography

These KEMs are trustworthy because super singular isogenies on elliptic curves are computationally difficult. Only SIKE stands out among these contenders as a KEM (alternative). The fact that it produces the shortest public key and ciphertext sizes among all PQC based KEMs is its main selling point, which makes it an excellent option for applications that have limited bandwidth. An important issue is that the runtimes are significantly slower compared to lattice-based KEMs, which is a tragic reality. While SIKE is susceptible to side channel attacks due to its resemblance to classical ECC-based encryption, solutions that mirror ECC's practical applications have been suggested[31-32]. Though additional studies on side channel and fault-injection analysis would be highly appreciated.

4. QUANTUM-ENABLED SECURITY: QUANTUM KEY DISTRIBUTION

Quantum key distribution (QKD) is an additional key-exchange approach that employs core quantum physics concepts [33]. Since it offers Information Theoretic Security (ITS), QKD is completely protected from an attacker with unlimited computational power. In stark contrast, traditional cryptographic techniques can only guarantee security under certain conditions, such as when an attacker has access to finite and well-defined computational resources. So, when up against a quantum opponent, QKD is a suitable alternative to conventional key exchange protocols. Keep in mind that a quantum computer is not required to set up a QKD system.

4.1 QKD's Fundamental Function

Quantum key distribution (QKD) security relies on the notion that nothing can be known about a quantum state without affecting it. The compromised bits can be removed after establishing the amount of communication channel eavesdropping. This lets any two entities send plaintext data across a quantum channel. Simple QKD connections are shown in Fig. 30.1.

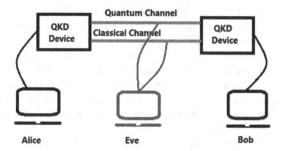

Fig. 30.1 Block diagram of quantum key distribution

Source: Author

Alice and Bob communicate via quantum and normal channels. Alice encodes a secret key into non-orthogonal light states to communicate with Bob via quantum channel. After receiving quantum states, Bob sends Alice measurements and a bitstream over the classical channel. No severe eavesdropping has been noticed if Alice's correlation reaches a threshold. Interconnected bit strings can produce a secret key. If not, restart until you can share a key. Figure 30.1 shows its ability to confirm an eavesdropper (Eve) or man-in-the-middle using computed correlation over communicated data. Thus, a QKD-based key exchange has two phases: the quantum phase, when the message is sent across the classical channel, and the classical phase, when the keys are reconciled. QKD needs a traditional channel since man-in-the-middle attacks are easier with an unauthenticated channel. QKD's authentication requires public-key or classical private-key cryptography.

4.2 Implementation Aspects of QKD

Both QKD system classification methods involve quantum communication channels and encoding. Encoding and decoding are fundamental. Encoding/decoding separates CVQKD, a continuous variable, from DVQKD, a discrete variable. While restricted in application, DVQKD quietly stores photon polarization [33]. CVQKD encrypts data across continuous variables in photon states [34] and is popular because telecom parts can be used. The key rate at a given distance is limited in DVQKD/CVQKD systems [35]. The technology to install quantum repeaters to overcome this constraint is lacking. The recently launched Twin-Field (TF) QKD technology avoids the key rate constraint [36].

Dark counts and photon losses affect the key rate at great distances, even if TFQKD works at 500 km. QKD may be deployed far thanks to TFQKD's range extension [37]. 2) Free space and optical fibre are QKD communication media. Despite their strength and straightness, optical fibre routes are not flexible or portable and are limited by propagation losses. Free-space communication is third. QKD also has signal transmission concerns in Earth's free space. However, satellite transmission of QKD to empty space could make it work anyplace. A recent 1Kbps key rate test demonstrated free-space satellite-based QKD over 1200 km [38]. More study is needed to prove longer lengths are possible. Currently, fiber-based QKD systems can only maintain speed over 100–150 km.

4.3 Usage of QKD for Secure Communication

Modern digital networks use two QKD methods to protect communication. QKD Keys and OTP make message encryption easy. The combination procedure is secure because QKD and OTP are always safe. This strategy fails because keys are hard to track and QKD slows transmission. It's not something you'd use daily, but it's a good option for government and trade secrets. 2) AES and HMAC can be used with QKD keys for more realistic authentication and encryption. This solution relies on the computational safety of the symmetric cryptography scheme. It supports old and modern internet security standards. Dedicated QKD lines provide safe keys, and upgrading them is as easy as instantiating QKD. This method guarantees forward secrecy, so retrieving one key won't undermine the security of other shared keys or future ones.

4.4 Side Channel Attacks on Quantum Key Distribution

The article discusses different types of side-channel attacks that can be used to target Quantum Key Distribution (QKD) technology [39]. The attacks can be specific to quantum mechanics or more general. The article emphasizes the need to protect QKD from both quantum and non-quantum level attacks. The article suggests using tried-and-true methods from SCA to secure QKD as well as developing cryptographic algorithms that are inherently immune to side-channel attacks[40]. Finally, the article explains that measuring device independent quantum key distribution (MDI-QKD) technology could offer a strong defense against QKD attacks, but its practical demonstration is unproven in the real world.

5. CONCLUSION

There has been a huge disruption in the field of security due to the quick development of large-scale quantum computers. We examined these impacts in this article. We started by outlining where quantum computing is at the moment, and then we estimated how big they would need to be in order to crack all of today's cryptosystems. Secondly, in order to counter the danger posed by an attacker with quantum capabilities, we provide a synopsis of two prominent research directions: post-quantum cryptography and quantum key distribution. A quick overview of additional quantum primitives, including quantum PUF and quantum random number generators, was included as a last section of the paper.

■ REFERENCES ■

1. Mark W Johnson, Mohammad HS Amin, Suzanne Gildert, TrevorLanting, FirasHamze, Neil Dickson, R Harris, Andrew J Berkley, JanJohansson, Paul Bunyk, et al. Quantum annealing with manufacturedspins. Nature, 473(7346):194, 2011.

2. IBM. Ibm announces advances to ibm quantum systems and ecosystem.https://www-03.ibm.com/ press/ us/en/ pressrelease/ 53374.wss.

3. IBM. Ibm quantum breaks the 100-qubit processor barrier. https://research.ibm.com/ blog/ 127-qubit-quantum-processor-eagle.

4. Google. A preview of bristlecone, google's newquantum processor. https:// ai.googleblog.com/ 2018/ 03/a-preview-of-bristlecone-googles-new.html.

5. Frank et al Arute. Quantum supremacy using a programmable superconducting processor. Nature, 574(7779):505–510, 2019.

6. Austin G. Fowler, Matteo Mariantoni, John M. Martinis, and Andrew N.Cleland. Surface codes: Towards practical large-scale quantum computation. Phys. Rev. A, 86:032324, Sep 2012.

7. Peter W Shor. Algorithms for quantum computation: Discrete logarithmsand factoring. In Foundations of Computer Science, 1994 Proceedings.35th Annual Symposium on, pages 124–134. IEEE, 1994.

8. John Proos and ChristofZalka. Shor's discrete logarithm quantumalgorithm for elliptic curves. arXiv preprint quant-ph/0301141, 2003.

9. Thomas Haner, Samuel Jaques, Michael Naehrig, Martin Roetteler,and Mathias Soeken. Improved quantum circuits for elliptic curvediscrete logarithms. In Jintai Ding and Jean-Pierre Tillich, editors,Post-Quantum Cryptography, pages 425–444, Cham, 2020. SpringerInternational Publishing.

10. Craig Gidney and Martin Ekera. How to factor 2048 bit RSA integers °in 8 hours using 20 million noisy qubits. Quantum, 5:433, April 2021.

11. Andre Chailloux, Maria Naya-Plasencia, and Andre Schrottenloher.An efficient quantum collision search algorithm and implications onsymmetric cryptography. Cryptology ePrint Archive, Paper 2017/847,2017. https:// eprint.iacr.org/2017/847.

12. Kyungbae Jang, AnubhabBaksi, Gyeongju Song, Hyunji Kim, HwajeongSeo, and AnupamChattopadhyay. Quantum analysis of AES.IACR Cryptol. ePrint Arch., page 683, 2022.

13. Zhenyu Huang and Siwei Sun. Synthesizing quantum circuits of AESwith lower t-depth and less qubits. IACR Cryptol. ePrint Arch., page620, 2022.

14. Kyungbae Jang, AnubhabBaksi, JakubBreier, HwajeongSeo, andAnupamChattopadhyay. Quantum implementation and analysis ofdefault. Cryptology ePrint Archive, Paper 2022/647, 2022. https://eprint.iacr.org/2022/647.

15. NIST. Post-quantum crypto project.http://csrc.nist.gov/ groups/ST/post-quantum-crypto/, 2016.

16. Dustin Moody, GorjanAlagic, Daniel Apon, David Cooper, QuynhDang, John Kelsey, Yi-Kai Liu, Carl Miller, Rene Peralta, Ray Perlner, Angela Robinson, Daniel Smith-Tone, and Jacob Alperin-Sheriff. Statusreport on the second round of the nist post-quantum cryptographystandardization process, 2020-07-22 2020.

17. The transport layer security (tls) protocol version 1.3 (may 2016). https://tools.ietf.org/html/draft-ietf-tls-tls13-13, 2016.

18. NIST. Post-Quantum Crypto Project - Round 3 Submissions. https://csrc.nist.gov/Projects/post-quantum-cryptography/round-3-submissions/,2021.

19. Prasanna Ravi, AnupamChattopadhyay, and AnubhabBaksi. Sidechannel and fault-injection attacks over lattice-based post-quantumschemes (kyber, dilithium): Survey and new results. Cryptology ePrintArchive, 2022.

20. Prasanna Ravi, Sujoy Sinha Roy, AnupamChattopadhyay, and ShivamBhasin. Generic side-channel attacks on cca-secure lattice-based pke andkems. IACR Transactions on Cryptographic Hardware and EmbeddedSystems, pages 307–335, 2020.

21. Prasanna Ravi, RomainPoussier, ShivamBhasin, and AnupamChattopadhyay. On configurable sca countermeasures against single traceattacks for the ntt. In International Conference on Security, Privacy, and Applied Cryptography Engineering, pages 123–146. Springer, 2020.

22. Joppe W Bos, Marc Gourjon, JoostRenes, Tobias Schneider, and Christine van Vredendaal. Masking kyber: First-and higher-orderimplementations. IACR Transactions on Cryptographic Hardware andEmbedded Systems, pages 173–214, 2021.

23. Robert J McEliece. A public-key cryptosystem based on algebraic.Coding Thv, 4244:114–116, 1978.

24. Brice Colombier, Vlad-Florin Dragoi, Pierre-Louis Cayrel, and VincentGrosso. Message-recovery profiled side-channel attack on the classicmceliece cryptosystem. Cryptology ePrint Archive, Paper 2022/125, 2022. https:// eprint.iacr.org/2022/125.

25. QianGuo, Andreas Johansson, and Thomas Johansson. A key-recoveryside-channel attack on classic mceliece, Cryptology ePrint Archive,Paper 2022/514, 2022.https:// eprint.iacr.org/2022/514.

26. Whitfield Diffie and Martin Hellman. New directions in cryptography. IEEE transactions on Information Theory, 22(6):644–654, 1976.

27. Dorian Amiet, Lukas Leuenberger, Andreas Curiger, and Paul Zbinden.Fpga-based sphincs+ implementations: Mind the glitch. In 2020 23rdEuromicro Conference on Digital System Design (DSD), pages 229–237. IEEE, 2020.

28. Laurent Castelnovi, AngeMartinelli, and Thomas Prest. Grafting trees: afault attack against the sphincs framework. In International Conferenceon Post-Quantum Cryptography, pages 165–184. Springer, 2018.

29. Matthias J Kannwischer, Aymeric Genet, Denis Butin, JulianeKr ˆ amer, ¨and Johannes Buchmann. Differential power analysis of xmss andsphincs. In International Workshop on Constructive Side-ChannelAnalysis and Secure Design, pages 168–188. Springer, 2018.

30. Ward Beullens. Breaking rainbow takes a weekend on a laptop. Cryptology ePrint Archive, Paper 2022/214, 2022. https://eprint.iacr.org/2022/214.

31. Brian Koziel, Reza Azarderakhsh, and David Jao. Side-channel attackson quantum-resistant supersingular isogeny diffie-hellman. In International Conference on Selected Areas in Cryptography, pages 64–81.Springer, 2017.

32. Aymeric Genet, NatachaLinard de Guertechin, and Novak Kalu ˆ derovic.´Full key recovery side-channel attack against ephemeral sike on thecortex-m4. In International Workshop on Constructive Side-ChannelAnalysis and Secure Design, pages 228–254. Springer, 2021.

33. Charles H Bennett and Gilles Brassard. Quantumcryptography: Publickey distribution and coin tossing. arXiv preprint arXiv:2003.06557,2020.

34. Christian Weedbrook, Stefano Pirandola, Raul Garcıa-Patron, Nicolas J ´Cerf, Timothy C Ralph, Jeffrey H Shapiro, and Seth Lloyd. Gaussianquantum information. Reviews of Modern Physics, 84(2):621, 2012.

35. Stefano Pirandola, Riccardo Laurenza, Carlo Ottaviani, and LeonardoBanchi. Fundamental limits of repeaterless quantum communications. Nature communications, 8(1): 1–15, 2017.

36. Marco Lucamarini, Zhiliang L Yuan, James F Dynes, and Andrew JShields. Overcoming the rate–distance limit of quantum key distributionwithout quantum repeaters. Nature, 557(7705):400–403, 2018.

37. Jiu-Peng Chen, Chi Zhang, Yang Liu, Cong Jiang, Weijun Zhang, XiaoLong Hu, Jian-Yu Guan, Zong-Wen Yu, HaiXu, Jin Lin, et al. Sendingor-not-sending with independent lasers: Secure twin-field quantum keydistribution over 509 km. Physical review letters, 124(7):070501, 2020.

38. Sheng-Kai Liao, Wen-Qi Cai, Wei-Yue Liu, Liang Zhang, Yang Li, JiGangRen, Juan Yin, Qi Shen, Yuan Cao, Zheng-Ping Li, et al. Satelliteto-ground quantum key distribution. Nature, 549(7670):43–47, 2017.

39. Vadim Makarov. Controlling passively quenched single photon detectorsby bright light. New Journal of Physics, 11(6):065003, 2009.

40. ArtemVakhitov, Vadim Makarov, and Dag R Hjelme. Large pulseattack as a method of conventional optical eavesdropping in quantumcryptography. Journal of modern optics, 48(13):2023–2038, 2001.

Challenges and Opportunities for Innovation in India – Dr. Shweta Mishra et al. (eds)
© 2024 Taylor & Francis Group, London, ISBN 978-1-032-99842-8

Multiscale Neural Network Approach—A Study

31

Brijesh Kumar Bhardwaj[1]

Associate Professor,
Dept of MCA, University Ayodhya, U.P.

Kavita Srivastava[2]

Associate Professor,
Dept of CSE, IET, Dr. RML Avadh KNIPSS,
Sultanpur, U.P.

Abstract

Purpose: A neuron's reaction to a sequence of stimuli emerges from intricate interactions involving enzymes, and ions and electrical channels. Late advances in learning have had a methodological and viable effect on cerebrum PC interface research. Among the different profound network structures, convolutional neural networks have been appropriate for spatio-spectral-temporal electroencephalogram signal portrayal learning. **Methodology:** This paper presents the methodology of building modules emulating a neural network loop. Emulated activities are qualitatively similar to diseases data set. **Try-outs:** We present a Multiscale Convolutional Neural Network approach for vision–based grouping of cells. In view of a Neural Networks acting at various goals, the proposed engineering maintains a strategic distance from the old-style handmade highlight's extraction venture, by handling highlights extraction and arrangement in totality.

Keywords

Neuron, Network, Model, Simulation

1. INTRODUCTION

Despite extensive exploration efforts spanning many years, investigating the brain at the atomic, system levels, cellular, and circuit, the operational of the human brain, largely remain elusive. Furthermore, effective treatments for prevalent severe mental disorders and dementia are still insufficient [1]. Different methodologies have been utilized to investigate how various kinds of tangible information and conduct are spoken to in the brain. In these undertakings the measurable relationship between's recorded neural movement, commonly activity possibilities from single neurons, and tangible incitement or conduct of the creature is registered [2]. From this, supposed engaging numerical

[1]wwbkb2012@gmail.com, [2]wwwksknipss@gmail.com

models have been inferred, representing, state, Recognizing that network nodes in actual individuals are far from homogeneous, the virtual brain catches the working of the sub-networks of the human brain through the novel idea of the space-time structure of the network couplings including implies for quantifiable coupling lattices inside and across areas [3]. In spite of the fact that product front-finishes can shroud the usage multifaceted nature of the hidden neuron models utilized in their network, the most widely recognized model improvement cycle in computational neuroscience research actually includes direct turn of events and simulation on a particular test system, yet not over front-ends.

1.1 Condensed Contribution

We verified the effectiveness of the proposed scheme through extensive experiments, which had been quite an increase.

- We achieved state-of-the-art results on the specific challenges.

2. NEURAL SYSTEM

The network engineering of the human brain has become a component of expanding interest to the neuro-academic network, to a great extent as a result of its capability to enlighten human insight, its variety over turn of events and maturing, and its adjustment in infection or injury. Conventional instruments and ways to deal with study this engineering have generally centered around sizes of topology, time, and space. A brain tumor is an unsafe and problematic illness on the grounds that the influenced cells can without much of a stretch split and spread to different districts [4]. Subsequently, it must be recognized as right on time as conceivable to dodge further outcomes. A little arrangement of adjoining handling component structure a layer. Most counterfeit neural networks mandatorily comprise of an info and yield layer, alongside some valuable layers called shrouded layers. The neural interconnection is prepared to acquire the ideal yield by playing out a specific capacity [5]. The estimate of the associations between the elements(weights) can be modified to cause the network to play out the ideal capacity. The interconnection of neurons prompts the arrangement of numerous pathways to arrive at the ideal yield and thus the associations decide the working and usefulness of the network.A multilayer network comprises of a few particular traditional networks, every one encoding a particular sort of data about the framework [6]. Review the issue of gaining according to mathematical perspective capacities performed by neural hubs should empower decoration of the info space in the most adaptable manner utilizing few versatile boundaries of parametric infections.

2.1 Experiments

In Fig. 31.1, imitate an artificial neural network, though drawing inspiration from biological neural systems, employs A simplified set of principles drawn from natural frameworks is employed in artificial neural networks. More specifically, these neural models imitate the electrical processes occurring in the brain and nervous system. Processing units, known as neurodes or perceptrons, form interconnections with other processing units. Typically organized in a layer or vector, neurodes in one layer produce output that functions as input for the subsequent layer, potentially extending to other layers. A neurode in a given layer may establish connections with all or a subset of the neurodes in the following layer, replicating the synaptic associations observed in the brain. Illustrated in Fig. 31.2, the weighted input signals entering a neurode mimic the electrical excitation of a nerve cell, thereby emulating the information exchange within the network or brain.

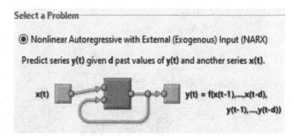

Fig. 31.1 Network structure

A multilayer network comprises of a few unmistakable old-style networks, every one encoding a particular kind of data about the framework. In the accompanying, we will quickly talk about various sorts of multilayer brain networks where layers' availability, estimated as for a particular meaning of closeness [7]. Move work (Fig. 31.4) originates from the name change and is utilized for change purposes for example, from input hubs to the yield of a neuron. This capacity maps the contribution to an incentive somewhere in the range of 0 and 1 (yet not equivalent to 0 or 1). This implies the yield from the hub will be a high sign (if the info is positive) or a low one (if the information is negative). This capacity is frequently picked as it is one of the least demanding to hard-code as far as subordinate. The simplicity of its derivative permits us to effectively perform back proliferation without utilizing any extravagant bundles or approximations. The way that this capacity is smooth, ceaseless (differentiable), monotonic and limited implies that back engendering will function admirably. These examinations give proof and backing to the theory that useful layers don't go about as free substances, recommending the presence of components for incorporation and isolation of brain action inside and

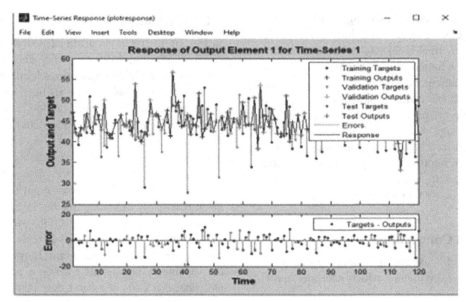

Fig. 31.2 Target behaviour

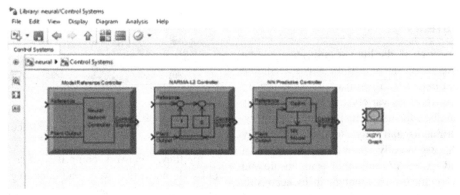

Fig. 31.3 Control system

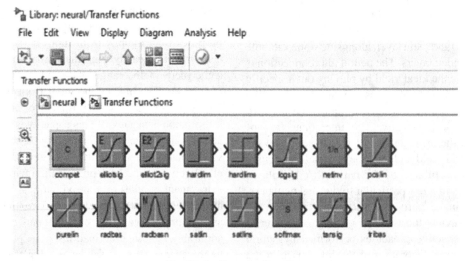

Fig. 31.4 Transfer function

across various bands of frequency. The enactment work decides the complete signal a neuron gets.

3. Conclusion

We have introduced a review of various exchange capacities utilized in multiscale neural network models and have also proposed a few new mixes of initiation and yield capacities reasonable for this reason. During the time spent neural networks preparing adaptable transfer functions are as significant as great designs and learning systems. Most number of network boundaries ought to take into account great adaptability. These functions utilize blended initiation to bring together the separation based, limited worldview with enactment works that are quadratic in inputs, and the non-neighbourhood approximations dependent on discriminant capacities that utilization just straight actuations. Reasonable examination of transfer functions would be extremely troublesome, if certainly feasible, on the grounds that outcomes rely upon the techniques, learning calculations, introduction, models and datasets utilized. Many transfer functions might be attempted with a solitary neural model, keeping all different elements consistent, hence in any event incomplete experimental correlation of the viability of transfer function should be conceivable.

■ REFERENCES ■

1. Minor DL Jr (2007) The neurobiologist's guide to structural biology: a primer on why macromolecular structure matters and how to evaluate structural data. Neuron 54(4):511–533.
2. Klassen T (2015) Epilepsy: abnormal ion channels. In: Jaeger D, Jung R (eds) Encyclopedia of computational neuroscience. Springer, New York, pp 1119–1121.
3. Park HJ, Friston K. Structural and functional brain networks: from connections to cognition. Science2013; 342(6158):1238411.
4. ZuoXN , Ehmke R, MennesMet al. . Network centrality in the human functional connectome. Cereb Cortex2012; 22(8):1862–75.
5. Van Den , Heuvel MP, Pol HEH. Exploring the brain network: a review on resting-state fmri functional connectivity. Eur Neuropsychopharmacol2010; 20(8): 519–34.
6. Ben Haim L., Rowitch D. H. (2017). Functional diversity of astrocytes in neural circuit regulation. *Nat. Rev. Neurosci.* 18 31–41.
7. Casali S., Marenzi E., Medini C., Casellato C., D'Angelo E. (2019). Reconstruction and simulation of a scaffold model of the cerebellar network. *Front. Neuroinform.*
8. Schwalger, T., Deger, M., and Gerstner, W. (2017). Towards a theory of cortical columns: From spiking neurons to interacting neural populations of finite size. PLoS Comput. Biol. 13, e1005507.

Note: All the figures in this chapter were made by the author.

Challenges and Opportunities for Innovation in India – Dr. Shweta Mishra et al. (eds)
© 2024 Taylor & Francis Group, London, ISBN 978-1-032-99842-8

Quantum-Resilient TLS 1.3: Challenges, Solutions, and Future Directions

32

Alok Mishra[1],
Jitendra Kurmi[2], Vipin Rawat[3]
Department of Computer Science and Engineering,
Ambalika Institute of Management and Technology,
Lucknow, India

Abstract

This paper discusses the significance of integrating post-quantum security measures in TLS 1.3 cryptographic protocol, emphasizing its role in ensuring long-term security against quantum attacks. It highlights the importance of collaboration between researchers, industry stakeholders, and standardization bodies for widespread acceptance and interoperability. The cryptographic algorithms used in TLS 1.3, including AES-GCM, ChaCha20-Poly1305, and secure key exchange algorithms, are discussed for ensuring confidentiality and integrity. Post-quantum security threats to TLS 1.3 are analyzed, and proposed solutions encompass hybrid encryption schemes, development of new post-quantum cryptographic algorithms, and quantum-resistant key exchange protocols. The paper concludes by underscoring the necessity of a comprehensive approach to post-quantum security in TLS 1.3 and cryptographic systems, emphasizing continuous research, collaboration, and adaptation to address evolving cybersecurity threats.

Keywords

TLS 1.3, Post-quantum security, Quantum-resistant cryptography, Standardization, Cybersecurity

1. INTRODUCTION

TLS 1.3 is the latest version of the cryptographic protocol that ensures secure communication over the internet. It provides enhanced security measures, improved performance, and stronger encryption algorithms compared to its predecessor, TLS 1.2 [1]. TLS 1.3 offers protection against attacks like eavesdropping, tampering, and man-in-the-middle attacks, ensuring that data transmitted over the internet remains confidential and intact. Moreover, TLS 1.3 introduces a feature called "forward secrecy," which enhances security by generating a unique session key for each session [2]. By incorporating forward secrecy, TLS 1.3 ensures that even if a long-term private key is compromised, past communications remain secure. TLS 1.3 also introduces a streamlined handshake process, reducing the time it takes to establish a secure connection. Additionally, TLS 1.3 incorporates stricter certificate validation, ensuring that only trusted and valid certificates are accepted, preventing potential man-in-the-

[1]meet.alokmishra17@gmail.com, [2]jitendrakurmi458@gmail.com, [3]vipinrawat6668@gmail.com

DOI: 10.1201/9781003606260-32

middle attacks. Overall, the adoption of TLS 1.3 is crucial in safeguarding sensitive information and maintaining the integrity of online communication.

1.1 Definition and Explanation of Post-Quantum Security

The concept of post-quantum security, which refers to cryptographic algorithms and protocols that are resistant to attacks from quantum computers. TLS 1.3 incorporates post-quantum secure algorithms and key exchange methods, ensuring that even if an adversary possesses a quantum computer, they would not be able to decrypt the encrypted data exchanged between a client and server. TLS 1.3 proves its commitment to staying ahead of evolving threats in the digital landscape and sets a new standard for secure communication in the age of quantum computing.

1.2 Importance of Addressing Post-Quantum Security in TLS 1.3

TLS 1.3 needs to integrate post-quantum security measures to protect sensitive information from the evolving threats posed by quantum computing. Traditional encryption methods are at risk of being broken, and by prioritizing quantum-resistant key exchange methods, TLS 1.3 can maintain its relevance and effectiveness. Incorporating quantum-resistant algorithms will help future-proof TLS 1.3 and enable it to adapt to the evolving landscape of cybersecurity threats shown in Fig. 32.1.

Organizations can safeguard their sensitive data and communications from potential quantum attacks by embracing post-quantum security measures, which also demonstrate a commitment to staying at the forefront of technological advancements and prioritizing the protection of user privacy [3].

1.3 Explanation of the Key Features and Improvements of TLS 1.3

TLS 1.3 is the latest version of the Transport Layer Security protocol that enhances the security and efficiency of online communications. It reduces the number of round trips required for a TLS handshake and removes support for outdated cryptographic algorithms while introducing stronger encryption algorithms. TLS 1.3 prevents downgrade attacks, enhances forward secrecy, and introduces zero round trip time resumption to save time and improve performance. It also incorporates encrypted SNI to prevent eavesdroppers from seeing the hostname of the server. TLS 1.3 provides better protection against potential vulnerabilities, making it an indispensable upgrade for anyone concerned about the confidentiality and integrity of their online communications [4].

1.4 Discussion on the Cryptographic Algorithms used in TLS 1.3

TLS 1.3 incorporates advanced encryption algorithms such as AES-GCM and ChaCha20-Poly1305 to ensure the confidentiality and integrity of data transmitted over the network. It also introduces secure key exchange algorithms like Diffie-Hellman and Elliptic Curve Diffie-Hellman (ECDHE) and perfect forward secrecy to prevent attackers from intercepting and deciphering encrypted data. TLS 1.3 improves the speed and efficiency of online communications while prioritizing security. Overall, TLS 1.3 sets a new standard for secure and private online communications,

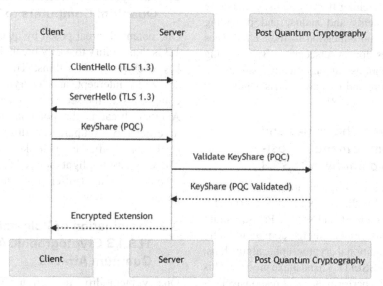

Fig. 32.1 TLS 1.3 with post quantum cryptography

Source: Author

giving users peace of mind when interacting with websites and applications [5-6].

2. POST-QUANTUM CRYPTOGRAPHY

2.1 Introduction to Post-Quantum Cryptography and its Motivation

Post-quantum cryptography refers to cryptographic algorithms that are resistant to attacks from quantum computers and aims to provide long-term security against quantum threats. The development of post-quantum cryptographic algorithms is crucial for safeguarding sensitive information and preserving the integrity of digital communication in the face of advancing technology. Implementing post-quantum cryptographic algorithms involves transitioning from current encryption methods to new ones that can withstand the power of quantum computers. This transition requires careful planning and coordination, as organizations need to ensure compatibility with existing systems and minimize disruption to operations [7].

2.2 Explanation of Different Post-Quantum Cryptographic Algorithms

The section, discusses the importance of post-quantum cryptographic algorithms in the era of advancing quantum technology. Organizations need to carefully evaluate which algorithm is best suited for their specific needs based on factors such as its resistance to quantum attacks, computational efficiency, and compatibility with existing systems. In addition, organizations need to assess the algorithm's level of security and its ability to withstand potential vulnerabilities. They should consider implementing a multi-layered approach to enhance their security posture, regularly updating and patching their systems, conducting regular security assessments and audits, and providing comprehensive training and education to their employees regarding best practices for cybersecurity. By adopting these measures, organizations can significantly strengthen their cybersecurity posture and mitigate the risks posed by advancing quantum technology [8].

2.3 Discussion on the Challenges and Limitations of Implementing Post-Quantum Cryptography in TLS 1.3

One of the main challenges in implementing post-quantum cryptography in TLS 1.3 is the computational overhead it may impose on both the client and server. Post-quantum algorithms are typically much more computationally intensive compared to traditional cryptographic algorithms, which can slow down the SSL/TLS handshake process. This can potentially impact the performance and responsiveness of secure communications, especially in high-traffic environments. Therefore, extensive research, testing, and collaboration within the cybersecurity community are necessary to address these challenges and ensure the smooth integration of post-quantum cryptography into TLS 1.3. Furthermore, the large key sizes required for post-quantum algorithms can also increase the computational load on servers and devices, leading to longer processing times. This could result in increased latency and reduced throughput for secure connections. In addition, the transition to post-quantum cryptography may require significant updates and modifications to existing systems and infrastructure, further adding to the complexity and potential disruptions during integration. Overall, while the development of post-quantum cryptography is crucial for ensuring the long-term security of encrypted communications, its deployment in TLS 1.3 poses various challenges that need to be carefully addressed and managed [9].

3. POST-QUANTUM SECURITY THREATS TO TLS 1.3

TLS 1.3 faces post-quantum security threats due to the vulnerability of current cryptographic algorithms to quantum attacks. The integration of new quantum-resistant cryptographic algorithms into TLS 1.3 requires careful planning and coordination to ensure compatibility with existing systems and infrastructure. The increased computational requirements of post-quantum cryptographic algorithms pose a challenge in terms of performance. The adoption of post-quantum cryptography in TLS 1.3 is essential for protecting encrypted communications against future quantum threats [10].

3.1 Analysis of Potential Threats Posed by Quantum Computers to TLS 1.3

One potential threat posed by quantum computers to TLS 1.3 is their ability to easily break the currently used public key encryption algorithms. This could allow malicious actors to intercept and decrypt sensitive information, compromising the security of encrypted communications. Another threat is the potential for quantum computers to efficiently compute the discrete logarithm problem, rendering Diffie-Hellman key exchanges vulnerable. These threats highlight the need for adopting post-quantum cryptography, as it offers algorithms that are resistant to attacks by quantum computers.

3.2 Examination of Vulnerabilities in Current TLS 1.3 Cryptographic Algorithms against Quantum Attacks

One vulnerability in current TLS 1.3 cryptographic algorithms against quantum attacks is the susceptibility of

RSA encryption. RSA relies on the difficulty of factoring large prime numbers, which can be easily broken by a powerful enough quantum computer. Another vulnerability lies in the elliptic curve cryptography (ECC) used in TLS 1.3. ECC is also vulnerable to attacks by quantum computers due to its reliance on the same discrete logarithm problem as Diffie-Hellman. Therefore, it is crucial to explore and implement post-quantum cryptographic algorithms to ensure the security of encrypted communications in the face of quantum threats.

3.3 Discussion on the Consequences of a Successful Quantum Attack on TLS 1.3

If a quantum attack were successful against TLS 1.3, it would render the encrypted communications vulnerable to eavesdropping, data tampering, and identity impersonation. This could have far-reaching consequences, as TLS 1.3 is widely used to secure sensitive data in various applications, including online banking, e-commerce, and secure communication platforms. The breach of TLS 1.3's security would undermine trust in online transactions and communication, potentially leading to financial losses, privacy breaches, and damage to businesses and individuals alike. Implementing post-quantum cryptographic algorithms is imperative to safeguard against such threats and maintain the integrity of encrypted communications in a quantum era.

4. Proposed Solutions for Post-Quantum Security in TLS 1.3

The solution discusses various approaches for integrating post-quantum security into TLS 1.3, which include using hybrid encryption schemes, developing new post-quantum cryptographic algorithms, and using quantum-resistant key exchange protocols. It also highlights the importance of ongoing research in quantum-resistant cryptography to ensure the confidentiality and integrity of communications in the face of future quantum threats. Finally, the text suggests that lattice-based cryptography and code-based cryptography hold great promise for providing long-term security for TLS 1.3.

1. *The advantages and disadvantages of using lattice-based cryptography in TLS 1.3:* Explore the specific security guarantees offered by lattice-based cryptography and discuss its potential drawbacks, such as computational overhead or key size limitations.

2. *The mathematical foundation of code-based cryptography:* Explain how error-correcting codes are utilised in code-based cryptography to create cryptographic schemes that are resistant against attacks from both classical and quantum computers.

3. *Comparing the performance of different post-quantum cryptographic protocols for TLS 1.3:*

Analyze various post-quantum cryptographic protocols, including lattice-based and code-based approaches, to evaluate their efficiency in terms of speed, memory usage, or bandwidth requirements when implemented in TLS 1.3.

4. *Challenges and open research questions related to implementing these new cryptographic solutions into TLS 1.3:* The adoption of lattice-based or code-based cryptography in TLS 1.3 introduces potential performance overhead due to computational complexity. Standardization and interoperability among TLS implementations is lacking, and transitioning to new algorithms requires careful planning and evaluation of post-quantum security. Developers and administrators require adequate training and awareness to implement these new cryptographic approaches, and resource constraints may necessitate specialized hardware or software support for optimal performance. The challenges of implementing post-quantum security measures in TLS 1.3 and similar cryptographic systems need to be addressed for successful and secure integration.

5. *The role of standardisation bodies like NIST in guiding the adoption of post-quantum secure algorithms for TLS 1.3:* Standardization bodies like NIST play a crucial role in ensuring the successful integration of new post-quantum secure algorithms into existing protocols such as TLS 1.3. Collaboration between researchers and industry stakeholders is imperative to address challenges like algorithm standardization and compatibility. NIST offers a structured process for evaluating and selecting post-quantum cryptographic algorithms, ensuring that the chosen solutions meet the stringent security requirements for the long term. This collaboration not only fosters trust in the security community but also streamlines the adoption process, minimizing fragmentation and facilitating a smoother transition to new cryptographic standards. Ultimately, this collaborative approach ensures that post-quantum secure algorithms integrated into protocols like TLS 1.3 are not only robust but also enjoy widespread acceptance and seamless interoperability across diverse technology ecosystems.

5. Implementation Challenges and Considerations

5.1 Analysis of the Challenges and Complexities in Implementing Post-Quantum Security in TLS 1.3

In order to successfully implement post-quantum security in TLS 1.3, various challenges and considerations need to be thoroughly analyzed. This includes evaluating potential post-quantum cryptographic algorithms and examining their performance and compatibility implications within the existing protocols. Additionally, stakeholders must also address the challenges and complexities that arise during the implementation process to ensure a seamless integration of post-quantum security measures in TLS 1.3.

5.2 Discussion on the Potential Impact on TLS 1.3's Performance and Efficiency

In order to assess the feasibility of incorporating post-quantum security. Balancing the level of security provided by the post-quantum algorithms with their potential impact on TLS 1.3's speed and resource consumption is essential to maintain optimal performance. Furthermore, extensive testing and benchmarking of different algorithm combinations and configurations is required to identify the most efficient solutions for real-world applications. Overall, a thorough analysis of performance and efficiency considerations is vital in ensuring that the implementation of post-quantum security in TLS 1.3 does not compromise the protocol's speed and usability.

5.3 Considerations for Backward Compatibility and Interoperability with Existing Systems

It is also critical in the implementation of post-quantum security in TLS 1.3. It is important to ensure that the new cryptographic algorithms and configurations can seamlessly integrate with older versions of TLS and other cryptographic protocols. This will enable smooth transitions and avoid any disruptions in communication between different systems. Therefore, careful consideration and testing of backward compatibility and interoperability are necessary to ensure a successful implementation of post-quantum security in TLS 1.3. Counterargument: However, implementing post-quantum security in TLS 1.3 may introduce compatibility issues and require significant adjustments to existing systems, potentially causing disruptions in communication and hindering widespread adoption.

6. CONCLUSION

The paper discusses the importance of addressing post-quantum security in TLS 1.3 to protect sensitive information and maintain trust in online communication. While there may be potential compatibility issues and disruptions in communication, the successful implementation of post-quantum security can ensure the overall security of the internet. However, the development and implementation

of post-quantum encryption algorithms may not be enough to mitigate the potential risks associated with quantum computing. It is crucial to explore other avenues of post-quantum security such as further research into quantum-resistant cryptographic protocols and the development of new techniques that can withstand attacks from quantum computers. Additionally, continuous monitoring and updating of security measures will be necessary to stay ahead of potential advancements in quantum computing technology. A comprehensive approach that combines multiple layers of defense is needed to ensure the security of TLS 1.3 and other cryptographic systems in the future.

■ REFERENCES ■

1. Kannojia, Suresh Prasad, and JitendraKurmi. "Analysis of Cryptographic Libraries (SSL/TLS)." International Journal of Computer Sciences and Engineering 9, no. 9 (2021): 59–62.
2. Kurmi, Jitendra, and Suresh Prasad Kannojia. "Comparative Study of SSL/TLS Cryptographic Libraries." International Journal of Innovative Research in Science, Engineering and Technology 10, no. 8 (2021): 11658–11662.
3. Xu, Guobin, Jianzhou Mao, Eric Sakk, and Shuangbao Paul Wang. "An Overview of Quantum-Safe Approaches: Quantum Key Distribution and Post-Quantum Cryptography." In 2023 57th Annual Conference on Information Sciences and Systems (CISS), pp. 1–6. IEEE, 2023.
4. Kannojia, Suresh Prasad, and JitendraKurmi. "An Approach for attack resistance nonce misuse Authenticated Encryption Cipher for Multi-Tenant Security." International Journal of Mechanical Engineering 7 (2022): 685–692.
5. Kannojia, Suresh Prasad, and JitendraKurmi. "Performance Analysis of SSL/TLS Crypto Libraries: Based on Operating Platform." Journal of Scientific Research 66, no. 2 (2022).
6. Kannojia, Suresh Prasad, and JitendraKurmi. "A Security Mechanism to Defend TLS Certificate against Vulnerabilities." Advances and Applications in Mathematical Sciences, Volume 21, Issue 6, April 2022, Pages 3553–3562, 2022.
7. Bennett, Charles H., and Gilles Brassard. "Quantum cryptography: Public key distribution and coin tossing." Theoretical computer science 560 (2014): 7–11.
8. Gnatyuk, Sergiy, TetianaOkhrimenko, SergiyDorozhynskyy, and AndriyFesenko. "Review of modern quantum key distribution protocols." SciPract Cyber Secur J 4, no. 1 (2020): 56–60.
9. Kong, Peng-Yong. "A review of quantum key distribution protocols in the perspective of smart grid communication security." IEEE Systems Journal 16, no. 1 (2020): 41–54.
10. Zhang, Qiang, FeihuXu, Yu-Ao Chen, Cheng-ZhiPeng, and Jian-Wei Pan. "Large scale quantum key distribution: challenges and solutions." Optics express 26, no. 18 (2018): 24260–24273.

Challenges and Opportunities for Innovation in India – Dr. Shweta Mishra et al. (eds)
© 2024 Taylor & Francis Group, London, ISBN 978-1-032-99842-8

A Methodological Framework of Containerized Microservices Orchestration and Provisioning in the Cloud: A Case Study of Online Travel Platforms

33

Biman Barua*

Department of CSE,
BGMEA University of Fashion & Technology,
Dhaka, Bangladesh

M. Shamim Kaiser

Institute of Information Technology,
Jahangirnagar University,
Dhaka, Bangladesh

Abstract

Cloud computing and Microservices are new paradigms in the new technological era. Due to functionality and modularity, many existing cloud applications are designed as microservices. This transformation to microservices is facing challenges for infrastructure orchestration. Integrating these combined technologies into the online travel platform is a great initiative and will bring the travel industry in a new direction. On the existing online travel platform, booking flights, hotels, and rental car facilities faces problems during the seasonal period when a large number of users hit the system. Integrating microservices and cloud computing can make the system scalable, flexible, and high-performance in processing requests. The microservices architecture breaks down the large program into smaller modules that can run independently and provide individual results with self-contained services. In microservices, each service is responsible for an individual responsibility, and it is also more suitable to build, deploy, and scale independently. The research utilizes a case study methodology to conceive, build, and implement a microservices architecture for online travel services. Technologies like containerization and orchestration are used in the construction of this architecture. The paper analyzes the efficiency of containerized microservices, and an analytical comparison is shown of the existing monolithic architecture. In addition, the research investigates the scalability, agility, resource usage, fault tolerance, and overall system performance advantages and downsides that are connected with adopting containerization and orchestration for online travel platforms.

Keywords

Kubernetes, Online travel platforms, Microservices architecture, Containerization, Orchestration, Cloud computing

*Corresponding author: biman@buft.edu.bd

DOI: 10.1201/9781003606260-33

1. INTRODUCTION

With the evaluation of internet technology, the travel business has dramatically changed the shape of travel and tourism. These sectors expanded a wide variety of support and services to the customers; those include airline ticket bookings, hotel reservations, car rentals, and vacation package reservations. As the number of customers is increasing rapidly, it has become more important to ensure high-class services, flexibility, scalability, and, moreover, security. To meet customers' expectations, the different vendors are facing challenges in the growing competitive markets. Programmers are facing great challenges in integrating new technologies into their applications as the size of the applications increases. In traditional application development, the existing monolithic applications are tightly coupled, which is very uncomfortable for software developers [1]. The main disadvantages of monolithic applications were extension and upgrade. To upgrade and change any module, you need to recompile the whole program. So, it becomes necessary to change the new technology to microservices. On online travel platforms, it is more important as the system is handled in different regions and countries.Online travel platforms are web-based technologies that provide customers with the capability to book different types of travel and tourism-related services, like hotel reservations and bookings, air ticket bookings, car rentals, tour packages, and vacation package reservations [2]. The advantages of this platform are that users can search for availability, compare pricing, and make reservations online by sitting at a desk. The popularity of online travel platforms has increased in the last few decades due to their flexibility, convenience, and low cost. Customers can book their tickets themselves using an OTA (online travel agent). According to Statista, in 2022, two-thirds of sales in the global market will be generated from online sales. The market size of online travel sales was around 475 billion US dollars, which is planned to reach over one trillion by 2030 [2]. As the travel industry is growing and challenges are also increasing in a current competitive market, it is needed to provide high-performance support with scalability, flexibility, and reliability to its customers. When questions arise about performance, it is important to provide a platform that will ensure trustworthy services in a timely manner. Performance also means how the system can process the user's request faster without a single error and in a trustworthy manner. Scalability ensures the platform accommodates all volumes of customer requests without affecting the system's performance. It also ensures that if the number of users increases, it will accommodate and handle all requests smoothly. To develop a better platform, flexibility is one of the more concerning issues, which will

ensure the ability to control shifting user performances, modify the requirements of the business, and change conditions according to the market.The best possible solution to overcome the challenges is to implement a microservices architecture for online travel platforms. In microservices architecture, a large program is broken down into smaller units or modules that can perform individual tasks; smaller modules are called services. The individual modules can be deployed and scaled separately. This architecture can increase the efficiency, flexibility, and performance of online travel portals by implementing autonomy, modularity, and parallelism. The modularity separates the services and acts as an independent service, which increases cohesion and reduces coupling. Parallelism means that multiple services execute concurrently. Which increases the throughput and responsiveness? Autonomy indicates the self-healing and self-management of each individual service, which increases fault tolerance and reliability (Fritzsch et al., 2019).

2. LITERATURE REVIEW

Microservices is one of the most popular technologies in the software industry for its different features in designing software with efficient, scalable, and smooth application development. The integration of microservices in the online travel platform will provide many advantages, like fault tolerance, modular development, and independent service execution. Implementing microservices in the cloud environment on an online travel platform mostly depends on efficient containerization and orchestration techniques. Saboor et al. [3] provided a conceptual framework for how the execution of microservices can reduce response time, energy costs, and execution costs. They also proposed a conceptual framework with four key agent services: intelligent partitioning, dynamic allocation, resource optimization, and mutation action. They show their framework service can reduce energy consumption, reduce the number of network calls, and also reduce carbon dioxide emissions. Sing et al. deployed a proposed microservices architecture on the Docker container and tested it as a case study using a social networking application. They showed that efforts and time were reduced during the deployment and integration of the application using their proposed design framework. [4] Rahman et al. showed a modeling of containerization and performance characterization of microservices in the cloud. Their model involved integrating cloud platforms, combining the use of resource matrices from multiple layers, and applying machine learning processes to predict the latency of microservice workflows. They used NSF's chameleon testbed for containerization using Docker engine orchestration and Kubernetes for KVM virtualization. [5]Zhong et al. [6] presented a review of container orchestration approaches based on existing machine learning techniques. It also showed an evaluation of container orchestration based on machine learning from 2016 to 2021, including objectives.

2.1 Overview of Microservices Architecture in Online Travel Platforms

A couple of studies have been done on the benefits of implementing microservice architecture in the field of online travel platforms. Garcia et al. discussed three applications: trip planning, the tourism marketplace, and heritage education. The integrated microservices architecture is a small service that runs independently. [7]

2.2 Containerization Technologies

All containerization technologies have become more popular nowadays, such as Docker, as they are more efficient and lightweight approaches for any packaging and deployment of applications. Docker encapsulates the microservices, and they include all dependencies within the portable containers, which ensures consistency within a variety of environments. Zhang et al. discussed Docker as a suitable containerization technique that is used for virtualization at an operating system level [11]. They discussed container placement and VM placement. In their findings, it has been shown that resource utilization was degraded due to the scattered distribution of containers in a data center. The three main entities were involved and named the "Container-VM-PM" architecture for the best placement of containers.

2.3 How do Containerized Microservices Work?

To keep isolated microservices from each other normally would run on individual physical servers, which is a waste of resources. In modern technology, a high-configuration server can run multiple operating systems, so a separate

Physical server isn't necessary for each microservice. Running multiple microservices on a single operating system is also risky, as they may conflict with each other due to their non-isolation. This problem can lead to the failure of conflicting services. If the different virtual machines (VMs) run multiple microservices, these techniques provide a unique environment to run each microservice autonomously. There is also the possibility of replicating the OS instance. Running a new OS is also a waste of resources. To overcome the situation, the best practice is to run microservices with the necessary libraries, which ensure every microservice executes autonomously, reducing interdependence with other microservices. Figure 33.1 shows the architecture of a virtual machine and container. In order to successfully manage complex deployments in cloud environments, having an orchestration of containerized microservices that is both effective and efficient is an absolute must. In the realm of business, orchestration solutions like Kubernetes and Docker Swarm are both well-known and widely utilized tools. An easy solution Docker Swarm is the best solution for orchestration deployments on a small scale. The deployment, scaling, and load balancing of microservices may all be automated to a greater extent with Kubernetes because of its rich feature set in this area. Research by Kaur et al. (2022) compared the performance and scalability of Kubernetes and Docker Swarm in the context of microservice architecture and found that both tools offer robust orchestration capabilities [21].

2.4 Existing Research on Containerization and Orchestration in Online Travel Platforms

There are a number of studies focused on how to deploy containerization and orchestration of microservices on online travel platforms. Shah et al. 2021 represented a case study on the online travel platform regarding orchestration and containerization [2]; they examined the performance of

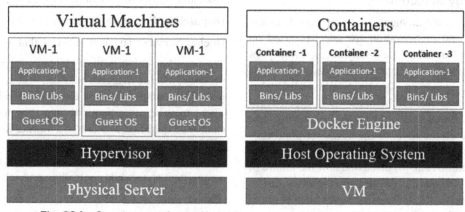

Fig. 33.1 Comparison of virtual machines and containers orchestration tools

scalability and fault tolerance. Yang et al., 2020 proposed a microservices architecture using the Unified Modeling Language for Group-CRM [10]. They applied Rabbit MQ and ELT in data communication with relevant services, which they proposed for large-scale airline companies. The main research that was conducted at this time normally emphasizes deploying a microservices architecture, the advantages of deploying containerization technologies like Docker, and effective tools of orchestration like Kubernetes and Docker Swarm in the field of online travel platforms [18]. In this research, our main goal is to integrate efficient technologies for containerization and orchestration of online travel.

3. METHODOLOGY

This section describes the methodology employed to investigate the containerization and orchestration of microservices in cloud environments for online travel platforms. The methodology encompasses the following steps:

- Selection of a case study
- Containerization and orchestration technology selection
- Deployment strategy
- Evaluation metrics

3.1 Selection of Case Study

The field of the case study that has been selected is an online travel platform. The functions are fully dependent on the Internet, where different types of Global Distribution Systems (GDS) and APIs from different vendors display airline information from all over the world [19]. As a large number of APIs are used in this field, it is more suitable for testing microservices containerized in the cloud.

3.2 Containerization and Orchestration Technology Selection

Depending on the requirements analysis and features, containerization and orchestration are selected based on different factors, including flexibility, compatibility of technologies, community support, and availability. The most popular technologies, Docker Swam and Docker for containerization and Kubernetes, are selected for orchestration in the case of online travel platforms. The selection is done on the basis of the needs for platforms. The architecture of modular and scalable is a lightweight virtualization. Rafino et al. [8] discussed how the failure of a single service doesn't affect system performance due to the availability and fault tolerance features of microservices when distributing the application.

Why Docker?

Docker is an open-source environment that executes applications and processes easily to develop and distribute applications [9]. Designing the application using Docker is packaged, including all relevant dependencies, into a single standard form, which is called the container.

3.3 Container Orchestration

Docker Swarm Architecture

Docker Swarm is the most popular clustering and orchestration tool for microservice containers that are built for distributed environments and has a built-in Docker engine where hundreds of containers are integrated. The main components of Docker Swarm are Docker Services, Docker tasks, and nodes.

Raft Consensus Group: It is a group of external and internal database states and a collection of workers' nodes.

Docker Node: It is an instance of the Docker engine built with Docker Swarm, there are two types of nodes:

Workers: The worker's node takes the instructions from the control node and works according to them. The worker's node sends its own status and the status of the task to the control node.

Manager Node: It maintains the system in a stable state by scheduling the services maintaining the cluster and service providing swarm mode HTTP endpoints. The manager node includes with below components-

API Server: Depending on the incoming commands it receives the commands from the client and creates new services based on the request [12].

Allocator: It assigns the IP addresses.

Orchestrator: It collects the details of services and creates new tasks.

Scheduler: The scheduler is responsible for scheduling the tasks and distributing them to worker nodes.

Dispatcher: It controls the services to the worker's nodes.

Docker Service: This is the service that will be executed.

The main key component of Docker swarm architecture is the node, where a manager node can be managed by another node. The manager node is elected by the Raft algorithm. There may be more than one manager node. A manager cannot be qualified to work as a worker node. To manage the internal cluster state, a manager node uses the Raft consensus algorithm so that all manager nodes maintain a consistent state while controlling and scheduling tasks.

The services we deploy are called Docker engines or nodes, a cluster of swarms [17]. At the primary stage, using a communication protocol, Docker involves a cluster management system called Beam. After that, it changed the name to Swarm, integrating more APIs. In Fig. 33.2 shows the Docker Swarm Architecture.RT-Kubernetes is the most popular architecture for real-time deploying components in the cloud infrastructure within the container [14]. It is more suitable for CPU scheduling with a real-time scheduler, which is based on Linux. A Kubernetes is built with a primary control plane that includes different nodes. All instances can be stored in the cloud as a VM (virtual machine) or on the host PC. For a large-scale deployment, usually the designer of the cloud provider manages the control plane.

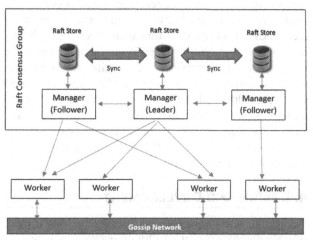

Fig. 33.2   The docker swarm architecture

Kubernetes Master Node Component

Kubernetes API server: The API server is positioned inside the master node, where all activities relating to administration are performed [15]. The rest of the API commands are sent to the API server, and the process is validated and processed on the server. Based on the request and the key value, the cluster's state is stored.

Scheduler: The scheduler provides a task to the worker's nodes and manages all requests that come from the API server. It also schedules the task in the form of pods and services. It is also ensuring service quality through anti-affinity, affinity, and data locality.

Control Manager: It is also identified as the controller. It works to manage different types of non-terminating control loops. It also works on collecting event garbage, node garbage, and cascade deletion garbage. The control manager also looks after the state of a managed object and manages its current state using an API server. In the case of failure to meet the desired state, the control loop positions the current state and sets the specified state to achieve the target.

ETCD: This component is used for distributing key values, which are used to store a cluster state. It can be a part of Kubernetes Master or externally configured. To write the code for ETCD "Go" programming languages are normally used.

3.4 Deployment Strategy

A deployment strategy is designed to place and deploy the containerized microservices effectively in the cloud environment that is chosen [17]. The selection is mainly based on the configuration of networking, infrastructure requirements, selection of suitable cloud providers, investigation of security issues, and analysis of the transformation of the monolithic patterns. The deployment strategy should be ensured and consider fault tolerance and resource utilization.

Key Considerations of Deployment

To effectively deploy the application to the cloud a number of key points should be considered.Should have knowledge of dependency management, many services, and interactions at application runtime make the project difficult to manage. Should have knowledge about distributed systems as communications between different services may make the application fail. The deployment team should have knowledge about load balancing and network latency. The team of developers has to choose suitable DevOps, select networking, and have much knowledge about network security skills to deploy microservice. There should be critical testing to deploy in a distributed environment. The coordination is needed between different teams to upgrade and roll out microservices.

Service Instance per Container

This is one of the most important models in the deployment strategy of microservices. In this model, each and every individual service instance is executed in its corresponding container, which is a virtualization device or technology within the operating system. The containers are called Docker and Solaris Zones. In this model, all relevant services, including the applications and libraries that are required to execute the service, are combined as a package with a file image. The image file is known as the container image. After packaging it, it needed to launch on different containers or single and multiple containers on a virtual machine or physical host. In this model for container management, Kubernetes can be used as a cluster manager. In Fig. 33.3, service instances per container are shown.

Define the Infrastructure Requirement

Selecting or building a microservices infrastructure is a challenging task. It needs to use appropriate tools and approaches. A few points are enumerated below:

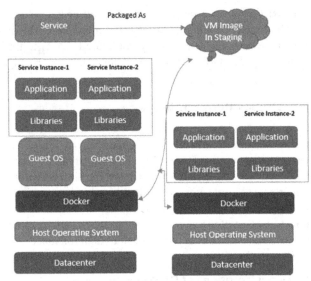

Fig. 33.3 Service instance per container

Requirement Analysis

It needs to identify the organization's specific requirements and goals. Also, it is important to identify the number of microservices and the nature of the microservices planned to be deployed. Needs to ensure the expected level of performance and scalability. It is also important to evaluate the factors to consider, like the complexity of the application, the required traffic pressure, and the need for high availability. It's fully dependent on the organization's requirements. The team of developers should be skilled enough to handle and maintain the infrastructure.

Choosing a Secure Networking Platform

When deploying a microservices application in a cloud environment, network security is an important issue. To evaluate the security of the network, one needs to check its scalability, security, and availability before deployment. It also needs to check the compatibility of the existing system and whether it is capable of handling the expected workload or not. Tests are needed about access control, secure channels, and the availability of encryption mechanisms.

Evaluation Metrics

The evaluation metrics provide a comparison between containerized microservices and traditional monolithic architectures. This type of comparison is identifiable. The metric-based or scenario-based evaluation is essential to finding out the quality of attributes in a software system and helps to lay the planning foundation [13]. The maximum identified metrics are applicable to centralization metrics. The number of coupling services can be measured by the number of services consumed. The main research objective and goal were to containerize and orchestrate microservices

in a cloud environment. There are also other evaluation metrics for the improvement of scalability, flexibility, and dependability to facilitate online travel reservations [10]. As different stakeholders like customers, developers, GDS providers, distributors, and operators are involved in the assessment techniques, both needs and requirements analyses are feasible to apply in the evaluation methods. This is possible because there are many facts and different methods of evaluation that are interconnected in the process.

3.5 Performance

The efficiency of microservices in the cloud environment refers to how efficiently the resources of the containerized microservices are used. The utilization metrics of resources include CPU uses (the CPU time used in percentage by the microservices), memory utilization (the amount of memory used by the microservices), disk utilization (the disk space used by the microservices), and network utilization (the bandwidth used at the network). The tools used for monitoring resources are Prometheus, Datadog, and Grafna. Grafana provides visualization and data analysis from different sources; on the other hand, Prometheus is famous for collecting metrics.

4. DESIGN AND DEVELOPMENT

We need to select an appropriate architecture that is more suitable for the application [20]. The selection is mainly based on how large the application is and what data are connecting to each other. After that, it is easy to choose the communication pattern, whether asynchronous, synchronous, or a hybrid.

5. IMPLEMENTATION AND RESULTS

Implementation of Microservices

- Need to identify the logical divisions of microservices like the total number of modules from start to end.
- Identifying what module of microservices is used for what purpose. It will be easy to update or modify later on and also will avoid unnecessary changes of code.
- Carefully look out for modules from monolithic before starting to split up all modules into microservices.
- Select the developers needed to distribute the responsibilities so that each developer can work on their specific task.

6. CONCLUSIONS

In this paper, we have explored the provision and orchestration of containerized microservices in the cloud environment for the specific platform of online travel. An analysis and investigation details are shown in this paper. We use different tools and techniques, like Kubernetes and Docker Swarm Architecture, for containerized orchestration in the cloud environment, including deployment strategy, infrastructure requirements, evaluation metrics, and resource utilization. Future research areas may provide a solution to a better microservices cloud framework that supports the online travel industry and its current evolution.

■ REFERENCES ■

1. Ren, Z., Wang, W., Wu, G., Gao, C., Chen, W., Wei, J., & Huang, T. (2018, September). Migrating web applications from monolithic structure to microservices architecture. In Proceedings of the 10th Asia-Pacific Symposium on Internetware (pp. 1–10).
2. Chaki, P. K., Sazal, M. M. H., Barua, B., Hossain, M. S., & Mohammad, K. S. (2019, February). An approach of teachers' quality improvement by analyzing teaching evaluations data. In 2019 Second International Conference on Advanced Computational and Communication Paradigms (ICACCP) (pp. 1–5). IEEE.
3. Saboor, A., Hassan, M. F., Akbar, R., Shah, S. N. M., Hassan, F., Magsi, S. A., & Siddiqui, M. A. (2022). Containerized microservices orchestration and provisioning in cloud computing: A conceptual framework and future perspectives. Applied Sciences, 12(12), 5793.
4. Singh, V., &Peddoju, S. K. (2017, May). Container-based microservice architecture for cloud applications. In 2017 International Conference on Computing, Communication and Automation (ICCCA) (pp. 847–852). IEEE.
5. Rahman, J., & Lama, P. (2019, June). Predicting the end-to-end tail latency of containerized microservices in the cloud. In 2019 IEEE International Conference on Cloud Engineering (IC2E) (pp. 200–210). IEEE.
6. Zhong, Z., Xu, M., Rodriguez, M. A., Xu, C., &Buyya, R. (2022). Machine learning-based orchestration of containers: A taxonomy and future directions. ACM Computing Surveys (CSUR), 54(10s), 1–35.
7. Garcia, L. M., Aciar, S., Mendoza, R., & Puello, J. J. (2018, July). Smart tourism platform based on microservice architecture and recommender services. In International Conference on Mobile Web and Intelligent Information Systems (pp. 167–180). Cham: Springer International Publishing.
8. Rufino, J., Alam, M., Ferreira, J., Rehman, A., & Tsang, K. F. (2017, March). Orchestration of containerized microservices for IIoT using Docker. In 2017 IEEE International Conference on Industrial Technology (ICIT) (pp. 1532–1536). IEEE.
9. Sun, L., Li, Y., &Memon, R. A. (2017). An open IoT framework based on microservices architecture. China Communications, 14(2), 154–162.
10. Yang, H., Dong, X., Wang, T., & Xiao, A. (2020, April). The Microservice Architecture of Airline's Group-CRM Based on UML. In 2020 3rd International Conference on Advanced Electronic Materials, Computers and Software Engineering (AEMCSE) (pp. 133–136). IEEE.
11. Zhang, R., Zhong, A. M., Dong, B., Tian, F., & Li, R. (2018). Container-VM-PM architecture: A novel architecture for docker container placement. In Cloud Computing–CLOUD 2018: 11th International Conference, Held as Part of the Services Conference Federation, SCF 2018, Seattle, WA, USA, June 25–30, 2018, Proceedings 11 (pp. 128–140). Springer International Publishing.
12. Moravcik, M., &Kontsek, M. (2020, November). Overview of Docker container orchestration tools. In 2020 18th International Conference on Emerging eLearning Technologies and Applications (ICETA) (pp. 475–480). IEEE.
13. Engel, T., Langermeier, M., Bauer, B., & Hofmann, A. (2018). Evaluation of microservice architectures: A metric and tool-based approach. In Information Systems in the Big Data Era: CAiSE Forum 2018, Tallinn, Estonia, June 11-15, 2018, Proceedings 30 (pp. 74–89). Springer International Publishing.
14. Fiori, S., Abeni, L., &Cucinotta, T. (2022, April). RT-kubernetes: containerized real-time cloud computing. In Proceedings of the 37th ACM/SIGAPP Symposium on Applied Computing (pp. 36–39).
15. Joseph, C. T., &Chandrasekaran, K. (2020). IntMA: Dynamic interaction-aware resource allocation for containerized microservices in cloud environments. Journal of Systems Architecture, 111, 101785.
16. Keni, N. D., &Kak, A. (2020, January). Adaptive containerization for microservices in distributed cloud systems. In 2020 IEEE 17th Annual Consumer Communications & Networking Conference (CCNC) (pp. 1–6). IEEE.
17. Rad, B. B., Bhatti, H. J., & Ahmadi, M. (2017). An introduction to docker and analysis of its performance. International Journal of Computer Science and Network Security (IJCSNS), 17(3), 228.
18. Vayghan, L. A., Saied, M. A., Toeroe, M., & Khendek, F. (2019). Kubernetes as an availability manager for microservice applications. arXiv preprint arXiv:1901.04946.
19. Barua, B., Whaiduzzaman, M., MesbahuddinSarker, M., Shamim Kaiser, M., & Barros, A. (2023). Designing and Implementing a Distributed Database for Microservices Cloud-Based Online Travel Portal. In Sentiment Analysis and Deep Learning: Proceedings of ICSADL 2022 (pp. 295–314). Singapore: Springer Nature Singapore.
20. Fritzsch, J., Bogner, J., Wagner, S., & Zimmermann, A. (2019, September). Microservices migration in industry: intentions, strategies, and challenges. In 2019 IEEE International Conference on Software Maintenance and Evolution (ICSME) (pp. 481–490). IEEE.
21. Kaur, K., Guillemin, F., &Sailhan, F. (2022). Container placement and migration strategies for cloud, fog, and edge data centers: A survey. International Journal of Network Management, 32(6), e2212.

Note: All the figures in this chapter were made by the author.

Challenges and Opportunities for Innovation in India – Dr. Shweta Mishra et al. (eds)
© 2024 Taylor & Francis Group, London, ISBN 978-1-032-99842-8

Diabetic Retinopathy Detection using: Machine Learning Approach

34

Amreen Fatma[1],
Saurabh Tiwari[2], Pawan K. Chaurasia[3]
Dept. of Information Technology, BBAU,
Lucknow

Abstract

The issue of Diabetic Retinopathy (DR) continues to be of great concern due to its capacity to result in permanent vision loss. The objective of this paper is to tackle the problem above through a comprehensive analysis of persons suffering from Diabetic Retinopathy (DR). The primary aim is to develop a reliable machine-learning model that can accurately forecast the emergence of symptoms in affected patients. By employing machine learning methodologies, to efficiently detect and rectify this situation. The suggested approach entails employing a Convolutional Neural Network (CNN) to examine retinal pictures, to precisely categorize the existence and extent of Diabetic Retinopathy (DR). By undergoing rigorous training using a wide range of data, this system exhibits a notable level of expertise in identifying tiny abnormalities in the retina that are suggestive of the initial phases of Diabetic Retinopathy (DR). The utilization of automated diagnostic techniques in diabetic eye care presents a potential opportunity to facilitate prompt treatments, eventually resulting in enhanced patient outcomes.

Keywords

Diabetic retinopathy, CNN, PDR, Machine learning

1. INTRODUCTION

Diabetes is a long-term medical problem. In the healthcare field, the treatment of disease is effective when detected at an early stage. Diabetes is a disease that increases the amount of glucose in the blood caused by a lack of insulin. It affects 425 million adults worldwide. Diabetes affects the Heart, Retina, Nervous system, and Kidney. Diabetes has Two Types. Type1 and Type2. Diabetic Retinopathy disease of Diabetes. DR is part of type 2 Diabetes. Diabetic Retinopathy is the leading cause of visual impairment among adults, with an estimated 37 million people globally with this DR disease. With the number of patients with Diabetes increasing from 422 million people in 2021 to 642 million people in 2024, DR usually has two types; Early and advanced DR. Early DR more common form called NPDR (Non-proliferative Diabetic Retinopathy). NPDR week the walls of blood vessels retinas. Advanced DR can progress to this more severe type, known as Proliferative Diabetic Retinopathy (PDR), In this type damaged vessels

[1]alishakazmi718@gmail.com, [2]Dtiwarisaurabh2028@gmail.com, [3]pkc.gkp@gmail.com

DOI: 10.1201/9781003606260-34

in the retina these new blood vessels are fragile and leak into the clear. jelly-like substance that fills the center of your eye[Vitreous]. New blood vessels interfere with normal blood flow which can cause the retina to detach from the back of your eyes. The objective of the paper is to develop a model with the help of machine learning that can detect diabetic Retinopathy and provide the stage of diabetic retinopathy in a diabetic patient [NoDR, DR, Mild, Moderate, Severe, PDR].

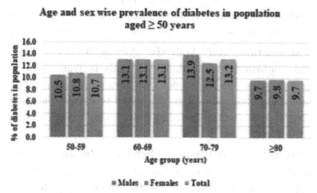

Fig. 34.1 Age–wise and sex–wise diabetes distribution in the population

Source: Author

2. LITERATURE REVIEW

Medical professionals can benefit greatly from deep-learning-based systems that automate the interpretation of retinal pictures and provide objective and consistent assessments of the severity of DR [21]. DL-based screening methods can test a large diabetic population for DR. The research paper summarizes the field of diabetic retinopathy classification through the application of machine learning and deep learning techniques, these research articles provide DR detection accuracy. Abeer Ahmed Ali, and Fateh Abd Ali Dawood [2023] classify the diabetic Retinopathy severity through fundus im-ages. The study aims to design an automated model based on deep learning. In this model, a convolutional neural network (CNN) and used the APTOS2019 Dataset [1]. Dolly das, saroj kr. Biswas and Sivaji Bandyopad-hyay [2022] give a review of the diagnosis of DR using machine learning and deep learning. this paper gives a detailed review of DR. Its features, causes, ml model, state of art Dl models, and challenges. Comparisons and future directions for early detection of DR [2]. Krishnan Sangeetha et. al., gives a broad study of machine learning and deep learning techniques for DR based on feature extraction, detection, and classification [3]. In this paper, classifies the DR's various stages like Mild non-proliferative retinopathy, moderate non-proliferative retinopathy, severe non-proliferative retinopathy, and proliferative diabetic retinopathy and diagnose with the aid of fundus images [4] [5]. M. B. Alazzam et.al. in the identification of DR through machine learning. A cross-sectional study of patients with suspected DR, who had an ophthalmological examination, and a retinal scan in the focus of research [6]. Specialized retinal images were analyzed and classified using OPF and RBM models (restricted Boltzmann machines). Classification of radio graphs was based on the presence and absence of disease-related retinopathy (DR) [7]. O. F. Gurcan et.al. perform a comprehensive study in machine learning methods on diabetic Retinopathy classification [8]. The study proposed an Automated DR clarification system based on pre-processing and feature extraction from a per-trained model by the transfer learning approach. It provides a data- cost-effective solution that includes comprehensive and fine-tuning processes [9]. Wejdan L. Alyoubi et.al. review about diabetic retinopathy detection through deep learning techniques [10]. In this review, various retinal dataset such as DIARETBD I, Kaggle, E aphtha, DDR, DRIVE, HRF, messier-2, STARE, CHASE DB-I, Indian diabetic Retinopathy image dataset (IDRID), ROC are review with its performance measures such as:

Specificity = TN/ (TN FP)

Sensitivity = TP/(TD'FN)

Accuracy = TN + TP /(TN+TP+ FN + P)

Nathan Zhang et. al. in predicting diabetic retinopathy using machine learning, violent plots were created to compare the distribution of diabetic [11]. Retinopathy diagnoses with gender plot showed that those with hypertension who were taking insulin were less likely to have DR. Multiple models were tested according to Nathan Zhang and the most accurate predicting DR with 80 percent accuracy [12]. R. Priya and P. Aruna in the diagnosis of DR using Machine Learning techniques. In this paper, diagnose diabetic retinopathy, three models like Probabilistic Nural Network (PNN), Bayesian classification and support vector machine (SVM) are described and their performance is compared [13]. The amount of the disease spread in the retina, features like blood vessel hemorrhages of NPDR Images, and exudates of PDR images are extracted from the raw images using the image processing techniques and fed to the classifier for classification [14].

3. METHODOLOGY

In this research, GoogleNet was decided for training and learning the model. After reviewing the literature about image classification using CNN architecture, GoogleNet has methods such as 1x1 convolution and global average pooling that can make the model getting deeper for learning.

CNN Architectures: GoogleNet is praised for its efficiency from input data, efficiency in achieving state-of-the-art accuracy. This efficiency removed unnecessary background and focus on the relevant is achieved through a combination of low-dimensional embedding and heterogeneous-sized spatial filters retinal region [15]. After cropping, the images were normalized with 2x2 layers. Normalization typically involves transforming pixel values [16].

GoogLeNet is a deep neural network capable of learning and extracting more complex features. The neural network normalization process to a standardized range to ensure consistent input data for which can lead to improved performance on tasks such as image classification. The use of batch normalization after each convolution layer helps in stabilizing and accelerating training. It can also reduce the sensitivity of the network to the choice of initialization and the learning rate. Max pooling with a 3x3 kernel size and a stride of 2 helps down sample the feature maps, reducing the spatial dimensions while retaining important features. The use of dropout during training helps prevent over-fitting. It randomly drops some neurons during training, which can improve the generalization of the model. The use of leaky rectified linear units (ReLU) with a gradient value of 0.01 can help mitigate the issue of "dead neurons" during back-propagation. Leaky ReLU allows a small gradient for negative values, preventing neurons from becoming inactive. The network employs L2 regularization in the convolutional layers to reduce over-fitting. This is a common technique to prevent the model from fitting the noise in the training data. The Xavier method is used for weight initialization. Proper weight initialization can help the network converge faster and avoid getting stuck in training.

Training and Testing Models: Deep Learning GPU Training System (DIGITS): DIGITS is an interactive system designed to facilitate the training of deep learning models, especially on GPU hardware. It provides prebuilt CNN models for image classification, data management, model prototyping, and real-time performance monitoring. DIGITS is a popular tool for deep learning tasks, and it simplifies the training and evaluation of models.

Data Splitting: The Messidor and MildDR fundus image folders were split into training and validation subsets, consisting of 1077 and 269 images, respectively. A separate test subset folder contained 400 images from Lariboisiere Hospital's Messidor partition data splitting is crucial to train,

Data Preprocessing: Images were cropped to a size of 256x256. Preprocessing often includes tasks such as resizing, normalization, and augmentation to prepare the data for model training. In this case, the images were prepared for input to models previously trained for generic classification tasks, likely based on the ImageNet dataset. Model Training: The training system was used to build model prototypes over 100 epochs. The training process required approximately 20 minutes for each epoch. A Tesla K80 GPU device powered the training, which is a common choice for deep learning tasks due to its high computational power. Early Stopping: An early stopping mechanism was employed to determine the optimal model epoch during training. Early stopping helps prevent overfitting and ensures that the model doesn't continue to train once its performance starts to degrade on the validation set.

Visualization and Analysis: Advanced visualization and confusion matrix statistical analysis were used to gain insights into the model's performance. Visualization tools help under-stand how the model is learning, and the confusion matrix provides information about classification performance.

TensorFlow and Custom Model Development: More refined models were developed using TensorFlow, a popular deep-learning framework. Modified versions of open-source packages were used for model development. Custom models are often created to better suit the specific requirements of the task.

Image Preprocessing Techniques: Additional digital image preprocessing techniques were employed to further enhance the quality and informativeness of the input data. Preprocessing can include techniques like noise reduction, contrast enhancement, and data augmentation. The overall workflow involves data preparation, model training, evaluation, and refinement. It also makes use of state-of-the-art tools and practices in the deep learning community, aking it a comprehensive approach to developing deep learning models for retinal image analysis.

Transfer Learning Pretrained Models: The pre-trained AlexNet and GoogLeNet architectures are well established convolutional neural networks that have been trained on a large and diverse dataset called ImageNet. These models have already learned valuable features from a wide range of images.

Last Fully Connected Layer Removal: In transfer learning, the last fully connected layer (the output layer responsible for classification) of these pre-trained models is removed. This layer is specific to the original ImageNet classification task and needs to be replaced with a new one for the target task.

Transfer Learning Scenario: The process follows a transfer learning scenario. In this scenario, the remaining layers of the pre-trained model are considered as a fixed feature extractor. This means that all the layers preceding removed the fully connected layer are retained, and their weights remain unchanged. These layers are responsible for extracting high-level features from the input images.

New Dataset: A new dataset is introduced for the target task. The pre-trained model is fine-tuned on this new dataset. Fine-tuning typically involves adding new layers, including a new output layer with the appropriate number of classes for the target task.

Retaining Pre-trained Model Weights: The weights of the initial pre-trained model are retained. These weights represent valuable knowledge learned from the ImageNet dataset, and they are preserved to help the model perform better on the new task. Feature Extraction: The retained layers act as a feature extractor. They process the images and extract features that are then used as input to the newly added layers, which are specific to the new task. Transfer learning is a powerful technique in deep learning, especially when you have limited data for the target task. By leveraging knowledge learned from a large and diverse dataset like ImageNet, the model can benefit from generalized features that are transferable to the new task. This often leads to faster convergence and better performance, compared to training a model from scratch. It is particularly useful when the target task shares some similarities with the original task for which the pre-trained model was created.

4. CONCLUSON

This paper presents a literature review of different machine learning styles for diabetic retinopathy detection. It discusses datasets and the selected papers based on image segmentation, traditional ML styles, DL methods, and the parameters used for quantifying the performance of various classification models. After analyzing, it was concluded that subdomains of machine learning such as neural networks(CNN), linear regression, and support vector ma-chines (SVM) have been used to identify and solve diabetic retinopathy. It also explores statistical data in DR detection and classification. It was observed that various research studies were carried out using supervised learning and, recently, deep learning. Future work can be focused on working with a balanced and multimodal dataset. The second point is to use semi-supervised, self-supervised, and co-learning techniques with deep neural networks. This paper may help researchers to narrow the research spectrum and form hypotheses by identifying the gaps.

■ REFERENCES ■

1. A Systematic Review on Diabetic Retinopathy Detection Using Deep Learning Techniques, f Computational Methods in Engineering (2023) 30:2211–2256.
2. Abeer Ahmed Ali, Faten Abd Ali Dawood, December. (2023). Deep Learning of Diabetic Retinopathy Classification in Fundus images".
3. Dolly Das, Saroj Kr.Biswas, sivaji Bandyopadhyay, (2022). "A critical on diagnosis of diabetic retinopathy using machine learning and deep learning",
4. "A broad study of machine learning and deep learning techniques for diabetic retinopathy based on feature extraction, detection and classification"
5. Suraj Kumar Gupta, Aditya Shrivastava, SP Upadhyay, Pawan Kumar Chaurasia (2021). A machine learning approach for heart attack prediction, International Journal of Engineering and Advanced Technology (IJEAT), 10(6), 1–11.
6. Krishnan sangeetha, K. Valarmathi, T. Kalaichelvi, S. Subburaj, 17 November 2023.
7. "Identification of Diabetic Retinopathy through machine learning" Malik Bader Alazzam, Fawaz Alassery, and Ahmed Almulihi, vol 2021, Article ID 1155116,8 page, 26 November 2021.
8. Vipin Kumar, Pawan Kumar Chaurasia, Prem Shankar Singh Aydav (2023). Deep multi-view learning for healthcare domain, Computational Intelligence Aided Systems for Healthcare Domain, CRC Press, 55–90.
9. "A comprehensive Study of machine learning methods on diabetic retinopathy classification"
10. Omar Faruk Gurcan, Omer Faruk Beyca, Onur Dogan, **Articale** in International Journal of Computational Intelligence Systems March 2021.
11. Neha Singh, P K Chaurasia, (2020). Machine Learning in Healthcare Industry: Tools and Techniques, Journal of Test Engineering and Management, Vol 82, ISSN: 0193–4120, Page No. 4146–4150.
12. "Diabetic retinopathy detection through deep learning techniques: A review" Wejdan L. Alyoubi , Wafaa M. Shalash, Maysoon F. Abulkhair, https://doi.org/10.1016/j.imu.2020.100377, 2352–9148/© 2020 The Authors. Published by Elsevier Ltd. 20 June 2020.
13. Nathan Zhang (2022). "Predicting Diabetic Retinopathy Using Machine Learning", Volume 11 Issue 2022.
14. P K Chaurasia, (2020). Paradigms of Machine Learning and Data Analytics Handling Priority Inversion in Time-Constrained Distributed Databases, IGI Global, 156–174.
15. R. Priya, p. Aruna, 2013. "diagnosis of diabetic retinopathy using machine learning techniques"

Challenges and Opportunities for Innovation in India – Dr. Shweta Mishra et al. (eds)
© 2024 Taylor & Francis Group, London, ISBN 978-1-032-99842-8

Evaluation Metrices in Stock Market Price Prediction

35

Satish Kumar Singh*, Sheeba Praveen

Department of Computer Science and Engineering,
Integral University, Lucknow

Abstract

The stock market price prediction has been a very challenging task in the recent times. The different models, algorithms and associated data sets based on Machine learning, deep learning and sentiment analysis have provided millions of the results to prove their accuracy but the efficiency is still the prime concern among the researchers. Any model and their results can only be verified and trusted if they are subjected to certain performance parameters that check their validity and accuracy of the results they provide. In this paper we are going to discuss some of the most popular evaluation metrices that have been extensively used in the stock market price predication methods. Also, we have tried to highlight the most frequently used techniques, their challenges and their benefits according to the accuracy based on the results provided.

Keywords

Metrices, Performance parameters, Evaluation metrices, Results analysis

1. Introduction

It is difficult to predict stock market prices without employing statistical or machine learning models and analyzing a variety of elements. Although it's crucial to remember that the unpredictability of financial markets makes it very difficult to predict stock prices with 100% accuracy, analysts and data scientists employ a variety of methods and strategies to produce well-informed forecasts. Some widely used techniques are:

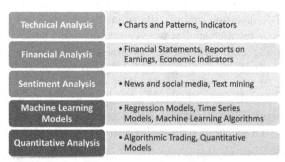

Fig. 35.1 Commonly used stock market price prediction techniques

*Corresponding author: satishkrsingh167@gmail.com

DOI: 10.1201/9781003606260-35

Because financial markets are inherently unpredictable, it's critical to approach stock market prediction cautiously. Past performance is no guarantee of future performance, and stock prices can be impacted by unanticipated circumstances, market sentiment, and outside events. In addition, rigorous validation and consideration of overfitting to historical data are necessary when using machine learning models. In the end, accurate stock market forecasting frequently combines various methods, accounting for both fundamental and technical aspects, and regularly modifying plans in response to shifting market conditions. The generic method for the stock market price prediction is as follows:

Fig. 35.2 Generic price prediction process

2. Performance Metrices used in Stock Market Price Prediction

In stock market price prediction using sentiment analysis and deep learning some most frequently used performance parameters were used [1]. These metrices are as follows:

2.1 Mean Absolute Error (MAE)

The arithmetic mean of the absolute errors, or MAE, is a very simple and uncomplicated measure to compute. By default, the values have equal weights when comparing the difference between the observation and the prediction. Even in the presence of outliers, good behavior is guaranteed by the analytic form's lack of exponents. The unit of measurement for the target variable is the one that represents the outcomes. Since MAE is a scale-dependent error metric, the observation's size is significant. This implies that it can only be applied to method comparisons in situations when all schemes include the same unique target variable, as opposed to distinct ones.

$$MAE = \frac{1}{n}\sum_{i=1}^{n}\left|y_{p_i} - y_{a_i}\right|$$

2.2 Mean Absolute Percentage Error (MAPE)

The mean absolute percentage error is known as MAPE. It is an error measure that is relative rather than absolute. When assessing the precision of forecasts, MAPE is frequently used. It is calculated by dividing the absolute value of the observation by the average of the absolute discrepancies between the prediction and the observations. This output can then be multiplied by 100 to get a percentage. When the real value is zero, it is impossible to calculate this inaccuracy. In actuality, it may accept values in $[0,\infty)$ rather than as a percentage. In particular, the MAPE output may be greater than 100% when the projections contain values that are significantly larger than the data.

$$MAPE = \frac{1}{n}\sum_{i=1}^{n}\frac{\left|y_{p_i} - y_{a_i}\right|}{\left|y_{a_i}\right|}$$

On the other hand, the metric's output may significantly diverge from 100% in situations where low values are present in both the prediction and the observation. This can also result in an inaccurate assessment of the model's predictive skills, leading one to assume that the mistakes are high while, in reality, they may be minimal. Cases where the anticipated value exceeds the actual value are given extra weight by MAPE. Larger mistakes are produced in these circumstances. Therefore, approaches with low prediction values are best suited for employing this metric. Finally, because MAPE is not scale-dependent, it may be applied to compare a wide range of variables and time series.

2.3 Mean Squared Error (MSE)

Mean squared error is abbreviated as MSE. It is a standard metric for evaluating forecasts. The average of the squares representing the variations between the actual and expected values is known as the mean squared error. The square of the unit of the variable of interest serves as its measuring unit. First, examining the analytical form, the non-negativity of the error is guaranteed by the square of the differences. Additionally, it renders data on little faults usable. Simultaneously, it is evident that greater deviations result in greater penalties, meaning a higher mean square error. Outliers, then, have a major impact on the error's output; that is, the presence of such extreme values has a major effect on the measurements and, in turn, the assessment.

$$MSE = \frac{1}{n}\sum_{i=1}^{n}\left(y_{p_i} - y_{a_i}\right)^2$$

Furthermore, and in a sense the other way around, when differences are less than 1, there is a risk of overestimating the predictive capabilities of the model. Given the error's differentiability, as one can observe, it can easily be optimized.

2.4 Root Mean Squared Error (RMSE)

Root mean squared error is referred to as RMSE. It is a widely used statistic to assess how estimated values and observations differ from one another. It seems that all it takes to compute it is to find the root of the mean squared error. The metric can be conceptualized as an abstraction that represents the average difference between the predicted and actual values, based on the numerical formulation. In other words, the formula can be observed as representing the Euclidean distance if the denominator is disregarded.

$$RMSE = \sqrt{\frac{1}{n}\sum_{i=1}^{n}\left(y_{p_i} - y_{a_i}\right)^2}$$

The division by the number of observations leads to the ensuing interpretation of the metric as a form of normalized distance. The output is significantly affected by the presence of outliers in this instance as well. The RMSE's application is straightforward since, unlike the MSE, it expresses error values in the same units as the target variable rather than in its square. Lastly, because the measure depends on scale, it can only be applied to compare different models or model variations in relation to a specific fixed variable.

2.5 Root Mean Squared Logarithmic Error (RMSLE)

Root Mean Squared Logarithmic Error is referred to as RMSLE. It appears that the RMSLE metric is an altered form of the MSE. When predictions show notable variances, it is preferable to use this change. The RMSLE use the logarithms of the observed and predicted values, making sure that the logarithms have non-zero values by adding the necessary simple units to the formula.

$$RMSLE = \sqrt{\frac{1}{n}\sum_{i=1}^{n}\left(\log(y_{p_i}+1) - \log(y_{a_i}+1)\right)^2}$$

This version has been adjusted to be resilient to noise and outliers, and it lessens the penalty that the MSE applies when predictions differ noticeably from observations. When there are negative values, the measure cannot be applied. The relative error between observations and forecasts is represented by RMSLE. Just applying the following property to the square root's radicand term will demonstrate this.

3. EVALUATION METRICES USED IN RECENT YEARS

The evaluation metrices discussed above has been extensively used in the recent years to validate the performance analysis of the different price prediction algorithms. The few of them utilized in the recent years have been discussed with their implementation details as follows in the given Table 35.1:

Table 35.1 Metrices used in performance analysis of algorithms

Contributors	Prediction target	Metrices	Performance	Year	Ref
Rana et al	Daily stock price	RMSE	0.0151	2019	2
Chen et al.	Direction of stock indices price		0.0143–0.0239	2017	3
Siddique et al	Predicting the next day close price		4.3	2019	4
Das et al	Prediction of 1,3,5,7,15,30 days ahead price		143.1104	2019	5
Li et al.	Predicting one-day ahead close price value	MAE	0.054	2022	6
Botunac et al	Direction of close price		0.01606	2020	7
Siddique et al	Next day close price		2.76	2019	8
Das et al	Prediction of 1,3,5,7,15,30 days ahead price		121.8011	2019	9
Farahani et al.	Close price		13.499	2021	10
Dami et al	Returns prediction		0.022–0.039	2021	11
Li et al.	Predicting closing priced on day advance	MSE	0.006	2022	12
Botunac et al	Direction of close price		0.00046	2020	13
Li et al.	Forecasting one day ahead closing prices	MAPE	1.092	2022	14
Chen et al.	Prediction of direction of stock indices		0.646–1.06	2017	15
Siddique et al	Next day close price		0.63	2019	16
Das et al	Prediction of 1,3,5,7,15,30 days ahead price		0.308	2019	17

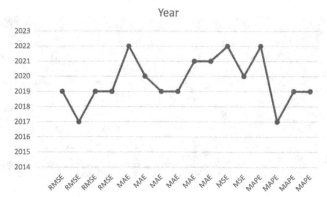

Fig. 35.3 Yearwise metrics selection for performance analysis

4. CONCLUSION

Stock market price prediction metrics involves a multifaceted approach that incorporates various indicators and techniques. While no method can guarantee absolute accuracy due to the inherent unpredictability of financial markets, a combination of fundamental analysis, technical analysis, and machine learning models can enhance the accuracy of predictions. The above data shows performance of price prediction algorithm is very important for the accuracy of the predicted model. The table above represents comparative analysis of all those algorithms. It clearly shows that RMSE and MAE was the most dominant metric for the performance evaluation for the given period. But since 2020 MSE have been a very popular metric and together with MAE it has been widely used for the performance analysis of the price prediction algorithms. In performance evaluation, accuracy criteria have been used extensively to evaluate the performance of prediction algorithms for short durations for less than 15 days. Other criteria RMSE, MAPE and MAE were very helpful in testing the algorithms in longer duration prediction process for 15 to 30 days in advance.

■ REFERENCES ■

1. Charalampos M. Liapis, Aikaterini Karanikola and Sotiris Kotsiantis, Investigating Deep Stock Market Forecasting with Sentiment Analysis, Entropy 2023, 25(2), 219; https://doi.org/10.3390/e25020219
2. Rana M, Uddin MM, Hoque MM (2019) Effects of activation functions and optimizers on stock price prediction using LSTM recurrent networks, CSAI, Beijing, China, pp 354–358.
3. Chen Y, Hao Y (2017) A feature weighted support vector machine and K-nearest neighbor algorithm for stock market indices prediction. Expert Syst Appl 80:340–355.
4. Siddique M, Panda D (2019) A hybrid forecasting model for prediction of stock index of tata motors using principal component analysis, support vector regression and particle swarm optimization. I J Eng Adv Tech 9:3032–3037.
5. Das SR, Mishra D, Rout M (2019) Stock market prediction using firefly algorithm with evolutionary framework optimized feature reduction for OSELM method". Expert Syst Appl X 4:100016.
6. Li G, Zhang A, Zhang Q, Wu D, Zhan C (2022)Pearson correlation coefficient-based performance enhancement of Broad Learning System for stock price prediction, IEEE Trans Circuits Syst II, (Early Access).
7. Botunac I, Panjkota A, Matetic M (2020) The effect of feature selection on the performance of long short-term memory neural network in stock market predictions, In 31st DAAAM ISIMA, Vienna, Austria, pp 0592-0598.
8. Siddique M, Panda D (2019) A hybrid forecasting model for prediction of stock index of tata motors using principal component analysis, support vector regression and particle swarm optimization. I J Eng Adv Tech 9:3032–3037.
9. Das SR, Mishra D, Rout M (2019) Stock market prediction using firefly algorithm with evolutionary framework optimized feature reduction for OSELM method". Expert Syst Appl X 4:100016.
10. Farahani MS, Hajiagha SHR (2021) Forecasting stock price using integrated artificial neural network and metaheuristic algorithms compared to time series models. Soft Comput 25:8483–8513.
11. Dami S, Esterabi M (2021) Predicting stock returns of Tehran exchange using LSTM neural network and feature engineering technique. Multimed Tools Appl 80:19947–19970.
12. Li G, Zhang A, Zhang Q, Wu D, Zhan C (2022)Pearson correlation coefficient-based performance enhancement of Broad Learning System for stock price prediction, IEEE Trans Circuits Syst II, (Early Access).
13. Botunac I, Panjkota A, Matetic M (2020) The effect of feature selection on the performance of long short-term memory neural network in stock market predictions, In 31st DAAAM ISIMA, Vienna, Austria, pp 0592–0598.
14. Li G, Zhang A, Zhang Q, Wu D, Zhan C (2022)Pearson correlation coefficient-based performance enhancement of Broad Learning System for stock price prediction, IEEE Trans Circuits Syst II, (Early Access).
15. Chen Y, Hao Y (2017) A feature weighted support vector machine and K-nearest neighbor algorithm for stock market indices prediction. Expert Syst Appl 80:340–355.
16. Siddique M, Panda D (2019) A hybrid forecasting model for prediction of stock index of tata motors using principal component analysis, support vector regression and particle swarm optimization. I J Eng Adv Tech 9:3032–3037.
17. Das SR, Mishra D, Rout M (2019) Stock market prediction using firefly algorithm with evolutionary framework optimized feature reduction for OSELM method". Expert Syst Appl X 4:100016.

Note: All the figures and table in this chapter were made by the author.

Challenges and Opportunities for Innovation in India – Dr. Shweta Mishra et al. (eds)
© 2024 Taylor & Francis Group, London, ISBN 978-1-032-99842-8

Imposing on Defy Protocol in Supply Chains Managements: A Comprehensive Study

36

Amit Kumar Jaiswal[1], Ajay Pal Singh[2]
University Institute of Engineering Chandigarh University
Mohali, Punjab, India

Abstract

This research paper explores the potential of utilizing Defy Protocol, a decentralized finance (DeFi) protocol, in supply chains managements to enhance transparency, efficiency, and security. The paper delves into the principles of blockchain technology, smart contracts, and their applications in supply chain operations. It also investigates the challenges and opportunities associated with integrating Defy Protocol into the traditional supply chain ecosystem. The study employs a mixed-method approach involving qualitative and quantitative data analysis, case studies, and interviews with industry experts to provide insights into the feasibility and benefits of adopting Defy Protocol in supply chains managements. Yet, traditional supply chain models often fall short in addressing the modern-day imperatives of transparency, efficiency, and security. This research seeks to offer an all-encompassing analysis of the transformative possibilities that the adoption of Defy Protocol can bring to supply chains managements

Keywords

Defy protocol, SCM, Data analysis, Data integration, Training & validation loss

1. INTRODUCTION

1.1 Background

In a rapidly evolving global business landscape, supply chains managements have emerged as a critical area of focus for organizations seeking to maintain competitiveness, traditional supply chain models often struggle to meet the demands of transparency, efficiency, and security in an era defined by interconnectivity, complex networks, and heightened consumer expectations this necessitates an exploration of innovative solutions, and among the promising technologies [1], blockchain and defi protocols like defy protocol have garnered significant attention. in this context, this research endeavors to delve deep into the potential transformation that the adoption of defy protocol can bring to supply chains managements supply chains of today are not the linear, monolithic structures of the past, they are intricate networks connecting suppliers, manufacturers, logistics providers, and consumers across borders and time zones, the pressures of an interconnected world demand greater transparency, efficiency, and security within these supply chains. These expectations are heightened by the digital age, where information flows at

[1]amitjaiswal939@gmail.com, [2]Apsingh3289@gmail.com

DOI: 10.1201/9781003606260-36

the speed of light, and the slightest disruption can have far-reaching consequences supply chain managers are faced with the unrelenting task of optimizing these networks, reducing operational costs, mitigating risks, and ensuring compliance with an ever-expanding web of regulations, the need for real-time visibility into the movement of goods, accurate traceability, and secure transactions has never been more pronounced these challenges necessitate a revaluation of traditional supply chain processes and the adoption of innovative technologies capable of reshaping how we manage, operate, and secure supply chains. it is in this context that we turn our attention to the potential of defy protocol[1], a decentralized finance (defi) protocol, as a transformative force in supply chains managements.

1.2 Problem Statement

Traditional supply chains managements systems are characterized by inherent challenges such as opacity, inefficiencies, data fragmentation, and trust deficits among stakeholders[1,2]. these challenges pose significant hurdles to the effective functioning of supply chains in the modern landscape the need for a solution that addresses these challenges and brings about substantial improvements in supply chain operations has never been more pressing. blockchain technology and defi protocols offer a promising path to addressing these challenges, making the adoption of defy protocol a subject of keen interest in the context of supply chains managements as the global business environment becomes more complex and interconnected, addressing these challenges becomes a priority businesses, governments, and supply chain participants must find innovative solutions that can offer improved transparency, traceability, security, and efficiency while navigating a regulatory landscape that continues to evolve.

1.3 Research Objectives

The primary objectives of this research are to comprehensively evaluate the feasibility of integrating defy protocol into conventional supply chains managements practices[3], to assess the multifaceted benefits it may offer, and to gain valuable insights into the challenges and complexities involved in such an integration, this research will equip businesses and policymakers with a holistic understanding of the implications of incorporating blockchain technology and defi protocols in supply chain operations.

1.4 Research Question

1. How can defy protocol be effectively integrated into supply chains managements processes to enhance transparency and traceability[4]?

2. What are the regulatory and compliance challenges that organizations may encounter when adopting defy protocol in their supply chains?

1.5 Scope of the Study

This research will explore multiple facets of supply chains managements, spanning various industries, sectors, and geographical regions, the case studies will be drawn from diverse industries to offer a well-rounded perspective, with global examples ensuring a comprehensive understanding. However, it is essential to recognize that the adoption and adaptation of blockchain technologies and defi protocols, including defy protocol, can vary based on regional regulations, industry-specific requirements, and technological infrastructure, the findings from this research are intended to provide valuable insights and inform strategic decisions for businesses and policymakers as they navigate the ever-changing landscape of supply chains managements by expanding upon each subsection of the introduction, you provide a thorough context for your research on leveraging defy protocol in supply chains managements, this not only sets the stage for your study but also engages your readers with a clear understanding of the challenges and opportunities in the supply chains managements landscape

2. LITERATURE REVIEW

2.1 Supply Chains Managements

The literature review will commence with an exploration of contemporary supply chains managements models and their intrinsic challenges. It will elaborate on the complexities of global supply chains, the need for real-time visibility, and the ever- increasing pressure on supply chain managers to enhance efficiency.

2.2 Blockchain Technology and Defy Protocol

The literature review will provide an extensive overview of blockchain technology, elucidating its core principles, including decentralization, transparency, immutability, and security. It will further delve into the workings of smart contracts, emphasizing their role in automating and optimizing processes within a blockchain network. Additionally, it will discuss Defy Protocol and its underlying mechanisms in detail[5].

2.3 Applications of Blockchain in Supply Chain

This section will explore the myriad applications of blockchain technology in supply chains, encompassing areas such as provenance tracking, authentication, and logistics optimization. Real-world examples will be highlighted to illustrate the tangible benefits that blockchain can offer to supply chain stakeholders.

2.4 Challenges in Traditional Supply Chains Managements

The literature review will dissect the challenges that have plagued traditional supply chains managements, with a particular emphasis on opacity, data fragmentation, trust deficits, and inefficiencies.

2.5 Benefits of Defy Protocol in Supply Chains Managements

The literature review will summarize the potential benefits of integrating Defy Protocol into supply chains managements, including cost savings, enhanced transparency, increasedtrust, and operational efficiency[6].

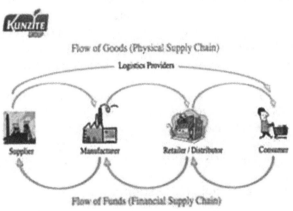

Fig. 36.1 Flow of funds

Designing a research methodology for your study on "Leveraging Defy Protocol in Supply chains managements" is a critical step in ensuring the research is structured and credible. Here's an elaboration of the research design section:

3. RESEARCH DESIGN

3.1 Research Approach

This study employs a mixed-method research approach to provide a comprehensive understanding of the integration of Defy Protocol in supply chains managements[7]. The mixed-method

A. Annotations

As previously stated, the class ID and traffic sign name are included in the dataset that we have chosen. 43 unique classes in all, with class IDs ranging from 0 to 42, are present. Every class in the dataset has a different distribution of the training data [1]. The graphic below displays the sample annotated image. The frequency of photos in each class is displayed in this histogram graph. design combines both quantitative and qualitative methods to achieve a well-rounded perspective on the subject.

3.2 Qualitative Research

The qualitative component of this research involves in-depth case studies and expert interviews to explore the nuances of Defy Protocol adoption in diverse supply chain settings. Case Studies: Multiple case studies will be conducted across various industries and sectors. The selection of case study

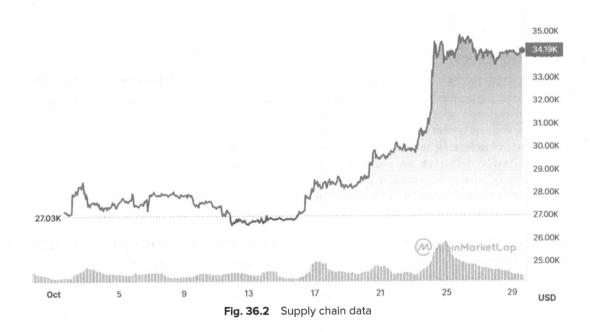

Fig. 36.2 Supply chain data

organizations will be based on specific criteria[8], such as the degree of Defy Protocol integration, geographical representation, and industry diversity. These cases will provide real-world examples of how Defy Protocol is applied in different supply chain contexts. Data collection for case studies will include interviews, documentation analysis, and on-site observations where feasible. Expert Interviews: A set of structured interviews will be conducted with industry experts, including supply chain professionals, blockchain developers, and policymakers. The experts will be selected based on their experience and expertise in areas relevant to Defy Protocol and supply chains managements. The interviews will be designed to delve into specific topics, including regulatory challenges, technology adoption issues, and the practical benefits of Defy Protocol integration.

3.3 Quantitative Research

The quantitative component of this research involves surveys distributed to supply chain professionals, blockchain technology experts, and business leaders involved in supply chains managements. The surveys aim to collect empirical data that quantifies the impact of Defy Protocol on various supply chain performance metrics. Survey Development: A comprehensive survey questionnaire will be developed based on insights gained from the qualitative research component. The questionnaire will be designed to capture data on a wide range of aspects, such as the extent of Defy Protocol integration, perceived benefits, challenges faced, and key performance indicators. The survey will be carefully crafted to ensure clarity, relevance, and the ability to yield meaningful data. Survey Distribution: Surveys will be distributed to a diverse sample of supply chain professionals and experts. To ensure a representative sample, a variety of distribution methods will be employed, including email surveys, online survey platforms, and direct outreach to industry associations. The sample will encompass participants from different geographical regions and industries to provide a broad perspective[9].

3.4 Data Analysis

Qualitative data collected from case studies and expert interviews will undergo rigorous analysis. The analysis process will involve thematic coding, content analysis, and the identification of recurring patterns and themes. The qualitative data analysis will aim to uncover insights into real-world applications of Defy Protocol, as well as the challenges and opportunities it presents in various supply chain settings. The results will be used to provide in-depth narratives for each case study and to complement the qualitative findings of the research.

3.5 Data Integration

Both qualisatives and quantitative data will be integrated to provide a holistic understanding of the impact and implications of Defy Protocol in supply chains managements. The findings from the case studies, expert interviews, and surveys will be synthesized to offer a comprehensive view of how Defy Protocol is being leveraged, the challenges faced, and the opportunities realized across different supply chain contexts. The integration of both data types will enhance the credibility and validity of the research findings.

3.6 Ethical Considerations

Ethical considerations will be of paramount importance throughout the research process. Informed consent will be obtained from all participants, including those involved in case studies, surveys, and expert interviews. Confidentiality and data security measures will be rigorously implemented to protect the privacy of participants and the proprietary information of the organizations involved. Ethical guidelines for research involving human subjects will be strictly adhered to, and all research activities will prioritize the welfare and rights of participants. By employing this comprehensive mixed-method approach and conducting rigorous qualitative and quantitative data collection and analysis, this research aims to provide a nuanced and well- supported understanding of the integration of Defy Protocol in supply chains managements. The combination of real-world case studies, expert insights, and empirical data from surveys will allow for a holistic exploration of the opportunities, challenges, and implications of Defy Protocol adoption in supply chains. Prediction using the recently created dataset and real-time webcam traffic sign detection are the project's two primary features. The ratio of accurate predictions to total predictions is known as accuracy. Accuracy = (The Number of Correct Predictions) / (Total predictions). The accuracy achieved on the test dataset is ~98%. Loss statistics after 30 epochs.

Table 36.1 Loss dataset

Sr No.	Dataset	Loss
1.	Training Loss	0.0096
2.	Validation Loss	0.0013

4. BLOCKCHAIN AND DEFY PROTOCOL MANAGEMENTS IN SUPPLY CHAINS

Peer-to-peer lending and borrowing of cryptocurrencies, including stablecoins. Unlike traditional financial systems, Defy Protocol operates without intermediaries, offering users the opportunity to lend and borrow assets directly from one another. The core mechanisms of Defy Protocol include liquidity pools, automated market makers (AMMs), and yield farming. Liquidity providers deposit their assets into these pools, and the protocol

4.1 Understanding Blockchains Technology

Blockchain technology is the foundational pillar of the Defy Protocol, and comprehending its core principles is crucial to understanding its role in supply chains managements. At its essence, blockchain is a distributed ledger technology that maintains a decentralized and immutable record of transactions. Unlike traditional centralized systems, where a single entity or authority controls the ledger, blockchain operates on a network of nodes, ensuring transparency and security. One of the primary attributes of blockchain is its immutability. Once data is recorded on the blockchain, it cannot be altered, making it a reliable source of truth in supply chain operations. Each transaction is linked to the previous one in a chain, creating a chronological and unchangeable history. This feature enhances the traceability of products and transactions, which is crucial for supply chains managements.

4.2 Role of Smart Contracts

Smart contracts are self-executing contracts with predefined rules and conditions directly written into code. They are integral to the functioning of blockchain technology, and their role in supply chains managements is transformative. Smart contracts automate and optimize various processes within a blockchain network, such as the verification of transactions, payments, and the enforcement of contractual agreements. In supply chains managements, smart contracts can be used to automate tasks like verifying the authenticity of goods, ensuring compliance with regulations, and executing payments upon the successful completion of milestones. This not only reduces the need for intermediaries but also minimizes the risk of errors or fraud. For instance, when goods are received at a specified location, the smart contract can automatically trigger payment to the supplier[12].

4.3 Defy Protocol: Overview and Mechanisms

Defy Protocol is a decentralized finance (DeFi) protocol that operates on the Ethereum blockchain. It is designed to facilitate uses these assets to facilitate loans and generate interest. Users can also participate in yield farming by staking assets in the protocol in exchange for rewards. Defy Protocol introduces the concept of decentralized finance into the supply chains managements landscape, allowing businesses to access capital more efficiently and transparently, while also enabling investors to earn returns by participating in the lending and borrowing activities. This novel approach has the potential to revolutionize the financing aspect of supply chains, reducing reliance on traditional financial intermediaries.

2.4 Defy Protocol in Supply Chain Operations

The integration of Defy Protocol into supply chain operations offers numerous advantages. It can streamline and optimize the financial aspects of supply chains, enabling more efficient working capital management and reducing the reliance on traditional banking institutions. With Defy Protocol, organizations can access liquidity from a global pool of funds, enhancing flexibility in managing their financial resources.

Furthermore, the transparency and security inherent in blockchain technology and smart contracts enhance the traceability and authenticity of products in the supply chain. Each step of a product's journey can be recorded [14] on the blockchain, from its origin to its final destination. This not only helps in preventing fraud and counterfeit goods but also facilitates compliance with various regulations, such as food safety standards or customs requirements.

By incorporating Defy Protocol and blockchain technology into supply chain operations, organizations can potentially reduce operational costs, enhance the trust and confidence of stakeholders, and improve the overall efficiency of their supply chains managements practices. The automation of various processes through smart contracts and the access to decentralized finance can drive innovation in the industry, ultimately leading to a more transparent, secure, and cost-

How does the
Smart Contract work?

Pre-defined Contract   **Business Logic**   **Execution**   **Settlement**

Fig. 36.3   Flow of smart contract work

effective supply chain ecosystem. In summary, blockchain technology and Defy Protocol offer a novel approach to enhancing supply chains managements. The decentralized and immutable nature of blockchain, coupled with the automation capabilities of smart contracts, has the potential to revolutionize various aspects of supply chains, including financial operations, transparency, and traceability. Defy Protocol, as a DeFi solution, introduces a new dimension of decentralized finance into the supply chain landscape, creating opportunities for more efficient and transparent financial transactions.

5. Case Study: Company XYZ - Enhancing Supply Chain Finance with Defy Protocol**

5.1 Background

Company XYZ, a global manufacturing and distribution company, faced common challenges in managing its supply chain operations, particularly in terms of working capital management. The company sought a solution to optimize its financial processes and enhance transparency across its supply chain. This case study explores how the adoption of Defy Protocol brought about transformative changes in their supply chain finance management.

6. Challenges

1. **Working Capital Constraints:** Company XYZ, like many organizations, often faced working capital constraints. Traditional financing methods were both time-consuming and came with high-interest rates.
2. **Opaque Supply Chain:** The lack of transparency in the supply chain made it challenging to track the movement of goods, verify product authenticity, and ensure compliance with regulatory requirements. Solution: Company XYZ decided to integrate Defy Protocol into its supply chains managements processes. Here's how they leveraged the technology:
3. **Decentralized Financing:** Through Defy Protocol, Company XYZ established a decentralized finance solution for its supply chain. They created a liquidity pool that allowed participants to provide capital directly to the supply chain, reducing the need for traditional financial intermediaries.
4. **Smart Contract Automation:** Smart contracts were employed to automate payment processes. When predefined supply chain milestones were reached, the smart contracts automatically triggered payments, reducing delays and eliminating the need for manual intervention.

5. **Blockchain-Based Traceability:** Company XYZ used blockchain technology to record each step of its product journey. From the manufacturing plant to the end consumer, every transaction and movement was recorded immutably on the blockchain. This increased transparency and ensured that product data was secure and tamper-proof.

6.1 Results

The integration of Defy Protocol yielded several significant outcomes for Company XYZ:

1. **Working Capital Optimization:** By accessing capital through the Defy Protocol's liquidity pool, Company XYZ was able to optimize its working capital. This reduced their dependence on costly loans and provided access to more affordable financing options.
2. **Supply Chain Transparency:** The blockchain-based system improved supply chain transparency significantly. This led to a reduction in product counterfeit and enhanced compliance with various regulations, thereby improving the overall integrity of the supply chain.
3. **Cost Reduction:** The elimination of intermediaries and the automation of payment processes reduced operational costs. Company XYZ experienced a measurable reduction in the time and resources required for financial transactions and product tracking.

6.2 Conclusion

The adoption of Defy Protocol in supply chains managements allowed Company XYZ to address working capital constraints[12], enhance supply chain transparency, and reduce operational costs. By leveraging decentralized finance and blockchain technology, they not only streamlined their financial processes but also established a more secure and transparent supply chain ecosystem. This case study illustrates the potential benefits of integrating Defy Protocol into supply chain operations for companies seeking to optimize their financial processes and improve transparency.

■ REFRENCES ■

1. Nakamoto, S. (2008). "Bitcoin: A Peer-to-Peer Electronic Cash System." Bitcoin Whitepaper. [Available online]
2. Tapscott, D., & Tapscott, A. (2016). "Blockchain Revolution: How the Technology Behind Bitcoin is Changing Money, Business, and the World." Penguin.
3. Mougayar, W. (2016). "The Business Blockchain: Promise, Practice, and Application of the Next Internet Technology." Wiley.

4. Iansiti, M., & Lakhani, K. R. (2017). "The Truth About Blockchain." Harvard Business Review, 95(1), 118–127.

5. Shen, Q., Nucci, A., Santoni, G., & Wang, Y. (2018). "Blockchain and supply chains managements: A review and research agenda." International Journal of Physical Distribution & Logistics Management, 48(3), 205–230.

6. Li, X., Wu, J., & Shi, Y. (2018). "A survey on the security of blockchain systems." Future Generation Computer Systems, 89, 641–658.

7. Cachin, C., Vukolić, M., & Zakhary, S. (2017). "Blockchain Consensus Protocols in the Wild." In Advances in Cryptology – CRYPTO 2017.

8. Fan, K., Wang, S., Ren, Y., Li, H., & Yang, Y. (2018). "MedRec: Using blockchain for medical data access and permission management." In 2018 17th IEEE International Conference on Trust, Security and Privacy in Computing and Communications/12th IEEE International Conference on Big Data Science and Engineering (TrustCom/BigDataSE).

9. Sarkar, A., & Bhattacharya, A. (2019). "A Blockchain-Based Smart Contract System for Healthcare Management." In 2019 IEEE Region 10 Symposium (TENSYMP).

10. Zohar, A. (2015). "Bitcoin: under the hood." Communications of the ACM, 58(9), 104–113.

11. Tapscott, D., & Tapscott, A. (2016). Blockchain revolution: how the technology behind bitcoin is changing money, business, and the world.

12. Mougayar, W. (2016). The Business Blockchain: Promise, Practice, and Application of the Next Internet Technology.

13. Swan, M. (2015). Blockchain: blueprint for a new economy.

14. Tapscott, D., & Tapscott, A. (2017). How blockchain is changing finance

15. Mallen, B. (2018). Smart Contracts for the Supply Chain

16. Zohar, A. (2015). Bitcoin: under the hood

Note: All the figures and table in this chapter were made by the author.

Challenges and Opportunities for Innovation in India – Dr. Shweta Mishra et al. (eds)
© 2024 Taylor & Francis Group, London, ISBN 978-1-032-99842-8

Design of Framework of Automatic Evaluation of Descriptive Questions using Text Summarization

37

Subhash Chandra Gupta[1], Noopur Goel[2]

Department of Computer Applications,
V.B.S. Purvanchal university,
Jaunpur, India

Abstract

As the use of internet is increasing day-by-day, most of the services/facilities are going to online. Education system is also gone online through e-learning, but evaluation of answer scripts are still performed in manually in manual evaluation system, the evaluator has to do tedious work of evaluation when a question does not have a definite answer and have multiple correct answers, these answers contains different sentences, but their key points are about same. In this paper a frame work of a evaluation model(AEDQ) is designed to perform automatic evaluation of descriptive questions. The model is based on text summarization and its supportive techniques such as text mining, information retrieval, information extraction and NLP. The paper briefly discussed the importance of automation of evaluation work and demerits of present evaluation. it also make a discussion about the technology used in model and make a detail discussion on the methodology of proposed model.

Keywords

Text summarization, Text mining, Evaluation of descriptive questions

1. INTRODUCTION

An examination plays an vital role in the life of a student, he has to face many examinations throughout his life at school, college or university level for his academic achievements or participate in national or international examination for his carrier opportunities. Generally these examination held in offline or online mode. At college or university level, where number of students comes in thousands most of the examinations are held in offline mode; while at the national level, examination are held in both offline and online mode due to huge number of participants, usually in millions, in exams. The patterns of examination may be in descriptive questions and /or multiple choice questions (MCQs). Since evaluation of examinations based on descriptive questions take much time, so the declaration of results take too much time, the delay in the process is bad, not only for the students, but also for the examination governing body. More than 50% sessions of university exams are suffered from this problem. To save the time of evaluation, to declare result on time, most of the examinations are held in MCQs patterns. The University Grant Commission, a

[1]csubhashgupta@gmail.com, [2]noopurt11@gmail.com

DOI: 10.1201/9781003606260-37

prominent body which performs UGC-NET at national level, had to divert the pattern of this examination from descriptive mode to MCQ mode to declare results of millions participants on time. But MCQs is not a better option to evaluate the performance of a participant. The examinations based on Descriptive answers may be helpful to check the overall growth, progress, and positive change of students[1] . Along with , it encourage the student to get in-depth knowledge about a topic in preparation of examinations. Taking exam on online examinations based on descriptive questions not only overcome the delay in conducting exams but also provide a leak proof systems for examinations. If it may have been supported by online evaluation system, it will be better for candidate and exam governing body, both also evaluation of descriptive mode answers is very difficult in online mode for an examiner due to the lengthy textual answer given by students. Biasness is another problem in evaluation. Two students may have got different marks of the same question with the same answer, evaluated by different evaluator or by the same examiner checked at different time.

2. OBJECTIVE

The main objective of this paper to focus on the design of framework to develop an automatic evaluation system for online descriptive questions examinations (AESODQE). The framework uses the concept of text summarization, Information retrieval, information extraction along with Natural language processing and machine learning algorithms. Application of artificial intelligence may even improve the performance and accuracy level of evaluation system. A brief introduction about different technology used in the framework is discussed in upcoming sections. The paper is divided into following sections- the first section made a discussion about the role of online and offline examinations, descriptive and MCQ based examination patterns and their importance and demerits. Second section is the objective of paper and lecture reviews related to works done in past are discussed in third section. Fourth section provides the theoretical backgrounds about the different technology used in framework. Fifth section is the main section of paper , in which the methodology of proposed model is discussed in detail. Sixth section is about the issues which may be faced by the model and seventh section is the last section discussed the conclusion and future scope of the paper.

3. LITERATURE REVIEW

Bhagat Gayval at el [1] has discussed the importance of evaluation of descriptive answers for the analysis of student's growth. They proposed a model for evaluation of descriptive answers of questions. The model used the

probability approach, cosine similarity approach and a pre trained model, and compared its performance with manual scoring by a subject expert. From the observations, got by the probability approach, cosine similarity approach and the pretrained model, they have concluded that probability approach is better in comparison to other two in the evaluation of descriptive answers. Birpal Singh et al [2] focus on differences of the evaluation work of short answered and long answered questions. Since in short questions, there are very few keywords, so evaluation of these answered required extra care during the calculation of the weighting score of the answers. They made a review of different methods for this purpose in their paper. G. Deepak et al [3] has proposed a model to evaluate the answer scripts of descriptive questions using Strategically Constructed Semantic Skill Ontologies. The model is created from a language model based on expected answer keys, and entity graph generated from the ontology model to evaluate the input answers. A survey paper is presented by T. A. Tayde at el [4] on effective way of online descriptive exams. the model consume a unstructured textual content to evaluate ,and is based on the concept of semantic similarity between the students' answers and faculty's answers. They also made a comparisons between different techniques used such as Term Frequency- Inverse Document Frequency (TF-IDF), NLP, Naive Bayes algorithm, LSA, SOM etc. Nandini V. et al [5] has proposed a model which contains the steps such as classification of questions in short answered and long answered questions; similarly answer is also categorized in short and long type of answers. To evaluate descriptive answers, they proposed a syntactical relation-based feature extraction technique that also adapted a syntactical relation-based feature extraction technique. For the evaluation of descriptive answer script, a machine should consider the important factor of evaluation such as an evaluator keeps in mind in manual assessment of answers. To solve the problem researchers, Vinal Bagaria et al [6], proposed a system which used the concept of grammar checking, graph, fuzzy string matching and other similarity metrics to evaluate answers. The model also paid attention on key parameters such as question's type, conceptual and structural aspects of answers and expected words and their synanyms. From the review of a number of papers, it is find that most the model is based either on statistical method such as huge information tongue process, Laten linguistics Analysis, Thomas Bayes theorem, Inverse Document Frequency (TF-IDF), NLP, Naive Bayes, LSA, SOM etc. or machine learning techniques such as K-nearest classifiers. In some paper natural language processing is also applied to enhance the model acuracy and efficiency. Statistical techniques based model is based on keywords matching and cannot handle appropriately the issues like the sysnonyms and the context of material. So these models are not considered as robust as required. In this paper, a framework of model is proposed to evaluate descriptive answer scripts, which based on the concept of extraction of information. This model uses the modern techniques for mining of knowledge like Information retrieval, information extraction, text mining and text summarization along with the natural language processing.

4. THEROTICAL SUPPORT

A. **Text Mining:** Text mining is the process of finding hidden patterns / information from unstructured data. An unstructured does not follow the structural concept/ schema architecture of datasets and are usually contains textual content. Extracting interesting and meaningful information from textual data source such as blogs, social media chats, reviews of products/ services, pdfs, web pages and text documents, is called text mining. Text mining is interdisciplinary approach which includes techniques like information retrieval, Information Extraction, text summarization and works with supporting techniques such as Natural language processing, Machine learning, computational linguistics and statistics [9].

B. **Information Extraction (IE):** The process of extracting relevant information about a topic / words from unstructured and /or semi-structured and transforming it a structured format is called Information extraction. IE is performed with a well defined objective since its inputs and target to be extracted, both are clearly defined [10].

C. **Information Retrieval (IR):** Getting the collection of one or more documents, usually in form of text / string, from huge volume of unstructured data , according to the given information in query / based on a specific filed of interest is called Information retrieval. The web search engine such as google, yahoo or bing is the example of information retrieval process in which a user pass his query or search words in search text box and search engine return a collection of documents which satisfy the query or containing the specified words [11]. IR and IE both are different things, IR is related with the retrival of those documents which satify the needs of a query, while IE is the process of extracting valuable information from one or more unstructured documents on a specific topic/ contents, and transforming them in a structured form.

D. **Text Summarization:** The process of summarizing the contents of one / more text documents which cover the relevant information from whole text and also have its length in less than the half of size of original text, is called text summarization. The automatic summarization technique provides the ability to a machine, that enables it behave like a human as he can read and understand the content of a file a produce a summarized view of documents[10] [12]. there are two approach to perform text summarization- extractive approach and abstractive approach, extractive methods generally use statistical method to find the most important words/sentences to measure the weightage and the summarized text contains those sentences whose weightage are relatively high in comparison to others. Abstractive approach uses the NLP, machine learning techniques to get the output and much better and advance approach in comparison to extractive approach.

E. **Natural Language Processing (NLP):** NLP is a modern techniques in language processing and provide the abilty to computer, by which it can understand the textual content as human can [3], [6].

5. METHODOLOGY OF PROPOSED FRAMEWORK

The proposed model perform automatic evaluation of descriptive questions and produce the final result. The major techniques used by the model is Text Summarization, Information Retrieval and information extraction along with the NLP. The model is named as Automatic Evaluation of Descriptive Questions (AEDQ). The working of model is start with the appearing of students in the online examination based on descriptive questions. The AEDQ first read a question from the paper and find the keypoints of possible answer of the question using these processes in a sequence –preprocessing of text : to produce topic words of question, information retrieval: for the given topic to get needed text documents, text summarization: to get the summarized view of possible answer text of question, and information extraction: to convert the relevant keypoints in dataset. This dataset contains the keypoints of answer text of a question, weightage of keypoints, and the associated marks to assign for the presence of that key points. In next stage the answer of given question is read by the AEDQ and generate a dataset having keypoints in answer and its weightage to do this job, AEDQ again follow the text ummarization and information extraction process in a sequence for the given answer script and finally get the keypoint dataset for student's answer. Now AEDQ try to match the both dataset, the keypoint dataset of answer of exam question and the keypoint dataset for student's answer, using content similarity index measures and assign marks to student for given answer of the question. the same procedure is repeated for evaluation of the each question and score the marks gained by student and finally declare/display his results. The detail process of methodology of AEDQ is given below:

Step-1: Submission of answer script of questions in digital form of Online Descriptive Questions Examination.

Step-2: Conversion of question-sentence into its related topic words:

- AEDQ read a question from exam question.
- Preprocess the questions:
  - Sentence-wise Segmentation-break the question into one or more sentence.
  - Tokenization of sentence
  - Removal of Stop Word
  - Stemming

Output: Get a list of topic words for the selected question.

Step-3: AEDQ performs Information Retrieval process for topic words of question sentence to get the list of document for the formation of answer of question. Documents can be provide to AEDQ considering the difficulty levels of question (materials according to the syllabus of exam).

Output: AEDQ get a list of document , related to the topic words of question, for answer formation.

Step-4: Use Text summarization techniques to get summarized text from the obtained documents to form the possible answer script of question.

Output: AEDQ get a summarized text of multiple documents which contain keypoints of the contents of all documents.

Step-5: Use Information Extraction techniques and transform the keypoints of summarized text into a structured dataset.

- Extract the relevant words form text.
- Rank the sentence/words with their weightage.
- Assign marks for its weighted sentence.
- Transform it into structured form to get the topic word, its weightage and assigned marks.

Output: a dataset having key points (name entity), its weightage and assigned marks for a topic of possible answer of a questions.

Step-6: Read the answer script of selected question submitted by student and apply Text summarization to get the summarized view/ text of answer script having important keypoints of answer.

- Read the answer of specified question.
- Preprocessed the answer script to remove anomalies and convert the text to its lemma.

- Get the summarized text of answer script using text summarization techniques.

Output: AEDQ got the summarized text of the answer of selected question.

Step-7: Perform Information Extraction on summarized text and transformed the keypoints (name entity) in structured dataset.

Output: AEDQ now have the student's answer in the form of a structured dataset.

Step-8: Evaluate the given answer and assign score to it.

- Find the similarity measures between the name entities (topic words) of a student's answer and exam question's answer.
- Assign marks to the answer according to the similarity measure index.

Output: AEDQ check the answer of question and assign marks to it.

Step-9: Calculate the marks earned by student and display his result by evaluating each question by repeating the process of step-2 to step-9.

6. ISSUES RELATED WITH PROPOSED AEDQ MODEL

AEDQ model is developed to evaluate the answer script of questions automatically and produce the result of student by evaluating the answers of all questions. Although, the AEDQ uses NLP, computational linguistics to improve and increase the performance of model, but there still exist some issues such as the language border, availability of multi-lingual text documents, availability of huge amount of text documents on a specific topics/ key words, categorization of questions in short answer and long answer, complexity of the same question at different levels of exam etc which may pull the performance down.

7. CONCLUSION

Evaluation of a descriptive question is affected from the biasness and emotions of evaluators, and it also take much time. In this paper, the design of framework for automatic evaluation of answer script is proposed. The proposed AEDQ model is to use to automatically evaluate the answer script of question available digitally. It can automate the tedious works of evaluating the answer scripts for a checker and save their a lot of his time. The AEDQ model uses the text summarization and text mining techniques to evaluate the answer. Information retrieval techniques is used to get a collection of relevant documents on a specific keywords while information extraction techniques is used to extract

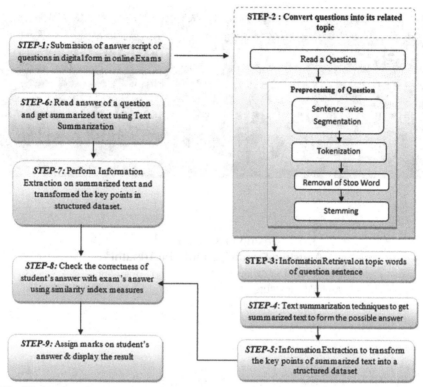

Fig. 37.1 Working methodology of automatic evaluation of descriptive questions model (AEDQ)

Source: Author

the valuable information from textual documents. Natural language processing may also applied to overcome the language obstacles.

There are some issues before the evaluation model such as language barrier, availability of huge amount of text data on a specific topic, difficulty level of answers of questions etc. these issues may diminish the performance of model. In this paper, only framework of automatic evaluation system is designed. In future, it is planned to implement the model in appropriate programming language such as python. AI may reduces the impacts of issues discussed above, so during model implementation suitable AI techniques may even apply for better performance.

■ REFERENCES ■

1. B. Gayval and V. Mhaske, "Evaluation of Descriptive Answer by using Probability Approach , Cosine Similarity and Pretrained model," vol. 67, no. 2, pp. 105–109, 2023, doi: 10.37398/JSR.2023.670212.

2. B. S. J. Kapoor, S. M. Nagpure, S. S. Kolhatkar, P. G. Chanore, M. M. Vishwakarma, and R. B. Kokate, "An Analysis of Automated Answer Evaluation Systems based on Machine Learning," pp. 439–443, 2020.

3. G. Deepak, A. K. A, S. Priyadarshini, and D. Singh, "Descriptive Answer Evaluation using NLP Processes Integrated with Strategically Constructed Semantic Skill Ontologies," 2022.

4. T. A. Tayde, "Descriptive Answer Evaluation System using Machine Learning," no. August, pp. 26–33, 2021.

5. P. U. Maheswari, "Automatic assessment of descriptive answers in online examination system using semantic relational features," *J. Supercomput.*, 2018, doi: 10.1007/s11227-018-2381-y.

6. V. Bagaria, M. Badve, and M. Beldar, "An Intelligent System for Evaluation of Descriptive Answers," pp. 19–24, 2020.

7. P. G. Deshmukh and P. K. R. Ingole, "Online Evaluation System for Descriptive Answers," pp. 2555–2556, 2021.

8. M. Jalgaon, I. Technology, and G. H. Raisoni, "AUTOMATED DESCRIPTIVE ANSWER EVALUATION SYSTEM USING MACHINE," no. 3, pp. 596–598, 2021.

9. H. Hassani, C. Beneki, S. Unger, M. T. Mazinani, and M. R. Yeganegi, "Text mining in big data analytics," *Big Data Cogn. Comput.*, vol. 4, no. 1, pp. 1–34, 2020, doi: 10.3390/bdcc4010001.

10. A. P. Widyassari *et al.*, "Review of automatic text summarization techniques & methods," *J. King Saud Univ. - Comput. Inf. Sci.*, vol. 34, no. 4, pp. 1029–1046, 2022, doi: 10.1016/j.jksuci.2020.05.006.

11. A. T. Sadiq, "English Text Summarization Using Statistical , Linguistics , Heuristics and Machine Learning Techniques," vol. 40, pp. 1–13.

12. N. Goel, "A study of text mining techniques: Applications and Issues," *Pramana Res. J.*, vol. 8, no. 12, pp. 307–316, 2020.

13. P. S. P. Raut, S. D. Chaudhari, and V. B. Waghole, "Automatic Evaluation of Descriptive Answers Using NLP and Machine Learning." vol. 2, no. 1, pp. 735–745, 2022, doi: 10.48175/IJARSCT-3030.

Challenges and Opportunities for Innovation in India – Dr. Shweta Mishra et al. (eds)
© 2024 Taylor & Francis Group, London, ISBN 978-1-032-99842-8

A Comprehensive Review of Innovations Improving Legal Procedures and Rehabilitation for Undertrial Prisoners in India

38

Jasmeen Kaur Arora[1],
Anushka Pandit[2], Samriddhi Tripathi[3]
Department of Computer Science and Engineering,
Ambalika Institute of Management and Technology,
Lucknow, India

Abstract

This comprehensive review examines the myriad innovations that have been introduced to enhance legal procedures and rehabilitation efforts for undertrial prisoners in India. The undertrial population faces unique challenges within the criminal justice system, including prolonged detention periods and inadequate access to rehabilitation services. The study explores a range of initiatives, spanning legal reforms, technological advancements, and social interventions, aimed at addressing these issues. This research paper examines the rights and status of prisoners who are awaiting trial from the standpoint of the Indian Constitution and relevant national and international human rights laws. By exposing the vulnerable state in which detained undertrial inmates find themselves, it is contended that further measures are desperately needed to protect their constitutionally guaranteed right to life and liberty. It assesses the impact of these innovations on the efficiency of legal proceedings, the rights of undertrial prisoners, and their successful reintegration into society post-release. By synthesizing current knowledge and highlighting gaps in existing research, this review contributes to the ongoing discourse on criminal justice reform and human rights in India. The main purpose of criminal law is to protect the human rights of every victim, prisoner, and prisoner facing trial. The days of a convicted criminal being sent to spend his days in a dark prison are over.

Keywords

Undertrial prisoners, legal procedures, rehabilitation, criminal justice system, technological advancements, social interventions, human rights, reintegration, detention periods, legal proceedings, prison reform.

1. INTRODUCTION

A person who has been held in custody while these legal procedures are pending and is still being looked into for the crime they are allegedly guilty of committing is known as an undertrial or pre-trial inmate. People placed under such custody are typically maintained there for a number of reasons, but most frequently, it's to maintain justice. The trial processes by keeping them from having any kind of influence over the proceedings. Social civilization has

[1]jasmeenkaurarora2003@gmail.com, [2]anushkapa04@gmail.com, [3]samyashi0513@gmail.com

DOI: 10.1201/9781003606260-38

historically promoted ever-more-important discussions about the State, its relationship to its people, and the acceptance of individual liberties, rights, and justice ideals. The rights of inmates have become increasingly important in these conversations as a result of this heightened focus. The Indian Express didn't start writing about it till 1979.

2. CHALLENGES FACED

The Indian criminal justice system, like many others worldwide, grapples with the intricate challenges posed by the detention and legal processing of undertrial prisoners. This vulnerable demographic often faces protracted periods of pre-trial incarceration, coupled with limited access to rehabilitation services, leading to significant human rights concerns. Recognizing the need for systemic improvements, a spectrum of innovations has been introduced in recent years, encompassing legal reforms, technological advancements, and social interventions. This comprehensive review endeavours to shed light on the evolving landscape of legal procedures and rehabilitation initiatives tailored for undertrial prisoners in India. As the nation seeks to balance the imperative of justice with the protection of individual rights, the examination of these innovations becomes paramount. This exploration encompasses the diverse facets of the undertrial experience, ranging from the efficiency of legal proceedings to the post-release reintegration of individuals into society. By synthesizing existing knowledge, this review aims to provide a nuanced understanding of the impact of these innovations, identify gaps in current strategies, and offer insights that contribute to the ongoing discourse on criminal justice reform and human rights in the Indian context.

3. SUGGESTIONS/APPROACH

Some years back when people started to understand the need for awareness of their human rights mentioned in a book of laws, which we call as THE CONSTITUTION Every person is inherently entitled to basic human rights, irrespective of any bias or discrimination. Simply by being part of the human race, individuals naturally possess these fundamental rights. Prisoners, whether in custody or awaiting trial, should be treated with respect. Since undertrials are not housed in a different prison, there is possibility that first-time and circumstantial offenders will become criminals due to the presence of hardened criminals and the lack of scientific categorization techniques to distinguish them from others. Most jails struggle to maintain the safe and healthy conditions of their inmates because of prisoner overpopulation and lack of suitable housing. The majority of inmates, even those awaiting

trial, are from socioeconomically deprived back grounds where it is typical to experience illness, malnutrition, and a lack of access to healthcare. Prisoners awaiting trial often encounter human rights violations, such as extended detention, inadequate legal representation, poor living conditions, presumption of guilt, and limited access to healthcare. Addressing these issues is vital for upholding their fundamental rights. Extended custody-Extended periods of pre-trial detention without a prompt and equitable trial process. Insufficient legal representation -Lack of proper legal representation hampers the ability to present a robust defence. Unsatisfactory detention conditions: Overcrowded and unhygienic facilities that violate the right to humane treatment. Presumption of innocence involves bias or mistreatment arising from assumptions of guilt before a verdict is determined. Access to healthcare: Refusal of essential medical care, encroaching upon the right to health.

4. TECH DRIVEN REMEDY

We can head up via a digital approach to get rid of this problem. We can develop a digital platform, an interface to seek quick access to legal authorities. Build an application, website to help the undertrial prisoners file their case, get access to lawyers, and hire one for themselves. Get knowledge about their rights and awareness of their crime and extent of punishment or rehabilitation period. Prisoners may get access to probono lawyers – the lawyers working for betterment of society for legal aid. They can get hold of their trial through the web application, and even check the status for their case.

They can communicate through video calls or chats with the lawyers and get their speedy trial.

5. CONCLUSION

In conclusion, an analysis of the Indian judiciary and judgments on the protection of human rights of prisoners shows that the judiciary fills the gap left by the executive and the legislature in important issues affecting the nation. The Supreme Court and the Supreme Court compensate citizens for damage caused by officials33in addition to awarding compensation related to the violation of rights. In these dark cells of the prison system are thousands of men and women seeking justice, which unfortunately is beyond their reach. Public awareness campaigns and government and legal oversight are needed to highlight these differences. In order to obtain favourable results in the preliminary investigation of, systemic changes must be made in the investigation, prosecution and prison administration. Achieving these lofty goals will take a lot of our time and resources, but the state should do its best to at least protect all the fundamental rights that are necessary during investigations and sub-trials.

■ REFERENCES ■

1. Baxi, Upendra. "Legal Assistance to the Poor: A Critique of the Expert Committee Report." Economic and Political Weekly, July 5, 1975: 1005–1013.
2. The lost souls. A study of undertrial prisoners in Karnataka and provision of legal aid. By Vikrant Singh. The centre for competition Law and Economics.
3. Right to bail. Right of undertrial prisoners. Probono India SocioLegally Yours. By Tejaswini Ramakrishna kle society's law college, Bengaluru. August 20, 2021.
4. Justice system in crises: The case of undertrial prisoners. www.orfonline.org/research
5. Bail and Incarceration: The state of Undertrial prisoners in India. www.papers.ssrn.com
6. www.google.com
7. www.mha.gov.in
8. www.law.cornell.edu
9. htttps://nhrc.nic.in
10. www.thehindu.com
11. www.researchgate.net
12. www.academia.edu
13. www.ijcrt.org/papers/
14. www.nliulawreview.nliu.ac.in
15. www.indianexpress.com

Challenges and Opportunities for Innovation in India – Dr. Shweta Mishra et al. (eds)
© 2024 Taylor & Francis Group, London, ISBN 978-1-032-99842-8

European Commissions' Directive Against Greenwashing—A Policy Review

39

Abhishek Mishra*

AIMT | Amir Raza, University of Warwick

Abstract

The term 'greenwashing' was first used by Jay Westerveld in 1980 to describe 'dishonest practices used by businesses to represent themselves as more sustainable; either by giving a false impression or providing misleading information as to the sustainability of a product or service' (Wagemans & Montens, 2023). The study explores the timeline of events, reports, legislatures and directives which led to the formation of the European Union's policy against greenwashing. In recent years green labeled products are found to be more in demand with a 71% rise in the search for sustainable products globally and over 80% EU consumers interested in durability of the products which contribute towards circular economy (EU, 2023). Survey conducted after the COVID-19 crisis in 4 EU countries found that between 66 – 76% consumers would buy products which are better for the environment even if they cost more (Hahnel, 2020). Many European citizens believe that 'changing the way we consume' is the most effective way to tackle environmental problems (Eurobarometer, 2020) European Commission (EC) explains green claims as ''Implicit, general or explicit practice of suggesting or otherwise creating the impression that a good or a service has a positive or no impact on the environment or is less damaging to the environment than competing goods or services. The study conducted by the EC in 2020 assessed 150 environmental claims and exposed 53.3 % of the claims as vague, misleading or based on unfounded information, 40% have no supporting evidence and over half of the labels offer weak or non-existent verification. There were 230 sustainability and over 100 green labels in the EU with vastly different levels of transparency. (EC, Green Claims, 2021) The proposal is in the advanced stage. Once approved by the European Parliament and the Council of the EU it will be adopted and the directive will be implemented in national legislation of all EU Member States.

Keywords

Greenwashing, European Commission, Sustainability, Environment

1. INTRODUCTION

The term 'greenwashing' was first used by Jay Westerveld in 1980 to describe 'dishonest practices used by businesses to represent themselves as more sustainable; either by giving a false impression or providing misleading information as to the sustainability of a product or service' (Wagemans & Montens, 2023). The study explores the timeline of

*Corresponding author: abhishekm2823@gmail.com

DOI: 10.1201/9781003606260-39

events, reports, legislatures and directives which led to the formation of the European Union's policy against greenwashing. In recent years green labeled products are found to be more in demand with a 71% rise in the search for sustainable products globally and over 80% EU consumers interested in durability of the products which contribute towards circular economy (EU, 2023). Survey conducted after the COVID-19 crisis in 4 EU countries found that between 66 – 76% consumers would buy products which are better for the environment even if they cost more (Hahnel, 2020). Many European citizens believe that 'changing the way we consume' is the most effective way to tackle environmental problems (Eurobarometer, 2020) European Commission (EC) explains green claims as ''Implicit, general or explicit practice of suggesting or otherwise creating the impression that a good or a service has a positive or no impact on the environment or is less damaging to the environment than competing goods or services. The study conducted by the EC in 2020 assessed 150 environmental claims and exposed 53.3 % of the claims as vague, misleading or based on unfounded information, 40% have no supporting evidence and over half of the labels offer weak or non-existent verification. There were 230 sustainability and over 100 green labels in the EU with vastly different levels of transparency. (EC, Green Claims, 2021) Such a scenario prompted EC to come up with a proposal for a 'Directive of the European Parliament and of the Council amending Directives 2005/29/EC and 2011/83/EU as regards empowering consumers for the green transition through better protection against unfair practices and better information' (EC, SWD, March 2022). Based on its evaluations and in line with the objectives of the 'European Green Deal' the proposal was updated in March 2023. The new proposal for the Directive of the European Parliament and the Council on substantiation and communication of explicit environmental claims (Green Claims Directive) was adopted by the Commission (EC, COM, March 2023) The proposed Directive will make it mandatory for the companies to disclose clear and comprehensive information regarding the environmental impact of their products and services. It will prohibit unsubstantiated or vague environmental claims and provide the need for the validation of green claims by the independent third parties. Additionally, it addresses the jungle of environmental labelling schemes by regulating green labelling schemes and any new scheme will have to prove its value in addition to the existing labels. (Watkins & Mason, 2023) The proposal is in the advanced stage. Once approved by the European Parliament and the Council of the EU it will be adopted and the directive will be implemented in national legislation of all EU Member States. Then the designated competent authorities in each Member State will have the powers to enforce the directive and offending companies will then be subject to penalties, exclusion from public procurement and funding systems apart from the reputational risk and damage to the company's image if a product or service offered as green turns out to be non-compliant. It is a landmark step in the fight against greenwashing and enabling consumers to contribute to the green transition (KPMG, 2023).

2. LITERATURE REVIEW

The European Green Deal was announced in December 2019 to reduce Greenhouse Gases (GHG) by 55% by 2030 compared to 1990 levels and make EU the first Net Zero continent in the world by 2050. To achieve this ambitious target, over 3 billion additional trees would be planted and over €600 billion will be invested to decouple economic growth from resource use. For the citizens, deal is expected to ensure fresh air, clean water, energy security, affordable healthcare, healthy food, protection of biodiversity, secure jobs, cutting edge innovation through research and development, reliable public transportation, skilled manpower, globally competitive industry and, long lasting products which can be repaired, recycled and reused. (EC, Green Deal, 2019) To achieve the objectives of the deal several amendments need to be made in the EU policies related to the production and consumption with the aim of influencing business as well as consumer behavior. The Circular Economy Action Plan (CEAP) and New Consumer Agenda were rolled out in 2020 to strengthen the partnership through collective actions and ensure all goods and services sold to EU adhere to the objectives of the European Green Deal (2019). They are integral to the European Commissions (EC) strategy for implementing the United Nations Sustainable Development Goals (UN-SDG, 2030) agenda. (EC, Environment, March 2020 & Consumer Strategy, November 2020)

3. INTERNATIONAL COOPERATION FOR SUSTAINABLE DEVELOPMENT

The Green Deal documents clearly state that 'The Green Deal will not be achieved by Europe acting alone. The drivers of climate change and biodiversity loss are global and are not limited by national borders. The EU can use its influence, expertise and financial resources to mobilize its neighbors and partners to join it on a sustainable path (Sultana, 2022). The EU will continue to lead international efforts and wants to build alliances with the like-minded. It also recognizes the need to maintain its security of supply and competitiveness even when others are unwilling to act'. (EU, Green Deal, 2019)

4. Report on Green Claims

Inception Impact Assessment (IA) conducted in 2020 received 77 responses, from business associations (30%), NGOs (25%) and companies (22%), public authorities (6%), consumer organizations (4%), EU citizens (4%), academic/research institutions (3%), environmental organizations (3%) and others (4%) and the report published in 2021 made startling revelations about 'Green Claims' by the companies. Two main problems identified in the report are that consumers lack reliable information and face misleading claims which prevent them from contributing towards green transition. The primary drivers for these problems are market failure and insufficiently adopted regulatory framework. Consequences being customer detriment including sub-optimal choices, manufacturers not improving the environmental performance of their products, loss of trust, risk of increased compliance cost and uneven playing field for those putting in sincere efforts. (EC, Impact Assessment Report, 2022)

5. Need for Ban on Greenwashing and Planned Obsolescence

The Commission has proposed amendments to the Unfair Commercial Practices Directive (UCPD) to cover the social impact and the durability of the products. It also considers the claims on the future environmental performance without verifiable data and independent monitoring mechanism. The 'blacklist' includes not informing the consumer durability, making generic claims especially when it concerns only an aspect of the product, labelling not based on a third-party or a public authority validation and not disclosing complete information about the consumables, spare parts, accessories etc. required for the proper functioning of the product. While there is a need to ensure legal certainty for businesses complying with the principles of CEAP, Consumer Strategy and Green Deal, there is also a need to stop greenwashing and immature obsolescence of products. (EC, Circular Economy, March 2022)

6. Proposal for the Directive on Empowering the Consumer for Green Transition (March 2022)

The general objectives of this proposal are to ensure smooth functioning of the single market, foster the role of consumption in achieving the EU's climate goal and protect the environment. The more specific objectives include enabling informed purchasing decisions, eliminating misleading practices and ensuring a better and coherent

application of the EU legal framework thanks to cleaner and more enforceable rules. The proposal explores the legal basis for the intervention of the EU in dealing with the business and consumer related issues affecting the sustainability targets expressed in the green deal. National and EU level Initiatives such as Green Initiative and Sustainable Initiative were adopted to incentivize businesses to provide information on environmental characteristics of their products and encourage the evolution of consumer interest in sustainable products. Article 169, of the Treaty on the Functioning of the European Union (TFEU) became the legal basis of intervention for the EU. The article states 'the EU shall contribute to protecting the economic interests of consumers as well as promoting their right to information and education for safeguarding their interests. Policy options available with the EU for intervention to tackle greenwashing by the companies included Consumer Rights Directive, Sale of Goods Directive and Unfair Commercial Practice Directive. Through these directives were exercised to ensure reliable information about the products from the manufacturers. For ensuring these obligations and provisions are honored by the businesses, amendments in the Consumer Rights Directive (CRD) and Unfair Commercial Practices Directives (UCPD) are required along with the other initiatives like Sustainable Product Initiative, Green Initiative and the Impact Assessment, a self-regulatory initiative which was announced in the New Consumer Agenda adopted in November 2020 by the EU (EC Consumer Strategy, January 2021). To address the problem of consumers facing misleading commercial practices related to the sustainability of products and unclear green claims in the proposal (EC, March 2022) Amendments in the Unfair Commercial Practices Directive along with the development of best practices guidelines and new legal provisions are required to safeguard the credibility of 'EU Ecolabel and EMAS'. Effectiveness, efficiency and coherence of the policy would be evaluated through the Inception Impact Assessment, Open Public Consultations, Targeted stakeholder consultations, Industry Survey, Consumer Survey and regular Workshops with various stakeholders and general members of the society.

7. Case Study: Proposal for the Green Claims Directive (March 2023)

The document provides a more specific set of rules and amendments to the Unfair Commercial Practices Directives. Supporting the 'European Green Deal's commitment to tackle false environmental claims by ensuring that buyers receive reliable, comparable and verifiable information to enable them to make more sustainable decisions and to reduce the risk of green washing'. Supporting sustainable consumption will also contribute to the SDG#12 (Responsible Consumption and Production) encouraging large corporates to adopt sustainability measures by integrating all relevant information in their regular ESG reporting. Such practices will have a net positive impact on global value chains involving production in developing countries. It will incentivize those firms to contribute to the transition, especially those operating in the EU. Multilateral, Bilateral and Regional Trade Agreements create massive opportunities for partnerships to scale such policies. Amendments to Unfair Commercial Practices Directive to address the problem of greenwashing includes (1) environmental or social impact, durability and reparability, (2) making an environmental claim related to future environmental performance without clear, objective and verifiable commitments and targets and an independent monitoring system and (3) practices associated with greenwashing. The proposal is limited to the environmental labels and is not in any way intended to change the existing or future EU sectoral rules. Its primary aim is to fight against greenwashing by the unregulated environmental communication on products by certain businesses. Amendments to the Unfair Commercial Practices Directive are expected to contribute towards a consistent policy framework and help the EU in facilitating the green transition by sustainably transforming the consumption patterns.

8. Actions Suggested in the Proposal for Green Claims Directives

Article 114 of the Treaty of the Functioning of the European Union (TFEU) is the basis of the proposal which ensures the functioning of the internal EU market with a high level of environmental protection. But there are different environmental compliance requirements which have been imposed by the member states through national legislation or private initiatives for the regulation of environmental claims. The variations and overlaps create confusion and burden for companies in cross border transactions. This negatively affects the ability of the businesses to take advantage of operating in the single market. (EU, COM, 2023) Since the proposal on empowering consumers for the green transition (March 2022) does not specify what the companies should do to properly substantiate their environmental claims, the proposal for Green Claims Directive (March 2023), deals with substantiation and communication of explicit environmental claims. It helps the EU with the value-added tools to bring in common approach and provides necessary instruments to limit the proliferation of labels and misleading environmental claims. The tools will support the assessment of environmental

claims, and the instruments provide a high degree of legal assurance and empower the council in the enforcement.

To explore the appropriate tools and instruments without any amendments to the existing legislature, 362 contributions were made in 2020 through open public consultations. Business associations, large corporations, citizens, public authorities, environmental and consumer NGOs participated in these consultations and registered their suggestions. It was then through the several rounds of stakeholder workshops to access overall feedback, communication options, practical challenges and reliability of information it was confirmed that greenwashing needs to be addressed through the harmonized approach. Drawing on the lessons learnt on the proliferation of ecolabeling schemes, I.e., the Ecolabel and EMAS needs to be revived along with the development of environmental footprint method.

9. EU Ecolabel and Eco-Management and Audit Scheme (EMAS)

Comprehensive policy framework for 'communications from the seller and information with the consumer' is required for transforming consumption patterns. EMAS and the EU Ecolabel were launched by the EU as part of the policy framework for sustainable consumption and production. Ecolabel was launched in 1992 and EMAS in 1995, both were relaunched in 2008 as part of the communication on sustainable consumption and production and the sustainable industrial policy action plan. The objective for EU Ecolabel is to promote products with a reduced environmental impact during their entire life cycle and provide consumers with accurate, science-based information on the environmental impacts of products. Eco-Management and Audit Scheme EMAS was launched to promote continuous improvements in the environmental performance of the organizations by establishment and implementation of environmental management systems (EMS). It requires objective and periodic evaluation of EMS, provision of information on performance, open dialogue with the stakeholders and active involvement of employees along with the proper training. EC, under the Better Regulation Guidelines, in 2013 undertook the Fitness Test of EU Ecolabel and EMAS regulations. The test examined the schemes in terms of relevance, effectiveness, efficiency, coherence and their value addition to the EU regulatory effectiveness. The report came out with the observations that Ecolabel and EMAS contribute to the reduction of environmental impact of consumption and production, promote EMS performance and the cost of compliance exceeds benefits discouraging the participation. With disproportionate impact on the SMEs.

A lower subscription of EMAS to ISO 14001 indicates the relatively unfavorable cost/benefit for the scheme.

10. DISCUSSION

With all their contributions and limitations, Ecolabel and EMAS are important instruments of EU policy responses to the environmental impact of production and consumption behaviors. The two regulations with crucial role in green public procurement and benchmarking company processes, hold the potential to address the environmental impact due to production and consumption which happens not only in EU but outside. Since many products consumed in the EU are manufactured elsewhere and many European products get exported to countries with minimum or no regulations. The regulations are integral tools of the EU production and consumption policy supporting Circular Economy, Consumer Strategy and the European Green Deal. The report acknowledges the limitations given their voluntary nature but suggests that the uptake can be improved through 'increased awareness and focused approach to maximize on the ground impact'.

11. EUROPEAN PARLIAMENT LEGISLATIVE RESOLUTION, AMENDMENTS (APRIL 2023)

Committee on the Internal Market and Consumer Protection in April 2023 proposed for a directive of the European Parliament and of the Council on amending Directives 2005/29/EC and 2011/83/EU as regards empowering consumers for the green transition through better protection against unfair practices and better information. The amendments include tackling practices that deceive consumers and false environmental claims ("greenwashing"), non-certified labels. It makes it clear that 'businesses have an important role in promoting a green transition and greater sustainability of the products they produce and sell on the internal market'. (Amendment 1) Green labels should not be solely based on carbon off-setting, but need to be supported by quantifiable, science-based and verifiable commitments including a detailed and realistic implementation plan to achieve environmental performance. The plan submitted by the company should also include objectives aligned with the EU policies, tangible targets consistent with the long-term commitments, properly backed by adequate funding provisions and allocation of necessary resources to ensure delivery of promised outcomes. The report also added 'reusability, repairability and recyclability' in dealing with the product life cycle and a ban on 'immature obsolescence'. (Amendment 2 & 3) The report suggests considering the needs of SMEs to keep the cost of acquiring the label to a minimum and aid in complying with the regulations. The award of the certification should be based on global standards taking the nature of the products, processes and businesses into account. Ensures that an independent and competent third party is responsible for the monitoring of compliance. The 'scheme owner and the trader', are also verified by the Member States. The process must include a complaints system available to all stakeholders and ensure the withdrawal of the sustainability label in cases of noncompliance. (Amendment 5, 32 & 36A)

Provisions have been explored through Article 12 of the EU to ensure that the appropriate measures are taken to help the SMEs, including credit support, access to funds, training managements with organizational and members of the staff with technical assistance. The proposed amendment clearly mentions that the label should be displayed prominently and in a clearly legible way in accordance with requirements under the EU and national law, in an official language of the Member State where the good is offered. (Amendment 22 & 23A)

12. CONCLUSION

'No force on earth can stop an idea whose time has come', said the French Philosopher Victor Hugo, which looks true for the EU Eco label and EMAS regulations launched in 1992 and 1995 respectively but never received the significance they now enjoy. They have always been important tools of the European Environmental Policy, but it took almost 3 decades for them to gain the centerstage in the action plan to deal with the unsubstantiated and vague' green claims. UN Millennium Development Goals (2015) followed by the Sustainable Development Goals (2030) have been instrumental in aligning the global forces (Weber, 2007). In the EU Green Deal (2019) and the COVID-19 crisis played the role of the catalyst in this transition toward sustainable future. CEAP and New Consumer Agenda were launched in 2020 to promote circular economy. Then the landmark 2021 EC report based on Inception Impact Assessment carried out 2020 lead to proposals for directive on empowering consumers (2022) and green claims (2023). The study highlights the role of and interlinkages between global events, environmental conditions, social movements, economic compulsions, political forces, intended and unintended consequences of the past policies and actions of members states and competing nations in shaping the national, regional and global policies. The process is dynamic and is generally the product of both intra- and inter-scalar socio-political contestation (Hameiri & Jones, 2017). Many factors play simultaneously some controllable and most uncontrollable by individuals, organizations and even the governments. It is evident from the study that most local or national policies are dictated by the global forces, but the cumulative national and regional policies too, decide the course of the major global policy shifts.

■ REFERENCES AND BIBLIOGRAPHY ■

1. European Commission, 2019. COMMUNICATION FROM THE COMMISSION: The European Green Deal https://eur-lex.europa.eu/legal-content/EN/TXT/?qid=1576150542719&uri=COM%3A2019%3A640%3AFIN

2. European Commission, 2021. Delivering the European Green Deal: The decisive decade https://ec.europa.eu/commission/presscorner/detail/en/ip_19_6691

3. European Commission, 2022. Proposal for a DIRECTIVE OF THE EUROPEAN PARLIAMENT AND OF THE COUNCIL amending Directives 2005/29/EC and 2011/83/EU as regards empowering consumers for the green transition through better protection against unfair practices and better information. https://eur- lex.europa.eu/legal-content/EN/TXT/?uri=CELEX%3A52022SC0085

4. European Commission, 2017. REPORT FROM THE COMMISSION TO THE EUROPEAN PARLIAMENT AND THE COUNCIL on the review of implementation of Regulation on the voluntary participation by organizations in a community eco-management and audit scheme (EMAS) and the Regulation (EC) No 66/2010 of the parliament and of the Council of 25 November 2009 on the EU Ecolabel https://ec.europa.eu/environment/emas/pdf/other/COM_2017_355_F1_REPORT_FROM_COMMISSION_EN_V5_P1_875286.pdf#:~:text=EMAS%20and%20the%20EU%20Ecolabel%20are%20part%20of,industrial%20policy%20action%20plan%20%28SCP%20action%20plan%291in%202008.

5. European Commission Green Claims, 2023. https://environment.ec.europa.eu/topics/circular-economy/green-claims_en#:~:text=With%20a%20proposed%20new%20law%20on%20green%20claims%2C,allow%20co nsumers%20to%20make%20better%20informed%20purchasing%20decisions.

6. European Union, 2020. COMMUNICATION FROM THE COMMISSION TO THE EUROPEAN PARLIAMENT, THE COUNCIL, THE EUROPEAN ECONOMIC AND SOCIAL COMMITTEE AND THE COMMITTEE OF THE

7. REGIONS: A new Circular Economy Action Plan, For a cleaner and more competitive Europe https://eur- lex.europa.eu/legal-content/EN/TXT/?qid=1583933814386&uri=COM:2020:98:FIN

8. European Commission, 2022. Circular Economy: Commission proposes new consumer rights and a ban on greenwashing https://ec.europa.eu/commission/presscorner/detail/en/ip_22_2098

9. European Commission, 2020. COMMUNICATION FROM THE COMMISSION TO THE EUROPEAN PARLIAMENT AND THE COUNCIL: New Consumer Agenda, Strengthening consumer resilience for sustainable recovery. https://eur-lex.europa.eu/legal-content/EN/TXT/?uri=CELEX%3A52020DC0696&qid=1605887353618

10. European Commission, 2023. Proposal for a DIRECTIVE OF THE EUROPEAN PARLIAMENT AND OF THE COUNCIL on substantiation and communication of explicit environmental claims (Green Claims Directive) https://eur-lex.europa.eu/legal-content/EN/TXT/?uri=COM%3A2023%3A0166%3AFIN

11. European Parliament, 2023. REPORT on the proposal for a directive of the European Parliament and of the Council on amending Directives 2005/29/EC and 2011/83/EU as regards empowering consumers for the green transition through better protection against unfair practices and better information https://www.europarl.europa.eu/doceo/document/A-9-2023-0099_EN.html

12. Hameiri, S. and Jones, L. 2017. Beyond Hybridity to the Politics of Scale: International Intervention and 'Local' Politics, International Institute of Social Studies, Development and Change 48(1): 54–77.

13. Hahnel, J, J. 2020. Mitigating climate change during and after COVID-19: Challenges and windows of opportunity, University of Geneva

14. Sultana, F. 2022. The unbearable heaviness of climate coloniality, Political Geography. https://www.sciencedirect.com/science/article/abs/pii/S096262982200052X?via%3Dihub

15. Wagemans, M. and Monten, W. 2023. European Commission proposes the Green Claims Directive: New EU regulations set to protect consumers and businesses from harmful greenwashing practices. KPMG https://kpmg.com/be/en/home/insights/2023/04/rr-the-green-claims-directive-by-european- commission.html

16. Watkins, D. and Mason, K. 2023. The Green Claims Directive – what's next for green claims in the EU? DWF Group https://dwfgroup.com/en/news-and-insights/insights/2023/3/the-green-claims-directive

17. Weber, H. 2007. A Political Analysis of the Formal Comparative Method: Historicizing the Globalization and Development Debate, Globalizations, 4:4, 559–572, https://www.tandfonline.com/doi/abs/10.1080/14747730701695828

Challenges and Opportunities for Innovation in India – Dr. Shweta Mishra et al. (eds)
© 2024 Taylor & Francis Group, London, ISBN 978-1-032-99842-8

A Review on Hybrid Approach on Textual Data for Emotion Detection Using Machine Learning

40

Er. Sanjeet Kumar,
Aditya Agrawal*, Khyati Singh, Yash Tripathi
Department of Information Technology,
U.I.E.T. C.S.J.M. University,
Kanpur, India

Abstract

The majority of people on the planet today have access to the Internet for text, image, audio, and video communication. On social media, people with different backgrounds share information about current events and express their opinions about them. Analysing people's emotions is necessary in order to comprehend and identify the behaviour of such vast amounts of textual data about them. Human interaction is greatly influenced by emotions. A person's speech, face gestures, body language, and sign actions can all be used to figure out their emotional state. These days, people communicate with each other via a variety of text-based devices, so extracting emotion from texts has become increasingly important. Therefore, it is essential that machines comprehend emotions in textual conversations in order to provide users with feedback on their emotional awareness.

Keywords

Machine learning, Emotion detection, Face gestures, Convolutional neural networks

1. INTRODUCTION

The six categories of emotions, according to Ekman, are: joy, sadness, fear, surprise, anger, and disgust. Moreover, there are many ways to characterise emotion, including love, optimism, and so forth. A person's mood and emotions are typically expressed through their speech, body language, gestures, and facial expressions. A text sentence loses its ability to define itself due to its tastelessness, unlike facial expression and speech recognition technology. Determining the emotions contained in a text can be challenging due to its intricacy and ambiguity. Identifying the emotion contained in a given text becomes challenging because words can have varying morphological forms and meanings.[3] Scholars have recently put forth a number of techniques—including keyword-based, lexical affinity, learning-based, and hybrid models—for identifying the text's emotions. According to the study, deep learning models outperform machine learning models in terms of accuracy when dealing with large amounts of text or data. However, machine learning provides us with greater accuracy for small data. However, none of the methods

*Corresponding author: adityaagrawal20202020@gmail.com

DOI: 10.1201/9781003606260-40

provided a comprehensive answer for identifying the emotion contained in a given text. In an effort to achieve high accuracy, numerous researchers have also begun to hybridise their approaches. Consequently, high accuracy is achieved by merging the deep learning and machine learning approaches.[3]

2. LITERATURE REVIEW

In [1] The field of emotion detection in user text has gained a lot of attention because of its applications in sentiment analysis, affective computing, and human-computer interaction. The paper "Affective Interaction based Hybrid Approach for Emotion Detection using Machine Learning" by Alice D. Souza and Dr. Rio D. Souza presents a hybrid model that combines lexical analysis and machine learning. Lexical-based approaches use SVM-like algorithms, while machine learning uses lexicons rich in emotions. The paper's approach combines the two methods in an attempt to increase accuracy through the capture of semantic relationships and emotional context. This synthesis highlights the potential for practical application and builds on previous research that supported hybrid approaches. In [2] The significance of textual emotion recognition is covered in the literature review section of the article. It looks at various approaches to emotion recognition that are currently in use, such as hybrid models, learning-based approaches, and keyword spotting. These approaches are limited by inaccurate emotion correlation and the malleability of emotional expression. Semantic analysis and ontologies have been researched by researchers to improve accuracy, particularly in real-world applications like the Happy Planet Index (HPI), which relies on emotion recognition. Even with these advancements, more accurate models are still needed. This leads the authors to propose a hybrid model that combines pre-trained models with natural language processing features to improve emotion detection. In [3] The literature review emphasises the usefulness of emotion detection and sentiment analysis in a variety of fields. It highlights how difficult it is to decipher emotions from text because there are no speech or facial expression cues. We primarily discuss three approaches: lexicon-based, machine learning, and keyword-based. Their shortcomings include issues with context extraction and vocabulary gaps. Recent advances in deep learning techniques, Convolutional Neural Networks (CNNs) and Recurrent Neural Networks (RNNs), are emphasised for their potential to enhance emotion recognition. The review does concede that a comprehensive solution is still required. The proposed hybrid model is introduced in order to address these limitations. It seeks to improve accuracy by fusing the advantages of machine learning

and deep learning. The study aims to progress the field by overcoming existing challenges and obtaining more accurate emotion recognition results from text data. In [4] Emotion recognition from speech and text is a rapidly developing field with applications in numerous industries. Researchers use natural language processing and machine learning techniques to decode human emotions. This facilitates tailored services and enhances human-computer interaction. Difficulties arise from a wide range of expressions and cultural nuances. Emotion detection has potential applications in better technology interfaces and mental health tracking. In [5] Textual emotion detection is an important application of affective computing. The first approaches focused on keyword-based tactics, but these methods struggled with word ambiguity. Subsequently, techniques based on machine learning emerged, leading to increased classification accuracy. Combining the two approaches, hybrid approaches have been developed to overcome present constraints in an effort to maximise advantages and minimise disadvantages. There are still challenges in identifying emotion indicators and developing standardised emotion categories. In response, a dynamic architecture that combined keyword and learning-based techniques was proposed, which may lead to an improvement in the accuracy of emotion detection. As this field advances, sentiment analysis and human-computer interaction may both benefit. In [6] The authors integrate textual and speech features to increase accuracy. They use techniques like SVM, SentiWordNet, WordNet Affect, and Natural Language Processing. The hybrid approach outperforms the use of text or audio alone. The paper highlights the importance of accurate emotion recognition for improved human-machine interaction and discusses potential uses in sentiment analysis. Subsequent studies ought to concentrate on broadening the examination of auditory characteristics. In [7] Affective interaction, or recognising and responding to emotions, is gaining popularity in computer-mediated communication. Affective computing uses machine learning and natural language processing (NLP) to analyse emotional text, often concentrating on Ekman's emotional categories. Machine learning and linguistic models are combined in emerging methods. In [8] Research on emotion recognition in NLP has accelerated due to the development of affective computing. This is an interdisciplinary field that investigates emotion models, text analysis techniques, and evaluation metrics. The often nuanced and context-dependent emotional expression in text has served as a catalyst for linguistic investigations of sentiment and intensity. [9] Hybrid approaches that integrate audio and video features for increased accuracy have gained attention due to the emphasis on emotion recognition in human-computer interaction (HCI). In audio-based emotion analysis, energy, pitch, and MFCCs are analysed. However, adding visual components to the audio analysis—particularly facial markers—makes sense. The proposed hybrid method uses both audio and video data and uses support vector machines (SVM) for classification. The results show a considerable increase in accuracy compared to traditional methods. This study improves emotion recognition by emphasising the advantages of a multimodal approach.

3. PROPOSED METHODOLOGY

The proposed method identified the emotions present in the input text and extracted the salient features from the general text using pre-trained machine learning and deep learning models. Emotion was generally extracted from text data using the Random Forest Algorithm, SVM, Hybrid Model, Multinomial Naive Bayes Algorithm [11] (MNB), and Decision Making Tree Algorithm. To do this, extract the features from the given input text corpus using the Natural Language Processing Tool Kit, then train the input dataset with each of these models. By downloading and analysing the dataset from the Kaggle website [12], each model's performance is thoroughly investigated. In general, the procedures to identify the emotion from the natural text are as follows: A Hybrid Approach To Emotion detection A Combination Approach to Emotion Identification The meaning and expression of the movements are unclear. Despite the emergence of several expressive models, there remains disagreement regarding the selection between a dimensional representation and a categorical representation. There is also dispute over the number of categories to select and the metrics to be applied in order to identify them. Predicted by Ekman, the Big Six model is one of the most well-known models. It considers six basic categories: joy, anger, surprise, disgust, sadness, and fear. The Ekman model has been used in this research since our main objective is to pinpoint the main emotions in real-time to enable mobile dialogue that shows emotional intelligence to its clients. Machine learning method We looked into machine learning for emotion classification because of the shortcomings in the lexicons and NLP tools that are currently available. By adding up the valences of related affective words, we were able to compute cumulative valences for emotional categories through supervised learning. Based on valence, the system determines which two emotions are the strongest. Choosing between opposing emotions of equal valence or when valences do not differ by 15% present difficulties. When SVM classifiers were tested, the polynomial kernel demonstrated effective real-time evaluation and balanced performance. Techniques for text pre-processing such as

root word extraction, stop word removal, and tokenization were used. By using chi-square statistics and information gain as filtering techniques, 608 informative features were generated, increasing the accuracy of the SVM classifier. This method improved feature representation for emotional annotation in testing occurrences by unifying training data. Random Forest Algorithm One popular machine learning algorithm is Random Forest, which is used in supervised learning techniques. It can be used for machine learning problems that involve regression and classification. Its basis is the concept of ensemble learning, which is the process of combining multiple classifiers to improve the functionality of the model and solve a difficult problem. As the name suggests, "Random Forest is a classifier that contains a number of decision trees on various subsets of the given dataset and takes the average to improve the predictive accuracy of that dataset." The random forest predicts the result based on the majority vote of projections from each decision tree, as opposed to relying solely on one. Because there are more trees in the forest, accuracy is higher and overfitting is avoided.

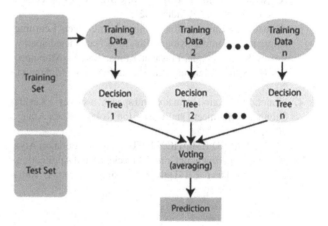

Fig. 40.1 Approach of machine learning

Source: Author

4. EXPECTED OUTCOMES

When employing a hybrid approach instead of just machine learning or deep learning separately, accuracy is probably going to be higher. By combining the advantages of both methods, the model is able to represent a greater variety of linguistic subtleties connected to various emotions. Textual emotions can be unclear and contingent on the situation. By fusing the structured representations of machine learning techniques with the context-awareness of deep learning models, the hybrid approach can help reduce ambiguity. Within [3], a possible increase in accuracy over the use of lone machine learning or deep learning models greater F1-score values, recall, and precision when compared to individual models. We obtain better results, but they're still not the best, just like with the ML and DL basic model. For various emotions, the ML approach and the DL approach will yield the highest accuracy. Thus, we obtain the maximum accuracy by combining the models [3]. [3] requires that the Deep Learning Model provide an accuracy of 77–80 and the Machine Learning Model provide an accuracy of 76–79. The accuracy we should obtain when combining the two models is between 79 and 82.

■ REFERENCES ■

1. "Affective Interaction based Hybrid Approach for Emotion Detection using Machine Learning", Alice D Souza Dm (Sr. Sadhana DM) and Dr Rio D Souza Research Scholar, St Raymond's PU College, Vamanjoor, Mangaluru Professor, Dept of CSE, St. Joseph Engineering College, Mangaluru, 2020.

2. "Detecting Emotion from Natural Language Text Using Hybrid and NLP Pre-trained Models", Simhadri Madhuri Dr. S. Venkata Lakshmi 2 Research Scholar, Department of CSE, GITAM (Deemed to be University), AP, India. Assistant Professor, Department of CSE, GITAM (Deemed to be University), AP, India, 2021.

3. "Text-Based Emotion Recognition Using Deep Learning Approach", Santosh Kumar Bharti, S Varadhaganapathy, Rajeev Kumar Gupta, Prashant Kumar Shukla, Mohamed Bouye, Simon Karanja Hingaa, and Amena Mahmoud, 2022.

4. "Emotion detection from text and speech: a survey", Kashfa Sailunaz · Manmeet Dhaliwal1 · Jon Rokne · Reda Alhajj, 2018.

5. "TEXT BASED EMOTION DETECTION", Poonam Arya Student, Department of Computer Science and Application, Chaudhary Devi Lal University, Sirsa, Haryana, India Shilpa Jain Asstt. Prof., Department of Computer Science and Application, Chaudhary Devi Lal University, Sirsa, Haryana, India, 2018.

6. "Hybrid Approach for Emotion Classification of Audio Conversation Based on Text and Speech Mining", Jasmine Bhaskar, Sruthi K, Prema Nedungadi, Department of Compute science, Amrita University, Amrita School of Engineering, Amritapuri, 690525, India Amrita Create, Amrita University, Amrita School of Engineering, Amritapuri, 690525, India, 2014.

7. "A Hybrid Approach for Emotion Detection in Support of Affective Interaction", Sonja Gievska Department of Computer Science, The George Washington University, Washington DC, USA. Kiril Koroveshovski, Faculty of Computer Science and Engineering, University of Ss. Cyril and Methodius Skopje, Macedonia. Tatjana Chavdarova Idiap Research Institute Switzerland EPFL Martigny, Switzerland, 2014.

8. "A Review of Different Approaches for Detecting Emotion from Text", Ashritha R Murthy, Anil Kumar K M, Assistant Professor, Department of Computer Science and Engineering, Sri Jayachamarajendra College of Engineering, JSS Science and Technology University. Associate Professor, Department of Computer Science and Engineering, Sri Jayachamarajendra College of Engineering, JSS Science and Technology University, 2021.

9. "PROPOSING A HYBRID APPROACH FOR EMOTION CLASSIFICATION USING AUDIO AND VIDEO DATA", Reza Rafeh, Rezvan Azimi Khojasteh, Naji Alobaidi. Centre for Information Technology, Waikato Institute of Technology, Hamilton, New Zealand Department of Computer Engineering, Malayer Branch, Islamic Azad University, Hamedan, Iran, Department of Computer Engineering, Unitec Institute of Technology, Auckland, New Zealand, 2019.

Challenges and Opportunities for Innovation in India – Dr. Shweta Mishra et al. (eds)
© 2024 Taylor & Francis Group, London, ISBN 978-1-032-99842-8

A Review on Data Mining and Techniques of Clustering Algorithms

41

Sandeep Kumar[1]
Information Technology, DSMNRU Lucknow

Vinodani Katiyar[2], Devesh Katiyar[3]
Computer Science, DSMNRU Lucknow

Abstract

In today's world information technology is everywhere, to maintain account records in banks, to maintain records of the patients in hospitals, to record academic performance of the students in educational institutes etc. In the late 1980s, a novel trend emerged to take intelligent and safe decisions from meaningful data gathered in information systems. The mining of data defined by a process which generates patterns or knowledge with the collected data for making a decision. It helps organizations to take right decisions at right time. Data mining provides techniques to process large amount of data efficiently and presents it in the required form. The predefined strategies and calculations that are utilized to separate these helpful examples are known as mining of Data. the various popular mechanisms used as mining of data. Several analysis algorithms can be used for mining of data like association rule, pattern identification, clustering, and classification.

Keywords

Data mining, Association rule, Pattern identification, Clustering, Classification

1. INTRODUCTION

In the current era of Information Technology, the markets are barrier less and the reach of businesses is expanding beyond cities to entire nation, and even across the globe. Large organizations in Banking, Automobile, Agriculture, Education etc. use huge amount of data and classify it to understand demographics, consumption, usage patterns etc. These businesses also generate huge amount of data themselves, which is increasing exponentially. For taking right decisions at right time, this big data can be analyzed and interpret for taking better decisions. This entire philosophy of storing, maintaining, classifying and interpreting data, to find patterns or trends for better business decisions, is an upcoming area of research.

2. DATA MINING

The mining of data defined by a process which generates patterns or knowledge with the collected data for making a decision. It helps organizations to take right decisions at right time. Data mining provides techniques to process

[1]sandeep.cse88@gmail.com, [2]drvinodini@gmail.com, [3]dkatiyar@dsmnru.ac.in

DOI: 10.1201/9781003606260-41

large amount of data efficiently and presents it in the required form. The predefined strategies and calculations that are utilized to separate these helpful examples are known as mining of Data. As an example of data mining methods are classification, pattern matching, rule analysis, clustering, and frequent Pattern Mining.

3. KNOWLEDGE DISCOVERY FROM DATA (KDD)

In today's world information technology is everywhere, to maintain account records in banks, to maintain records of the patients in hospitals, to record academic performance of the students in educational institutes etc. In the late 1980s, a novel trend emerged to take intelligent and safe decisions from meaningful data gathered in information systems. Information mining or KDD is known as the extraction cycle for valuable examples or information (Han et al. 2011). The knowledge discovery process is shown in Fig. 41.1 in data mining.

Thus, data retrieving process using data mining techniques for significant information from a database having current and historical data, using predefined methods and algorithms. These methods and algorithms together are called data mining techniques. Data mining uses approaches and methods from multi-disciplinary areas like Statistics and Artificial Intelligence (AI). So Data Mining can be considered as a set of computer-assisted method to explore the data statistically and intelligently.

4. DATA MINING TECHNIQUES

The next section gives brief overview of the various popular mechanisms used as mining of data. Several analysis algorithms can be used for mining of data like association rule, pattern identification, clustering, and classification.

4.1 Analysis of Association Rules and Mining of Pattern

In Frequent Pattern Mining the patterns that appear in the dataset frequently are extracted. The association among these frequent patterns is found out by rules for association. The Analysis of shopping basket is the most popular example of this technique. In this example, the buying habits of the customers are analysed and the items frequently purchased are recorded. Using this information of frequent itemsets, association rules are generated. The example of automatically generated rule may be like: buys(X, "computer") => buys(X, "printer") [support=20%, confidence=60%] This rule shows that a person who buys "computer" tends to buy "printer" at the same time. There are two measures to guess the relationship between association rules and the patterns. These measures are expressed in %. In the above example, a support of 20% shows that 20% of the customers purchase "computer" and "printer" together. Similarly, a confidence of 60% reflects the possibility that the customers who have purchased computer may purchase printer also. Using this association rule, the manager of the store can offer some scheme so that the persons buying "computer" are prompted to buy the "printer" also. This will in turn lead to increase of sale of "printer". The Apriori algorithm is one of commonly used technique for finding frequent itemsets from the given dataset, from these itemsets Association rules can be generated (Han et al. 2011).

4.2 Classification

The similar kind of data can be grouped as the classification technique or in a similar group of classes. For performing

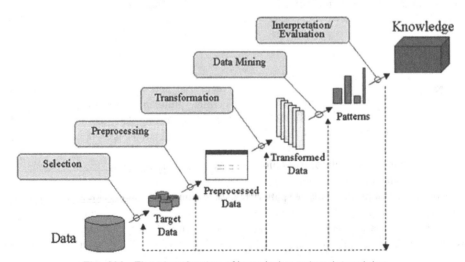

Fig. 41.1 The identification of knowledge using data mining

classification on a given dataset, the dataset should have at least one attribute as categorical attribute which will represent the class. This technique is then applied to divide the given dataset into groups. The attribute which are categorical can be determine the groups and the values. The process of classification in groups has two steps:

I. Generation of Classification Rules

II. Classification of data using Classification Rule

The input parameters and output parameters can be defined as the attributes in the dataset other than the attribute representing the class and the attribute which represents the class respectively. This concept can be better understood with the example shown in Table 41.1.

Table 41.1   Dataset for classification

Age	Income	Buys computer
Senior	Low	No
Middle-aged	Low	Yes
Senior	High	Yes
Middle-aged	High	Yes

In this example, "Age" and "Income" are Input parameters and "Buys computer" is Target parameter.

The first step of classification generates two rules:

- If Age = Senior and Income = High Then Buys computer = Yes
- If Age = Middle Aged Then Buys computer = Yes

The first step is also called Supervised Learning as it is known to which class each object in the dataset belongs. The second step classifies the data whose class is unknown. Suppose a new object is added in the dataset with value of **Buys computer** as unknown are representing in Table 41.2.

Table 41.2   Predicting the class as dataset

Age	Income	Buys_computer
Senior	Low	No
Middle_aged	Low	Yes
Senior	High	Yes
Middle_aged	High	Yes
Senior	High	?

Using the classification rules generated above, missing value will be predicted as **"Yes"**.

4.3 Clustering

Clustering is a cycle by which the informational collection is isolated into gatherings or groups with the goal that the articles in a single gathering have a more prominent comparability between themselves than the items in the other. It differs from Classification in a way that it is unsupervised while Classification is supervised. Clustering is not monitored as it does not depend on predefined classes and on training dataset rules generation. Some of the clustering methods are discussed below:

Partitioning Method

In this method, the given dataset containing n objects is divided into required number of clusters, K, where K ≤ n such that these clusters must be non-empty and mutually disjoint. This is an iterative method and the clusters once created are further refined with the movements of objects. This movement of objects is done based on value of some objective function.

Hierarchical Method

In this method, the objects in the given dataset are organized into a tree of clusters. There are two ways of using this method: Agglomerative method: This method starts by putting every object in the dataset into a separate group. The groups which are having similar functionalities can be merged into large clusters and formed a large cluster which contains all objects. AGNES (Agglomerative Nesting) algorithm is an example of this approach (Han et al. 2011). Divisive method: This method starts by putting the similar objects into a cluster which is a reverse of Agglomerative approach. This cluster is then divided into smaller clusters until the unit clusters are obtained. DIANA (Divisive Analysis) comes under this category (Han et al. 2011). The advantage of Hierarchical method is that a tree of clusters is obtained and user can see the tree for clusters at different levels with all clusters. This approach works well when the clusters are globular. Also, algorithms following this approach are sensitive to noise and outliers.

Density–Based Method

As the name recommends, the technique requires an underlying contribution of thickness boundaries like least number of articles expected to make a group and the base distance between objects inside a cluster. The algorithms under this category produce clusters of arbitrary shape and can handle noise. The limitation of this approach is that the algorithms require some input parameters which sometimes become difficult to predict. The famous algorithms of this category are: DBSCAN and OPTICS (Han et al. 2011).

Grid-Based Method

The objects in the dataset are segregated as n cells of finite numbers. The density of each cell is calculated and then cells are sorted according to their densities. The major advantage is that this method is efficient for evaluating the complexity in terms of computational resources. The major problem with this approach is that it generates a very low quality of clusters. The famous algorithm of this category is: STING (Han et al. 2011).

Clustering Algorithm K-Means

The K-Means estimation is a dividing that is iterative. This estimation secludes the given dataset into the vital number of packs (K). The technique starts with a discretionary assurance of K centroids, one for each gathering. The centroids are recalculated as the items are moved starting with one group then onto the next, until the entirety of the articles in each bunch are inside a specific distance of their centroids. As shown in Equation 1, the distance calculation used in this technique is Euclidean distance.

$$d(x, c) = \sum_{i=1}^{n} (xi - ci)^2 \qquad (1)$$

The representation of symbols can be explained as x indicates distinguished value like $(x_1, x_2, \ldots \ldots x_n)$ for objects and c represent the clusters centroid for clusters such as $(c_1, c_2, \ldots .. c_n)$.

K-means algorithm must follows the some criteria in k-means algorithm.

- It produces high cohesiveness in data.
- It is less expensive as compared to other algorithms used for data analytics purpose.
- There are a few issues with the k-implies calculation, for example,
- Since the initial centroids are selected at random, the final clusters formed are extremely sensitive to them.
- Since still up in the air as the mean of the qualities in a cluster, the calculation is touchy to exceptions.
- The calculation needs an underlying contribution of K. Since the individual utilizing the calculation can't be an area master, offering this benefit might be troublesome now and again.

Algorithm used for Clustering K-Modes

K-Modes calculation is utilized to improve the usefulness of k-implies calculation for certain focuses, for example,

- Instead of Euclidean distance, a Simple Matching Dissimilarity work appropriate for straight out information is utilized.
- Instead of utilizing Mean qualities, modes are utilized to depict centroids.
- In every emphasis of the calculation, a recurrence based methodology is utilized to find centroids.

Since it follows the same iterative mechanism as K-Means, the K-Modes algorithm inherits the advantages and drawbacks of K-Means. Various extensions of K-Modes have been proposed in the literature to address these

limitations (Bai et al. 2012; Cao et al. 2013; Gan et al. 2009; Huang 1997, Won et al. 2005).

Algorithm used for Clustering K-Prototype

Clustering calculations recently focused on a solitary kind of dataset, like all mathematical or all out ascribes. As blended datasets become more normal, all things considered, bunching calculations are being created to group them. The K-Prototype rendition of K-Means is intended to work with blended datasets. Following the fundamental meaning of the K-Means, K-Prototype utilizes Euclidean distance for numeric characteristics and Binary distance for downright qualities. In certain real-life situations, categorical values will differ by more than just 0 or 1. Using the binary distance for categorical attributes, on the other hand, does not provide accurate results.

5. Scope of the Study

In the present thesis, the extended algorithms are compared with the original algorithms and various other algorithms based on the purity or accuracy of the clusters. However, the time taken by the new algorithms is somewhat high as compared to the original algorithms. This is due to the increase in the computational steps in the extended algorithm. This increase in computational complexity is natural due to weak assumption and high dimensionality of the dataset. In future work, efforts may be made to decrease the time taken by modifying the algorithms, if possible. Also, the proposed algorithms can be coded in Scala language to make them work in distributed environment given by Apache Spark's framework. Apache Spark is a popular open-source framework for performing data analytics on distributed computing.

6. Research Gap

There are several gaps on the basis of past work done by several researchers which works on k-means algorithms. In this kind of algorithms, there is one of the major issues was to identify the value of k and can be applied for distinguished datasets like categorical, numerical, and mixed to apply any clustering algorithm. For the optimization purpose, k-prototype and k-modes algorithms can be used. The real-world datasets with high dimensionality pose a considerable challenge to the efficiency of K-Means clustering. The algorithm becomes computationally expensive and quality of the clusters is reduced with the increase in dimensions. Several past works have been done to overcome the gaps of numerical datasets but not much work has been done for categorical and mixed datasets. In the improved version of the algorithm, we also modify the existing k-mode algorithm and generate better results in case of high dimension datasets.

7. Objective of the Study

- To extend the K-Means algorithm for numerical datasets to improve the performance of k-means algorithm.
- To modify the K-Modes algorithm to make a cluster for categorical datasets so as to conquer the limitation by providing the cluster number in advance and work efficiently for high dimension datasets.
- To transform the K-Prototype algorithm for mixed datasets to conquered the limitation of providing the cluster number in advance.
- Finally, we compare the results for distinguished clustering algorithms with variable datasets.

8. Contribution of the Study

It makes a contribution by presenting enhanced algorithms for distinguish datasets such as numerical, categorical, and mixed datasets. The algorithms are partition-based which includes efficient data pre-processing, and generation of clusters automatically. The developed algorithms also generate clusters that are comparable to the clusters generated by the original algorithms and various other algorithms. An algorithm that extends the K-Modes algorithm that does not requires K as input and also works efficiently for high dimension datasets is also presented.

9. Conclusion

The focus of the present study has been to develop efficient clustering techniques. Clustering has its applications in variety of domains like psychology, statistics, medicine, engineering, computer science etc. For example, in an organization, grouping and identifying the products which are not in high demand may help in reducing their production to cut losses. It makes a contribution by presenting new algorithms for numerical, categorical, and mixed datasets that are based on the partition-based clustering algorithms K-Means, K-Modes, and K-Prototype, but with advanced features such as efficient data analysis and automatic generation of the appropriate number of clusters. The developed algorithms also generate clusters that are in general better than the clusters generated by the original algorithms and various other algorithms.

10. Limitations and Future Scope of the Study

In the present thesis, the extended algorithms are compared with the original algorithms and various other algorithms based on the purity or accuracy of the clusters. However, the time taken by the new algorithms is somewhat high as compared to the original algorithms. This is due to the increase in the computational steps in the extended algorithm. This increase in computational complexity is natural due to weak assumption and high dimensionality of the dataset. In future work, efforts may be made to decrease the time taken by modifying the algorithms, if possible. Also, the proposed algorithms can be coded in Scala language to make them work in distributed environment given by Apache Spark's framework. Apache Spark is a popular open-source framework for performing data analytics on distributed computing.

■ REFERENCES ■

1. Abubaker, Mohamed, &Ashour, Wesam 2019, 'Efficient Data Clustering Algorithms: Improvements over Kmeans', International Journal of Intelligent Systems and Applications, vol. 5, no. 3, pp. 37–49.
2. Agha, El, Mohammed, & Ashour, M., Wesam 2019, 'Efficient and Fast Initializtion Algorithm for K-Means Clustering', I. J. Intelligent Systems and Applications, vol. 4, no. 1, pp. 21–31.
3. Ahmad, A. & Dey, L. 2003, 'A K-mean clustering algorithm for mixed numeric and categorical data set using dynamic distance measure', Proceedings of Fifth International Conference on Advances in Pattern Recognition.
4. Ahmad, A. & Dey, L. 2007, 'A K-Mean Clustering Algorithm for Mixed Numeric and Categorical Data', Data & Knowledge Engineering, vol. 63, pp. 503–527.
5. Ahmad, A. &Dey, L. 2007, 'A Method to Compute Distance between Two Categorical Values of Same Attribute in Unsupervised Learning for Categorical Data Set', Pattern Recognition Letters, vol. 28, no. 1, pp. 110–118.
6. Leela, V., Sakthipriya, K. & Manikandan, R. 2013, 'A Comparative Analysis between KMean and Y-Means Algorithms in Fisher's Iris Data Sets' , International Journal of Engineering and Technology, vol. 5, no. 1, pp. 245–249.
7. Yuepeng, Sun, Wu, Cheng & Liu, Min 2011, 'A Modified k-means Algorithm for
8. Clustering Problem with Balancing Constraints', Third International Conference on Measuring Technology and Mechatronics Automation, pp. 127–130.
9. Zhang, Kang &Gu, Xingsheng 2014, 'An Affinity Propagation Clustering Algorithm for Mixed Numeric and Categorical Datasets', Mathematical Problems in Engineering.
10. Zhao, Hua-long 2008, 'Application of OLAP to the Analysis of the Curriculum Chosen by Students', 2nd International Conference on Anti-counterfeiting, Security and Identification, pp. 97–100.

Note: All the figure and tables in this chapter were made by the author.

Challenges and Opportunities for Innovation in India – Dr. Shweta Mishra et al. (eds)
© 2024 Taylor & Francis Group, London, ISBN 978-1-032-99842-8

Significance of Professional Communication in Changing Practices of Human Resource Management

42

Priyanka Singh*

Associate Professor,
Ambalika Institute of Management and Technology,
Lucknow

Abstract

In any organization, the prime objective of Human Resource Management is to find and cultivate professional capabilities among the employees. This is achieved through good communication skills which in turn is developed through the use of Professional Communication. Professional Communication helps in right decision making, skillful planning, resource optimisation, providing motivation and conflict management. Through the use of modern technological advancements like Metaverse and various social media platforms and apps, Professional Communication has revolutionized the field of Human Resource Management. In addition to making organizations more technological friendly, it has enabled a more emotionally stable working environment in them. Good communication skill is the backbone of any Human Resource activity. Be it selection of candidates, their training, work allocation among them or team management, Professional Communication provides significantly useful tools to the Human Resource field through its various communication skill sets. Today's Human Resource Management demands dynamism, speedy conflict resolutions and global connectivity for any organization to flourish. Professional Communication has made this possible for HR managers. An HR professional, with his expertise in communication skills and by the use of modern technological advancements, can cater to the needs of modern day organizations. And this is what Professional Communication aims to provide.

Keywords

Smooth functioning, Good communication skills, Professional communication, HR managers, Productivity

1. INTRODUCTION

At present Human Resource Management is considered as a powerful tool to create and manage policies of an organization. Not only it helps and supports the smooth functioning of an organization, but also fosters a working culture which encourages the employees to display their whole potential. It adds value and productivity to the organization. The prime objective of human resource management is to find and cultivate professional capabilities among the employees. Since good communication and team spirit among employees are essential parameters

*Corresponding author: priyanka_31781@rediffmail.com

DOI: 10.1201/9781003606260-42

of an organization's success, the HR professionals focus on developing these skills among the employees. While making several policies, motivating employees, recruiting eligible candidates, preparing feedbacks of the employees on the basis of their performance and several other activities that are important for the growth of the organization, HR professionals need good command over communication skills. Good communication skills play a significant role in taking right decisions, understanding the real situation, engaging the employees in various tasks as per their capabilities, optimizing their productivity, motivating them to perform a difficult task, managing their conflicts and dissatisfactions and taking regulatory actions well. The organizational works demand proficiency in professional communication which is the sum total of all the communication within the different parts of the organization as well as of the organization with the external environment. Professional communication includes both oral and written modes. Good oral communication helps managers in convincing the employee, salary negotiation and settling disputes at the workplace whereas being good in written professional communication is helpful in documenting the policies and data with utmost accuracy, clarity and conciseness.

2. Traditional HR Practices

The rules and policies followed by the traditional HR managers were mainly Job Evaluation, Compensation, Workforce planning, Compliance based works and employee relations etc. All such duties demanded great command over professional communication since official notices, reports and several other official documents needed careful attention. Along with that, professional communication always remained an effective tool to manage employee's conflicts and issues and for measuring outputs. In the absence of technological advancements, HR professionals mostly depended on face-to-face communication or on written messages on papers. Due to the lack of advanced technology, it was a challenge for the HR professionals to build a network chain and for recruiting the suitable candidates, they had no other choice except costly advertisements and their own personal networking.

3. Modern HR Practices

In the fast changing modern world, as new practices are replacing the age old conventions, Human Resource Management is also not an exception. Though the HR managers are still holding the responsibilities of planning, coordinating and supervising, now they have started using advanced methods like working in the metaverse,

using people analytics, using the hybrid work model for collaboration and several other practices to uplift the performance of employees so that they can contribute well in the growth of the organization. During the pandemic period, when every organisation was struggling with smooth conduction of work, HR professionals adopted a hybrid work force model which ensured the completion of several essential activities like planning for projects, recruitment, making a comfortable environment for the employees, etc. Many activities of professional communication started running through online mode. With the help of several online platforms like zoom, google meet, teams, etc. it became possible to recruit new employees, arrange periodical meetings, and resolving office and staff problems on regular basis. Online communication has not only enabled HR managers to remain connected with the employees personally, but has also sensitized them to their emotional needs as well. These factors have led to an increase in employees' productivity in favour of the organization. Now the HR professionals realise that good communication skills can make them more efficient in their roles. In modern times, metaverse is being used as a useful tool to communicate better. Metaverse is a virtual world where people interact with each other in three-dimensional forms. It's a powerful communication tool that makes professional communication more effective even when people are not in a face-to-face contact. It is useful in performing many HR duties like training and development, conducting interviews, recruitments and engaging employees in several official activities. Not only HR managers can arrange an official board meeting through it, but also if the need arises, they can avail a separate virtual room for private conversations. Latest and advanced means of communication have made it possible to build network globally. With the help of modern means of communication now HR managers can easily transfer huge amount of data, images or videos within few seconds to a person sitting in any corner of the globe. Now HR managers are not confined to search candidates only through newspaper ads, they are using social media as an effective tool of communication. Many social media platforms like LinkedIn, Freshersworld.com, Indeed, Naukri, Glassdoor and Monster are being used by HR professionals to hire the best employees for their organizations. These are the platforms where HR managers connect with the candidates and can fix their interviews. With the effective use of communication an HR manager can post his requirements and the eligible candidates can apply. Through these portals, HR managers can not only connect with the candidates but also can update about their organization's events and activities which help to project a positive and progressive image of the organization.

For completing several tasks HR managers need to build several teams occasionally. Communication plays a vital role in building and managing a team. Good communication establishes trust among the team members and it increases their credibility as well. In the present scenario when the businesses are spreading globally, virtual teams are made which are not only performing well but also saving time and energy. Sometimes when the issues related to wages, working conditions or working hours, trade union issues etc. arise, an HR manager can prove his calibre in addressing the grievances of the workers by the apt use of his good communication skills. Now complaints can be filed through email, audio or video recording on mobiles or through some portals which are specially prepared for people's convenience. These modes of communication are safer, faster, trusted and more convenient than earlier methods. Productivity and smooth functioning largely depends on the decisions taken by the HR managers. For knowing everyone's opinion and avoiding conflicts, nowadays HR managers do not hesitate to create a poll using smart technology. They simply communicate their message to the other members and create a poll through google forms on mobiles which is quick and reliable.

4. Conclusion

In the fast changing business world, now the HR professionals' role has become more challenging since now it's their responsibility to train and educate the new recruits about their roles and responsibilities. Effective communication works as a backbone to any organization and by employing good communication skills with the use of advanced means, an HR manager can achieve the company's goals easily and effectively.

■ REFERENCES ■

1. Julie Beardwell, Tim Claydon, "Human Resource Management: A Contemporary Approach," Prentice Hall, 6th edition, pp.120–122, 2010.
2. K Aswathappa, Sadhna Dash, "Human Resource Management: Text and Cases," McGraw-Hill, 9th edition, pp. 25–29, 2022.
3. Raman Preet, "Future of Human Resource Management: Case studies with Strategic Approach," Wiley, pp. 101–111, 2019.
4. Ian Tuhovsky, "Communication Skills Training," Createspace Independent Pub, 1st edition, pp.68–70, 2015.
5. Thich Nhat Hanh, "The Art of Communicating," Rider & Co, pp. 93–108, 2013.

Challenges and Opportunities for Innovation in India – Dr. Shweta Mishra et al. (eds)
© 2024 Taylor & Francis Group, London, ISBN 978-1-032-99842-8

Trade Horizons: Navigating Globalization in the Era of Industry 5.0

43

Anshuman Mishra,
Jaibeer Pratap Singh, Deepak Kumar Srivastava
Professor, KIPM College of Management,
Sector-9, GIDA Gorakhpur

Abstract

The transition towards Industry 5.0 revolutionizes international trade and globalization by integrating advanced technologies like artificial intelligence, block-chain, 3D printing, and the Internet of Things into manufacturing and supply chain processes. This change fundamentally alters global trade dynamics and has significant economic implications. The study of international commerce has long been intertwined with political, social, and economic debates. As we approach the Industry 5.0 revolution, it is crucial to understand how these technologies are changing the nature of international commerce and the interconnectedness and dynamics of economic success across countries. Digital trade is a key aspect of Industry 5.0, focusing on specialized, personalized, high-quality products. It also includes digitally-enabled products, services, and indirect digital services. Digital trade has significant economic implications for domestic sectors, such as financial services, agriculture and food, infrastructure, and consumer and retail.

Keywords

Industry 5.0, International trade, Digital trade, Industry 4.0, Global trade

1. INTRODUCTION

The continuous transition towards Industry 5.0 redefines the fundamental underpinnings of international trade and globalisation in the modern global economics and business environment. Industry 5.0 is ushering in a new industrial paradigm, integrating cutting-edge technologies, such as artificial intelligence, block-chain, 3D printing, and the Internet of Things, into conventional manufacturing and supply chain processes as the world races towards unprecedented technological innovation. This revolutionary change transforms how goods are created, manufactured, and disseminated, fundamentally altering global trade dynamics. The limits of globalisation are changing as a result of Industry 5.0, and this has significant economic ramifications.

The study of international commerce has long been intertwined with political, social, and economic debate. However, as we approach the Industry 5.0 revolution, it is

*Corresponding author: director.mba@kipm.edu.in

DOI: 10.1201/9781003606260-43

crucial to comprehend how these cutting-edge technologies are changing the nature of international commerce and, in turn, the interconnectedness and dynamics of economic success across countries. In the Age of Industry 5.0, global trade has many different facets. This research paper explores these facets, examining how technological breakthroughs accelerate globalisation while presenting new possibilities and challenges to countries and enterprises worldwide. In this paper, we'll look at the revolutionary dynamics sparked by Industry 5.0, how they may affect established trade practices, how automation and digitalisation may play a part, and how these changes may affect economies, companies, and labour markets. We seek to shed light on the changing nature of globalisation and the extensive economic ramifications that will define the future of our linked world by examining the intersection of Industry 5.0 and international commerce. Understanding these processes is crucial to developing strategies for economic development, trade policy, and international collaboration when the world economy is set for unprecedented upheaval.

2. Literature Review

Saniuk, S., Grabowska, S., & Straka, M. (2022) interest in industrial humanisation, sustainability, and resilience has increased due to the digitalisation and dehumanisation of the fourth industrial revolution. This essay examines Industry 4.0 and Industry 5.0, pointing out conceptual flaws, especially with regard to the place of people in smart manufacturing and sustainable development. It also emphasises the necessity of employee skill development and the Industry 5.0 framework.

Breque et al., (2021) participants from research and technology firms were organised by the Directorate "Prosperity" of the DG Research and Innovation European Commission EC to discuss the idea of Industry 5.0 from July 2 to July 9, 2020. The EC publication has presumptions about the "Industry 5.0" idea. This document's main points are important changes that should be made to the industry to make it more human-centred and sustainable.

Mustafin, A. N., & Makhmutova, D. I. (2019) International cooperation and globalisation positively impact the market economy, leading to cultural, moral, social, political, and economic unification. This integration of countries into international trade plays a crucial role in developed countries' economies. The paper presents foreign trade indicators in China, Russia, the United States, and Germany, ranking them in order of importance for their economies.

Knobel, A. (2019) The report examines globalisation trends and their impact on trade, revealing a shift in economic balance between developed and developing countries.

Despite the dominance of developed economies, trade rules and conditions were formed, leading to structural problems and protectionism instead of liberalisation. The report also assesses the impact of trade wars in 2018 and proposes three options for future developments.

Paliu-Popa, L. (2008) This paper discusses the importance of active participation in the international division of labour for a country's development, focusing on foreign trade as a distinct economic branch and the relationship between internationalisation stages and international transactions, highlighting the role of international business development in globalisation.

Objectives

- To study the elements of Industry 5.0 and its impact on global trade.
- Explore the rise of digital trade, e-commerce, and cross-border data flows in Industry 5.0.
- To analyse the upcoming challenges of globalisation and Industry 5.0.

3. Research Methodology

To obtain a thorough understanding of the subject, we adopted qualitative approach through a literature study and investigated the current condition of industries and their digital transformation activities. Furthermore, a comprehensive systematic literature review methodology is performed. Aside from the foregoing, Casual Research was carried out to investigate the cause-and-effect links between digital transformation and industry sustainability.

4. Important Aspects of Industry 5.0 and their Possible Impact on Trade

Building on the innovations of Industry 4.0, Industry 5.0 is the next stage in the evolution of industries and manufacturing. It integrates cutting-edge ideas and technology that could greatly impact world trade. Here are some significant aspects of Industry 5.0 and how they might affect global trade.

- **Cooperative Human-Machine Systems:** A more integrated and cooperative approach between humans and robots is emphasised by Industry 5.0. More specialised, personalised, and high-quality products may result, giving manufacturers a competitive edge in markets abroad.

- **Decentralised Production:** Distributed production networks and decentralised manufacturing may become more common. Smaller businesses may find it simpler to engage in international trade due to the potential reduction in the requirement for central

Fig. 43.1   Important aspect of industry 5.0

production canters and decreased transportation expenses.

- **3D Printing and Additive Manufacturing:** The two main components of Industry 5.0 are additive manufacturing and 3D printing. They enable localised, on-demand manufacture, which can significantly affect global supply chains and save shipping and inventory costs.

- **Sustainable Manufacturing:** Industry 5.0 places a high priority on environmental issues and sustainability. International trade agreements are projected to emphasise sustainable practices, such as cutting back on waste and energy use, which may also impact trade patterns and regulations.

- **Artificial Intelligence and Machine Learning:** Using AI and machine learning for predictive maintenance, quality control, and supply chain optimisation can improve efficiency, reduce errors, and enhance the competitiveness of businesses in international markets.

- **IoT and Connectivity:** There will be a greater prevalence of the Internet of Things (IoT), enabling real-time tracking and monitoring of cargo while it is in transit. This can lower the chance of loss or damage during international trade and increase supply chain visibility.

- **Blockchain Technology:** Blockchain technology can potentially improve the security and transparency of global commerce transactions. Trade may be automated in a number of ways with smart contracts, which eliminates the need for middlemen and boosts confidence in international trade agreements.

- **Customisation and Personalization:** A higher level of product personalisation and customisation is made possible by Industry 5.0. Niche marketplaces and distinctive products that satisfy the varied tastes of global consumers may result from this.

- **Digital Twins:** The idea of "digital twins," which entails building digital copies of actual goods or procedures, can help with quality assurance, testing, and design. This may result in shorter time-to-market and faster product development in international trade.
- **Cybersecurity:** Industry 5.0's increased connectedness makes cyber security a top priority. International trade agreements may need to consider cybersecurity best practices and standards to protect intellectual property and digital assets during international trade.
- **Regulatory Harmonization:** In an Industry 5.0 world, countries may need to harmonise rules pertaining to cybersecurity, data privacy, intellectual property, and technology standards to facilitate international trade and foster a more welcoming corporate environment.
- **Green Markets:** A green market, sometimes known as a "green economy" or a "sustainable market," is a type of economic structure that prioritises goods, services, and business methods that are socially and environmentally conscious while remaining commercially feasible. Green markets prioritise sustainability and work to mitigate the harm that economic activity causes to society and the environment while promoting long-term economic prosperity. A green market has the following essential components.

5. Role of Digital Trade in Economic Implication

There is currently disagreement over what constitutes digital trading. The continually evolving nature of the digital economy contributes to the difficulty of characterising digital trade. Various international organisations have adopted different definitions. Instead of using the word "digital trade," the World Trade Organisation (WTO) has typically used "electronic commerce," which it defines as "the production, distribution, marketing, sale, or delivery of goods and services by electronic means."

Trade in goods and services is made possible by digital means. This consists of three parts:

Fig. 43.2 Digital services

- **Digitally-enabled products:** These pertain to digital and physical goods exchanged digitally over the Internet, such as digital downloads of local apps from abroad or physical goods sold to foreign markets via cross-border e-commerce platforms.
- **Digitally-enabled services:** These are services rendered through the use of digital technologies. This is a sizable area since most industry sectors have embraced digital technologies and offer e-services to varied degrees. This covers digital information-technology business process outsourcing (IT-BPO), online advertising viewed from overseas, data processing exports, and online software consulting services. It also covers commerce in other direct e-services, like online travel reservations and electronic banking; however, the lack of granularity in the available data makes it difficult to quantify these categories robustly.
- **Indirect digital services:** These are digital services that are imported and utilised to export other goods and services. Examples include voice over internet protocol (VOIP) services, email, video conferencing, digital file sharing, and other telecommunication services that a mining company exporting to another country uses.

The digital trade's economic value for domestic sectors:

- **Financial Services:** Thanks to their ability to increase financial inclusion rates, digital technologies drive significant advancements in this area. The government introduced "Cashless India," a plan to raise awareness and adoption of cashless transactions by promoting 10 different cashless payment mechanisms, such as mobile wallets, prepaid cards, and digital banking services, as part of its "Digital India" strategy.
- **Agriculture & Food:** Digital technologies like IoT, precision farming, and mobile internet have the potential to significantly increase information, improve yields, reduce waste, and increase income for Indian farmers.
- **Infrastructure:** Digital technologies can potentially improve the efficiency of building new infrastructure and its use and upkeep.
- **Consumer & Retail:** By 2034, domestic e-commerce sales are anticipated to have risen at a sharp annual pace of 31%, overtaking the US to take second place in the world's e-commerce industry.[1] Online retailers like Flipkart, based in India, are expanding quickly. During a significant sales event known as "Big Billion Day" in 2018, Flipkart sold over 3 million smartphones in a single day and 1 million in an hour, setting a record for the most smartphones sold in a single day by an Indian retailer.[2]
- **Education & Training:** Digital technologies promise to raise the standard of instruction, boost labour supply

and demand matching, and increase the productivity of teaching and support personnel.

- **Manufacturing:** While real-time data on inventory levels and shipments in transit can help manufacturing organisations manage their supply chains, big data and IoT can be used to improve demand forecasts and production planning to improve customer service levels. Given the cross-border nature of supply chains, digital trade is essential to manufacturing. It will become more so as the government's "Make in India" initiative seeks to draw in more global corporations.

- **Health:** Digital trade-enabled technologies can provide affordable ways to raise the standard and accessibility of healthcare in India. Thus, digital trade is essential to developing and providing high-quality, reasonably priced healthcare services for Indian physicians and patients. It is also essential since some applications like IoT to track medications (and stop tampering) along the supply chain, are cross-border.

- **Resources:** India's resource environment may offer more prospects to be discovered using clever exploration techniques utilising big data. However, consolidating its fragmented geophysical database would take some time. Digital trade is essential for resources sector technology since it allows global Indian resource corporations to pool data from their various foreign operations to identify areas for performance improvement and the necessity for affordable storage solutions.

Challenges of Industry 5.0

Approximately, industry 5.0 makes it simpler to ignore the possible difficulties. The business is identifying and resolving the obstacles to the success of industry 5.0 innovations.

- In order to work with sophisticated robots, humans must acquire competency skills. They must also learn how to collaborate with smart machines and robot makers. For human workers, acquiring technical skills is a challenge in addition to the soft skills needed. In the new roles, coordinating translation and programming to the industrial robot are challenging duties demanding high technical expertise.

- Human workers will need more time and effort to adopt new technologies. Industry 5.0 requires customised software-connected factories, internet of things, collaborative robotics, artificial intelligence, and real-time information.

- Investing in advanced technology is necessary. The costs of retraining human labour for new positions are increased. Upgrading production lines for Industry 5.0

has proven to be challenging for companies. Adopting Industry 5.0 is costly since it requires highly trained workers and intelligent machinery to boost output and efficiency.

- Industry 5.0 has security challenges since ecosystem trust is essential. In order to defend against potential quantum computing applications and facilitate the deployment of Internet of Things nodes, authentication is employed on a large scale in the business. Industry 5.0 uses automation and artificial intelligence, which poses risks to the company and necessitates reliable security. Because Industry 5.0 applications are centred on ICT systems, stringent security regulations are necessary to avoid security issues.

- The rise of the Authoritarian economy refers to the economic structures and regulations established by autocratic or dictatorial governments. These economies are typified by a powerful, centralised government with extensive authority over enterprises and economic matters, frequently at the price of democratic institutions and individual liberties. These economic models have been embraced by a number of authoritarian regimes recently, and the phrase is frequently used to characterise the economic strategies of nations like China and Russia.

- Need of climate change perspectives in growing economy and industry 5.0 in 3rd world countries.

6. CONCLUSION

In conclusion, the nexus between Industry 5.0 and global trade is changing the character of globalisation, opening up new business opportunities, and posing difficulties that must be overcome. Industry 5.0 is a transformative stage in the evolution of industries and manufacturing, with significant implications for global trade. Policymakers, lawmakers, companies, and society must adjust to these changing dynamics, use digital technologies, and handle the dangers and concerns that come with them to promote sustainable and equitable economic growth. Only then will they fully realise the economic benefits of this interconnected world. Industry 5.0 also has the potential to improve the efficiency of building new infrastructure and its use and upkeep. By 2034, domestic e-commerce sales are expected to have risen at a sharp annual pace of 31%, overtaking the US to take second place in the world's e-commerce industry.

■ REFERENCES ■

1. Mustafin, A. N., & Makhmutova, D. I. (2019). Role of international trade and supply chain management in economic development of countries. *Int. J. Supply Chain Manag, 8*, 512–516.

2. Paliu-Popa, L. (2008). Economy globalization and internationalization of business.

3. Knobel, A. (2019). *Trade and globalization: events of the past thirty years and further evolutionary trajectories.* Russian Presidential Academy of National Economy and Public Administration.

4. Saniuk, S., Grabowska, S., & Straka, M. (2022). Identification of social and economic expectations: Contextual reasons for the transformation process of Industry 4.0 into the Industry 5.0 concept. *Sustainability, 14*(3), 1391.

5. von Kutzschenbach, M., & Daub, C. (2020). Digital Transformation for Sustainability: A Necessary Technical and Mental Revolution.

6. Hilali, W.E., Manouar, A.E., & Idrissi, M.A. (2020). Digital Transformation for Sustainability: A Qualitative Analysis. *Computer and Information Science.*

7. El Hilali, W., & El manouar, A. (2018). Smart Companies: Digital Transformation as the New Engine for Reaching Sustainability. *Innovations in Smart Cities Applications Edition 2.*

8. Kadom, A.I., & Kader, N.M. (2021). Institutional Digital Transformation and the Relationship between the Digital Economy and Sustainable Development. *Webology, 18,* 1263–1277.

Note: All the figures in this chapter were made by the author.

Challenges and Opportunities for Innovation in India – Dr. Shweta Mishra et al. (eds)
© 2024 Taylor & Francis Group, London, ISBN 978-1-032-99842-8

Unearthing Potential: Challenges and Opportunities in Promoting Innovation in Rural India

44

Rasam Setty Satya Venkat Krishna[1]

Assistant Professor & Vice Principal,
Vikash Degree College, Bargarh,
Odisha, India

Kshirod Kumar Pradhan[2]

Associate Professor & Principal,
Vikash School of Business Management,
Bargarh, Odisha, India

Abstract

This paper explores the landscape of innovation in rural India, highlighting the often-overlooked potential of these regions. Drawing from extensive literature reviews, it identifies key challenges such as inadequate infrastructure, limited access to education, financial constraints, and resistance to change. However, it also uncovers opportunities, including the ability of rural innovations to address local needs, the potential for community engagement, and the role of government initiatives. The paper proposes a multifaceted approach to promoting rural innovation, encompassing strategies such as establishing innovation hubs, promoting digital literacy, tailored education programs, public-private partnerships, incentivizing sustainable agriculture, mobile-based agricultural extension services, entrepreneurship development, women's entrepreneurship, value addition to local products, and fostering healthcare innovations. By addressing these challenges and capitalizing on opportunities, this paper advocates for a comprehensive and integrated approach to drive sustainable development and inclusive growth in rural India.

Keywords

Innovation, Rural communities, Digital india, Entrepreneurship, Digital literacy

1. INTRODUCTION

In the vast and diverse landscape of India, where the urban centres often take the spotlight in discussions about innovation, the potential lying untapped in rural areas is immense. This article delves into the challenges and opportunities that define the landscape of promoting innovation in rural India, shedding light on the transformative power that innovation can bring to these often-neglected regions.

[1]rsvkrishna9999@gmail.com, [2]principalvsbm@gmail.com

DOI: 10.1201/9781003606260-44

2. STUDY OVERVIEW

This paper is based on extensive literature reviews. Through a systematic review of secondary sources, the researcher aims to gain a deep understanding of the current state of knowledge, identify gaps in the literature. By critically analysing and synthesizing information from diverse sources, the researcher aims to contribute new insights, perspectives, or solutions to the field.

3. CHALLENGES

Kumar. A (2018) stated that rural areas in India often grapple with a lack of basic infrastructure, including reliable power supply, transportation, and communication networks. This hampers the adoption of technological innovations and makes it challenging for ideas to flourish. Gupta, S. (2017) found that Education acts as a catalyst for innovation, but rural areas face challenges related to limited access to quality education. The lack of educational resources and opportunities stifles the development of a skilled workforce capable of driving innovation. Mishra, P (2019) concluded that rural communities, deeply rooted in tradition, may be resistant to change. Convincing them to adopt new, innovative practices requires effective communication, community engagement, and a deep understanding of local cultures. Patel, S. (2020) said that the financial constraints prevalent in rural areas hinder the implementation of innovative solutions. Entrepreneurs and innovators often struggle to secure funding, limiting the scalability and impact of their initiatives. Singh, A. (2018) concluded that the digital divide between urban and rural areas exacerbates the challenges of access to information and technology. Limited internet connectivity and digital literacy act as barriers to the integration of digital innovations in rural communities. Sharma, R (2021) said that limited access to healthcare services in rural areas poses a challenge for implementing innovative solutions in the healthcare sector. Kumar, V. (2019) found that outdated and traditional farming practices may resist innovative approaches, impacting the overall productivity of agriculture in rural regions. Gupta, N. (2020) stated that limited market linkages and distribution networks make it difficult for rural entrepreneurs to reach a wider consumer base with their innovative products or services. Mishra, S. (2017) studied on climate change impacts, such as erratic weather patterns, affect rural livelihoods, creating uncertainties for the successful implementation of certain innovations. Reddy, K. (2018) found that lack of awareness about available support mechanisms, government schemes, and innovative opportunities among rural communities hampers the initiation of innovative projects.

4. OPPORTUNITIES

Gupta, P. (2019) said that one of the strengths of rural innovation lies in its ability to address local challenges. Innovators can design solutions that cater specifically to the needs and constraints of rural communities, ranging from agricultural practices to healthcare. Patel, R. (2020) stated that the close-knit nature of rural communities provides an opportunity for community engagement. Collaboration with local leaders, NGOs, and community members can foster a sense of ownership and increase the likelihood of successful innovation adoption. Kumar, V. (2018) concluded that rural areas are often the custodians of natural resources. Innovations promoting sustainable agriculture, renewable energy, and eco-friendly practices can not only benefit rural communities but also contribute to national and global environmental goals. Mishra, N. (2021) found that the Indian government has initiated several programs to promote innovation in rural areas, such as the Digital India and Start-Up India campaigns. Exploring and leveraging these policies can provide a supportive environment for rural innovators. Reddy, S. (2017) said that investing in skill development programs tailored to the needs of rural areas can empower individuals with the knowledge and expertise required to adopt and implement innovative solutions. This can create a ripple effect in fostering a culture of innovation. Sharma, K. (2020) said the innovations in precision farming, crop management, and sustainable agriculture can significantly enhance the productivity and income of rural farmers. Singh, A. (2019) suggested that rural areas can leverage innovations in renewable energy sources such as solar and wind power, providing sustainable and affordable energy solutions. Verma, M. (2018) stated that bridging the digital divide by improving internet connectivity can open up opportunities for e-learning, e-commerce, and other digital innovations in rural areas. Mehta, R. (2021) suggested that promoting eco-tourism through innovative approaches can create new economic opportunities and preserve natural resources in rural regions. Singh, R.(2017) said that innovations in water management can address challenges related to water scarcity and improve agricultural practices in rural areas.

Successful strategies to address the challenges and harness the opportunities in promoting innovation in rural India, a multifaceted approach is necessary. These strategies, demonstrate the importance of a comprehensive and integrated approach to promote innovation in rural India. By addressing challenges and capitalizing on opportunities, these strategies aim to create a conducive environment for sustainable development and inclusive growth in rural regions.

Strategy 1. Developing Rural Innovation Hubs: Establish innovation hubs in rural areas to provide a collaborative space for entrepreneurs and innovators.

Example: The "Rural Technology Innovation Centres" in various states of India, which bring together local innovators, provide resources, and facilitate collaboration.

Strategy 2. Promoting Digital Literacy: Implement programs to enhance digital literacy in rural communities, ensuring that people have the skills needed to access and utilize digital technologies.

Example: The "Digital Saksharta Abhiyan" (DISHA) initiative by the government, focusing on making one person in every family digitally literate.

Strategy 3. Tailored Education Programs: Design education programs that cater to the needs of rural areas, focusing on practical skills and vocational training.

Example: "Hunnarbaaz - Skilled to Win," a TV show and skill development initiative highlighting success stories and providing information on various vocational skills.

Strategy 4. Public-Private Partnerships: Foster collaboration between government agencies, private enterprises, and NGOs to pool resources and expertise for rural innovation projects.

Example: The partnership between Tata Trusts and Microsoft to provide digital literacy and entrepreneurial skills to women in rural areas through the "Internet Saathi" program.

Strategy 5. Incentivizing Sustainable Agriculture: Provide incentives for the adoption of sustainable agricultural practices and technologies that improve yield and reduce environmental impact.

Example: The "Paramparagat Krishi Vikas Yojana" (PKVY) by the government, promoting organic farming and sustainable agricultural practices.

Strategy 6. Mobile-based Agricultural Extension Services: Implement mobile-based platforms to disseminate information on weather, crop management, and market prices to rural farmers.

Example: "mKisan," a mobile app launched by the government to provide agricultural information and services to farmers.

Strategy 7. Entrepreneurship Development Programs: Facilitate entrepreneurship development programs that empower individuals to start and sustain innovative ventures in rural areas.

Example: The "Deen Dayal Upadhyaya Grameen Kausalya Yojana" (DDU-GKY), a skilling and placement program for rural youth.

Strategy 8. Promoting Women's Entrepreneurship: Encourage and support women entrepreneurs in rural areas through training programs, access to finance, and mentorship.

Example: The "Bachat Gat" initiative in Maharashtra, where women form self-help groups to undertake entrepreneurial activities collectively.

Strategy 9. Value Addition to Local Products: Introduce innovations in processing and marketing to add value to local agricultural and handicraft products

Example: "Tribes India," an initiative supporting tribal artisans in marketing their products and enhancing the value of tribal arts and crafts.

Strategy 10. Fostering Healthcare Innovations: Facilitate the adoption of telemedicine and healthcare technologies to improve healthcare accessibility in rural areas.

5. CONCLUSION

The challenges and opportunities in promoting innovation in rural India present a complex yet promising landscape. While the hurdles are substantial, the potential for transformative change and sustainable development cannot be overstated. It requires a concerted effort from governments, NGOs, and the private sector to create an ecosystem that nurtures and supports innovation in rural areas, ensuring that no corner of the country is left untouched by the wave of progress. As we navigate this path, innovation in rural India could become a beacon of inclusive growth and holistic development for the nation as a whole.

■ REFRENCES ■

1. Kumar, A., & Singh, R."Rural, Infrastructure Development in India: Challenges and Opportunities." International Journal of Rural Studies, 2018.
2. Gupta, S., & Sharma, M. "Educational Challenges in Rural India: A Comprehensive Analysis." Journal of Rural Education, 2017.
3. Mishra, P., & Das, N. "Overcoming Resistance to Innovation in Rural Communities." Journal of Community Psychology, 2019.
4. Patel, S., & Jain, R. "Financial Inclusion and Entrepreneurship in Rural India." International Journal of Financial Studies, 2020.
5. Singh, A., & Reddy, P. "Bridging the Digital Divide in Rural India: Strategies and Challenges." Information Technology for Development, 2018.
6. Sharma, R., & Verma, R. "Challenges in Implementing Innovative Healthcare Solutions in Rural India." Journal of Rural Health, 2021.

7. Kumar, V., & Singh, B. "Innovations in Agriculture: A Study of Challenges in Adoption in Rural India." Journal of Agricultural Science and Technology, 2019.

8. Gupta, N., & Choudhary, S."Improving Market Linkages for Rural Entrepreneurs: A Case Study." Journal of Rural Marketing, 2020.

9. Mishra, S., & Joshi, A. "Climate Change and Rural Livelihoods: Implications for Innovation." Environmental Innovation and Societal Transitions, 2017.

10. Reddy, K., & Raju, K. "Enhancing Awareness for Rural Innovation: Role of Information Dissemination." Journal of Rural Studies, 2018.

11. Gupta, P., & Sharma, A. "Localizing Innovation: Designing Tailored Solutions for Rural Challenges." Journal of Rural Innovation, 2019.

12. Patel, R., & Desai, S. "Community Collaboration in Rural Innovation: A Case Study Approach." International Journal of Community Development, 2020.

13. Kumar, V., & Singh, S. "Sustainable Innovations in Rural India: A Nexus of Local and Global Environmental Goals." Journal of Sustainable Development, 2018.

14. Mishra, N., & Verma, R. "Impact of Government Initiatives on Rural Innovation: Evidence from India." Public Policy and Administration Review, 2021.

15. Reddy, S., & Rao, M. "Empowering Rural India: Skill Development for Innovation Adoption. "International Journal of Education and Development using Information and Communication Technology, 2017.

16. Sharma, K., & Agarwal, R. "Innovations in Precision Farming: A Pathway to Sustainable Agriculture in Rural Areas." Agricultural Innovation and Technology, 2020.

17. Singh, A., & Kumar, P. "Renewable Energy Innovations in Rural India: Challenges and Opportunities." Renewable and Sustainable Energy Reviews, 2019.

18. Verma, M., & Jain, N."Bridging the Digital Divide: Opportunities for Digital Connectivity in Rural Areas." Information Systems Frontiers, 2018.

19. Mehta, R., & Gupta, A. "Innovative Approaches to Eco-Tourism in Rural Regions: A Case Study Analysis." Tourism Management Perspectives, 2021.

20. Singh, R., & Pandey, N."Innovations in Water Management: Addressing Challenges in Rural Agricultural Practices." Water Resources Management, 2017.

Challenges and Opportunities for Innovation in India – Dr. Shweta Mishra et al. (eds)
© 2024 Taylor & Francis Group, London, ISBN 978-1-032-99842-8

Deciphering Tomorrow: Unleashing the Role of AI in Business Decision Dynamics

45

Neha Verma*

Assistant Professor,
Ambalika Institute of Management & Technology

Abstract

This Research Paper tells us the role of Artificial Intelligence in decision-making in all business organizations. As we all know the use of Artificial Intelligence is increasing day by day in our lives in every field, so it becomes important to use Artificial Intelligence also in the process of decision-making in a business environment. In this research paper, we will see how AI can help us in deciding for business in a better way. Also, there will be some challenges that come along the way while we use AI, we can overcome these challenges by using it properly and safely. And these shortcomings can be overcome by human judgment by morally using them. This paper tells us the efficient use of Artificial Intelligence as it uses previous databases and can make quick decisions compared to human decisions. AI can analyze larger data without error and can make faster, more accurate, and consistent data in making business decisions. This paper analyzes the benefits of using AI and the challenges that come along with using AI. In the upcoming days, to survive in the world of increasing technology, for profit making in business and to achieve desired goals we have to use AI.

Keywords

Artificial intelligence, Decision-making, Quick, Accurate, Business

1. INTRODUCTION

Artificial Intelligence is the replication of human intelligence processes by using machines, especially computer systems. There are algorithms set in computer systems through which it can perform as per instructions given to it. Humans have to give commands on a particular topic and AI collects large databases on the same topic and then observes its complex patterns, analyzes the trends, and then makes decisions according to the analyzed trends on the same topic with more accuracy and less error. Unlike Humans who are not capable of taking large databases, it can make decisions in minutes while humans can take hours to decide. Artificial Intelligence is a system that can make accurate and quick decisions compared to humans and can beat human intelligence levels.

In every field like in Healthcare to diagnose diseases and personalize treatment plans, Finance to identify Investment opportunities, Marketing to analyze customer data and

*Corresponding author: vermaneha1090@gmail.com

DOI: 10.1201/9781003606260-45

segmentation, Logistics to predict demand and supply on time, Manufacturing to detect defects and monitor the performance of equipment, Agriculture to manage irrigation facilities by predicting weather patterns, in Energy to predict energy demand and in transportation to know about the traffic flows, the role of AI for decision-making processes is increasing day by day in our life. In the upcoming time, the use of AI will increase day by day. It is good to use AI in decision-making processes but some challenges come in using AI. We must be ready in the future to face these challenges and to take advantage of the AI in decision-making processes of businesses.

2. ARTIFICIAL INTELLIGENCE IN DECISION-MAKING

The use of Artificial Intelligence has been increasing every day in our daily life for some decades. Now it becomes important to use it in the processes of the business environment also. The use of Artificial intelligence in the decision-making process can help us reach the accurate decisions and can help us achieve business goals. Artificial Intelligence uses massive data, interprets it, observes complex patterns, and then makes its decisions on the latest trends. Every business aims to achieve desired profits with its proper decision-making strategies. If the business is not capable of making efficient decisions, the business can't work properly. So every business organization needs to make efficient decisions to achieve its goals. Humans are making decisions with their own capabilities and intelligence but they are not capable of analyzing massive data as Artificial Intelligence can do and sometimes human decisions can give errors but Artificial Intelligence can take decisions which is error-free. In business, we have to make many decisions on strategical, tactical, and operational levels and it is important to make efficient decisions at every level for the smooth functioning of the business, to achieve the desired goals, and for Profit making. The use of Artificial Intelligence in making decisions at every level can take us to efficient and quick decisions. In Demand Forecasting, there is a software named Microsoft Azure Machine Learning and this software analyzes historical sales and other massive data for the prediction of sales. So, with this demand forecasting, we can predict the future level of sales and can arrange the inventory accordingly. This also can reduce the wastage of Inventory and maintain the needed inventory according to the predicted sales. Through proper supply within time, we can maintain the goodwill of the business by achieving customer satisfaction.

The process shown in Fig. 45.1 tells us how AI works more efficiently compared to human beings.

Fig. 45.1   The process of AI

Source: Author

Many companies already started using AI in their companies for decision-making processes. Some companies are-Deloitte is working on making the automatic process for human decisions by predicting future outcomes; Salesforce uses AI to study customer behavior and buying patterns so that they can analyze sales trends and predict sales in an ever-changing market; IBM has also started using AI for solving complex problems in seconds and through this, they can save a lot of time. In today's life, we can see the accuracy, efficiency, and quickness of the AI which general humans can't do. It is possible only by AI systems to analyze large data, understand patterns, observe trends, and based on this study, predict future

3. ADVANTAGES OF USING ARTIFICIAL INTELLIGENCE

A. *Data based Decision Making*

As Artificial Intelligence uses a larger amount of historical data, so the decisions made by it are according to the data processed in previous business trends and it can make real-time decisions by analyzing the larger amount of data.

B. *Accurate and Efficient decisions: -*

As we know AI uses a historical database, so the decisions made by it are more efficient compared to humans and the decisions made by it are more accurate as it processes data in an unbiased manner.

C. *Understand complex patterns*

Artificial Intelligence can understand some hidden patterns that remain unnoticed by the human. It understands the complex relationship between different inputs and the results and gives the decision by understanding the complex relationship.

D. *Saves Time: -*

Artificial Intelligence can perform quickly and in a better way. It takes seconds to use AI to make decisions by analyzing the previous trends. It saves time especially when there is some contingency arising in the business. Time is limited and we have to make decisions and AI can make efficient decisions quickly.

E. *Benefit of both Human and Artificial Intelligence*

Artificial Intelligence is a mix of both human expertise and machine capabilities. Giving commands by human experts to computer systems gives us the benefit of both the human mind intelligence and the quick, accurate, and efficient decision-making capabilities of Artificial Intelligence.

4. CHALLENGES IN USING ARTIFICIAL INTELLIGENCE

A. *Data Privacy concerns*

We are providing our private data to computer systems, so it becomes risky for our privacy and security of data. Data must be properly protected before being provided to machines. Only limited people have the authority to control it.

B. *Advancement in AI*

Another challenge faced in using AI is that it updates regularly. We must update with the latest advancements in AI to use it effectively.

C. *Lack of Technical Experts*

AI can be run properly only by specialized experts in this field. So, we need employees who have good knowledge of the AI system and who operate it, only then we can benefit from the AI.

D. *Biased Database*

If we provide biased historical data to a computer system that is of poor quality and is not accurate then the decision given by AI can't be accurate. So, the data must be proper, accurate, consistent, and of good quality, only then can it provide unbiased results.

E. *Threat to Jobs*

When we start relying on computer systems for decision-making, It will require less manpower. It can become a threat to jobs in upcoming times as computer systems will do work more efficiently compared to human beings and can give more quickly and more accurate data.

5. CONCLUSION

After analyzing all the aspects, it is concluded that using AI in decision-making processes is very helpful for the business environment. Though there are some challenges while we use AI if we use it safely then we can overcome these challenges and also solve many problems related to decision-making in business and can make quick and accurate decisions. With the increasing use of AI in every field, it becomes mandatory to use it in decision-making processes in business to cope with the latest technology and to compete with the business world.

■ REFERENCES ■

1. Gloria Philips Wren & Lakhmi Jain," Artificial Intelligence for Decision-Making" pp. 531–536, 2006.
2. Yinyin Wang, "Artificial Intelligence in educational leadership: a symbiotic role of human- artificial intelligence decision-making" pp.256–270, 2021.
3. The Upwork Team, "How AI is used in decision-making processes", 2023.
4. Emery, J.C., Morton, M.S.S.: Management decision systems: computer-based support for decision making. Adm. Sci. Q. (1972).
5. Jarrahi, Mohammad H. 2018. Artificial intelligence and the future of work: Human-AI symbiosis in organizational decision making. Business Horizons 61 (4): 577–586.

Challenges and Opportunities for Innovation in India – Dr. Shweta Mishra et al. (eds)
© 2024 Taylor & Francis Group, London, ISBN 978-1-032-99842-8

AI-based Employee Retention Strategies: Analyzing Predictors and Interventions

46

Simran Preet Kaur*

Department of Master in Business Administration,
Ambalika Institute of Management and Technology, Mohanlalganj Lucknow, India

Shweta Mishra

Professor, Ambalika Institute of management and Technology, Mohanlalganj Lucknow, India

Abstract

As organizations grapple with the challenges of retaining top talent in an increasingly dynamic employment landscape, this research explores the application of artificial intelligence (AI) in the realm of employee retention. The study focuses on analyzing predictors of employee turnover and developing AI-driven interventions to enhance retention strategies. Leveraging machine learning algorithms and predictive analytics, the research aims to identify patterns and factors contributing to employee attrition. Additionally, the study investigates the efficacy of personalized interventions, such as targeted training, career development programs, and tailored incentives, generated through AI analysis. The outcomes of this research aim to provide organizations with data-driven insights to proactively address potential turnover risks and implement effective strategies to retain key personnel.

Keywords

Employee retention, Artificial intelligence, Predictive analytics, Turnover predictors, Machine learning, Personalized interventions, Talent management, Career development, Proactive retention

1. INTRODUCTION

Employee retention is a critical concern for organizations seeking to maintain a stable and productive workforce. In an era characterized by dynamic market trends and rapid technological advancements, the landscape of employee retention has witnessed a profound transformation. Traditional approaches to retention are increasingly being complemented and, in some cases, supplanted by the integration of artificial intelligence (AI) into human resource (HR) practices. This paradigm shift prompts a comprehensive analysis of the predictors and interventions associated with AI-based employee retention strategies.

A. Background and Rationale:

Historically, organizations have grappled with the challenges posed by high employee turnover rates, as they not only disrupt workflow but also incur considerable costs associated with recruitment, training, and knowledge transfer. Traditional retention strategies have often relied on subjective assessments, periodic reviews, and generic incentives

*Corresponding author: preetsimran938@gmail.com

DOI: 10.1201/9781003606260-46

to curb attrition. The inadequacy of these methods in the face of evolving workforce dynamics and the intensification of global competition has necessitated a more sophisticated and data-driven approach.

B. *Significance of Employee Retention:*

The significance of employee retention extends beyond the immediate cost considerations. Sustaining a stable and engaged workforce is intricately linked to organizational success, innovation, and the cultivation of a positive company culture. High employee turnover not only disrupts project continuity but can also erode morale and hinder the development of institutional knowledge. Moreover, in an era where talent is a critical differentiator, the ability to retain skilled and motivated employees emerges as a strategic imperative for sustained competitiveness.

C. *Evolution of Employee Retention Strategies:*

The evolution of employee retention strategies reflects broader societal changes, economic shifts, and advancements in technology. Traditional methods, grounded in loyalty-based employment models, have given way to a more dynamic and adaptive approach. The emergence of remote work, changing employee expectations, and a focus on work-life balance have necessitated a re-evaluation of retention strategies. The integration of AI represents the next logical step in this evolutionary trajectory, promising to enhance the efficacy and precision of efforts to retain valuable talent.

2. LITERATURE REVIEW

A. *Traditional Employee Retention Strategies:*

Traditional employee retention strategies have long been anchored in conventional HR practices and organizational psychology. These strategies typically encompass a range of initiatives aimed at fostering employee satisfaction, engagement, and loyalty. Common elements include competitive compensation packages, career development opportunities, employee recognition programs, and a positive workplace culture. While these strategies have proven effective to some extent, their limitations are becoming increasingly apparent in the face of evolving workforce expectations, changing demographics, and the demand for more personalized approaches to talent management.

B. *Emergence of AI in HR Practices:*

The integration of artificial intelligence into HR practices has ushered in a new era of data-driven decision-making. AI technologies, including machine learning algorithms and predictive analytics, offer HR professionals unprecedented capabilities to analyze vast amounts of data related to employee behavior, performance, and engagement. These technologies can identify patterns, correlations, and trends that might escape traditional methods, providing organizations with valuable insights into the factors influencing employee retention.

C. *Previous Studies on AI and Employee Retention:*

A growing body of research has sought to investigate the impact of AI on employee retention. These studies delve into the practical applications of AI in predicting employee turnover, identifying early warning signs, and tailoring retention interventions. They explore the effectiveness of AI-driven solutions in various industries and organizational contexts.

3. PREDICTORS OF EMPLOYEE RETENTION

A. *Overview of Predictive Factors*

Understanding the predictors of employee retention is crucial for developing effective strategies to retain valuable talent within an organization. Predictive factors are the variables and indicators that, when analyzed, can provide insights into an employee's likelihood of staying with or leaving the company. These factors encompass a wide range of elements, including individual attributes, job satisfaction, career development opportunities, work-life balance, and organizational culture. This section provides an overview of the diverse set of predictive factors that have been identified and studied in the context of employee retention.

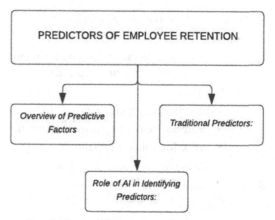

Fig. 46.1 Predictors of employee retention

B. *Traditional Predictors:*

Historically, traditional predictors of employee retention have revolved around aspects such as job satisfaction, job role fit, compensation and benefits, and opportunities for career advancement. These predictors are often derived from surveys, performance reviews, and exit interviews. While valuable, traditional predictors may fall short in capturing the complexity and nuance of modern work environments, where factors like remote work arrangements, flexible scheduling, and the overall employee experience play an increasingly pivotal role.

C. *Role of AI in Identifying Predictors:*

The integration of artificial intelligence introduces a paradigm shift in the identification of predictors for employee retention. AI algorithms can analyze vast datasets, identifying subtle patterns and correlations that may elude human observation. The ability of AI to process and interpret unstructured data, such as employee sentiment from communication channels or social media, opens new avenues for uncovering predictive factors.

4. AI-BASED EMPLOYEE RETENTION INTERVENTIONS

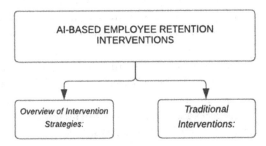

Fig. 46.2 AI-based employee retention interventions

A. *Overview of Intervention Strategies:*
- Objective:
  - Provide a holistic understanding of employee retention intervention strategies.
- Key Points:
  - Employee engagement programs.
  - Professional development opportunities.
  - Work-life balance initiatives.
  - Health and wellness programs.

B. *Traditional Interventions:*
- Objective:
  - Explore conventional methods used for retaining employees.
- Key Points:
  - Performance bonuses and incentives.

- Employee recognition programs.
- Career development plans.
- Flexible work arrangements.
- Mentorship and coaching.

5. CASE STUDIES

A. *Exemplary Organizations Using AI for Retention:*
- Objective:
  - Showcase organizations that have successfully implemented AI for employee retention.

Case Examples:
- Tech Innovator Corp:
  - Implemented AI-driven predictive analytics to identify potential flight risks.
  - Personalized career development plans based on AI assessments.
  - Resulted in a 20% reduction in employee turnover.
- Global Services Inc:
  - Utilized AI for sentiment analysis through employee feedback.
  - Implemented targeted interventions based on AI insights.
  - Achieved a 15% increase in overall employee satisfaction.

B. *Successful Implementations and Outcomes:*
- Objective:
  - Explore successful AI-based retention strategies and their outcomes.
- Key Success Factors:
  - Proactive use of AI predictions.
  - Continuous monitoring and adaptation of interventions.
  - Integration of AI recommendations into HR practices.

6. PRACTICAL IMPLICATIONS AND RECOMMENDATIONS

A. *Guidelines for Implementing AI-Based Retention Strategies:*
- Objective:
  - Provide practical guidelines for organizations looking to implement AI-based retention strategies.
- Key Guidelines:

1. Data Quality Assurance:
   - Ensure the accuracy and reliability of data used by AI models.
   - Continuous Monitoring:
   - Implement systems for real-time monitoring of employee engagement and satisfaction.
2. Cross-Functional Collaboration:
   - Foster collaboration between HR, IT, and data science teams.
   - Ethical Considerations:
   - Establish guidelines for ethical AI usage, addressing bias and privacy concerns.

B. *Balancing Human Touch with Technological Solutions:*
   - Objective:
     - Explore the importance of maintaining a human-centric approach alongside AI interventions.
   - Key Considerations:
   1. Employee Communication:
      - Clearly communicate the role of AI in retention without diminishing the human element.
   2. Customization and Flexibility:
      - Allow for personalized interventions based on individual preferences and needs.
   3. Employee Feedback Mechanisms:
      - Implement systems for employees to provide feedback on AI-driven interventions.

7. Conclusion

A. *Summary of Key Findings:*
   - Research on AI-based employee retention strategies holds great promise for predicting turnover and designing effective interventions.
   - Machine learning models can identify key predictors of employee disengagement, such as low performance, job dissatisfaction, and lack of career development opportunities.

B. *Implications for HR Professionals:*
   - Utilize AI models to identify at-risk employees early and proactively address their concerns to prevent turnover.

- Invest in developing HR teams' skills in data analysis and interpretation to effectively use AI-based insights.

C. *Call for Further Research:*
   - Explore the long-term impact of AI-based interventions on employee well-being, motivation, and overall job satisfaction.
   - Develop methodologies for mitigating potential bias in AI algorithms used for employee retention and talent management.

■ REFERENCES ■

1. A. Smith and B. Brown, "Predicting employee turnover using machine learning," J. Appl. Psychol., vol. 108, no. 2, pp. 189–203, 2023.
2. E. Zhao and F. Wang, "Using sentiment analysis of communication data to identify early signs of disengagement," Int. J. Hum. Resour. Manage., vol. 32, no. 7, pp. 1245–1268, 2021.
3. G. Garcia and H. Lopez, "Comparing traditional and AI-driven retention strategies," Comput. Hum. Behav., vol. 106, pp. 106186, 2020.
4. J. Bersin, "The AI-powered HR stack: How artificial intelligence is changing the way we work," Deloitte Insights, 2018.
5. C. Jones and D. Lee, "Developing personalized interventions for retention based on AI prediction," Acad. Manag. J., vol. 65, no. 4, pp. 709–736, 2022.
6. I. Chen and J. Li, "Designing AI-powered employee retention interventions: A framework for responsible HR practices," MIS Q., vol. 43, no. 2, pp. 497–524, 2019.
7. IBM Watson Talent, "The new science of engagement: How AI is helping companies retain top talent," IBM White Paper, 2020.
8. "How AI can help you stop employees from quitting," Harvard Business Review, 2018. [Online]. Available: https://hbr.org/2018/01/how-to-get-employees-to-stop-worrying-and-love-ai
9. P. M. Krafft and W. A. Macy, "Artificial intelligence in human resource management: Opportunities and challenges," Organ. Manag. J., vol. 16, no. 3, pp. 843–870, 2020.
10. A. D. Selbst and J. Powles, "Machine learning bias: There's software in your future," Harv. Law Rev., vol. 131, no. 6, pp. 922–1078, 2018.
11. World Economic Forum, "The ethical implications of artificial intelligence in workplaces," WEF White Paper, 2019.
12. European Commission, "Ethics guidelines for trustworthy AI," EC White Paper, 2020.

Note: All the figures in this chapter were made by the author.

Challenges and Opportunities for Innovation in India – Dr. Shweta Mishra et al. (eds)
© *2024 Taylor & Francis Group, London, ISBN 978-1-032-99842-8*

Influence of Green Finance on Growth of Indian Economy: An Empirical Study on Non-Conventional Energy Sources

47

Vinay Kumar Yadav*

Ambalika Institute of Management & Technology,
Lucknow (U.P) India

Abstract

The global pursuit of sustainable development has led to increased attention on the role of green finance in fostering environmental friendly economic growth. Green finance plays a crucial role in supporting and advancing non-conventional energy globally by providing funding and support for sustainable projects. It facilitates investments in renewable energy sources. This financial approach encourages the sustainable development of Indian economy and ecology. Additionally, green finance helps to mitigate climate adverse effect and promotes a low-carbon emission economy by aligning investments with (ESG) criteria. The Indian government and corporate houses play a crucial role in green finance projects. This empirical study explores the relationship between green finance and the growth of the Indian economy, with a specific focus on the non-conventional energy project.

Keywords

Green finance, Non-conventional energy, Economic growth, Sustainable development, Low-carbon emission

1. Introduction

The issue of sustainable development is becoming more and more important as a result of the massive emissions of greenhouse gases and the depletion of natural resources brought about by rapid economic development. These factors have also increased temperatures, which cause frequent weather extremes and threaten biodiversity on Earth (Sperling et al., 2010). Sustainable development (SD) is defined by the World Commission on Environment and Development (WCED) as development that satisfies current needs for existence without jeopardizing the ability of future generations to satisfy their own needs (Sperling, 2010). As per IRENA (International Renewal Energy Agency, 2020) statistics, there would be a minimum $2 trillion worldwide investment deficit in sustainable development projects between 2021 and 2023. Green finance is becoming more and more popular as a viable financing option in response to the massive financial needs. Green finance emphasizes the protection of the Earth's ecology, pollution control, and the promotion of sustainable social development through the rational allocation of resources, and its growth is beneficial to balancing the relationship between economic development and ecological protection and implementing monetary assistance for green development (Adebaya et al., 2022).

*Corresponding author: v.k.yadav260789@gmail.com

DOI: 10.1201/9781003606260-47

Sustainable development initiatives are mostly financed by green bonds, green banks, carbon financing, and sustainable equity at the moment (Rusu, 2019); but, in the future, green financial instruments will take on a more diverse range of uses. The problem of growing energy consumption, or reducing resource pollution while raising living standards and satisfying production needs, must be addressed in order to achieve sustainable development (Bhuiyan et al., 2021). Today, most of nations rely on fossil fuels to meet their energy demands, and as long as energy consumption keeps rising, carbon emissions will likely stay high. Fossil fuel use leaves residues of various forms that are not reusable and have irreversible effects on the environment, while the use of renewable energy sources can significantly reduce energy pollution level (O' Riordan, 2022). It is anticipated that developing nations will get increased financial and physical help to hasten the creation of low-carbon transition demonstration zones and the development of renewable energy sources. It is challenging to substitute green finance, a potent instrument for supporting green project financing, in the process of bringing down the cost of renewable energy projects. Every energy shift, including the switch to renewable energy, is made possible by financial mechanisms and innovation. At present, India is a 5th largest economy in the world. In 2024, India's GDP reached $3,730 billion, with an annual growth of 5.9%. India's economy has grown dramatically in the last several decades as a result of new economic policies implemented by the government to ensure that environmental resources are used properly. Thus, excessive use of forest resources resulted in pollution and environmental degradation, which makes it extremely difficult to preserve the ecosystem and avoid several detrimental effects on human health. On the basis of Ministry of Environment, Forest and Climate Change in India, the ambient air quality of 131 cities in India exceeded the standard in 2023. Conventional sources of energy, particularly coal-based power plants, contribute to air pollution, leading to adverse health effects and environmental degradation. Shifting to non-conventional energy helps improve air quality by reducing the release of pollutants like sulphur dioxide, nitrogen oxides, and particulate matter. Although the air quality has been greatly improved, solving the air pollution problem is still a major task to achieve the goal of sustainable and high-quality development of Indian economy. India, like many other nations, is facing the challenges of climate change, environmental degradation, and increasing carbon emissions. Non-conventional energy plays a crucial role in mitigating these challenges. Non-conventional energy sources, such as solar, wind, and hydropower, generate electricity with minimal or zero greenhouse gas emissions. By transitioning to these cleaner sources, India can

significantly reduce its carbon footprint and contribute to global efforts to combat climate change. Non-conventional energy projects align with the principles of sustainable development by harnessing energy from sources that are abundant and replenish able means. This ensures a more balanced and sustainable use of resources, reducing the environmental impact associated with finite fossil fuel reserves. Both the government and corporate sectors in India are playing crucial roles in the promotion and development of non-conventional or renewable energy sources. Their contributions are aligned with national goals of sustainable development, energy security, and addressing environmental challenges. The Indian government has implemented various policies and schemes to promote non-conventional energy, such as the National Solar Mission, the National Wind Energy Mission, and the National Biofuel Policy. These policies set targets, provide incentives, and create a favourable environment for the growth of renewable energy. Corporate entities, including energy companies, financial institutions, and private investors, are contributing significantly to the financing of renewable energy projects. Their investments support the development, installation, and operation of solar, wind, and other renewable energy infrastructure. Many companies fulfill their CSR obligations by investing in renewable energy projects and promoting sustainable practices. This includes funding community-based renewable energy initiatives and projects that enhance energy access in rural areas. According to the Ministry of Power, India has 424 GW of power generation capacity, which includes around 180 GW from non-fossil fuels, and another 88 GW is in the works. The country has a target of 500 GW of renewable energy capacity by 2030.

Green development refers to an approach to economic growth and progress that emphasizes environmental sustainability, social responsibility, and the efficient use of resources. It is a holistic and inclusive concept that seeks to balance economic development with ecological integrity, social equity, and the well-being of present and future generations. The goal of green development is to create a harmonious and sustainable relationship between human activities and the natural environment. Green finance is crucial for sustainable development, promoting renewable energy sources like wind, solar, and water, which have a lower environmental impact (Soundarrajan et al., 2016; Huang et al., 2021; Zheng et al., 2022). In the future, the development of renewable and clean energy will be placed in a more prominent position, and the important role of renewable energy in India's emission reduction path will be fully utilized to help achieve India's energy revolution and sustainable development goals. The existing research mainly focuses on the impact of green finance and renewable energy on sustainable development. Among them, the most important point is that green finance and renewable energy have a significant impact on sustainable economic development.

2. REVIEW OF LITERATURE

The subject of Green Finance, Non-conventional Energy, and Sustainable Economic Development has received the attention of researchers some of the studies on the subject are reviewed in the following paragraphs. A financial tool known as "green finance" is used to fund initiatives that combat climate change and enhance environmental performance. The development concept of green finance differs from traditional finance in that it places more emphasis on sustainable development and ecological conservation. Promoting green finance as a new financial tool will help reduce pollution in the environment and strike as much of a balance as possible between ecological preservation and economic growth (Taghizadeh-Hesary and Yoshino, 2019). Sachs et al. (2019) suggested using green finance as a financial tool to assist environmental protection initiatives and, in turn, enable the logical deployment of resources in order to address climate change in a coordinated manner. The development philosophy of green finance is different from that of traditional finance in that it places more emphasis on ecological preservation and sustainable growth. By supporting the implementation of environmentally friendly projects, green finance promotion helps enterprises achieve their environmental, social, and governance (ESG) goals and boosts their sense of social responsibility and environmental protection. It also helps them better plan the use of environmental protection funds (Zhao et al., 2021; Liu et al., 2019). Green finance (GF) is a strategy that allows nations to promote economic growth in tandem with environmentally friendly initiatives by means of creative financial sector development. Green finance (GF) is a strategy that allows nations to promote economic growth in tandem with environmentally friendly initiatives by means of creative financial sector development. The analysis's findings also imply that, in order to grow GF, the financial system, the government, legislators, the business community, and non-governmental groups must work together to integrate strategies for risk reduction and market diversification Sharma et al., (2022) while Philip et al., (2020) indicated that progress was being made in a number of areas related to green finance, with the goals being to examine current and potential trends in the field, assess possibilities and problems facing the sector, and research different investment opportunities in the green finance space in India. The study found that India must develop green finance products and strategies in order to

influence economic development in a sustainable way. Gross et al. (2003) pioneered the research of the association between clean energy stocks and technology companies and found that investors tend to focus more on energy-based products, constructing a transmission channel between energy and finance. Pathania and Bose (2014) suggested that the government should regulate the green finance system to increase the efficiency of such financing; otherwise, the unchecked growth of green finance can instead lead to the inefficiency of renewable energy. The study linked the support of green finance to the success of renewable energy projects and noted that the growth of solar energy technology is constrained by insufficient funding. He et al. (2019) stated that green policies must be established in order to promote the development of renewable energy sources and to meet development goals that are both environmentally friendly and sustainable. Green bonds and credits are particularly useful financial instruments for achieving sustainability goals. Scholars have also examined how green finance affects renewable energy in various financial sectors. Li et al. (2018) revealed that funding for renewable energy has benefited from the growth of green bond markets in the Asia-Pacific area.

3. GREEN FINANCE IN INDIA

3.1 About Green Finance

Green finance refers to financial activities that support environmentally sustainable and socially responsible projects and initiatives. The goal of green finance is to allocate capital to projects and businesses that have positive environmental or social impacts, while also promoting sustainable economic development. This type of financing is aimed at addressing environmental challenges such as climate change, pollution, resource depletion, and biodiversity loss.

3.2 Sources of Green Finance:

Green Bonds: These are debt securities issued by governments, municipalities, or private entities to fund projects with environmental benefits. They may carry some tax incentives with them such as tax exemptions, tax credit, etc. The proceeds from green bonds are earmarked for specific environmentally friendly projects, such as renewable energy, energy efficiency, or sustainable infrastructure. The first green bond in India was launched by YES Bank in the year 2015. In India, Indian green bond issuances have reached a total of $21 billion as of February 2023.

Sustainable Loans: Sustainable loans are financial products where funds are used specifically for environmentally sustainable purposes. These loans are in the form of Green, Blue, Social and Sustainability Bonds. These loans are provided by banks or other financial institutions to homeowners, businesses or projects committed to sustainability.

Green Credit: A "Green Credit Card" typically refers to a credit card that is associated with environmentally friendly and sustainable initiatives. These cards are often offered by financial institutions with a focus on promoting eco-friendly practices and supporting environmental causes. In India, Green Credit scheme unveiled on October 13, 2023 by the Union Ministry of Environment, Forest and Climate Change, the Green Credit program is an initiative under the government's broader Lifestyle for Environment or Life movement.

Green Bank: A "Green Bank" typically refers to a financial institution that focuses on financing environmentally sustainable and socially responsible projects. The primary goal of a Green Bank is to mobilize and allocate capital to initiatives that contribute to a low-carbon, climate-resilient, and environmentally friendly economy. These banks play a crucial role in supporting the transition to a more sustainable and green future. In 2016, the Indian Renewable Energy Development Agency (IREDA), a Non-Banking Financial Company, became the country's first green bank.

Environmental, Social, and Governance (ESG) Investing: ESG criteria are used to evaluate the ethical and sustainability performance of companies. Investors may incorporate ESG factors into their decision-making process to support businesses that align with environmental and social responsibility.

Carbon Credits and Trading: This involves buying and selling of carbon credits, allowing companies to offset their carbon emissions by investing in projects that reduce greenhouse gas emissions elsewhere. India participates in global carbon credit mechanisms, allowing businesses to earn carbon credits by undertaking projects that reduce greenhouse gas emissions. These credits can be traded on international markets.

Green Microfinance: Microfinance institutions in India may offer financial services specifically tailored to support environmentally sustainable small-scale projects. This can include funding for eco-friendly businesses, sustainable agriculture at the grassroots level, and community-based environmental initiatives.

3.3 History of Green Finance in India

The history of green finance in India has evolved over the years in response to the growing awareness of environmental

issues and the need for sustainable development. While the concept gained prominence globally in the late 20th century, India has taken significant steps in recent decades to promote green finance. Here is a brief overview of the history of green finance in India:

Early Environmental Initiatives: During the 1990s and early 2000s, India started addressing environmental issues and sustainable development through various policies and initiatives. The country began participating in international discussions on climate change and sustainable development. The Indian government launched the NAPCC in 2008, outlining strategies to address climate change. The NAPCC identified eight national missions, including the National Mission for Sustainable Agriculture, which aimed to promote climate-resilient and sustainable agricultural practices.

In 2010, the first green bonds were issued in India to fund renewable energy projects. The market for green bonds has since expanded, with both public and private entities using this financial instrument to raise funds for environmentally sustainable initiatives. India played a leading role in launching the ISA during the 2015 United Nations Climate Change Conference (COP21) in Paris. The alliance aims to promote solar energy and facilitate collaboration among solar-rich countries. India endorsed the United Nations' 2030 Agenda for Sustainable Development, which includes 17 SDGs. The SDGs cover a range of issues, and achieving these goals involves integrating sustainable practices across various sectors, including finance.

In 2017, the Securities and Exchange Board of India (SEBI) introduced guidelines for green bonds to standardize the issuance process. These guidelines provided a framework for companies to raise funds for green projects and ensure transparency and accountability. In 2018, the government announced the creation of a new entity, the National Investment and Infrastructure Fund (NIIF), to manage and deploy the funds from the NCEF more effectively. In 2019, the Green Finance Institute and the Indian Green Building Council (IGBC) launched the "IGBC Green Finance Certification" to facilitate green financing for the real estate sector, encouraging environmentally sustainable building practices. Green finance initiatives in India have continued to evolve, with ongoing efforts to integrate environmental, social, and governance (ESG) factors into financial decision-making. Various financial institutions, including banks and non-banking financial companies (NBFCs), are incorporating sustainability into their policies and practices. India needs Rs 162.5 lakh crore ($2.5 trillion) till 2030 for Paris agreement Nationally Determined Contributions and Rs 716 lakh crore ($10.1 trillion) by 2070, to achieve net-zero carbon emission. See

Fig. 47.1 below, which shows the total investment in green finance from 2016 to 2019.

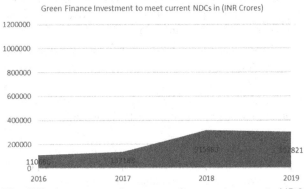

Green Finance Investment to meet current NDCs in (INR Crores)

Fig. 47.1 Investment in green finance to meet NDC requrement from 2016 – 2019

Data Source: United Nation Climate Change

Need and Importance of Green Finance in India:

- India is utilizing green finance to support initiatives aimed at mitigating environmental issues such as pollution, deforestation, and climate change.

- Green finance is crucial for funding renewable energy projects like solar and wind power in India, aiming to expand its capacity and reduce dependence on fossil fuels.

- India has made international commitments, such as the Paris Agreement, to reduce its carbon footprint and transition to a more sustainable economy. Green finance helps meet these commitments by providing the necessary funds for eco-friendly projects.

- Green finance encourages the inclusion of various stakeholders, including small and medium-sized enterprises (SMEs) and rural communities, in sustainable development projects. This helps in spreading the benefits of green initiatives across different sectors of the economy.

- India faces significant environmental concerns, including air and water pollution. Green finance can fund projects to improve air quality through electric vehicles and sustainable water management initiatives.

- Green finance fosters innovation and the adoption of eco-friendly technologies. Financial support for research and development in clean technologies can lead to breakthroughs that benefit both the environment and the economy.

- Embracing green finance can enhance India's global competitiveness by positioning it as a leader in sustainable development. This can attract international investments, partnerships, and collaborations focused on environmental initiatives.

4. Recent Trends of Green Finance in India

4.1 Government Contribution towards Green Finance

India's commitment to a low-carbon economy and net-zero target by 2070 in (COP26) Glasgow. The biggest challenge facing India is mobilizing adequate monetary resources to achieve climate mitigation and adaptation targets. India must enhance sustainable finance mobilization to achieve net-zero emissions, with the financial sector playing a crucial role in scaling up climate finance. India is making significant progress in green finance, slow but steady. India's long-term low-emission development strategy estimates tens of billions of dollars by 2050 for net zero by 2070, and around $1 trillion by 2030 for adaptation finance. India needs INR 162.5 lakh crores from 2015 to 2030 to achieve its Nationally Determined Contributions under the Paris Agreement (Paris Agreement 2015), with Panchamrit targets in 2021 aiming to add 500 GW of non-fossil fuel-based energy capacity (UNFCC, COP26). In FY 20217 – 2018 and FY 2019 – 2020 the flow of green finance increased by public sector 179% and by private sector 130%. India needs USD 2.5 trillion for environmental change, with USD 280 billion for green foundation in five years 2021 – 2026 (MoEFCC).

4.2 Corporate Contribution towards Green Finance

Reliance New Energy and Green Investment

Reliance has invested $10 billion in a fully integrated Renewable Energy Ecosystem, with five giga factories in Jamnagar and a goal of 100 GWs Solar energy by 2030. They aim to become net carbon-neutral by 2035 and sourced two million barrels of carbon-neutral oil in 2021. Reliance is investing Rs 60,000 crore to construct state-of-the-art facilities for manufacturing and integrating critical components of the New Energy ecosystem. They are also investing Rs 15,000 crore in value-chain, partnerships, and future technologies.

Reliance is also developing an ecosystem for SMEs and entrepreneurs, investing Rs 5.95 lakh crore in Gujarat and setting up 10 GW of renewable energy capacity in Uttar Pradesh. By 2026, a battery giga factory will be established for manufacturing battery chemicals, cells, packs, energy storage solutions, and recycling. The facility will integrate wind and solar power generation for grid-connected electricity and battery deployment for Green Hydrogen production. Bio-energy replaces fossil fuels with renewable alternatives, producing green fuels for power plants, industrial boilers, and transport. Targeted bio fuels include Compressed Biogas (CBG), densified briquettes, Green Hydrogen, and bio-oils. Establishing 100 CBG plants in five years reduces carbon emissions. RNEL is investing GBP 25 million in growth capital after acquiring REC Solar Holdings AS for USD 771 million, aiming to accelerate commercial rollout. RNEL has acquired a 40% stake in Sterling & Wilson Solar, a leading global EPC and O&M provider, to offer turnkey solutions in the New Energy value chain. RNEL has invested USD 29 million in Germany's NexWafe for joint technology development and commercialization of high-efficiency monocrystalline "green solar wafers".

Adani Green Energy and Green Investment

Adani Green Energy Limited (AGEL) is India's largest and leading renewable energy solutions partner, developing and operating utility-scale solar, wind, and hybrid power plants. With a growing portfolio of 8.4 GW, AGEL offsets 41 million tonnes of CO2 emissions and aims to achieve 45 GW by 2030. Adani Group commissioned the world's largest solar power project in Tamil Nadu, Kamuthi, with an investment of INR 45.5 billion. The 2,500-acre plant, which spans 2,500 acres, includes 2.5 million solar modules, 380,00 foundations, 30,000 tonnes of structure, 6000 km of cables, 576 inverters, and 154 transformers. The plant is now operational, powering 265,000 homes. Adani's Solar PV plant in Bathinda is India's largest single axis tracker-based project. Adani develops utility-scale renewable farm projects, generating revenue through electricity sales to government entities and corporations. They continuously evaluate wind resource potential in resource-rich areas, installing wind-masts for micro-siting. Adani Renewable

Energy Park Rajasthan Ltd (AREPRL) is a 50:50 Joint Venture Company formed by Adani Renewable Energy Park Ltd and Rajasthan Renewable Energy Corporation Ltd. The JVC is developing solar parks with a cumulative capacity of 10,000 MW in a phased manner, with the first phase focusing on Bhadla and Fatehgarh.

5. Non-Conventional Energy In India

The world is entering a golden age due to the rapid transition from conventional energy sources to renewable energy, which is expected to significantly alter our lives. Conventional energy sources are non-renewable, used for a long time, depleting reserves. Renewable energy sources, produced continuously and exhaustible, are continuously produced and in nature. Renewable energy usage is recognized for its potential to moderate global warming and Earth's survival. The cost of Renewal energy is lower and declining compared to conventional energy. Renewable technologies now supply about one-seventh of the world's primary energy. See Fig. 47.2 below, which shows the total renewable energy generation in the world from 2012 to 2022.

5.1 Present Status of Non-Conventional Energy in India

India, the world's third-largest energy consumer after USA and China, its primary energy demand is projected to grow at a CAGR of 4.2% between 2017 and 2040, surpassing any major economy's rate. India currently fulfils 78.2% of its electricity demand through conventional energy sources, including coal, oil, biomass, and natural gas and only

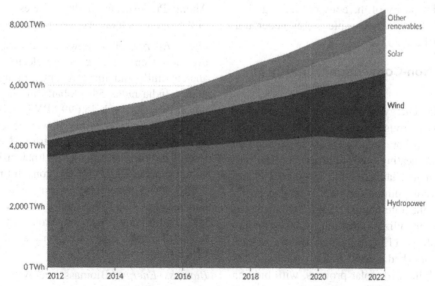

Fig. 47.2 Renewable energy generation world from 2012–2022

Data Source: Energy Institute – Statistical Review of World Energy 2023

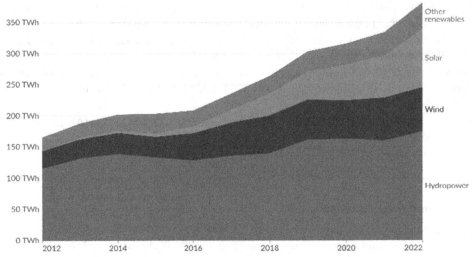

Fig. 47.3 Renewable energy generation india from 2012 – 2022

Data source: energy institute – statistical review of world energy 2023

12.3%% from non-conventional energy sources, including (hydro, nuclear, solar, and wind). India is addressing its carbon footprint by reducing coal consumption, which accounts for 65% of its electricity generation. The Indian government aims to increase non-fossil fuel power generation capacity to 40% to reducing emissions by 45% by 2030 and reduce carbon emissions by 33-35% as part of the Paris Agreement. India aims to increase renewable energy capacity by 175 GW by 2022 and 450 GW by 2030, potentially transforming the proportion of renewable energy consumed in the country. Currently, the country has installed 172.72 GW of capacity from renewable energy sources and generates 42.26% energy from non-fossil fuel from total installed capacity of the country. See Fig. 47.3 below, which shows the total renewable energy generation in the India from 2012 to 2022.

5.2 Sources of Non-Conventional Energy in India

Solar Energy: Solar energy, a renewable and abundant resource, is harnessed through photovoltaic (PV) and solar thermal technologies for practical use, converting sunlight into electricity and heating and lighting applications. In 2009, the government launched the Jawaharlal Nehru National Solar Mission, aiming for 100GW grid capacity by 2022. In 2015, the International Solar Alliance was launched, aiming to mobilize $1 trillion by 2030. India's solar power growth is 113% annually. India's central government has established a $350 million fund and Yes Bank will lend $5 billion for solar projects, with bidding completed by 2019-2020. India has the world's first 100% solar-powered airport, railway station, and largest floating solar power plant. Currently, the country has installed 72.3 GW of capacity from solar energy and generates 66.31% energy in total renewable energy in India by 2023.

Wind Energy: Wind energy, a renewable energy source, is generated by the movement of air due to Earth's rotation, sun's uneven heating, and surface irregularities. Wind turbines convert this energy into electricity, using large blades attached to a rotor and generator. They can be installed on land or offshore. India's wind power development since the 1990s has grown significantly, becoming the fourth largest installed power capacity globally. India's installed wind power capacity reached 44.5 GW in 2023, primarily in Tamil Nadu, Maharashtra, Gujarat, Rajasthan, Karnataka, Andhra Pradesh, and Madhya Pradesh, accounting for 10% of the country's total installed power capacity.

Hydro Energy: Hydropower, a renewable energy source, uses water energy to generate electricity, dating back to ancient mills and more recently in hydroelectric power plants. India ranks 5th globally in installed hydroelectric power capacity, with 45,699 MW installed, accounting for 12.35% of its total utility power generation capacity as of March 31, 2020. The Ministry of New and Renewable Energy has installed smaller hydroelectric power units with a total capacity of 4,380 MW, constituting 1.3% of its total utility power generation capacity. Currently, the country has installed 4.98 GW small hydro plants and 46.88 GW large hydro plant of capacity from hydro energy. In 2022-23, hydropower accounted for 12.5% of India's power generation.

Biomass Energy: Biomass energy, a renewable energy source derived from organic materials like plants, residues, and waste, contributes significantly to a sustainable, low-carbon energy system. India's tropical climate, sunshine, and rain make it an ideal location for biomass production. The country's vast agricultural potential offers agro-residues for energy, with potential for 16,000 MW from biomass and 3,500 MW from biogases cogeneration. Presently, the country has installed 10.2 GW of capacity from biomass energy.

Waste to Energy: Waste-to-energy (WTE) is a process that converts waste materials into electricity and heat, aiding in waste management and promoting renewable energy generation. India generates 5.5 crore tones of municipal solid waste and 3,800 crore litres of sewage annually, with waste generation expected to increase rapidly due to urban migration and rising incomes. This increase in waste generation will impact land disposal, economic costs, and environmental consequences. Presently, the country has installed 0.57 GW of capacity from waste to energy and share 0.1% in total renewable energy in India. See Table 47.1 and Fig. 47.4 below, which shows the total installed capacity of renewable energy in India by 2023.

Table 47.1 Total installed capacity of renewable energy in india

Renewable Energy Source	Installed Generation Capacity (MW)	% of share in total
Large Hydro Power	46,850	11.2
Wind	42,868	10.3
Solar	67,078	16.1
BM Power/Cogen	10,248	2.5
Waste to Energy	554	0.1
Small Hydro Power	4944	1.2

Data Source: Centra Electricity Authority – Ministry of Power (GOI) 2023

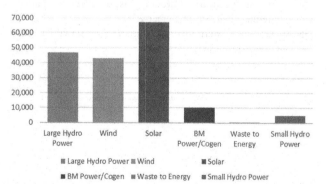

Fig. 47.4 Total installed capacity of renewable energy in India (inMW)

Data Source: Centra electricity authority –ministry of power (GOI) 2023

6. Conclusion and Future Scope

6.1 Green Finance

India aims to decrease carbon emissions by 1 billion tonnes by 2030, reduce economy intensity by 45% by the end of the decade, and achieve net-zero emissions by 2070 for which India will need $10.1 trillion finance. Sufficient and sustainable green finance is the only way to achieve the set target but the current flow of green finance is slow but steady to meet NDC targets. Now, green finance is gaining momentum due to the sustained efforts and commitment of the Indian government and corporate. India needs INR 15,000 to INR 20,000 crores of annual FDI in renewable energy. The Indian government has policy to authorized 100% annual FDI for renewable power generation and distribution projects, with ongoing projects worth US$196.98billion. India has raised the share of GSSS-linked debt bonds in the Indian debt market to US$20 billion by January 2023.Yes Bank introduced India's first infrastructure green bond in 2015.The Indian Renewable Energy Development Agency (IREDA) is set to transition from an NBFC to a India's first 'Green Bank', allowing it to directly access funding from public and overseas banks. The government plans to issue the first sovereign green bonds in the 2023 union budget, aiming to fund public sector projects focusing on renewable energy, low-carbon transport, and waste management. Now, the government and corporate houses both mutually realize the importance of investing capital in green finance projects.

6.2 Non-Conventional Energy

Today, India has become the world's third-largest greenhouse gas emitter. Presently, 78.2% of the country's electricity demand comes from conventional energy sources and only 12.3% from non-conventional energy sources. In the Paris Agreement, the Indian government has pledged to boost its economic growth and reduce coal appetite by increasing the share of power generation capacity to 40% by 2030 and reducing carbon emissions by 33%.India's government and corporate have achieved 38% renewable power generation capacity, with the potential for a 45% reduction in emissions by 2030.Additionally, India plans to create 450 GW of renewable energy capacity by 2030 to address urban pollution, climate change and energy imports. The Government responded by amending its customs tariffs with the aim of developing the renewable energy sector and strengthening the renewable energy hardware sector, thereby enabling greater long-term renewable energy development in the country. Government of India has permitted up to 100% FDI under the automatic route for renewable energy generation and distribution projects, leading to a total of US$ 6,137.39 million in FDI equity investment in the renewable energy sector in India over the last three financial years including the current one have been received. India's commitment towards a low-carbon economy and net-zero target by 2070 is reflected in the fact that India ranks fourth globally in government and corporate renewable energy, wind energy and solar energy capacity. Overall, with the continuous efforts of the government and the private sector, it seems that India will achieve its target of net zero carbon emissions before 2070 and will be able to move the country towards green and sustainable economic growth.

■ REFERENCES ■

1. Adebayo, T. S., Bekun, F. V., Rjoub, H., Agboola, M. O., Agyekum, E. B., and Gyamfi, B. A. (2022). Another look at the nexus between economic growth trajectory and emission within the context of developing country: Fresh insights from a nonparametric causality-in-quantiles test,6 1–23. doi:10.1007/s10668-022-02533-xEnviron. Dev. Sustain.

2. Bhuiyan, M. A., An, J., Mikhaylov, A., Moiseev, N., and Danish, M. S. S. (2021). Renewable energy deployment and COVID-19 measures for sustainable development. Sustainability 13 (8), 4418. doi:10.3390/su13084418

3. Gross, R., Leach, M., and Bauen, A. (2003). Progress in renewable energy. Environ. Int. 29 (1), 105–122. doi:10.1016/S0160-4120(02)00130-7

4. He, L., Liu, R., Zhong, Z., Wang, D., and Xia, Y. (2019). Can green financial development promote renewable energy investment efficiency? A consideration of bank credit. Renew. Energy 143, 974–984. doi:10.1016/j.renene.2019.05.059

5. Li, Z., Liao, G., Wang, Z., and Huang, Z. (2018). Green loan and subsidy for promoting clean production innovation. J. Clean. Prod. 187, 421–431. doi:10.1016/j.jclepro.2018.03.066

6. O'Riordan, T. (2022). COP 26 and sustainability science (Taylor & Francis), 64, 2–3. doi:10.1080/00139157.2022.1999748

7. Parvadavardini Soundarrajan, Nagarajan Vivek (2016): Green Finance for sustainable green economic growth in India, Agric. Econ - Czech,62 2016(1): 35–44, 10.17221/174/2014-AGRICECON

8. Rusu, E. (2019a). A 30-year projection of the future wind energy resources in the coastal environment of the Black Sea. Renew. Energy 139, 228–234. doi:10.1016/j.renene.2019.02.082

9. Sperling, K., Hvelplund, F., and Mathiesen, B. V. (2010). Evaluation of wind power planning in Denmark–Towards an integrated perspective. Energy 35 (12), 5443–5454. doi:10.1016/j.energy.2010.06.039

10. Sumedha Bhatnagar, Dipti Sharma (2022): Green Investment in Renewable Energy Projects: A Path to Cleaner Revival in Post-pandemic India, Sage Journal, 10.1177/09722629221132066

11. Taghizadeh-Hesary, F., and Yoshino, N. (2019). The way to induce privateparticipation in green finance and investment. Finance Res. Lett. 31, 98–103. doi:10.1016/j.frl.2019.04.016

12. Zhao, J., Zhao, Z., and Zhang, H. (2021). The impact of growth, energy and financial development on environmental pollution in China: New evidence from a spatial econometric analysis. Energy Econ. 93, 104506. doi:10.1016/j.eneco.2019.104506

13. https://chat.openai.com/c/bd69c5b7-2ee7-4356-8c55-6dcda06d50f6

14. https://unfccc.int/sites/default/files/NDC/2022-08/India%20Updated%20First%20Nationally%20Determined%20Contrib.pdf

15. https://ourworldindata.org/renewable-energy

16. https://climateactiontracker.org/countries/india/targets/

17. https://www.ey.com/en_in/climate-change-sustainability-services/green-finance-is-gaining-traction-for-net-zero-transition-in-india

18. https://www.investindia.gov.in/sector/renewable-energy

19. https://pib.gov.in/PressReleasePage.aspx?PRID=1885147

20. https://moef.gov.in/moef/resource/publications/index.html

21. https://www.ril.com/businesses/new-energy-materials

22. https://www.adani.com/businesses/renewable-power-generation

23. https://cea.nic.in/?lang=en

24. https://unfccc.int/conference/glasgow-climate-change-conference-october-november-2021

25. https://www.energyinst.org/statistical-review/resources-and-data-downloads

Innovation Led by World Bank in India—An Empirical Study of Rural Productivity

48

Arachana Mohanty*,
Shweta Mishra, Aradhana Misra
Ambalika Institute of Management & Technology,
Lucknow (U.P) India

Abstract

The World Bank Group (WBG) over seven decades long partnership with India is strong and enduring. The world bank group partners with India to maximize technological gains, such as promoting post-harvest and processing technologies to modernize farm production and increase rural productivity with the help of sustainable transport,digital development, technical education, blended financing, renewable energy etc. In this research paper author represents an empirical study about how the world bank helps in development of rural India with its recent and upcoming projects in agriculture sector, energy efficiency sector, state highway project, sustainable development projects and directly affects the rural productivity in India.

Keywords

Smart technologies, Rural productivity, Sustainable development projects, Innovations, Digital development, Renewable technology

1. INTRODUCTION

The world bank is an international financial institution that provides loans and grants to low and middle income countries for the purpose of pursuing capital projects .The world bank is the family of five groups International bank for reconstruction and development (IBRD), International Development Association (IDA), International Finance Corporation(IFC), Multilateral Investment Guarantee Agency (MIGA),International Centre for settlement of Investment Disputes (ICSID).India has been accessing funds from the World Bank for various development projects. World bank assistance of started from 1948 when a funding for Agricultural Machinery Project. World bank provides fund for India to invest in many projects for the upliftment and development of rural sector. As India is predominantly a rural country. As per the census, 68.8 percent of country's population and 72.4 percent of workforce resided in rural areas. However, steady transition to urbanisation over the years is leading to decline in the rural share in the population workforce. Between 2001 and 2011. India 's urban population increased by 31.8 percent as compared to 12.18 percent increase in the rural population. This paper is organised in 4 major sections. the first section

---

*Corresponding author: soniyamohanty1997@gmail.com

DOI: 10.1201/9781003606260-48

discusses the challenges in rural sector. The second section discusses the programmes and projects which were run by both India and world bank and discuss its importance for rural economy. The third section provides the future growth perspectives in rural India by some upcoming initiatives of world bank. And the last section discusses the increasing rural productivity after the initiatives of world bank.

2. LITERATURE REVIEW

In literature, According to U.S Bureau of labour statistics productivity refers to economic performance compares the amount of goods and services produced over the input used in production. Rural productivity refers to the output that are generated by farm and non-farm activities in the rural India. Few authors in their research paper (Farm productivity and rural poverty in India) Gaurav Dutt and Martin Ravalli on suggests the idea about agriculture productivity in India and (Migration from rural areas of poor countries: The impact on rural productivity and income distribution) Michael Lipton. These two research papers help to read out about rural productivity.

3. CHALLENGES IN RURAL INDIA

- *Poverty*—Poverty is the bigger challenge for the rural areas. According to world bank poverty has reduced by 12.3% between 2011-2019 from 22.5% in 2011 to 10.2% in 2019.The current poverty line in rural areas is 1059.49 INR per month. World bank invest in India to overcome this challenge by initiating various programmes.
- *Migration*—In rural areas peoples migrate to urban areas in search of jobs and good standard of living. According to world bank net migration is the number of immigrants minus the number of emigrants, including citizens and non-citizens. People migrate to urban areas for increasing their living standard and to enhance their income level *Unemployment and Underemployment*- Unemployment refers to the situation when the people is capable of doing work but he is not getting the work whereas underemployment is the situation when person is working in less than their capability and skills. Rural India is facing the problem of unemployment and underemployment in India.
- *Education*—Rural India is facing the problem of secondary and higher education in India. Schools and colleges are far away from their homes and problems in transport facility leads to move towards urban areas.
- *Infrastructure*—Infrastructure facilities in rural areas are at narrow conditions that creates hindrance in rural livelihood.
- *Health*—Rural India faces challenges of health conditions and mechanized medical equipment's.
- *Transportation*—Rural India faces challenges of transportation due to poor conditions of roads and highways facilities.

According to above problems faced in India World bank started some programmes and initiatives that directly creates innovation and leads to increase the rural productivity.

4. PROGRAMMES AND INITIATIVES OF INDIA AND WORLD BANK

Innovation in Solar Power and Hybrid Technologies

Financial Support: Through a $150 million IBRD loan, a $28 million loan from the Clean Technology Fund (CTF), and a $22 million grant from the CTF, the World Bank has given financial support. The purpose of this significant contribution is to support India's attempts to increase the amount of power it generates from cleaner, renewable energy sources. *Government Commitment:* The agreement's signature demonstrates the Indian government's resolve to address the issues posed by climate change. India has demonstrated its commitment to reaching its 2030 objective of 500 gigawatts (GW) of renewable energy by obtaining financial backing from foreign institutions such as the World Bank. *Goals for Renewable Energy:* The target of 500 GW of renewable energy by 2030 is audacious and consistent with international initiatives to shift to a cleaner energy source.

Odisha Higher Education Program for Excellence and Equity

Government of India and the World Bank are working together to improve the governance, equity, and quality of higher education institutions in the state of Odisha through the Odisha Higher Education Program for Excellence and Equity. The $119 million loan arrangement is intended to address the different issues that the state's institutions face and put reform measures into place. Here are a few of the project's essential elements. The project's main goal is to raise the standard of instruction at connected colleges. Grants for institutional development are one way to assist colleges in becoming independent. Colleges with autonomous status have more control over their administrative and academic operations. Higher education institutions will work to improve their examination system.

Maharashtra Project on Climate Resilient Agriculture

In order to address the difficulties faced by small and marginal farmers in Maharashtra, India's rural areas, the World Bank Board of Executive Directors approved the

US$ 420 million project. Over 25 million people will benefit from the Maharashtra Project for Climate Resilient Agriculture, which seeks to improve the climate resilience of agriculture in these sensitive areas. The project focuses on the rainfed agriculture-heavy Marathwada and Vidarbha areas, which are among the top 15 districts in Maharashtra most vulnerable to climate change. Impact Scope: 5,142 communities and more than 3.5 million hectares of land will be affected, demonstrating a wide geographic and demographic reach.

AP Integrated Irrigation and Agriculture Transformation Project

The Andhra Pradesh Integrated Irrigation and Agriculture Transformation Project is a noteworthy endeavour that endeavours to tackle fundamental obstacles encountered by impoverished and disenfranchised farmers in the area. Based on the data you submitted, the following are some salient features of the project: Funding and Approval: A $172.20 million project for the initiative has been approved by the World Bank Board of Executive Directors. The project's goals: The project's main objectives are to increase poor and marginalized farmers' agricultural output, profitability, and climate resilience. Making ensuring farming stays financially viable is the goal. Target Beneficiaries: It is anticipated that more than 200,000 households of underprivileged and marginalized farmers, women, and other vulnerable groups will gain from the project.

NHAI Technical Assistance Project

The World Bank has approved a $45 million loan for technical assistance to India, with the primary goal of enhancing the National Highways Authority of India's institutional capacity (NHAI). Given the nation's growing road traffic and vehicle population, the emphasis is on enhancing the administration and functioning of the National Highway (NH) network. According to the data, the NH network carries 40% of all traffic on Indian roads, and this percentage is expected to rise. Nevertheless, with 30% of the NH network being single-lane, 53% being double-laned, and only 17% being four, six, or eight lanes, a major section still need improvement and extension. The National Highway Development Project (NHDP) was launched by the Indian government in 2000 to address these issues and guarantee sustainable growth. Its implementation.

PMGSY Rural Roads Projects

The Prime Minister's Rural Roads Program, also known as the Pradhan Mantri Gram Sadak Yojana (PMGSY) of the Indian government, has been building all-weather roads to connect villages with 500 or more residents since 2000. About 16,000 km of rural roads have been constructed and

improved by the PMGSY with assistance from the World Bank since late 2004. N The Second Rural Roads Project in Jharkhand, Bihar, Rajasthan, Uttar Pradesh, Meghalaya, Uttarakhand, Himachal Pradesh, and Punjab is a $1.5 billion project funded by the World Bank. Each of these states has a different set of difficulties due to differences in their topography, people, and implementation capacities. Road surfaces in Jharkhand have been replaced with stronger concrete ones that can withstand heavier vehicles transporting minerals from the mining regions. These rural roads are frequently used by these vehicles. It appears that you have given us some information.

Maharashtra Rural Water Supply and Sanitation Program

The project's goals were to improve the way Maharashtra's sector institutions managed the program for rural water supply and sanitation. This is a big project with a lot of objectives to increase access to sustainable and high-quality services, especially in semi-urban communities and places where there are problems with water stress and water quality. Improving the efficacy, efficiency, and general capacities of the organizations in charge of developing, carrying out, and overseeing the Rural Water Supply and Sanitation Program is probably the main goal of this purpose. It could involve adopting best practices, training, and capacity building.

5. RECENTLY APPROVED PROJECTS

World Bank Approves $255.5 Million Loan for Education in Government Institution

A sizeable loan of USD 255.5 million has been authorized by the World Bank to raise the standard of technical education at Indian government-run schools. The Multidisciplinary Education and Research Improvement in Technical Education Project appears to be all-encompassing, with the goal of providing support to multiple government-run technical colleges in a few states throughout the nation. The project intends to help a large number of students— roughly 350,000 annually—during the next five years. It is imperative that students' employability and skills be improved, with a focus on innovation, entrepreneurship, and research. The project also seeks to improve technical institution governance, which is critical to the general efficacy and long-term viability of educational initiatives.

Tamil Nadu Climate Resilient Development

The $300 million IBRD loan had been accepted. It appears that the details you have shared are to a particular loan agreement between the International Bank for Reconstruction and Development (IBRD) and an Investment Project Financing (IPF) method in conjunction with a Program-for-Results (PforR). The International Bank for Reconstruction and Development (IBRD) is the source of the loan.Financing Instruments: The loan combines the Investment Project Financing (IPF) and Program-for-Results (PforR) instruments in a blended financing approach.Program-for-Results (PforR): This strategy directly ties the distribution of funding to the accomplishment of predetermined goals or objectives. This is meant to guarantee that the money is utilized wisely in order to accomplish the stated objectives.

Sikkim Integrated Service Provision and Innovation for Reviving Economic Operation

Approved by the World Bank's Board of Executive Directors, the Sikkim: Integrated Service Provision and Innovation for Reviving Economies (INSPIRES) Operation is a major project meant to assist the Indian state of Sikkim. The project's main goals are to up skill, train, and place women and young people in priority and high-growth industries Known for having a varied economic environment, Sikkim is one of the fastest-growing states in India. Even though a large percentage of young people work in agriculture, the manufacturing and service sectors are expanding in the state. Sikkim wants to provide its women and youth with skills applicable to non-farm industries like renewable energy, information and technology (IT) services, tourism, hospitality, wellness care, and more in order to maintain and accelerate this growth.

Himachal Power Sector Development

Cooperative initiatives to advance power sector changes and raise the proportion of renewable energy in Himachal Pradesh involving the governments of India, Himachal Pradesh, and the World Bank. This project is in line with Himachal Pradesh's bold plan to become a "Green State" by 2030, when it hopes to meet all of its energy needs from renewable and environmentally friendly sources.Supported by a $200 million World Bank investment, the Himachal Pradesh Power Sector Development Program seeks to expand the state's renewable energy portfolio while optimizing the use of already-existing renewable energy resources, particularly hydropower. Through the program, 150 megawatts of additional solar capacity will be added, greatly reducing annual greenhouse gas emissions by about 190,000 metric tons.

Manipur Infotech Enabled Development Project

The World Bank is going to provide Manipur a lot of money to help them develop their digital capabilities and establish a solid platform for activities related to digital government. With a $46 million commitment from the World Bank, the Manipur Infotech eNabled Development Project seeks to use digital technology for better e-service delivery in the rural sector and economic change. The program is expected to cost $67.50 million in total, which represents a significant investment in the development of digital infrastructure and skills. In its 2017 Industrial and Investment Policy, the Manipur government acknowledged the significance of information technology (IT) and IT-enabled services (ITeS). Furthermore, equal access to digital technology has been given top priority by the Manipur Vision 2030 for a number of industries, including trade facilitation, agriculture, and education.

6. HOW RURAL PRODUCTIVITY INCREASED AFTER WORLD BANK INITIATIVES

Resource Effective Growth in Rural Sector

With a focus on boosting entrepreneurship and job access, particularly for vulnerable populations, the World Bank Group supports government initiatives at all levels to encourage participation in enterprise development in the agricultural and other non-farm sectors. Ways and means by which the World Bank Group is aiding the agriculture industry. The main ideas are broken down as follows: A Transition to Income Growth: The World Bank Group is in favour of agriculture placing more of an emphasis on income growth as opposed to production targets alone. Agribusiness and High Value Crops: To increase farmers' financial returns, agribusiness and high-value crops are prioritized. Inclusive Value Chains: The Group wants to create chains of inclusive value that help farmers and advance the regional, national, international etc.

Agriculture and Rural Development

Improving agricultural production is essential for reducing poverty, particularly as a large proportion of the world's impoverished live in rural regions and depend on farming as their primary source of income. In order to comprehend the ongoing transformation and direct investments and policies aimed at boosting productivity in the agriculture industry, take into consideration the following. Encourage agricultural research and development to bring new and improved seeds, cutting-edge technologies, and productive farming methods. Access to Finance and Credit: Make sure that farmers may purchase fertilizer, cutting-edge farming equipment, and other inputs that can increase production by having access to credit and financial resources.

Infrastructure Development

Putting money into environmentally friendly infrastructure that improves livelihoods, opens doors for people, and spurs economic progress. Additionally, it gives nations a framework for integrating their development and climate change objectives by funding initiatives like digital ecosystems, renewable energy, and green transportation that lower carbon footprints. To promote social inclusion and human development, the World Bank wants to increase the availability of sustainable transportation options, particularly in low-income or vulnerable communities. Digital Development: Establishing a strong basis for digital economies requires a concentration on digital data infrastructure and broadband connections. Sustainable Infrastructure Finance: To promote excellent, sustainable projects that optimize benefits for people, the economy, and the environment, the World Bank strives to encourage increased infrastructure investment.

7. CONCLUSION

In this research paper, it was conveyed that world bank initiatives and programmes increase the rural productivity of country. The world bank develops the infrastructural sector, agricultural sector etc to develop the country's GDP. Rural Development needs more attention than urban areas. Rural productivity increased by the initiatives of World Bank because the various programs increase the per capita income and gross development product of country.

Infrastructure Development:

- The World Bank plays a significant role in developing the infrastructure sector of countries. This likely includes projects related to transportation, energy, water supply, and other essential facilities.
- Improved infrastructure in rural areas can enhance connectivity, accessibility, and the overall quality of life for rural communities.

Agricultural Sector Development:

- The paper suggests that the World Bank focuses on developing the agricultural sector. This could involve initiatives to modernize farming practices, improve irrigation systems, provide access to technology, and support sustainable agricultural methods.
- Enhancements in the agricultural sector are crucial for rural development, as agriculture often forms the backbone of rural economies.

GDP Growth

- By investing in infrastructure and agriculture, the World Bank aims to contribute to the overall economic growth of the country. This is reflected in the increase in the Gross Domestic Product (GDP).
- Rural development is seen as a key driver of overall economic progress, and the World Bank's initiatives are acknowledged for their role in stimulating growth.

Focus on Rural Development:

- The paper argues that rural development requires more attention than urban areas. This might be due to the recognition that a significant portion of the population resides in rural areas, and their development is crucial for achieving national economic goals.
- The World Bank's targeted efforts in rural development are seen as instrumental in addressing the specific challenges faced by rural communities.

Income and Productivity:

- The paper highlights that World Bank programs contribute to the increase in per capita income. This is likely tied to the idea that improved infrastructure, agricultural practices, and overall economic development lead to higher income levels for individuals in rural areas.
- Increased productivity in rural areas is mentioned as a positive outcome of World Bank initiatives, indicating a more efficient use of resources and improved economic conditions.

In summary, the research paper appears to endorse the idea that the World Bank's initiatives, especially in infrastructure and agriculture, play a crucial role in fostering rural development. The focus on rural areas is emphasized as a key strategy for overall economic growth, with tangible impacts on per capita income and GDP.

■ REFERENCE ■

1. Gaurav Dutt and Martin Ravallion (1998) Farm productivity and rural poverty in India
2. Michael Lipton (1980) Migration from rural areas of poor countries: The impact on rural productivity and income distribution.
3. https://www.worldbank.org/en/home
4. https://www.worldbank.org/en/cpf/india/project
5. https://www.worldbank.org/en/cpf/india/cross-cutting-themes/high-impact-technology
6. https://www.business-standard.com/education/news/world-bank-approves-255-5-mn-loan-to-improve-technical-education-in-india-123062500046_1.html
7. https://documents.worldbank.org/en/publication/documents-reports/documentdetail/099655010312240959/p17918903affca0309eaf0058cf2143337
8. https://www.businessworld.in/article/World-Bank-Approves-100-Mn-INSPIRES-Operation-For-Skill-Development-In-Sikkim-/22-12-2023-503193/

Online Media and its Impact on Consumer Behavior

49

Manish Chandra Mishra*, Shweta Mishra
Ambalika Institute of Management & Technology,
Lucknow (U.P) India

Abstract

Online media is playing a phenomenal role in today's time in the marketing field. Now through the online media, marketers can interact with our customers 24*7 and 365 days in the 21st century without the use of online media in the market is very tough to survive, where competition exists as a bottleneck, every movement of customers are important for marketers and their brand. Online advertising had a significant effect on consumer purchasing decisions. Thus, among other recommendations, it was proposed that companies increase their use of internet advertising to encourage customers to make profitable purchases. Online media makes customers more efficient and saves time to make decisions. Online media is a boon for marketers.

Significance of this study -

1. To maintain existing customers.
2. To create customers.
3. To spread awareness about products and services.
4. Customers can easily purchase.
5. Customers can easily compare products with substitute products.

Methodology - we are taking both qualitative and quantitative, we are taking data through the questionnaire, report, survey, and interview. Primary research involves collecting new data directly from individuals or sources.

Conclusion - Through this research we find that online marketing is much easier than offline and, we found that this is beneficial for both marketers and customers to find suitable products and services. Who buy product online they are often young between 25 to 35.

Keywords

Online media, Primary research, Internet, Substitute product

---

*Corresponding author: manish91chandra@gmail.com

DOI: 10.1201/9781003606260-49

1. INTRODUCTION

The purpose of this study is to examine and evaluating consumer behavior after print media to online media, in 21ˢᵗ century, this is incorrect to say behavior of customer has changed drastically, but main aim of this study is to know behavior of customer has changed permanently or short time. Will the consumers permanently change their consumption habits once? Will the new rules pertaining to flying, shopping at malls, and going to sporting events and concerts cause consumers to develop new habits? This is looking like a hassle to attend a store, and shopping malls for purchasing. Therefore online marketing has become very popular and convenient for customers and consumers. To some extent it has happened due to covid-19 pandemic, and there are many factors which directly and indirectly influence consumer buying habits. There are many consumer predictive models through use of this model till to some extent marketers can find out preferences of customers and their likeness and attitude of customers and what they think before taking decision to purchase and product and services.

Buying behavior of customers are affected by many factors like location, nature of products and requirement of products and economic conditions of country as well as world. There are many contexts which influence buying habits of customers and that is categorized mainly in four major parts, which govern and disrupt consumers' habits, the first is change in the societal context by such life events as festivals, marriage, having children and moving from one city to another. The second context is technology, and as new and innovative technologies are developed, traditional practices are altered. The most significant technological advances in recent years have been in e-commerce, smart phones, online marketing, and internet ordering. These advancements have a significant impact on how consumers purchase goods and services. The third context that impacts of consumption habits is rules and regulations especially related to public and private space, especially addictive products are not available at anywhere because of government rules and regulations , this is obvious rules and regulation of products are also impacting on demand of products, in other hand public policy can also encourages some types of products and services like electric car, mandatory life insurance, solar energy , insurance for old people and vaccine for children.

2. LITERATURE REVIEW

Online media provides consumers with easy access to vast amounts of information, influencing their decision-making process. Scholars (Smith & Taylor, 2002; Li, 2007) have noted that consumers actively seek product information, reviews, and comparisons online before making purchase decisions. Social media platforms play a crucial role in shaping consumer opinions and behaviors. Researchers (Mangold & Faulds, 2009; Smith et al., 2012) have explored the impact of social media on brand perception, highlighting the power of user-generated content and the role of influencers in influencing consumer choices. Online reviews have become a significant source of information for consumers. Studies (Cheung & Thadani, 2012; Duan et al., 2008) emphasize the role of online reviews in building trust and credibility, affecting consumers' attitudes and purchase intentions. The growth of e-commerce platforms has revolutionized the way consumers shop. Research (Liang & Huang, 1998; Wolfinbarger & Gilly, 2003) has explored factors such as website design, security, and ease of use, demonstrating their impact on online consumer behavior and satisfaction. Online media allows for personalized advertising based on user preferences and behavior. Scholars (Li et al., 2014; Davenport & Beck, 2001) have examined the effectiveness of targeted advertising in influencing consumer attitudes and purchase decisions.

The proliferation of mobile devices has further transformed consumer behavior. Studies (Bauer et al., 2005; Okazaki, 2008) have investigated the impact of mobile technology on consumer mobility, exploring how location-based services and mobile apps influence purchasing behavior. Online brand communities provide consumers with a platform to engage with like-minded individuals. Research (Muniz & O'Guinn, 2001; Dholakia et al., 2004) has delved into the role of brand communities in shaping consumer loyalty and brand advocacy. Emerging technologies such as virtual reality (VR) and augmented reality (AR) have started to influence consumer experiences. Scholars (Grewal et al., 2017; Fiore et al., 2005) have explored the impact of immersive technologies on consumer perceptions and decision-making.

2.1 Advertising Efficiency

According to Rimoldi (2008), advertising effectiveness is defined as consumers' preference for ads that lead to PUR behaviour. Effectiveness of advertising is one of the key elements to be examined in PI analysis. The effectiveness of advertising is positively impacted by customers' participation with media, as demonstrated by Calder Malthouse and Schaedel (2009). Mehta (2000) pointed out that a variety of elements, including the consumers' engagement with the media and the medium of choice, influence how effective advertising is. According to Nysveen and Breivik's (2005) theory, the commercial's efficacy is greatly influenced by the media's calibre and content. According to Bishnoi and Sharma's (2009) research, TV commercials have a greater impact on teenagers in rural areas than in metropolitan areas. Madhavi and Rajakumar (2004) suggested that analysing the efficiency of Internet advertisements could be done with ease. Mehta (2000) discovered that, in comparison to print ads, Internet advertisements are less effective since users have more control over them. According to Numberger and Schwaiger (2003), using print and online media in tandem maximises the effectiveness of advertising. However, AWR and purpose have an impact on PURDEC in addition to advertisement efficacy (Bendixen, 1993; Siegel & Ziff-Levine, 1990).

2.2 Reasoned Action Theory

Reasoned action theory was presented by Ajzen and Fishbein in 1980. This theory states that one of the key indicators of behavioural intention is attitude towards behaviour. "An internal evaluation of an object, such as a branded product," is the definition of attitude. According to Lutz (1985), a range of cognitive and affective processes influence how consumers feel about an advertisement, which in turn influences their exposure to, attention on, and response to it. In consumer behaviour research, the constructs attitude towards the brand, attitude towards the advertisement, and PI are frequently employed to forecast the efficacy of marketing communications across various media (Trivedi, 2017b).

2.3 Consciousness

AWR was defined by Aaker and Equity (1991) as the level of customer awareness of a specific brand. According to Rowley (1998), this is the time to introduce the product to the clients. According to Baca, Holguin Jr., and Stratemeyer (2005), the objective of advertising at this point should be to convey the benefits and features of the product. According to Rossiter, Percy, and Donovan (1991), creating PI requires brand AWR. Numerous researchers have found a direct correlation between brand AWR and buyer behaviour (Hoyer, 1984; Nedungadi, 1990). Advertisers should therefore continuously tell consumers about new items and provide updates on current products in order to increase AWR in the market (Meyrick, 2006).

2.4 Interest

In a commercial, INT can be generated from people by creatively displaying the benefits and qualities of the product. Sachdeva (2015) found that the degree of INT in commercials is influenced by relevant ads based on the viewer's INT. The association between INT and TV commercials was found by Farooq, Shafique, Khurshid,

and Ahmad (2015). Tang and Chan (2017) studied an online advertisement in a similar manner. They came to the conclusion that, in contrast to the necessity for a product, generation Y pays more attention to those commercials that align with their INT. According to Rajagopal (2010), radio commercials that are amusing have a greater effect on boosting customers' INT. Businesses spend money on a variety of marketing initiatives to increase customer penetration (Baca et al., 2005; Broeckelmann, 2010; Rowley, 1998).

Objectives of the Study-

1. To comprehend the fundamental idea behind online advertising.
2. To study the effect of Online Advertising on Consumer Behavior.
3. To know the importance of Online Advertising.
4. How Online media affects purchasing decision of consumers.

2.5 Types of Online Advertisement

Search Engine Advertising (SEA) & SEM (Search Engine Marketing) Search engine marketing, or SEM, is a general phrase that covers all methods of increasing visibility in search results. Included in this is sponsored advertising, or SEA, which tops search engine results pages (SERPs). You can successfully draw in the attention of your target audience by making an advertisement with an attention-grabbing title, description, and clear call to action. The display of your advertisement will depend on the standard of your website and the predetermined CPC (Cost Per Click). If you're searching for a quick and simple approach to connect with a big audience of potential clients, SEM is a great choice.

Display Advertising

In this format, graphic advertisements are posted on social media sites, websites, and other online spaces. The reason they are called "display ads" is because they are put prominently in particular portions of websites, such blogs. You can get these advertising directly from Google Adwords or through other platforms. You can select the pricing model that best fits your campaigns by choosing from CPC (Cost Per Click) or CPM (Cost Per Thousand Impressions), which are the usual methods used to calculate the cost.

Advertising on Mobile

Given the widespread use of smart phones and tablets, mobile advertising is essential to any successful marketing strategy. Use a responsive design that makes your ads seem great on all devices, or adapt them to mobile platforms to get the most out of them. Investing in mobile platforms broadens your audience, enhances user engagement, and boosts your website's search engine optimization (SEO) according to Google's Mobile First algorithm. Adopting mobile advertising can help your business in a number of ways.

Advertising on Social Media

Social media is a necessary component of our daily existence. Developing advertising campaigns on these platforms is crucial for increasing brand recognition and attracting possible new clients. Social networks are perfect for targeting particular groups with new products and services because they provide a wealth of segmentation options. Social media advertising is a terrific option whether you want to implement a branding plan or just start conversations.

Video Marketing

You may utilize video content as a very exciting and engaging tool to connect with your target audience. You can collaborate with You Tubers that talk about and showcase you're good or service. To raise your website's traffic and SEO position, you can also provide original video content. You may improve your videos' chances of going viral by posting them on social media. Video is a strong tool that you can't ignore, with an estimated 89% of internet users accessing video-based content online.

Email Marketing

Email marketing is a tried-and-true method of reaching your target audience and generating leads. It is also a cost-effective way to advertise, as you only pay when someone opens your email. With the right tools and strategy, you can see a high return on investment from your email marketing campaigns.

2.6 Advantages of Online Media

Development of Brands

A firm is more than just its brand and line of goods. Instead, the brand's voice and message must become well-known in the marketplace in order for consumers to regard the company as reliable and for the brand to have a wider audience. The primary benefit of digital marketing is its ability to strengthen a brand through targeted advertising and tailored content, which draws clients in and allows them to understand the company's value and distinctive selling point.

Greater Reach

Online media gives the brand a platform to reach a large number of consumers while also assisting in brand expansion. The brand goes global as a result of digital marketing's provision of the global display platform, which puts upstarts and newcomers on an even playing field with large, well-established businesses that control the traditional market.

Availability

The benefit of online media is that it puts the brand in the customer's hands because past consumers are always likely to want to suggest the store to their friends and give reviews for a positive experience. As a result, digital marketing gives clients a place to write feedback. In addition, potential customers might also be interested in learning about the brand's general areas of expertise, store hours, availability, and location.

Increased Involvement

Online media is useful since it gives a brand the opportunity to capture consumers' attention till they have successfully built a respectable reputation and brand loyalty. More brand recognition makes it easier for a brand to survive. This may be accomplished through digital marketing, which includes consistent blog postings, timely and relevant social media material, and the usage of customer-engaging posts like surveys, event promotions, and promotional offers.

Reduced Price

Online media is very cost-effective, which is quite beneficial for businesses. Compared to traditional marketing campaigns, very little is spent on digital marketing. Since small firms have a limited budget for advertising, the digital marketing process is more straightforward than the old approach.

2.7 Disadvantages of Online Media

Fierce Rivalry

The online media campaign needs to be well-planned, distinctive, attention-grabbing, and impactful on the intended audience because the competition has gotten much fiercer lately. Any repetitive strategy or tactic will quickly push the brand out of the competition. Campaigns for digital marketing are now highly competitive. As a result, brands need to be responsive and pertinent to their customers' requirements.

Assurance in Technology

The internet is prone to faults, and online media relies solely on technology. Sometimes landing pages don't load, links don't function, and page buttons don't just do their thing. This causes potential buyers to move to different brands. Thus, a website test is required to prevent this. It also becomes crucial to proofread the material and make sure the advertising will be effective in the chosen niche.

Time-consuming

Online media campaigns' time-consuming nature is one of their main drawbacks. It can be tough to dedicate the necessary time to the campaign when tactics and strategies are disorganized and take up a lot of time. This will ultimately have unfavorable effects. As a result, it has been advised to concentrate on the approach that the business most needs, then plan and curate the content in that manner. To get beyond the possible obstacles, digital marketing tools like Ahrens, Hub Spot, and social media posting, along with scheduling tools like Hoot suite and Tweet deck, should be employed.

Concerns about Security and Privacy

For any brand, security is the most important necessity. Therefore, as an online media, website protection is something that should be taken carefully. Using firewalls and encryption software, such as VPNs, to secure and protect network connections is always advised. The best course of action is to use a competent antivirus program. Legal considerations must be taken into account while collecting consumer data for digital marketing initiatives and all necessary procedures must be followed. Since consumer information might be compromised during data breaches, protecting it should be of utmost importance.

3. METHODOLOGY

3.1 Data and Sample

Using a convenience sample, a structured questionnaire was developed and administered to a group of 529 students. The respondents were students, both male and female, enrolled in graduation and post-graduation programmes in Uttar pradesh, India's five largest cities (Lucknow, Noida, Kanpur, Gaziabad, pryagraj). Online administration was used to administer the survey. Every student was only allowed to submit one response. 397 responses were deemed suitable for additional analysis after partial replies were excluded from consideration owing to incompleteness. The research methodology is a major section for the study. The part has significant value for researcher to indentify techniques and appropriate tools to deliver the complete report. These kinds of research are based on mixed finding and adapt two research methods i.e. qualitative and quantitative. The findings are necessary to undergone both the methods has got spontaneous and logical approach to bridge the gap between qualitative and quantitative research technique (Van Dijck, 2013). The methods are 9 helping out the researcher to draw complete study at each and every angle. The researchers have preferred descriptive research design. The technique is valuable for quantitative researches. While undertaking the

research, while collecting the data from primary resources the surveyor and interview techniques should be grasped by investigator. This could include sales information, online reviews, website traffic, and online media interaction analytics (likes, shares, and comments). Gather pertinent information from online resources including customer surveys, e-commerce websites, and social media platforms. Design of Questionnaires Our questionnaire is designed with multiple choice questions as its format. This is carried out in order to enable the researcher to determine how social media affects customer purchasing behavior.

3.2 Research's Scope

Conducting the study from the perspective of the consumer would be the best strategy, taking the research's aims into consideration. The purpose of the study, according to the researcher, is to assist users in determining why social media. Altered the purchases they made. Since analyzing customer demands is the primary goal of marketing, the information gathered via the questionnaire is viewed from the perspective of the customer in order to yield fresh insights. The study additionally seeks to elucidate to prospective readers the significance of social media platforms and applications in the customer decision-making process. The behavior of final consumers is the main focus of the study.

4. EXAMINATION OF DATA

4.1 Overview

An analysis of the information gathered from the questionnaire is presented in the section that follows. The series of inquiries were delivered to people who presently reside in Uttar Pradesh, India. Given that 499 people participated in the survey out of 529 recipients, the overall response rate was 94.32 percent. The questionnaire consists of 12 items in total.

4.2 Findings and Result

1. Because they are the age group that spends the most hours on social media, the majority of responders were between the ages of 15 and 25.
2. According to survey data, about half of the population shops online once or twice a month.

   This could imply that they are members of the working class, who typically purchase in bulk from online platforms yet do not have a lot of free time.
3. Nearly half of the population uses social media platforms for between one and two hours each day, according to poll statistics. Social media is essential for fostering connections and building relationships,

both of which help us advance professionally and take advantage of new opportunities.

4. According to survey data, about 60% of participants follow brands on social media. Consumers follow brands on social media in order to be informed about new products, sales, and other updates.

5. According to study data, nearly 61% of respondents consider social media to be an electronic kind of word-of-mouth recommendation, with many consumers basing purchasing decisions on recommendations from social media.

6. According to poll data, about 47% of participants think that social media Page/website had an impact on their brand vision. Since the majority of internet shoppers read brand evaluations before making a purchase, this could have an impact on how people perceive a given brand.

7. According to study data, 46% of participants said that social media had an impact on their choice. This is due to the fact that many consumers frequently check internet reviews and comments about a product before deciding on the best brand and pricing.

8. According to survey data, nearly 88% of participants think social media is crucial for brand promotion since it increases visibility, which in turn helps a brand generate leads and boost sales.

Results

Overall from this study, we got that online advertising is very popular and effective among young people, especially in india, because young people are spending at least 2 to 3 hours per day on social sites and online media is very helpful for improving brand loyalty. Through this online media, Consumers can easily access a vast amount of information about products and services online. Reviews, ratings, and testimonials play a crucial role in shaping consumer perceptions.Online media provides consumers with the tools to compare products and services before making purchasing decisions.Social media platforms often serve as a source of recommendations and opinions from peers.Brands use online media for marketing, creating awareness, and engaging with their audience.Social media platforms allow for direct communication between brands and consumers, fostering a sense of community.

Online ads, especially retargeting ads, remind consumers of products they have shown interest in, encouraging them to complete the purchase. Online platforms use algorithms to personalize content, ads, and product recommendations based on consumer behavior. This personalization enhances the overall online shopping experience. The ubiquity of smartphones has made online media accessible anytime,

anywhere. Mobile apps and websites influence on-the-go purchasing decisions.

5. CONCLUSIONS

After the analysis of collected information, we got this result that maximum buyers are laying between 25 to 35 years age, and without using of internet and online media, in 21st century in any area of business is very tough to survive, The emergence of digital media has significantly altered consumer behavior and reshaped the conventional framework for trade and communication. Online platforms have a pervasive influence on everything from personalized experiences to information accessibility. The volume of information available online has given consumers the ability to do research, compare, and make well-informed decisions that they never had before. Social media platforms function as powerful spaces where marketers interact with their audience directly, taking advantage of influencer marketing and peer recommendations. Thanks to e-commerce platforms, online purchasing has become effortless and frequently impulsive, with mobile devices serving as constant companions throughout the consumer journey. Of course, the following is a condensed assessment of how internet media affects consumer behaviour:

6. IN SUMMARY

The emergence of digital media has significantly altered consumer behaviour and reshaped the conventional framework for trade and communication. Online platforms have a pervasive influence on everything from personalised experiences to information accessibility. The volume of information available online has given consumers the ability to do research, compare, and make well-informed decisions that they never had before. Social media platforms function as powerful spaces where marketers interact with their audience directly, taking advantage of influencer marketing and peer recommendations. Thanks to e-commerce platforms, online purchasing has become effortless and frequently impulsive, with mobile devices serving as constant companions throughout the consumer journey. Online media has essentially brought to the emergence of a dynamic, networked marketplace characterized by the combination of trade, entertainment, and information. It has ushered in a new era of consumer empowerment, in which people navigate a broad digital world and make decisions affected by both traditional marketing and the opinions of their online community as a whole. The relationship between online media and consumer behaviour will probably change as technology develops, bringing with it new opportunities and difficulties for companies hoping to prosper in the digital era.

■ REFERENCES ■

1. Researchers (Mangold & Faulds, 2009; Smith et al., 2012) have explored the impact of social media on brand perception,
2. Social media platforms play a crucial role in shaping consumer opinions and behaviors. Researchers (Mangold & Faulds, 2009; Smith et al., 2012) have explored the impact of social media on brand perception,
3. Online reviews have become a significant source of information for consumers. Studies (Cheung & Thadani, 2012; Duan et al., 2008)
4. The proliferation of mobile devices has further transformed consumer behavior. Studies (Bauer et al., 2005; Okazaki, 2008).
5. The proliferation of mobile devices has further transformed consumer behavior. Studies (Bauer et al., 2005; Okazaki, 2008).
6. Roland Berger, 2010, Social networks are changing consumer behavior, http://www.rolandberger.com/media/press_releases/Socia l_networks_are_changing_consumer_behavior.html Accessed 20 April 2013.
7. GFK, Social media influences how we shop, http://www.gfk.com/uk/documents/thoughtpieces/social%20media%20influences%20how%20we%2 0shop.pdf Accessed 4 April 2013.
8. Constantiniades E., (2004) Influencing the online consumer's behaviour, Internet Research journal, vol. 14, issiue 2, pp. 111–126;
9. Darley, W.K., Blankson, C., Luethge, D. (2010), "Toward an integrated framework for online consumer behavior and decision making process: a review", Psychology and Marketing, Vol. 27 No. 2, pp. 94–116.

Challenges and Opportunities for Innovation in India – Dr. Shweta Mishra et al. (eds)
© 2024 Taylor & Francis Group, London, ISBN 978-1-032-99842-8

Impact of Artificial Intelligence in Organized Retail Sector: An Exploratory Study of India

50

Gaurav Shukla*, Shweta Mishra

Ambalika Institute of Management & Technology,
Lucknow (U.P) India

Abstract

The organized retail sector in India has witnessed significant technology upgradation over the years, transforming the way retailers operate, engage with customers, and manage their businesses. The continuous technology upgradation in the organized retail sector of India reflects the industry's commitment to embracing innovation and meeting the evolving needs of consumers. As technology continues to advance, retailers are likely to explore and integrate more cutting-edge solutions to stay competitive and provide enhanced shopping experience. In continuation with the upgradation with technology, the integration of Artificial Intelligence (AI) technologies with Indian organized retail has indeed brought about significant changes, revolutionizing various aspects of the industry. The transformative era marked by AI adoption has influenced operations, customer engagement, and the overall trajectory of the sector. The importance of Artificial Intelligence (AI) in the organized retail sector is noteworthy, as it brings about numerous benefits and opportunities for retailers to enhance their operations, improve customer experiences, and stay competitive in a rapidly evolving market. As technology continues to advance, AI is expected to play an increasingly crucial role in shaping the future of the retail industry. The below article depicted and analyzed the importance & growth of AI in the Indian organized retail sector.

Keyword

Supply chain optimization, Operational efficiency, Automation, Customer engagement, Predictive analytics, Data analytics, Technology integration

1. INTRODUCTION

Artificial Intelligence (AI) refers to the development of computer systems that can perform tasks that typically require human intelligence. These tasks include learning, reasoning, problem-solving, perception, natural language understanding, and speech recognition. AI aims to create machines that can mimic cognitive functions and adapt to new situations, making them versatile in handling a variety of tasks.

Here are some key aspects and components of AI:

- **Machine Learning (ML):** Machine Learning is a subset of AI that focuses on developing algorithms

*Corresponding author: gauravshukla@ambalika.co.in

DOI: 10.1201/9781003606260-50

and statistical models that enable computers to learn from data. ML algorithms can identify patterns, make predictions, and improve their performance over time without explicit programming.

- **Deep Learning:** Deep Learning is a type of machine learning that involves neural networks with multiple layers (deep neural networks). This approach is particularly effective for tasks like image and speech recognition. Deep learning models attempt to simulate the way the human brain works.

- **Natural Language Processing (NLP):** NLP is a branch of AI that enables machines to understand, interpret, and generate human language. It is used in applications like language translation, chatbots, and sentiment analysis.

- **Computer Vision:** Computer Vision involves enabling machines to interpret and make decisions based on visual data. This includes image and video recognition, object detection, and facial recognition.

- **Robotics:** AI plays a crucial role in robotics, allowing machines to perceive their environment, make decisions, and carry out tasks. This is applied in various fields, including manufacturing, healthcare, and autonomous vehicles.

- **Expert Systems:** Expert Systems are AI programs that mimic the decision-making ability of a human expert in a specific domain. They use rules and knowledge bases to provide solutions to problems.

- **Reinforcement Learning:** Reinforcement Learning is a type of machine learning where an agent learns to make decisions by interacting with an environment. The agent receives feedback in the form of rewards or penalties, allowing it to learn optimal strategies.

- **AI in Business and Industry:** AI is widely used in various industries for tasks such as predictive analytics, process automation, and customer service. In business, it can optimize operations, improve decision-making, and enhance overall efficiency.

- **AI in Healthcare:** AI is utilized in healthcare for medical image analysis, disease diagnosis, drug discovery, and personalized medicine. It has the potential to improve patient outcomes and enhance the efficiency of healthcare systems.

- **AI in Finance:** In the financial industry, AI is used for fraud detection, risk management, algorithmic trading, and customer service. It can analyze vast amounts of financial data and make rapid decisions in real-time.

- **AI Research and Development:** AI research continues to advance, with ongoing efforts to improve algorithms, increase computational power, and explore new applications. OpenAI, DeepMind, and other organizations contribute to the cutting-edge developments in the field.

The organized retail sector refers to a segment of the retail industry characterized by a more structured and formalized approach to business operations. In organized retail, retailers operate in a planned and systematic manner, often using modern management and technological practices. This is in contrast to the unorganized or traditional retail sector, where businesses may be smaller, less formalized, and often lack advanced systems and processes. Examples of organized retail include well-known chains of supermarkets, department stores, and specialty retailers that operate with a structured and organized approach to serving customers. The organized retail sector is a key driver of economic growth, offering employment opportunities, contributing to tax revenues, and playing a vital role in the overall development of the retail industry in a region or country. The organized retail sector has been increasingly adopting Artificial Intelligence (AI) technologies to streamline operations, enhance customer experiences, and gain a competitive edge. The application of AI in organized retail spans various areas, offering benefits such as improved efficiency, personalized customer interactions, and data-driven decision-making. Here are several key applications of AI in the organized retail sector like Inventory Management, Demand Forecasting, Supply Chain Optimization, Personalized Marketing and Recommendations, Chatbots and Virtual Assistants, Dynamic Pricing, Facial Recognition for Security, Customer Behavior Analysis, Predictive Maintenance, Augmented Reality (AR) and Virtual Reality (VR), Fraud Detection in Online Transactions, Predictive Analytics for Trends etc.

2. LITERATURE REVIEW

The rise of Artificial Intelligence (AI) has indeed sparked a range of perspectives and opinions, reflecting the complexity and potential consequences of this transformative technology. Ginni Rometty expresses an optimistic view on AI, emphasizing that AI technologies are meant to augment human intelligence. She envisions a partnership between humans and machines, where AI enhances human capabilities, making us better at what we do. This perspective sees AI as a tool to complement and amplify human potential, fostering a symbiotic relationship between humans and intelligent machines. Stephen Hawking and Bill Gates, in contrast, express caution and concern regarding the potential risks associated with the development of full artificial intelligence. Hawking goes as far as suggesting that the development of strong AI could pose a threat to the existence of the human race. Bill Gates also emphasizes the need for caution and raises awareness about the potential threats that AI could pose to humanity. Their remarks reflect a more cautious and speculative stance, considering the broader implications and risks associated with highly advanced AI systems.

These varying viewpoints highlight the ongoing debate surrounding AI and its societal impacts. The optimistic perspective envisions AI as a force for positive change, while the cautionary views underscore the importance of ethical considerations, responsible development, and potential risks associated with the rapid advancement of AI technologies. As AI continues to evolve, finding a balance between harnessing its potential benefits and addressing ethical and safety concerns will be crucial in shaping the future relationship between humans and AI. In their study, Taguimdje, Wamba, Kamdjoug, & Wanko (2020) identified the different kinds of AI applications that are being used by business entities. These include chatbots, neural networks, machine learning, deep learning, cognitive, natural language processing, robotic personal assistants, pattern/visual recognition, and virtual companions. Oosthuizen, Botha, Robertson, and Montecchi (2020) examined the deployment of AI in the retail sector from four angles: 1. gaining clients' trust through personalization; 2. controlling inventories in accordance with demand; 3. increasing efficiency by lowering costs and raising quality; and 4. exchanging, using, and processing data. It is advised that in order to benefit their companies in the long run, retail managers should implement AI techniques.

3. EVOLUTION OF ORGANIZED RETAIL IN INDIA

In the beginning there were only kirana stores called Mom and Pop Stores, the Friendly neighbourhood stores selling every day needs. In the 1980s manufacturer's retail chains like DCM, Gwalior Suitings, Bombay Dying, Calico, Titan etc started making its appearance in metros and small towns. Multi brand retailers came into the picture in the 1990s. In the food and FMCG sectors retailers like Food world, Subhiksha, Nilgris are some of the examples. In music segment Planet M, Music world and in books Crossword and Fountainhead are some others. Shopping Centres began to be established from 1995 onwards. A unique example was the establishment of margin free markets in Kerala. The millennium year saw the emeregence of super markets and hyper markets. Now big players like Reliance, Bharti, Tatas, HLL, ITC are entering into the organized retail segment. The big international retail bigwigs are waiting in the wings as the present FDI guidelines do not allow them to own retail outlets in the country. Walmart is testing the waters by agreeing to provide back end and logistic support to Bharti for establishment of retail chains with a view to study the market for future entry when the FDI guidelines change and to establish a backbone supply chain. Table 50.1 shows the different phases in the growth of organized retailing in India. The historical evolution of organized retailing in India in highlighting key milestones as below:

Initial Phase (Pre-1980s): The retail landscape was dominated by small, independently-owned kirana stores,

Table 50.1 Regulations and phases of development of retail sector

A. Regulator (State/ Central)	Players (Foreign/Indian)	Provisions
State	Indian	Organized retailers in India are regulated by state governments
Central	Foreign	Regulated by the central Government
B. Phases	**Characteristics**	
Pre-1990s	• Mainly dominated by unorganized players like traditional mom-and-pop stores, street markets, and local bazaars • Organized retail was limited. • Main formats of retail shops were kirana stores, weekly markets, street shops, hawkers	
2000s (Post-1990s)- Rise of modern trade	• Rise of shopping malls in major cities • Malls having mix of national and international brands • Still retail sector was dominated by unorganized sectors	
2000s-2010s (Evolution of different formats of Modern Trade	• Large-format retail stores like Big Bazaar, Reliance Retail, and others introduced modern retail concepts, • They offered a large variety of products under one roof. • Stores focused on convenience, value, and a range of options.	
2010s and onwards (E-Commerce Booms)	• The popularity of the internet made the rise of e-commerce platforms like Flipkart, Amazon, and Snapdeal • It brought a drastic change to the retail landscape.	

*Source:*Author

often referred to as "Mom and Pop Stores." These neighborhood stores catered to everyday needs.

Manufacturer's Retail Chains (1980s): In the 1980s, manufacturer-driven retail chains such as DCM, Gwalior Suitings, Bombay Dying, Calico, and Titan began emerging in metros and small towns. These chains marked a departure from the traditional kirana stores.

Multi-Brand Retailers (1990s): The 1990s saw the entry of multi-brand retailers into the Indian retail sector. Examples in the food and FMCG sectors included stores like Food World, Subhiksha, and Nilgiris. In music, Planet M and Music World, and in books, Crossword and Fountainhead, were some of the notable players.

Shopping Centers (From 1995 Onwards): Shopping centers started to be established from 1995 onwards, providing a centralized location for various retail outlets. These centers offered a variety of shopping options to consumers.

Margin-Free Markets in Kerala: A unique development in Kerala was the establishment of margin-free markets, providing consumers with a retail model that aimed to eliminate profit margins.

Supermarkets and Hypermarkets (2000s): In the early 2000s, super and hypermarkets emerged, offering a wide range of products under one roof. This marked a shift towards larger retail formats, providing customers with more choices and convenience.

Entry of Big Players (Present): Major Indian conglomerates such as Reliance, Bharti, Tatas, HLL (Hindustan Unilever Limited), and ITC have entered the organized retail segment. These companies are leveraging their resources to establish a significant presence in the retail industry.

International Retail Players (Restricted Entry): As of the provided information, big international retail giants are waiting to enter the Indian market. However, existing Foreign Direct Investment (FDI) guidelines restrict them from owning retail outlets directly in the country.

Walmart's Entry Strategy: Walmart is mentioned as a company testing the Indian market by providing backend and logistic support to Bharti for establishing retail chains. This strategic move allows Walmart to study the market and assess opportunities for future entry when FDI guidelines may change. The overall narrative reflects the dynamic evolution of the retail sector in India, transitioning from small independent stores to the emergence of organized retail formats with the participation of both domestic and international players. It also highlights the role of regulations, such as FDI guidelines, in shaping the industry landscape.

4. The Rise of Artificial Intelligence in Organized Sector

Against this backdrop, the infusion of AI technologies into the organized retail sector has brought about a revolutionary change. AI, encompassing machine learning, natural language processing, and computer vision, is enabling retailers to leverage data-driven insights, automate operational processes, and deliver personalized services at scale. The rise of Artificial Intelligence (AI) in the organized retail sector has been a transformative journey, bringing about significant changes in the way retailers operate, interact with customers, and manage their businesses. Several factors have contributed to the increasing adoption of AI in organized retail. AI enables retailers to analyze large volumes of data quickly and extract valuable insights. This includes customer behavior, purchasing patterns, and market trends. By leveraging advanced analytics, retailers can make informed decisions to improve operations and enhance customer experiences. AI algorithms analyze customer data to understand individual preferences, shopping habits, and demographics. This information is used to provide personalized recommendations, promotions, and targeted marketing, creating a more engaging and tailored experience for customers. AI plays a crucial role in optimizing inventory management through predictive analytics. Retailers use AI algorithms to forecast demand, manage stock levels efficiently, and minimize the risk of stockouts or overstock situations. This results in improved supply chain performance. AI-driven automation is employed to streamline routine operational tasks, such as inventory replenishment, order processing, and data entry. This reduces manual efforts, minimizes errors, and allows retail staff to focus on more strategic and customer-centric activities. AI enables retailers to implement dynamic pricing strategies by analyzing real-time market conditions, competitor pricing, and customer demand. This flexibility in pricing helps retailers optimize margins and respond quickly to market changes. AI-powered chatbots and virtual assistants are integrated into online and offline retail channels to provide real-time customer support. These conversational AI systems assist customers with inquiries, product information, and problem resolution, enhancing the overall shopping experience. AI-based facial recognition technology is utilized for security purposes in retail stores. It helps prevent theft, monitor store activities, and enhance overall security measures. AI is applied to optimize supply chain processes, including logistics, transportation, and warehousing. Machine learning algorithms help retailers predict potential disruptions, improve route optimization, and enhance overall supply chain efficiency. AI-driven AR and VR technologies create immersive shopping experiences. Customers can virtually try on products, visualize furniture in their homes, and engage with interactive displays, driving customer engagement and influencing purchasing decisions. AI assists retailers in predicting consumer trends and market shifts. By analyzing historical data and external factors, AI algorithms provide valuable insights that help retailers stay ahead in a dynamic and competitive market. AI is used for fraud detection and prevention, especially in online transactions. Machine learning models analyze transaction patterns to identify and block potentially fraudulent activities, ensuring secure financial transactions. The rise of AI in the organized retail sector signifies a paradigm shift in how retailers leverage technology to enhance efficiency, improve decision-making, and deliver more personalized and engaging experiences for customers. As technology continues to advance, the integration of AI is expected to play an increasingly pivotal role in shaping the future of organized retail.

5. Indian Retailing Sector now become AI Savvy

The adoption of Artificial Intelligence (AI) in the Indian retail sector reflects a growing trend in leveraging advanced technologies to enhance business operations and improve decision-making Over time, the business of selling consumer goods and services through retail channels has seen an interesting transformation, ranging from hawkers to roadside stalls to branded showrooms to ecommerce platforms. It is important to note that the task has become more specialist and sophisticated with each refinement, necessitating the sellers to use novel strategies. As the final link in the supply chain, retailers play a crucial role in the era of customer-centric enterprises. For businesses that interact directly with consumers, this eliminates any room for mistakes or inaccuracies. In a highly competitive market where consumers have an abundance of options, brands need to adopt artificial intelligence (AI) and data-driven solutions to provide optimal customer service while maintaining cost effectiveness. These five case studies highlight creative and efficient An AI-based video analytics system was implemented by the footwear retailer Bata to enhance in-store sales, customer happiness, and operations. Utilising the store's current video infrastructure, Agrex.ai's solution generated insights on audience segmentation and smart conversion through data gathering. The quantity and kind of items that clients were displaying interest in was determined by a "Emotions Chart." The retailer evaluated the feedback received from customers to identify the items that made them feel content or joyful. Blackberrys, a male clothes chain, used artificial intelligence (AI)

to increase revenue through omnichannel interaction. Capillary Technologies used its in-house AI technology, Zero AI, to power the Engage+ platform for Blackberrys. The most effective Blackberry campaigns were produced via the use of AI and machine learning algorithms. The platform's sophisticated algorithm evaluated a number of variables, including Reachability, Responsiveness Score, and Conversion Probability, to determine the optimal channel mix for each consumer automatically. Blackberrys were able to automate interactions with customers throughout their purchase lifetime and deliver the most relevant message thanks to Journey Builder. The Tata conglomerate's eCommerce division, Tata Cliq, implemented Vue.ai's Personalisation Suite to facilitate product discovery for its online shoppers. The solution allowed the marketing, product, and cataloguing teams to obtain actionable insights by extracting catalogue data, analysing it with user behaviour, and applying image recognition and data science. These discoveries decreased expenses, increased conversions, and enhanced consumer experiences. To generate distinct profiles for each customer, product and customer intelligence were integrated. In order to devote more time to other crucial areas of the customer experience, Nykaa made the decision to automate its customer service. Consequently, Nykaa partnered with Verloop.io to enhance consumer engagement through chat-based problem-solving. Nykaa was able to employ bot-qualified queries to handle recurring requests, such as cancellations, returns, shipping questions, replacements, refunds, and payment concerns, thanks to a system put in place by Verloop.io. Both the automation and the Natural Language Understanding (NLU) modules of Verloop were constructed using both contemporary deep learning concepts and traditional machine learning techniques. Improved customer loyalty and post-purchase consumer pleasure are the outcomes of the solution.

6. Futuristic Impact of AI in Indian Retail Sector

The retail industry is undergoing a significant transition as we approach 2024, partly due to the impressive rise of artificial intelligence (AI). Our AI and data firm specialises in assisting retailers in streamlining their business processes and improving customer satisfaction. We'll explore the rapidly changing landscape of artificial intelligence (AI) in retail in this blog post, providing analysis, trends, and forecasts that will influence the sector going forward.

AI has already had a profound impact on the retail industry. Artificial intelligence (AI) is having a huge impact on everything from inventory control and personalised product suggestions to loyalty programmes and improved customer service. But it's important to realise that this is only the start. As AI continues to advance, new opportunities will arise, giving merchants the chance to establish distinction, value, and a competitive advantage. Modern consumers need a flawless and uniform purchasing experience, whether they purchase on their mobile devices, in-store, or online. Retailers will be able to synchronise and integrate operations, systems, and data across all touchpoints thanks to artificial intelligence. As a result, every step of the consumer journey is served with relevant and personalised content, goods, and services. Consumers seek to feel appreciated and understood by merchants. Retailers will be able to create dynamic consumer profiles and segments with the aid of artificial intelligence (AI) by gathering and analyzing customer data from various sources. Based on each customer's behaviour, intent, and mood, this data will enable customized communications, promotions, and experiences. AI will be essential for optimizing pricing and promotion strategies in a world where consumers shop around for the best offers. Data-driven algorithms will make sure that clients are presented with offers that they find attractive by taking into account a number of aspects, such as supply, demand, competition, and customer value. It will also become commonplace to make changes in real-time in response to shifting market conditions and consumer feedback. For customers, finding the appropriate products quickly and conveniently is of utmost importance. Using computer vision and natural language processing to better comprehend client requests and preferences, artificial intelligence (AI) will transform product search and discovery. Additionally, clients will have a thorough understanding of products through immersive product visualisation alternatives including AR, VR, and 3D models. Modern customers want orders to be delivered quickly and reliably. Artificial intelligence (AI) will intervene to improve fulfilment and inventory management procedures by using predictive analytics to precisely estimate supply and demand. Automation from robotics, drones, and self-driving cars will simplify warehouse operations and increase their effectiveness and economy. For merchants, providing exceptional customer service and loyalty programmes will be essential. Chatbots, voice assistants, and social media platforms powered by AI will offer prompt, amiable, and customised assistance. In order to encourage consumer loyalty and advocacy, AI will also assist merchants in developing and managing loyalty programmes, prizes, discounts, gift cards, referrals, and more. The future of retail is brimming with potential and promise, and AI is the catalyst.

7. Conclusion

AI is the spark that will ignite the vast potential and promise that await retail in the future. Artificial intelligence (AI)

will make shopping even more smooth and fluid, making it harder to distinguish between real-world and virtual retail environments. Artificial intelligence (AI)-powered chatbots and virtual assistants will be a crucial component of customer support, improving problem solving and response times. AI will be essential in forecasting trends, allowing merchants to stock the appropriate goods and meet customer wants. AI-driven privacy tools to safeguard consumer data will be developed in response to data security and privacy concerns. Artificial intelligence (AI) is transforming the retail sector by empowering companies to make knowledgeable decisions about hiring and stockpiling. AI is increasing sales, decreasing out-of-stock scenarios, and optimizing labour and replenishment costs. AI is therefore changing the retail employment landscape and increasing company efficiency. Retailers should think about how these technologies can affect their workforce and take action to make sure that their employees have the knowledge and training necessary to thrive in a sector that is changing quickly. As technology advances, retail companies are proactively investigating the ways in which artificial intelligence is revolutionizing the sector. With its embrace of innovation and digital transformation, India's retail sector is well-positioned to prosper in the dynamic market environment.

■ REFERENCES ■

1. https://www.indianjournals.com/ijor.aspx?target=ijor:ajrbem&volume=9&issue=2&article=001

2. https://www.researchgate.net/profile/G-P-Dang/publication/369559461_Impact_of_AI_on_Businesses_of_Organised_Retailers/links/64228820315dfb4cceb23fc7/Impact-of-AI-on-Businesses-of-Organised-Retailers.pdf

3. https://segwitz.com/the-impact-of-artificial-intelligence-on-the-retail-industry/#:~:text=AI%20is%20rapidly%20revolutionizing%20the,%2C%20accuracy%2C%20and%20customer%20experience.

4. https://www.linkedin.com/pulse/evolution-ai-retail-market-upcoming-years-all-the-research/?trk=article-ssr-frontend-pulse_more-articles_related-content-card

5. https://www.forbes.com/sites/forbestechcouncil/2017/11/03/the-evolution-of-retail-the-effect-of-automation-and-ai/?sh=a5c055314a1a

6. https://www.sciencedirect.com/science/article/abs/pii/S0268401219300581

7. http://dspace.iimk.ac.in/xmlui/bitstream/handle/2259/645/603-612.pdf?sequence=1&isAllowed=y

8. https://cio.economictimes.indiatimes.com/news/next-gen-technologies/how-indian-retailers-are-getting-ai-savvy/87717041

9. https://www.communicationstoday.co.in/71-of-indian-retailers-plan-to-adopt-gen-ai-in-the-next-12-months/

Challenges and Opportunities for Innovation in India – Dr. Shweta Mishra et al. (eds)
© 2024 Taylor & Francis Group, London, ISBN 978-1-032-99842-8

Spiritual Accounting: A Study of Human's Inner Mind as Element of Spiritual Accounting and its Various Benefits Aids in Decision Making Power of Accounting Professionals

51

Vineet Kumar
Ambalika Institute of Management & Technology,
Lucknow (U.P) India

Abstract

This paper offers views on attributes of human 's inner mind. This paper depicts the various attributes of Human's inner mind which is one of the main element forms of spiritual accounting. Spiritual accounting is method leading from darkness to light. Spiritual accounting is initiative to conquer or control over the inner mind. The core objective of spiritual accounting is to keep accounting professionals in tranquillity state & right trajectory of achieving mission and vision of company, to descend our inner mind into spiritual wisdom, to expand your consciousness to unvaried dimensions for saturation of mind which reduces the chances of manipulation, frauds and committing mistakes in company. The knowledge of various attributes of inner mind builds the mechanism to deal with complicated problems prevails in inner mind of accountant and financial managers and useful in managing the stress. Spiritual accounting is initiative from known to unknown dimension of life pursuits & to develop business, financial acumen, maintain fraternity among different genre of people. Spiritual accounting is initiative to make balance within people. Spiritual accounting tends to arise the feeling of right understanding for work, people, our nature & other species.

Keywords

Spiritual accounting, Inner mind, Accounting professionals, Decision making power, Mindset

1. INTRODUCTION

According to ICAEW nearly a third of accountants (30.4%) suffer from mental health issues, with more than half (51%) admitting depression and anxiety leaves them dreading going to work. More than two in five (43.5%) accountants believed their job was a key contributor to their poor mental health. A need arises to develop the right understanding and awareness about balanced mental conditions of accounting professionals and maintaining balance state of our inner mind. Human resources in office possess the various personality traits and all personality traits comes from choosing the different kinds of thoughts which is coming from Human's Inner mind. So, a need arises first to understand our anatomical, philosophical and psychological features of our inner mind to cope up with different issues occurs in workplace related to human beings. Accountant and finance managers face a demanding schedule, constantly monitoring transactions, reconciling differences, and rectifying mistakes. This leads to tedious

Corresponding author: pitventurepvtltd@gmail.com

DOI: 10.1201/9781003606260-51

tasks like formulating statements, tax compliance, and matching balance sheets. Mistakes can lead to confusion and missed deadlines, affecting relationships and causing chaos in the minds of accounting professionals. Spiritual accounting helps in company's sustainability for long-term period and become the epitome for humanity. Spiritual accounting removes the toxicity of Human 's inner mind and helps to get off from emotional baggage, provide clarity about our goal on future corporate success without losing sight of spiritual values. The questions arise how we knows either mistakes are done intentionally or unintentionally, both leads to inconvenience, often the accountant and finance manager get tired and faces the lots of psychological problems but due to lacking of proper conscience and in putting all your efforts on organization goals, they forget to saturate their mind which increases the possibilities of making mistakes, frauds and manipulation. In the race to earn a profit, everyone is trying to get ahead of the other, on putting stake of ethics and human moral values which becomes weak and the mental health of humans. Spiritual accounting is an initiative to make balance between the chaos degraded minds of people through spiritual ways. Spiritual accounting is an initiative to control the greed and develop the spiritual mechanism for long-lasting sustainability of companies without harming other humans and other species. Spiritual accounting is a practice or conditioning to retain the richness of thoughts for most of the time. Spiritual accounting is an initiative to control and maintain the inner mind, which is connected to our body, brain, and heart. Spiritual accounting is the keeping track of yourself in accordance with life and is way to know your refine form. Spirituality one aspects which is seen and able to proven is called scientific and other non –physical abstract things are considered the non-scientific which is not able to be proven. Spiritual Accounting offers the various benefits:

- It is very important to know about our's negative aspects of thinking patterns which resides inside us for a several years. It will be helpful in reaching our higher self.
- It helps us to timely raise our balanced thinking and helps in maintaining our balanced consciousness, discretion against lots of adverse situations.
- It makes a rational Human.
- This accounting helps us to live organized life. Spiritual accounting leads us to extract the reality of life and the mechanism and process of eternal energy.
- It helps in functioning of our mind at highest level.
- Spiritual Accounting is based on known to unknown, it provides mechanism to control restlessness of our inner mind.

- It raises the capabilities of mind to conceptualize abstract or subtle things, pervades the world.
- It helps in understanding the psychology of human.
- It gives illuminating insights into spiritual matters and provide practical, existing circumstances-based solutions to inner mind.
- It helps in controlling the rising of mind into ripples. Equilibrium (balanced state is the state of happiness and peace.
- It is used in workplace and useful for self-analysis. Inner mind acts as catalyst in your life.
- we can differentiate between shirkers and diligent people, between goodness and badness which plays relevance role in efficiency of business.
- It helps in developing understanding about people's inner mind and their personality traits and will leads to refine decision making, acute observation for goal attainment with a view to earn profit. It reduces the cost of organization.
- In Spiritual Accounting organization can rightly evaluate the person and could assign the work according to that evaluation to save the capital of the company. We can recognize the person's perception by their personality traits for example one who possess guns for birds and one who possess water for birds. A need arises to analysis of inner mind and to know the various attributes of our human 's inner minds.

In this study we are exploring the attributes of human's Inner mind which is one of the main elements of spiritual accounting. Human's inner mind is full of thoughts with consciousness, all human 's actions is based on their selection of types of thoughts. Consciousness includes wisdom, conscience &intelligence. Human is always surrounded by their inner mind. Most of the negative aspects which happens within seconds comes when our wisdom & conscience gets deteriorated or when you hold the negative/inhumane thoughts and leads to deterioration of selection of our productive thoughts. Depletion of our inner mind is due to non- control on our inner mind. To control on our inner mind is possible through the practice of consistent habits of productive and right-thinking style. For directing and controlling purpose, firstly we need to understand various the features of Human inner mind. This paper involves the different features of Human's Inner mind.

2. REVIEW OF LITERATURE

(AnantawikramaTunggaAtmadja, et al, 2014) propounded the concept of Emotional Spiritual Quotient (ESQ) & Tri Hita Karana (THK) and their impact on accounting profession culture through ethical behaviour. ESQ is merger of emotional intelligence and spiritual control. According to them both concept is a way of living life, part of society, basis of human relations with God, with environment, with other human and it's a main element to make accounting process peaceful and cooperative. This concept helpful in smooth running and expansion of business. (Dr Naveen K Mehta, et al, May 2017) propounded that Accounting Scams are the reasons from where the need of ethical issues arises. They proposed the model on cross-cultural conceptual framework for integrating, ethical and spiritual practices. Ethics are foundation of cross-cultural professional accountants to develop the ethical and spiritual sense. Ethics and spiritual values are the factors helpful for accountant in decision making. (Melissa A. Donald, et al, 8 December 2020) elaborated the mental illness in accounting profession due to hectic working style of accountants. They said accounting is a complex and long process, so managers and authority should ensure the better stressful ambience. They suggested to ponder on factors which arises stress, to make organized systematic process so that accountant get motivated to come from home to workplace and go back to home without stress. (Nisar Ahmad, et al, December 2020) portrait the importance of personality type to understand the state of mind. They study the different factors to understand the financial manager's mindset. They suggested the motivational seminars, back-to-back meetings, personality tests, four themes for the expansion of Capital budget.

Attributes (Features) of Human 'S Inner Mind:

- Inner mind act as traveler from top to bottom of human 's spine comprises of various points /chakras. Every point experiences the different dimensions of life. Inner mind is came from brains and through spine its travels with help of energy. In sleep it travel around the universe as inner mind is the fastest abstract element. Different point include fire, water, soil and air element in body. Human personality traits are reflected by its inner mind, keeping the inner mind under our control is the condition of equilibrium. Spiritual accounting is initiative to conquer or control over the inner mind, Inner mind is resides in brain that why when our brain is healthy we feels good in our inner mind also. Our brain is under body & body is prevails on earth. The trajectory of inner mind is limited to body only. It is not difficult to connect your inner mind to eternal energy with purity of thoughts, with full veneration to exchange your inner voice to them and gets the solution and make your situations according to your desires. Many successful entrepreneurs acknowledge the spiritual values, and believes it's a way to become your best version among human race. Nature (trees, rivers air water, fruits, etc) doesn't discrimination between any species it is accessible to everyone but human does for greed of profits. Spiritual accounting is a initiative to control the greed and develop the spiritual mechanism for long-lasting sustainability of companies without harming other humans and other species. Deer is not aware about their musk 's aroma from where is coming from, in same way human is not aware about their power which resides within him. This helps you in uncovering your higher existence which was covered in a blanket of dust of materialistic upbringing with some prevailing beliefs. Its inner mind which control the decision, and give directions to your life.its inner mind which resume when you wake up from bed and Our inner mind is not active during sleep and when we wake up it takes time to activate its consciousness through body, brains, heart. it is inner mind which when you adopt the habit of doing same things consistently then it leads to form your personality type in society. Spiritual accounting is an initiative to control and maintain the inner mind, which is connected to our body, brain, and heart. Depletion of the inner mind leads to loss, while upgradation results in gain. Spiritual accounting helps in company's sustainability for long-term period and become the epitome for humanity.

- Inner mind is the mirror image or reflection of your imagination, intentions & thoughts. Inner mind is experiential element of life, you cannot conceal your personality from your inner mind. True treasure of inner mind is higher than treasure of materialistic world. Human's inner mind comprises of desire to buy product & services which leads to Inner mind 's vibration or ripple effects, where buyer send the vibrational thoughts to buy the product will reached to person who have desire to sell it and thus connects to each other's inner mind, whole world is running on above concept of need vibrational format. Through this we can say inner mind possess communicative traits.

- When we start thinking of doing some work from your inner mind, then we involve yourself to do it, but because the inner mind distracts you and pulls you out from that work and this is the reason why your energy does not focus at one place and leads to failure. Inspite of focusing on more number of work focus on one should have to focus on one work. If dullness prevails in human 's inner mind then only by lifting up will benefits it, and its your choice where you want your inner mind 's position.

- Every human has different thoughts and inner mind, you have different physiognomy from each other in terms of learning and accumulation of wealth, so don't compare yourself to others because mango tree can't produce all fruits, i.e. you have your own skills, knowledge which will leads to journey of thrive and success. When you compare with others you can't recognize your higher self. Individuality refers to state of knowing your own strength. When human is with their family and friends, there is a chemical release in the brain and body which gives good physical and mental health. Human is made for oneness but in inner mind and spiritual point of view we all are different, other human as family, friends, relative etc can help for some time but not for longer time then human 's inner mind become alone at some time, then the need arises to help your own & correcting yourself, it can be corrected by our own efforts to achieve our higher self.

- *Inner mind developed with the development of Chetna /Consciousness* - It's always lean towards materialistic things, attracts towards wealth, power and status, luxury, looks or other temptations needs because inner mind originated from body and it want pleasure by hook and crook. It fluctuates often for example in illness or problem times. It is not fixed at one point. Inner mind formulates truth from our surroundings, through our six organs like eyes (vision), ear, (hearing) nose(smell) skin(touch), tongue (taste) insight (pineal gland) experiences the world and create their learning and make memories and set its goal to achieve in life. Inner mind fluctuates and through awareness we can control it.

- *Inner mind is subject matter of developing mechanism for conditioning, right understanding and perception* – Inner mind of human need to develop the ability to transform state into desired state which helps you to achieve your desired goals. Conditioning refers to ways to infuse your goods thoughts into your daily habits and consistently maintaining them. Inner mind needs continuous improvement and efforts to reach at balance, higher is based on exploration self-actualization or self –learning.

- *Inner mind is easily attachable & sticking in nature, based on arbitrariness* – When inner mind gets attached to one zone, it does not accept change quickly, and unable to shift towards other zone of higher self which include pain for new learning. Pain ends with human change of personality ie hriday parivartan. Pain is that process which ends with new learning and experiences. Pain is our friend which aids us in uplifting us and this leads to profitable in terms of productivity and cooperative environment for business.

- *Inner mind is mirror of inbuilt ethical values /Inner mind oftenly behaves on its inbuilt ethical values*-Inner mind is often likes the things which at early stage of human childhood like. The thoughts and thinking style which a person keeps thinking since childhood becomes his permanent habit of thinking even in adulthood and it gets used through his inbuilt thinking and beliefs, principles. and likelihood to recognized what is right and what is wrong. when you help other without reason you feel good but once you are stealing something from someone your heart pumps and you feel guilt and fear of caught by someone.

- *Inner mind is connecting link between transient and eternal energy* –Thoughts are portable from transient energy to eternal energy.

- *Inner mind is energy box without energy, human will get collapse* - Body need sleep, rest and some sort of healthy pleasure i.e. your hobbies you like most.

- *Inner mind is based on newness, more efficiently work can be done when new ways is explored and created* – Inner mind likes the new and different ways to do work and try other element of earth or materialistic world but when inner mind decides something to achieve desperately but it didn't achieve then it goes down by refusing food which results in debility, in that situations pills are suggested but pills is also made from nature extracted materials, it means then earth and nature heals you and makes you reach at equilibrium zone. After recovery person forget all of it and start degrading nature once again. Nature is our spiritual parents and feed our body. For example, light of sun aid trees to prepare food which is our basic need, our clothes are came from nature. So, we should have to preserve nature to attain prosperity and peace.

- *Inner mind is experience box of life through senses* – Human achieves different experiences from world and make memories from happening of different events occurred on earth that's retain in inner mind i.e Experience box.

- *Inner mind is hub of all imagination & based of communication* – All imaginations, thoughts come from inner mind. Inner mind through brain it thinks the word, speech and it weighs that word and speech from heart and through body expression its speak and listen by sensory organs. Person who are indulge in antisocial activities depleting their peace and inner mind. Through this attribute we can recognized that type of anti-social person.

- *It is transient in nature as inner mind born with your life and ends with your death* - Human have limited time on earth with their body which is a transient in nature. Hence, we can conclude that Human's inner mind is transient in nature.

- It is the base of all works/actions/thoughts.
- Inner mind can be both aid in achieving your goals and can be reason of ruining your goals or dead ends.
- *Inner mind is base for developing intellect and helps in our survival* – Inner mind is trained right after birth of human by their experiences which is gained by brain, heart, body 's elements. Human is putting all his efforts on reaching zenith of their intelligence to achieve more wealth. Through attributes the human can easily develop understanding and recognized his and others personality traits & eliminate the unnecessary cost of the company.
- *Real place of Human 's inner mind is upper zone of higher self* - People who accumulate a lot of wealth, dominate and control others human, do illegal activities they are not happy for long time because they are unaware about the upliftment of their inner mind which provides peace and unaware from their real source of energy i.e eternal energy.
- *Inner mind is form of oneness* - Human belongs with different profession is having their different thoughts process. But we all are linked with each other with oneness basis, we look different, our life 's purpose are different but our soul is same which is a part of eternal energy, living with each other and support other species to maintain balance in nature.
- *Inner mind is based on breathing* - All thoughts are coming from our breathing and breathing is pulling force which receives different thoughts from universe.
- *Other species have also inner mind* - Other species have also a inner mind those have human like features for example Chimpanzee, Gorilla rats etc.
- Inner mind is contradicted on various points other, lives in environment and claim superior from each other.
- *Be the master of your Inner mind* - Give as much freedom you can but do not forget about to control to your inner mind but it is not easy to control inner mind for longtime, its needs a rigorous firm determination and sword of ceaseless practice then you can conquer it. After conquering yourself you become the master of controllable factors that is utilizing your present time and spend your life with at equilibrium (balanced) state of inner mind.
- *Inner mind possesses both constructive and destructive qualities* - Always involve your inner mind in continuous productive work otherwise inner mind spoils your conscience and so inner mind is always

be a matter of control in organization which helps in maximizing the profits, controlling is one of the functions of management.

- *Inner mind 's oblivion in nature* – Human 's Inner mind is too materialistic in nature which somehow helps us to come out from the extreme sadness of demise of loved one or partner, adverse situations like bankrupt, or other. Human 's inner mind seeks the happiness around us through sensory organs and from our surroundings happenings/ events and with passage of time that sadness is lessen. As such desires/ wants are unlimited in nature same our inner mind never gets filled, but can only be controlled at some satisfied points.
- *Inner mind at isolation becomes easily monotonous* – It is very important to keep yourself busy in some work otherwise in situation of isolation inner mind ponder the past and pull out the different old life's events which gives either the feeling of pain or pleasure.
- *Inner mind is imitating in nature* – The child is white blank canvas who learns from others by imitating and with uses of its sensory organs and builds their perception and deals and react in world according to that. With passage of time child's perception becomes rigid. A person's thoughts are shaped by his family's, community's, society's beliefs. Then they spend most of his life with those beliefs, and he does not listen to others' views against their views because the base of their whole life seems to be shaken because of reality of eternal energy, that is why people sometimes do not even accept the truth, because their beliefs and hopes are the face of their genes and heredity.
- *Inner mind movement starts with the seeds of any thoughts* – If you do no action with one's thought, then thoughts revolve in universe when you give again and again attention to your thoughts then its activate otherwise its is lost in universe.
- *Inner mind is highly impactful/sticky in nature* - Negative attracts and spread easily than positive but differences come in regards with consequences. Negative send hard frequency/signals in universe than positive.
- *Inner mind is highly transferrable / Recognizable by other Human's inner mind* – As we know that every thoughts have different chemicals collision with neurons released by brains.for example I gave you the slang with anger traits then you recognize the person and its your choice either you response in that person's harsh way or other gentle way.if you response or react in harsh way then its is a transferrable of emotions from one to other. Through words, thoughts, gesture,

facial expressions we can know the other's inner mind whether it is in happy or sad state.

- *Inner mind 's weight on movement* - Inner mind becomes heavy when you lift towards upward movement and on contrary it becomes lite towards downward movement but consequences differs at the end. Inner mind which becomes heavy & afterward ends with lite feel. On other hand inner mind first feel lite will ends with heavy. The above statement is described with context of crime and inhuman activities. When you uplift your inner mind, it pulls towards down because of gravity or materialistic vibes that's why inner mind feels heavy. Inner mind is that traveller of your vehicle (body) which gain experiences on earth & react, deals with different peoples according to that experience and knowledge.

The true existence of human lies in living with each other's in a shared manner. Human beings seem to be subjugated from body's phenomenon like sleep, hunger, thirst or, human have no control on their body's phenomenon and it seems like we are visitors on this earth but through mutual cooperation we can explore ways and methods to live our life better and will able achieve happiness and peace.

3. USAGE FOR ACCOUNTING PROFESSIONALS

- It helps in achieving the purpose in life i.e. Ikigai,
- It enhances the decision-making power of accounting professionals.
- It helps Accountant and finance managers to overcome their psychological problems & helps to achieve the conscience to attain the saturation of their mind which reduces the possibilities of making mistakes, detects frauds and manipulation. All human achievement is worthless without having spiritual conscience.
- Helps to achieve the calmness and tranquility of inner mind, builds egoless character.
- Helpful in acumen, boosts our decision-making power. It helps in reducing the feeling of discrimination. It accelerates your feeling of cooperation in company. Holding each other in storm of adverse situations & living together under one belt is means of prosperity and peace. For example, in feast employer put a condition to eat all luxuries food items without bending elbow. Everyone tried but fails to feed our self but at the end they explore that by feeding each other's will leads to appeasement of their hunger is epitome of cooperation & humanity.
- Helps in achieving the state of clarity in our thoughts, work, highly efficient inner mind & working together to uplift each other in organization

- It makes strong will power, feels self -motivated towards our work, good relations and harmonious ambience in company, explore the problem handling techniques & solution –oriented behaviour.
- Increases the quality of thinking and life's perception & leads towards meaningful life.
- Able to achieve mental health, Strong mechanism to deal with problems, eliminates fear of survival, can recognize human possessing traits of doing manipulation and frauds.
- To develop the mechanism to deal with complicated problems prevails in inner mind of accountant and financial managers.
- To keep accounting professionals in tranquility state & right trajectory of achieving mission and vision of company.
- To develop business, financial acumen, maintain fraternity among different genre of people.
- To avoid hasty decision which can leads to reduction of loss & destruction.
- Spiritual accounting is a initiative to make balance between the chaos & degraded minds of people through spiritual ways. It is helpful in smooth running and expansion of business.
- Spiritual accounting helps in taking decisions for different problematic issues of accounting and & to develop situational based accounting research.
- Spiritual accounting reduces the workforce's pressure.
- It removes the toxicity of Human 's inner mind and helps to get off from emotional baggage, provide clarity about our goal on future corporate success without losing sight of spiritual values.
- Building cordial employee's relationship and help them in their growth and survival.
- It leads to putting efforts to make our environment a better place to live, protecting the environment, like renewable energy, and reducing waste and carbon dioxide emissions.
- It is a way to make work meaningful and respecting the abilities of workers. It improves quality of our self-thinking, gives a sense of interconnectedness and oneness.
- It is helpful in training the next generation of students for building the refine human's Inner mind.
- Human beings should the value the nature and should considered the ways to extract their profits without depleting of nature and other species.
- It enlightens the accounting professionals (the accountant and finance mangers) to avoid the illegitimate ways to manipulate all users of accounting.

- In the race of maximizing profit, everyone is trying to get ahead of the other, on stake of human values which weakens human's inner mind and tending towards facing the negative consequences in life.

4. CONCLUSION

We can conclude that spiritual accounting gives us sense of interconnectedness and oneness and enhance our decision-making power. The attributes of human 's inner mind leads to human's holistic development, which provide insights for sustainability of company without depletion of our environment and will become efficient to live sorted life. It results in working together for betterment of each other and encourage each other in their growth in organization. The feeling of excess greed for money will leads us to imbalance in nature results in self –destruction of life and property of human. Human will able to control restlessness of mind, extracts positivity from negative aspects of life through this study. This study is based on Indian cultures & ethics only. We can use these conclusions as tools for definitive evidence in the future through quantitative measurements.

■ REFERENCES ■

1. https://www.researchgate.net/publication/361717857_Spiritual_Accounting_and_Corporate_Financial_Reporting_A_Study_of_Micro_Finance_Banks_in_Delta_State_Nigeria
2. https://core.ac.uk/reader/234629880 ((AnantawikramaTunggaAtmadja, et al, 2014))
3. https://digitalcommons.sacredheart.edu/cgi/viewcontent.cgi?article=1690&context=acadfest ((Melissa A. Donald, et al, 8 December 2020)
4. https://www.academia.edu/45187462/SPIRITUAL_PRACTICES_AND_ACCOUNTING_PROFESSIONALS_EMERGING_SCENARIO ((Dr Naveen K Mehta, et al, May 2017))
5. https://www.researchgate.net/publication/350521777_Role_of_Personality_and_Psychological_Attributes_of_Financial_Managers_in_Capital_Budgeting_Decisions_Case_of_Spinning_Industry_of_Pakistan (NisarAhmad, et al, December 2020)
6. https://www.cyresourcing.com/article/mental-health-for-accountants
7. https://www.researchgate.net/publication/361717857_Spiritual_Accounting_and_Corporate_Financial_Reporting_A_Study_of_Micro_Finance_Banks_in_Delta_State_Nigeria
8. https://www.researchgate.net/publication/357849647_Reverting_Consciousness_in_Mind_to_Inner_'Self'

Challenges and Opportunities for Innovation in India – Dr. Shweta Mishra et al. (eds)
© 2024 Taylor & Francis Group, London, ISBN 978-1-032-99842-8

Technology Adoption and Utilisation in Small Business

52

Shubhangi Gupta, Divyanshi Pal

MBA 1st Year, Ambalika Institute of Management and Technology

Shweta Mishra*

Professor, Ambalika Institute of Management and Technology

Abstract

Technology adoption may have a big impact on a small business's ability to earn a profit and withstand a recession. In particular, green technology may save energy expenses while also lessening the impact on the environment. However, implementing new technology could come at too high of a cost for the typical small- to medium-sized company. Adoption costs include things like buying new machinery, updating old industrial equipment, and even covering the cost of intellectual and other property rights. Using a database of small businesses, the researchers produced and sent a survey questionnaire to 2,000 small businesses nationally. Out of the 475 questionnaires that were returned, 397 had legitimate responses, yielding a 20% response rate. The results of this study could be quite important. The study's conclusions could be important in determining whether owners of small businesses will use innovative energy-saving technologies to protect the environment, cut expenses, and increase profits.

Keywords

Small business, Green technology, Legitimate responses, Neighborhood effect

1. INTRODUCTION

All over the nation, small business owners are constantly looking for fresh approaches to boost revenue and maintain their position as market leaders. Simultaneously, an increasing number of small business owners aspire to be more environmentally conscious, both for the sake of the environment and because many of them grew up in an era when environmental concerns and awareness among Americans became more widespread. As green technology advance, astute company leaders understand that current investments may yield substantial returns down the road. Even though energy prices are low right now, the long-term picture indicates that energy costs may have a significant impact on many firms' capacity to remain profitable. Will small business owners implement new energy-saving technologies on their own, or will the government need to provide grants, tax breaks, and other measures? Will small firms take on debt in order to buy these new technologies, seeing technology an investment in their company's future?

*Corresponding author: shwetamishra@ambalika.co.in

DOI: 10.1201/9781003606260-52

- The nation's small and medium-sized enterprises (SMBs) are gradually moving toward broad technological adoption.
- In India, 35% of SMBs currently spend more than 10% of their income on technology, and 26% have embraced emerging technologies earlier than their peers, according to a Microsoft survey.
- Meanwhile, during the next two to three years, 35% intend to go toward the cloud. The Microsoft SMB Voice and Attitudes to Technology Study 2022 featured these observations.
- This Microsoft study encompassed approximately 3,000 organizations with between one and three hundred people in each of the five top industry groups across ten of the world's most important markets, including India. According to the report, 27% of SMBs are already situated on the cloud, and this percentage is expected to rise to an average of 2–3 years globally.
- Simultaneously, Indian SMBs dominate the world in terms of technological expenditures. Moreover, 10% more money will be spent on technology in 2023, according to 22% of SMBs.

2. Definition of Terms

Gazelles - is a company that began operations in 1990 and has grown its revenues by at least 20% annually since then, with a minimum base of $100,000. As stated by Case (1996).

Green technology - often known as clean technology or cleantech, is new technology and associated business models that address global issues and offer investors and customers competitive returns (Bloomberg Business Exchange, 2010).

Energy smart grid - A digitally-enabled electrical network is known as an energy smart grid. By employing two-way digital communications to manage appliances at consumers' homes, a smart grid distributes electricity from suppliers to consumers, saving energy, cutting prices, and enhancing dependability and transparency. It adds an information and net metering system—which includes smart meters—overtop of the standard electrical infrastructure. Numerous governments are promoting smart grids as a solution to the problems of energy independence, global warming, and emergency preparedness. Energy Department, 2010).

Neighborhood effect - One of the contextual factors that explains a person's propensity to vote a specific way based on the interpersonal influences of the neighbors is the "neighbor effect." A neighborhood's voting preferences are typically established by consensus, with residents generally following the neighborhood's overall voting tendency. The interpersonal relationships a person makes in a community help to build this consensus. Voting behavior has also been predicted using what appears to be a socioeconomic association to voting trends.

Smart Meters - A smart meter is a digital gadget that communicates with your utility supplier to record and transmit the quantity of gas or energy you consume. Your utility bills will always be based on actual readings rather than guesses thanks to smart meters, which also enable flexible tariffs to be applied based on usage patterns.

3. Literature Review

The U.S. economy is still dominated by small businesses in terms of employment and the creation of new jobs. According to the U.S. Small Business Administration, all net new job creation in the most recent reporting year, 2004 (U.S. Census Bureau, 2007), was accounted for by businesses with 500 or less employees. These small businesses provide slightly over half of the GDP and employ slightly more than half of the labor population in the United States (U.S. Census Bureau, 2007).Technology adoption could be a major driver of small firms' expansion and development as well as a way for them to outcompete competitors that are less inclined to use particular technologies. The Corporate Research Board looked at gazelles, or high-growth entrepreneurial endeavors, in research for the U.S. Small Business Administration (quoted in Henreksen & Johansson, 2010). According to this study, gazelles can be found in both high-tech and low-tech industries. Within every industry, nevertheless, the more recent and efficient businesses displace the more established and inefficient ones. Efficiency can be attained in part through technologies that improve quality and decrease waste, produce goods and services more quickly, or provide other efficiencies. Henrekson and Johansson (2010) looked at gazelles, or high-performing, fast-growing small enterprises in another study and discovered that these companies were overrepresented in the service sector and underrepresented in high-technology industries. Henrekson and Johansson (2010) assert that gazelles are especially significant because, despite their typical younger age, they typically generate more net new jobs. Even while gazelles are present in every industry, the authors' research revealed several interesting distinctions between technology-based and non-technology-based enterprises. Fast-paced technological advancements frequently present a financial hardship for small businesses that are either underfunded or have restricted access to loans. Small businesses might not use the internet or other standard technologies used by larger companies. In order to support small businesses with their financial services needs, the Credit

Union National Association created a number of creative solutions (Help Small Business Prosper, 2009). One of the suggestions is remote deposit capture, which enables companies to use an internet connection and a scanner to deposit checks from a distance. Small businesses who would put up a booth at a county fair, roadside stand, or special event might find this very helpful. Using business credit cards and conducting bill payments online are more recommendations. Technologies can exist in many different forms. Larger businesses adopted Total Quality Management, or TQM, years ago, while smaller businesses frequently lag behind in adopting new technology because of resource or budgetary limitations. Hoang, Igel, and Laosihongthong (2010) investigated the adoption of Total Quality Management (TQM) methods by small and medium-sized manufacturing and service organizations in Vietnam. The study discovered that companies who had greater success with TQM adoption were typically more competitive globally.

3.1 What Early Technological Adoption can do for SMBs

SMBs can benefit greatly from early technology adoption. Some important takeaways are as follows:

- Early adopters are likely to have four times more business confidence and two times better possibilities of higher revenue growth.
- It is anticipated that SMBs with larger IT budgets will allocate more than 10% of their total sales to technology.
- They have greater aspirations for the future implementation of cloud-based technology and are already five times as likely to rely on it.
- Every year, 82% of early adopters of technology also submit reports on ESG and CSR issues.
- Compared to their peers, they are likely to believe that technology is seven times more important to achieving corporate objectives.

3.2 Hurdles Towards Technological Adoption

For SMBs, however, the future is less straightforward. Adopting new technologies comes with a number of challenges. Among them are the following:

- For 47% of SMBs, the expense of more modern technologies is a barrier.
- 38% struggle with making decisions and comparing solutions.
- 38% of respondents are worried about technical matters, and 35% are having trouble finding or doing research.
- Additionally, 29% are not open to change.

3.3 Using Technology to Make Decisions

SMBs are stimulated to make technical decisions by a number of factors. Among them are the following:

- While 45% of people rely on outside partners or consultants, 77% of people have committed internal staff members.
- New technology recommendations are desired by 51%, while updated and enhanced security is desired by 47%.
- Twenty-three percent assess the CSR goals of technology partners, and thirty percent believe that partner technologies should align with company priorities.
- Additionally, 31% favor alliances with MSPs or CSPs.

4. RESEARCH DESIGNATION

The following questions were the focus of the study's investigation. First, is there a connection between the age of the company and energy-saving technology? Secondly, is there a relationship between a company's debt-to-asset ratio and its use of energy-saving technologies? Lastly, are firms in major cities and towns more likely than those in smaller cities and towns to employ energy-saving technologies? A small company database that the researchers assembled had information on 2,000 small enterprises located all throughout the nation. Subsequently, the researchers created a survey questionnaire that encompassed inquiries aimed at obtaining fundamental business demographic information, like the firm owner's age and gender. Prior to sending out a pilot study of 25 questionnaires to small business owners to ensure survey instrument reliability, the researchers had the questionnaire reviewed by a panel of experts for validity purposes. The results of the pilot study were not used to modify the current questionnaire. To boost the total response rate, the researchers then emailed the survey questionnaire and two follow-up emails. A randomly chosen sample of small business owners received two thousand questionnaires; 397 of them were returned, representing a 20% response rate. We used an interpretive research approach to create a model of IT adoption for small companies in emerging communities, ideas in the model and a methodical approach to creating constructs that would allow the model to be operationalized. Because it generates qualitative insights inside the strict confines of a quantitative model, this approach is distinct. Information systems research, according to, can be categorized as interpretive if it is predicated on the idea that social constructions including language, consciousness, shared meanings, records, tools, and other artifacts are how we come to understand reality.

The process of generalizing from empirical claims and qualitative descriptions to theoretical claims is how theory is generated in interpretive research. They contend that this allows measurements, observations, or other descriptions to be more broadly applied theory as well as the capacity of the developed theory to be used outside of the sample or the area of observation for the researcher. Formal and hypothetico-deductive logic principles are used to establish structures by using our interpretive understanding to create a model. According to Lee, theoretical entities have observable effects even while the entities themselves are not, and this may be demonstrated through the use of hypotheticalo-deductive reasoning. This makes it possible to create a model that meets the requirements for a solid theory. We created an open-ended questionnaire using the propositions from the literature and the case studies from journals for an independent study student who was multilingual in Spanish and English, utilized in Omaha, Nebraska, to conduct interviews with nine Hispanic small business owners. The instrument, which is available from the authors and contains questions taken from empirical studies looking into Ajzen's Theory of Planned Behavior (described on his website) as well as from empirical studies of ethnic identity and learned styles cited elsewhere in the paper, is not published in this article due to space constraints. Nine further case studies featuring Hispanic small business owners were created based on these interviews. As a result, we decided to use these groups as the foundation for developing a global IT adoption model that may subsequently be evaluated in non-US environments. While our case studies did not account for specific industry effects, a larger scale, multi-ethnicity empirical investigation would undoubtedly match the industries of the enterprises polled in order to control for those effects. Nevertheless, the majority of the investigated firms were in the service sector, which includes establishments like pawn shops, restaurants, and day care centers. These businesses are probably going to have comparable requirements for information technology.

4.1 Outcomes and Advantages Over Time

Even in tiny organizations, the need for a comparative advantage over rivals typically drives the adoption of technology, particularly in the case of computer as well as online technologies. On the other hand, green technologies might not offer a significant competitive edge; instead, they might lower long-term energy expenses, which would increase profitability. Over time, new technology diffusion can be a challenging process. Problems frequently arise as a result of adoption expenses that could be prohibitive for the average small firm, plant equipment changes, or even the purchase of new machinery. If the government

wants to embrace new technologies, it should think about using tax breaks and other incentives to encourage this adoption. Just this past year, the federal government offered tax incentives to buy new, more energy-efficient cars through the "cash for clunkers" program and a $1500 tax credit for home energy-saving technologies like wood stoves, programmable thermostats, and windows as part of The American Recovery and Reinvestment Act of 2009 (Agency Group, 2010). Nations all across the world are working to implement green technologies. For instance, Malaysia offers tax incentives to builders whose projects satisfy new government regulations as part of that nation's attempts to minimize carbon emissions (Peterson, 2008). Incandescent light bulbs have already started to be phased out in the US and the EU as part of their efforts to save energy through new technologies. The IDC Asia-Pacific poll (cited in Peterson, 2008) reveals that, despite the fact that green technology adoption in Asia and some other regions of the world lags behind that in the United States and the European Union, 75% of small businesses surveyed cited adoption costs as a driver of technology adoption, while 60% cited cost reduction. The ordinary small business's competitiveness is greatly impacted by this circumstance. The American Recovery and Reinvestment Act of 2009 may be particularly advantageous to larger companies, such as energy providers, because it places a strong emphasis on replacing energy smart meters and smart grids to assist lower peak energy consumption. However, when implementing new technologies, small and medium-sized enterprises also gain as energy consumers. Additionally, companies who manufacture energy-efficient devices or their components profit from the rise in demand for connected products like meters and batteries. According to Hall and Khan's 2003 report, the adoption of new technologies has a major impact on our economy's growth, mostly through determining the rate of growth and increasing productivity. Furthermore, there is little to no environmental damage associated with economic growth facilitated by green technologies. Although family businesses were not the focus of this study, Huang, Ding, and Kao (2009) note that family businesses are more likely to use environmentally friendly business methods. Some intriguing results on family businesses come from more research. Gallo (2004) discovered that the average family firm is more socially responsible due to the distinctive characteristics that are frequently present in family enterprises. While Stavrou and Swiercz (1998) claim family enterprises are more attentive to quality of life issues effecting themselves and employees, Deniz and Suarez (2005) found family firms likely to have a strong dedication to philanthropic causes and activities. Lastly, family business values influence corporate conduct with relation to downsizing, and this is a significant point in this economic cycle (Stavrou, Kassinis & Filotheou, 2007).

5. DISCUSSION

An age of maturity may also greatly increase energy-conserving habits among entrepreneurs, according to the first hypothesis, which examined whether there was a significant association between age and energy-conserving technologies. Even while new technology has the potential to conserve energy and lower operating costs, an older business owner may not be open to implementing them. The researchers discovered a strong positive correlation between age and energy-conserving technologies, according to data analysis. The second hypothesis investigated the possibility of a significant correlation between debt to asset ratio and energy-conserving technology. The scientists discovered a significant correlation between debt to asset ratio and energy-saving technology, which may indicate that business owners took out loans to buy new equipment they thought would help them run their companies more profitably. They would also benefit financially from their investment. In the third hypothesis, the researchers looked into the possibility of a connection between the local population and the use of energy-saving technologies. Would digital adoption by business owners be higher in larger towns and cities? According to statistical findings from hypothesis 3, there is no correlation between population (urban vs. rural) and the adoption of energy-saving technologies.

6. SUMMARY AND CONCLUSION

It seems that younger business owners are more eager to implement energy-saving technology. Their generation may have grown up with the green technology paradigm, which could explain this. Alternatively, younger business owners can see a longer payback period from their energy savings and hence gain more from it. More research in this field may give light on the true factors that spur younger entrepreneurs to embrace technology. Small business owners appear more eager to take on debt in order to invest in new technologies, as evidenced by their greater debt-to-asset ratio. One significant conclusion here could be to offer tax breaks, low-interest loans, and grants to small and medium-sized businesses (SME's) in order to encourage their adoption of green technology, particularly as the government works to revive the economy. There is no discernible variation in business placement between urban and rural areas, according to survey replies. This

finding may surprise some people because it suggests that urban company owners to accept technologies with greater openness. The "energy-savings" component of adopting new technologies may hold the key to the solution. The findings of this study may encourage smaller companies to implement energy-saving technologies for the practical reasons of cutting costs and increasing profitability, rather than only as a way to help the environment. We can create "best practices" as we explore this subject more, which could help small and medium-sized businesses succeed in the more cutthroat business environment. Some fascinating and practical information on small firms and technology adoption was found by this study. The study's conclusions, however, pose other issues, and more investigation may be able to shed light on the driving forces behind a small business's decision to embrace energy-saving technologies or not. Future studies could also determine which technology, in terms of adoption costs, potential cost savings, or motivating factors, small business owners find more important.

■ REFERENCES ■

1. Agency Group (August 2, 2010). Department of Energy announces $188 million for small business technology commercialization. FDCH Regulatory Intelligence Database, Retrieved from Business Source Premier Database.
2. Baerenklau, K. (2005). Toward an Understanding of technology Adoption: Risk, Learning and Neighborhood Effects. Land Economics, 81 (1): 1-19.
3. Bloomberg Business Exchange (December 27, 2010). http://bx.businessweek.com/green-technology/ Case, J. (May 15, 1996). The age of the gazelle. Inc. Magazine. (http://www.inc.com/ magazine/19960515/2084.html).
4. Déniz, D & Suárez, M.K.C. (2005). Corporate social responsibility and family business in Spain, Journal of Business Ethics 56(1): 27-36.
5. Department of Energy website. Retrieved December 26, 2010 from http://www.oe.energy.gov/SmartGridIntroduction.htm.
6. Gallo, M.A. (2004). The Family Business and its Social Responsibilities. Family Business Review 17, 2, 135-149.
7. Thollander, P., & Dotzauer, E. (2010). An energy efficiency program for Swedish industrial small- and mediumsized enterprises. Journal of Cleaner Production, 18(13), 1339-1346.
8. U.S. Census Bureau data and the U.S. Small Business Administration, Office of Advocacy contract, The Small Business Share of GDP, 1998-2004, submitted by Kathryn Kobe, Economic Consulting Services, LLC, April 2007.

Role and Relevance of Schools, NGOs and 'Applications' in Managing Menstrual Health and Hygiene in Developing Contexts Like India*

53

Prajwal Arora[1]

BIT Mesra, Off-Campus Noida Masters in
Computer Applications Sem II

Suparna Dutta[2]

Associate, Professor,
Department of Management BIT Mesra,
Off-Campus Noida

Arnav Saxena[3]

BIT Mesra, Off-Campus Noida Masters in
Computer Applications Sem II

Rudra Pradhan[4]

Associate Professor,
Vinod Gupta School of Management Indian Institute of
Technology Kharagpur

Abstract

In the contemporary world, women have demonstrated their indispensable role in society, making diverse and multifaceted contributions that are equally vital. It is imperative to acknowledge their importance as it is essential for fostering equality, well-being, and progress for all members of the community. However, when we make a comparison with rural areas, the empowerment and well-being of women often remain obscured by cultural taboos and stigmatization, hindering their ability to advocate for their rights. This is particularly evident in areas related to menstrual health, where it may not be immediately evident that women who menstruate encounter numerous challenges. Some of these challenges may appear unrelated, such as mental health, yet menstruation exerts a significant impact on it. Menstrual Health Management (MHM) plays a vital role in the quality of life of menstruating women. This research paper explores various aspects of MHM, aiming to provide insights into effective strategies for promoting menstrual health, reducing stigma, and improving access to necessary resources via a medium that can be provided to those with fewer facilities and a less understanding environment. Overall, this research paper aims to contribute to the ongoing dialogue on Menstrual Health Management, offering valuable insights to researchers, policymakers, and organizations who are working towards Menstrual Hygiene and well-being for all.

Keywords

Menstrual Health, Stigmatization, Hygiene

*This Paper is Part of the Investigation and Study Being Carried out Under the DST-SRI Project at BIT Mesra, off Campus Noida

[1]prajwal26082002@gmail.com, [2]s.dutta@bitmesra.ac.in, [3]saxenaarnav2001@gmail.com, [4]rudrap@vgsom.iitkgp.ernet.in

DOI: 10.1201/9781003606260-53

1. INTRODUCTION

1.1 Overview

Menstrual health management covers a wide variety of practices, products, and aspects related to the menstrual cycle It is a natural and fundamental biological process experienced till menopause by adolescent girls, women, and individuals with a uterus. (Dutta & Mehta ;2019) Clinically speaking, this monthly occurrence, commonly known as a woman's 'period' is the periodic discarding of the uterine lining experienced during the reproductive years that is accompanied by a plethora of physical and emotional changes. It is no secret that even today across the world, women from all walks of life face challenges on multiple fronts. Menstruation is one fundamental challenge that frequently becomes a battle for the marginalized ones. (Dutta & Mehta 2019) For these girls and women, living generally in remote areas deprived of modern facilities the initial hurdle is still exposure to scientific knowledge and rightful awareness on the matter. No doubt, sustained initiatives, drive, and efforts made by the government, non-governmental agencies, and the faceless good Samaritans for decades have percolated much knowledge, (Dutta & Das 22) but still looms before us the 'last mile' challenge of connecting with those still carrying and wearing their proverbial albatross. With this, the next big challenge for most menstruating individuals in the underprivileged section is their access to and being able to afford essential female hygiene products (FHPs) like sanitary products and functional, affordable & clean underwear. In addition, secure, hygienic, and private facilities with functional fittings, doors, disposal bins, adequate and easy access to water, and drying washed wear further complicate the poor women's struggle to manage their menstrual health. Additionally, in many rural areas, even now women lack access to private clean, and functional toilets in their households. With this, the cultural and societal norms & taboos that prompt and encourage the concealment of menstruation frequently escalate menstruation as an existential battle.

2. BACKGROUND

2.1 Social Taboos

The challenges confronted by women during menstruation are by and large deeply rooted in their cultural norms and economically weaker women especially from remote places suffer more due to the lack of or the absence of congenial, scientific, and 'happy' infrastructure. (Mehta Dutta 2015) Unfortunately, there still exists in contexts like India the pervasive belief that menstruating women are impure, unholy, and unclean and hence to be ostracised till the bleeding stops. (Dutta & Das; 2022) Additionally, such taboos and stigmas surrounding menstruation have mostly contributed to the culture of silence on this topic. Consequently, information about menstruation and menstrual hygiene is inadequately discussed in mainstream conversations. This significantly impacts the daily lives of numerous women, reinforcing the exploitation, deprivation, and consequent suffering of menstruating women and girls and other individuals with uterus in society. It is now a widely documented fact that the inability of women to manage their menstrual hygiene in schools effectively leads to increased absenteeism, resulting in significant economic loss for these individuals, their families, and the nation as a whole. Many girls even today in tier 2 and 1 city in India refrain from using public toilets due to inadequate facilities, which restricts their access to proper sanitation, especially during their menstruation days. The biggest casualties are the big city hospitals, busy markets, government offices, and so on. This makes the situation stark when we realize that available data indicates that only 12% of the 350 million women between the ages of 12 and 45 have the financial means to afford sanitary towels. (S.Foundation; 2023)

2.2 Environmental Impacts

Unmanaged MHM in contexts like India has a stark environmental impact that has the potential to hurt even the non-menstruating population, cattle, stray animals, pets, and birds. The first in this order is the disposal of the used and blood-soiled cloth, pad, or any other material that the menstruating girls and women use. Though as per the available data FHP (and even the most commonly used sanitary pad) usage is at less than 18%, only our urban areas witness the disposal of approximately 58 million used menstrual pads annually, leading to a significant environmental issue with non-biodegradable menstrual waste overwhelming our cities (Dutta & Das 2022). Hence, it is exemplary that organizations like the non-governmental organization Goonj, are making remarkable efforts wherein they repurpose old and unused cloth to make very affordable menstrual pads and distribute these and other affordable reusable pads in rural and remote regions. The difference such efforts are making has made it clear that it is time we realize as responsible citizens that it is crucial to recognize that menstrual hygiene extends beyond being solely a public health concern; it involves complex socio-economic implications that women, therefore their families and hence their nation grapple with.

2.3 Status of MHM In India

Redundant as it may be, it nevertheless needs to emphasize an overwhelming socio-economic reality or even a challenge that India is home to over 355 million women and girls who menstruate. Despite this, many women in India are still facing significant obstacles when it comes to maintaining a comfortable and dignified MHM routine. A study has revealed that 71% of girls in India claim to have had no prior knowledge of menstruation before experiencing their first period. When girls in Jaipur, Rajasthan, start menstruating, they commonly express feelings of shock (25%), fear (30%), anxiety (69%), guilt (22%), and frustration (22%). Additionally, 70% of women in India mention that their families cannot afford sanitary pads. In 2012, 40% of government schools in the country did not have a functioning standard toilet, and another 40% still lacked a separate toilet for girls. (Geertz & Iyer; 2016). The pandemic we have so hard to overcome globally has ravaged the menstrual ecosystem as well. The Lockdowns due to COVID-19 have massively disrupted human lives. Despite continuous efforts to restore other services, women's health has faced significant challenges. And many of which affected their reproductive and menstrual system as well. The availability of menstrual hygiene products like sanitary pads, menstrual cups, reusable napkins, pain relief medications, soaps, and so on too has been starkly affected. But most ironically it needs to be realized that the pandemic had further increased mobility restrictions for women.6 (S.Foundation; 2023) It is now widely acknowledged that a woman's struggles, especially those who come from the lower rungs of the social order have been made worse by the psychological problems induced by menstruation, pregnancy, childbirth, social isolation, and unstable financial conditions which in turn has a detrimental effect on the menstruation health creating often a monstrous vicious circle. Further, women are prone to and are usually found to prioritize food and essentials above their personal hygiene products due to economic instability, even in the absence of the epidemic. On Menstrual Hygiene Day, a senior UNICEF official underlined that "every girl has the right to manage her period safely and with dignity; don't stop for pandemics."(UNICEF; 2018) The WASH Poverty Diagnostics conducted by WHO provide valuable insights into the challenges of Menstrual Health Management (MHM) across different countries and their repercussions on human development This is supported by data from multiple sources. For Example, in Nigeria, 25% of women face a lack of sufficient privacy for defecation or MHM. In Bangladesh, merely 6% of schools offer education on MHM, and over one-third of surveyed girls in Bangladesh state that menstrual issues negatively impact their school performance. Data also indicates that nearly 23% of girls drop out of school, and some are coerced into early marriages due to these challenges. (World Bank; 2018)

Fig. 53.1 Sanitary pads

2.4 Period Poverty

Period poverty is a common professional parlance indicating what financially challenged women to encounter in obtaining or affording menstrual hygiene products. It also encompasses the lack of awareness and information on this issue which contributes to the persistence of outdated traditions, customs, and narrow-minded beliefs regarding menstruation that affect the wellness of menstruating individuals in general and society at large, Data shows that one out of every five girls drop out of school annually due to her inability to access safe sanitary products. Further, among those who stay in school, 40% have to miss classes during their menstrual period, which significantly hampers their education and classroom performance as mentioned earlier. The same is the case for older individuals who are part of the working and wage-earning population (Vashisht et al., 2018). It is common knowledge that misinformation about women's menstrual cycles is still widespread with 70% of the unlettered and semi-lettered mothers regarding menstruation as unclean even today. These problems are further compounded by the financial constraints faced by women from economically disadvantaged backgrounds as mentioned earlier. (S.foundation; 2023) A common period poverty fact is that approximately 50% of women in India still rely on clothes during their menstrual periods, while it is just 1.7% from the elite class who use products like tampons. Additionally, the usage of sanitary napkins can directly be linked to the income levels of families indicating that only around 53% of women in the poorest households are currently using hygienic menstrual products in India today (S.Foundation; 2023). Another study reveals that 71% of girls in India have no previous knowledge of the female period cycle or menstruation before their first menstrual cycle. (Kalita, D., & Pathak, G. ;2019) In rural

India, proper menstruation hygiene is often not practiced due to challenges such as inadequate restroom facilities, and limited access to menstrual products, and clean water. Official statistics show that 15,000 out of the 10.83 lakh government schools in India lack restrooms, compounding the issue for many teenage menstruators due to the glaring absence of sanitary facilities (Gohain; 2021).

2.5 Role of the Government

The Indian government still plays a pivotal role in addressing the healthcare needs of over 280 million menstruating women. The Ministry of Health and Family Welfare introduced the 'Menstrual Hygiene Scheme' under the National Health Mission's Menstrual Hygiene Management Programme to tackle menstrual health hygiene. The initiative aimed to boost awareness, improve access to sanitary napkins, and establish effective disposal methods. However, challenges have impeded the scheme's success.

Fig. 53.2   Reduced efficiency: A concern for all

Originally, the plan intended to distribute sanitary napkins directly through government channels to 107 districts, while empowering self-help groups to produce and sell them at a cost below ₹8 per pack in 45 other districts. Unfortunately, irregular and inefficient supply disrupted the distribution chain, and the absence of a proper disposal system for used pads further complicated matters. To address these challenges, the National Guidelines on Menstrual Hygiene Management delineate the specific responsibilities of each stakeholder involved in tackling this issue.

- *Rashtriya Kishor Swasthya Karyakram (RKSK) (2014) (Rana, 2022):* RKSK is a holistic initiative with a primary emphasis on advancing the sexual and reproductive health of adolescents. Within the framework of this scheme, Peer Educators, also

Fig. 53.3   Helping and educating

known as Saathiyas, are trained and identified at the village level to effectively communicate information about adolescent health issues. This program operates in both urban and rural areas, addressing the diverse needs of adolescents across different settings. A key sub-component of RKSK involves the acquisition of sanitary napkins as part of the Menstrual Hygiene Scheme (MHS), highlighting a commitment to addressing menstrual health challenges and ensuring access to sanitary products for adolescent girls within the program.

- *Scheme for Promotion of Menstrual Hygiene (also known as the Menstrual Hygiene Scheme) (2011) (Rana,2022):* Functioning in rural areas, this initiative strives to raise awareness and facilitate access to safe menstrual practices for adolescent girls. The primary emphasis of the scheme is on acquiring sanitary napkins, particularly in districts, to ensure the effective implementation of menstrual hygiene practices.

- *Jan Aushadhi Suvidha Sanitary Napkin (SSK) (2019) (Rana, 2022):* Biodegradable and environmentally friendly pads are now accessible at just ₹1 per pad at over 8,000 Pradhan Mantri Bhartiya Jan Aushadhi Pariyojana (PMBJP) centers throughout India. The government encourages private partnerships to operate these centers.

2.6 Menstrual Hygiene Education

To improve menstrual health and cleanliness, schools are not only essential but they have a critical role to play. It is a cliché that although half of the world's population experiences this natural process of menstruation, little is known about it, especially in the context of underdeveloped and developing economies. (DFID; 2016) Schools can help reduce knowledge gaps by providing instruction-based education on menstruation. This is best in terms of the selection of FHPs, cleanliness habits, and clinical knowledge of the menstrual cycle. This knowledge can make the girls more aware of their bodies, practice better hygiene habits to lower their risk of falling prey to serious, fatal but avoidable infections and other health issues for which not only these hapless individuals, but their financially struggling families and the nation at large end up paying a great price. In these lines, it is the schools, which are the first line of contact with this target audience that should guarantee access to the FHPs within their grounds in addition to providing vital education. Further, It is also very critical to draw the attention of the policymakers, perhaps our media, to the unique difficulties experienced by girls with disabilities. Missed school days and a drop in academic performance usually result from this. Educational institutions have the scope to ensure that girls win their battle against menstruation with ease and elan. However, in recent years, menstrual hygiene management (MHM) in schools has witnessed enhancements through collaborative efforts from various ministries like Health and Family Welfare, Human Resource Development, Rural Development, and Women and Child Development, etc As a result, progressively. Indian schools are providing safe drinking water and sanitation and, in some states, even FHPs to the registered girls. Their policies and initiatives are beginning to play a crucial role in this improvement, raising hopes for a more significant impact across India. However, to sustain and expand these positive changes, there is a need for improved coordination among government agencies involved in MHM activities. The authors also feel that. More planned, documented, and continuous monitoring to assess progress and effective budget allocation and utilization will be to augment progress in this domain.

2.7 Case Study

Contribution of Smile Foundation

It is now a documented reality that girls who previously talked about menstruation in hushed tones have now gained the confidence to prompt and participate in open and detailed discussions on school assemblies and within their homes. This transformation has had a ripple effect, as many adolescent girls have started joining these conversations, influenced by what they've learned from their peers at school and friends in the community creating a domino effect that is positively affecting their community as well. This is the result of priceless efforts made by non-governmental organizations like the Smile Foundation. Furthermore, the Smile Foundation has tried to ensure access to menstrual products by distributing over 100 million sanitary pads to girls in both rural and urban areas. The foundation has also taken several significant steps to address the challenges related to menstruation. Some salient ones are:

1. *Breaking Cultural Taboos:* The foundation has organized awareness-raising campaigns and workshops to dismantle the cultural taboos associated with menstruation.

2. *Providing Menstrual Education:* Over 10,000 community health workers and teachers have been trained by the foundation to impart knowledge on menstrual hygiene and management.

3. *Addressing Poverty:* Collaborating with schools and other organizations, the foundation offers financial support to girls who are unable to afford menstrual products.

4. *Eliminating Gender Discrimination:* The foundation has actively worked this help them to ensure that girls have equal access to education and healthcare, irrespective of their menstrual status.

2.8 Workshops Conducted by Smile Foundation

The 'Swabhiman' program organized a three-day workshop focused on menstrual hygiene and safe practices and was designed for the program's community health educators and health volunteers. Approximately 123 participants, aged 12 to 42, from Swabhiman centers 'Adhaar' (Shashi Garden), 'Sahyogita Samaj Vikas Sansthan' (Chhattarpur), and 'Health & Care Society' (Indira Camp) actively engaged in the workshop, which was conducted by Dr. Uzma Bano." (S.foundation; 2023). In addition to the workshop mentioned earlier, other workshop topics included:

1. Emphasizing the Significance of Menstrual Hygiene
2. Exploring Various Menstrual Products
3. Instruction on the Proper Use of Menstrual Products
4. Safe Disposal of Menstrual Products
5. Awareness of Health Risks Linked to Inadequate Menstrual Hygiene
6. Understanding the Social and Economic Consequences of Poor Menstrual Hygiene
7. Strategies to Break Down the Stigma Surrounding Menstruation
8. Empowering Girls to Effectively Manage Their Periods with Safety and Hygiene

3. THE DIGITAL ROUTE REQUIREMENT ANALYSIS

Fashion, fads, and useful, applications or 'Apps' are galore in every domain. The menstrual ecosystem is hence no exception. Hence, to speculate on what a pragmatic App should cover is not rocket science anymore. Further, with the fiercely spreading digital literacy, Apps are now the order of the day both for content creators as well as content consumers. Hence, it is now not only pragmatic but welcome to encourage the development of full-stack Applications which would prove highly beneficial as an instructor, counselor, confidant, and certainly as one's first line of defense. In a very simplistic term, an application that does not require heavy bandwidth and with the following specifications is recommended:

3.1 Hardware requirement
- RAM: 2 GB or more
- OS: Android 5.1+

3.2 Software requirement
- Stable network connection

3.3 System requirement
3.3.1 Client's side requirements
- Android 5.1+
- Smartphone
3.3.2 Server's side requirements
- Database connectivity

4. ABOUT THE APP AND FEATURES

4.1 Scope of the App

The app's scope includes the following essential elements:

1. *Menstrual Hygiene Education:* The app will offer educational materials and resources to raise awareness and understanding of menstrual hygiene practices, primarily aimed at girls and young women who may lack knowledge in this area.

2. *Distribution of Menstrual Hygiene Products:* The app will streamline the distribution of menstrual hygiene products, particularly to individuals in need, with a focus on underprivileged or underserved communities.

3. *Blockchain Integration:* To ensure data integrity and security, the app will incorporate blockchain technology for storing crucial information related to product distribution and educational resources. This integration will make the data tamper-proof and resistant to corruption.

4.2 Major Features

The application should include the following key features and components:

1. *How-to/Instructions:*
   Provide clear instructions for users of all backgrounds on how to navigate and utilize the application effectively.

2. *Education:*
   Target users who may not be well-informed about menstrual hygiene and related issues, particularly those in rural areas that consist of marginalized adolescent girls.

3. *Comprehensive Guides:*
   Offer detailed guides on managing menstrual challenges, including pain relief, mood management, dealing with irregular cycles, symptom tracking, and dietary recommendations tailored to different age groups and households.

4. *Menstrual Cycle Tracker:*
   Provide an interactive and informative menstrual cycle tracker that enables users to better understand their body's functions, track their menstrual cycles, and identify potential problems.

5. *Medical Support:*
   Incorporate features such as 24/7 call assistance and a map for locating nearby government medical centers or dispensaries that are cost-effective and dependable.

6. *Product Delivery:*
   Implement a product delivery service to distribute affordable menstrual hygiene products to individuals across the country, particularly those in rural areas, in line with the World Bank's findings regarding the economic impact of improved menstrual hygiene.

7. *Additional Content:*
   - The application includes a variety of content formats, such as videos, animations, cartoons, and games.
   - Consider implementing a reward system to motivate users.
   - Provide content cards, FAQs, and other supplementary materials to enhance user experience and knowledge.
   - By integrating these features, the application can serve as a comprehensive resource for menstrual health education, support, and access to essential products, ultimately improving the well-being and empowerment of girls and women.

4.3 Security Features

Blockchain technology is mostly famous for its robust security features, which allow the developers to keep the user's data safe making it a proffered choice while building an application these days.

Here's how blockchain is useful for security features:

1. *Immutability:* Once data is registered on a blockchain, it remains unchanged and cannot be

Fig. 53.4 Blocks and a blockchain

deleted or modified without the agreement of the network's consensus algorithm. This immutability makes it highly secure against data tampering and fraud. In a world where data breaches and hacks are commonplace, the immutability of blockchain can be a significant security advantage.

2. *Decentralization:* Blockchain functions on a network of computers distributed across various locations, thereby reducing vulnerability to individual points of failure. Unlike centralized systems that are vulnerable to attacks on a central server or authority, The decentralization of blockchain significantly bolsters its security. It presents a formidable challenge for malicious entities to compromise a significant portion of the network's nodes simultaneously.

3. *Cryptography:* Strong cryptographic techniques are used to secure data on the blockchain. Each transaction or data block is encrypted, and users have cryptographic keys that provide access. This encryption ensures the privacy and confidentiality of data and makes it difficult for unauthorized parties to access or decrypt the information.

4. *Consensus Mechanisms:* Blockchain utilizes consensus mechanisms such as Proof of Work (PoW) or Proof of Stake (PoS) to authenticate and incorporate transactions into the chain. These mechanisms necessitate participants to either solve intricate cryptographic puzzles or stake tokens, rendering it economically impractical for attackers to manipulate the network.

5. *Smart Contracts:* Smart contracts are autonomous agreements where the agreement terms are encoded into software. They are triggered automatically upon meeting specific conditions, eliminating the necessity for intermediaries. This reduces the likelihood of fraud, disputes, or errors typically encountered in traditional contract enforcement.

6. *Permissioned Blockchains:* In some use cases, especially in enterprise environments, permissioned blockchains are used. These blockchains restrict access to a defined set of participants, enhancing control and security. Participants are usually vetted, making it more challenging for malicious actors to enter the network.

7. *Transparency:* Blockchain offers transparency by providing a public ledger of all transactions. While this may seem counterintuitive to security, transparency is an essential feature. It allows all participants to independently verify transactions, reducing the risk of fraud or manipulation.

8. *Audit Trails:* The ability to trace every transaction and data entry back to its source is a powerful security feature. It simplifies the auditing process and can deter malicious actions, as they can be easily traced.

9. *Data Recovery:* In a traditional centralized system, data can be lost due to server failures or data breaches. Blockchain's decentralized and distributed nature ensures data is stored redundantly across multiple nodes, making data recovery more reliable.

10. *Digital Identity:* Blockchain is primarily employed to create a secure digital identity system, safeguarding against identity theft and fraud.

11. *Supply Chain Security:* Blockchain technology is applied in supply chain management to trace the journey of products and data from manufacturer to consumer. This robust system guarantees authenticity and diminishes the likelihood of counterfeit goods entering the supply chain.

Overall, blockchain technology's security features, especially its immutability, decentralization, and strong cryptographic techniques, make it a powerful tool for various applications where data security and integrity are paramount. However, it's important to note that while blockchain technology enhances security, it is not immune to all types of threats, and proper implementation and best practices are essential for its effectiveness.

5. Conclusion and Future Scope

In conclusion, this paper has shed light on the critical issues surrounding menstrual health management in India. The challenges faced by menstruating individuals are multi-faceted, encompassing social taboos, environmental impacts, and the dire need for menstrual hygiene education. This comprehensive overview has shown that addressing these challenges is not only a matter of public health but also one of socio-economic importance, impacting the education and well-being of millions of women and girls. The role of the government and various schemes aimed at improving menstrual hygiene in India has been discussed, highlighting both the progress made and the need for more efficient implementation. Additionally, the significant contributions made by organizations like the Smile Foundation in breaking down cultural taboos, providing education, addressing poverty, and eliminating gender discrimination have been emphasized. Furthermore, the proposed menstrual health application, which combines education, product distribution, and blockchain technology, shows great promise in addressing these challenges comprehensively. Its potential to empower women and girls with knowledge, support, and access to menstrual products could be a game-changer in the field of menstrual health management. Incorporating blockchain technology as a security feature in the application adds an extra layer of trust and integrity to the data, ensuring the privacy and reliability of information related to menstrual health. In summary, while the challenges are substantial, this paper underscores that menstrual health management is not only an achievable goal but also a fundamental right for individuals with a uterus. Through coordinated efforts, innovative solutions, and a commitment to breaking down taboos, India can pave the way for improved menstrual health, education, and empowerment, ultimately benefiting the well-being and progress of its women and girls.

■ REFERENCES ■

1. L. I. P. K. F. M. a. K. P. Alexandra Geertz, "Menstrual Health in India | Country Landscape Analysis," fsg.org, Mumbai, 2016.

2. S. Foundation, "Why Period Poverty In India Needs A Proper Discussion?," Smile Foundation, 20 November 2023. [Online]. Available: https://www.smilefoundationindia.org/blog/why-period-poverty-in-india-needs-a-roper-discussion/#:~:text=Data%20shows%20that%20around%2050,women%20use%20hygienic%20menstrual%20products.

3. S. Foundation, "How Important Is Women's Menstrual Health?," 1 September 2021. [Online]. Available: https://www.smilefoundationindia.org/blog/how-important-is-womens-menstrual-health/.

4. S. Foundation, "Importance of Menstrual Hygiene for Girls in Schools," Smile Foundation, 1 April 2023. [Online]. Available: https://www.smilefoundationindia.org/blog/importance-of-menstrual-hygiene-for-girls-in-schools/.

5. i. team, "Common misconceptions and taboos surrounding menstruation," Ichhori, 28 April 2023. [Online]. Available: https://www.ichhori.com/2023/04/common-misconceptions-and-taboos.html.

6. Swetha, "The Oscars, Period. Let's talk about it.," 25 February 2019. [Online]. Available: https://capriciousnomad.wordpress.com/2019/02/25/the-oscars-period-lets-talk-about-it/.

7. T. Rana, "Menstrual Health Services in India: A Comprehensive Overview of the Public System," accountabilityindia.in, 2 September 2022. [Online]. Available: https://accountabilityindia.in/blog/menstrual-health-services-in-india-an- verview/#:~:text=Through%20these%20various%20initiatives%2C%20menstrual,IV%20(2015%2D16)..

8. S. Foundation, "Menstrual Hygiene at the Forefront of Indian Women's Growth Story," Smile Foundation, 4 July 2023. [Online]. Available: https://www.smilefoundationindia.org/blog/menstrual-hygiene-at-the-front-of-indian-womens-growth-story/.

9. A. D. Suparna Dutta, "Gender issues and New Governance: Managing Menstrual Health and Hygiene with Emerging Multimedia Options for a Progressive Economy".

10. D. &. P. G. Kalita, "International Journal of Medical Science and Public Health," *Study on hygiene practice among adolescent girls with special reference to menstrual hygiene in Barpeta, Assam.*, 2019.

11. N. M. Suparna Dutta, "Dutta Suparna, Mehta Niket (2019), Multimedia Communication as a Means to Address Teen Pregnancy: A Perspective of Behavior Change Communication," in *ICECEICTamil Nadu*, Enathur, Kanchipuram, Tamil Nadu, 2019.

12. A. Vashisht, R. Pathak, R. Agarwalla, B. N. Patavegar and M. Panda, "School absenteeism during menstruation amongst adolescent girls in Delhi, India," 25 Sep-Dec 2018. [Online].Available: https://www.ncbi.nlm.nih.gov/pmc/articles/PMC6130156/.

13. S. House, T. Mahon, and S. Cavill, "Menstrual Hygiene Matters," WaterAid, 2016.

14. TNN, "42k of 11 lakh govt schools lack drinking water, 15k toilets | India News - Times of India," timesofindia, 19 March 2021. [Online]. Available: https://timesofindia.indiatimes.com/education/news/42000-govt-school-lack-drinking-water-supply-15000-have-no-toilet/articleshow/81572756.cms.

Note: All the figures in this chapter were made by the author.

Challenges and Opportunities for Innovation in India – Dr. Shweta Mishra et al. (eds)
© 2024 Taylor & Francis Group, London, ISBN 978-1-032-99842-8

Thermodynamic Comparison of Conventional and Hybrid Power Cycle

54

Abhinav Anand Sinha[1]

Mechanical Engineering Department PDPM
Indian Institute of Information Technology Design and
Manufacturing Jabalpur, India

S. P. Pandey[2]

Engineering Roorke,
(Formerly known as University of Engineering and
Technology Roorkee), India

Kriti Srivastava[3], Tushar Choudhary[4]

Mechanical Engineering Department PDPM
Indian Institute of Information Technology Design and
Manufacturing Jabalpur, India

Abstract

Rapid increase in population, the demand for energy consumption increases. The existing conventional power plants are performing well but are not enough to fill the gap between energy demand and supply. To fill this gap a hybrid power generation system is proposed which is compared with the conventional system. A hybrid system is the integration of a high-temperature fuel cell, called a Solid Oxide Fuel Cell (SOFC) to the conventional gas turbine (GT). A thermodynamic comparison between these two configurations is presented at a pressure ratio of 6 and a turbine inlet temperature of 1250 K. The energy efficiency and exergy efficiency of the hybrid system are found to be increased significantly and simultaneously the network output increases, which helps to minimize the gap between the demand and supply.

Keywords

Exergy, Gas turbine, SOFC, Thermodynamics

1. INTRODUCTION

India is a developing country, and its energy consumption increases continuously. Since the population is also increasing simultaneously, therefore there is a need to supply power at the same rate as required. The gap between power production and requirement is one of the major challenges in India [1]. Conventional power generation

[1]s.abhinav17@gmail.com, [2]drsppandey1966@gmail.com, [3]kritiarivastava.17@gmail.com, [4]tushar.choudhary@iiitdmj.ac.in

DOI: 10.1201/9781003606260-54

systems have some limitations due to which the power production rate is insufficient as per the requirement. The challenges in India are the power gap between demand and supply. To minimize this gap the government takes several initiatives such as to promote the utilization of renewable energy or to adopt alternative means of power production.

There are various renewable energy sources such as solar, wind, etc. but the major challenge is still associated with conventional systems until these sources are not directly or indirectly integrated with conventional systems. In this regard, a fuel cell which is working on the principle of electrochemical reaction, is found to be suitable for direct integration with conventional gas turbine power generation systems. Since the fuel cells are directly integrated with conventional systems, therefore it is important to know about the fuel cell. It is an electrochemical fuel cell with three major components, anode, cathode, and electrolyte. Fuel is supplied to the anode and oxygen is supplied to the cathode. The selection of electrolyte is very important, generally, the YSZ (Yttria-stabilized zirconia) is used, because it has high ionic XXX-X-XXXX-XXXX-X/ XX/$XX.00 ©20XX IEEE conductivity [2]. This accelerates the oxygen ion from the cathode to the anode. There are a variety of fuel cells available in the market, which are categorized based on their working temperature. Some of the common fuel cells are given in Table 54.1.

Table 54.1 Operating parameters [3]

Types	Operating temperature
AFC- Alkaline fuel cells	90-100 °C
PAFC- Phosphoric acid fuel cells	150-200 °C
PEMFC- Polymer electrolyte membrane fuel cells	50-100 °C
MCFC- Molten carbonate fuel cells	600-700 °C
SOFC- Solid oxide fuel cells	600-1000 °C

Conventional gas turbine power cycle is running at high temperatures; therefore, the high temperatures fuel cell is suitable to directly integrate with it. The maximum temperature of a gas turbine is decided by the maximum possible temperature sustained by the blades of the gas turbine. The turbine blades have some materialistic constraints due to which some temperature-based limitations must be taken into consideration [4]. Kumari and Sanjay [5] presented a parametric study to estimate the exergetic and emission-based performance of basic and conventional intercooled gas turbines. Dabwan et al. [6] presented a novel inlet air cooling system for the intercooled gas turbine and reported that the proposed system is capable of improving efficiency by 8-18%. Rathore et al. [7] presented the thermodynamic analysis of an internal convection air-cooled based intercooled gas turbine. For this, they have

considered the wide range of TIT (from 1300 K to 2000 K). and achieved a maximum efficiency of 46.93% for a superalloy-bladed gas turbine at a pressure ratio of 48 and TIT = 1900 K. Carcasci and Winchler [8] suggested that organic Rankine cycle (ORC) is a good choice of integration with intercooled gas turbine to for waste heat recovery. Candra et al. [9] presented an intercooled gas turbine with ORC. This ORC is attached to the intercooler to reduce the losses in the intercooler and achieve the optimum exergy efficiency of 33%. Musharavati et al. [10] carried out the numerical modeling for the waste heat utilization from the intercooled gas turbine system. Leal et al. [11] performed an analysis of SOFC integrated with a gas turbine and achieved a maximum exergy efficiency of 58.7% at 1100 °C. Rupiper et al. [12] investigated the performance of fuel cell integrated gas turbine cycles with six different fuels. Hydrogen fuel was found to be the best fuel followed by CH_4. Previous literature covers the intercooled gas turbine cycle and the fuel cell with the gas turbine cycle, but not with the intercooled system. This paper provides a performance comparison in terms of energy and exergy for the intercooled conventional gas turbine and fuel cell intercooled gas turbine.

2. OPERATING PARAMETER

Figure 54.1 Shows the configuration of an intercooled fuel cell gas turbine hybrid system. This paper compares the performance of two configurations. Case A: intercooled gas turbine without fuel cell and Case B: intercooled gas turbine with fuel cell. In a conventional intercooled gas turbine, inlet air enters the low-pressure compressor and then into the highpressure compressor through the intercooler. This way the power consumed by the compressor is reduced. A fuel cell is placed in between the recuperator and the combustion chamber. Because the unutilized fuel leaving SOFC is combusted into the combustion chamber. The operating parameter for the proposed system is given in Table 54.2.

Table 54.2 Operating parameters [13], [14]

Parameter	Value
Pressure Ratio	6
Turbine Inlet temperature	1250 K
The mass flow rate of air	4.123 kg/s
Isentropic efficiency of the compressor	81%
Isentropic efficiency of gas turbine	84%
Isentropic efficiency of power turbine	89%
The efficiency of the combustion chamber	98%
Pressure loss in recuperator	4%
Pressure loss in the combustion chamber	5%
Ambient temperature	288 K
Ambient pressure	101.3 kPa

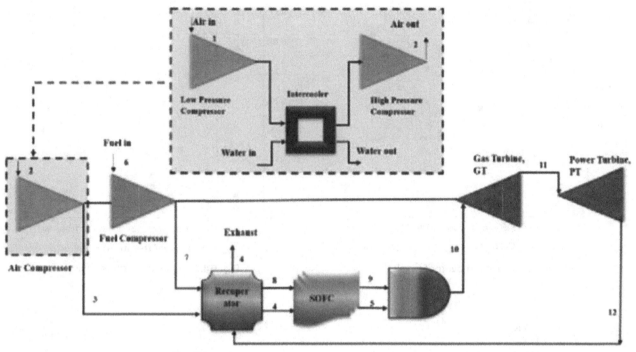

Fig. 54.1 Configuration of hybrid intercooled gas turbine

3. MODELING EQUATIONS

The energy analysis is based on the first law of thermodynamics. Therefore, the steady flow energy equation is used to analyze the thermodynamic performance of each component and the overall energetic performance of each configuration.

The steady flow energy equation is given as follows:

$$Q - W + \sum \dot{m}_{in}\, h_{in} - \sum \dot{m}_e\, h_e = 0 \qquad (1)$$

For exergy calculations

$$Ex = \dot{m}\left((h - h_0) - T_0(s - s_0)\right) \qquad (2)$$

Enthalpy: $h = \int_{T_0}^{T} Cp(T)dT$ \qquad (3)

Entropy: $s = \int_{T_0}^{T} Cp(T)\dfrac{dT}{T} - R\ln\left(\dfrac{p}{p_0}\right)$ \qquad (4)

The modeling details for the fuel cell is given in Table 54.3

4. RESULTS AND DISCUSSION

The two systems are taken into consideration for the comparison of thermodynamic performance. Case A is for the conventional intercooled gas turbine power cycle whereas Case B is for the hybrid gas turbine power cycle. For the thermodynamic analysis, the energetic and exergetic performance of both systems were compared.

Table 54.3 Modeling equations for fuel cells

Nernst Potential	$V = V_o + \dfrac{RT}{nF}\ln\left(\dfrac{P_{H_2} \times P_{O_2}^{0.5}}{P_{H_2O}}\right)$
	Where, V_o is reversible cell potential [15]
	$V_o = 1.253 - 2.4516 \times 10^{-4}T$
Activation overpotentials [16]	V activ = (0.001698RTT − 1.254)F sinh-1
	* (id 4))
	2(13.087T − 1.096 * 10
Ohmic overpotentials [17]	$V_{ohm} = \delta A^k \exp\left(\dfrac{B^k}{T}\right) \times i_d$
Concentration overpotentials [17]	
Net cell potential	Vnet = V − Vact − Vohm − Vconc

But before this, the few results of fuel cells are also discussed. As we already discussed in modeling, the fuel cell is associated with the three different overpotentials as a function of temperature. Therefore, the performance of those overpotentials at different operating temperatures is given in Fig. 54.2–54.5. Increasing current density, all three overpotentials are increased. In activation overpotentials are a function of the inverse of the sin hyperbolic function therefore the overpotentials follow the same trend. Ohmic overpotentials follow the linear trend. Whereas in concentration overpotential it follows

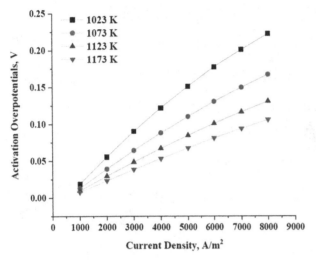

Fig. 54.2 Activation overpotentials

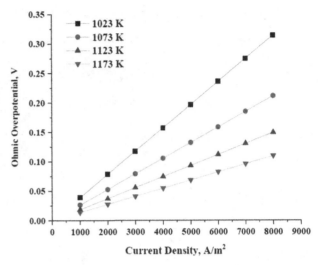

Fig. 54.3 Ohmic overpotentials

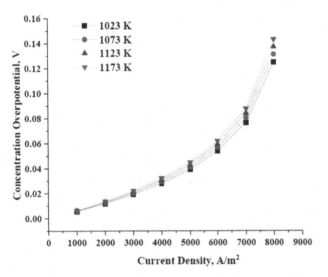

Fig. 54.4 Conventional overpotentials

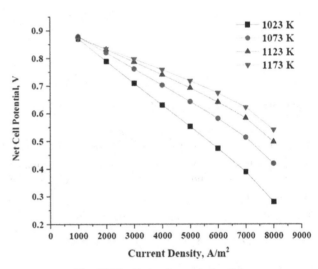

Fig. 54.5 Net cell overpotentials

the logarithmic trends. One important thing that is to be noted is that when the temperature change is considered, the trends in overpotential are the reverse of activation and ohmic overpotential. It means that as the working temperature of the fuel cell increases the activation and ohmic overpotential decrease whereas the concentration overpotential decreases. This is due to a reduction in the decrease in the concentration of ions available at the anode. Because at higher temperatures the rate of reaction increases and to maintain the reaction rate a large number of ions is needed at the anode electrolyte interface.

Table 54.4 represents the combined effect of Nernst potentials and the three discussed overpotentials. The net effect shows that as the current density increases the net

cell potential decreases, and as the temperature increases the net cell potential increases for the same current density only. For energy analysis first law of thermodynamics is used which gives us quantitative results of energy analysis. For qualitative results, the second law of thermodynamics is used, called exergy analysis. As the pressure ratio increases, the energy and exergy efficiency of the conventional gas turbine initially increases and after achieving optimum value it will start decreasing. The optimum value is reported at a pressure ratio of 6. For the hybrid system, the energy efficiency is approximately doubled, due to the integration of SOFC with the conventional gas turbine power cycle.

Figure 54.6 and Fig. 54.7 represent the exergy destruction of each component used in conventional (case A) and hybrid

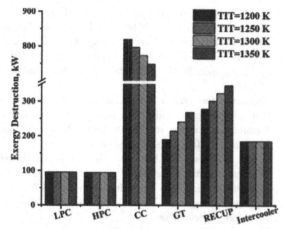

Fig. 54.6 Exergy destruction for Case A

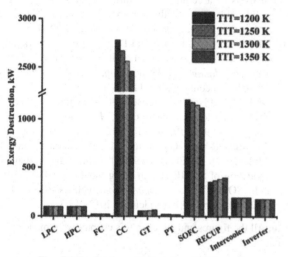

Fig. 54.7 Exergy destruction for Case B

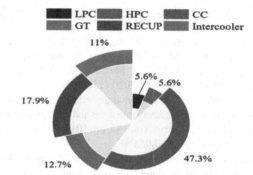

Fig. 54.8 Percentage-based exergy destruction for Case A

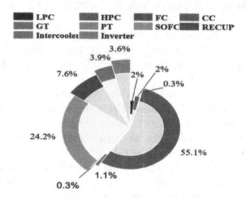

Fig. 54.9 Percentage-based exergy destruction for Case B

systems (case B), respectively. In case A the maximum exergy destruction is found to be in the combustion chamber, this is due to the combustion of fuel and chemical reactions in the combustion chamber. Similarly, in case B the maximum exergy is destroyed again in the combustion chamber, followed by SOFC. These are the two components that directly interact with fuel due to which maximum exergy destruction is found in that component.

Figure 54.8 and Fig. 54.9 represent the details contribution of exergy destruction for conventional and hybrid system, respectively. 47.3 % of exergy destruction is found in the combustion chamber for conventional systems whereas 55.1% of exergy is destroyed in CC followed by 24.2% in recuperator only.

Since these components have large exergy destruction, they are the least efficient. It means if the irreversibilities associated with these components are minimized then the performance of the overall system is significantly improved.

Therefore, instead of focusing on each component, just focus only on the combustion chamber and recuperator.

5. CONCLUSIONS

Conventional and hybrid configuration of gas turbines is thermodynamically compared. The energy and exergy efficiency of hybrid systems is found to be more compared to conventional systems. The Energy efficiency of the hybrid system is 40% more than conventional system. The quality of energy is also assessed. The exergetic efficiency of the hybrid system is 36% more than a conventional system. This improved performance of the hybrid system is one of the possible ways to improve the efficiency of existing power plants in India. This way the gap between demand and supply of electricity is minimized readily.

■ REFERENCES ■

1. *India Energy Outlook.* 2021. doi: 10.1787/ec2fd78d-en.
2. B. Zhu, "Solid oxide fuel cell (SOFC) technical challenges and solutions from nano-aspects," *Int. J. Energy Res.*, vol. 33, no. 13, pp. 1126–1137, 2009, doi: 10.1002/er.1600.
3. O. B. Inal and C. Deniz, "Assessment of fuel cell types for ships: Based on multi-criteria decision analysis," *J. Clean. Prod.*, vol. 265, Aug. 2020, doi: 10.1016/j.jclepro.2020.121734.

4. R. Kumar, V. S. Kumar, M. M. Butt, N. A. Sheikh, S. A. Khan, and A. Afzal, "Thermo-mechanical analysis and estimation of turbine blade tip clearance of a small gas turbine engine under transient operating conditions," *Appl. Therm. Eng.*, vol. 179, no. March, p. 115700, 2020, doi: 10.1016/j.applthermaleng.2020.115700.

5. T. Choudhary, "Thermodynamic assessment of SOFC-ICGT hybrid cycle : Energy analysis and entropy generation minimization," *Energy*, vol. 134, pp. 1013–1028, 2017, doi: 10.1016/j.energy.2017.06.064.

6. Y. N. Dabwan, L. Zhang, and G. Pei, "A novel inlet air cooling system to improve the performance of intercooled gas turbine combined cycle power plants in hot regions," *Energy*, vol. 283, no. May, p. 129075, 2023, doi: 10.1016/j.energy.2023.129075.

7. S. S. Rathore, V. R. Kar, and Sanjay, "Thermodynamic Analyses of an Intercooled Gas Turbine from Ceramic Material," *Arab. J. Sci. Eng.*, 2023, doi: 10.1007/s13369-023-07855-0.

8. C. Carcasci and L. Winchler, "Thermodynamic analysis of an Organic Rankine Cycle for waste heat recovery from an aeroderivative intercooled gas turbine," *Energy Procedia*, vol. a. 101, no. September, pp. 862–869, 2016, doi: 10.1016/j.egypro.2016.11.109.

9. O. Candra *et al.*, "Thermal and environmental optimization of an intercooled gas turbine toward a sustainable environment," *Chemosphere*, p. 139624, 2023.

10. F. Musharavati, S. Khanmohammadi, A. Pakseresht, and S. Khanmohammadi, "Waste heat recovery in an intercooled gas turbine system: Exergo-economic analysis, triple objective optimization, and optimum state selection," *J. Clean. Prod.*, vol. 279, p. 123428, 2021, doi: 10.1016/j.jclepro.2020.123428.

11. E. M. Leal, L. A. Bortolaia, and A. M. Leal Junior, "Technical analysis of a hybrid solid oxide fuel cell/gas turbine cycle," *Energy Convers. Manag.*, vol. 202, no. July, p. 112195, 2019, doi: 10.1016/j.enconman.2019.112195.

12. L. N. Rupiper, B. B. Skabelund, R. Ghotkar, and R. J. Milcarek,

13. "Impact of fuel type on the performance of a solid oxide fuel cell integrated with a gas turbine," *Sustain. Energy Technol. Assessments*, vol. 51, no. August 2021, p. 101959, 2022, doi: 10.1016/j.seta.2022.101959.

14. C. O. Colpan, I. Dincer, and F. Hamdullahpur, "Thermodynamic modeling of direct internal reforming solid oxide fuel cells operating with syngas," *Int. J. Hydrogen Energy*, vol. 32, no. 7, pp. 787–795, 2007, doi: 10.1016/j.ijhydene.2006.10.059.

15. Y. Haseli, I. Dincer, and G. F. Naterer, "Thermodynamic analysis of a combined gas turbine power system with a solid oxide fuel cell through exergy," *Thermochim. Acta*, vol. 480, pp. 1–9, 2008, doi: 10.1016/j.tca.2008.09.007.

16. M. Ni, M. K. H. Leung, and D. Y. C. Leung, "Parametric study of solid oxide fuel cell performance," *Energy Convers. Manag.*, vol. 48, no. 5, pp. 1525–1535, 2007, doi: 10.1016/j.enconman.2006.11.016.

17. M. Rokni, "Plant characteristics of an integrated solid oxide fuel cell cycle and a steam cycle," *Energy*, vol. 35, no. 12, pp. 4691–4699, 2010, doi: 10.1016/j.energy.2010.09.032.

18. J. Pirkandi, M. Ghassemi, M. H. Hamedi, and R. Mohammadi, "Electrochemical and thermodynamic modeling of a CHP system using tubular solid oxide fuel cell (SOFC-CHP)," *J. Clean. Prod.*, vol. 29–30, pp. 151–162, 2012, doi: 10.1016/j.jclepro.2012.01.03

Note: All the figures and tables in this chapter were made by the author.

Challenges and Opportunities for Innovation in India – Dr. Shweta Mishra et al. (eds)
© 2024 Taylor & Francis Group, London, ISBN 978-1-032-99842-8

Experimental Procedure of Copper Electroplating on Tungsten Powder

55

Beena Rizvi*

Assistant Professor,
Department of Mechanical Engineering,
Ambalika Institute of Management & Technology,
Lucknow

Abstract

Reinforcing, safe and protecting properties, to give some examples, can be accomplished by carrying out a surface material covering onto a designing part. Different components of these intensified parts can expand the usefulness of the part, for example, expanded life time and more intuitive surfaces. Tungsten has demonstrated to be a test to plate with different metals, yet whenever done accurately, the outcomes can consider the virus shower of tungsten. Cold showering tungsten particles alone gives a test in light of the fact that the powder is excessively hard and on second thought of sticking, it disintegrates the surface it is endeavoring to plate. Covering tungsten in a gentler metal, similar to copper, will consider the particles to stick to the surface and make a fortified and radiation safeguarded part. It likewise yields a superior surface to electroplate onto from now on, as tungsten itself is difficult to plate onto, so the copper layer gives the capacity to plate different metals without any problem. The reason for this exploration paper is to exemplify tungsten powder inside copper, then, at that point, increase the cycle to create mass measures of the material in a cluster cycle. The particles will be encased utilizing an electroplating strategy, that has been transformed into a semi-independent interaction for the simplicity of delivering mass powder. While electroless testimony has recently shown positive outcomes for accomplishing a uniform covering, making it a semi-group process for mass material would have a super expense in contrast with electrolytic statement. The tungsten particles have been effectively encased in copper by electrolytic statement here of trial and error utilizing a HF electro-scratch pretreatment and ultrasonic disturbance during electroplating. Further trial and error will incorporate superior techniques for blending and moving powder, as the exchange takes too lengthy between the engraving and the beginning of plating and the mixing strategy is massive and decreases the region that can be productively plated on.

Keywords

Resistant, Tungsten, Coating, Electrolytic deposition

*Corresponding author: beenarehan@gmail.com

DOI: 10.1201/9781003606260-55

1. INTRODUCTION

Presently Metal plating has been utilized in various applications over numerous years, similar to wear obstruction, consumption opposition, and improved designing properties. Tungsten covering has likewise started to arise in the insulating and hostile to radiation ventures, as it has a higher thickness than other well known enemies of radiations materials, like lead. In any case, its expense is a lot higher, prompting the utilization of tungsten just when the space for the radiation security is less positive for lead [3]. Concerning insulating, tungsten has the most elevated dissolving point among all metals, in addition to the progress metals, and it can hold its solidarity at those high temperatures. By and large, tungsten's hardness and high thickness give it many capabilities, for general and military purposes, as a covering layer on a part. Cold splash is a strong state testimony process in which metal powder is moved at high speeds and temperature well underneath the softening purpose in the material, causing molecule disfigurement on influence that outcomes in a solid metallurgical bond. The critical plastic twisting experienced by the particles shapes an adiabatic shear insecurity upon contact, separating surface oxides. Because of this break, shear is created at the contact point of interaction and material is ousted from the contact. This shear among particles and at the shower contact interface causes the strong state metallurgical holding [4].

Plasma, explosion and HVOF all work at higher temperatures than cold splash, yet explosion and HVOF have some speed cross-over with cold shower, while plasma is totally low speed application [5] There are numerous advanced metal splash procedures utilized all through industry, Figure 55.1 exhibits the functional edge for every one of the strategies. The virus splash process works at the most reduced temperature of all the customary shower procedures and the most noteworthy speed. Plasma, detonation, and High Velocity Oxygen Fuel (HVOF) all produce melted particles that shrink when they cool. As a result, high tensile residual stresses remain. Because of the low temperatures of cold splash, the particles are not liquefied, bringing about a lot more modest, and compressive, leftover pressure, in contrast with different techniques. In contrast to the particles of higher temperature depositions, which tend to change their crystalline structure upon resolidification [5], in cold spray deposition, the crystalline structure largely remains unchanged. The appearance of the coating is affected in different ways by these various coating methods. The higher temperature coatings show a lot higher porosity in contrast with cold splash, which has <1% porosity. This distinction is displayed in Fig. 55.2, a high temperature

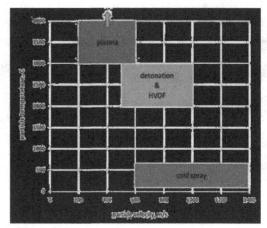

Fig. 55.1 A view at the operating ranges for metal deposition coatings

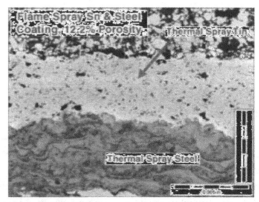

Fig. 55.2 Flame spray deposition of Sn and Steel, with a coating porosity of 12.2%. This image was created using backscattered electron (BSE) imaging [5]

fire splashed Sn covering, and Figs. 55.3, which are cold shower covering models.

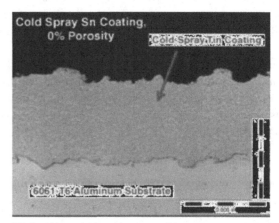

Fig. 55.3 Aluminum substrate cold spray coated with Sn displaying a 0% porosity, viewed in a BSE image [5]

2. Experimental Procedure

2.1 Purpose

Positive material properties can be acquired as the consequence of covering a part with a surface material. These surface coatings may, in some instances, offer a variety of capabilities, including increased strength, the capacity to solder, and wear resistance. The reason for this paper is to investigate different strategies for plating tungsten (W from Bison Tungsten), with copper, for an exclusive application. The grains of powder are being encased utilizing an electroplating technique, designed by Pay Yih (patent # 5,911,865) in 1997 [1]. A copper covering on the tungsten powder will allow it a superior opportunity to cling to a metal surface in a virus shower process. Copper is a milder metal that makes the misshapening of particles better, which is a key to the accomplishment for holding in the virus splash covering process. Metals have been applied to the outer layer of materials because of multiple factors, such as changing the erosion coefficient of the surface and to give another layer of wear safe material [2].

2.2 Method of Coating Particles

Powder particles should be covered in copper to permit the twisting required for fruitful clinging to one more metal during a virus splash process. Electroplating was looked into as a method for making the coating a semi-batch process on a large scale. Electroplating has numerous benefits These saved coatings can be accomplished in alternate ways other than electroplating, like electroless plating, and substance and actual fume statement (CVD and PVD, separately) processes. Electroless plating explicitly can be exceptionally viable for accomplishing a uniform covering on the powder, nonetheless, practically speaking, the technique brings about excessively high of an expense to be cutthroat in an enormous scope covering process. Concerning CVD and PVD, there is a restricted arrangement of covering materials, matched with much greater expenses and a lower statement rate.

2.3 Electroplating

In order to electroplate copper, a direct current must flow between two electrodes that are immersed in a copper salt solution in water. The cathode acts to diminish the Cu2+, copper particles, that are available in the arrangement. The copper particles gain electrons and show up at their impartial metal state to become saved on the substrate. All the while, the Cu at the anode is being oxidized by the current, changing Cu to Cu2+ particles, and recharging its fixation in the electrolyte arrangement. Electrons set free from the anode follow a way through the power supply to the cathode, where they connect with the copper particles

at the cathode surface. Tossing power gives a proportion of an arrangements capacity to plate complex designs with intrinsic surface intricacies. The tossing force of a still up in the air by the ionic conductivity of the arrangement, current productivity, and applied current thickness. High tossing power is related with almost equivalent plating thickness all through the surface, no matter what the intricacy. To build the tossing force of the copper electrolyte arrangement, there are different measures that can be taken. They incorporate, expanding the electrical conductivity of the arrangement, raising the pH, bringing down the ongoing thickness, expanding the temperature, and expanding the distance between the anodes.

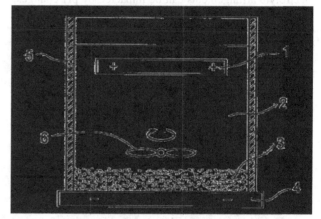

Fig. 55.4 Method of coating particles

Figure 55.4 Dr. Pay Yih's electroplating device. Powder (3) is confined to a container (5), in this case a beaker, that contains an electrolyte solution (2) to connect the anode (1) and cathode (4) by direct current. When the particles settle on the cathode, a metal stirrer (6) disperses the particles to allow for an even plating of the powder [1]. A third way to deal with electroplating utilizing the contraption is a crossover between the first and second and hypothetically would boost plating proficiency. This strategy was introduced to go with the gadget in the patent [1,8]. After the particles have been stirred and settled, only enough direct current is applied in this method to completely cover the cathode. The initial layer will receive a coating when the current is applied, and the subsequent layers will gradually receive a coating as they settle and come into contact with the powder pile. This means that multiple layers can be coated in a single cycle. The approximately settled powder will have the caught particles, similar as in technique two, notwithstanding, these particles will actually want to exist in more prominent amounts, nearer to the cathode due to the falling particles proceeding to trap them whenever plating has started. This strategy will likewise consider the electrolyte answer for stay present in the interparticle spaces dissimilar to previously. This permits the trial to have an ideal thickness of sedimented W, that will consider a maximal statement on the powder, rather than the cathode. The ideal sedimentation thickness is determined by the throwing power and covering power of the copper salt solution, the distance between the powder's top layer and the submerged anode's base (usually greater than 5 mm), and the particulate's density, morphology, and conductivity. The electroplating system can be firmly impacted by the electrolyte arrangement that it happens in. Electrolyte arrangements can be influenced to be higher tossing power arrangements or lower in view of focuses and measures of explicit parts in arrangement. The electrolyte arrangements can be impacted by pH changes, comparing to the shower sythesis change, and temperature vacillations.

3. RESULTS AND DISCUSSION

Utilizing the thickness computation introduced the thickness covering on a coin and W foil had the option to be approximated under the suspicion that the statement was 100 percent effective. Figure 55.5 shows a backscattered electron picture of one of the coins that was electroplated for roughly two hours in the HCl electrolyte shower. Utilizing the most extreme plating thickness showed in Fig. 55.6, 15.12 μm, Table 55.1 was developed to show the hypothetical estimation and the noticed benefits of plating thickness.

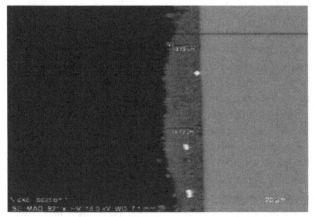

Fig. 55.5 This figure depicts the variable thicknesses of copper plated on a nickel coin for approximately 2 hours

Table 55.1 portrays the determined thickness esteems that were normal on a nickel coin following 2 hours. Note that the genuine worth is marginally lower than the normal because of copper misfortunes to the cathode during plating, so the proficiency was just 72%. The pace

Table 55.1 Thickness of Nickel plating

Thickness of Nickel Plating	Calculated value after experiment	Observed value	Effi-ciency
Thickness (micrometer/min)	0.4	N/A	N/A
Thickness (micrometer/2 min)	24.30	16.13	72%

of testimony during the examination was not consistent, which can be credited to the additional plating onto the cathode. Figure 55.6 delineates the statement of copper onto the cathode with little dendrites shaping on the top during the electrolytic testimony during a perceptible substrate test, for this situation W foil, however the nickel coins had similar outcomes.

Fig. 55.6 This figure depicts copper deposition and dendritic growth on the cathode, while showing the shadow of where the HF pretreated foil was during the deposition

The shadow towards the focal point of the cathode is where the HF pretreated foil refreshed, different tests had comparative engravings for W foil and nickel pieces. The principal action item is the copper testimony onto the cathode. Dendrite development should be visible on the cathode away from the foil spot, showing that a portion of the copper was consumed by the dendrites rather than the nickel or W foil, prompting the lower effectiveness esteem. A second illustration of a post-experiment beaker that highlights the foil imprints for testing the various foil types can be found in Fig. 55.6. Every one of the pictures were assessed similarly, BSE imaging with a 20 μm scale. Figure 55.7 portrays a powder test led at a lower direct current. The figure shows a great deal of copper agglomeration and an incredibly restricted measure of clinging to the

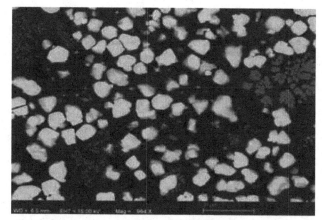

Fig. 55.7 This figure depicts the W powder without a pretreatment at a current of 0.6 A

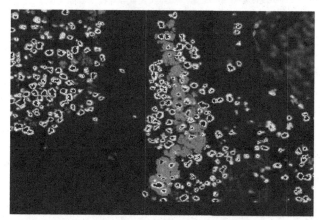

Fig. 55.8 A section of the HF pretreated W powder electroplated at a current of 0.25A

W powder surface. The copper agglomeration itself shows up in dendritic structure, demonstrating that it might have developed from the cathode at a high nearby current thickness spot. Copper stores where the electrolyte arrangement meets electrons. An exposed metal surface would be plated consistently for a moderate current thickness. A surface covered in non-conductive oxide would be plated exclusively at holes in the oxide covering. Ensuing affidavit would happen just on the recently kept copper, bringing about this high neighborhood current thickness, making the dendrite morphology happen.

The figure shows a current density of 2.12 A/dm2 and a current of 0.6 A. This exists in the ideal reach for plating in a corrosive copper shower, for this situation, the H2SO4 rendition, in any case, no plating is apparent, demonstrating that something is banning the copper from storing on a superficial level. Considering this, it was speculated that there was an oxide layer on the W powder forestalling the conduction of current to the surface. Every

one of the pictures contain comparable 20 µm scale bars. Allowed the 2-hour plating time, just few the particles were expected to be plated and assuming they were plated, there was a potential that they wouldn't be plated consistently, as not every one of their sides might have had the chance to be uncovered in the abbreviated examination. Figure 55.8 presentation areas of the HF pretreated and covered powder. The outcomes shown are reliable, in term of value, with the powder that the support provided as the objective.

4. Conclusion

- Starter tests showed effective electrodeposition of Cu on W on a naturally visible and minute scale. A few circumstances detailed in the writing as accommodating achievement didn't work for either W foil or powder, yet one set worked.

- For both macro and microscopic substrates, the combination of HF pretreatment with the copper sulfate and sulfuric acid bath solution produced the best results.

- Nitric corrosive wash and nonpretreated powders were precluded, as they didn't deliver effective coatings. This was ascribed to an oxide layer staying on the particles, where for the HF tests, it was effectively eliminated.

- Writing reports that a ultrasonic shower is important to keep particles disturbed all through the investigation to restrict agglomeration. In accordance with the literature, tests revealed that ultrasonic agitation significantly reduced agglomeration in HF-pretreated powderplated samples. Tests were not performed to segregate the impacts of these two changes.

- The HF pretreated powder permitted great plating and showed guarantee for imitating the modern powder that is as of now not accessible. Moreover, the technique for electrolytic testimony is a minimal expense plating strategy that gives vow to use to get industry standard particles.

■ REFERENCES ■

1. P. Yih, "Method for Electroplating of micron Particulates with Metal Coatings". United States Patent 5911865, 11 April 1997.
2. M. Schlesinger and M. Paunovic, "Electrodeposition of Copper," in Modern Electroplating, fifth edition, John Wiley & Sons, Inc., 2010, pp. 33–78.
3. A guide to the use of lead for radiation shielding. (2017). Lead Industries Association, Inc.doi:10.18411/a-2017-023
4. Hall, Aaron Christopher., et al. "Deposition Behavior in Cold Sprayed Copper- Tungsten Metal Matrix Composites." Deposition Behavior in Cold Sprayed Copper-Tungsten

Metal Matrix Composites. (Conference) | OSTI.GOV, 1 Jan. 2015, www.osti.gov/servlets/purl/1244889.

5. Army Reasearch Lab Center for Cold Spray, "ARL Center for Cold Spray - Advantages," United States Army Research Laboratory, 19 May 2015. [Online]. Available: http://www.arl.army.mil/www/default.cfm?page=371. [Accessed 11 March 2018].

6. "Properties of Tungsten." Buffalo Tungsten Inc. Tungsten Powder Homepage, www.buffalotungsten.com/index.html.

7. Safety Data Sheet Tungsten Powder; Buffalo Tungsten Inc., Depew, NY, Aug 16, 2016. (accessed Mar 11, 2018).

8. Xu, Jiudong, et al. "Preparation of Copper Coated Tungsten Powders by Intermittent Electrodeposition." Powder Technology, vol. 264, 2014, pp. 561–569., doi:10.1016/j.powtec.2014.06.005.

9. G. DiBari, "Electrodeposition of Nickel," in Modern Electroplating, Wiley & Sons, Inc., 2010, pp. 79–110.

10. B. Nejad, "Role of PH & temperature in bright nickel(Watts) plating," Linkden, 14 July 2014.

11. Rigali, J.R. (2017). ELECTROLESS DEPOSITION & ELECTROPLATING OF NICKEL ON CHROMIUMNICKEL CARBIDE POWDER (Master's thesis).

12. K. C. Wilson, G. R. Addie, A. Sellgren and R. Clift, "Chapter 2 Review of fluid and particle mechanics," in Slurry Transport Using Centrifugal Pumps, Springer US, 2006, pp. 15–50.

13. Lashmore, D. and Kelley, D. (1995). PROCESS FOR ELECTRODEPOSITING METAL AND METAL ALLOYS ON TUNGSTEN, MOLYBDENUMAND OTHER DFFICULT TO PLATE METALS. US5456819.

Note: All the figures and tables in this chapter were made by the author.

Challenges and Opportunities for Innovation in India – Dr. Shweta Mishra et al. (eds)
© 2024 Taylor & Francis Group, London, ISBN 978-1-032-99842-8

A Review of Advances in Design and Technologies for Solar Panel Cleaning Systems

56

Madhav Kumar Mishra[1],
Prashant Sharma[2], Jitendra Verma[3]
Department of Mechanical Engineering,
Institute of Engineering and Technology, Bundelkhand University,
Jhansi, (U. P.), India

Vandana Pathak[4]
Department of Mechanical Engineering,
Ambalika Institute of Management & Technology,
Lucknow, (U. P.), India

Abstract

This comprehensive review paper aims to thoroughly analyze the latest developments, solutions, and future opportunities in the area of solar panel cleaning robots over the last decade. The key focus will be examining emerging technologies, from early methods utilizing essential components to more innovative solutions integrating advanced mechatronics and sensors. The paper will also evaluate different panel cleaning techniques studied through experiments and their suitability under changing environmental conditions. The review seeks to identify current trends and applications of these automated cleaning systems while highlighting promising research directions that can optimize their operations and maximize returns on investments for solar farm owners.

Keywords

Solar farm, Solar panel cleaning, Dust accumulation, Cleaning techniques

1. INTRODUCTION

Solar energy presents a reliable, carbon-free solution to meet the world's growing power needs. This industry's core to expansion is photovoltaic solar panels, which utilize the photovoltaic effect to transform sunlight into electricity directly. Modern PV cells employ a semiconductor material typically crystalline silicon at the microscale fashioned with an intricate arrangement of billions of p-n junctions. Each junction is primed to initiate a cascading reaction of electron activity when struck by photons. However, a leading sustainability challenge for solar has emerged

[1]madhavkumarmishra285@gmail.com, [2]bholapandit9149@gmail.com, [3]jitendravermajss@gmail.com, [4]vp9415809167@gmail.com

DOI: 10.1201/9781003606260-56

dust accumulation inhibiting consistent yields. Particulate matter deposited from environmental vectors like wind, rain, and passing wildlife impedes irradiation levels, impacting p-n junction activity [1]. Experimental research has demonstrated the power reductions this causes, with even a minuscule 0.5 mg/cm^2 layer capable of 10-20 % degradation [2]. More severely, prolonged exposure without cleaning under arid conditions can exceed 50 % diminishment after only half a year due to the static dust film developing [3]. The reduction in the solar intensity due to dust accumulation is presented in Fig. 56.1. Therefore cleaning the solar panel is regularly needed. However, manually dusting encompassing solar sites poses logistical difficulties. The process proves labor-intensive, unsafe on elevated structures, and cost-prohibitive at the plant scales required [3].

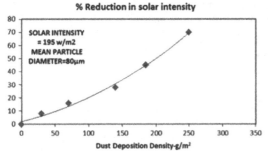

Fig. 56.1 Solar intensity reduction versus amount of dust deposition density [4]

This is where automated cleaning robotics demonstrate promise if engineered with reliable, low-cost functionality. Following earlier designs utilizing basic controls [1], technological refinements now leverage mechatronics, sensors, and solar tracking to autonomously navigate complex terrain while scrubbing each panel thoroughly. This review paper describes the various techniques used for cleaning the solar panel in detail.

2. METHODOLOGIES USED TO CLEAN SOLAR PANELS

Maintaining clean photovoltaic surfaces is paramount to maximizing solar energy generation. Researchers have developed and evaluated various cleaning techniques suitable for deployment scales and environments.

2.1 Manual Cleaning Methods

One of the simplest and earliest solar panel cleaning methods involves manual cleaning using cloth, brush, or water. Hegazy [5] studied the impact of dust accumulation on the transmittance of sunlight through glass covers. The researcher noted that manual wet cloth cleaning restored

80-90 % of the power loss but required significant time and labor.

However, manual cleaning has its limitations. A study by Ghazi et al. [4] highlighted that it is inefficient for large solar farms due to labor intensiveness. Other shortcomings include the potential for scratches or damage to the panel surface during the process. It also cannot be effectively used in locations with rugged terrains or high-rise installations.

2.2 Chemical Cleaning Methods

Chemical cleaning involves specialized solutions/agents that can dissolve or remove dirt, dust, and other contaminants from the solar panel surface. Jaswal and Sinha [6] discussed various chemical cleaning formulations and mechanisms that have been investigated. Super-hydrophobic and self-cleaning coatings are examples of chemical cleaning methods gaining popularity. When applied to the glass surface of solar panels, they enable easy roll-off of dust and water during rains without leaving any residues behind. However, concerns regarding the long-term stability of such coatings and compatibility with all panel types need further evaluation [4]. Tayel et al. [7] developed a hydrophobic Nano coating solution combining PDMS and SiO2 that can be applied on photovoltaic surfaces. Under outdoor conditions, tests demonstrated a 57 % lower dust density accumulation on coated panels than on reference panels after 40 days of exposure. Water droplets also removed up to 74 % of deposited dust through rolling action, enabled by the coating's hydrophobicity. As a result, the Nano coated panels showed 30.7 % higher energy conversion efficiency. The coating's visible light transmittance ensures minimal optical losses as well. Compared to previous chemical formulations, the functional stability exceeds over longer durations. The passive self-cleaning mechanism circumvents manual labor, significantly lowering operating costs. In another study, Park et al. [8] developed an environmentally friendly aqueous cleaning formulation featuring plant-derived surfactants that showed superior dust removal efficiency from solar panels without causing surface damage compared to traditional alkaline cleaners. This opens up new eco-friendly options for chemical cleaning. The Super hydrophobic coating is depicted in Fig. 56.2. Together,

Fig. 56.2 Super hydrophobic coating Kleen-Boost [8]

these studies began validating options for chemical-based passive cleaning that are complementary to manual efforts and suitable for large-scale deployments. However, long-term performance and environmental effects require further research.

2.3 Semi-Automatic Cleaning Methods

Collectively, such work moved manual processes toward higher productivity through mechanization tailored for large ground-mounted PV farms, seeing savings in water, cleaning chemicals, and labor over the long run. Standardized models require further cost reductions to compete commercially worldwide, however. Semi-automatic cleaning systems utilize mechanical mechanisms assisted by water/chemical agents for cleaning. A study by Kazem et al. [9] proposed a semi-automatic cleaning concept involving wiper blades and water spray nozzles installed on the module frame. The wiper can be electrically operated once or twice a day for cleaning. Thomas et al. [10] fabricated a battery-powered automated cleaning robot with rotating nylon brushes and onboard water storage for wet scrubbing. The locomotion relies on motorized wheels traversing rails installed at the site. Automatic operation occurs through an interval timer, and the limit switches to the reverse direction at the row end. While requiring considerable fixed infrastructure, the design focuses on water conservation and reuse, which provides environmental benefits. Tests gave promising improvements but lacked quantified efficiency gains. Ongoing enhancements envision complete energy self-sufficiency through solar charging. Sagar et al. [11] studied a unique dual-axis solar tracker integrated with a water-dispensing cleaning mechanism that travels across the length and breadth of solar arrays atop the tracker platform periodic activation of sprinklers and wipers aided in the removal of thick dust layers. While effective, synchronizing cleaning movements with sun-tracking added complexity. Moreover, water scarcity is a hurdle in many solar-rich regions.

2.4 Fully Automatic Cleaning Methods

Researchers have explored fully automated cleaning solutions using alternative techniques to tackle the issues associated with water usage. Among the feasible choices, electrostatic-based, fully automated cleaning systems have recently gained significant attention. As Derakhshandeh et al. [12] proposed in their work "Investigation of an electrostatic solar panel cleaning concept", the application of high voltage electrostatic fields can remove over 95 % of dust particles by electrostatic attraction within seconds without using water. Rapid cleaning cycles ensure higher annual energy outputs. Zatsarinnaya and Amirov [13] developed an automated system utilizing a linear actuator

design powered by a stepper motor. Their proposed solution features a carriage with a mounted nylon spiral brush that traverses horizontally across solar panel surfaces along a threaded rod and aluminum guide rail. The brush rotation coupled with linear motion removes dust particles upon periodic activation without human intervention. Custom microcontroller code controls the cleaning cycles while monitoring sensor feedback on solar irradiation changes. A key advantage is the system retrofits onto existing panel arrays as an autonomous add-on module. The simplicity also enables cost-effective adoption. However, the long-term reliability of the mechanics and sensors remains invalidated. The study served as an initial proof of concept for the approach.

Seeking to address efficiency losses in solar street lights from dust accumulation, Maindad et al. [14] developed a self-cleaning solution leveraging electromechanical actuators. The system features two gear motors coupled to rotate nylon brushes that scrub panels while traversing horizontally along a rail. Linear motion comes from additional motors driving a belt-pulley mechanism. Onboard microcontroller code triggers automated periodic activation, with limit switches reversing direction at the end of each row. A separate water pump sprays panels ahead of the brushes, supporting wet cleaning. The modular design enables retrofitting onto existing installations. Tests gave improved energy yields compared to uncleaned panels, confirming the concept's viability as given in Table 56.1. Ongoing work looks to enhance reliability using sensors for fault diagnostics. While constrained to small-scale structures, the study demonstrates that automation can effectively liberate labor and boost solar asset productivity. Commercially available examples include the robotic cleaning system using electrostatic charge induction technique and PVD solar's dust free DF-50 using triboelectric charging technology. Both systems claim less than 10 minutes cleaning speeds for megawatt-scale solar farms with easy retrofitting on existing installations [15].

As technologies mature, standalone cleaning stations will provide round the clock sanitation for large MW-scale parks through networked artificial intelligence and Internet of Things connectivity [16]. Future standardization may stimulate further cost reductions, enabling worldwide adoption as discussed in Table 56.2.

Overall, solar panels have become essential in sustainable energy and water supplies globally, thanks to multifaceted research that has systematically improved performance year after year. While technical hurdles remain around prolonged low-maintenance operations, the exponential growth trajectory indicates solar power backed by efficient cleaning solutions will only become more integral

Table 56.1 The given below tables shows the impact of the cleaning system [14]

Day	Power output reading before installation of cleaning system			Power output reading after installation of cleaning system		
	Voltage(volts)	Current(amp)	Power(watt)	Voltage(volts)	Current(amp)	Power(watt)
1	15.60	1.25	19.5	16.00	1.25	20
2	15.27	1.24	18.93	15.98	1.24	19.81
3	15.12	1.14	17.23	15.98	1.23	19.85
4	15.04	1.08	16.24	16.01	1.24	19.82
5	15.01	1.09	16.36	15.99	1.26	20.14
6	14.92	1.06	15.81	15.97	1.25	19.96
7	14.70	1.01	14.84	15.99	1.24	19.95

Table 56.2 Comparison between various cleaning methods [9]

Method	Manual	Automatic				Coating method	
	Washing & brushing	Water Spray Machine	Static Robotic Cleaning	Portable Robotic Cleaning		Super hydrophilic coating	Super hydrophobic coating
Operational Cost	High	Medium	Low	Low "		Low	Low
CO2 Emissions	Medium	Medium	Low	Nil		Low	Low
Labor costs	High	Low	Nil	Nil		Low	Low
Water wastage	High	High	Medium "	Low		Low	Low
Air pollution	Medium	Medium	Medium	Medium		Low	Low
Fuel consumption	High	High	Low "	Low		Low	Low
Human safety	Low	High	"High "	High		High	High
Major Advantage	Reliable	Sustainable and requires almost no human intervention				Easier method to remove dust, especially for titled PV's	
Major Disadvantage	Slow and labor-intensive	High costs of maintenance				Reduced electrical efficiency due to reduced solar irradiance absorption	

worldwide. With pollution rising along with electricity demands, harnessing the sun's bounty presents a bright future, energizing lives cleanly.

3. CONCLUSION

Two major discussion points emerge looking ahead. First, further work must validate chemical treatments, coatings, and other passive approaches to self-cleaning under real-world weathering over more extended periods. Confirming multi-year durability remains a challenge delaying widespread adoption. Second, fully autonomous cleaning machines still require cost reductions comparable to human labor before competing commercially at utility scales. Continued mechatronics advancements may accelerate such competitiveness.

Researchers have made strides in advancing effectiveness, efficiency, and scalability when considering the various cleaning techniques explored across manual, chemical,

semi-automatic, and fully automated methods. From 3D printed wiper prototypes to sensor-driven controls, each new study incrementally moves the industry closer to reliable, low-maintenance solutions optimized for diverse environments worldwide. While manual cleaning remains practical for distributed applications, automation appears essential to economically serving vast ground-mounted "solar farms" of the future.

■ REFERENCES ■

1. A. Makalesi *et al.*, "A Solar Panel Cleaning Robot Design and Application," *Eur. J. Sci. Technol.*, vol. 3, pp. 343–348, Oct. 2019.
2. A. K. Mondal and K. Bansal, "A brief history and future aspects in automatic cleaning systems for solar photovoltaic panels," *Adv. Robot.*, vol. 29, no. 8, pp. 515–524, Apr. 2015.
3. M. K. Swain, M. Mishra, R. C. Bansal, and S. Hasan, "A Self-Powered Solar Panel Automated Cleaning System: Design and Testing Analysis," *Electr. Power Components Syst.*, vol. 49, no. 3, pp. 308–320, 2021.

4. S. Ghazi, A. Sayigh, and K. Ip, "Dust effect on flat surfaces – A review paper," *Renew. Sustain. Energy Rev.*, vol. 33, pp. 742–751, May 2014.

5. A. A. Hegazy, "Effect of dust accumulation on solar transmittance through glass covers of plate-type collectors," *Renew. energy*, vol. 22, no. 4, pp. 525–540, 2001.

6. A. Jaswal and M. K. Sinha, "A Review on Solar Panel Cleaning Through Chemical Self-cleaning Method," *Lect. Notes Mech. Eng.*, pp. 835–844, 2021.

7. S. A. Tayel, A. E. Abu El-Maaty, E. M. Mostafa, and Y. F. Elsaadawi, "Enhance the performance of photovoltaic solar panels by a self-cleaning and hydrophobic nanocoating," *Sci. Reports 2022 121*, vol. 12, no. 1, pp. 1–13, Dec. 2022.

8. Y. B. Park, H. Im, M. Im, and Y. K. Choi, "Self-cleaning effect of highly water-repellent microshell structures for solar cell applications," *J. Mater. Chem.*, vol. 21, no. 3, pp. 633–636, Dec. 2010.

9. H. A. Kazem, M. T. Chaichan, A. H. A. Al-Waeli, and K. Sopian, "A review of dust accumulation and cleaning methods for solar photovoltaic systems," *J. Clean. Prod.*, vol. 276, p. 123187, Dec. 2020.

10. S. K. Thomas, S. Joseph, T. S. Sarrop, S. Bin Haris, and R. Roopak, "Solar panel automated cleaning (SPAC) system," *2018 Int. Conf. Emerg. Trends Innov. Eng. Technol. Res. ICETIETR 2018*, Nov. 2018.

11. B. S. Sagar, B. Bairwa, Ganavi M, N. Arshiya, B. Sharavani, and Jayashalini, "Microcontroller based automatic dual axis solar tracking and cleaning system," *AIP Conf. Proc.*, vol. 2461, no. 1, Aug. 2022.

12. J. Farrokhi Derakhshandeh *et al.*, "A comprehensive review of automatic cleaning systems of solar panels," *Sustain. Energy Technol. Assessments*, vol. 47, p. 101518, Oct. 2021.

13. Y. N. Zatsarinnaya and D. I. Amirov, "Automated system for cleaning solar panels based on a linear actuator," *IOP Conf. Ser. Mater. Sci. Eng.*, vol. 1035, no. 1, p. 012001, 2021.

14. N. Maindad, A. Gadhave, S. Satpute, and B. Nanda, "Automatic Solar Panel Cleaning System," *SSRN Electron. J.*, Apr. 2020.

15. A. Bari, P. C. M, U. Student, and A. professor, "Automatic Solar Panel Cleaning System," *Int. J. Adv. Sci. Res. Eng. (IJASRE), ISSN2454-8006, DOI 10.31695/IJASRE*, vol. 4, no. 7, pp. 26–31, Jun. 2018.

16. N. Khadka, A. Bista, B. Adhikari, A. Shrestha, D. Bista, and B. Adhikary, "Current Practices of Solar Photovoltaic Panel Cleaning System and Future Prospects of Machine Learning Implementation," *IEEE Access*, vol. 8, pp. 135948–135962, 2020.

Challenges and Opportunities for Innovation in India – Dr. Shweta Mishra et al. (eds)
© 2024 Taylor & Francis Group, London, ISBN 978-1-032-99842-8

Benchmarking of Regression Algorithms on Major Evaluation Criteria for Stock Price Prediction

57

Satish Kumar Singh*

Research Scholar,
Department of CSE, Integral University,
Lucknow, U.P.

Sheeba Praveen

Associate Professor,
Department of CSE, Integral University,
Lucknow, U.P.

Abstract

It's challenging to forecast stock market values with any degree of accuracy due to the financial markets' complexity and volatility. Although several approaches, including technical and fundamental analysis, have been employed, none of them can provide perfect accuracy. But other techniques, including deep learning and machine learning algorithms that are trained on past data, can produce projections that are more realistic and accurate within given confidence intervals. In order to confirm the correctness of various regression algorithms, we are benchmarking them in this study using their R2 score and RMSE values. According to our findings, linear regression offers superior accuracy and outperforms all other methods in terms of R2, RMSE, and R2.

Keywords

Stocks, Machine learning, Deep learning, Price forecasting, Accuracy

1. INTRODUCTION

Stock market price prediction entails employing different approaches and methodologies to predict the future movement of stock prices. These may include fundamental analysis, technical analysis, machine learning and deep learning with sentiment analysis based quantitative models [1] [2]. Regression analysis is a typical statistical technique for predicting stock market prices. It entails using a mathematical model to historical data to determine the links between independent factors (such as economic indicators, firm performance measurements, or technical indicators) and the dependent variable (stock prices) [3]. The following Fig. 57.1 represents the steps involved in the regression process.

*Corresponding author: satishkrsingh167@gmail.com

DOI: 10.1201/9781003606260-57

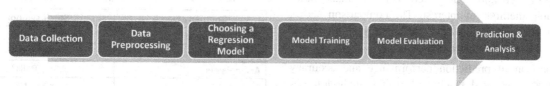

Fig. 57.1 Steps involved in regression process

The most popular regression techniques are highlighted below [4]. However, the accuracy is the major factor that decides the effectiveness of the algorithm used.

1.1 Machine Learning Algorithms

A. Linear Regression: A dependent variable, sometimes referred to as the response variable or outcome, and one or more independent variables, such as predictors, repressors, or traits, are modeled statistically using linear regression. Finding the best-fitting linear regression (for simple linear regression) or hyperplane (for multiple linear regressions) that best represents the dependent variable's variation with changes in the independent components is the goal [3].

B. Polynomial Regression: Regression analysis known as polynomial regression uses a polynomial of degree n to represent the relationship between the independent variable (y) and the dependent variable (x). In comparison to straightforward linear regression, this indicates that the model can handle more intricate, nonlinear relationships.

C. Support Vector Regression (SVR): It functions effectively for both linear and non-linear interactions. The concepts of Support Vector Machines (SVM) are applied to the field of regression analysis through the regression approach known as Support Vector Regression (SVR). Similar to SVM for classification, SVR is based on the notion of finding a hyper plane that maximizes the margin while offering the greatest fit to the data.

1.2 Evaluation Criteria

The major evaluation criteria that have been used in earlier works are given as follows [5]. The accuracy has been a major issue in the stock market price prediction. The following metrices are the important parameters to check the accuracy of the regression algorithms.

A. R-squared (R^2): The coefficient of determination, or R-squared, is a statistical metric used to evaluate the quality of fit of a regression model. It shows the percentage of the dependent variable's variance that can be explained by the independent variables. Put

simply, R-squared displays the percentage of the dependent variable's overall variation that can be accounted for by the model's independent variables. It has a range of 0 to 1.

B. Root Mean Squared Error (RMSE): The Root Mean Squared Error (RMSE) is a commonly used statistic to evaluate the performance of a regression model. It is effectively the square root of the Mean Squared Error (MSE) and provides a measure of the average magnitude of the errors between planned and actual values, with the benefit of being in the same units as the target variable [9].

2. Literature Review

Several researchers used their work to produce precise solutions to this dynamic problem, and they proposed several ways for predicting the stock market. In earlier work Awan et al. [3] concluded that Liner regression produced much precise results compared to other machine learning models like decision tree which was unbale to produce accuracy in the prediction. Panwar et. al. [6] also evaluated the importance of Linear regression and proved better than SVM. In the work of Eka et al. [7] on Indonesian market they found that, the linear regression model can generate accurate predictions which may help investors to determine what to buy or sell in the share market. Bhuriya et. al. [8] also used liner regression and found it best for price prediction on different criteria.

In another work of Kong [9], The share price of the Tesla company was predicted using six machine learning algorithms. These algorithms are used to analyze and forecast the stock of Tesla, a pioneer in the field of new energy vehicles, and include linear regression, polynomial regression, XGBoost, ARIMA, Prophet, and LSTM. He used the RMSE metric to evaluate the performance and fount that polynomial regression was the second-best algorithm to predict the price after the LSTM.

Based on historical datasets, Dash et al. [12] suggested a new Support Vector Machine (SVM) based model. The suggested approach is utilized to analyze several stock market performance metrics. The computed root mean square error and mean absolute percentage error of the suggested approach are compared to many other comparable methods of interest. The comparison shows that, for the chosen datasets, the suggested technique predicts stocks with greater accuracy.

A comparison of prediction performance and accuracy between statistics and machine learning methodologies was carried out, as is also clear from earlier works by Bhattacharjee et al. [13]. The results showed that machine learning approaches are more accurate than statistical approaches for predicting stock prices.

3. METHODOLOGY

In this work, we are benchmarking different regression algorithms based on historical data of different stock prices of last 20 years. The objective is to find the few of the best regression algorithm by calculating and analysing Root Mean Square Error (RMSE) and R^2 score. The detailed methodology has already been discussed in the Fig. 57.1. However, the details of the dataset used and tools and techniques implemented for study are as follows:

3.1 Datasets

We collected historical data sets of stock prices for five different well-known companies for last 20 years. These datasets were gathered via Google Dataset Search, Kaggle.com, and Yahoo Finance, among other sources. These figures can include a company's close, high, open, and low prices. Closing prices are the stock values at the conclusion of a trading day or session when the stock market closes. Opening prices are the prices at which stocks trade when a stock market opens. The stocks and their code, we selected for our study are given in Table 57.1 and the sample data set used in the study have been represented by Table 57.2 as follows:

3.2 Tools and Techniques

Three regression algorithms—linear regression, polynomial regression, and support vector regression (SVR)—which are already covered in section 1.1—were employed to analyse historical stock price data over

Table 57.1 Company names and stock symbols

Company Name	Stock symbol
Adani Enterprises	ADANIENT
Apollo Hospitals	APOLLOHOSP
Asian Paints	ASIANPAINT
Axis Bank	AXISBANK
Bajaj Finance	BAJFINANCE

Table 57.2 Historical dataset sample for study

Date	Open	High	Low	Close
07-02-2002	22.383	22.383	21.403	21.697
08-02-2002	22.67	22.92	22.667	22.677
09-02-2002	21.37	22.783	21.37	22.52

the previous 20 years. As mentioned in section 1.2, the implementation was carried out to determine the model's accuracy by computing the associated errors on Root Mean Squared Error (RMSE), and R2 score. Google Colab is a hosted Jupyter Notebook service that requires no setup and delivers free computing resources like GPUs and TPUs, especially well-suited for machine learning, data research, and teaching. These models are used in Python and panda libraries utilizing this service.

4. RESULTS AND DISCUSSION

In order to estimate the model's accuracy, we applied four distinct regression algorithms: support vector regression (SVR), polynomial regression, lasso regression, and linear regression. We also computed the associated evaluation metrics. The graph that follows depicts these.

4.1 R2 Score

R-squared is a statistical metric used to evaluate a regression model's goodness of fit. It shows the percentage of the dependent variable's overall variation that can be accounted for by the model's independent variables. It has a range of 0 to 1. The R2 score of the five stocks was determined using four distinct algorithms, as shown below:

STOCK/MODEL	LR	PR	SVR
ADANIENT	0.9651	0.9612	0.963
APOLLOHOSP	0.9658	0.9628	0.961
ASIANPAINT	0.966	0.9652	0.9635
AXISBANK	0.9585	0.9568	0.9572
BAJFINANCE	0.9541	0.9521	0.9507
Average	0.9619	0.95962	0.95908

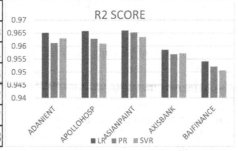

Fig. 57.2 Calculated R2 score on three different algorithms for five different stocks

We can observe that in individual stock calculation, LR, PR and SVR have approximately equal values but when we compare the average values of the individual algorithm/ model, the LR is emerging as the best algorithm/model in the experimental results.

4.2 Root Mean Squared Error (RMSE)

With the advantage of being in the same units as the target variable, it is the square root of the Mean Squared Error (MSE) and gives an indication of the average size of errors between projected and actual values. The following are the RMSE values that were determined for ten stocks using various algorithms:

STOCK/MODEL	LR	PR	SVR
ADANIENT	10.2520	10.2624	10.2725
APOLLOHOSP	10.3564	10.3675	10.3785
ASIANPAINT	10.2914	10.2915	10.3018
AXISBANK	10.3456	10.3417	10.3710
BAJFINANCE	10.2638	10.2614	10.2810
Average	**10.3018**	**10.3049**	**10.3210**

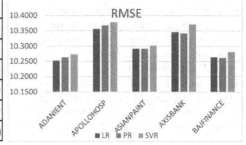

Fig. 57.3 Calculated RMSE score on three different algorithms for five different stocks

It is evident form the above data that RMSE is minimum for LR in almost all the individual stocks and even in the average RMSE for all the stock again, LR is producing the minimum RMSE i.e. 10.3018 and clearly emerging as the best model for the price prediction based on historical data.

The calculated average values of different metrices have been given below Fig. 57.4.

5. CONCLUSION

The individual average values of the all the metrices for each algorithm show that Linear regression (LR) is leading in its performance in R2 score. Therefore, it is concluded that LR is the best algorithm for the price prediction based on historical data among the above used algorithms.

After analysing the ten different stocks on four different algorithms, we concluded that Linear Regression (LR) is the best for predicting the stock prices based on historical data with more accuracy than other algorithms. LR also

performed comparatively better than on all the considered criteria i.e. R2, RMSE, MSE against all the other models implemented i.e. PR and SVR. Any other factors effecting stock prices like market sentiments and company performance, have not been considered in this work. The other models based on CNN, RNN and LSTM can be implemented in future with other factors effecting stock market to improve the prediction process.

■ REFERENCES ■

1. Idrees, S.M.; Alam, M.A.; Agarwal, P. A prediction approach for stock market volatility based on time series data. IEEE Access 2019, 7, 17287–17298.
2. Nti, I.K.; Adekoya, A.F.; Weyori, B.A. A systematic review of fundamental and technical analysis of stock market predictions. Artif. Intell. Rev. 2020, 53, 3007–3057.
3. Mazhar Javed Awan et. al., Social Media and Stock Market Prediction: A Big Data Approach, Computers, Materials & Continua, DOI:10.32604/cmc.2021.014253

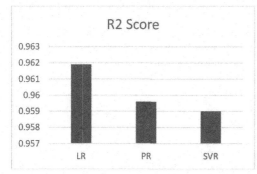
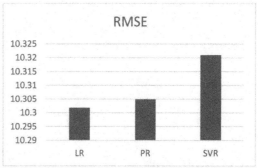

Fig. 57.4 Average R2 and RMSE score of above implementation

4. Mahinda MailagahaKumbure, Christoph Lohrmann, Pasi Luukka, Jari Porras, Machine learning techniques and data for stock market forecasting: A literature review, Expert Systems With Applications 197 (2022) 116659, https://doi.org/10.1016/j.eswa.2022.116659

5. Dattatray P. Gandhmal, K. Kumar, Systematic analysis and review of stock market prediction techniques, Computer Science Review 34 (2019) 100190, https://doi.org/10.1016/j.cosrev.2019.08.001

6. B. Panwar, G. Dhuriya, P. Johri, S. Singh Yadav and N. Gaur, "Stock Market Prediction Using Linear Regression and SVM," 2021 International Conference on Advance Computing and Innovative Technologies in Engineering (ICACITE), Greater Noida, India, 2021, pp. 629–631, doi: 10.1109/ICACITE51222.2021.9404733

7. Andi PrimafiraBumandava Eka, Asri Ady Bakri, Leny Yuliyani, Utilizing linear regression to forecast the stock price fluctuations of top-rated companies, Jurnal Info Sains :Informatika dan SainsVolume 14 , Number 01, 2024, DOI 10.54209/infosains.v14i01

8. D. Bhuriya, G. Kaushal, A. Sharma and U. Singh, "Stock market predication using a linear regression," 2017 International conference of Electronics, Communication and Aerospace Technology (ICECA), Coimbatore, India, 2017, pp. 510–513, doi: 10.1109/ICECA.2017.8212716.

9. Kong, Y. (2024). Machine Learning in Tesla's Stock Price Prediction. Highlights in Business, Economics and Management, 24, 272–277. https://doi.org/10.54097/f4psd953

10. Roy, S.S., Mittal, D., Basu, A., Abraham, A. (2015). Stock Market Forecasting Using LASSO Linear Regression Model. In: Abraham, A., Krömer, P., Snasel, V. (eds) Afro-European Conference for Industrial Advancement. Advances in Intelligent Systems and Computing, vol 334. Springer, Cham. https://doi.org/10.1007/978-3-319-13572-4_31

11. Shijie Li and Mingyu Si "A comparison between linear regression, lasso regression, decision tree, XGBoost, and RNN for asset price strategies", Proc. SPIE 12330, International Conference on Cyber Security, Artificial Intelligence, and Digital Economy (CSAIDE 2022), 123301A (23 August 2022); https://doi.org/10.1117/12.2646634

12. Dash, R.K., Nguyen, T.N., Cengiz, K. et al. Fine-tuned support vector regression model for stock predictions. Neural Comput&Applic 35, 23295–23309 (2023). https://doi.org/10.1007/s00521-021-05842-w

13. I. Bhattacharjee and P. Bhattacharja, "Stock Price Prediction: A Comparative Study between Traditional Statistical Approach and Machine Learning Approach," 2019 4th International Conference on Electrical Information and Communication Technology (EICT), Khulna, Bangladesh, 2019, pp. 1–6, doi: 10.1109/EICT48899.2019.9068850.

Note: All the figures and tables in this chapter were made by the author.

Challenges and Opportunities for Innovation in India – Dr. Shweta Mishra et al. (eds)
© 2024 Taylor & Francis Group, London, ISBN 978-1-032-99842-8

A Novel Inhibitory Kinetic Spectrophotometric Method for the Determination of Famotidine

58

Sushil Kumar Singh Tomar[1]

Department of Applied Sciences,
Ambalika Institute of Management and Technology,
Lucknow

Abhas Asthana[2]

Department of Chemistry, Govt. M. J.S PG College,
Bhind, M.P

Joy Sarkarc[3]

Department of Chemistry, University of Lucknow,
Lucknow

Abstract

A kinetic spectrophotometric method for the determination of famotidine, based on its inhibitory effect on Hg(II) catalyzed substitution of cyanide ion, by 4-cyanopyridine in hexacyanoferrate (II) is described. Famotidine ions form strong complexes with Hg(II) catalyst which is used as the basis for its determination at trace level. The progress of reaction was monitored, spectrophotometrically, at 477nm (λmax of [Fe(CN)5CNpy]3–, complex) under the optimum reaction conditions at: [Fe(CN)64-] = 5×10-3 M, [4-CNpy] = 2.5×10-4 M, [Hg2+] = 2×10-5 M, pH = 2.8 ± 0.02, I = 0.02 M (KNO3) and temperature = $25 \pm 0.1°C$. A linear relationship obtained between absorbance (measured at 477nm at different times) and inhibitor concentration, under specified conditions, has been used for the determination of [famotidine] in the range of $0.2 - 2.0 \times 10$–5M with a detection limit of 5.2×10–7 M. The standard deviation and percentage relative standard deviation have been calculated and reported with each datum. A most plausible mechanistic scheme has been proposed for the reaction. The values of equilibrium constants for complex formation between catalyst–inhibitor (KCI), catalyst–substrate (Ks) and Michaelis–Menten constant (Km) have been computed from the kinetic data. The influence of possible interference by major cations and anions on the determination of famotidine and their limits has been investigated.

Keywords

Kinetic, Spectrophotometric method, Catalyst–inhibitor (KCI), Michaelis–Menten constant,pharmaceutical dosage

Corresponding author: [1]skstomar@gmail.com, [2]abhasasthana1234@gmail.com, [3]dr.jsarkar4@gmail.com

DOI: 10.1201/9781003606260-58

1. INTRODUCTION

Famotidine, chemically 3-([2-(diaminomethyleneamino) thiazol-4-yl]methylthio)- *N'*-sulfamoylpropanimidamide is an H2-receptor antagonist and is widely used in short term treatment of duodenal ulcer and in the management of hypersecretory conditions [1]. It acts by blocking histamine receptors which are present on the cells in the stomach lining. Ranitidine binds to H2 receptors, replacing some of the histamine. As a result, the amount of stomach acid produced by these cells is decreased. Ranitidine decreases the amount of acid in the stomach and duodenum. As a result, ranitidine helps relieve the symptoms of indigestion and aids the healing of ulcers. It is also used to depress acid production in various other conditions. Several methods have been reported for the determination of ranitidine in bulk, pharmaceutical dosage forms, and/or biological fluids. These methods include kinetic spectrophotometry [2, 3], HPLC [4-8], coulometry [9], capillary electrophoresis [10, 11], fluorimetry [12], HPTLC [13], voltammetry [14], potentiometry [15] and polarography [16]. But, such techniques are time consuming because of extensive sample pretreatment, require expensive instrumentation and beyond the reach of small laboratories, particularly in under developed and developing countries. There are several reports of the determination of Famotidine by spectrophotometry involving the use of Folin-Ciocalteu reagent [17], N-bromosuccinimide [18], Cerium (IV) [19], 3-methyl-2-benzothiazoline hydrazone-iron (III) [20], 7, 7, 8, 8 tetracyanoquinodimethane [21], 2, 6- dichloroquinone chlorimide [22], bromothymol blue [23], potassium dichromate [24], perchloric acid [25], DDQ [26], $Hg(SCN)_2$ [27]. These methods are based on redox, coupling, charge-transfer complexation, and ion pair complexation reactions. Already reported spectrophotometric methods suffer from one or other deficiency such as heating or extraction step, critical dependence on acid/pH condition, use of non-aqueous medium/expensive chemicals, poor sensitivity and/or narrow range of linear response. It has also been reported that an addition of thio-compounds to the metal ion catalyzed reaction inhibit the rate of reaction to a considerable extent [28-33]. Such rate inhibition has formed the basis of the quantitative application for the determination of thio-compounds [28, 30-33]. Few studies have been conducted on the kinetic determination of inhibitors or complexing agents based on their inhibitory effect on the rate of metal ion catalyzed reactions [30-33]. In the present paper, this fact is successfully utilized for the quantitative determination of famotidine by monitoring the said indicator reaction on UV-visible spectrophotometer. For this purpose the selected indicator reaction must be such that the stability of the catalyst–inhibitor complex

formed is very high so that the formation of this complex may take place even at low concentrations, hence, the kinetics and mechanism of Hg(II) catalyzed exchange of coordinated cyanide in $[Fe(CN)_6]^{4-}$ by 4-CNpy has been chosen.

2. EXPERIMENTAL

2.1 Reagents and Equipments

The chemicals $K_4[Fe(CN)_6] \cdot 3H_2O$ (E. Merck), $HgCl_2$ (AR, Galaxo Laboratories, India) 4-cyanopyridine (SD Fine Chemicals Ltd., India), and famotidine (Aldrich Chemical Co., USA) were used for present work. All other chemicals used were of analytical grade. Deionized water was used throughout this study. The pH value was kept constant by use of potassium hydrogen phthalate buffer as described in literature [34]. The ionic strength was kept constant by adding KNO_3 (E. Merck) of analytical grade. The progress of the reaction was monitored at 477 nm at constant temperature ($25 \pm 0.1°C$) by following the increase of absorbance of $[Fe(CN)_5 4\text{-CNpy}]^{3-}$, the final product of the reaction, at different intervals of time with the help of DIGI-110DUV-Visible spectrophotometer having a circulatory system to maintain temperature of the cell compartment. The pH of the reaction mixture was measured on a Toshniwal digital pH-meter model, CL-46. The standard BDH buffers were used to standardize the pH meter. A fixed time procedure was adopted to record the absorbance changes as a function of varying concentration of inhibitor and the data obtained were used to plot the calibration graphs for further applications.

2.2 Determination of Famotidine

The concentration of famotidine was varied by changing the mole ratio [I]/[C] from 0.10 to 1.10 keeping other variables at optimum conditions (*cf.* Chapter II) except the concentration of Hg(II) which was fixed at 2.0×10^{-5} M. The absorbance change, recorded as a function of concentration of Famotidine at fixed time intervals were used to achieve the calibration curves for the determination of Famotidine.

3. RESULT AND DISCUSSION

3.1 The Indicator Reaction

The cyanide substitution reaction between $[Fe(CN)_6]^{4-}$ and 4-CNpy has been found to be catalysed by the Hg(II) ion. The product formed, $[Fe(CN)_5(CNpy)]^{3-}$, as a result of this reaction has wavelength of maximum absorption in the visible region at 477 nm corresponding to metal to ligand charge transfer (MLCT) transition. The Famotidine was found to inhibit this reaction. The inhibition of reaction rate by the addition of thio-compound i.e. Famotidine in the present case may be attributed to the formation of complexes of high stability between Hg(II) catalyst and the inhibitor leading to the decrease in free catalyst concentration which ultimately mask the catalytic activity of Hg(II) catalyst. The subsequent decrease in the rate of inhibited reaction is directly proportional to the concentration of inhibitor added to the reaction system. Therefore, a linear relationship between the rate of the indicator reaction and the concentration of inhibitor added may be obtained empirically by the simple treatment of rate equation/data. The inhibitory effect depends upon their [inhibitor]/ [catalyst] ratio in the reaction system.

3.2 Calibration Graph and Precision in Determination of Famotidine

The plots of A_t (taken as a measure of initial rate) *versus* [inhibitor] were found to be linear as shown in Fig. 58.1,

and serve as calibration curves. The linear plots provide a basis for the determination of Famotidine. The relevant expressions which relate the change of absorbance A_t (t = 5, and 10 min) to that of the concentration of inhibitor Famotidine in reaction mixture for these calibration curves are given by Eqs. (1) and (2).

$$A_5 = 0.228 - 9.18 \times 10^3 \text{ [Famotidine]} \tag{1}$$

$$A_{10} = 0.275 - 9.24 \times 10^3 \text{ [Famotidine]} \tag{2}$$

The linear regression coefficients and standard deviations for A_5, and A_{10} versus [Famotidine] plots are 0.9973, 0.9976 and 0.005, 0.004 respectively. The recovery experiments were performed for the determination of Famotidine in aqueous solutions in the range of $0.2 - 2.0 \times 10^{-5}$ M. The recovered amounts along with the standard deviations and the percentage errors in case of Famotidine are given in Table 58.1. The detection limits for Famotidine were calculated to be and 5.2×10^{-7} M.

Table 58.1 Quantitative determination of famotidine (Famotidine) at temperature = $25 \pm 0.1°C$

[Famotidine] × 10⁵ M (taken)	A₅			A₁₀		
	[Famotidine] × 10⁵ M (found)ᵃ ± s.d.	RSD (%)	Recovery (%)	[Famotidine] × 10⁵ M (found)ᵃ ± s.d.	RSD (%)	Recovery (%)
0.25	0.26 ± 0.01	4.00	104.00	0.24 ± 0.01	-4.00	96.00
0.42	0.41 ± 0.01	-2.38	97.62	0.43 ± 0.02	2.38	102.38
0.94	0.93 ± 0.03	-1.06	98.94	0.93 ± 0.03	-1.06	98.94
1.24	1.25 ± 0.02	0.81	100.81	1.26 ± 0.04	1.61	101.61
1.56	1.57 ± 0.03	0.64	100.64	1.54 ± 0.02	-1.28	98.72
1.92	1.91 ± 0.02	-0.52	99.48	1.93 ± 0.01	0.52	100.52

ᵃmean of three determinations ± s.d values represent standard deviation of the mean for three determinations.

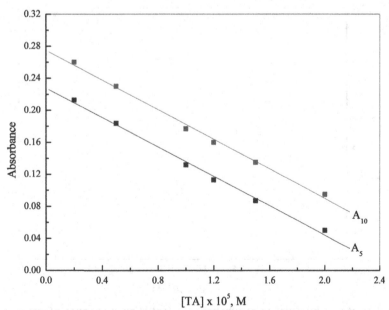

Fig. 58.1 Calibration curve for the determination of famotidine at $[Fe(CN)_6^{4-}] = 5 \times 10^{-3}$ M, [4-CNpy] = 2.5×10^{-4} M, $[Hg^{2+}] = 2 \times 10^{-5}$ M, pH = 2.8 ± 0.02, I = 0.02 M (KNO₃) and temperature = $25 \pm 0.1°C$

Reaction conditions are $[Fe(CN)_6^{4-}] = 5 \times 10^{-3}$ M, $[4\text{-}CNpy] = 2.5 \times 10^{-4}$ M, $[Hg^{2+}] = 2 \times 10^{-5}$ M, pH = 2.8 $\pm$ 0.02, I = 0.02 M (KNO$_3$).

3.3 Mechanism of Inhibition

The inhibition caused by Famotidine containing sulfur donor atom to the Hg(II) catalysed CN$^-$ substitution of $[Fe(CN)_6]^{4-}$ with 4-CNpy may be understood by modifying the mechanistic scheme for this reaction system without inhibitor and may schematically be represented as shown in **Scheme 1**.

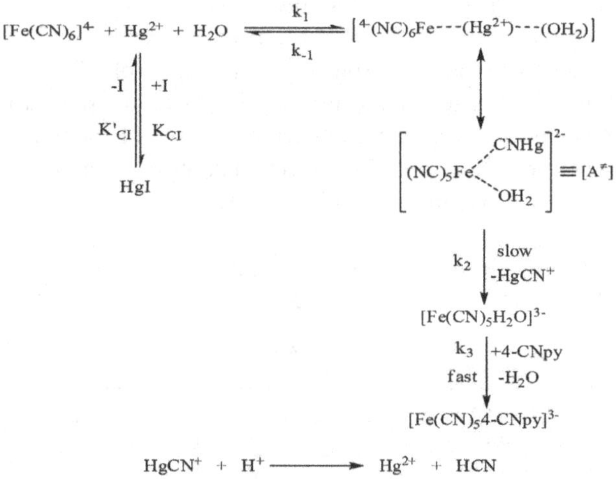

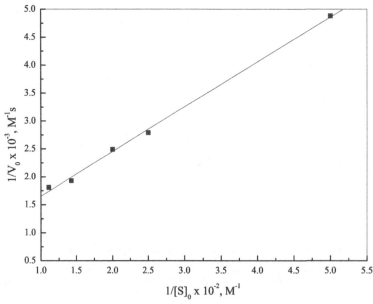

Scheme 1

In the above mechanistic scheme, the uncatalyzed reaction path has been ignored for simplicity. If the non-rate

limiting concentration of $[Fe(CN)_6]^{4-}$ is represented by [S] and its initial concentration by $[S]_0$, then it is simple matter to derive a kinetic formulation by a treatment similar to one followed for an enzyme catalyzed reaction involving a single substrate in the presence of an inhibitor. The reaction velocity, in the presence of catalyst only, can be given in the form of Eq. (3):

$$V_0 = \frac{V_{max}}{1 + \dfrac{K_m}{[S]_0}} \quad (3)$$

Double reciprocal plot of the reaction rate can also be constructed by inverting Eq. (3), which results in the Lineweaver–Burk's [35] form as shown in Eq. (4):

$$\frac{1}{V_0} = \frac{1}{V_{max}} + \frac{K_m}{V_{max}}\frac{1}{[S]_0} \quad (4)$$

In Eq. (4), V_0 represents the initial rate in the presence of catalyst only, V_{max} denotes the maximum attainable rate at a particular catalyst concentration in the presence of non-rate-limiting amount of substrate, and K_m ($K_m = (k_{-1} + k_2)/k_1$) is equivalent to the Michaelis–Menten constant, which is approximately equal to dissociation constant of the catalyst–substrate complex (vide-supra). A plot of $(1/V_0)$ versus $(1/[S]_0)$ in the absence of an inhibitor yielded a straight line (R $\geq$ 0.9719, s $\leq$ 0.3493) as shown in Fig. 58.2. From the plot in Fig. 58.2 (cf. Eq. (4)); it is seen that one can get V_{max} from the intercept and K_m from the slope intercept ratio. It is further to be noted that the values

Fig. 58.2 The determination of V_{max} by variation of substrate concentration in absence of inhibitor at [4-CNpy] = 2.5×10^{-4} M, $[Hg^{2+}] = 2 \times 10^{-5}$ M, pH = 2.8 $\pm$ 0.02, I = 0.02 M (KNO$_3$) and temperature = 25 $\pm$ 0.1°C.

of K_m and V_{max} are also referred as the kinetic parameter of a catalyst and serve to characterize catalyst acting on a substrate. The values of K_m of catalyst depend on particular substrate and also on experimental conditions such as pH, ionic strength, temperature and solvent used.

In the presence of inhibitor, the rate of reaction can be expressed in the form of Eq. (5):

$$V_i = \frac{V_{max}}{1 + \left(\dfrac{K_m}{[I]_0}\right)\left(1 + \dfrac{[I]_0}{K'_{CI}}\right)} \qquad (5)$$

Comparison of Eq. (5) to the corresponding expression for the uninhibited case, i.e., Eq. (3) illustrates that with competitive inhibition, a new apparent Michaelis–Menten constant (K'_m) can be defined through Eq. (6) [36]:

$$K'_m = K_m\left(1 + \frac{[I]_0}{K'_{CI}}\right) \qquad (6)$$

In Eq. (5), V_i denotes the reaction rate in the presence of the inhibitor (at a fixed catalyst concentration), K_{CI} is the dissociation constant of catalyst–inhibitor (C–I) complex. Eq. (5) was derived on the basis of assumption that $[S]_0$ is large and $[I]_0 > [CI]$. Eq. (3) is formally similar to the rate equation for heterogeneously catalyzed gas phase reactions proceeding by Langmuir mechanism. A supportive reference to a similar case of inhibition was also made by Klockow et al. [37] who investigated the inhibition of zirconium catalyst for the determination of fluoride.

In order to obtain Lineweaver–Burk plot, Eq. (5) can be transformed to Eq. (7):

$$\frac{1}{V_i} - \frac{1}{V_{max}} = \frac{K_m}{V_{max}[S]_0} + \frac{K_m}{V_{max}[S]_0}\frac{[I]_0}{K'_{CI}} \qquad (7)$$

Although V_{max} used in Eq. (7) is not an experimental quantity, yet it can be evaluated from the intercept of the plot of $1/V_0$ *versus* $1/[S]_0$ using Eq. (5) in absence of inhibitor as shown in Fig. 58.2. The slope of this plot yields the value of K_m which was found to be 9.48 mM in the present case. For the validity and good results from Eq. (7), inhibitor 'I' must form a complex of the type (C–I) with catalyst 'C'. There should be no S–I type complex formed. The plot of $1/V_i - 1/V_{max}$ versus $[I]_0$ for famotidine was found to be linear and shown in Fig. 58.3. From the intercepts of the plot, the value of K_m in the presence of inhibitor was evaluated. This value was again found to be in agreement with its previously calculated value from $1/V_0$ versus $1/[S]_0$ plot. The slope of this plot gives the value of K'_{CI} corresponding to the complexes of Hg(II) with Famotidine. The value of K'_{CI} for Famotidine was found to be 4.61×10^{-6}.

At last, a general mechanistic scheme describing the role of inhibitor may be represented as Scheme 2

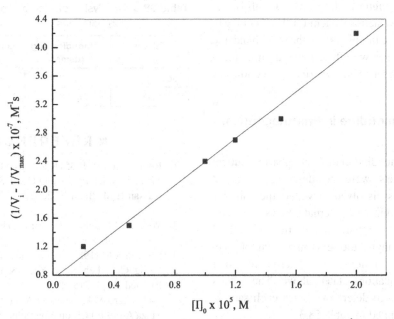

Fig. 58.3 Determination of K'_{CI} and K_m in the presence of inhibitor Famotidine at $[Fe(CN)_6^{4-}] = 5 \times 10^{-3}$ M, [4-CNpy] = 2.5 × 10^{-4} M, $[Hg^{2+}] = 2 \times 10^{-5}$ M, pH = 2.8 ± 0.02, I = 0.02 M (KNO$_3$) and temperature = 25 ± 0.1°C

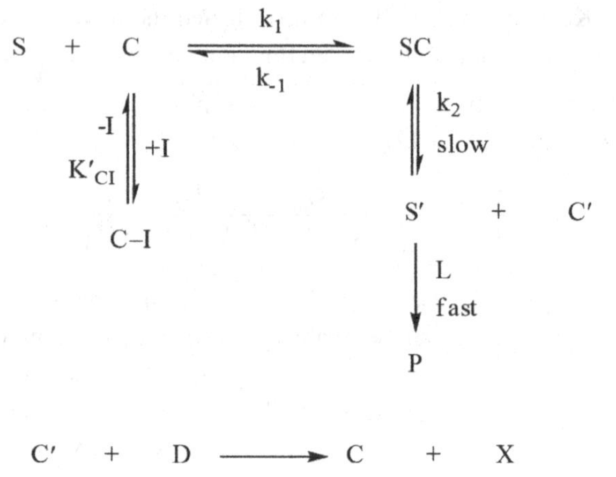

$$S \ + \ C \ \underset{k_{-1}}{\overset{k_1}{\rightleftharpoons}} \ SC$$

Scheme 2

where, S, C, I, SC, L and C–I are substrate, catalyst, inhibitor, substrate–catalyst complex, ligand and catalyst–inhibitor complex respectively. S′ is a species which on reaction with a reagent gives the final product P, while C′ is a species which on reaction with D (usually H^+, OH^- or H_2O) regenerates the catalyst C.

3.4 Interferences Caused by Foreign Substances

The interferences caused due to the presence of different cations, anions and organic molecules have been studied and the maximum limits are presented in Table 58.2. It is important to mention here that no complexing agent which may form a complex of high stability constant with Hg(II) should be present in the reaction system for the accuracy in the determination of these inhibitors. On the other hand, the metals which may complex with these two inhibitors more strongly than Hg(II) under these experimental conditions must also be absent.

3.5 Analysis of Famotidine in Pharmaceutical Preparations

For the analysis of Famotidine in different pharmaceutical preparations, ten tablets were powdered. A weighed amount of powder was dissolved in water; the samples were centrifuged for 5 min, the supernatant was separated and water was added to prepare the solution of desired concentrations. Accordingly, the amount of Famotidine, contained in aqueous solutions, was determined using standard calibration equations stated above. The results obtained on three repeated determination of each sample on Famotidine are compiled in Table 58.3.

Table 58.2 Effect of different foreign ions on the determination of Famotidine at $25 \pm 0.1°C$

Foreign ions	[Foreign ion] M, limit	Comment on interference
Sn^{2+}	6×10^{-4}	Non interfering
Pb^{2+}	3×10^{-4}	Non interfering
Sr^{2+}	3×10^{-4}	Non interfering
Cu^{2+}	4×10^{-4}	Non interfering
Co^{2+}	2×10^{-5}	Inhibition due to the formation of Co–L complex
Mg^{2+}	3×10^{-4}	Non interfering
Cd^{2+}	3×10^{-4}	Non interfering
Cr^{3+}	6×10^{-4}	Non interfering
Fe^{3+}	4×10^{-4}	Non interfering
Al^{3+}	2×10^{-4}	Non interfering
Na^+	6×10^{-5}	Interfering
Br^-	5×10^{-4}	Non interfering
I^-	4×10^{-4}	Non interfering
NO_3^-	3×10^{-4}	Almost non interfering
$(COO)_2^{2-}$	6×10^{-4}	Almost non interfering
SO_4^{2-}	4×10^{-4}	Interfering significantly
EDTA	2×10^{-4}	Interfering significantly
IDA	3×10^{-4}	Interfering significantly
NTA	2×10^{-4}	Interfering significantly
HEDTA	4×10^{-4}	Interfering significantly

Table 58.3 Analysis of famotidine in pharmaceutical preparations

Tablets	Famotidine, mg (taken)	Famotidine, mg (found)	% RSD
Facid 40	168.00	167.24 ± 3.2	1.07
Facid 20	168.00	169.02 ± 4.4	0.73

■ REFERENCES ■

1. Remington J P (1985) Remington Pharmaceutical Sciences, 17th ed., Mack Publishing Co.: USA, p.798.
2. Hassan E M, Belal F (2002) J. Pharm. Biomed. Anal. 27: 31.
3. Walash M I, Belal F, Ibrahim F, Hefnawy M, Eid M (2002) J. AOAC Int., 85: 1316.
4. Rustum A M (1988) J. Liq. Chromatogr. 11: 3447.
5. Wong C F, Peh K K, Yuen K H (1998) J Chromatogr Biomed. Appl. 718: 205.
6. Campanero M A, Lopez O A, Garcia Q E, Sadaba B, dela Maza A (1998) Chromatographia 47: 391.

7. Farthing D, Brouer KLR, Fakhry I, Sica D (1997) J. Chromatogr. Biomed. Appl. 688: 350.

8. Dasgupta V (1988) Drug. Dev. Ind. Pharm. 14: 1647.

9. Nikolic K, Stankovic B, Bogavac M (1995) Pharmazie, 50: 301.

10. Shou-Mei Wu, Yu H H, Hsin L W, Su H C, Hwang S K (2001) 22: 2717

11. Kelly M A, Altria K D, Grace C, Clark B J (1996) J. Chromatogr., 798: 297.

12. Lopez C E, Vinas P, Campillo N, Hernandez M C (1996), Analyst, 121: 1043.

13. Khadiga M K, Azza M A, Maha A. Hegazy, Laila A F (2002) J AOAC International, 85: 1015

14. Parviz N, Mohammad R G, Parandis D (2007) Journal of pharmacological and toxicological methods, 15:289

15. Yousry M, Badawy S S, Mutair A A (2005) Anal Sci. 21: 1443.

16. Richter P, Tora I, Munoz V F (1999) Analyst 119: 1371.

17. Basavaiah K, Nage G P (2004) Ind. Pharm. 3: 60.

18. Sastry C S P, Rao S G, Rao J S V M L, Naidu P Y (1997) Anal. Lett. 30: 2377.

19. Amin A S, Ahmed I S, Dessouki H A, Gouda E A (2003) Spectrochim. Acta Part A, 59: 695.

20. Rao E V, Rao J J, Murthy S S N, Rao G R (1987) Indian J. Pharm, Sci., 49:143.

21. Al-Ghannam S, Belal F (2002) J. AOAC Intl. 85: 1003.

22. Emmanuel J, Haldankar S D (1989) Indian Drugs, 26: 249.

23. Ozsoy Y, Guvner B (1987) Acta Pharm. Turc. 29:13.

24. Basavaiah K, Somashekar B C (2007) J. Iran. Chem. Soc. 4: 78.

25. Basavaiah K, Nagegowda P, Ramakrishna V (2005) Science Asia, 31: 207.

26. Walash M, Sharaf-EL Din M, Etawalli M E S, Reda S M (2004) Arch. Pharm. Res., 27: 720.

27. Basavaiah K, Somashekar B C (2007) Ecl. Quím. 32: 19.

28. M.H. Cordoba, P. Vinas, C. Sanchez-Pedreno, Talanta 32 (1985) 221.

29. A. Giannousios, C. Papadopoulos, Analyst 121 (1996) 413.

30. M.S. Garcia, C. Sanchez-Pedreno, M.I. Albero, Analyst 115 (1990) 989,

31. S. Prasad, Microchem. J. 85 (2007) 214 (and references cited therein).

32. R.M. Naik, J. Sarkar, S. Prasad, Microchem. J. 88 (2008) 45 (and references cited therein).

33. R. M. Naik, B. Kumar, A. Asthana, Spectrochim. Acta, Part A 75 (2010) 1152.

34. R.C. Weast, CRC Handbook of Chemistry and Physics, 49th ed; The Chemical Rubber Co.: Cleveland, OH (1969) D-79.

35. H. Lineweaver, D. Burk, J. Am. Chem. Soc. 56 (1934) 658.

36. I. Tinoco Jr., K. Sauer, J.C. Wang, Physical Chemistry, Principles and Applications in Biological Sciences, Prentice-Hall Inc., New Jersey, 1978, p. 351.

37. D. Klockow, J. Auffarth, C. Kopp, Anal. Chim. Acta 89 (1977) 37.

Note: All the figures and tables in this chapter were made by the author.

Challenges and Opportunities for Innovation in India – Dr. Shweta Mishra et al. (eds)
© 2024 Taylor & Francis Group, London, ISBN 978-1-032-99842-8

Social Media Impact on Consumer Trust on FMCG Brands in North India

59

Sandeep Rai[1],
Nuwoo E. Doe[2], Yogesh Kumar Sharma[3]
Mittal School of Business, Lovely Professional University,
Jalandhar, Punjab

Abstract

Purpose: The purpose of this article is to conduct an analytical investigation on the impact of social media and the specific social media platform on consumers' trust in FMCG brands. The extent to which social media alters experiences is examined in a quantitative survey. Outsiders in senior positions are now gradually surpassing insiders in understanding of customers and services, which might have an impact on results in unrelated roles. Because advertisers have no influence over the content, timing, or recurrence of online customer discussions, web chat draws customers. According to the findings, social media use has an impact on customer satisfaction during the information-seeking and other assessment phases. This effect gets stronger as customers proceed to make their final decision and conduct post-purchase analysis. The findings demonstrate that marketing initiatives have a favorable effect on people. Method.70 participants with at least six months of social media exposure were chosen at random for this study, which will be carried out using google analytics. Google Forms will be used to distribute an online survey to collect data. To cover the distribution of the North Indian population, consumer data will be gathered using the Google Form, and questionnaires will be used for analysis. Finding This research will show the consumer's trust affected to what degree by the social media platform in FMCG brands. The study will be done in the part of North India to see the effect of the social platform using SEM to which extent the trust varies, of the consumer. We will take well known platforms like Instagram, Twitter, and YouTube.

Keywords

Social media, Factors, Loyalty, Trust, Brand

1. INTRODUCTION

Social media enables the sharing of ideas and information and ideas through virtual collaboration. From Facebook and Instagram to Twitter and YouTube, social media includes a variety of apps and platforms that allow users to share content, interact online, and build communities. More than 4.7 billion people use social media, which corresponds to 60% of the world's population. Social media chat apps and platforms are the most used websites worldwide. In

Corresponding author: [1]sa15114136@gmail.com, [2]nuwooed@gmail.com, [3]yogeshsharmame355@gmail.com

DOI: 10.1201/9781003606260-59

early 2023, 94.8% of users visited chat and messaging apps and websites, followed by social media with 94.6%. This was followed by search engine sites with 81.8% of users. Statista estimates that around 3.96 billion people worldwide will use social media from 3.6 billion in 2020 to 2022. This number should increase to 4.41 billion by 2025. Online advertising is a fantastic way for businesses of all sizes to reach potential buyers and customers. People discover, learn, follow, and buy names on social networks, so if you are not on platforms like Facebook, Instagram, and LinkedIn, you are missing out! A good understanding of social media can lead to enormous success for our business, build brand loyalty and even increase goodwill and sales. With over 80% of consumers reporting that social media – especially social media content – has a significant impact on their purchasing decisions, marketers in the industry have driven social media marketing (SMM) to evolve from a representative tool to a versatile marketing tool. the field of marketing intelligence and growing audiences. Social media reviews have a massive impact on consumer behavior. Social media is a powerful source of social proof, which is important when shopping. More than half of consumers (51%) read reviews on forums or SM to evaluate a product or service before purchasing it. The FMCG industry is the most important and largest in media today. The use of social media can be beneficial for businesses by increasing sales, expanding their customer base, and opening new business opportunities. However, reputation management has become a prominent issue for management, as social media can reveal both positive and negative features of the products and people used against it. Businesses must be aware of the risks of negative feedback and respond promptly. The company's reputation has been hit hard, as they took so long to respond to questions asked on social media.

1.1 Objective

- To study the impact of social media on FMCG brands through SEM Methodology.
- Which FMCG brands are more affected by social media in terms of trust?

2. Literature Review

2.1 The Effect of Social Media Marketing on Brand Trust, Brand Equity and Brand Loyalty

Author: - Haudia, Wiwik Handayanib*, et al.

Published: - 29/January/2022

The purpose of this study is to ascertain how social media marketing affects brand equity, trust, and trust in social media. The findings demonstrate that marketing initiatives have a favorable impact on trust, brand loyalty, and business loyalty. SME performance is positively impacted by corporate trust, business value, and brand trust. Instagram's social media advertising can help to increase trust among media users. Instagram has the potential to raise awareness of the Instagram brand and offer a deeper understanding of the image brand. With Instagram's growing advertising business, user loyalty is rising as well. Another thing to keep in mind is that brand loyalty and customer loyalty can both act as mediators in the interaction between social media marketing and brand loyalty, as well as between social media marketing and product loyalty.

2.2 Charismatic Inclination of Social Nexus on Brand Endorsement of FMCG Merchandize

Author: - Renuka Devi

Published: - 2016

Social media links information in a cooperative way by utilizing the "Wisdom of population." Social media is the information community that turns users from content consumers into content producers. Content developed or uploaded by non-media professionals is referred to as User Generated Content (UGC) or Consumer Generated Media (CGM). It could be a hashtag, a remark you made on Twitter, or an Instagram picture. The whole market has changed since the introduction of social media in marketing. A new market has been opened for the producers and the sellers. In the case of FMCG products favorable comments can increase the brand loyalty, purchase more, and repurchase, and its endorsement. An unfavorable comment of the product or service can be creating a no demand, no repurchases which will finally lead to switching brands. Through this study the purchase behavior of consumers studied in accordance with the social media platform.

2.3 Social Media Brand Communication Impact on CBBE Dimensions

Author: - Aaker, D.

Published: - 1991

Over time, the standards set by the CBBE have changed and gained controversy. According to Aaker (1991), CBBE is a collection of factors that includes trust, consensus, market share, and brand recognition. besides other advantages like a competitive edge. The two dimensions of the original CBBE model, developed by Keller in 1993, are brand awareness and brand image. According to this viewpoint, brand loyalty happens when customers are aware of the brand and have some strong, memorable connections with it. A five-pronged strategy, comprising performance, relationship, value, trust, and commitment, was put forth by Lassa et al. (1995). Furthermore, Yoo et al. (two thousand) highlighted that brand awareness, brand loyalty, and brand awareness and brand association are among the CBBE dimensions.. The reliability of the CBBE dimension has been the subject of several research recently due to its significance. For instance, trust is a potential CBBE dimension that comprises cooperation, consensus, dependability, and trustworthiness, according to Atılgan et al. (2009). Brand awareness, brand recognition, brand differentiation, brand integration, brand trust, and type relationship are among the CBBE dimensions, according to Kimpakorn and Tocquer (2010). According to Bruno and Dabrowski (2015), product exposure, brand trust, and awareness/interest are CBBE aspects. Numerous researchers have proposed different sizes of CBBE that could be connected to the species, according to earlier study. There is a difference with this CBBE. In other words, there is a positive relationship between BBQ dimensions (Yoo et al. two thousand; Atilgan et al. 2005; Tong and Hawley 2009; Xu and Chan 2010; Torres et al. 2015). According to the literature, using Aaker's (1991) model, the overall dimension for each model is one or more dimensions. The overall dimension specifically includes brand awareness, brand recognition, brand collaboration, and brand trust. Therefore, the researchers examined the effects of dimensions (brand awareness, brand associations, brand awareness, and brand loyalty) in addition to trust as a means of reducing risk to help customers, such as trust.

2.4 Consumers Attitude Towards Product Harm Crisis

Author: - Garg, Ebha

Published: -2021

Organizations can experience product damage at any stage of the supply chain at any time. In addition, most FMCG companies and retailers today manage many brands and brand names, which can easily cause bad information to pass from relevant products to irrelevant products in the market. When consumers encounter negative information about a brand/product, they also change their perception of the organization's entire product, and the behavior of competing names in the affected category is also affected. This study provides marketers in the FMCG space with useful information for hiring companies and strategies to protect other brands from product disruption. It also shows how competitors can protect their brands by subverting their competitors' brands using different strategies. The finding of this study can also be generalized to other sectors.

2.5 A Study on Brand Loyalty Behavior in FMCG Market

Author: - Sudha, R

Published: - 26 November 2018

Building brand loyalty is decisive for FMCG products where consumers profoundly depend on the brand for the product category in a competitive and brand sensitive market. The Researcher has found Product Quality, Price and Promotion, Brand Awareness, Brand Image are building brand Loyalty. Brand Name, Price, and Promotion are three dimensions that have a positive impact, demonstrating the key role of awareness and belief in building brand loyalty. Creating a brand is not easy, but brand management is especially important for competitive advantage. The consumer knows everything. They should provide quality products at an affordable price. Marketers and business leaders must always put materials in the right packaging. If customers believe the product is valuable and know its quality, then price is not a measure of their trust. Most importantly, businesspeople need to be incredibly careful about "packaging and labeling." Respondents gave the highest average score in the study. Packaging and labeling are the company identity of each product. In general, the product needs to be stylish, traditional, good, and healthy to retain the customer.

2.6 Influence of Social Media Strategies on Consumer Decision Making Process an Empirical Study of Selected FMCG Goods

Author: - Menka

Published: - 2020

It has been found that, albeit to varying degrees, social media initiatives have a significant impact on the different stages of the decision-making process for consumers. Even with the advent of social media as a means of marketing communication, the consumer still needs to go through each step of the decision-making process before completing a purchase. Furthermore, the study's findings indicate that marketing professionals must acknowledge the importance of customer involvement in mediating the interaction between social media techniques and the decision-making process of consumers, which in turn motivates them to frame their choice of FMCG items for purchase. The study's findings will aid managers in comprehending the value of social media tactics as a crucial component of marketing communication plans.

2.7 The Impact of Social Media Brand Communication on Consumer-based Brand Equity Dimensions through Facebook in Fast Moving Consumer Goods: The Case of Egypt

Author: - Heba Sadek, et al.

Published: -25th June 2017

The aim of this paper is to investigate how the five-consumer business model (CBBE) lengths of the Egyptian FMCG industry are affected by the design of the company and the social media communication style of the users on Facebook. Our article's findings demonstrate that co-branding only directly improves the four CBBE dimensions—trust, joint ventures, product quality awareness, and brand awareness. However, brand approval, brand trust, and brand trust were not significantly impacted by user-generated brand communication experiences. Additionally, it has been demonstrated that marketing organizations and brand recognition suffer when user-generated social media brand communication is used.

2.8 Impart of Social Media on Consumer Behavior and Buying Behavior

Author: - Abdelkader, et al.

Published: - 2021

This finding shows that a small number of people produced or contributed to the material, according to the results, consumers in large numbers consume the content. One hundred and twenty-one of the sample's activities were associated with consumption, forty-one were related to consumption, and the rest were with the product. Abdelkader, A. A., & Ebrahim, R. S. (2021). Separating user interaction effects between marketer and user-generated content and repurchase insights in an online airline service community. International Journal of Online Marketing.

2.9 Understanding Consumer's Trust in Social Media Marketing Environment

Author: - Irshad, et al.

Published: - 2020

Recognizing the level of consumer confidence in the social media marketing landscape. The International Journal of Distribution and Retail Management. This study aims to investigate how consumer incentives—rewards, connections, and empowerment—that stem from social media store trust affect online shopping behavior. The findings demonstrate that incentives and rewards from society have a direct impact on customers' intentions to shop online and can confidently influence those intentions. On the other hand, trust moderates the association between consumers' intentions to make online purchases and motivational support.

2.10 Impact of Social Media Marketing Features on Consumer's Purchase Decision in the Fast-Food Industry: Brand Trust as a Mediator

Author: - Jalal Rajeh Hanaysha

Published: -19/July/2022

Investigating the impact of four marketing advertisement characteristics on customers' purchasing decisions in the fast-food industry is the primary goal of this study. Determining whether the trust type heals their connection is another objective. An online survey was used to gather qualitative data from customers of various fast-food establishments in the United Arab Emirates. According to the findings, social media platforms play a significant role in helping fast food companies accomplish their marketing objectives, which include influencing consumer behavior and developing brand trust. The four dimensions of the marketing efforts examined in this study are interactive, entertaining, visually striking, and educational. With the exception of entertainment, all of these factors were shown to matter when making purchases.

2.11 The Impact of Social Media on Consumer-Brand Loyalty: A Mediating Role of Online Based-Brand Community

Author: - Abdul Bashiru Jibri

Published: - 09 October 2019

Considering the interaction of the buyer's behavior in the virtual environment, this article aims to analyze the results of online communication (OBBC) through a social media platform (SMP). To make a link between online business use of social media and consumer brand loyalty (CBL), we used an online survey to gather their thoughts. The survey included 122 social media users connected to at least one online community list. Results from partial least squares and structural equation modeling (PLS-SEM) show that OBBC of social media platforms helps create a relationship between business customers and their respective business customers. And OBBC does not directly support CBL's Consumer Brand Promise and Trust (CBPT) through SMP.

2.12 Using Social Media for Generating Trust-A Study of FMCG Brands

Author: - Harshita Singh Chandrapuri

Published: - October 2020

"Using Social Media to Build Trust - A Study on FMCG Brands" appears to be the title of the study to which you are referring. As to the survey, eight distinct FMCG companies promote their brands and products on social media platforms like Facebook and Twitter. This exemplifies how FMCG firms can leverage social media platforms like Facebook and Twitter to enhance user engagement and brand awareness. The Indonesian ready-to-eat tea market provides evidence on how Instagram marketing affects consumers' intent to purchase.

2.13 Effect of Social Media Marketing on Instagram Towards Purchase Intention: Evidence from Indonesia's Ready-to-Drink Tea Industry

Author: - Prasetyo Matak Aji, et al.

Published: - 19 March 2020

This study shows that a company's or brand's mass media marketing (SMMA) positively impacts customers' propensity to buy, e-WOM exposure on social media, and brand equity. In order to give readers and other researchers more insightful findings, the researchers in this study examine the findings of earlier investigations. An online survey with the purpose of gathering research data was completed by 114 Instagram users in Indonesia. The outcomes of the equation modeling demonstrate that SMMA positively affects brand equity and validate the existing model's validity. Furthermore, e-WOM is positively impacted by product quality, and this in turn positively influences consumers' purchase intentions. SMMA has a limitless direct impact on client needs.

2.14 In Brands We Trust? A Multicategory, Multicounty Investigation of Sensitivity of Consumers' Trust in Brands to Marketing-Mix Activities

The authors investigate whether brand marketing mixes—which include advertising, new product releases, distribution, price, and promotional expenses—have an impact on CTB. Using a range of data, including survey data, the authors propose and demonstrate how customer, category, and national variables affect CTB's sensitivity to marketing mix performance. the biggest marketplaces combined, home to half of the world's population. Employ advertisements to boost gold brick and accomplish multiple goals at once. Firstly, it's an additional method by which advertising raises a product's value. Secondly, CTB is directly impacted by BRIC.

2.15 Consumers' Trust in a Brand and the Link to Brand Loyalty

Author: - Geok Theng Lau & Sook Han Lee

Published: - 1999

Perhaps helpful is a research titled "The Role of Trust in Consumer Brand Loyalty." This study demonstrates the significance of trust and how it contributes to the development of this kind of trust. Specific attributes of the product, the firm, and the client are chosen in a way that will boost brand trust. The poll comprised a diverse range of Singaporean consumers as participants. The findings indicate that consumer trust in a brand is significantly influenced by the brand. The results also demonstrate that brand loyalty and brand trust are positively correlated. Thus, while developing trust, businesses should focus on the brand.

2.16 Effects of Customer Equity Drivers on Customer Loyalty in B2B Context

Author: - B. Ramaseshan, Fazlul K. Rabbanee, et al

Published: - April 2013

I think reading the research article "Customer Loyalty Driving and Customer Success in a B2B Environment" would be beneficial. This study demonstrates that in a business-to-business setting, loyalty value and relationship quality are impacted by the mediating function of customer trust. Nonetheless, research indicates that the impact of brand loyalty on customer loyalty and trust is negligible. The report states that in order to win over their customers' trust, managers need to put the importance of their relationships ahead of their work.

2.17 Social Commerce – E-Commerce in Social Media Context

Author: - Linda, Sau-ling LAI

Published: - 5 April 2013

This study investigates a novel approach known as business marketing in light of the way e-commerce makes use of Web 2.0 technologies and online media. The nature of human and professional contacts is evolving as a result of the World Wide Web's continued usage of cutting-edge technology to connect individuals at home and at work. an extensive analysis of Facebook's rise to prominence as a medium for commercial marketing. A triple relational model that describes the financial dynamics of the modern Internet community is presented as the study's conclusion.

Together, Web 2.0 technology, e-commerce, and online media have created a worldwide community that is beginning to transform social and corporate life. The findings and their explanation indicate that social economy is feasible since people, irrespective of place or identity, benefit differently from working together. This article's primary goal is to help readers comprehend the Web 2.0-based social media industry's explosive growth and the ensuing effects on emerging economies.

2.18 Consumer's Trust in the Brand: Can it Be Built through Brand Reputation, Brand Competence and Brand Predictability

Authors: - Muhammad Aslam Khan, Kashif ur Rehman

Published: - 1 January 2010

It will be beneficial to read a study named "The Impact of Brand Name, Brand Competition, and Marketing Activity on Consumer Brand Trust". The study investigates the relationship between reputation, product competitiveness, and product predictability in the context of consumer trust in brands. Participants were given a self-administered questionnaire to complete to gather data. The results were assessed using regression analysis and correlation, and all models were significant at the 5% level. The results of the survey indicate that the product raises customer trust from 30% to 60%.

The research's findings indicate that the factors influencing a customer's trust are brand awareness, competition, and product reputation.

2.19 The Impact of Brand Trust and Satisfaction on Retailer Repurchase Intentions

Author: - James J. Zboja, Clay M. Voorhees

Published: -1 October 2006

This study aims to show that consumers' perceptions of health and safety mean consumers' evaluations of stores and their repurchase intentions. Structural equation models are used to develop and evaluate hypotheses. Standard methods were used to measure direct and mediator effects. The results show that customer satisfaction and store trust play a mediating role between product trust and satisfaction and the customer's willingness to purchase again. The results show that managers need to understand that stores selling these products are affected by the same kind of perception.

2.20 How Large U.S. Companies can use Twitter and Other Social Media to Gain Business Value

Author: - Mary J. Culnan Bentley University (U.S.), et al.

Published: - 04 December 2010

This article begins by discussing how Fortune 500 companies use four of the best-known social media platforms to engage with customers: Twitter, Facebook, blogs, and guest posts. The authors argue that for businesses to take advantage of social media, the implementation strategy should focus on three aspects: social development, positive thinking, and absorptive capacity. Next, they present a case study of three

Fortune 100 companies to illustrate how each company operates its own network of social media platforms. Finally, they give advice on how to use social media.

3. Research Methodology

3.1 Research Design

The questions the researcher will pose are outlined in the research design. It lays forth the measurement protocols, sample plan, analytical framework, and time frame in a logical order. Three categories of study designs exist:

1. **Exploratory research design:** When the problem is ambiguous, this type of research design is employed, with the primary goal being to investigate and gain understanding of the problem scenario. It mostly entails a qualitative inquiry.

2. **Descriptive research design:** When a thorough and in-depth explanation is needed for the study's problem, this design is employed. There are various ways to go about doing it.
   - Longitudinal Study.
   - Cross sectional study.

3. **Casual research design:** When a researcher modifies one or more causal variables to evaluate their impact on a dependent variable, they employ this kind of research design. There is typically a probability component to this cause-and-effect relationship.

The research design used for this paper is Exploratory since we are trying to gain insight on the Impact of social media on consumer trust in FMCG brands through surveys and published papers with relevant information.

3.2 Data Collection Method

There are two methods of gathering data: primary and secondary. We used the Google Forms platform, a free web-based survey tool, to administer surveys and gather the core data. We looked through other research papers on related themes and spoke with other people about their purchasing decisions to gather secondary data.

Exploratory research is defined as an analysis conducted to investigate a challenging problem that isn't clearly defined. It leads to a better understanding of the existing problem, but it won't produce results that are compelling. Usually, this kind of analysis is conducted when the problem is still in its early stages.

3.3 Sampling Design

Sample universe: The sample universe includes students at Lovely Professional University.

Sample size: The sample size will be 100.

3.4 Questionnaire Design

The type of question used in questionnaire are structured multiple choice question. This is done so that we can find, is the consumer trust get effected by social media influence on FMCG brand.

3.5 Scope of Research

Considering the goals of the research, it would be best to conduct the study from the perspective of the consumer. We conduct this study to assist consumers in identifying the reasons behind how social media changed their trust on various FMCG brands. Since the primary goal of marketing is to analyze consumer needs, the data gathered through the questionnaire is from the consumer's point of view to determine new insights. The research also aims to assist potential readers in understanding the significance of social media websites/apps in the consumer decision-making process. The research focuses on end-user behavior.

Research Gap

- The research gap we found after reading many literatures was that the study on consumer's trust which is impacted by social media content has been never done in North India.

- We have found that by reading research papers on shod ganga and as well as on Google Scholar, that research which has done in India are mostly on brand trust, brand Loyalty, and repurchase but, it is not related to both social media, North India combined with FMCG brands. So, for this reason we want to research this topic.

4. GOOGLE FORM DATA

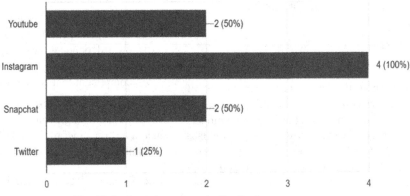

Fig. 59.1 Social media use distribution

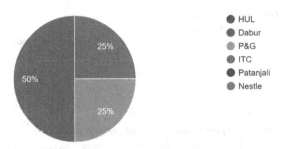

Fig. 59.2 Advertisement data

Which FMCG brand you trust more?
4 responses

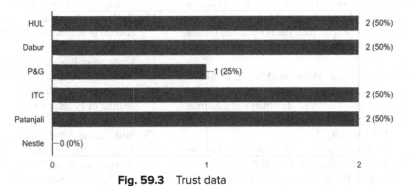

Fig. 59.3 Trust data

Which FMCG brand you are loyal to?
4 responses

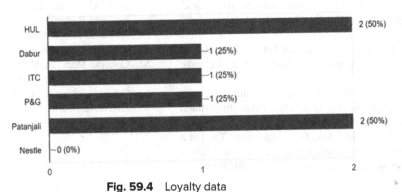

Fig. 59.4 Loyalty data

What you like about the product?
3 responses

Fig. 59.5 Product characteristics distribution

Did you switch to any product after Seeing ads on Social Media?
3 responses

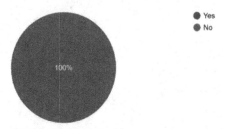

Fig. 59.6 Product switching data

■ REFERENCES ■

1. Haudi, H., Handayani, W., Musnaini, M., Suyoto, Y., Prasetio, T., Pitaloka, E., ... & Cahyon, Y. (2022). The effect of social media marketing on brand trust, brand equity and brand loyalty. International Journal of Data and Network Science, 6(3), 961–972. Haudia, Wiwik Handayanib*(2022) Received in revised format: November 26, 2021, Accepted: January 29, 2022. International Journal of Data and Network Science · February 2022
2. Aaker, D. (1991), Measuring Brand Equity: Capitalizing on the Value of a Brand Name, The Free Press, New York, NY.
3. Garg, Ebha: Consumers Attitude Towards Product Harm Crisis, 2021 page- xv123
4. Pradhan, Jyoti & Misra, Devi. (2015). Consumer Brand Loyalty: A Study on FMCGs-Personal Care Products in Rural and Urban Areas of India.
5. Title of Thesis: Influence of social media strategies on consumer decision making process an empirical study of select FMCG products, Name of the Researcher: Menka, Name of the Guide: Sharma, Sanjeev Kumar, Completed Year: 2020, Name of the Department: University Business School, Name of the University: Panjab University
6. Heba Sadek Email addresses for corresponding author: heba_sadek@yahoo.co.uk First submission received: 25th

June 2017 Revised submission received: 30th August 2017 Accepted: 28th September 2017

7. Abdelkader, A. A., & Ebrahim, R. S. (2021). Decomposing Customer Engagement Effect Between Marketer- and User-Generated Content and Repurchase Intention in the Online Airline Service Community. International Journal of Online Marketing, 11(4), 1–22.

8. Irshad, Madeeha & Ahmad, Muhammad Shakil & Malik, Omer. (2020). Understanding consumers' trust in social media marketing environment. International Journal of Retail & Distribution Management. ahead-of-print. 10.1108/IJRDM-07-2019-0225.

9. Jalal Rajeh Hanaysha, School of Business, Skyline University College, 1797 Sharjah, United Arab Emirates, received 10 May 2022, Revised 19 July 2022, Accepted 19 July 2022, Available online 28 July 2022, Version of Record 28 July 2022.

10. The impact of social media on consumer-brand loyalty: A mediating role of online based-brand community, Article: 1673640, Published online:09 Oct 2019, Author: Abdul Bashiru Jibri

11. Chandpuri, Harshita & Ahuja, Vandana. (2020). Using social media for generating trust-a study of FMCG brands. 5.

12. Prasetyo Matak Aji, Vanessa Nadhila, Lim Sanny, Accepted: March 19, 2020, Keywords: Social Media Marketing, Brand Equity, e-WOM, Purchase Intention

13. Geok Theng Lau & Sook Han Lee, Consumers' Trust in a Brand and the Link to Brand Loyalty, Journal of Market-Focused Management volume 4, pages341–370 (1999)

14. Lau, G.T., Lee, S.H. Consumers' Trust in a Brand and the Link to Brand Loyalty. Journal of Market-Focused Management 4, 341–370 (1999).

15. B. Ramaseshan, Fazlul K. Rabbanee, Laine Tan Hsin Hui, Journal of Business & Industrial Marketing, Volume 28 (4): 12 – Apr 5, 2013

16. Linda, Sau-ling LAI, Journal of Business & Industrial Marketing, Volume 28 (4): 12 – Apr 5, 2013, World Academy of Science, Engineering and Technology International Journal of Economics and Management Engineering Vol:4, No:12, 2010

17. Muhammad Aslam Khan, Kashif ur Rehman. Consumer's Trust in the Brand: Can it Be Built through Brand Reputation, Brand Competence and Brand Predictability, Vol. 3, No. 1 January 2010

18. Hasan, Afzal & Khan, Muhammad & ur Rehman, Kashif & Ali, Imran & Sobia, Wajahat. (2009). Consumer's Trust in the Brand: Can it be built through Brand Reputation, Brand Competence and Brand Predictability. International Business Research. 3. 10.5539/ibr. v3n1p43.

19. James J. Zboja, Clay M. Voorhees, Journal of Services Marketing, Volume 20 (6): 10 – Oct 1, 2006

20. Culnan, Mary & McHugh, Patrick & Zubillaga, Jesus. (2010). How Large U.S. Companies Can Use Twitter and Other social media to Gain Business Value. MIS Quarterly Executive. 9. 243–259

Note: All the figures in this chapter were made by the author.

Challenges and Opportunities for Innovation in India – Dr. Shweta Mishra et al. (eds)
© 2024 Taylor & Francis Group, London, ISBN 978-1-032-99842-8

Gender Equality in Trade: Laws and Trends in India

60

Ratan Singh Yadav[1]
Assistant Professor,
AIHE, Lucknow, Uttar Pradesh, India

Om Prakash[2]
Assistant Professor,
AIMT, Lucknow, Uttar Pradesh, India

Abstract

Gender equality refers to equal access to resources and equal participation in social and economic spheres. Women's participation is crucial for trade to enhance. However, despite measures by the Indian government, their participation is very low. This paper provides an overview of legislation related to women prevailing in India and analyses the trend of their status on three themes- preparedness, safety and security and participation. The results reveal that despite the decrease in the gender gap in education, mortality rate, and labour force participation, they are inadequate. Further, the women are highly anaemic, their participation in politics is very low and crimes against them are alarming situation. Therefore, Governments to enhance women's preparedness by developing their skills, and health along with providing safety and security to participate in economic and political arenas of the economy. This paper contributes to academicians, policymakers and businesses in identifying needs and challenges faced by women and developing policies and products for developing women's human capital.

Keywords

Gender gap, Preparedness, Safety and security, Participation

1. INTRODUCTION

The relationship between gender equality and trade is a two-way interaction. A reduction in the gender gap would help the economy and foreign trade. But whether the economic well-being of a nation promotes gender equality has mixed experience in the world. Global and national shocks increase the gender gap, which is evident from the economic recession of 2008 and the pandemics of COVID-19 in 2020 and 2021. Whenever economies are hit hard, the impact is transferred to women, making them suffer the most. However, the literacy rate of females has improved gradually. The government's schemes of gender equality have been fruitful, yet the expected results are below. Self-help groups have uplifted many women as access to financial services increased, women's

Corresponding author: [1]2913ratan@gmail.com, [2]omprakashnep1@gmail.com

DOI: 10.1201/9781003606260-60

empowerment. across the world. Several studies confirm the role that trade can play in reducing gender inequality and vice versa ([1]. Simultaneously, empirical results tell the story to be different from what common findings are. In most developed countries, gender equality is closely associated with trade, while in some developing countries, the association between them is found to be either negative or absent. Despite these mixed results, the role of gender equality cannot be neglected. Gender equality reduces the gap between males and females in various arenas of life. The existence of a gap in developing countries hints towards the under-developed and untapped human resources. In a globalised world, governments and society cannot afford to lose the opportunities that can be made available by the participation of females in the labour force. The global value chain has enabled developing and underdeveloped nations to engage the labour force in different stages of production and supply chain. The digital revolution has opened new avenues for development and good governance. Digital dividends—benefits derived from the use of digital technologies [2]—have transformed a variety of economies. Leaving the female workforce away from the opportunities accrued will surely cause the country to be left behind. India has the largest young population, with more than 374 million people between the ages of ten and twenty-four. She has one of the largest young workforces which shows India has a huge untapped labour force. However, female work participation declined over the years. The wage, and employment gap remained widened. Female young workforce participation is very low. The primary sector remained the highest breadwinner for females. Despite the increased female literacy rate, the total workforce participation is low. This paper focuses on the economic aspects of gender equality in India which build the barrier for women playing a crucial role in trade enhancement. The study analyses challenges and opportunities through three main dimensions viz. **preparedness** of female, **safety** measures for their **participation**, and the actual status of their participation.

2. LITERATURE REVIEW

Research shows that gender equality has a significant impact on trade. In a study by [3], the impact of various measures of gender inequality on comparative advantage was investigated. The study found that a reduction in inequality in labour force participation is associated with an improvement in the comparative advantage of labour-intensive sectors. The panel data were collected from 29 countries over six years. However, the relationship loses statistical significance when high-income countries are excluded from the sample. This is surprising given

that women are disproportionately employed in labour-intensive exports, particularly in most developing countries such as Mauritius, Mexico, Peru, the Philippines, and Sri Lanka. [4] reports that there is some evidence of a positive relationship between women's employment share and aggregate exports in these countries. [5] emphasizes that gender-specific provisions in trade policies are crucial to promoting equality. [6] suggests the use of gender and trade indicators to monitor the consistency between trade and gender policies. However, [7] highlights the negative impact of trade openness and gender inequality on economic development in developing countries. Despite the contrary observations, Inclusive female labour force participation has positive effects on comparative advantage, import demand, and can be a source of welfare gains. As, Women's labour force participation is closely linked to falling fertility rates and rising life expectancy, as well as increased educational opportunities.

3. RESEARCH METHODOLOGY

Determining the Dimensions of Gender Equality We used three popular reports- the McKinsey Global Institute (MGI) report of 2015 on gender equality, the World Economic Forum (WEF)'s Global Gender Gap Report2021 and the Gender Inequality Index of the United Nations Programme to arrive at our own set of indicators. In its report "The power of parity: How advancing women's quality can add $12 trillion to global growth", MGI used four categories of 15 indicators. Similarly, WEF used four categories of indicators while the United Nations Programme calculates the Gender inequality index on three dimensions viz. health, empowerment, and labour market. We summated all the indicators under three categories- Preparedness, Safety and Participation. The lists are in Table 60.1 and Table 60.2.

Further, we collected secondary data for trend analysis from the International Labour Organisation (ILO), the United Nations Conference on Trade and Development (UNCTAD), the World Trade Organisation (WTO), https://ncrb.gov.in/, https://www.startupindia.gov.in/, https://data.gov.in/, https://www.eci.gov.in and https://www.mospi.gov.in/

4. DATA ANALYSIS, RESULTS AND DISCUSSION

4.1 Dimensions

1. Preparedness

Education: The literacy rate of women has increased over the years. In 1901 it was only 0.8 percent which became

Table 60.1 Dimensional similarity

Organisation/ Institution	Title of Report / Study	Dimensions /categories	This can be clubbed with the themes of this paper
McKinsey Global Institute (MGI)	The power of parity: How advancing women's quality can add $12 trillion to global growth	Equality in work	Participation
		Essential services and enablers of economic opportunity	Preparedness
		Legal protection and political voice	Safety Participation
		Physical security and autonomy	Safety Participation
World Economic Forum	Global gender gap report 2021	Economic opportunities	Participation
		Education	Preparedness
		Health	Preparedness
		Political Leadership	Participation
United Nations Development Programme	*Gender inequality index* in *Human development report 2020*	Health	Preparedness
		Empowerment- Education	Preparedness
		Empowerment- share in parliament seats	Participation
		Labour market	Participation

Source: Authors based reports of McKinsey Global Institute (MGI) 2015, World Economic Forum (WEF) and Human Development Report 2020.

Table 60.2 Final dimensions and indicators for assessing gender equality

Preparedness	Safety and Protection	Participation
Education	Legal Protection	Labour Market Participation
Health	Physical Security and Autonomy	Political Participation
Skill Development programmes		
Financial and economic upliftment programmes and Laws		

Source: Authors

65.46 percent in 2011 and the literacy gap remained increasing till 1981. After 1991 the gap started declining. This can be attributed to the steps taken by GOI and the assistance from the World Bank. The gap has further dwindled to 12.9 per cent in 2020 from 16.68% in 2011 [8]. The male literacy rate increased by 2.26 % while the female literacy rate increased by 6.04% during this period (Fig. 60.1).

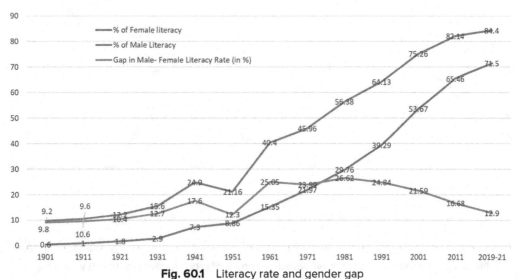

Fig. 60.1 Literacy rate and gender gap

Source: Census 2011 and National Family Health Survey (NHFS-5) 2019–21

Health: About 105 major schemes are under health and family welfare by the central government and state government ranging from primary health care centres to ASSHA, AYUSH and many more. Under the Ministry of Women and Child Development, major schemes are Mission Poshan 2.0, Mission Shakti, and Mission Vatasalya. These provisions and schemes have resulted in a declining mortality rate and increased health services. However, still, the dream of India being a healthy nation seems to be distant away. Although the mortality rate has been dwindling for both male and female infants, the mortality rate has been slightly higher for female infants as compared to male infants since 2000 but the trend seems to have reversed since 2019. In 2000 male and female mortality rates were 66 and 67 respectively while in 2020 the rates became 27 for each per 1000 live births (Fig. 60.2).

The prevalence of anaemia among women is not still a big challenge for the Government to tackle. Fig. 60.3 shows that the prevalence of anaemia among women is decreasing

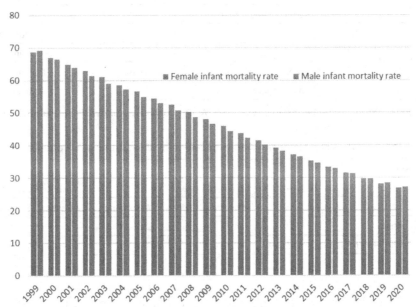

Fig. 60.2 Mortality rate (Male and female)

Source: UNICEF

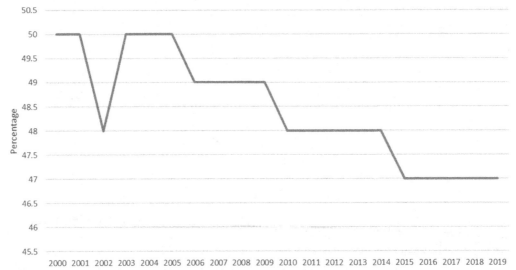

Fig. 60.3 Anaemia prevalence (all types) in women of reproductive age (15-49 years) (%)

Source: UNICEF

slightly. However, it is still high for women. The prevalence is 25.0% in men (15-49 years) while 57.0% in women (15-49 years), and 52.2% in pregnant women (15-49 years). Similarly, it is 31.1% in adolescent boys (15-19 years) and 59.1% in adolescent girls. [Ministry of Health and Family Welfare[8]

Skill Development Programmes: For women's skills development, the Ministry of Women and Child Development, run training programmes for gender budgeting and provides grants for internships for women students, scholars, social activists, and teachers between the ages of 21 and 40 years old in association with a university, academic and non-academic institution. Further, the ministry has given guidelines for gender-inclusive communication.

Financial and economic upliftment programmes and Laws: Under the Ministry of Skill Development and Entrepreneurship vocational training is provided to women to stimulate employment skills. Women's Vocational Training Programme (WVTP) was launched in 1977 to bring women into economic activities with the assistance of the Swedish International Development Authority (SIDA) and the International Labour Organization (ILO) in March 1977. Under this project, vocational trades were identified that were particularly suitable for women and their implementation planned.

Several other programmes and schemes are run by the Government and banks. Some major programmes and schemes are discussed below.

- **Skill Upgradation and Mahila Coir Yojana** Focused on women artisans in coir fibre-producing regions, the coir board under the Ministry of Micro, Small and Medium Enterprises provides two months of exclusive skill development training programmes with a stipend of Rs 3000 per month.

- **Mahila Samriddhi Yojana**: It is a micro-finance scheme for women belonging to backward classes under the Ministry of Social Justice and Empowerment. Women get financial assistance up to Rs 1, 40,000.

- **Women Entrepreneurship Platform (WEP)-** The initiative by NITI Ayog is aimed at building an ecosystem for women across India to realize their entrepreneurial aspirations, scale-up innovative initiatives and formulate sustainable, long-term strategies for their businesses. The three pillars on which WEP is built: Ichha Shakti (motivating aspiring entrepreneurs to start their enterprise); Gyaan Shakti (providing knowledge and ecosystem support to women entrepreneurs to help them foster entrepreneurship); Karma Shakti (providing hands-on support to entrepreneurs in setting-up and scaling up businesses).

- **Trade Related Entrepreneurship Assistance and Development (TREAD) -** The scheme envisages economic empowerment particularly for illiterate & semiliterate women of rural and urban areas through trade-related training, information and counselling extension activities related to trades, products, services etc.

- **Mudra Yojana for Women/ Mahila Udhyami Yojana -** Women entrepreneurs engaged in manufacturing and production business but not belonging to any corporate or farming or agribusiness, may get loans up to Rs 10 lakhs without any collateral by the department of financial services of the ministry of finance.

- **Nai Roshni- Scheme for Leadership Development of Minority Women-** This scheme aims to empower and enhance confidence in Minority women by providing knowledge, tools and techniques for Leadership Development of Women.   It is a six-day non-residential or five-day residential training programme conducted for women belonging to a minority community between the age group of 18 years to 65 years. The training modules cover areas related to Programmes for women, health and hygiene, legal rights of women, financial literacy, digital Literacy, Swachh Bharat, life skills, and advocacy for social and behavioural changes.

- **Mahila Udyam Nidhi Yojana-** Women entrepreneurs get assistance in setting up new projects or expansion, modernisation, technology upgradation and diversification in the tiny or small-scale sector and rehabilitation of viable sick SSI units with a soft loan limit of 25 per cent of the project cost subject to a maximum of Rs 2.5 lakhs.

- **Dena Shakti Scheme-** It is the combination of the term loan (term 1-3 years) and working capital which is provided to women entrepreneurs, who are involved in retail, service and manufacturing activities holding the business all by themselves or at least have more than 50 per cent stake in the business and a part of or pursuing the Entrepreneurship Development Programs (EDP), at 25 per cent concessional rates in the loan.

- **Stree Shakti Package for Women Entrepreneurs-** It is the Scheme of the State Bank of India (SBI). Under this scheme, SBI provides term loans or working capital based on the borrower profile with concessions or relaxations in the margin built into the scheme along with the low floating rate of interest, linked to the base rate of the bank [9].

4.2 Safety and Protection

Legal Protection, Physical Security and Autonomy

The enabling environment is not enough to bring women into the mainstream and boosting trade, safety and protection is also important. The government of India has enacted several laws addressing the issues. The prominent laws are described below.

- **Dowry Prohibition Act, 1961,** enumerates the social and legal consequences of practising dowry along with its other various aspects.
- **The Immoral Traffic (Prevention) Act, 1956** called as All India Suppression of Immoral Traffic Act (SITA), describes sexual exploitation of any male or female as a cognizable offence. This law was intended to limit and eventually abolish prostitution in India by gradually criminalising various aspects of sex work.
- **The Indecent Representation of Women (Prohibition) Act, 1986,** prohibits indecent representation of women through film, web series, advertisements or in publication, writings, paintings, figures or in any other manner and describes these activities as a punishable offence leading to banning all of them or the platform.
- **The Commission of Sati (Prevention) Act, 1987,** mandates the prevention of *sati*, the voluntary or forced burning or burying of a widow and prohibits glorification of this action through the observance of any ceremony, participation in any procession, creation of a financial trust, construction of a temple or any actions leading to honouring the memory of a widow who committed sati.
- **The National Commission for Women Act, 1990** recommends remedial legislative measures, facilitates redressal of grievances and advises the government on all policy matters affecting women.
- **The Protection of Women from Domestic Violence Act, 2005,** a civil law in nature, protects women from domestic violence, of all forms whether it is physical violence or other forms of violence such as emotional, verbal, sexual and psychological abuse.

- **The Prohibition of Child Marriage Act, 2006 prohibits** marriage below the age of 21 for boys and below 18 for girls as an illegal child marriage calling for punishment.
- **The Sexual Harassment of Women at Workplace (Prevention, Prohibition and Redressal) Act, 2013** protects women and safeguard their rights at workplace
- **The Trafficking in Persons (Prevention, Care and Rehabilitation) Bill, 2021,** specifies penalties for various offences including (i) trafficking of persons, (ii) aggravated trafficking (such as, for bonded labour and begging), and (iii) promotion of trafficking. Further, the Bill punishes an owner if he knowingly allows the offence of trafficking to be carried out on his/her premises.
- **The Protection of Children from Sexual Offences Rules, 2020** is a reviewed and amended form of the Protection of Children from Sexual Offenses (POCSO) Act, 2012 which was enacted to safeguard children below the age of 18 years from sexual abuse and sexual offences.

Despite the severe laws to protect women and children, the offences are rampant. For example, as per Table 60.3, the cases of criminal offences registered under the Dowry Prohibition Act were 10366 in 2020 which increased to 13479 in 2022. Similarly, criminal offence cases registered related to the Immortal Traffic (Prevention) Act, The Protection of Women from Domestic Violence Act, and The Indecent Representation of Women (Prohibition) Act were 1497, 468 and 28 respectively in 2022 as compared to 1294, 446 and 12 respectively in 2020. Altogether crimes against Women – Related Acts were 15472 in 2020 as compared to 12118 in 2020. Though registered cases under the four categories were higher in 2021 as compared to 2022. Furthermore, crime registered against women in a year has been increasing as compared to the previous year. From 2018 to 2022, the highest increment (15.3%) was in 2021 as the steep fall in crime was observed in 2020. This fall in 2020 can be attributed to the lockdown imposed by the government of India to prevent Covid-19. The highest

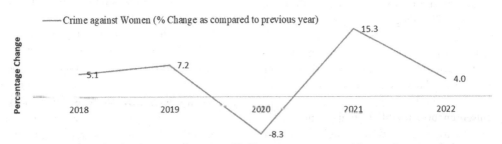

Fig. 60.4 Crime against women (% Change as compared to previous year)

Source: Authors based on National Crime Records Bureau, Ministry of Home Affairs, GOI

registered cases have been in the category of domestic violence [10]

Table 60.3 Crime registered under various laws and acts during 2020-2022

Crime Head	2020	2021	2022
The Dowry Prohibition Act	10366	13568	13479
The Immoral Traffic (Prevention) Act	1294	1678	1497
The Protection of Women from Domestic Violence Act	446	507	468
The Indecent Representation of Women (Prohibition) Act	12	28	28
Crime Against Women – Related Acts	**12118**	**15781**	**15472**

Source: National Crime Records Bureau, Ministry of Home Affairs, GOI

3. PARTICIPATION

3.1 Labour Market Participation

Despite the rising violence against women, the participation of women in the workforce has been rising. Figure 60.5 shows that the Female labour force participation rate in 2017-18 was 23.3% which went up to 37.0% in 2022-23 with about 59 increases. The rate improved by 4.2% in 2022-23 as compared to 2021-22 (rate=32.8%).

This is the result of numerous government measures to assist women in various spheres of life, including education, skill development, business encouragement, and workplace safety for girls. Policies and laws in these sectors have fuelled the government's aim for "women-led development".

3.2 Political Participation

Despite increasing women's participation in the labour force, political participation is dismal. Table 60.4 shows that in the General election (Lok Sabha) from 1999 to 2019

women's political participation increased by a meagre percentage (5.4%). In the 1999 general election, only 9% of women were elected to the Lok Sabha, which increased to 14.4% in 2019. Similar is the case with elections in five states in 2019. The percentage of women elected in Goa, Manipur, Punjab, Uttarakhand and Uttar Pradesh was only 7.5%, 8.33%, 11.11%, 11.43% and 11.66% respectively

Table 60.4 Women's political participation in elections

Name of the State (Election year-2019)	Elected - Women (In %)	Year of General Election	Elected - Women (In %)
Goa	7.5	1999	9
Manipur	8.33	2004	8.3
Punjab	11.11	2009	10.9
Uttarakhand	11.43	2014	11.4
Uttar Pradesh	11.66	2019	14.4

Source: Election Commission of India

5. CONCLUSIONS AND LIMITATIONS

Gender equality has become necessary for economic development. It gives opportunity to women to contribute in the well-being of society. Their participation will bring unutilised human resources into productive activities in the economy. On one hand, they create demand and, on another hand, they participate in the supply of the labour force. For Innovation, women's participation in all walks of life is a must. This can be possible if they are prepared, safety and security are provided to them and allowed to participate in social, economic and political arenas. The government of India has enacted several laws for women's protection, development and participation. This study provides an overview of legislation for women in India and trends of women's status on three themes- preparedness, safety and security and participation in trade using secondary data.

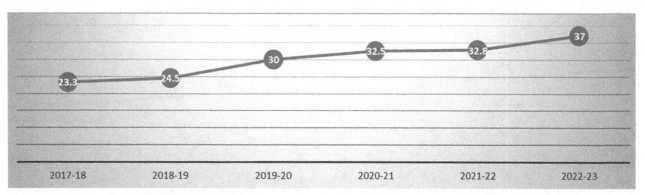

Fig. 60.5 Women labour force participation rate (%, 15 years and above, usual status)

Source: Annual National Sample Survey Report 2022-23

Results show that the literacy gap and mortality rate have decreased, and participation of women in the workforce has increased, however, malnutrition and crime against women are still are still embedded with challenges. The government needs to take steps to improve these parameters.

The study is limited to a few themes and indicators related to women's challenges which address gender equality to boost trade.

■ REFERENCES ■

1. L. Woetzel *et al.*, "How advancing women's equality can add $12 trillion to global growth | McKinsey," Sep. 2015. Accessed: Feb. 20, 2024. [Online]. Available: https://www.mckinsey.com/featured-insights/employment-and-growth/how-advancing-womens-equality-can-add-12-trillion-to-global-growth

2. World Bank, "World Development Report 2016: Digital Dividends," Washington, DC, 2016. Accessed: Feb. 20, 2024. [Online]. Available: https://www.worldbank.org/en/publication/wdr2016

3. M. Busse and C. Spielmann, "Gender Inequality and Trade*," *Rev Int Econ*, vol. 14, no. 3, pp. 362–379, Aug. 2006, doi: 10.1111/J.1467-9396.2006.00589.X.

4. H. K. Nordås, "The impact of trade liberalization on women's job opportunities and earnings in developing countries," *World Trade Review*, vol. 2, no. 2, pp. 221–231, 2003, doi: 10.1017/S1474745603001381.

5. A. Frohmann and S. Researcher, "Gender Equality and Trade Policy", Accessed: Feb. 20, 2024. [Online]. Available: www.wti.org

6. I. van Staveren, "Monitoring Gender Impacts of Trade," *Eur J Dev Res*, vol. 15, no. 1, pp. 126–145, Jun. 2003, doi: 10.1080/09578810312331287405.

7. Farooq *et al.*, "How do trade liberalization and gender inequality affect economic development?," *Pakistan Journal of Commerce and Social Sciences*, vol. 13, no. 2, pp. 547–559, 2019, Accessed: Feb. 20, 2024. [Online]. Available: http://hdl.handle.net/10419/201005

8. Ministry of Health and Family Welfare, "National Family Health Survey (NFHS-5) 2019-21."

9. GOI, "Women Entrepreneurship." Accessed: Feb. 20, 2024. [Online]. Available: https://www.startupindia.gov.in/content/sih/en/women_entrepreneurs.html

10. GOI, "Crime In India Year Wise | National Crime Records Bureau." Accessed: Feb. 20, 2024. [Online]. Available: https://ncrb.gov.in/crime-in-india-year-wise.html?year=2022&keyword=

Challenges and Opportunities for Innovation in India – Dr. Shweta Mishra et al. (eds)
© *2024 Taylor & Francis Group, London, ISBN 978-1-032-99842-8*

Abrasion Resistance of Hooked Steel Fiber Silica Fume Concrete Using Recycled Aggregate

61

Raushan Kumar[1], Lavkush Gupta[2]
Assistant Professor,
Department of Civil Engineering, Gaya College of Engineering,
Gaya, Bihar, India

Alok Mishra[3]
Professor,
Department of Physics, Gaya College of Engineering,
Gaya, Bihar, India

Saurabh Kumar[4]
Assistant Professor,
Department of Civil Engineering, Purnea College of Engineering,
Purnea, India

Abstract

In present experimental study, the effect of silica fume and hooked steel fiber in concrete on abrasion resistance is investigated. Six concrete mixtures containing 0, 5,7.5, 10, 12.5, and 15% silica fume as cement replacement in mass basis were prepared. Another, four fiber-reinforced ordinary Portland cement (OPC 43 grade) concrete mixtures containing different fiber content (0 to 1.25 %) were prepared for hooked steel fiber in volume basis and 10% by replacing with cement mass basis were prepared for recycled aggregate. Water-cement/cementitious ratio was kept constant in all the concrete mixes. Compressive strength, flexural strength and surface abrasions of the concrete mixtures were measured at 28 days. The results of the laboratory work showed that replacement of cement with Silica Fume increase abrasion resistance, compressive strength, flexural strength and split tensile strength of concrete. Addition of hooked steel fiber improved the abrasion resistance of concrete. The comparison between the relation of abrasion to compressive strength and abrasion to flexural tensile strength, made in terms of R2 of the linear regression on log scale, showed that a stronger relation existed between abrasion and flexural tensile strength than between abrasion and compressive strength of the concrete containing either silica fume or silica fume and fibers both.

Keywords

Flexural strength, Abrasion resistance, Silica fume, Hooked steel fiber, Experimental studies, Recycled aggregate

Corresponding author: [1]raushanmit2k8@gmail.com, [2]guptalavkush1990@gmail.com, [3]dralokmishra72@gmail.com, [4]saurabhk.phd19.ce@nitp.ac.in

DOI: 10.1201/9781003606260-61

1. INTRODUCTION

Concrete is most widely used Civil Engineering construction material. Concrete is a composite material made up of cement, fine aggregate, coarse aggregate, water and occasionally admixture in their standard proportions to improve its strength and durability. Several industrial by-products are used as an alternative of Steel nowadays. Many industrial by-products are hazardous to environment and to dispose them is a major concern. Researches are being carried out to check the efficacy of various admixtures and waste material in construction industry. The waste material produced from construction activities can optimally be utilised when it is reused as recycled aggregate (RA) as a replacement of conventional coarse aggregate in production of concrete. In-depth discussions on it could potentially found in the available research. As per the (Sagoe-Crentsil, Brown, and Taylor 2001), the abrasion loss of RCA made with ordinary Portland cement increases by about 12% compared to conventional concrete without coarse RA (crushed concrete).The addition of steel fibres to concrete enhances its toughness and strain at peak stress, but can slightly reduce the Young's modulus (Neves and Fernandes de Almeida 2005). De Brito (2010) investigated that there is no loss of abrasion resistance with the incorporation of recycled aggregate rather it is improved. Abdallah et al. (2017) examined mechanical behaviour of steel fibres concrete using various cementaneous material as cement replacement. Concretes produced with a higher quality recycled concrete aggregate (RCA) and those containing slag and steel fibres exhibit reduced water absorption and shrinkage compared to plain natural aggregate concrete (Afroughsabet et al. 2017). Flexural strength of steel fibre reinforced concrete containing multiple hooked-end fibres is proportional to square of the number of hooks at the fibre ends (Venkateshwara et al; 2018). Patil et al. (2017) investigated how the exposure to a chloride solution affects concrete mixtures made with different proportions of fly ash and silica fume-based High-Performance concrete mixes. Testing for acid attack has been done to gauge the toughness. Reddy and B.D.K. (2018) examined that Concrete possesses a number of advantageous qualities, including a high compressive strength, rigidity, and durability. Presence of hooked-end steel fibres in reinforced concrete improves material properties for both the pre and post cracking phase in steel fibre hybridisation (Okeh et al. 2019). Reinforcing glass fiber in concrete and replacing the cement with silica fume enhances the strength of the concrete as compared to conventional concrete by improving its mechanical properties (Kumar et al. 2020). Micro steel fibres have the potential to improve the tensile strength, flexural strength and modulus of elasticity

increases the concrete strength and reduce the cost of concrete mix (Hakeem et al. 2022). In the present study the compressive strength, flexural strength, split tensile strength and abrasion test result of hooked steel fibre silica fume recycled concrete is check in case of M35 grade of concrete. For the abrasion resistance of hooked steel fibre silica fume recycled aggregate, no researchers used a regression analysis technique with various proportions of hooked steel fibre having the optimum value of silica fume concrete.

2. MATERIALS AND EXPERIMENTAL STUDIES

2.1 Cement

Ordinary Portland Cement of Grade 43 brand prism obtained from a single batch was used throughout this investigation. The Physical properties of OPC as determined are and values confirm to the requirement of IS 8112-1989. Its normal consistency, initial setting time, final setting time specific gravity and 28 days strength are found to be 30 %, 65 minutes, 255 minutes and 43.50 respectively.

2.2 Aggregate

Aggregate is classified as fine and coarse aggregate. Fine aggregates are material passing through IS sieve size 4.75 mm. The most important function of the fine aggregate is to provide workability and uniformity in the mixture. In case of close reinforcement spacing and fibre reinforced concrete 10mm size aggregate also used.

Fine Aggregate

It passes through 4.75 mm sieve size and considering specific gravity of 2.71 and water absorption of 0.9 %. Sieve analysis has been caried out and it has been found that fineness modulus of 2.05. It lies in Zone-III as per IS 383-1970.

Natural Coarse Aggregate

It retained on 4.75 mm sieve size and considering specific gravity of 2.65. Sieve analysis has been caried out for the 10 mm coarse aggregate. It has been found that fineness modulus of 6.26.

Recycled Aggregate

It retained on 4.75 mm sieve size and considering specific gravity of 2.52. sieve analysis has been caried out for the 10 mm coarse aggregate. It has been found that fineness modulus of 6.02

2.3 Aluminium Oxide Powder

White aluminium oxide (or white aluminium oxide) grit is a 99.5% ultrapure grade of blasting media, which was procured from V.S Chemical Trading Co. Kanpur. White aluminium oxide is increasingly being used in critical, high-performance micro abrasion equipment. It is most widely used abrasive in blast finishing and surface preparation because of its cost, longevity and hardness.

2.4 Silica Fume

Silica Fume supplied by KGR AGRO Pvt Ltd from Ludhiana was used in the present study. The specific surface of 1800000, cm^2/gm. Silica fume is a by-product of the manufacture of silicon metal and Ferro-silicon alloys. The process involves the reduction of high purity quartz (SiO2) in electric arc furnaces at temperatures in excess of 2,000°C. Silica fume is a very fine powder consisting mainly of spherical particles or microspheres of mean diameter about 0.15 microns, with a very high specific surface area (15,000–25,000 m2/kg). At a typical dosage of 10% by mass of cement, there will be 50,000–100,000 silica fume particles per cement grain.

2.5 Advantage of Silica Fume

The following advantage of silica fume is listed below:

- It helps to increased compressive and flexural strength of the concrete.
- It reduces the permeability and efflorescence of the concrete structure.
- It is observed that using silica fume as pozzolanic material as cement replacement to help increasing resistance to chemical attack and reduced shrinkage.
- It helps to improve finish ability, colour and Appearance.
- Silica fume concrete increases surface resistance & split tensile strength.

2.6 Hooked Steel Fibre

The hooked steel fibre used in this work was procured from STEWOLS INDIA (P) LTD, Nagpur; hooked steel fibre used are shown in Fig. 61.1 with the specification of fibres. Such as length, least lateral dimension and aspect ratio of the fibre is 36 mm, 0.45 mm and 80 respectively. The density of glass fibre is 7850 kg/m3.

2.7 Experimental Procedures

The test setups for abrasion resistance, flexural strength, compressive strength and split tensile strength are shown in Fig. 61.2. The load was increased in stages up to failure. To test the flexural strength of concrete three-point loading was used. The abrasion test was performed as per the guideline given in IS: 1237-1980[10]: First fix the specimen in the holding device with the surface to be ground facing

Fig. 61.1 Hooked steel fibre

Fig. 61.2 Abrasion test machine

the disc and loaded at the centre with 300 N (30 Kg-f); the grinding disc shall then be put in the motion at a speed of 30 rev/min. and the abrasive powder is continuously fed back on the grinding path so that it remains uniformly distributed in a track corresponding to the width of the test piece. After every 22 revolutions, the disc was stopped and the powder was removed from the disc and fresh abrasive powder (20 g) was applied each time. After 22 revolutions, the specimen was turned about its vertical axis through an angle of 90^0 in the clockwise direction. This procedure was repeated 9 times there by giving total number of revolutions of 220. The decrease in height and weight were measured after 220 revolutions.

2.8 Mix Design

With the help of IS 10262, mix design has been performed for the M35 grade of concrete containing recycled concrete. Now, using an optimum value of silica fume as a replacement with cement and along with hooked steel fibre.

Mix Proportion Using Recycled Aggregate

Design Stipulations

- Max size of coarse aggregate-10 mm
- Degree of quality control- good
- Type of exposure- mild
- Test data for materials
- Specific gravity of cement-3.15
- Specific gravity of coarse aggregates-2.52
- Specific gravity of fine aggregate-2.71
- Fineness modulus of recycled aggregate-6.02
- Fineness modulus of fine aggregate-2.05
- Water absorption of fine aggregate- 0.90%
- Water absorption of recycled aggregate-3.75%
- Quantity of super plasticizer -1.5% of the weight of cement content

Table 61.1 Final mix proportions obtained per m^3 of concrete

Ingredients	Water	Cement	F. A (Kg)	RC. A (Kg)
Quantity	184 lit	460 kg	578.5	1126.2
Ratio	0.40	1	1.26	2.45

3. Results and Discussion

Numerous Mix design involving the direct compressive strength, flexural strength, split tensile strength and abrasion resistance of M35 grade of concrete are prepared using recycled aggregate. The mix design is tested in the laboratory in the present work. Furthermore, the replacement of cement as silica fume is investigated and optimum value is achieved. In addition to a hooked steel fibre of various proportion by volume is added in the whole silica fume concrete.

3.1 Workability

The effect of silica fume on workability of concrete using recycled aggregate is shown in Table 61.2. The slump value is recorded at silica fume content varies from 0 to 15%. The present investigation is carried on M35 grade of concrete.

Table 61.2 Workability of concrete at different % of Silica Fume using recycled aggregate

% Silica fume replacement	0	5	7.5	10	12.5	15
Slump (mm)	96	90	84	75	68	59

3.2 Effect of Silica Fume on Abrasion Resistance of Silica Fume Mix Concrete with Hooked Steel Fibre Having Natural Aggregate

Compressive strength by NDT and destructive compressive strength, Flexural, split tensile strength & surface abrasion resistance results for concrete at 28 days with and without hooked steel fibre are presented in Table 61.3. In this study replacement of silica fume with OPC was 10% and addition of glass fibre from 0.5 to 1.25 %. It is evident from this table that compressive strength, flexural strength, split tensile strength and abrasion resistance increases with the addition of glass fibre and it is optimum at 1 %. It is observed from Table 61.3, that increase in compressive, flexural, split tensile strength and abrasion resistance is 13.6, 20, 10 and 10% respectively with referral concrete. The relation between the abrasion and compressive strength and abrasion & flexural strength is shown in Fig. 61.3 and Fig. 61.4 respectively. The regression analysis is made to establish a general relationship between abrasion value & compressive strength and abrasion value & flexural strength using the data given in Table 61.3 with and without glass fibre. The results are plotted on log scale in Fig. 61.3 and Fig. 61.4 with the best fit curve. The regression coefficient

Table 61.3 Compressive, flexural and abrasion test result of hooked steel fibre silica fume recycled concrete

S. No.	% Hooked Steel Fiber	28 days Comp. Strength (MPa) by NDT	28 days comp. strength (MPa)	28 days Flexural Strength (MPa)	28 days Abrasion (cm^3/50cm^2)	Split Tensile Strength (MPA)
1	0	39.50	44	7.25	6.40	4.50
2	0.50	42.60	45.75	7.60	6.10	4.65
3	0.75	45.20	48.20	8.10	5.95	4.85
4	1.00	48.50	50.00	8.70	5.75	4.95
5	1.25	46.80	48.50	8.50	6.05	4.80

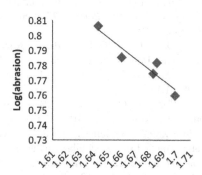

Fig. 61.3 Abrasion vs compression strength

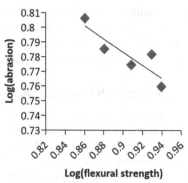

Fig. 61.4 Abrasion vs flexural strength

R^2 are found 0.8840 and 0.7639 for the relationship between surface abrasion to compressive strength and surface abrasion to flexural strength respectively. It observed from the graph that relationship between abrasion & flexural strength proved lower R^2 than R^2 value of compressive strength and abrasion relationship. In Table 61.4 Abrasion value is calculated with each proportion of glass fibre by volume and it is observed that 1 % hooked steel fibre reinforcement is optimum value.

4. CONCLUSION

The abrasion resistance of the fibre-reinforced silica fume recycled aggregate concrete is investigated. Some of the potential research areas in this fascinating field are listed below:

- Study of few properties of concrete made using all the three type of aggregates at optimum Silica Fume

content and by including different fibres in varying proportions.

- The optimum Silica Fume content is 10 %, for concrete made using, recycled coarse aggregate (RCA).
- The non destructive compressive strength is found lesser in the range of 8 to 10% from destructive testing in Silica fume mix concrete with recycled concrete aggregate.
- The increase in compressive, flexural, split tensile strength and abrasion resistance is 2.4, 9.8, 32 and 5.8% respectively, as compared to the optimum Silica fume concrete for the Silica fume mix concrete with recycled concrete aggregate using hooked steel fibres.
- The non destructive compressive strength is found lesser in the range of 13 to 16% from destructive testing in silica fume mix concrete with recycled concrete aggregate using hooked steel fibres.

Table 61.4 Abrasion test result of silica fume mix concrete with glass fibre using natural aggregate

S. No	No. of cycles	0.50% steel fibre		0.75% steel fibre		1.00 % steel fibre		1.25% steel fibre	
		Depth of abrasion (mm)	Loss in weight (gm)	Depth of abrasion (mm)	Loss in weight (gm)	Depth of abrasion (mm)	Loss in weight (gm)	Depth of abrasion (mm)	Loss in weight (gm)
1	0	0.00	0.00	0.00	0.00	0.00	0.00	0.00	0.00
2	22	0.14	1.69	0.13	1.43	0.09	1.04	0.13	1.56
3	44	0.29	3.51	0.27	3.12	0.20	2.34	0.26	3.12
4	66	0.41	5.07	0.39	4.68	0.33	3.90	0.39	4.94
5	88	0.53	6.63	0.51	6.37	0.40	4.68	0.50	6.50
6	110	0.63	7.80	0.60	7.54	0.52	5.85	0.63	8.06
7	132	0.72	9.10	0.69	8.71	0.60	6.50	0.75	9.62
8	154	0.92	11.70	0.89	11.31	0.69	9.10	0.90	12.48
9	176	1.04	13.13	0.98	12.61	0.86	10.14	0.98	13.52
10	198	1.12	14.17	1.07	13.52	0.95	11.70	1.09	14.17
11	220	1.22	15.86	1.19	15.47	1.15	14.90	1.21	15.73

- The non destructive compressive strength is found lesser in the range of 13 to 16% from destructive testing in silica fume mix concrete with recycled concrete aggregate using hooked steel fibres.

■ REFERENCES ■

1. Abdallah, Sadoon, Mizi Fan, and Xiangming Zhou. 2017. "Pull-Out Behaviour of Hooked End Steel Fibres Embedded in Ultra-High Performance Mortar with Various W/B Ratios." *International Journal of Concrete Structures and Materials* 11(2):301–13. doi: 10.1007/s40069-017-0193-8.

2. Afroughsabet, Vahid, Luigi Biolzi, and Togay Ozbakkaloglu. 2017. "Influence of Double Hooked-End Steel Fibers and Slag on Mechanical and Durability Properties of High Performance Recycled Aggregate Concrete." *Composite Structures* 181:273–84. doi: 10.1016/j.compstruct.2017.08.086.

3. De Brito, Jorge. 2010. "Abrasion Resistance of Concrete Made with Recycled Aggregates." *International Journal of Sustainable Engineering* 3(1):58–64. doi: 10.1080/19397030903254710.

4. Hakeem, Ibrahim Y., Mohamed Amin, Bassam Abdelsalam Abdelsalam, Bassam A. Tayeh, Fadi Althoey, and Ibrahim Saad Agwa. 2022. "Effects of Nano-Silica and Micro-Steel Fiber on the Engineering Properties of Ultra-High Performance Concrete." *Structural Engineering and Mechanics* 82(3):295–312. doi: 10.12989/sem.2022.82.3.295.

5. Kumar, R. Sanjay, D. S. Vijayan, P. A. Mubara. Manzoor, N. Subinjith, and Stagain Santhosh. 2020. "Effect of Silica Fume on Strength of Glass Fiber Incorporated Concrete." *AIP Conference Proceedings* 2271(September). doi: 10.1063/5.0024775.

6. Neves, R. D., and J. C. O. Fernandes de Almeida. 2005. "Compressive Behaviour of Steel Fibre Reinforced Concrete." *Structural Concrete* 6(1):1–8. doi: 10.1680/stco.2005.6.1.1.

7. Okeh, Clifford A. O., David W. Begg, Stephanie J. Barnett, and Nikos Nanos. 2019. "Behaviour of Hybrid Steel Fibre Reinforced Self Compacting Concrete Using Innovative Hooked-End Steel Fibres under Tensile Stress." *Construction and Building Materials* 202:753–61. doi: 10.1016/j.conbuildmat.2018.12.067.

8. Patil, Sachin, H. M. Somasekharaiah, and H. S. Pruthviraj. 2017. "Resistance of Fly Ash and Silica Fume Based Glass Fiber Reinforced High-Performance Concrete Subjected to Acid Attack." IV(Vii):30–33.

9. Reddy, B. Dileep Kumar. 2018. "Experimental Studies on Mechanical Properties of Glass Fibre Reinforced Concrete." 4(10):78–81.

10. Sagoe-Crentsil, K. K., T. Brown, and A. H. Taylor. 2001. "Performance of Concrete Made with Commercially Produced Coarse Recycled Concrete Aggregate." *Cement and Concrete Research* 31(5):707–12. doi: 10.1016/S0008-8846(00)00476-2.

11. Venkateshwaran, Akshay, Kiang Hwee Tan, and Yi Li. 2018. "Residual Flexural Strengths of Steel Fiber Reinforced Concrete with Multiple Hooked-End Fibers." *Structural Concrete* 19(2):352–65. doi: 10.1002/suco.201700030.

Note: All the figures and tables in this chapter were made by the author.

Printed in the United States
by Baker & Taylor Publisher Services